Teaching Music through Performance in Band

Volume 4

Also available from GIA Publications, Inc:
Teaching Music through Performance in Band, Volume 1
Teaching Music through Performance in Band, Volume 2
Teaching Music through Performance in Band, Volume 3
Teaching Music through Performance in Beginning Band
Teaching Music through Performance in Orchestra

G-6022

Teaching Music through Performance in Band

Volume 4

Larry Blocher
Eugene Migliaro Corporon
Ray Cramer
Tim Lautzenheiser
Edward S. Lisk
Richard Miles

Compiled and Edited by Richard Miles

GIA Publications, Inc.
Chicago

G-6022

Copyright © 2002 GIA Publications, Inc.
7404 S. Mason Ave.
Chicago, IL 60638
www.giamusic.com
ISBN: 1-57999-202-1
Printed in the United States of America

Table of Contents

ACKNOWLEDGEMENTS

The following research associates are gratefully acknowledged for outstanding scholarly contributions to the "Teacher Resource Guides":

Michael Alexander
Conductor
Waukesha Area Symphonic Band • Waukesha, Wisconsin

Dennis Beck
Director of Bands
Unionville High School • Markham, Ontario, Canada

Robert Belser
Associate Professor of Music and Director of Bands
University of Wyoming • Laramie, Wyoming

John Bleuel
Assistant Professor of Music
State University of West Georgia • Carrollton, Georgia

Thomas Bough
Southern Illinois University • Carbondale, Illinois

C. Kevin Bowen
Director of Bands
Wake Forest University • Winston-Salem, North Carolina

Sheryl A. Bowhay
Director of Bands
Thornhill Secondary School • Markham, Ontario, Canada

Andrew Boysen, Jr.
Director of Bands
University of New Hampshire • Durham, New Hampshire

Gordon R. Brock
Director of Bands and Assistant Chair
University of North Florida • Jacksonville, Florida

Marcellus Brown
Boise State University • Boise, Idaho

Michael Burch-Pesses
Director of Bands
Pacific University • Forest Grove, Oregon

John C. Carmichael
Director of Bands and Associate Professor of Music
Western Kentucky University • Bowling Green, Kentucky

Scott Carter
Director of Bands
East Carolina University • Greenville, North Carolina

Patrick F. Casey
Director of Bands
Central Missouri State University • Warrensburg, Missouri

James Chesebrough
University of Connecticut • Storrs, Connecticut

Rod M. Chesnutt
Director of Bands
Mississippi State University • Mississippi State, Mississippi

Jim Colonna
Laramie County Community College • Cheyenne, Wyoming

Lynn G. Cooper
Director of Bands
Asbury College • Wilmore, Kentucky

Jeff Cranmore
Director
Dowell Middle School • McKinney, Texas

Susan Creasap
Assistant Director of Bands
Morehead State University • Morehead, Kentucky

Joan deAlbuquerque
Doctoral Conducting Associate
University of North Texas • Denton, Texas

Wayne F. Dorothy
Director of Bands
Hardin-Simmons University • Abilene, Texas

Mark Duker
Scullen Middle School • Naperville, Illinois

Thomas C. Duffy
Director of Bands and Deputy Dean, School of Music
Yale University • New Haven, Connecticut

Patrick Dunnigan
Florida State University • Tallahassee, Florida

Jeffrey Emge
University of Texas at Tyler • Tyler, Texas

Bradley P. Ethington
Associate Professor of Music
Syracuse University • Syracuse, New York

Dennis W. Fisher
Associate Director of Wind Studies
University of North Texas • Denton, Texas

Sean Flanigan
Assistant Director of Bands
Drake University • Des Moines, Iowa

Thomas George Caracas Garcia
State University of West Georgia • Carrollton, Georgia

Bradley Genevro
Associate Director of Bands
Oklahoma State University • Stillwater, Oklahoma

Jay W. Gilbert
Doane College • Crete, Nebraska

Richard A. Greenwood
Director of Bands
University of Central Florida • Orlando, Florida

Monte Grisé
Master's Conducting Associate
Oklahoma State University • Stillwater, Oklahoma

Edward C. Harris
San Jose State University • San Jose, California

Glen J. Hemberger
Director of Bands
Southeastern Louisiana University • Hammond, Louisiana

Leslie W. Hicken
Director of Bands
Furman University • Greenville, South Carolina

Paul Hinman
Director of Bands
Leander High School • Leander, Texas

Paula Holcomb
Director of Bands and Professor of Music
State University of New York College at Fredonia • Fredonia, New York

Diana Hollinger
DMA Student
Arizona State University • Tempe, Arizona

L. Kevin Kastens
Associate Director of Bands
University of Iowa • Iowa City, Iowa

Eric Rombach-Kendall
Director of Bands
University of New Mexico • Albuquerque, New Mexico

Keith Kinder
McMaster University • Hamilton, Ontario, Canada

Daryl W. Kinney
Assistant Professor of Music Education
Kent State University • Kent, Ohio

James L. Klages
School of Music
University of Central Oklahoma • Edmond, Oklahoma

Kenneth Kohlenberg
Director of Bands and Professor of Music
Sinclair Community College • Dayton, Ohio

Barry E. Kopetz
Director of Bands
Capital University, Conservatory of Music • Columbus, Ohio

Brian Lamb
Director of Bands
University of Central Oklahoma • Edmond, Oklahoma

Jeremy S. Lane
Doctoral Graduate Assistant, Music Education
Louisiana State University • Baton Rouge, Louisiana

John M. Laverty
Director of Bands
Syracuse University • Syracuse, New York

Donald G. Lovejoy
Director of Bands
Winona State University • Winona, Minnesota

Richard Lundahl
Assistant Director of Bands
University of Wisconsin–Milwaukee • Milwaukee, Wisconsin

John A. Lychner
Western Michigan University • Kalamazoo, Michigan

Matthew Mailman
Director of Bands and Associate Professor of Music
Oklahoma City University • Oklahoma City, Oklahoma

Victor A. Markovich
Professor of Music and Director of Bands and Winds/Percussion Studies,
School of Music
Wichita State University • Wichita, Kansas

Andrew Mast
Director of Bands and Music Department Chair
St. Ambrose University • Davenport, Iowa

Jennifer McAllister
University of Saskatchewan • Saskatoon, Saskatchewan, Canada

Wendy McCallum
Doctoral Conducting Associate
University of North Texas • Denton, Texas

Captain Keelan Edward McCamey
Deputy Commander, United States Air Force in Europe Band
Sembach, Germany

Robert Meunier
Director of Bands
Drake University • Des Moines, Iowa

Joseph P. Missal
Director of Bands
Oklahoma State University • Stillwater, Oklahoma

Linda R. Moorhouse
Associate Director of Bands
Louisiana State University • Baton Rouge, Louisiana

Richard Anthony Murphy
Middle Tennessee State University • Murfreesboro, Tennessee

Ryan Nelson
Doctoral Conducting Associate
University of North Texas • Denton, Texas

Paul Nickolas
Director of Bands
Sam Barlow High School • Gresham, Oregon

Doug Norton
Director of Bands
Batesville Community Schools • Batesville, Indiana

Craig T. Paré
Associate Professor of Music and Director of University Bands
DePauw University School of Music • Greencastle, Indiana

Douglas A. Peterson
Music Program Manager
Daytona Beach Community College • Daytona Beach, Florida

James Popejoy
Director of Bands
University of North Dakota • Grand Forks, North Dakota

Edwin C. Powell
Director of Bands
McLennan Community College • Waco, Texas

R. Mark Rogers
Director of Publications
Southern Music Company • San Antonio, Texas

Darin Schmidt
Director of Bands
Lakeview School District • Battle Creek, Michigan

Kevin L. Sedatole
Associate Director of Bands
University of Texas • Austin, Texas

Deborah A. Sheldon
Ester Boyer College of Music
Temple University • Philadelphia, Pennsylvania

Philip G. Simon
Doctoral Conducting Associate
University of North Texas • Denton, Texas

Frederick Speck
Director of Bands
University of Louisville • Louisville, Kentucky

Gary Speck
Professor of Conducting
Miami University • Oxford, Ohio

Mark J. Spede
University of Texas at Austin • Austin, Texas

Jack Stamp
Director of Band Studies
Indiana University of Pennsylvania • Indiana, Pennsylvania

Scott A. Stewart
Emory University • Atlanta, Georgia

William Stowman
Director of Bands
Messiah College • Grantham, Pennsylvania

Ibrook Tower
Instrumental Music Instructor
Milton Hershey School • Hershey, Pennsylvania
Wind Ensemble Director
Pennsylvania Academy of Music • Lancaster, Pennsylvania

Frank C. Tracz
Director of Bands
Kansas State University • Manhattan, Kansas

Bruce Yurko
Wind Ensemble Conductor
Cherry Hills High School East and West • Cherry Hill, New Jersey
Princeton University • Princeton, New Jersey

William K. Wakefield
Director of Bands
University of Oklahoma • Norman, Oklahoma

Jason Worzbyt
Assistant Professor of Bassoon and Conductor of Concert Band
Indiana University of Pennsylvania • Indiana, Pennsylvania

PART I

THE TEACHING OF MUSIC

CHAPTER 1

Teaching for Moments That Matter

Larry R. Blocher

"The important thing is not to stop questioning. "
··· Albert Einstein ···

Teaching and Learning in Music

Someone much wiser than me once said that teaching and learning are two sides of the same coin. As I begin my twenty-fifth year of teaching music, I could not agree more with this statement. (For the countless numbers of you who are saying, "He doesn't look that old"—thank you!) We are all teachers and students every day!

This introductory chapter will offer a brief look into my own ongoing experiences as a teacher/student. The ideas presented here (and many others) continue to be important to me and to my own development as a teacher/ conductor. As you are reading this chapter, think about your own teaching/ learning experiences. Make personal transfers where possible. Focus on the special teachers and students who make these opportunities possible for you.

Summer Experiences

Sometimes the summer offers special opportunities to be both a teacher and a student. I have always had a special place in my heart for music teachers who choose to become "formal" students in the summer. Now I realize that students participate in these summer opportunities for a variety of reasons: some students are working on an advanced music degree; some students need recertification credit; some students are attempting to recharge their professional batteries; some students need to get away from home; some students are trying to earn credit hours for a "bump" in pay (usually not a very big bump); some students are doing all of the above; and no doubt a few students simply wander into the wrong room and don't realize it until it's too late. Over the years, I have "been" all of these students.

One of the things I enjoy most about the professional part of the summer these days is the opportunity to offer a class/workshop, invite really good folks to teach with and for me, and watch these amazing teachers "do their stuff." In a sense, I get paid (not very much—there is a recurring theme here) to be a student without the worry of formal homework or a grade. This has been and continues to be a wonderful experience for me!

As I watch some of the best and brightest music teachers that I know interact with students at all levels, I am amazed that these outstanding music teachers/conductors—band directors who seem to have their individual teaching behaviors so together—have a personal interest in continuing to learn. They ask questions. They listen. They observe. They evaluate. They read. They research. They practice. They make informed choices. They become students so they can be better teachers.

IDEA #1:
It is what you learn after you know it all that matters.

Post-Summer Experiences

Like many other students, I usually finish the summer with a case of "information overload." During the summer academic season, I almost always fill several new yellow notepads with fresh "summer wisdom." Sometimes these new yellow notepads join growing piles of handouts, journal articles, books, and older yellow notepads that occupy special places in my office. I have an amazing collection of academic office "piles." No doubt at least some of these piles contain some great information. Sometimes I sort through the piles and prioritize them, making several smaller piles. Sometimes (especially when we have campus guests) I move the piles around and/or file them under the general heading of "getting ready to get ready to look at really soon." Much of the information in these files is suffering from what I call *permanent potential*.

Sometimes, however, I actually read through the latest summer collection before I pile/file it. Now while it generally takes me a while to sort/read through the information, it is this sorting/reading task that allows me to think about and process what I consider to be the most important ideas. These are the ideas that may have the potential for personal application. This activity of "processing" often helps me begin to think if there are specific ways to apply these ideas to my teaching…to make them my own. However, it is the actual application step—the transfer step—the step where I attempt to make the ideas "fit" the context of my own teaching situations by actually using them. That is the real test and many times the "payoff" for me.

IDEA#2:
Getting started may be the most important (and sometimes hardest) part of an activity.

Learning by Doing

At one point in my career as a student, I enrolled in what I thought was an introduction to computers class. I remember that for the first six weeks of the semester-long course, we learned *about* computers. We studied computer history. We read material on "bits" and "bytes." We took tests on how computers worked. We looked at pictures of lots of different computers. We became "experts" on the theory of computer technology. I remember thinking during this six weeks of computer "orientation" that all I wanted to do was turn on a computer—any computer (we had not seen a computer in class up to that point)—and have it "beep" at me just one time. As more and more time went by in the class, I found myself needing to do something that involved hands-on contact with a real computer. I simply wanted to do what people who use computers in the real world do with computers on a regular basis: use them in some meaningful way.

IDEA #3:
Many people may learn best by "doing."

Knowledge, Good Intentions, and Desire

Looking back on the computer class now, I have no doubt that the teacher of the class intended the class to be wonderful (I don't know any teacher who intentionally designs a class to be "awful," and this class was not awful.) I also have no doubt that the information we "learned" was important, especially for students who could use it then or who could look ahead and see opportunities when they might use it at some future point. Unfortunately, I was not one of those students. Therefore, the first six weeks of the class did not "function" for me as it was intended to function.

Perhaps I signed up for the wrong computer class. Perhaps I could have tried harder. At this point, it doesn't really matter. What does matter about the computer class experience for me is what I learned about my own learning (and later teaching) as a result of taking the class.

I realize now that although the computer teacher had lots of computer knowledge and good intentions, neither of those things was "enough." I also realize now that while I had a strong desire to learn to use a computer, at least in the beginning, that also was not enough. I now believe that the teacher of the computer class and I started the class in different "places," and we remained in different places for a number of weeks. Because we were not on the same "learning page," the "timing" of the information presented was not right for me. As a student, I wanted to *do* something with computers early on in my study (the "beep" mentioned earlier would have served as a powerful motivation for me to keep working). Additionally, the information seems to me to have been presented out of context. There was no direct in-class opportunity for me to apply/use what was being taught, and I wasn't "ready" to seek out this opportunity on my own (I never even thought about doing this). As a result, it did not take long for me to become bored with the class. The class didn't seem to fit my needs (after all, I wasn't a computer technology major). I just wanted to learn how to turn the computer on and off and then learn how to use the computer better. I did not understand the need to learn anything else.

Now I realize that most folks who are reading this chapter probably do not teach computer technology classes. However, I also believe that many of us who teach music through performance in band sometimes teach students who do not come to us with an automatic understanding of what skills and knowledge they need for practical music-making, or why they need to acquire them. As music teachers—band directors—we not only get to decide what our students need to know and be able to do to make music, but we also get to teach these ideas through performance.

IDEA #4:
Start where the students are, take them where you want them to be, help them understand why they need to be there, and show them where they might go next.

Deciding Where Students Need to Be

Deciding what is important and meaningful for students to learn through performance in band can be challenging, especially given performance demands. Robert Duke suggests that one way to decide what is important for our students is to *begin with the end in mind*. To understand what it means to begin with the end in mind, consider the following question:

IDEA #5:
What do we want our students to "look like" as accomplished learners at any educational level?

(Perhaps the answer will be based, at least in part, on your personal philosophy of music teaching.)

Depending on the "level" of our students, the amount of time we have to

teach, and our own individual philosophy, we could decide to help our students learn to perform with good tone, play in tune, play together with the notes in the right place, and/or perform musically. Additionally, within the context of actual music making (rehearsals), we could also teach our students "about" the music and music in general by including information about the composer, the composition, the music's form and style, and how to "listen" during performance so individual parts fit together to make music.

Our job as band directors—music teachers—would be much easier if our music students would learn all this music "stuff" on their own as a result of being in the band. Some students might. Most students, however, may not learn what we want them to learn without our specific direction. The following story makes this point:

> A young lady walks into a public library, strolls up to the circulation desk, and says, "I'd like a Big Mac, large fries, and a large Diet Coke." The librarian looks at the young lady and says, "Madam, this is a public library." The young woman, looking somewhat embarrassed, replies, "Oh, I'm sorry," and then whispers, "I'd like a Big Mac, large fries, and a large Diet Coke."

IDEA #6:
Some folks (students) just won't get the "it" that we want them to get without our planned efforts to help them get it.

The Band (Music) Curriculum

As music teachers/conductors, we can teach all of the musical concepts listed previously, some of the concepts listed, or none of the concepts listed. We get to decide. If we decide that our students as accomplished learners should be able to play *"in tune,"* appropriate to their level of performance, then our teaching techniques in our rehearsals will need to include opportunities for students to become aware of what playing in tune means. Additionally, we will need to help them understand how to play in tune and provide opportunities for them to practice playing "in tune" on a regular basis. Likewise, if we want our students to learn about *form* in music, then once again our teaching strategies in our music rehearsals must include opportunities for students to become aware of, understand, and apply ideas taught/learned about the concept of form. This process would be the same for any concept.

IDEA#7:
Teach for student awareness, understanding, and application.

At this point you may want to stand up, stretch, and take a few deep breaths (we have been at this for a while). If education jargon tends to make you a little drowsy, you may want to read on with caution (unless you need the rest). However, please read on, because if we want to be regarded as an academic discipline in the schools, then we must deal with at least a little jargon.

The "big ideas" that we decide to teach and reinforce over time could be looked at as the beginning of a band curriculum. For me, the term *curriculum* indicates that these big ideas have been organized in some way. A curriculum, then, is a planned sequence of big ideas. One way to start the process of curriculum development is to begin with the end in mind. Begin with what you think an accomplished learner should know and be able to do (think about real students in your program when possible). Start from the "end" and work backwards. If you are unsure of what an accomplished learner should "look like," you could ask your colleagues, observe excellent programs, and/or read, research, and evaluate in order to make informed decisions. In other words, *you could become a student in order to be a better teacher.*

Once you have an idea of what you want your students to know and be able to do (the end result), you can begin the process of organizing learning objectives into learning sequences designed to help students become accomplished learners over the time you have with them. In designing these sequences, you might want to consider this concert, this semester, this year, next year, and even the next four years of band. You could organize your learning sequences around selected elements of music, styles of music, historical periods of music, the National Standards, or any combination of the above. As you develop your objectives and learning sequences, keep in mind where your students "are" with regard to their skill and knowledge levels. (For a detailed discussion of ways to organize a band curriculum, see Volume 1 of *Teaching Music through Performance in Band*, Chapter 7, written by Richard Miles.)

Your objectives and learning sequences should help you select the band literature you will perform and/or study, because many of the concepts you will teach will come from the music. The literature you choose will become your textbooks for band. The literature you select will also provide a basis for assessment tasks that will lead to evaluation

IDEA #8:
What you teach will come, in large part, from the music you select to rehearse/perform.

What Good Teachers Do

At the 1999 MENC National Biennial In-Service Conference, Jane Cassidy outlined what good teachers do as identified in our music research literature. According to Jane and her research overview, good teachers:

1. Give/provide accurate information;
2. Have an effective delivery system; and
3. Have an effective system of classroom management.

Jane was careful to point out that if any one of these three ideas was missing, the teacher might not be as effective. She also suggested that good teachers:

*   Avoid extra "stuff" in their teaching that would cause student "off task" behavior;
*   Provide enough information for student success;
*   Are not unnecessarily redundant;
*   Present information clearly;
*   Avoid inappropriate movements or behaviors that would distract;
*   Practice engaging behaviors such as enthusiasm, eye contact, movement around the room;
*   Include variety in their teaching;
*   Have routines and rules that are commonly understood;
*   Use contingent academic and social praise; and
*   Make forward progress with little transition time.

IDEA #9:
Good teaching rarely happens by chance alone.

Providing Accurate Information

If the band literature we select for rehearsal and/or performance serves as our textbooks, then it would seem important to have a thorough understanding of what is in each text (music selection) before attempting to teach music using it (provide accurate information). Of course, *score study* is a method that many band directors use to acquire a thorough understanding of the music. There are many wonderful approaches to the score study process. Ultimately, however, score study is a personal process that requires the development of a "system" that works for each individual.

Some band directors go through a period of "orientation" as part of score study; some do not. I use this part of score study as a "look for" time. This is a time following my decision to rehearse/perform the music. At this point, I have already determined that the selection fits my ensemble and my educational goals for the ensemble. During this time, I look for practical information that comes from the music: title page, composer, dedication/commission, instrumentation, key signature/key changes, range demands, dynamic indications, melodic roles, rhythmic demands, technical demands, solo/chamber/ *tutti* sections, and structure/form (what is the same and what is different as I work through the piece). I will highlight key signatures, meter changes, tempo markings, and musical indicators at this point with a marker. Some band directors listen to recordings of the music at this time; some do not. I try to find a number of good recordings of the selection, and I listen to them throughout my score study. For me, this is a way to get the overall sound of the music "in my head," not a way to learn how the music goes. It is an important part of my score study process.

The orientation phase of score study can be followed by a more detailed analysis of the music. I use this time to discover who does what, where, when, and why. I borrowed this idea from Maud Hickey, who presented a session on rehearsal planning at the Midwest a few years ago. She suggested that one approach to planning would be to do what the composer did. I made the connection to score study and began this music detective approach.

At this point, I generally mark important entrances, cues, instruments that play a similar role, and anything else that I feel will help me to be a more effective teacher/conductor. I am aware that many conductors do not put any markings in the score. I have no problem with this. I mark what I need to mark. I have a wonderful colleague, Victor Markovich, whose scores are marked in such detail and with so many colors that they could qualify as works of art. Vic sometimes takes some good-natured kidding from guest conductors on our campus when they see his colorful scores. I have asked Vic on many occasions why he marks his scores in this way. His answer is always the same: "I mark what I need to mark to be an effective conductor/teacher." Vic is an effective conductor/teacher. He has found a system that works for him.

I try to find formal analyses of the pieces that we are studying in my band, and I compare these analyses with my own. I use dissertations, master's theses, articles from journals, units from Garofalo and the *Teaching Music* series when available, and Vic's scores (many of which are now in my office—just kidding, Vic). Remember that I want to give my students the best and most accurate "information" possible. This is a major goal of my score study.

The above steps in the score study process help me make the piece my own. Many times, due to performance demands and time limitations, I do not have all the pieces to the musical puzzle in place before the first few rehearsals. This does not mean that I learn the score on the podium. Sometimes, reading

the piece with the band will help me clarify ideas I am considering in my score study. For me, score study is an ongoing process.

IDEA #10:
Good teachers provide accurate information.

An Effective Delivery System

Like score study, rehearsal techniques (delivery systems) are also personal; one size does not fit all. Eugene Corporon says that students should not come to rehearsal to learn their own parts. They should come to rehearsal to learn everyone else's part. I have often thought that as the conductor, I am the luckiest person in the rehearsal hall because I have a full score containing all of the individual parts. This allows me to see and hear what should be going on in the music—a total picture. Students must learn to listen to see how their individual part fits the whole musical picture. If we decide that we want our students to become intelligent listeners as a result of their time in band, then once again we must provide opportunities for students to become aware of how to listen, understand what to listen for, and practice "good listening" in the context of rehearsal. Borrowing an idea from the score study process, we could structure our rehearsals so students are given opportunities to figure out who does what, where, when, and why through listening. I call this *being aware of their musical role.*

Of course, students must be able to play their parts with a good sound, in tune, together with other parts, with right notes in place, and musically. Additionally, students may need information about the music as well: composer, composition, form…the list seems almost endless. Maintaining a careful balance between skills and knowledge seems important. In every rehearsal, there is an important relationship between teacher values and techniques. For every idea that a teacher/conductor believes is important (values), there are a number of ways (techniques) to help students get the information.

IDEA #11:
What the teacher/conductor does in each rehearsal is what the students get.

It seems important to look inside actual band rehearsals to see what band directors do in rehearsals (Volume 3, Chapter 1, of *Teaching Music through Performance in Band* contains detailed analyses of what band directors do in rehearsals). What follows are short transcriptions of two high school band directors in actual rehearsals. As you follow what happens in each rehearsal, try to imagine yourself as a student in each rehearsal.

Rehearsal #1

(The band director is speaking)

— Make sure you rest six counts before you start to play. Only *mezzo forte*. (band plays, short)

— (director) Stop! Horns down please. May I hear measures 38, 39, and 40, please? Clarinets and anyone who has 1a2&1&2. First note. Breathe. (group plays one measure)

— (director) Thank you to the person who just played B-natural. Somebody played B-natural instead of B-flat (group plays the measure again)

— (director stops the group and sings) doo da, ready and (group plays)

— (director stops the group and sings) doo da, again and (group plays)

— (director stops the group and says) Okay, good! Horns down. Second and third clarinets play your low A (gives the beat and students play). B-natural. B-flat. Sorry. (Gives second beat and students play). Now, 1&2 ready &. (clarinets play, director stops them shortly after they begin)

— (director) Now there is a *decrescendo* underneath that. Now you start loud and get softer. Ready and (clarinets play that measure)

— (director) Again and (clarinets play the same measure)

— (director) Sit up, please. Everyone who has the 1&2 at measure 40. Ready and (group plays, short)

— (director) Flutes you're not tuning! It's sounding very badly out of tune. I'm not going down individually to tune it. You fix it! Ready and (group plays, short)

— (director) OK, everybody, 37. Trumpets are nice. That's a good balanced sound. Make sure that when you get to the harmony you break it up evenly. Firsts soft, seconds a little louder, and thirds even louder. 37, 1&2, 37 and (group plays)

— (director) Stop! Wrong note in the flutes. Someone played an A-natural instead of A-flat. 1&2 ready breathe (group plays, short)

— (director) Stop! Horns down please. Could you please put a *crescendo* in measure 42? Take your pencils out and put a *crescendo* in measure 42. 37, ready, 37…Hope you have pencils. Hope you have pencils. 37, watch E-naturals in trombones, watch E-naturals. Flutes, you are all right now, you are all on A-flat. 37, 1&2, 37 and (group plays, short)

— (director) No! Stop! Horns down. That was not good! That was not good! That was overblown by all the flutes. 37, 1&2, 37 and (group plays, short)

— (director) Horns down please. Baritone, 1&2, 45 and (baritone plays, short)

— (director) Come on, Michael! Ready and (baritone plays while director counts)

— (director) Stop! Haven't worked on it enough. Correct? Gotta work on it. I want it perfect, nothing less than perfect by tomorrow.

(tape ends)

Rehearsal #2

(The director is speaking)

— Okay! That's the idea! Second trumpets, play your first note. It's C-sharp. Make sure I can hear just one voice instead of individuals. Ready. (trumpets play C-sharp)

— (director) Bravo! Next note (trumpets play the next note)

— (director) Great job! We're almost all of the way done. Now when we get to the rhythm dee da du du da, I hear a nice second trumpet player do this: la la la la la. Look up here. Remember this from yesterday? Dee da du du da. Again. I like your sound, and it's even better when you play all the notes. Ready (trumpets play)

— (director) Bravo! Great! You've got that rhythm pretty well. What a neat chord change at 144. Here we go. Baritone and horns, you guys have a great moment there! The trumpets are talking, "I'd like to sing this song." "Yeah, me too!" Okay? That's how important that is. You're part of the conversation. Ready (group plays)

— (director) Good! Low brass get ready to play at 144. Folks, look at two before 144. How many eighth notes does a quarter note get? If you were going to subdivide, your heart would go (demonstrates). How many eighth notes does the next note get? So your heart would go (demonstrates). And the next note? Sing and pat that with me (students sing and pat rhythm)

— (director) Now finger it. Don't blow (students do as instructed)

— (director) Play it. Ready, go (group plays)

— (director) Good! Now let's give it some energy, some separation and some style (group plays)

— (director) Yes, yes, yes, yes! Bravo, Bravo, Bravo. Thanks! Everybody at 144. Folks the style is better here and the notes (group plays)

— (director) Low brass look at the board. Remember to keep your foot on the gas all the way through the note. I'm hearing 55 miles an hour 30. 55 miles an hour 30. 55...56...56...57...Instead of growing, I'm hearing decay. Get physical with it. Hold on to the

note. Woodwinds, act like you are flirting with a male or a female. Flutter your eyelids really fast. Ready, go. Ever had butterfly kiss-es? Anybody who has ever had butterfly kisses knows how light and gentle those are, and how fast they are. That's how light and gentle those should be. Just float across the trills. Just float. A fast float, a hummingbird float. Here we go trombones. The strength is in the separation. Got it? 144 (group plays)
(tape ends)

If you had been a music student in each band, what would you have liked/disliked about each rehearsal? What opportunities would you have had to "learn music" through performance? How would you have felt at the end of each rehearsal segment? Now videotape and analyze your own rehearsals. Ask yourself the same questions as you review yourself in rehearsal.

IDEA #12:
An effective delivery system includes a variety of effective rehearsal techniques that are directly related to teacher values.

Teaching for Moments That Matter

Over the last several months, I have been looking at ways to make exercise a daily activity. For a long time, I was convinced that walking on a treadmill was the best and only exercise that would work for me. Not too long ago, I hit a plateau in my exercise program. My daily routine had become boring and less effective. I found myself spending more and more time on the treadmill and enjoying it less. I decided to try other exercise equipment. I began reading about exercise and watching other folks who seemed to be successful. One specific method suggested working for moments that matter during exercise. The moments that matter concept involved getting more payoff for exercise in less time by making the most of the time used.

More payoff by making the most of the time used—the transfer to teach-ing/learning in music is direct. We all may want a variety of different things for the music students in our bands. Ultimately, however, we want to help our students acquire the "tools" to be able to function as independent music learners who are capable of "doing music" on their own, without us. The challenge to teach for *moments that matter* in our band rehearsals continues for all of us.

CHAPTER 2

Making a Difference
with Your Dash

Ray E. Cramer

The word "dash" has many meanings and connotations. It can be constructive or destructive. Positive definitions include such words as *speed, drive, spice, swell, energy, spirit, gift,* and *élan* (which means *exuberance, ardor,* or *enthusiasm*). Negative definitions would include words like *bolt, hurl, pelt, ruin, slam, crush, fling, spurn, throw, collide,* or *hurdle*. The title of this chapter and the use of the word 'dash' also have a duel meaning. In addition to the above definitions, it also relates to a punctuation mark indicating a break. In the following pages, I wish to discuss "dash" as it covers the positive and negative implications in day-to-day living and "dash" as it represents the time line of our lives.

Every day we all face responsibilities requiring decisions that may be as far-reaching as choosing a life partner or as simple as to what to wear to work. The fact remains that as we make these decisions, factors come into play that can impact our lives in ways that seem simple and practical on the surface, but when combined with other obligations can create unbelievable stress. That is why it is so important to "see the big picture" as we are so often told. It is an easy statement to make but one that takes a great deal of thought and creative vision. The younger we are, the more difficult the task to be able to recognize who we are and what our role is going to be in life. As we gain experience and confidence in our chosen field, we begin to formulate goals and expectations of what can be attained during a career. As these elements of your life begin to fall into place, other areas will assume new responsibilities, which will ultimately change how you deal with time commitments throughout your working life.

All of us would like a crystal ball to show how our life will unfold. We want to know how important we will be to our family, friends, students, colleagues and, of course, ourselves. However, that is only fantasy, for we all must live life day by day. We need to remember that the important thing is to each day *make a difference in someone's life*.

How Do You Live Your Dash

I read of a man who stood to speak
At the funeral of a friend.
He referred to the dates on her tombstone
From the beginning...to the end.
He noted that first came her date of birth
And spoke the following date with tears,
But said what mattered most of all
Was the dash between those years.

For that dash represents all the time
That she spent alive on earth...
And now only those who loved her
Know what that little line is worth.
For it matters not, how much we own;
The cars...the house...the cash.
What matters is how we live and love
And how we spend our dash.

So think about this long and hard...
Are there things you'd like to change?
For you never know how much time is left
That can still be rearranged.
If we could just slow down enough
To consider what's true and real,
And always try to understand
The way other people feel.

And be less quick to anger,
And show appreciation more
And love the people in our lives
Like we've never loved before.
If we treat each other with respect,
And more often wear a smile...
Remembering that this special dash
Might only last a while.

So when your eulogy's being read
With your life's actions to rehash...
Would you be proud of the things they say
About how you spent your dash?

—Author unknown

Family Obligations

In a lecture early in my teaching career, a speaker said, "Don't major in the minors." This was a catchy and clever statement meant to elicit a chuckle from those listening. However, as I began to assume more responsibilities, the phrase took on a whole new meaning. I fully understand that there are many different kinds of family responsibilities. Some of you are single, some married, and others married with children. Regardless of your personal situation, family obligations, in any form, are part of your daily routine.

The life of a band director, as you well know, can become all-consuming if you let it. What you must do is establish priorities that will allow you to function in a manner conducive to a stable and effective home life and to being an effective teacher. It is possible! Yes, it takes work and cooperation, but more importantly is the decision to *make it work*.

If you are married with family obligations, then you will experience the wide-ranging demands placed on you by your employer and your family. It is quite easy to become so engulfed in your job that everything else becomes less important. Of course, this can be devastating to your marriage and family. Your family obligations demand as much work and energy as your job to be successful.

Your wife or husband, along with your children, needs to connect with you each day. I personally believe you cannot be effective in your job without a strong and loving home environment. As your children grow up, their requirements change, and with that comes serious decision-making on your part.

Our children are now grown, married, and have careers of their own, but I clearly remember their middle and high school years. They became quite involved in music and sports events, which involved a lot of weekend activities. I was very involved in weekend work myself with professional obligations I felt important to my developing career. I realized my children were only going to be in the house for a limited number of years before they went to college and on to their own careers. If I wanted to truly invest in their lives, then I had to decide which weekend events were the most important to attend.

My teaching career would extend well past the school-age years of my children, so for me the decision was easy to make. I wanted to be able to attend as many of their functions as possible, knowing full well that if I did not, many special moments would only be afforded me vicariously through my wife or related to me secondhand by my children. Even with all the fantastic audio and video equipment available today, none of those recorded events would have the same impact as my being there. Therefore, I wrote my children's events into my calendar first, thus avoiding the temptation to accept professional engagements that would mean missing any event in which my children were involved. While I fully understood I would miss many professional engagements, I was never sorry for being present at our children's activities. Later, they both expressed how much they appreciated our support, interest, and presence at these events during their school years.

Setting Priorities

What it boils down to is setting priorities that you know and believe will make a difference in the lives of your spouse, children, or other family members. It is a little frightening to think what I would have missed had I not decided to become immersed in my family life rather than become someone who only showed up to eat, sleep, or occasionally engage in some form of conversation. Please do not misunderstand me; there are times when job requirements unavoidably demand our undivided attention and energy. However, when you are with your family, make the time you share quality time. Give them your full attention and support. The *quality* of time spent with your family is more important than the *amount* of time...that means give them your undivided attention. If you are lounging in your favorite chair reading the paper or watching TV while your children attempt to get your attention, then even though you are in the same room, you are not making a connection.

Role Models

Perhaps you did not grow up in a home where family life was a top priority. Then it is very important that you identify role models who do place this kind of priority in their lives. My wife and I were fortunate to grow up in homes with parents who were supportive and interested in what we were doing during our school years. There were times, I am sure, when we felt like our parents were being too involved by not allowing our participation in some of the "fun" things we felt our friends were being allowed to do. But in retrospect, we know our parents only had our best interest at heart and wanted to protect us from those things that would be damaging to our personal well being.

Only through love and trust does this kind of connection develop within the family. Love is an ingredient that contains such power and inspiration that lives can be transformed in a way unparalleled by any other emotion. A home without love is a home likely destined for pain, stress, conflict and, usually, failure. I am saddened by the number of fractured lives created by a home environment devoid of love. For as Paul says in I Corinthians:

If I speak in the tongues of men and of angels, but have not love, I am only a resounding gong or a clanging cymbal. Love is patient, love is kind. It does not envy, it does not boast, it is not proud. It is not rude, it is not self-seeking, it is not easily angered, it keeps no record of wrongs. It always protects, always trusts, always hopes, always perseveres. And now these three things remain: faith, hope, and love. But the greatest of these is love.

Probably most of us have former teachers to thank for exciting and motivating us to seek a similar career. What was it about this person who turned us on so we just had to pursue a similar field of endeavor to find personal happiness and satisfaction? Perhaps we saw fame, fortune, glory, prestige, honor, or other attractive benefits that we felt only would come through a similar experience for ourselves. All of these could be a factor, but I can assure you it usually is not fortune. I know of few people in our profession who have become rich, but then again, being rich is relative, and personally speaking, the experiences I have had in teaching far outweigh the monetary rewards I may have missed by not being in a more lucrative profession.

So what did these people have in common that we all wanted to emulate? Assuredly, all included several of the following: enthusiasm about their work and profession, energy, vision, creativeness, passion, desire to share thoughts and feelings, knowledge of subject, sensitivity, positive attitudes, the ability to bring others into the glow of music-making. Most teachers I have known over the years want nothing more than to try to inspire in students their love for music. If you are lucky, perhaps you have had contact with one or more of these teachers during your school years. When this occurs, then you are never the same. We are so moved by the magnetism of these special people that our lives are changed in dramatic and positive ways forever. I can think of no greater way to say thank you to a former teacher who influenced your life than doing your best to become one yourself.

For us to be able to accomplish our goals, we have to make sure we do those things that will allow us to establish positive relationships on a daily basis with our families and with other people. This, of course, involves making correct decisions—decisions that influence how others perceive our existence.

1: Don't be a "loner"!

Most successful people in any profession grow in effectiveness by involving others in their work. If we become self-absorbed, we begin to think that our way is the only way. We are then on the path to ineffective work. Those around us strengthen us in a sharing, collaborative effort that benefits all concerned.

2: Don't try to be someone you are not!

Young students—and people in general—are quite perceptive when it comes to "seeing who we really are." Our society tends to place a high priority on helping individuals become someone they are not. Too often young people are sold a bill of goods, being told they are not good enough, smart enough, pretty or handsome enough to become "popular." All sorts of mechanisms are devised to "assist" them in establishing a different image. Adults are very good at this also. Why is it that who or what we are is not good enough? Who makes those distinctions? Certainly our culture and the media, in all forms, help to create these doubts in our minds. Our most effective manner of establishing good relationships with people is to be ourselves. Be real! We are who we are, and to try and make ourselves into something or someone else only compounds the problems involved in building strong personal relationships.

3: There are no shortcuts!

We see all the time in advertising how important it is to have something now. My wife and I have discussed on several occasions how it seems the younger generation has this fixation on having to have everything now. It is made so easy for us with time payments, long-term loans, or no money down—the pay-later syndrome. This is fine, but in the end we all have to pay, and if we cannot, then we lose all of those things we felt were so important. Most tasks or goals will take time and effort to come to successful conclusions. Patience is a wonderful thing, for with it comes the pleasure of expectation, anticipation, and realization. Don't try to hurry the process, for usually the result is far less satisfying than if we just exercised patience.

4: Avoid the lingering feeling of contentedness!

During any period of our lives, we can quickly become complacent if we fall into a pattern of familiarity and routine. Nothing ever stays the same. So we must be flexible enough to identify those things in our work and daily routine that inhibit our growth and effectiveness. Most people are afraid of change because it represents the unknown or unfamiliar. However, truly outstanding educators establish their effectiveness with their ability to change and their creativity. One of my favorite quotes of the late Will Rogers simply states, "Even if you are on the right track, you'll still get run over if you just sit there." So don't fear change; it can be the vehicle to even greater rewards as we press forward in our teaching career.

Professional Responsibilities

Most people are constantly searching for the perfect job, which means all the pegs in the right holes and the wrinkles carefully ironed out. As a colleague of mine once said, "There is no Mecca" (referring to finding the perfect job). Every job, regardless of the level, has drawbacks and flaws that, on first inspection, may be hidden from view. Only when we are on the job do we find the imperfections. The immediate question, of course, is how to deal with those problems. Usually what one discovers is that most of the difficulties can be overcome with thorough planning and a cooperative attitude. If, over a period of time, it is impossible to solve or remedy the difficulties, then a decision must be made regarding professional goals and the ability to achieve them in this situation.

When considering a job, make sure to find out as much about the responsibilities as humanly possible. That may mean investigating the job beyond the publicized listing. The important element is that you feel your strengths and abilities match those expected by the employer. A team of oxen only works together if they are equally yoked.

As you become more and more involved in the music field, you soon discover how easy it is to become inflicted with the "of course I will do it" disease. This can cause all sorts of pain and strain. There are certainly activities and responsibilities that we want to and must become involved with professionally. However, when the activities outside your regular job become too consuming of time and energy, then it is time to re-evaluate your professional obligations. It is important to be involved in the profession, but not at the expense of job and family stability.

Stress Management

The amount of money spent dealing with stress-related issues in our society today is truly astounding. Stress creates such damage to our health that we need to do everything in our power to alleviate its harmful effects. Just what is stress? People have differing views and opinions on this topic ranging from simple to complex answers. The dictionary defines stress as "a strain or straining force, mental or physical tension, a reaction to resisting such a force." Throughout time, human beings have learned to defend themselves against all kinds of stress assaults. These "assaults" create changes that may include increased heart rate, blood pressure, rate of breathing, muscular tension, and general metabolic rate. It is important to identify the stress in our life and decide if that stress is excessive. If it is, we must learn how to reduce the rate of "wear and tear" being experienced by decreasing the load being carried or increase our ability to carry it. We often need to do both.

How do you handle stress? In general, most people find their own best method to deal with stressful situations. However, some people either do not realize what is causing stress in their life or do not understand the symptoms. Do any of the following questions pertain to how you feel or what you do to deal with stress?

- Is it hard for you to unwind during your free time?
- Do you need a drink or tranquilizer to relax?
- If you're upset about something, do you find that your thoughts race through your mind so you can't sleep?
- When tense or anxious, do you feel the need to smoke or eat?
- Do you often get so worried that you have indigestion, diarrhea, or nausea?
- Are there people or situations in life that make you feel uptight just by thinking about them?
- Do you feel that you're always racing against the clock?

If you answered yes to one or more of these questions, then you ought to think about making some changes in your lifestyle to deal with the situation and your stress level. I will discuss practical ways to help release stress levels and improve your overall health.

Time Management

Work! Work! Work! Go! Go! Go! Hurry! Hurry! Hurry! Does this sound familiar? How many people do you know that remind you of a dog chasing his tail? Round and round they go, and in the end, what did they accomplish? I believe that some people can exist only if they are constantly busy. Perhaps frantic is a better description of their routine. They believe that unless they live a life in frenzy they must be wasting their time. Hurry becomes a way of life. I often get tired just thinking about the hectic pace that some people seem to enjoy. Or do they really? Perhaps the important question is what are they accomplishing? Some folks just have to be busy, because if they're not, then they must be lazy. If you are anything like me, I become uncomfortable around such people. Often, busy people are not accomplishing nearly as much as the illusion they create. All that seems to be accomplished is physical and mental fatigue. After all, if people are not worn to a frazzle, they must not be dedicated to their profession. I do not think we are called to live like this and still be effective in our work and personal relationships. The world would have us believe that being busy, fatigued, and stressed out is a normal lifestyle. Tim Hansel in his book *When I Relax I Feel Guilty* puts it well:

We are called to be faithful, not frantic. If we are to meet the challenges of today, there must be integrity between our words and our lives, and more reliance on the source of our purpose.

We live in a workaholic society. There never seems to be enough time to do the things we really desire to do. We are too busy living as fast as we can. Studies show that the average American household works many more hours per week than twenty years ago. Advanced technology has not helped in this matter; it has only added to the problem. We need to make sure we maintain control of how we use our time. I have taken an excerpt from a poem I read in the monthly publication *Guidepost*, which made great sense to me and maybe to you also.

"Take Time..."

Take time for friends...they are the source of happiness.
Take time for work...it is the price of success.
Take time to think...it is the source of power.
Take time to read...it is the foundation of knowledge.
Take time to laugh...it is the singing that helps with life's loads.
Take time to love...it is the one sacrament of life.
Take time to play...it is the secret of youth.

—Author Unknown

Some people are blessed with more energy than others. I happen to be a person who has always enjoyed the ability to sustain a high energy level for prolonged periods of time. However, that does not mean I do not enjoy those times of quiet relaxation. I also know people who cannot relax anytime, even while on vacation. None of us wish to experience the displeasure of a personal power failure. However, without adequate time to refresh and rejuvenate, we soon begin to fade in the stress of day-to-day existence. What "refills" your tank? I will later share a few ideas for maintaining one's energy and physical stamina.

Our constant battle is that of balancing personal and professional commitments. It is a difficult task. Unfortunately, our society usually recognizes success only as it pertains to our work. However, be aware that any habit or activity that promises short-term satisfaction can be costly in the long run, as we all too often trade the things that are most important for those that are least important. Define early in your career what is important. Make lists with professional goals on one side and personal relationship goals on the other. If one side or the other becomes unbalanced, then you should probably take careful stock of what is going to be the dominant priority in your life. This takes constant personal evaluation and examination. Now just to make certain we understand each other, it is important to work and work hard. We

are expected to work and to be productive. However, this should not be at the expense of maintaining a healthy lifestyle.

To gain another perspective on this subject, I would like to refer to a couple of paragraphs taken from a book titled *Your Work Matters to God*, by Doug Sherman and William Hendricks. They are discussing Rocky Balboa, who as a fighter embodies the careerist vision and articulates its ultimate slogan: "Go for it!" The "it" means what? A boxing championship? Lasting fifteen rounds, "going the distance"? The adulation of an adoring public? Defiance—a refusal to "throw" the fight? All this and more for Rocky. His battle, like ours, is to authenticate himself: "It" means whatever it takes to make certain that "self" really does matter. "It" requires determination ("There are many starters, but few finishers"), discipline ("Creativity is two percent inspiration and ninety-eight percent perspiration"), the right goals ("If you aim at nothing, you'll hit it every time"), savvy ("Success in life comes not from holding a good hand, but in playing a poor hand well"), perseverance ("Tough times never last; tough people do"), and vision ("Some people dream dreams and ask, Why? I dream dreams and ask, Why not?"). There is no end to the qualities that supposedly account for success. But all of them reflect human power to somehow "go for it" and get the job done: "Our rewards in life will depend on the quality of the contributions we make."

Developing a Healthful Lifestyle

To achieve positive results in work and life, we must discipline ourselves to develop minds and bodies that will be able to carry out the responsibilities required of our jobs and our families. Without planning and prioritizing these elements of our lives, then we are nothing more than a vessel without a GPS to guide us—of course, I am talking about a Global Positioning System. Aircraft and ships have enjoyed this technology for years, but now we are finding this guidance system in every kind of vehicle. I am amused by watching this system in cars as the system guides you through the most distressing array of streets in the most crowded cities. If you begin to make a wrong turn, a voice will tell you not to turn just yet and to please wait for further instruction. Perhaps as educators we need such a device we can strap on our backs that can tell us when we should say no, yes, right, left, up, down, or give other helpful hints to avoid the traffic jam of over-commitment.

For me, it is important to respect and rely on my faith to guide my decisions. This is my GPS, and it does not require batteries or any other contrived power source. Also, all my life I have tried to stay in good physical condition. It takes time and a consistent effort to maintain a relatively healthy conditioning routine. The effort is well worth the result in how I feel on a day-to-day basis. There are many exercise routines you may choose to fol-

low to assist in keeping you on a regular routine. The one I have used for over thirty years takes little time and does a marvelous job in maintaining fitness and muscle tone. It is the exercise manual developed for the Royal Canadian Air Force. These exercises can be completed in twelve minutes for women and eleven minutes for men. They are simple to do and progress at a rate through charts from 1 (being the easiest) to 6 (usually for advanced athletes only). I believe in this exercise program wholeheartedly. Here are a few passages taken directly from this exercise manual.

Why should you be concerned about physical fitness?

Mechanization, automation, and work-saving devices to make life easy are depriving us of desirable physical activity. As a result, we are in danger of deteriorating physically.

Here are the pertinent facts.

Muscles, unless adequately exercised or used, will become weak and inefficient. Let's look at some of the evidence, which shows why regular vigorous exercise is so essential to physical well-being.

Weak back muscles are associated, in many cases, with lower back pain. It has been estimated that increasing the strength of the back muscles through exercise may eliminate 90 percent of these backaches.

A bulging, sagging abdomen resulting from weakened abdominal muscles is detrimental to good posture.

The efficiency and capacity of your heart, lungs, and other organs can be improved by regular vigorous exercise.

A fit person is less susceptible to common injuries, and, if injured, recovers more rapidly.

The incidence of degenerative heart diseases may be greater in those who have not followed a physically active life.

Regular vigorous exercise plays an important role in controlling your weight.

You are never too old to begin and follow a regular exercise program.

Why You Should Be Fit

Research has shown that:

- The physically fit person is able to withstand fatigue for longer periods than the unfit;

- The physically fit person is better equipped to tolerate physical stress;

- The physically fit person has a stronger and more efficient heart; and

- There is a relationship between good mental alertness, absence of nervous tension (stress), and physical fitness. Physical fitness makes us work better, look better, and feel better.

As I stated earlier, in addition to good physical health through exercise, there are other equally effective ways to relieve stress in our lives. Hobbies and recreational activities can be important in stress management. They take your mind off your worries and give you outlets for your energy. Make a list of the stresses in your life. Cross out the ones out of your control and let go of them. If they are out of your control, don't waste energy on them. Do what you can to reduce the stress in the items left. Here are some additional suggestions to help you reduce the stress levels in your life.

1. Adjust your attitudes and goals. Decide that you're not going to let unimportant things or situations beyond your control bother you. Set realistic short-term and long-term goals. Discuss these goals with others you trust to see if they agree that your goals are realistic and obtainable.

2. Rehearse stressful situations. Visualizing a situation might help you to organize your time, identify what you want, and reduce your anxiety. Even if the situation goes differently than the way you rehearsed, you will be more relaxed about it.

3. Avoid stressful situations. When possible, avoid situations that are likely to make you tense or uptight.

4. Manage your time carefully. Use a planning book, a two- or three-year calendar, or other popular electronic devices to help organize your schedule.

5. Make a "to do" list of the things you want to accomplish everyday.

6. If you are on a tight schedule, allow time for unexpected problems, phone calls, student consultations, and e-mail.

Sometimes the best way to reduce stress is to take a short walk and listen to the wonderful sounds being produced in the great outdoors. In fact, my wife and I find walking one of the very best exercises to keep in shape, release stress, allow for meaningful conversation, and keep life in perspective.

To conclude this section on stress and physical well-being, I would like to quote a few statements from the book *Is It Worth Dying For?*, by Robert B. Eliot, M.D., and Dennis L. Breo. I quote:

Follow your feelings. If you are dissatisfied or want to improve your situation, recognizing that is the first step toward understanding what you do want and moving toward a new goal.

Visualize the future. Dream a little; see yourself where you would like to be (but be realistic, don't make it an impossible dream). Think about what you would like to have written on your tombstone. Define attainable goals, the kind that are achievable and realistic but still require you to stretch. As the poet Robert Browning said, "A man's reach should exceed his grasp." But be practical enough that you can take hold of something.

Concentrate on the few key areas that are most important to you. Don't undermine your efforts by trying to be all things to all people at all times.

In retrospect, look to where you have been to determine your strengths and weaknesses.

Use your time wisely. Make a thorough study of how you spend your time and ruthlessly eliminate the things that you need not be doing. Remember, though, time spent doing "nothing" is often time well spent.

Learn how to delegate. Consider the value of this motto: "Much can be accomplished if you don't care who gets the credit."

Simplify, simplify, simplify. Thoreau said it, "Our lives are too often mired in detail." More true today than in his time. Less really is more.

Take time to plan. Set aside one week or more a year to assess where you've been where you'd like to go, and how you're going to get there.

Conclusion

All of us want to be the best we can be in whatever we do. This is a wonderfully positive attitude and goal. Here are a few other areas that will help us expand our effectiveness as teachers, conductors, fathers, mothers, brothers, and sisters.

Broaden your vision.

It is so easy to become burdened with tunnel vision. We must see around us in all directions. When I was taking flying lessons many years ago, one of my least favorite requirements was to practice flying the aircraft and executing various maneuvers "under the hood." This was a device the instructor placed over your head, which allowed you to only see the instrument panel. The purpose of this exercise was to develop confidence and trust in flying the plane based only on what the instruments were telling me to do. Without the ability to see the horizon, I often felt like the plane was doing something other than what the instruments were reading. My instructor said I was "flying by the seat of your pants." I often found myself "correcting" a problem that did not exist. Of course, when I made a correcting maneuver, then a real problem was created. How often do we do this in real-life situations? We perceive many things incorrectly "flying by the seat of our pants" and only create a more troubling situation by overcorrecting. Trust those things that you have grown to rely on and found to be steady and true. Those tried-and-tested instruments of sensitive communication will keep you flying straight, level.

Involve yourself in as many multi-cultural experiences as you can.

When we see, experience, and understand other cultures, there is renewal, vitality, and freshness in our teaching and music that stretches us to new levels of understanding and competence. Our own personal experience of working with our friends in Japan has brought about a new sensitivity in communicating and expressing thoughts and ideas.

Establish friendships "outside the field."

In each location we have lived, we have worked diligently to develop friendships with people from every walk of life. You get an entirely different perspective on your work by sharing your life with people who have nothing to do with your profession. I have grown personally by observing and understanding the vision and perspective of others.

View the students with whom you work as people, not a name on the class list.

Consider how much time is spent with students over a given length of time in their school career. We may well spend as much quality time with them as will their parents in many situations. While it is important to maintain a student/teacher relationship, there is absolutely nothing wrong with the students seeing that you truly care about them as people and musicians. Respect is a street that clearly runs in two directions. We can only gain the respect of our students by respecting them first. One of the great benefits of any teaching career is the student who returns after graduation to express his/her gratitude for the experience he/she had under your leadership.

Evaluate your "gifts" and search for the most effective ways in which you can share them with the people in your life that mean the most to you, your family, your students, and your colleagues. All of us have been given special gifts. The only way to perpetuate these gifts is to give them away, as this quote of Waite Phillips so aptly states: "The only things we keep permanently are the things we give away."

I would imagine most of you reading this book are involved in a job related to music in some fashion. What a marvelous profession it is. I am now beginning my fortieth year in teaching. Many people ask me what I like most

about teaching. It really is quite simple. I love music and the kind of people I have had the pleasure of being associated with all these years. I have been blessed with a wonderful wife who is also my best friend. I am thankful for our children and the wonderful relationship we were able to establish with them at every phase of their formative years. We continue to enjoy them even more as adults with lives and careers of their own. Finally, I am thankful for all the outstanding students whose paths have crossed mine for whatever length of time. We are all impacted by the closeness, intimacy, and passion of music as it is shared by human contact. As David, the writer of Psalms, says, "Praise Him with the sounding of the trumpet, praise Him with the harp and lyre, praise Him with tambourine and dancing, praise Him with the strings and flute, praise Him with the clash of cymbals, praise Him with resounding cymbals."

Day by day strive to make a difference in the lives of the people with whom you come in contact. It is not easy. It is a task that is most difficult and demanding as we attempt to maintain that tenuous balance between faith, home, and work. We must not allow our own schedules, professional engagements, family obligations, job demands, and the time crunch we all feel to become our own worst enemies. Like the ship at sea or the airplane in flight, we must stay straight and level to be effective. There is nothing wrong with "going the extra mile." But when the extra mile begins to disrupt our effectiveness in teaching and life, then it is time for careful and honest personal evaluation. I love this simple thought of Albert Einstein: "There are two ways to live your life. One is as though *nothing* is a miracle. The other is as though *everything* is a miracle."

In the end, we want to be remembered not only as an outstanding educator but also as a person who was well rounded, cooperative, concerned about others feelings, and a loving individual.

So once again—just what is it you want people to remember about **how you spent your dash?**

CHAPTER 3

Beyond the Page
The Natural Laws
of Musical Expression

Edward S. Lisk

"The written note is like a strait jacket, whereas music, like life itself, is constant movement, continuous spontaneity, free from any restrictions… There are so many excellent instrumentalists who are completely obsessed by the printed note, whereas it has a very limited power to express what the music actually means."
··· Pablo Casals ···

"What is best in music is not found in the notes."
···Gustav Mahler ···

Musical expression…one of the more difficult areas that must be addressed when preparing a band for a concert. For artistic expression and meaning to occur, we must look beyond the symbols of musical notation. Simply responding only to the specifics of notation leaves little room for one's imagination when expressing the composer's intent. Expressive musical performance is more than a "paint by number" experience.

Frequently, when a teacher requests a student *to play with more feeling,* the mystery enters and the student searches for solutions. The question the student has is, How should the melody feel when playing my instrument? Feeling comes from within the individual and not from notation. The secret lies in interpreting and projecting *feeling* through the nuance and inflection of notes to create meaning and worth for the musical event. However, one must remember that feelings come first (before the notes, rhythm, etc.). If one is hesitant or fears expressing personal feelings, one will have difficulty in expressing feeling through music or words. Better stated by notable conductor and author James Jordan in his superb text, *The Musician's Soul,* "If you believe that music is self-expression, then you must have some self to express" (p. 51, required reading for every music educator).

For feeling and meaning to occur, it cannot be an imitation or a contrived response to musical notation (too often the case). Meaning occurs when a student experiences ownership through his or her personal subtle inflections and nuances surrounding artistic expression. Author Donald Barra, states in his publication, *The Dynamic Performance,* "Feeling arises from our inhibited or suppressed desires and expectations. This inhibited energy, or tension, forms the basis of our emotional response" (p. 28). This is the special moment when a musical performance sends a tingling chill through musicians and audience...the spontaneity of felt response. This magical moment occurs when music *contacts* or *connects* with our emotional center and is not consciously dominated by an analytical thought process. The subtleties of nuance and inflection surrounding the notes of a phrase enhance musical expression creating meaning, value, and understanding for the listener. Notes remain trivial until they are animated through passion, feeling, and spirit.

Feeling is an ever-changing emotional response or reaction that is unique to every individual and musical ensemble. If reading a text more than once, would we read with the same inflections and tone each time? If so, the statement becomes sterile or boring. It is the spontaneity and subtleties of word nuance and inflection triggered by our emotional center that creates interest for reader and or listener. Word nuances, inflections, and rhythmic flow play an important role in our understanding and comprehension. It is impossible to retain or duplicate a feeling for something that occurred at a previous time. Moreover, it is impossible to feel something precisely as another person. The uniqueness of musical thought is projected through the subtle rhythmic nuance and inflection of note patterns that make up a musical line or phrase. As Pablo Casals stated, "We can never exhaust the multiplicity of nuances and subtleties which make the charm of music." Therein lies the secret or mystery of musical expression!

How Do We Exercise "Expressive" Playing?

We must develop rehearsal techniques that activate the students' emotional center, allowing "feeling" to flow through their instrument. Furthermore, the emotional center determines the communicative actions of the conductor's baton. Our emotional center (mid-brain area) consists of the amygdala, thalamus, and prefrontal lobes controlling and releasing human feelings. The question is, can we develop instructional techniques that access this area controlling expressive emotions? Is this the location of the mysterious world of musical expression that has eluded us for so many years? At this point, I leave you with those two questions in anticipation to read on, participate, and experience the following exercises.

I discovered when applying word prosody with the rhythmic flow and lyricism of musical phrases and patterns that our deep emotional expressive center can be accessed, releasing "felt expression" without being mechanically contrived. Why prosody? Everyone possesses the language of expression! It is natural. Prosody is the science of poetic meters and versification. The word originates from the Greek word *prosoidia*, meaning accent, modulation, and all features that characterize speech. Students immediately connect with this technique and quickly discover the meaning of "feeling" and how easily it becomes a part of their musical performance.

When presenting this instructional procedure, early attempts will be uncomfortable for students. Moreover, this is typically a learning experience never before encountered. Feeling of inhibition and/or silliness are apparent, as students do not connect this with music-making. (I also discovered a similar reaction with many band directors who have participated in my clinic workshops.) Be patient and encouraging—students see this as a risk to their identity with friends, although students experienced with theater or drama events have no reservations participating.

Discovering Our Emotional Center

This simple exercise provides an entrance into the students' expressive center as they freely attempt to shape the meaning and expressive characteristics of the statement found below. When proceeding through this exercise, remember Pablo Casals's statement when guiding your students to become expressive: "We can never exhaust the multiplicity of nuances and subtleties which make the charm of music" (words are used for this exercise). The exercise immediately connects awareness and feelings through the multiplicity and subtleties of voice nuance and inflection.

Step 1:

Select a student to recite the following verse. Encourage the student to feel free to shape the statements (phrases) in a way he/she believes will project *his/her* special message. Do not impose any expectations in the way you would like to hear the statement presented. Refer to this recitation as "Concert #1."

The text/verse is taken from Stephen Melillo's composition, *Erich!* You are encouraged to use other examples or folk song lyrics appropriate for the grade level of your program.

> *It was a time of turbulence...*
> *When sea-faring men dared to claim the waters of the earth...*
> *A time when the crimson blade of treacher,*
> *slashed across trusting heats.*

—Stephen Melillo, composer

Have several students recite the above verse to hear the unique differences with each student. Refer to each student recitation as Concert #1, Concert #2, #3, etc.

As each student reads the statement, you will hear how reserved and restricted students become when trying to be expressive. The same is true when they play their instrument. Such freedom is unusual, as students expect teacher-defined boundaries for correctness. This is their fear of risk, which stifles or inhibits their expressive potential—and is similar when playing musical phrases. The exercise activates the same neuro-signals (emotional center) used for musical expression. Musical imagination atrophies if not used or exercised.

Step 2:

The next exercise makes a significant statement regarding what I refer to as "the unadorned markings of musical notation." The intent of this exercise is to demonstrate the difficulty of being expressive while focusing upon the dynamic markings (usually creates smiles and laughter). Again, have several students recite the verse. Refer to each recitation as Concert #1, Concert #2, #3, etc.

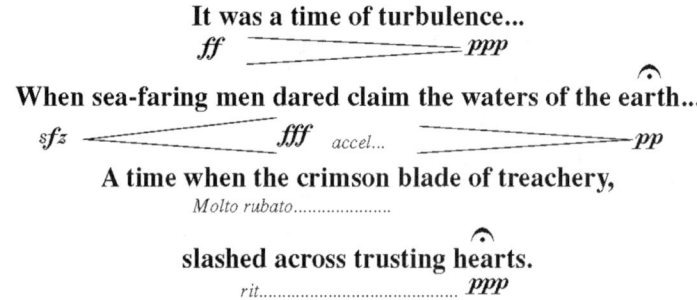

Step 3:

After several students have recited the above exercise, return to Step #1. The students quickly recognize the ease and freedom to be expressive when not responding to musical markings. It should not be misunderstood: musical markings are important and not to be overlooked. Once students have experienced the freedom of expression through Step #1 of this exercise, they will more easily apply such expressive subtleties when responding to the unadorned markings of musical notation.

Speaking Rhythm Patterns

We tend to be inhibited by the printed score with its scarcity
of expressive markings.
—Pablo Casals

The next phase of expressive musical development builds upon the preceding expression exercises by applying the process to rhythm patterns. It is important *not* to have students count rhythm patterns in a monotone response with very little voice inflection. This uncharacteristic counting sterilizes rhythm patterns and hampers stylistic interpretation as musical skills develop. I discovered that my students had no problem with rhythmic comprehension when I emphasized the nuance, inflections, and rhythmic flow through the language of subdivision. I quickly realized that this was the missing ingredient when expecting students to count and remember subdivided rhythm patterns. By stressing the nuance and inflections of this rhythmic counting process, students retain and recall patterns immediately.

To begin the exercise, have the students count the subdivided rhythm pattern in a conventional manner. The first step will not be difficult since this is something they are comfortable doing. I have included a few rhythm pattern variations as examples.

Step 1:

Count the subdivision in tempo (1–2–3&, etc.) in the same conventional manner as method books illustrate. Students should count the exercises twice, as you will compare the counting with Step 2.

Step 2:

This is the point of departure from conventional counting of rhythm patterns. Add the nuance and inflection of expressing personal feeling and meaning to the rhythm syllables, much like making a statement (exclamation and question marks indicate voice rise or fall), similar to the introductory verse recitation the students experienced earlier. Apply using the descriptors on the following page:

   a. By using the language of subdivision, make a very deliberate rhythmic statement (using the above rhythm pattern) projecting a feeling of suspicion or question of something being discovered.

   b. Make a very deliberate rhythmic statement expressing joy and happiness.

   c. Make a very deliberate rhythmic statement as in a profound announcement, without question, very forceful, dramatic!

Step 3:

Change the language of subdivision to articulation or nonsense syllables such as Di, Do, De, Ta, or Ti. Apply the same rhythmic nuance and inflections with the syllables. Do not try to learn a set of pre-programmed syllables, as this would be a mechanical repetitive process emphasizing something different from expression or articulation. This exercise establishes a natural connection between mind and felt expression (emotional center) through rhythmic voice utterance.

Speak the rhythm patterns several times and exaggerate the expression. Once beyond their first reserved attempts, students realize and enjoy this process as they have discovered one of the mysteries of musical expression. Experiment with and exaggerate the different inflections, nuance, emphasis, volume, and spoken tempo. Remember that we can never exhaust the multiplicity of rhythmic nuance and inflection.

This experience and exercise leads naturally to Step 4.

Step 4:

Using F concert, play this same "felt expression" with the rhythmic nuance and inflection into the instrument (beginning exercise for a student to artistically style a musical phrase).

Step 5:

Apply this process to any band literature phrase or solo for stylistic interpretation.

I am sure there will be varied reactions to these procedures. I am not encouraging in any way that we overlook or ignore dynamic markings or other musical indicators. However, none of these symbols connect to the musician's expressive emotional center. We can develop musically expressive organizations by bringing out the expressive inner feelings through the subtle nuance of voice inflections. By animating musical symbols with feeling, we are better able to communicate through musical performance. For so many years, we assumed that by emphasizing tempo, notes, dynamics, and rhythmic accuracy, *somewhere-sometime-someplace*-musical feeling would be a part of performance.

Three Natural Laws of Musical Expression

All music is nothing more than a succession of impulses
that converge towards a definite point of repose.
—Igor Stravinsky

Natural forms of expression are difficult concepts to teach. Because musical expression is not simply an objective occurrence, it requires conceptual teaching and learning beyond musical notation. As stated earlier, notes remain trivial until they are animated by a musician coupled with the conductor's feeling and spirit. The listener responds to the subtleties of inflection surrounding musical phrases for meaning and understanding. The beauty of a phrase comes from the musician/conductor's internal focused energy and not necessarily from volume expansion or contraction. ***Focusing is a matter of the mind and the movement of thought within the mind.***

Artistic expression is the movement of thought within the musician's mind that activates a musical phrase to a point of repose. The word *repose* has significant meaning when teaching musical expression. Repose is the act of resting or the state of being at rest; calmness; tranquility; freedom from worry; peace of mind (*American Heritage Dictionary*). Repose is an absence of motion or disturbance—calm, calmness, inactivity, breathing spell, lull, peace, peace-fulness, peace of mind, peaceableness, placidity, quiescence, quiet, rest, serenity, stillness, tranquility, and ease (*Roget's Thesaurus*).

As we continue our journey through the world of musical expression, the following simple concepts will compliment your rehearsal procedures when teaching and connecting the notes for direction and movement of a phrase...from the beginning of the journey and into the point of repose with mind and sound connected as one. It is the mind's internal motion, action, and feeling that determines the life of a musical composition!

Low Searches for High!

A very simple statement...low searches for high! The concept implies that whatever is low moves and begins a search for something that is above or higher. The mind energizes the movement of notes in a forward direction (journey) as it searches for a high note and its *point of repose* (reflecting briefly before motion continues). This thinking energy, moving in a forward direc-tion, becomes "whole" and eliminates note-by-note playing. The perception of this slight feeling of arrival before the point of repose or discovery of the high note is what communicates the subtle nuance of felt meaning occurring in the musician's mind.

I suggest singing a major scale in the described manner to remove the technical restrictions of an instrument (range, etc.).

1. Sing an ascending scale (see examples) and begin to think about the top note as soon as you start singing.

2. As you are ascending, feel free to stretch or slightly exaggerate the notes.

3. Slightly anticipate (*rubato*) arriving at the top note—the point of repose—the key to your artistic statement.

4. Sing through several times, experimenting with different inflections and speed before playing the same exercise on your instrument.

Musical examples: *Low Searches for High*

*As you sing/play the scale, gradually anticipate (rubato) arriving at the top note. Start to think about the top note as soon as you start the scale. Feel free to stretch the notes as you ascend.

*Suspend the thought (flow of notes) and feel how the subtle change in thought determines the movement (speed) of notes ascending to their resolution.

*The feeling that occurs just before the arrival of the top note (2-4 notes) is the sound arriving at its point of repose.

*The longer the delay (tension) before the point of *repose*, the greater the emotional reaction from the individual musician, ensemble and audience.

This simple exercise that activates the thought/flow of notes (phrase) determines the movement (speed) of notes ascending to their resolution. The feeling that occurs just before the arrival of the top note (resolution or discovery) is the artistic cradling of sound arriving at the point of repose. The longer the delay (tension) before the point of repose (top note), the greater the emotional reaction from the individual musician, ensemble, and audience. As stated by author Donald Barra, "It is not the development

of tension, but the prolongation of tension, that is the basis of our deeply felt emotional experience" (p. 29).

High Searches for Low!

The same holds true for this very simple statement...high searches for low! The concept implies that whatever is high moves and begins a search for something that is below. The mind's forward thought movement energizes the movement of notes as it searches for a low note as a point of repose (reflect) before motion continues. The pause may be so slight or insignificant (prolonging tension), but meaning occurs because it was the perception of this feeling by the musician's mind that communicated the subtle nuance of felt meaning.

Similar to the previous exercise, I suggest singing a major scale in the described manner to remove the technical restrictions of an instrument (range, etc.).

1. Sing a descending scale (see examples) and begin to think about the bottom/lowest note as soon as you start singing.

2. As you are descending, feel free to stretch or slightly exaggerate the notes.

3. Slightly anticipate (*rubato*) arriving at the bottom note—the point of repose—the key to your artistic statement.

4. Sing through several times, experimenting with different inflections and speed before playing the same exercise on your instrument.

Musical examples: High Searches for Low

*As you sing/play the scale, gradually anticipate (rubato) arriving at the bottom note. Start to think about the bottom note as soon as you start the scale. Feel free to stretch the notes as you descend.

*Suspend the thought (flow of notes) and feel how the subtle change in thought determines the movement (speed) of notes descending to their resolution.

*The feeling that occurs just before the arrival (2-4 notes) of the bottom note is the sound arriving at its point of repose.

point of repose 1

*The longer the delay (tension) before the point of *repose*, the greater the emotional reaction from the individual musician, ensemble and audience.

This is identical to low searching for high. The feeling that occurs just before the arrival of the bottom note (resolution or discovery) is the artistic cradling of sound arriving at the point of repose. The longer the delay (prolonging tension) before the point of repose (bottom note), the greater the emotional reaction from the individual musician, ensemble, and audience.

The following folk song example illustrates the combination of low searches for high and high searches for low concepts. Allow the students to experiment with different inflections with note and melodic direction, especially just before the arrival of high or low (point of repose). Place emphasis upon the energy and direction of thought moving with the flow of notes while being tempered by the individual's feeling. Resist the need to maintain the rigidity of tempo...it is the flow and beauty of the melodic line and contour (arrival points) that needs to be exercised before being placed into a fixed tempo.

Short Looks for Long!

The appearance and notation of a rhythm pattern on a printed page have an effect upon its interpretation and performance. Standard notation and manuscript divide note values within beats and measures to indicate rhythm patterns. Visually, the patterns can create different meanings for the musician when interpreting rhythmic flow and direction. It is the musician's or conductor's responsibility to look beyond the appearance of a notated rhythm pattern. Give special consideration and analysis with the grouping or direction of notes forming rhythm patterns divided equally over beats and measures. When reading a rhythm pattern, consider the note values without the indicated beaming connections to arrive at a musical conclusion or statement.

The best example is the interpretation of a dotted-eighth and sixteenth note. The notes beamed together indicate that it requires one beat to play this pattern. The two examples below illustrate the conventional way it appears in notation, which would be much as if saying "day-to" (which does not make any sense). Too often, rehearsal techniques spend considerable amounts of time addressing this pattern and continue to insist that it is "day-to" by teaching three tied sixteenth notes followed by one sixteenth. The result is the "to" becoming longer and longer until the rhythm becomes a compound pattern (6/8) of a quarter and an eighth.

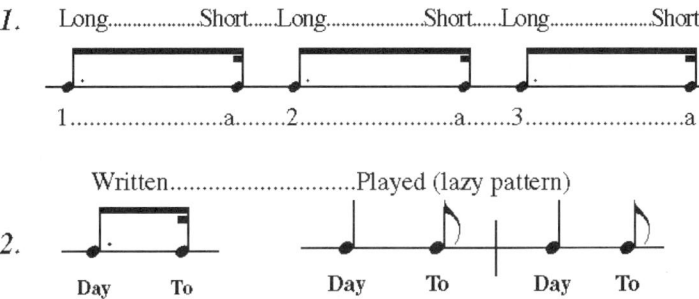

By applying the concept of short looks for long, the sixteenth is no longer a part of the dotted-eighth note. The dotted-eighth should be thought of as being connected to the note that precedes it. Therefore, the sixteenth note becomes the important note that points to the dotted-eighth. Much like saying "today" or "teday"(the "to" is the sixteenth and "day" is the dotted-eighth). When this concept is in place, the frequently heard lazy pattern of a quarter/eighth is removed and gives complete control over the length and placement of the sixteenth note. The ensemble or section articulation and interpretation are immediately unified and executed with accuracy.

- *The 'long' note is related to the*
  short note that came before !!
  The *long note* is much like a
  point of repose
  similar to the concept of
  "low searches for high."

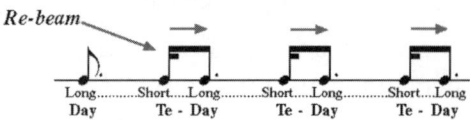

The length variation when speaking the syllable "to" determines the style and characteristic of the sixteenth note. Changing the length of the syllable "To" to "T" (as in "Tday"), can shorten the sixteenth to a thirty-second note. Practice the following examples so students realize the number of variations with their interpretation. The ensemble or section is to speak the word "To-Day" several times to unify articulation. Follow this by playing the spoken word.

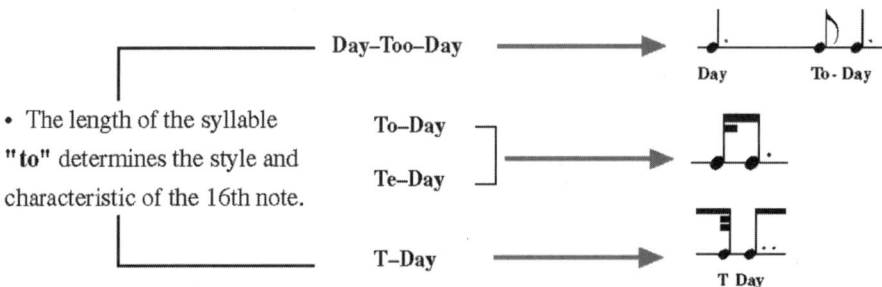

- The length of the syllable "to" determines the style and characteristic of the 16th note.

The concept is simple. It creates meaning and musical connection while eliminating many restrictive unmusical barriers that often enter the daily rehearsal or practice when reading this rhythm pattern.

The following examples illustrate various rhythm patterns based upon this *natural moving* concept...short looks for long! The important consideration is given to the "long" note. It is always related to the short notes that come before. The long note is the point of repose, similar to the concept of low searches for high and high searches for low. It is important to recognize the direction in which the rhythm pattern is moving. The arrows below each pattern indicate the direction of thought, which will always lead to the long note (as in resolution or discovery).

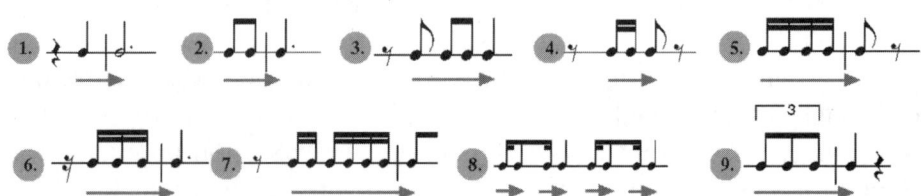

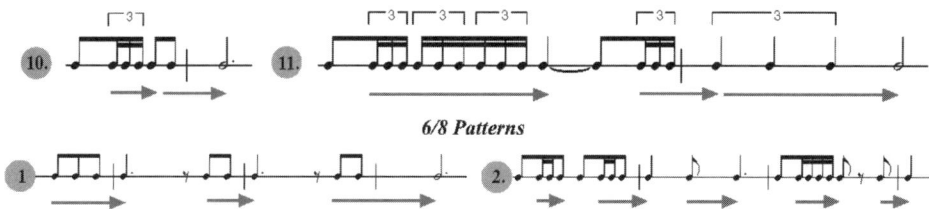

6/8 Patterns

As you read the above rhythm examples, treat the long note as if you discovered or found someone you were searching for—as in "Aha, there you are!" Just before the arrival of the long note, experiment with a very slight delay. It is ever so slight, but apparent, as it creates meaning and interest with the rhythm pattern (the life of musical expression).

In H. A. Vandercook's publication, *Expression in Music* (original copyright 1926 and later published by Rubank, Inc.), Chapter 1 illustrates the importance of accent and emphasis through the use of a sentence. The illustration repeats a sentence five times, each time placing the accent or emphasis on a different word. When reading each line, emphasis is on the word in capital letters. I have taken the liberty of placing a rhythm beside each sentence (not found in the publication). The arrows indicate the rhythmic flow and direction of the statement, or short looking for long.

Conclusion

The rehearsal techniques in this chapter can be applied to all the selected literature found in this four-volume publication. My intent is to provide a different rehearsal perspective when dealing with the unadorned markings we use when making music. For those who feel such musical techniques may be too complex for young musicians, I encourage reconsideration. As a teacher, I found that after students experienced these approaches, they were excited and totally absorbed when playing their instrument expressively—with feeling!

I am frequently asked about how adjudicators may respond or evaluate a program that has taken some of the musical liberties described in this chapter. Too often, many believe an adjudicator responds only to the specifics of notation and its markings. This is an untruth. An adjudicator will always encourage and respond favorably to the artistic and expressiveness of a musical organization. To be an adjudicator requires musicianship that is not only analytical but that is supported by musical sensitivity and integrity when responding to the expressive beauty of a musical performance. Music directors must have confidence in their musical decisions and interpretive sense when preparing their ensemble for performance or adjudication.

Our career ambitions and professional responsibility continue to consume countless hours and years with study and practice while observing the "masters" of our profession. State, national, and international instrumental events showcase many of our superb band programs. We listen and respond to those who have played the "exercise" but are captivated by those who have ventured beyond into the world of artistic and expressive beauty. For those who direct such organizations, obviously they have learned to fly and soar through the universe of musical expression. Perhaps an ancient Chinese question may be appropriate at this point: How can a caged man teach you to fly? Someone who does not know music cannot teach music. If we teach music, we must venture outside the "cage" to experience the truth of musical expression.

The most notable educator, Mortimer Adler, made this important statement in his 1988 publication, *Reforming Education:* "The primary cause of all learning is the activity of the student's mind. The best that the best teacher can do is to assist that activity" (p. 278). This statement emphasizes the importance for teachers to be knowledgeable about how students learn through thoughtful, intelligent actions. It is the thoughtful/timed thinking energy (neuro-signal) connected to the body (eyes, ears, fingers) that allows one to produce music. Playing a musical instrument requires an intricate combination of intellectual, visual, physical, and auditory control coupled with a perceptive decision-making process (intelligence in action). The best we can do is to assist and guide the students' thinking process as they play their instrument.

When teaching music, our responsibility is to develop outstanding expressive musicians. This can be accomplished by understanding that a musician's mind constantly moves in time, synchronized with other music-makers, creating an ensemble of musical expression through the lyricism of melodic, harmonic, and rhythmic sounds moving in and out of silence. This musically timed thinking energy elevates the musician to the mysterious summit

experience and continues to bring us back repeatedly to create and become part of a music-making experience.

Notes

Adler, Mortimer. *Reforming Education*. New York, NY: Macmillan Publishing Co., 1988.

Barra, Donald. *The Dynamic Performance*. Englewood Cliffs, NJ: Prentice-Hall, Inc., 1983.

Blum, David. *Casals and The Art of Interpretation*. Los Angeles, CA: University of California Press, 1977.

Goleman, Daniel. *Emotional Intelligence*. New York, NY: Bantam Books, 1995.

Jordan, James. *The Musician's Soul*. Chicago, IL: GIA Publications, 1999.

Lisk, Edward S. *The Creative Director: Beginning and Intermediate Level*. Galesville, MD: Meredith Music Publications, 2001.

Lisk, Edward S. *The Intangibles of Musical Performance*. Galesville, MD: Meredith Music Publications, 1996.

H. A. Vandercook. *Expression in Music*. Miami, FL: Rubank, Inc., 1942.

CHAPTER 4

Music's Hidden Message

Eugene Migliaro Corporon

Introduction

In 1969, my first year of teaching, I had the great fortune to meet a wonderful couple, Jack and Esther Hopkins. They served as chaperone chairs for the instrumental music parent group at Mt. Miguel High School, where I was Director of Instrumental Music. Esther was a perceptive and gifted elementary school teacher, and Jack taught a variety of art courses at San Diego State University. Their son, David, was a member of my orchestra and band, and was following the example of his sister, Ann, who had gone before him in the program. The Hopkins invited me to dinner one September evening after a long rehearsal. They became my friends and I became a semi-permanent guest in their home. It did not take me long to realize that these nurturing and enlightened people had a great deal to offer. It was clear from the outset that Jack and Esther had made a decision to live their lives in a very special way. Their humanity and sensitivity defined who they were and influenced the life choices they made. I was fortunate indeed to have been their welcomed and frequent guest, and have always treasured my time with them. Their home was a compassionate and creative place that provided a rich environment for self-reflection and artistic introspection. In every way imaginable, they lived with a passion and spirit that still influences me thirty-three years later. Every visit was a joyous lesson in how to be in the world. They showed me that one could construct a life that was loving and artistic, and that those qualities could be at the center of everyday experiences.

Jack's father had been a furniture maker, a fine craftsman. Jack always found it somewhat ironic that his art had aligned itself so closely with his father's craft. Jack was drawn to multiple areas of art, which included design, watercolor painting, jewelry making, and wood sculpting. His ability to create at a micro or macro level was impressive indeed. He could focus for days on the smallest piece of precious metal—or "finger sculpture" as he used to call it—and then redirect his attention and energy to devise a "wood sculpture" of tremendous size. The hours that I observed him taught me about form and function. Jack put his eloquently diverse craft in the service of art. His creations, no matter what form they took, were powerful pieces of absolute art that were also functional. They were intended to be used, to be experienced, and to become integrated into daily life. The "finger sculpture" doubled as a ring, and the "wood sculpture" was actually a very comfortable chair. While all of his works were extraordinary, his wood pieces were nothing short of astonishing.

I learned a great deal about the importance of the imagination and the genesis of an idea by watching Jack. Whenever he contemplated a new sculpted wood project, he would hold a small piece of material in his hands. It was important to him to make a physical connection with that sample of exotic wood and get a feel for what the fragment was trying to say to him about its future. When the message began to materialize in his mind, he would set the wood aside and reach for his sketchbook. The ideas would just stream onto the page. I was perfectly content to become a silent observer as an explosion of creative energy would interrupt our conversation. Everything would stop as Jack rushed to capture the thoughts that had been fermenting.

I am still discovering the gifts of knowledge that I received during those early years of my career. Jack taught me the importance of letting an idea simmer, the necessity of heating up the physical and emotional connection, and the value of trusting one's intuition when things come to a boil. Above all, he showed me that ideas could give birth to feelings, and that both ideas and feelings could present themselves in a work of art that people could inter-act with and enjoy.

Jack's design process was patiently fluid. He would move back and forth from the wood samples to the sketchbook, allowing both to freely influence his decision-making. At first glance, his method appeared to be completely intuitive, but I came to realize that a great deal of study and experience had led Jack to this point in his art making. It became obvious that he had done his work. What seemed a natural gift had been the result of years of dedicated preparation, persistent exploration, and meaningful discovery. There was no doubt that Jack had a gift. There was also no doubt that he had chosen to do something with it. While there was a strong sense of discipline in his method, he was very relaxed and allowed things to flow and follow their own natural course. He focused his full attention on the task at hand. No matter how subjectively involved he became in the piece, he would reserve time for honest and objective evaluation of his progress. Jack was always the first one to know if things were not working. As incredible as Jack's accomplishments were, I never detected any ego or pettiness. He was only doing what he loved to do and felt compelled to do. Jack did not have time to be critical of others work because he was too busy doing his own.

The production stage was a very physical one for Jack. It was hard work, always accompanied by classical music. Music was very clearly a catalyst in his process. I watched him methodically and thoughtfully assemble one piece of wood at a time into large architectural masses with a wood welder that heated the glue but did not damage the material. In the early stages, the pieces would resemble the skeleton of a great whale. You could see how the work was put together and supported on the inside. As the process proceeded, the piece was closed up, and it became impossible to view the technique that supported it. Once the cubist idea was glued together in front of him, Jack would begin working on the exterior by shaving away what did not belong. In effect, he was sculpting wood into organic shapes that seemed more the result of nature than of a person's imagination. He saw possibilities in these uneven blocks and was able to free the smooth curved lines from their angular framework. Watching his process helped me to understand that structure was fundamental to but not the purpose of great art. When he finished, the technique that brought the piece forth had completely hidden itself in the flowing seamless shapes.

For those of us in music, this process offers a very worthwhile model. To experience success, we must be sure a supportive structure is in place, take away what does not belong, heat up the process without damaging the ingredients, free what is naturally inherent in the piece, and put technique completely in the service of the work of art. On occasion, I was asked to help with this process. It was an honor. Applying oil to the finished product was my particular specialty. It was also the safest way to involve a rank beginner. I was always made to feel that my efforts were contributing to the success of the project and that my work was valued. That was the mark of a great teacher. Jack's approach involved a perfect blend of intensity and integrity mixed with intellect and intuition. I was privileged at a very formative age to spend time with a master artist and teacher. I continue to draw upon those lessons every day. They are a vital part of this chapter.

Teaching as a Creative Act

Is music an art or is it a trade? We must answer this question to be effective advocates for our discipline. Craft is admittedly a key component of the creative process. However, it is incumbent upon us as professional artists to project a clear message that teaching and performing music should be considered art, not craft. We must do so much more than develop skill through training; we must enlighten human beings and instill in them a creative spirit. Our fundamental charge as teachers is to create artists, not craftsmen. If we succeed, our students will be able to do nothing less than experience the significance of music for life. While a certain amount of craft must be in place, one does not need to perform at a professional level to participate artistically. A resourceful teacher leads students to artistic independence and makes himself or herself obsolete in the creative experience. I recently saw a video clip of Barbara Cooke, a famous Broadway singer, coaching students from The Juilliard School. Her advice was full of wisdom:

> Your singing is too much about I can sing. So you can sing; now what are you going to do with it? Let your singing reflect what life has done to you. You must reach deep down inside yourself to your *core*. It is about communicating from one person's *core* to another.

Musicing for an artist-teacher is more about sending a message than demonstrating ability. The quintessential goal is to move beyond mechanics to meaning. The true purpose of our work should be to produce musicians who can perform individual and independent acts of creativity.

How can we develop creative musicians? The answer lies in allowing one's intuition to lead to a more creative and compelling style of teaching. We must become the models for what we want students to be. A student recently handed me a message that he found in a fortune cookie on a dinner break at a recording session. It said, "The best teacher is also a student." I keep this little scrap of paper in my wallet to remind me that all of the master teachers whose creativity I admire have remained students of their art. They are curious people who have not lost interest in how their art functions. They are expressive people who are on a mission to interject their feelings into their work. They are thinking people who welcome and explore new ideas. They are perceptive people who pay attention to their intuition. They are giving people who willingly share their time and energy. They are modest people who show reverence for the mysteries of music. Most importantly, they are compassionate people who respect and value their students. They do not have all the answers because they are still working on the questions. They have come to a simple realization that the teaching of music is a selfless act that takes time and has nothing to do with immediate success or instant gratification.

Teaching is all about broadening, deepening, and enriching a person's existence by giving them something to love throughout life. The truth is that great musicing puts one in touch with civilization and helps to reveal an understanding of what it means to be a member of the human community. Great teachers work to design and implement experiences for students that are genuine and diverse. They understand that every composition of value provides exhilarating opportunities for unrestrained interactions. Observing and learning from great teachers is indeed necessary. Imitating those same sages leads to sure disaster. The challenge remains the same for all of us: learn from the work of others without copying the work of others while creating a significant relationship between the composer, the work of art, the performers and the listeners. One must develop and protect his/her individuality while

progressing through one's career. It is important to value who you are and what you have to offer. To do authentic and distinctive work, each of us must function as a one-of-a-kind original.

The Four Stages of Musical Development

I believe that we experience four discernible levels of development as we study and perform music. Each of these stages informs our ability and enriches our experience. Musical growth is a lifetime endeavor to be sure. Students become teachers, teachers become students, and so the cycle continues. Music can be imagined, made, and heard. The challenge is to decipher the message contained in the work of art. We must do more than uncover the message; we must unleash the power of its meaning.

Our primary duty as music educators is to help others experience a composition as a meaningful and memorable series of ideas and emotions. All of us start out with the same goal: to become the most sensitive and complete musician possible. Additionally, we have all found somewhere deep down inside our soul a need to share the wonders of music with others. Becoming a complete musician is a very complicated process that relies on receptivity and adaptation. The following breakdown represents the cumulative stages of development I have observed:

Beginner – Novice – Performer – Artist

Beginners . . . . .practice the patterns
Novices . . . . .play the part
Performers . . . . . . .project the piece
Artists . . . . .personify the message

On the surface, it would seem that the most important thing for someone to do who is starting to study music would be to develop technique and control. While one cannot progress very far without these physical attributes, there is a more important issue to address. The most significant thing we can accomplish early on is to help the students make an emotional connection with the sound. The sooner this is done, the more likely a student of music is to succeed in making music an integral part of his or her life *for life*.

Technique alone does not lead us to artistry. Artistry is a combination of technical mastery (which is the result of self-discipline) and human expression (which is the result of emotional maturity). With most great artists, the instrument is secondary to the message they send. One can be equally expressive and communicative with the voice, the violin, the euphonium, the cello, the saxophone, the marimba, or the piano. It is not the medium that makes artists great. It is their ability to communicate the message through their medium. Expression does not have to be the prerogative of a select group; it is accessible to all who aspire to make music.

If the true purpose of teaching and facilitating music is to help people find, understand, feel, and send the message, then we must do a whole lot more than teach students to be excellent technicians. We must facilitate their ability to comprehend and connect with the real stuff of music, the message. It is never too early to plug into the messages that are represented by the sounds. This must be a primary goal of our approach from the outset. We must make glorious sounds that express human thoughts and feelings in unique and uninhibited ways as early as possible because that is the true purpose and real gift of music.

Beginner (Enthusiasm and Celebration)

All musicians share one thing. At some point in time, they were beginners. Beginners are truly wondrous creatures. They show unbridled enthusiasm for what they are doing. Every day is full of discovery. They exhibit boundless possibilities. The smallest accomplishment is something to celebrate and represents a giant step forward. Starting an instrument should be a positive and exciting experience. It takes a very special teacher to maintain and focus enthusiasm. I have always believed that the closer a teacher is to the beginning of the learning process, the more effect he/she has on the student and the outcome. In addition to passing on fundamentals to beginners, we must instill a love of music and respect for the individually creative act that making music represents. The foundation for interpersonal interaction with the work of art and others must be put in place early on. This is every bit as important as teaching the pedagogically correct method. If we fail to make this connection, we run the risk of creating skilled automatons that are unaware of the existence of a message. This is no different than teaching people to speak a language flawlessly and failing to tell them what they are saying.

When students begin making sound, they are embarking on a journey that should last a lifetime. One can continue to be involved in music, whether actively participating in the creation of sound or not. Music can become a powerful and positive force in one's life. Once someone has allowed music to permeate his/her spirit, that person can be changed forever. Life-changing experiences do not happen because of technical achievement alone. We must help young musicians decipher messages as well as formulate their own. In the beginning stages, it may be more important that we "share the substance of music" rather than "teach the syntax of music." All beginners struggle along the way; the effective teacher will find ways to de-emphasize the struggle and help students discover the joy of musicing. I think it is important to hold on to the wonderment that we experienced as beginners. As one matures and develops greater abilities, it is all too easy to become overly critical and even cynical about our work. We must continue to celebrate accomplishment every

time as though it were the first time. One should stay in touch with what it felt like to make those early discoveries and how truly breathtaking they were. Enthusiasm and celebration remain integral to great music-making and should never be left behind.

Novice (Perspective and Listening)

A novice shows signs of developing skill and consistency. Technique emerges and a certain degree of accomplishment is realized. The ability to detect and decipher the message may still be formulating and may not always be discernible. It is important for the novice to make the connection that facility may not be the final goal. It is at this stage that the concepts of shape and movement become advantageous allies in the creative process. Novices begin to realize that they can sculpt the sound and control its motion. A paramount aspect of development is learning how to listen to a work of art. Novice musicians are fully capable of establishing listening priorities that make the listening goals clear. Their music-making experience expands to include larger and more diverse groups of musicians.

Novices should learn to accept the responsibilities that come with being in an ensemble. They can discover that expressive musicing is made up of collective as well as individual experiences. Every ensemble experience provides an opportunity to create a community. Students must be guided to the idea of becoming a contributing member of that community. At this point, things may still revolve around the individual rather than the work of art. Because novices are so focused on improving their skill, they often become isolated from the strength of the message. Good teachers find ways to broaden their perspective and involve students in the deciphering process. They help students develop patience and direct them towards understanding the value of the collective experience. Novice vision can be limited to what is most difficult rather than what is most significant. Novices can be somewhat myopic, relating to a piece of music only through the perceived difficulty of their part. If their part is technically challenging then the piece is "good." If their part is less challenging, then the piece is "bad." Informed teachers know that difficulty is never an indicator of value. Broadening the listening to encompass the entire piece is key to leading students to this realization as well.

Novices must learn the importance of listening beyond the bounds of their immediate sphere of involvement if they are to progress to the next phase. Expanded hearing helps them relate to the intricacies and respond to the subtleties of great music. While the mind seeks to bring order to the sounds, the heart must be encouraged to search for meaning. Once novices recognize the logic and expressions inherent in the sounds, they can become willing recipients of the ideas and feelings imbedded in the work by the creator. To participate fully in an ensemble, a novice must come to the realization that no single part can possibly contain all of the thoughts and emotions that make up a masterpiece.

Performer (Soul and Expression)

Performers enjoy a relatively high level of skill and consistency. Additionally, they begin to see that their music-making affects other people and can elicit powerful emotional responses. Good performers demonstrate a broad grasp of the music-making process. They understand that technique is not an end in itself but a means to a greater purpose...**expression**. Performers have the ability to expand their involvement beyond their part and relate to the piece as a whole. They become aware of the fact that large ensembles are quite flexible and are made up of a number of smaller chamber groups that are constantly re-inventing themselves. They can understand and appreciate the entire work of art. They find that the music can be incredibly intriguing even if their part is not continuously engaging. Performers participate in the experience in a holistic way. They give themselves over to the power of the message in the music. They begin to expect the music to have something to say and become impatient and even frustrated if it does not.

It is critical that the teacher helps the performers to embrace the idea that the purpose of a performance is to transmit ideas and feelings from soul to soul. While perfection is sometimes thought to be the purpose of performance, I find it a lesser achievement than expressive musicing. At this stage, each instrument can become a tool. Performers know how to use those tools to build environments that allow the essence of humanity to thrive and grow. They create a "sonic conservatory" that becomes a musical greenhouse for the spirit. This place preserves and propagates ideas and feelings, and allows all who enter to experience the very best that our civilization has to offer. It is most important for the teacher to help the performers recognize and appreciate the contribution they are making to others through music. The performers come to realize that expression is the reason for the sound, not an accidental by-product of perfection. Several concepts that are central to becoming a performer who is expressive, aware, and productive are:

1. Always give your best effort. Be sure to invest your energy and attention if you are going to give your time.

2. Make each rehearsal or performance better than the last. Be honest about your preparation and sincere about your motivation.

3. Be a positive force in the interaction. You are either adding to or taking away—there is no neutral in music.

4. Stay curious. Look beyond the obvious technical details of the part to find meanings in the music.

5. Be willing to do the unwritten. Think outside of the box that is created by the page.

6. Explore options responsibly and allow the composer to speak through you. Believe that there is more to the music than you can see.

7. Stay connected to what you see, hear, feel, know, and can imagine. Do more than listen to the sound; feel the vibrations.

8. Acknowledge the sanctity of the musical experience. Take yourself and others seriously but have fun.

9. Realize that interpretation is not the sole prerogative of the conductor. Have something to offer and be willing to contribute.

10. Understand that succeeding is more about doing than wanting. It takes individual action to improve.

Artist (Possibilities and Creativity)

The word "artist" is usually reserved for those who have achieved the ultimate level of accomplishment in the profession. One can be an artist performer, teacher, or both. It seems to me that artistry is all about one's ability to transfix people and transmit the message. A great artist is able to use his/her extraordinary skill to reach people through their musicing and teaching. Artists create transcending experiences. They operate at the upper limits of creativity, expression, sensitivity, and communication. Artists demonstrate a keen ability to conceive, conspire, convert, and connect. They are able to conceive ideas, conspire with colleagues to bring those ideas to fruition, convert symbols into feelings, and connect others to the experience. To an artist, the whole point of preparation is to enlarge the number of musical choices within the composer's acceptable range. They are fully aware that preparation yields possibilities. The goal is to be so well prepared that something of value will happen that has never happened before. Therefore, the music-making can be fresh every time. The ideal is to always get beyond the notes to the message, which can and should be read with a variety of inflections. An artist knows that there can be great value in focusing the listening on something other than the written page. He works from the inside out and realizes that what goes on above, below, around, and between the symbols is what makes musicing and teaching come alive.

To become an artist, one must do the "un-stuff." We must be willing to experience the unfamiliar, venture into the unknown, risk being uncomfortable, summon the power to be unrelenting, and above all dare to be unpredictable. Artists seek to capture the very soul of the composer and release the composer's spirit into the room at will. Artists appreciate that they are the sum total of their experiences. Limited experience yields limited artistry. Many believe that the reason we practice and study is so we can do it just right. They think there is one and only one way to perform a certain passage or piece. I believe that the reason we practice and study is so we can develop the artistic flexibility to do it differently every time. The goal is to find appropriate new messages and new meanings that bring relevance to the current performance. The "ultimate technique" allows for variance of expression and original thought to emerge. The entire process for an artist is about discovering options and revealing choices.

It is true that in performance one must choose from among the many options that have been uncovered, but that choice is not for **all** time—it is for **that** time. A performance represents one moment **in** time. Performing in a parallel universe, you may have made another equally appropriate choice. The choices we make are not the only ones that are valid. Being sensitive to and receptive of the ideas and feelings of others is a mark of artistic strength. It is important to contemplate alternatives if we are to expand our creativity. Artists embody just the right amount of skill and soul. They come to value uniqueness, diversity, and freedom. Their goals are altruistic. The admonition of American composer Vincent Persichetti seems appropriate here. He once said, "I have always thought that a composer shouldn't want to be a composer, they should want to be an artist-musician." This is great advice for all of us involved in music. Our ultimate goal should be to become artist-musicians.

Moving from Message to Meaning

In the first part of this chapter, I referred to the messages that I believe are contained in or preserved by a piece of music. It seems to me that the primary purpose of musicing is to broadcast those messages. There is no doubt that the messages reach across numerous historical periods and encapsulate a variety of civilizations past and present. Music's messages embody the thoughts and feelings of the human race. Music communicates beyond language and has the capability to convert messages from a multitude of cultures into a form of interaction that can be accessed, experienced, and understood by all.

The messages I am speaking about are written in a very sophisticated and complex code called *notation*. In the beginning, music was passed from one person to another via an aural tradition without the benefit of this code. As time passed, a written system developed that allowed a record or blueprint of the composition to be kept. The aural traditions and notational symbols have become equal partners in the decoding process. These allied means of saving the past make it possible to find, recall, and project the implied meanings that are contained in the sounds and silences. It is important to keep in mind that

unlike a painting, the notated form of a musical work of art is not the *actual* work of art. It is merely a plan of action that allows thoughts and feelings to materialize.

It is truly a paradox that while the message is written in black and white, it is heard in a myriad of vivid colors. The composition leaves behind a series of colorful after-images that are trapped in the mind's imagination. While the colors seem to fade the fastest from our memories, the message can remain long after the timbres of the sound have been forgotten. I think it is these after-images that compel us to return to the composition for multiple hearings. A piece that holds up to repeated listening must have a very powerful message hidden somewhere inside.

To become an artist-musician, it is not enough to love music. If you aspire to be a medium for the message, you must know about music. Developing a vivid imagination is key to beginning the process. The regular contemplation of timbres within the sound is too often left out of our preparation. Connecting physical movement to the sound is a critical part of any conductor's preparation. It is equally important to attach color and link style to the sound. Conductors need to have a glossary of appropriate styles and accurate sounds stored in their memory banks. This is why it is so important for teachers to be "well listened." To be effective, teachers need to be able to reference model sounds and suitable styles in their mind's ear. One cannot build musicianship within an individual or an ensemble if a characteristic tone that is stylistically accurate is not in place. The importance of consistent style and quality sound cannot be overstated.

When presented with a score, we have to believe that the composer has filled it with important and valuable messages from the past that need to be decoded and sent along. We have to understand that the goal of the work is to make a connection. A great performance is one in which the full strength of the message can be heard, felt, and perhaps even understood. I have organized the process of decoding the composer's message into four stages, which include:

1) Translate – 2) Transfer – 3) Transmit – 4) Transcend

Each of these stages requires a necessary set of sophisticated skills. Our ability to impact our culture through our messages is directly related to the depth of our development in all of these categories.

Translate (Decode and Discover)

If we can agree that the score contains encoded messages from the past, then it is clearly our job to translate these messages before we can begin to share them with others. There are two ways to translate a message: *study* and *practice*. Score study for the conductor is equivalent to practice for the performers. One is done in the mind; the other is done on the instrument.

Having a powerful aural vision is important to the conductor, whether or not the conductor is a skilled pianist who can reduce and perform a score at sight. To create a complete picture of the sound in the mind, we must be able to imagine timbre as well as sound. It is very important to study in color, which includes conceptualizing and contemplating the individual and combined timbres of the various instruments. *Instrumentation*, *scoring*, and *tessitura* create the character of the music and are front-line elements that should continually influence the conductor's decision-making process.

As I study and audiate the score, I am always in the question of how the choices made by the composer will effect my translation of the work. If you cannot recreate the sounds in your imagination, you cannot make decisions about their presentation. Clarifying *function* and revealing *form* are basic to organizing an appropriate and perceivable version of the message. As I begin my work on a score, I spend time categorizing the ideas that are presented into one of four groups: *new*, *repeated*, *varied*, or *developed*. This facilitates the understanding of points of *unity* and *contrast*. I am mindful of the process of *statement*, *digression*, and *return*. I pay attention to *growth* created by *shape*, *movement*, *direction*, and especially *patterns*. I focus on the use of *sound* and *silence*, and how that determines the *phrasal structure*. I observe *emphasis*, *accent*, *inflection*, and *contour*, and how they correlate to influence *note grouping*. I investigate the *horizontal*, *vertical*, and *diagonal* aspects of the music. I take special note of *timbres* and *textures* that weave together to create the fabric of the piece. I explore *energy*, *volume*, *speed*, *note length*, *range*, *note morphology*, and any of the other *instructions for reconstruction* that were important enough to the composer to leave behind in the printed message.

As I translate the score—or code book, as I think of it—I rely on a system of marking. It is quite simple, but the marks help to trigger my memory when I am rehearsing and performing. I use only three colors: red, blue, and green. In addition to the colors, I employ a set of symbols that have meaning to me. In a way, my process is about putting a code on top of a code. The colors and symbols can be used alone or in various combinations depending on the determined function of the various lines, chords, rhythms, or scoring choices. Score marking is a very personal thing. Some believe it should not be done at all, that it gets in the way of the composer's message. While I keep it to a minimum, marking has become a vital part of my process. Each person must determine the degree to which they will mark their own code book. Marking the score helps me move the message from the colorless page into my imagination and contributes to my efficiency and effectiveness.

One other word about the score may be appropriate at this point. Conductors should work from their own score. It is essential that teachers collect a personal library of code books. The score is the place to record one's ongoing discoveries and decisions. We need to keep a personal record so we

can reference what we have learned from previous study to build upon our cumulative knowledge of the repertoire while strengthening and diversifying our musicianship. The score is a sacred document, the most tangible link we have to the composer and his message. Therefore, it is important to treat a score with respect and reverence. It is difficult, if not impossible, to remember the thousands of decisions that have been recorded in the score. Even composers refer back to their own scores to help them recall the choices they made and the messages they intended to send.

Three components contribute to the perception of style in the composition: *tradition, performance practice,* and *interpretation.* Each of these supplies important information that influences the understanding of the work. The usefulness of that information will depend on the knowledge, preparation, ability, and integrity of the translator.

Tradition is grounded in the past and plays an important role. For centuries, music has been handed down from one person to the next in private sessions, called "lessons." This continues to be an integral and profound way to learn about music. Mentor teachers spending one-on-one time with conductors and performers is still a vital component of the decoding process. They pass along the unwritten secrets that have become central to the heritage of masterful performance. I believe that passing music from person to person will always remain a viable means of perpetuating the art.

Performance Practice is most often overseen by musicologists and theorists. Their work documents various musical events and practices for future study by chronicling what is going on or what has gone on. One must have a working knowledge of theory and history to gain a proper perspective of any work of art. It is crucial to our credibility that we seriously consider these aspects and allow them to influence our preparation. Researching the past can give us a significant glimpse of the future.

Interpretation in an ensemble is often thought to be the primary prerogative of the conductor. However, every conductor approaches this differently. Some share the decision-making with the performers, while others insist on a predeveloped plan that does not leave room for collaboration. Whatever the approach, thoughts and feelings must be projected if the message is to have any hope of being perceived. There is no doubt that a great deal of implied meaning can and must be distilled from the written message. As one extracts the essence of the message, opinions are formed. Those opinions will eventually yield an interpretation. It is no secret that interpretations can vary. A great work allows for a variety of interpretations. The diversity of opinion makes it incredibly interesting to hear works performed by various ensembles and artists. We must understand that no matter how much we believe in our interpretation, it is only *an* interpretation—not *the* interpretation. I would rather be challenged by an interpretation that I do not agree with than experience a performance that avoids decision-making. Every time we make a decision, we run the risk of upsetting someone. That should never stop us from having an informed opinion. When I hear an ensemble perform, I want to know who they are, what they understand, and how they feel about the music. Performances that lack character, are uninformed, and seem disconnected, are truly a cure for insomnia.

Maintaining an awareness and understanding of all of these elements is essential to the success of the final presentation and serves to refine the focus of the translator while sharpening the projection of the message. It is, of course, possible to come up with an incorrect translation, to be on the wrong track. This is why one needs to keep an open mind and continually seek input. In my opinion, a great translation is the result of an ongoing collaboration between the composer, the performer, the conductor, and the work of art. The interaction needs just the right mixture of subjective and objective ingredients. The development of informed intuition is the goal of the translation process. One must remain vigilant and be true to the message of the composer, without totally sacrificing his or her own creative spirit.

It is important to note that the process of translating is an ongoing one. A great work demands constant examination and interaction, which extends beyond each performance. The composition can take on a life of its own as it contributes to the lives of others. Losing oneself in a masterpiece is like escaping to another world or dimension. There is much to be gained from being suspended in time inside a great work of art. The more often we travel through the piece, the more familiar we become with the structure of those special places that we have found so intriguing. No matter how interesting the means of construction is, one should never lose sight of the fact that the music's message is more important than any system that organizes its presentation. Ross Lee Finney, a leading American composer offers this:

> I have always wanted my music to sing whatever devices or systems I might use in composing it. Beneath the surface, however, is a complexity of memories, functions, and abstractions that give depth to the musical experience but only if the music *flows* and *sings* without interruption from beginning to end.

Transfer (Teach and Empower)

For most of us, the art of transferring the message to others is a lifetime endeavor. Teaching the message that we have translated requires an entirely different set of skills than those we used to solidify our "point of view." While the ensemble is made up of a variety of secret decoders, each with its own unique set of instructions for operation, the goal remains the same for all. Unscramble the message and send it along. For the conductor, having the ability to transfer the message to performers in rehearsal is essential to bringing the music to life. What we do requires the commitment and cooperation of others, and because of that we must have good people skills.

Our ability to work with and motivate others cannot be detached from our music-making because one surely impacts the other. The use of anger, fear, intimidation, or sarcasm can endanger the entire process. It is only through positive collaboration that we can transmit the best possible version of the message. We should continually be refining and rethinking our approach to involving people with the composers' messages in ways that protect their souls and nurture their spirits. One must not lose sight of the fact that this is a shared experience. Performers need to have access to the message to appreciate, validate, and enjoy the process.

Transferring the message has the power to transform individual lives. Understanding the message empowers people to experience the universe through another person's heart and soul. Rehearsals should be thought of as transfer sessions. In a very real sense, we are downloading the thoughts and feelings of the composer into the ensemble. Everyone is integral to the experience because anyone can impact that experience in a positive or negative way. No matter how limited the time, the process must allow for experimentation and mistakes. Mistakes are a sign of learning in progress. New mistakes present opportunities for exploration and discussion. I have a simple charge regarding mistakes. If you are going to make a mistake, be sure it is a good one and a new one. It is unproductive to come to rehearsals and make the same mistake repeatedly. To progress we must learn from our mistakes.

Being in a productive rehearsal environment is akin to being in a laboratory filled with multiple experiments that are in various stages of progress. All sorts of elements are being simultaneously combined, observed, and evaluated throughout the room. Some things will work better than others, but there is no way to discover what works best unless you explore options. Experiments are only a waste of time if they never yield solutions. In fact, one could argue that a failed experiment is not a waste of time at all. Keep in mind that success may come next time because of the failure you experienced this time. At the very least, you have more knowledge coming out of a failure than you did going in. Trusting the ensemble and your teaching enough to experiment will yield multiple solutions to the problems you encounter. It is important to understand that the translation of the work is an overpowering process that should build up and reach out like a tidal wave, engulfing all who are in its path. The message will soak in during transfer as long as you are willing to take risks, let go, and trust the strength of the wave to carry you to safety.

Playing music is a game that has no losers. Everyone wins when involved in a sensitive, meaningful, and humane process. The reason we rehearse and perform music is for the moments of magic yet to be revealed. Rehearsals filled with revelation require intent and focus, but they need not be constricting. They must remain free-flowing and allow for ideas and feelings to be uncovered, exchanged, and pursued. Many mistakenly believe that rehearsals are about perfection. I never plan to perfect anything. I hope to apprehend something. There is a marked difference between the two. The goal is to **capture the moment** *and* **preserve the discovery** by retaining the thoughts and feelings of the composer in our minds so they can be accessed and disseminated when most appropriate and helpful. A flexible framework will yield more positive results than a highly controlled interaction that is too rigid and overly systematic. The best plan is pliable and has the ability to literally bend in the wind. Structure and pliability are not divided constructs. Discipline and self-control can yield flexibility and elasticity. Well-structured and inventive rehearsals help the group to become an ensemble. It is important to acknowledge the distinction between a group and an ensemble. A group is made up of individuals who are not yet relating to the message, are not connected to one another, and do not have anything to say. An ensemble is really tuned into the message, thinks and acts as one, and has the collective ability to express the thoughts and feelings of others to others.

Our purpose in the rehearsal should be to design a creative and appropriate listening plan that exposes the invisible meanings in the music. Good rehearsals allow ideas and feelings to be freed from the page and set into motion. When translating the work, we move the sound from the page to our mind's ear. When transferring the ideas and feelings, we move the "designed aural image" from our imagination to theirs. Movement is a primary tenet of expressive musicing. Composer Roger Sessions writes eloquently on the subject of movement in *The Musical Experience of Composer, Performer, Listener*:

> The basic ingredient of music is not so much sound as move-
> ment...I would even go a step farther, and say that music is
> significant for us as human beings principally because it
> embodies movement of a specifically human type that goes to
> the roots of our being and takes shape in the inner gestures
> which embody our deepest and most intimate responses.

The importance of natural and fluid movements from the conductor that "...take shape in the inner gestures which embody our deepest and most intimate responses..." (to the messages) cannot be over-stressed. The conductor must remain mindful of how the sound looks and the vibrations feel. All performers form silent links through vibration, movement, and breath when musicing. Motion and breathing are particularly important to the conductor's ability to communicate. Motion allows the conductor to draw designs in the air that represent his/her discoveries and decisions. Breathing allows the conductor to stay connected to the act of making sound by identifying the moment just before the sound comes to life in the ensemble. The breath sets the vibrating sound into motion. It is important to understand that sound and air are in continuous motion and that the conductor has the

responsibility to portray that motion through his/her movement. To guide the flow of movement within a piece, you must develop a keen sense of where you are, where you have been, where you are going, and when you have gotten there. If the conductor understands flow and direction, he or she will be able to lead others to sensitive responses that reveal the essence of sound in motion. In *Music and the Mind*, Anthony Storr observes that:

> The designation movement for a section of a symphony, concerto, or sonata attests to the indissoluble link between music and motion in our minds....

While finding answers surely advances the cause of moving the message on, worthwhile musicing is not always about answers. Sometimes the questions left unanswered are much more thought-provoking. An unanswered question is a very exciting and stimulating thing because it might lead to a new discovery. The Italians call a rehearsal a *probe*. This is exactly what should be going on during the transfer. All those involved should continue to probe for answers as they explore ideas and feelings. A great piece is a complex amalgam of thought, expression, and experience portrayed in movement. It is a revelation of the human condition in all of its manifestations and never fails to deeply reward one's investment of time, energy, and attention.

Transmit (Send and Engage)

Once the message has been translated by the conductor and transferred to the ensemble, the collective transmission of the message to others can begin. If you have done your work, the signal carrying the message will be clear and strong. Great transferring is all about eliminating the static and amplifying the message. For the message to reach its target, the audience, their receivers have to be on. A receptive audience is the final component of a delicately balanced relationship that includes the creator, the message, the transmitters, and the receivers. We have to help our audiences understand how to participate in this process. When people attend a concert, they have to assume responsibility for what they will take away from the interaction. They may need to be introduced to the concept that passive entertainment is not the primary goal of every performance. While entertainment can be a by-product, our presentations have a deeper and more important purpose. That purpose is to enlighten and inform, to connect and contribute, and to make life more rich and rewarding.

Assistive strategies such as program notes, narration, and intriguing presentation at concerts really help to make the interaction rich, informative, and enjoyable. It is important, though, to know how much information is enough. Too much can work against the process and overload the listeners. As conductors, we have to show the audience where, when, and how to attach their listening to the composition. They do not have the same advantage of repeated hearings that the ensemble has, so it is all the more important to guide and facilitate their experience. The audience should never feel like they are being lectured. Instead, they should just feel that they are being included. Never hesitate to let them in on the secrets that you have found encoded in the message—they love it.

A listener's goal at a concert should be to become engaged. The listeners must become active and join in the fun. We must help them understand that contemplation is central to the quality of their experience. The audience must do more than simply give their time. They must invest their energy and direct their attention as well. They have a part to play that can affect the outcome. We really need their contribution to achieve our goals, and they may not be aware of that. It is important to make it clear to the audience that their involvement is indispensable and appreciated. We cannot assume they understand what we are about. There is nothing more exciting than learning something new. We must find ways to include the listeners in the learning process so they feel like collaborators rather than observers.

The challenge of live performance is to help listeners understand the uniqueness of the event and how it differs from a recorded one. Actual people are present, making music in real time. Live music necessitates respectful and attentive interaction. If communication and exchange are to transpire, three things need to be present: a great message, a clear transmission, and willing receivers. All must acknowledge the symbiotic relationship that exists between the music, the artists, and the audience. They need our guidance as much as we need their energy. They want to understand and be moved by the messages we send. I am convinced that a concert can be more than something an audience hears and watches from a distance. With any luck at all, the audience will become co-conspirators who are guilty of aiding and abetting the creation of an aesthetic act.

Transcend (Elevate and Enlighten)

The final stage of this process is actually what the entire process is all about. Our goal is to operate beyond the daily routine of life, to reach through the reality of a sometimes-senseless world and grasp the intangible experience that enlightens and empowers our civilization. What is wonderful about this life-journey is that we can take others with us. To enable others to have a transcending experience and reach an ethereal plane of enlightenment, we must live inside the work of art as though it were our home. We should become so familiar with the space that we can walk around in the dark without stubbing our toe. A home should be an inviting place that nourishes our spirit and provides a safe haven for thinking, feeling, and especially dreaming. We want to be able to take pride in our surroundings and feel good about sharing them with guests. If the dwelling does not provide a quality environment worth inhabiting or visiting, then we surely should not move in.

The artist-composer seeks to evoke feelings and images with music. Pulitzer Prize winning composer John Harbison says, "The after-image that a piece leaves behind is more important than the performance itself." This statement suggests that the composer is counting on an interaction between the piece and those who hear it. The significance of that interaction cannot be underestimated. Cindy McTee, another remarkable composer, puts it this way, "We need new books, new art, and new music to provide a lens through which following generations can see our souls in this time and place. I wish to both enlighten and to entertain, to communicate wholeness, and above all, to celebrate life!"

It is abundantly clear from these statements that understanding the message and feeling its full force is what transcending is all about. We have the opportunity through our work to become transcenders. We can make soul-to-soul connections that change the way all of us relate to our world and the people we share it with. Transcending creates alternative realities that allow those involved to experience their deepest emotions in the safety of the concert hall with friends and facilitators. This process must be about impacting rather than impressing. The more honest the message, the less it has to do with those who are presenting it. Artists are mediums that resonate and amplify the composer's messages. They facilitate the listeners' experience so they can become transfixed and be transported to new worlds of value, truth, and beauty.

As we make our way through our creative life, we must strive to be **translators** who decode the message and discover its meaning, **transferers** who teach the message and empower the experience, **transmitters** who send authentic messages and engage all listeners, and **transcenders** who elevate the message and enlighten the human condition.

Coda

As this chapter concludes, I would like to return to those responsible for the influences I have been exploring. In reflecting on my development, it is clear to me that my experiences with Jack and Esther those many years ago deepened my sense of what life is all about and profoundly transformed my music-making. A very dear friend recently made me aware of this wonderful quote by Nikos Kazantzakis:

> Ideal teachers are those who use themselves as bridges over which they invite their students to cross; then having facilitated their crossing, joyfully collapse, encouraging them to create bridges of their own.

In retrospect, it seems that the Hopkins built many bridges for me, some of which I have yet to cross. They helped me learn to think and question, to explore and discover, and to acknowledge that if one is not willing to fail, one cannot experience success. They showed me a way to live artistically and responsibly in the world. They lead me to know that questions are just as important as answers. They inspired me to treasure ideas and make connections. They directed me to the concept that lifelong learning was my responsibility. They convinced me that diligent preparation and hard work are essential to creative growth. They focused me on the ideal that discipline and self-control are the partners of creative work. They encouraged me to hold on to original thoughts and to believe in the value of being different. They nurtured my spirit and taught me to trust my feelings. They proved to me that teaching was an honorable and noble profession that could have a tremendous impact on the outcome of people's lives. They guided me to an understanding that craft should be appreciated and art should be revered. Their mentorship focused me on my life's goal to become a creative artist.

I have always felt guilty about not doing a better job of staying in touch with the Hopkins. Perhaps what kept me from contacting them was the fear that they might not be there. Setting that fear aside, I recently called them. Jack answered the telephone with that friendly energetic voice I remembered so well. I had forgotten that his mind works faster than he can talk. The lessons took up exactly where they had left off. I was immediately transported back in time to those wonderful days we spent together. Jack and Esther are eighty now. Both are still living active and artistic lives, which are full of commitment for one another. Jack is deeply involved in ceramics and painting, and he and Esther are kept very busy passing on their creative spirits to their grandchildren. Jack reports that Esther is still the best wife any man could have. Additionally he had this to say:

> All my life I have been trying to break through my basic ignorance. I want ideas to come from my mind based on the times that I failed. Success doesn't teach you anything. As I look back on my life, I guess what I did might have been what I have had to do. Work and love are the same. Passion is what makes *everything* happen.

Artists are charged with the task of making the world a worthwhile place to be. We have the ability and responsibility to create experiences that remind people of the value of truly living life within the arts. There are challenges to face, but this is something that must be accomplished. We are called to make a difference, to leave a legacy that adds to the collective spirit of humankind. With the essence of humanity at risk and civilization under attack, we need artist-teachers now more than ever. When we transcend, we go to a place that contains the best the human spirit has to offer. In that place, we are able to achieve heights of nobility, sensibility, and compassion that define the value

of our world community. Hatred, violence, hostility, and prejudice are not welcome in this place. In fact, they cannot survive there. Our goal must be to go to this sanctuary as often as possible with as many people as we can take along. We must make connections that link our spirit to the spirits of others. I am confident and have great faith in the premise that the musical experiences we create and the bridges we build can make a difference. The world in which we live will be made whole again through music because music validates and distinguishes our species.

CHAPTER 5

Strategies for Teaching Music in the Rehearsal

Richard Miles

The purpose of this chapter is to present ideas and methods to assist with the organization and instruction in the rehearsal. Three areas are presented:

Planning – Steps to Teaching and Rehearsing
Ideas to Assist with Managing Time
Incorporating Resources That Enhance Instruction and Learning

Planning – Steps to Teaching and Rehearsing

If one were to start on a journey across a vast country, one would likely develop a *plan* for travel. Many aspects would be considered. One would likely locate and use a map and develop a travel plan. This would be especially important if one wanted to get to the final destination in the most economical time and travel the least miles. So it is in the organization of instruction in performing arts classes. Rehearsals require direction and planning is essential.

There are many possibilities in planning for rehearsals. Here are four basic stages: the organization and development of 1) curriculum, 2) units of study, 3) lesson plans, and 4) rehearsal outlines.

Curriculum

The first step in the overall planning for teaching musicianship is to develop a ***curriculum***—"a long-range guide for teaching music." Volume I, pages 44–56, of *Teaching Music through Performance in Band* outlines four basic curricular models based on literature selection. The literature serves as the primary text for which basic musical ideas and concepts for musicianship development are presented in a cyclic period. Here are the four curriculum plans:

1. The Basic Band Curriculum
2. The Comprehensive Music Curriculum
3. The Three- or Four-Year Cyclic Curriculum Based on the "Menu Principle"
4. The Four-Year "Hybrid Cycle"

Units of Study

The second recommended step in rehearsal planning involves the development of a ***unit of study*** that adapts to a multi-year curriculum. The purpose of the unit is to provide a balanced, comprehensive, and sequential program of instruction while preparing for performance. Sequential lessons would be developed that present particular concepts or objectives (e.g., melody, rhythm, harmony, form, historical perspective, etc.) and technical development.

An example of a unit of study would be to select one "masterwork composition" to study in depth. The selected work would then be the source for teaching and introducing music concepts.

Excellent examples of units of study are presented in Robert Garofalo's *Blueprint for Band, Guides to Band Masterworks,* and *Instructional Designs for Middle/Junior High School Band.* Here is an outline of possible items to include in a unit of study:

Unit Contents:

LEARNING GOALS
Each unit could include Core Concepts for Arts Assessment unique to your state and could be referenced with the *National Standards for Arts Education.*

ASSIGNMENTS
Special projects and assignments could be included for added learning opportunities:

Listening assignment
Practice assignment
Worksheet assignment
Creative projects

HISTORICAL NOTES
Connections that assist students in understanding the relation to history and culture with the music being studied and performed.

GLOSSARY OF MUSICAL TERMS
A listing of musical terms could be prepared that may or may not include definitions. Students could be responsible to look up the terms.

IMPORTANT TEACHING/LEARNING INFORMATION
Musical Elements (melody, rhythm, harmony, timbre, etc.)
    Composer
    Composition
    Historical Perspective
Technical Considerations (alternate fingerings, articulation
    requirements, range development, etc.)
    Stylistic Considerations
    Form and Structure
    Suggested Listening
    Additional References and Resources

ASSESSMENT STRATEGIES
A listing of methods of student assessment, which may include projects, reports, definitions, performance tests, constructed tests, etc. (see Chapter 4 by Larry Blocher in Volume 1, *Teaching Music through Performance in Band*, pp. 27–29)

Lesson Plans

The third step in the recommended planning process is to develop a **lesson plan**. This area seems to be universally accepted as an appropriate stage but seems to be omitted by some directors. Regardless of the reasons directors provide for not doing lesson plans, they are helpful in the planning and implementation stage of the curriculum and unit of study.

Lesson plan formats and contents vary tremendously. Here are several formats for consideration with the understanding that each director should adapt the format that seems best for his/her specific need.

FORM 1

LESSON PLAN FORMAT

*(Adapted from the Kentucky Education Professional Standards Board
KTIP Program "Resource Guide")*

Name: _____ Date: _____ Age/Grade Level: _____
Subject: _____
# of Students: _____
Major Content: _____ Unit
Title:_____

ACTIONS

Goals and Objectives
Clearly state your broad goals and specific objectives, which identify the
content and skills/processes to be taught and formally assessed. Identify
essential questions you want to address.

Connections
List targeted learning objectives and explain how your objectives relate to
standards for learning content established by professional organizations.
(Note: Do not simply list the related goals and/or standards.)

Resources
List resources (i.e., all materials including specific technology applications)
that will be used during the lesson.

Procedures
Describe the strategies and activities you will use to involve students and
accomplish your objectives, including how you will trigger prior knowledge
and adapt strategies to meet individual student needs and the diversity in
your classroom.

Student Assessment
Clearly state how you will assess student progress in meeting the above
objectives, including performance criteria you will use.

IMPACT
(prepared after the lesson)

Reflection/Analysis of Teaching and Learning
What did students learn and what were the indicators of achievement?

REFINEMENT
(prepared after the lesson)

Lesson Extension/Follow-Up
Based on your reflection, what are your plans for subsequent lessons to
reinforce and extend understanding, particularly for students who did not
make satisfactory progress?

FORM 2

Daily Lesson Plan
Performing Arts Class
(Adapted from *Scheduling and Teaching Music*,
GIA Publications, p. 49)

Date_____

Class_____

Compositions_____

_____

Objectives_____

_____

_____

Introduction/Warm Up _____

_____

_____

Teaching/Learning Strategies and Activities _____

_____

_____

_____

Assessment Strategies _____

_____

_____

Rehearsal Summary/Closure _____

_____

_____

_____

_____

Resources and Enrichment Activities _____

_____

_____

_____

_____

FORM 3

Daily Planning Guide

(KMEA Bluegrass Music News, Volume 52/2, p. 15, December 2000, Contributed by Gary L. Parker)

Date_____ Mo Tu We Th Fr Period/Class_____

Objectives

Formal Musical Concepts_____

KERA Learning Goals (circle)   2.22   2.23   2.24   2.25   2.26
                                    Production   Form   Apprec.   HeritageDiversity
                                           Analysis Aesth.

Others:

Warm-up   Begin Time_____   Formal Concepts as prelude to rehearsal Yes No

Rehearsal Outline

Sightreading?_____ Do concepts relate to main rehearsal Yes No

Selection #1	Selection #2	Selection #3
_____	_____	_____
Begin time: (Run-through at beg./end)	Begin time (Run-through at beg./end)	Begin time (Run-through at beg./end)
Anticipated Problem Spots ➤ ➤ ➤	Anticipated Problem Spots ➤ ➤ ➤	Anticipated Problem Spots ➤ ➤ ➤
Important Questions Concepts ⇨ ⇨ ⇨	Important Questions Concepts ⇨ ⇨ ⇨	Important Questions Concepts ⇨ ⇨ ⇨

Assessment *(circle all used)*

   Performance   On-Demand   Open-response   Portfolio   Written Test

   Musical process   Rehearsal   Practice   Listening Logs   Other
       folio   Critiques   Journal

Announcements on Board:

FORM 4

Rehearsal Planning Form

(Adapted from *Scheduling and Teaching Music*, GIA Publications, p. 50)

Date_____

Class_____

Compositions_____

Announcements to Post and Rehearsal Line-Up of Selections _____

_____

_____

_____

Tuning, Warm-Up, and Technical Development _____

_____

_____

_____

Musical Concepts/Objectives _____

_____

_____

_____

Composition – Specific Rehearsal Outline

Time Line   *Composition/Section/Measures*   *What to Rehearse/How to Fix*

_____

_____

_____

_____

_____

_____

_____

_____

_____

_____

_____

_____

_____

_____

_____

_____

Ideas to Assist with Managing Time

Use of Rehearsal Time

Ed Lisk in Volume 1 of *Teaching Music through Performance in Band* (pp. 40–43) presents helpful suggestions relating to the rehearsal period. He recommends a varied use of time.

> The question of how much rehearsal time a warm-up consumes has been a longtime concern for band directors. Approximately 20% of the rehearsal period should be devoted to warm-up exercises based upon the musical complexities of the literature being prepared... The remainder of rehearsal time can be devoted to literature preparation, study, and analysis as outlined in the model Units found in this text... The established curriculum serves as the driving force and guidance system... The concert performance is the result of a curriculum based upon band "masterworks"... (p. 43)

Scheduling and Developing a Long-Range Rehearsal Calendar

Many directors have found it beneficial to provide a long-range calendar that lists daily rehearsals and includes special events and functions. The use of this idea may assist with preparation and be useful in eliminating unnecessary reminders of upcoming special rehearsals, sectionals, and other functions. The following serves as an example.

FORM 5

Wind Orchestra Rehearsal Calendar
September & October
(Rotating Day Rehearsal Schedule)

Sunday	Monday	Tuesday	Wednesday	Thursday	Friday	Saturday
S E P T E M B E R 1	**R** Sightread New Concert Program 2	3	**R** 4	5	**R** Rehearsal & Listening Day to Recorded Excerpts 6	7
8	9	**R** Small Sectionals: Individual Sections 10	11	**R** Student Glossary Guide Due 12	13	14
15	**R** 16	17	**R** Large Sectionals: Brass WW Percussion 18	19	**R** Student Rhythm Assignment Due 20	21
22	23	**R** #1 Recorded Playing Excerpts Due Today 24	25	**R** Section Leaders: Record & Critique 26	27	28
29	**R** Student Critique Day 30	**O C T O B E R** 1	**R** Guest Clinician 2	3	**R** Small Sectionals: Individual Sections 4	5
6	7	**R** Large Sectionals: Brass WW Percussion 8	9	**R** Guest Band Concert 8:00 pm *Required Attendance* 10	11	12
13	**R** Run-Through & Recording Session - #2 Recorded Playing Excerpts Due 14	15	**R** Dress Reh Recording Session 16	**Concert 7:30 pm** Photos: 6:45 Warmup: 7:00 *Reception after Concert* 17	Check Out NEW MUSIC before the weekend 18	19

Concert Preparation Time Line

The following idea may assist students and directors in preparing for specific music for specific days. Often, some music selections require varied instrumentation (one percussionist versus the full section, etc.), small ensemble usage (a chamber work, work for one on a part, etc.), full band, or sectionals. Planning in advance may eliminate unnecessary conflicts, provide additional supervision or instruction that may be needed, help students know they need to have different instruments for a specific rehearsal, and assist in helping students know to prepare specific music and excerpts for specific rehearsal times and days. Here is an example of a *concert preparation time line*.

FORM 6

Concert Preparation Guide and Time Line Wind

Please note the instrumentation needs and varying set-up arrangements for each selection. If you do not perform on one of the works being rehearsed, please be ready when it is your time. Transitions should last no more than *two minutes* between works if the instrumentation and set-up varies. Please be prompt, efficient, and prepared.

Monday, Jan. 7
An Outdoor Overture
Third Symphony
Percussion Concerto
Awayday
Colonial Song
Emblem of Unity
and the mountains

Wednesday, Jan. 9
An Outdoor Overture
Third Symphony
Percussion Concerto

Friday, Jan. 11
Awayday
Colonial Song
Emblem of Unity
and the mountains

Tuesday, Jan. 15
An Outdoor Overture
Third Symphony
Percussion Concerto
and the mountains

Thursday, Jan. 17
Awayday
Colonial Song
Emblem of Unity

Monday, Jan 21
An Outdoor Overture
Third Symphony
Percussion Concerto

Wednesday, Jan. 23
Awayday
Colonial Song
Emblem of Unity
and the mountains

Friday, Jan. 25
An Outdoor Overture
Third Symphony
Percussion Concerto

Tuesday, Jan 29
Awayday
Colonial Song
Emblem of Unity
and the mountains

Thursday, Jan. 31
An Outdoor Overture
Third Symphony
Percussion Concerto
　and the mountains

Monday, Feb. 4
Awayday
Colonial Song
Emblem of Unity

Wednesday, Feb 6
An Outdoor Overture
Third Symphony
Percussion Concerto

Friday, Feb. 8
Awayday
Colonial Song
Emblem of Unity
and the mountains

Tuesday, Feb. 12
All compositions
"Run through
　and record"

Thursday, Feb 14
"Run-through"
CONCERT
7:30 p.m.

Daily Rehearsal Guide and Time Line

Those directors who are interested in saving time and staying on task with rehearsals will want to consider this idea. Many of the finest and most organized directors incorporate this type of organization. Of course, each situation dictates what is most appropriate for each class. Save time by providing students a daily rehearsal guide and time line for each rehearsal. List each selection to be rehearsed and provide a listing for the next rehearsal as well. This will eliminate the need to "call each selection aloud" and "wait" on the students to find the music and get ready. Include other information on the daily outline also (e.g., instrumentation needs, seating adjustments, etc.). Include general comments from the previous rehearsal, the time line for the current rehearsal, the concepts to be presented and, most importantly, include ALL of the announcements. Avoid using rehearsal time for any announcements—fund-raising included. Students will soon learn to "read the outlines" and be more prepared, thus potentially saving more time. Here is an example of a *daily rehearsal guide and time line.*

FORM 7

Daily Rehearsal Guide and Time Line

Please note the time line for today's rehearsal as well as the instrumentation needs and varying set-up arrangements (Schwantner).

TIME LINE FOR TODAY:

1:00   **Warm Up & Tune**

1:20   **Toccata**
(sight-read)

1:30   **Homage to Perotin (from *Medieval Suite*)**
(note the instrumentation needs cornets & trumpets –
percussion)

1:50   **Variations on America**
(beginning – Letter N)

2:15   **Set-up for the Schwantner**
(see the special set-up chart)

2:20   **In evening's stillness**
(beginning, m. 36)

MUSIC FOR THE FIRST CONCERT:

An Outdoor Overture   *Toccata*
Variations on America   *Masquerade for Band*
Emblem of Freedom   *In evening's stillness*
Medieval Suite
     Homage to Leonin
     Homage to Perotin
     Homage to Machaut

GENERAL COMMENTS FROM LAST REHEARSAL:

- All need to play with more expression and musical shape to each line.
- Soft sections need to be much softer by ALL.
- The balance of the band is pretty good generally; however, there is a tendency for the 1st cornets, piccolo, and snare to dominate the volume – back off slightly and listen into the ensemble.
- 3rd clarinets need to play stronger on clarinet choir sections.
- Harmonic passages with long tones need more attention with listening to the intonation (especially where the saxophones and horns double).
- The low brass are sometimes phasing with the ensemble (tubas are noticeably behind sometimes).
- Percussion need to play together on the start of the 4th movement.
- All soloists need to play more expressively and use appropriate vibrato – listen also for the releases and pitch matching at the release points.

ANNOUNCEMENTS:

Concert Reception
A reception will be held following the upcoming concert for friends and parents. Special slides from our recent concert tour will be shown during the serving. Please invite them to attend.

U.S. Marine Band Concert
University of Kentucky – Tuesday, October 5
We have 40 free tickets (only) and have reserved one charter bus for transportation – please sign up today if you want a ticket and a ride.

Reminder to ALL
Audio recordings and full music scores of those works on our first concert are on reserve in the Music Listening Library – Have you been to listen?

Rehearsal Calendar
Note: The rehearsal calendar for the semester includes our *two concert dates:* October 12 (10 rehearsals) and December 8.

Incorporating Resources that Enhance Instruction and Learning

The following examples are models to be adapted to fit each director's individual needs to enhance instruction and learning. The use of these types of resources may lead students to be more informed musicians.

Student Information Guides

Students can be provided information for each composition being prepared. Some directors provide this information in handout form, and some have created special websites designed specifically for student interaction and research.

Directors are encouraged to use the material provided in the *Teaching Music through Performance in Band* texts. When using the information, please properly credit the text and the contributors of the guides. The **student information guides** could include any unit from the Teacher Resource Guides.

FORM 8

DIVERTIMENTO IN "F"

Student Information Guide

(Guide Material from Teaching Music through Performance in Band,
Volume 2, pp. 584–587)

Divertimento in "F"
Jack Stamp
(b. 1954)

Unit 1: Composer

Jack Stamp was born in Washington, DC in 1954, and grew up in the nearby Maryland suburbs.　He received a BS degree in Music Education from Indiana University of Pennsylvania in 1976, a MM degree in Percussion Performance from East Carolina University in 1978, and a DMA degree in Wind Conducting from Michigan State University in 1988 where he studied with Eugene Corporon. His primary composition teachers were Robert Washburn and Fisher Tull. More recently he has worked with Joan Tower and David Diamond.

Stamp is currently Professor of Music at Indiana University of Pennsylvania where he conducts the Wind Ensemble, Symphony Band, and Concert Band, and teaches courses in conducting and percussion. He is founder and musical director of the Keystone Wind Ensemble, a professional recording group dedicated to the advancement of American concert band music.

Unit 2: Composition

Divertimento in "F", composed in 1994, was commissioned by Frank Wickes and the Louisiana State University Bands in celebration of their seventy-fifth anniversary.

The title does not refer to key centers, but to the fact that the movement titles all begin with the letter "F": "Fanfare," "Fate," "Fury," "Faith," and "Frolic." Each movement is dedicated to a person or persons important to the composer. The "Fanfare" is dedicated to Fisher Tull (one of Stamp's composition teachers); the "Fate" movement is subtitled "In Memoriam William Schuman" (Stamp calls himself a "Schumaniac", and learned much about composition from studying his scores); "Fury" is dedicated to Joan Tower (the movement was written during Stamp's brief study period with her); "Faith," the only movement not dedicated to a musician, is dedicated to four North Carolina Baptist ministers who Stamp considers influential

in his spiritual life; and "Frolic," dedicated to the great American composer David Diamond (written during a brief study period with the composer).

Unit 3: Historical Perspective

The *divertimento*, an instrumental composition dating back to the Classical era, is rooted in the wind music of Haydn and Mozart. The form, usually entertaining in design, is comprised of rather short, contrasting movements.

Unit 4: Musical Elements

This work is filled with a wide variety of compositional techniques which will educate the players to the creative process of the music of their time.

"Fanfare" explores a variety of textures and styles including quartal and quintal harmony, "wrong note" bass techniques, canon and fugue, minimalism, and augmentation.

"Fate" explores the *passacaglia* and is a study in polychords. There is also a brief quote from William Schuman's *Third Symphony*.

"Fury" is an adventure in rhythm. The illusion of *accelerando* and *ritard.* is created through meter change and the even distribution of a rhythmic pattern within those changes.

"Faith" is based on the Scottish hymn "Dundee." It is a chorale with five variations and a coda. The movement is treated much like a *chaconne* with each variation presenting a different compositional setting of the hymn tune. Variation 4 (m. 38) is an example of a modal harmonization.

"Frolic" returns to the contrapuntal texture of the first movement. A *fugato* section based on the "Frolic" theme ensues. The device of "cyclicism" appears where the theme of the "Fanfare" appears as a double *fugato* with the "Frolic" theme. The minimalistic section of the "Fanfare" also returns with the "Fanfare" theme in augmentation while the trumpets play the "Frolic" melody.

All information in this guide was contributed by the composer.
Jack Stamp
Conductor of University Bands
Professor of Music
Indiana University of Pennsylvania
Indiana, Pennsylvania

Student Glossary Guide

Following is an example of a *glossary guide* intended for students to complete. The information could be presented and filled out during the class, or students could obtain the information from out-of-class research.

FORM 9

Student Glossary Guide
Divertimento in "F"
by Jack Stamp

Students are to complete this guide in the next two weeks. All terms and definitions will be presented during the daily rehearsals. Additional information may be found in the Band Library. Resources and recordings are available for checkout. Please do not hesitate to "ask" if you cannot find the information.

Movements:
I: Fanfare
Quartal Harmony
Quintal Harmony
Canon
Fugue
Minimalism
Augmentation

II: Fate
Passacaglia
Polychords
Schuman's 3rd Symphony

III: Fury
Metric Modulation
Rhythm Complexities

IV: Faith

    Scottish Hymn: *Dundee*

    Chorale of Five Variations and Coda (treated like a
        Chaconne")

    (Where do each of the variations and the coda begin?)

        Var. 1

        Var. 2

        Var. 3

        Var. 4

        Var. 5

    Coda

Chaconne

Modal Harmonization

V: Frolic

    Minimalistic Section of Fanfare Returns

    Frolic Melody

    Fugal Section

    Combined Section: minimalistic section rhythm/frolic
        theme/ augmentation of the Fanfare theme

Composers:

Please provide some information about each of the following
composers—e.g., Why are they important to this work? How may
their compositions relate to the *Divertimento in F?*

Jack Stamp

Fisher Tull

William Schuman

Joan Tower

David Diamond

Rehearsal Critique

Directors who take the time to prepare a ***rehearsal critique*** may find the investment a significant and important teaching aid and time-saver. This idea works well when the goal of the rehearsal is to run through and record the music. Students could review the critique prior to the start of the next rehearsal.

FORM 10

Rehearsal Critique–Wind Orchestra

From the last rehearsal – Please review the comments and mark YOUR parts if needed. Each section leader is to record the rehearsal tomorrow from his/her area and provide a written critique similar to the one provided today. Cassettes and tapes will be available for checkout in the Band Office.

The Soaring Eagle
- Brass and snare need to be together more one before 8.
- Percussion – please check your parts (one voice is missing "humm" –there should be percussion 1, 2, 3, and timpani).

Four Scottish Dances
Movement 1
- Letter C needs to be more crisp and brilliant with the fanfares (one 1st cornet remain on the trumpet part until measure 30 (one before D) less 1st cornet 6 before D.
- More bass drum sting last note Movement 1.

Movement 2
- Opening needs to be more together.
- Letter E, softer accompaniment.
- Careful with the releases in the last 3 measures.

Movement 3
- Letter B less cornet and more mellow with the sound.
- Letter C needs to be more connected at the ends of the phrases (singing style).
- Less volume with the accompaniment voices at letter E.

Movement 4
- Woodwinds need to be stronger and more precise on the barn dance theme.
- Coda – who has the *fp?* – please do it.
- Last three bars can be stronger with the chords.

In Memoriam
- Careful to count woodwinds and piano, don't miss the entrance at 58.
- *Lento* to the end – listen more for entrance and release precision.

Canzona
- Please review the form. If you do not have one of the themes –you probably play a *secondary role* with the balance.
- Letter H is too loud (especially whole-note parts).
- Clarinets play slightly softer in the extended register where you parallel the unison melody.
- Much less piccolo on all unison lines.

Dance Movements
Movement 1
- The opening needs to be more rhythmically solid (some are hesitating on entrances and creating a phasing problem –especially mm. 1–4).
- Horns, saxes, and euphonium need to match pitch more on the opening theme.
- Measure 73 – rehearsal 8 (horns need more precision with your part).

Movement 2
- Non eighth-note theme needs to be softer.
- Play stronger on the fragment ending.

Movement 3
- COUNT and listen so that you do not miss your entrance after 39.
- All brass need to play in a more singing "dolce" style – even in the *ff* sections.

Movement 4
- Percussion, please play together at the beginning.
- Work for more overall rhythmic precision and note accuracy – "Make *Music* Together."
- Don't miss the transition entrance – 56 needs to be a bit stronger.
- More sting on the last note – timpani and bass drum.

With Quiet Courage
- Much SOFTER from everyone in the beginning (melody needs to be more in tune) – "Playing in TUNE is Matching the Pitch WITH Your Friends."
- Avoid any HARSH and strident tone (more "DOLCE" in style).

Dance of the Jesters
- Lock into the tempo at the beginning.
- Remember that the quarter note gets more emphasis in the melody on count 2 (measures 2, 3, 4, etc.).
- LOOK, Listen, and DO the Volume changes.
- More precision is needed 33–49.
- Clarinets, more precision is needed measures 210–212 in the exposed feature area.
- 229 – is out of tune in the half note chords (bassoons, saxophones, euphonium and horns in accompaniment).

Form and Structure Guides

Often seeing the ***structure and form*** presented visually assists students in comprehending the design of the compositions being performed. Here are two examples.

FORM 11

Form and Structure Guide
Dance of the Jesters

Dance of the Jesters was composed by Peter Ilyich Tchaikovsky and has been arranged by Ray Cramer. This composition is taken from the play, *The Snow Maidens*. It is also important to note that this work is also referred to as "Dance of the Tumblers."

Mark the Form (MODIFIED RONDO FORM)
A   #1–74
B   #75–122
A   #123–196
C   #197–228
D   #297–342
Transition (using D motive) #327–342
A   #343–358
(serves as coda)

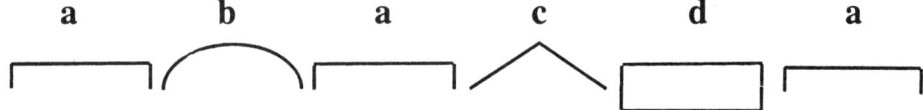

Canzona
Canzona was commissioned by the famous American band conductor, Edwin Franko Goldman, and premiered by the Goldman Band in 1951. This is the only work for band composed by Peter Mennin.

Mark the Form (ROUNDED-BINARY FORM)
A   Beginning–Letter H
B   Letter H–Letter P
A1   Letter P–Q
Codetta   Letter Q–end

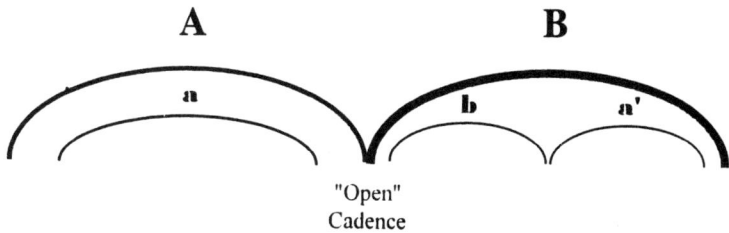

"Open"
Cadence

Rhythm Guide

In some compositions, certain rhythms are very intricate and difficult to understand and visualize, especially regarding the subdivision. Consider providing students with a reference guide for those areas. Precision and understanding is likely to improve. Here are two examples.

FORM 12

Rhythmic Flowchart
"Armenian Dances, Part 1" by Alfred Reed

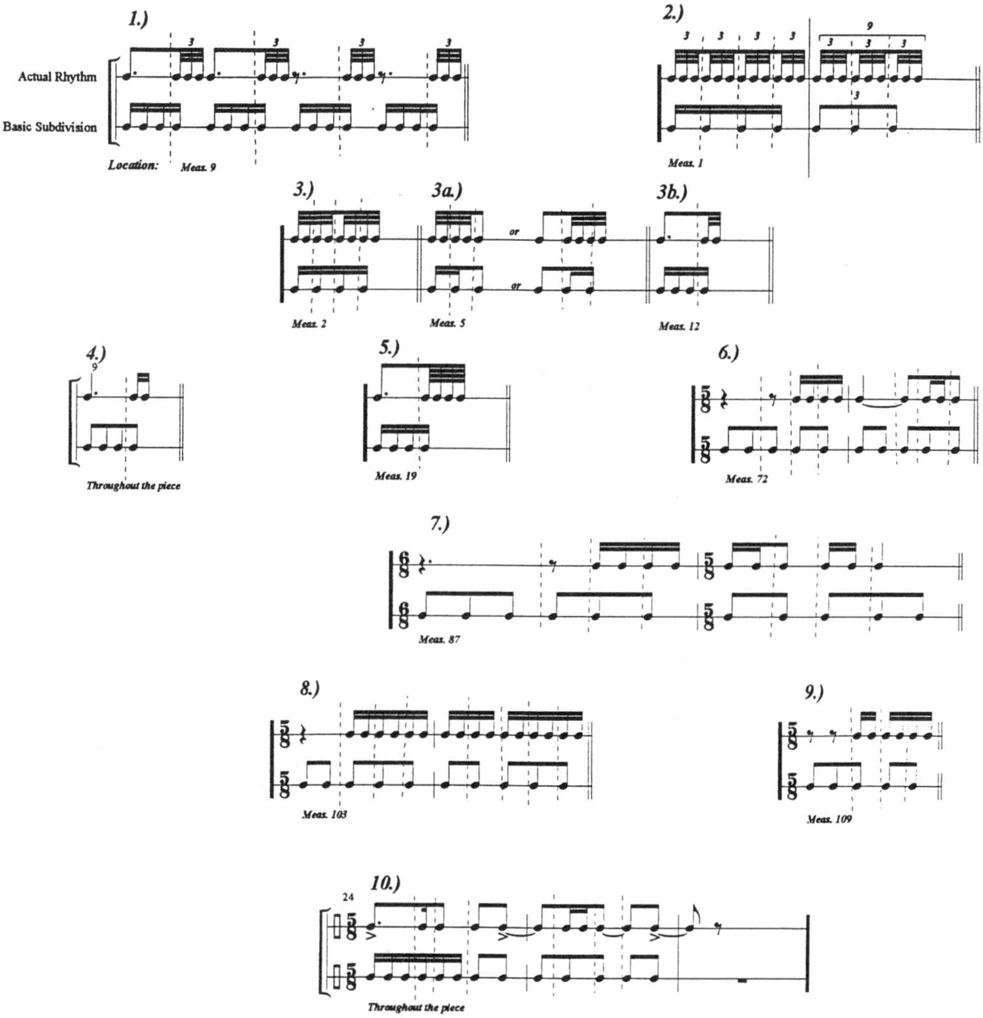

FORM 13

Rhythmic Flowchart
"Divertimento in F" by Jack Stamp

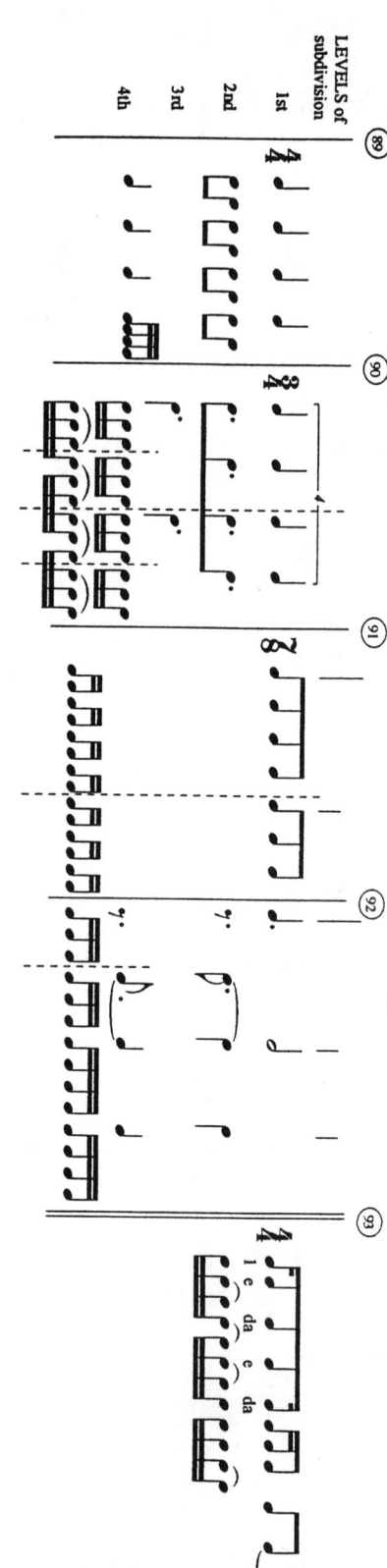

Note: "Illusion of accelerando and ritards . . . ." "Tempo changes through meter and rhythm equals much like metric modulations but occur without a change in the basic pulse. . . ."

Recording Reference Guide

Consider providing a master discography that lists recommended reference recordings of the works being performed. If encouraged, students may purchase those recordings, and if available in the school library, they may also listen to the recordings. The following is an example of a *recording reference guide*.

FORM 14

Recording Reference Guide
Wind Orchestra

The following resources are recommended references for obtaining recordings of works being performed. If you need toll-free numbers or addresses for the suppliers, please see the listing posted on the bulletin board outside the Listening Library. Order early so that the recordings will arrive prior to our concert.

Suite Francaise	Darius Milhaud	Cincinnati Wind Symphony	KCD-11058
		London Wind Orchestra	LWO-629
		Tokyo Kosei Wind Orchestra	KOCD-3101
		United States Army Field Band	
Trauermusik	Richard Wagner/ Votta/Boyd	Tokyo Kosei Wind Orchestra	KOCD-7507
		Indiana State University	BOCD-7507
		Wisconsin Wind Orchestra	MCD-2483
Armenian Dances, Part I	Alfred Reed	Senzoko Gakuen Symphonic Winds	WFR-140
		Tokyo Kosei Wind Orchestra	KOCD-3016
		Tokyo Kosei Wind Orchestra	KOCD-3502
		UNCG Wind Orchestra	CD-104
		University of Illinois	MCD-1210
The Gum-Suckers March	Percy Grainger	Cincinnati Wind Symphony	KCD-11065
		Michigan State Wind Ensemble	DE-3101
		United States Coast Guard Band	MW91MCD-8
		University of Illinois	MCK-1865
From a Dark Millennium	Joseph Schwantner	Baden Wurtemburg Wind Ensemble	MAS-279
		Ithaca College	MCBS-35891
		North Texas Wind Symphony	KCD-11089

Note: All discography references are taken directly from the following:

Teaching Music through Performance in Band, Volume 3. Chicago: GIA Publications. Discography compiled by Edwin C. Powell, pp. 771–792.

Summary

Teaching musicianship involves more than "rehearsing the notes." It requires detailed planning and advanced organization. As a result, students may experience an increase in their appreciation and understanding of the music being rehearsed and performed. The ultimate goal: to **teach music** (about the music—using quality music) while preparing for **performance in band.**

Selected References

Blocher, Larry, and Richard Miles. *Scheduling and Teaching Music*. Chicago: GIA Publications, 1999.

Durante, Leonard P., et. al. *Band Music That Works*, Volumes I and II. Burlingham, CA: Contrapuntal Publications, 1988.

Dvorak, Thomas L., Cynthia Crump Taggart, and Peter Schmaltz. *Best Music for Young Band*. Brooklyn, NY: Manhattan Beach Music, 1986.

Ericksen, Connie M. *Band Director's Curriculum Resource*. West Nyack, NY: Parker Publishing Company, 1998.

Garofalo, Robert. *Blueprint for Band*. Ft. Lauderdale, FL: Meredith Music Publications, 1983.

Garofalo, Robert. *Guides to Band Masterworks*. Ft. Lauderdale, FL: Meredith Music Publications, 1992.

Garofalo, Robert. *Instructional Designs for Middle/Junior High School Band*, Volumes I and II. Ft. Lauderdale, FL: Meredith Music Publications, 1995.

Hawaii Music Program, Curriculum Research and Development Group, College of Education, and the University of Hawaii. *Comprehensive Musicianship Through Band Performance*. Zone 4, Book A, by Brent Heisenger. Menlo Park, CA: Addison-Wesley Publishing Company, 1973.

Labuta, Joseph A. *Teaching Musicianship in the High School Band*. Ft. Lauderdale, FL: Meredith Music Publications, 1997.

Lisk, Edward S. *The Creative Director: Alternative Rehearsal Techniques*. Ft. Lauderdale, FL: Meredith Music Publications, 1991.

Lisk, Edward S. *Intangibles of Music Performance*. Ft. Lauderdale, FL: Meredith Music Publications, 1996.

Miles, Richard, and Larry Blocher. *Block Scheduling: Implications for Music Education*. Chicago: GIA Publications, 1996.

Miles, Richard, editor. *Teaching Music through Performance in Band*, Volumes 1, 2, 3. Chicago: GIA Publications, 1996, 1998, 1999.

National Band Association, *Selective Music List for Bands*. Third edition. Nashville, TN: National Band Association, 1990.

Rehrig, William H., *The Heritage Encyclopedia of Band Music*, Volumes I and II. Westerville, OH: Integrity Press, 1991.

Rehrig, William H. *The Heritage Encyclopedia of Band Music*, Volume III Supplement. Edited by Paul Bierley, Westerville, OH: Integrity Press, 1996.

Stycos, Roland. *Listening Guides for Band Musicians*. Portland, ME: J. Weston Walch Publishers, 1991.

The University of the State of New York, The State Education Department, Bureau of Curriculum Development. *Music in the Middle/Junior High School: Syllabus/Handbook*. Albany, NY: New York State Education Department, 1988.

Waley, Garwood. "*A Comparison of the Unit Study and Traditional Approaches for Teaching Musical Concepts and Skills through School Band Performance*." DMA dissertation, The Catholic University of America, 1991.

Wisconsin Department of Public Instruction. *A Guide to Curriculum Planning in Music Education*. Madison, WI: Wisconsin Department of Public Education, 1986.

CHAPTER 6

The Selection and Development of Effective Student Leaders

Tim Lautzenheiser

"You cannot teach a man anything.
You can only help him discover it within himself."
··· Galileo ···

Author's Note

Over the past two decades, I have enjoyed the tremendous opportunity to present leadership seminars to students, teachers, administrators, and business professionals throughout the nation. Leadership, unlike many disciplines, is constantly shifting, evolving, changing, and "becoming." In fact, the more we learn about the art of leadership, the more puzzling and mysterious it becomes. Modern-day leadership experts continue to highlight the importance of developing *leadership values* along with the understanding of systemic leadership techniques. The shift from *people control* to *group empowerment* is a common theme in today's contemporary leadership training; ultimately, the welfare of the people is the primary concern. The *process* becomes equally as important as the *product*.

Bands (music programs) are perfect settings for leadership training. The band culture represents a microcosm of the community environment and requires a cast of leaders to teach, explain, create, and serve the various members of the musical society. Student leaders are not a luxury but a necessity; therefore, the selection, training, and guidance of these young leaders is a crucially important aspect of every band director's daily responsibility. The following chapter is a leadership blueprint dedicated to helping you and your students develop a positive and productive student leadership curriculum that will serve the band in achieving excellence in every aspect of the band program.

By design, the following pages are sequenced in subchapters:

Character Traits of a Student Leader
A view of the six character traits desirable (and necessary) for the selection of the leader candidate are presented.

A Paradigm Shift for Today's Leaders
The emphasis on intrinsic motivation as opposed to extrinsic rewards becomes the charge for every young leader; to this end, the expectations of the leader are outlined in a clear and concise approach.

The Personal Values of a Student Leader
Simply put, *giving* and *forgiving* become the key factors in creating a safe, encouraging, and challenging environment to foster the growth of the members of the band.

Choosing Leaders: Maturity Is the Key
If there is one absolute in the leader selection process, it is the measurement of the candidate's maturity. Is he/she prepared to assume the additional responsibilities and assigned tasks?

Solution-Driven Leaders: The Ultimate Choice
Many people can recognize the problem, the successful leader is the person who offers the solution. It is vitally important the student leader understands that the key to quality is determined by the collective work ethic of his/her followers.

Reading all of the subchapters at one time may not be as valuable as looking at each one as a separate template of leadership training. May I suggest you have your student leader candidates study these various areas of leadership development as they launch on their leadership journey; the benefactors of this exercise will be *everyone*.
    Strike up the band!

Character Traits of a Student Leader

Student leaders are no longer a luxury in our educational world but rather a necessity, particularly in the field of music. Any successful ensemble is made up of a strong director and a committed group of responsible and dedicated student leaders. We count on these extraordinary young people to offer their time and energy in the ongoing growth and development of our programs; without them, much of the daily work simply would not be completed.

Students are usually eager to assume the leadership roles, but are they *capable* of assuming the responsibilities that accompany the real leadership agenda? Do they truly understand the personal price of leadership? The selection process cannot be taken lightly, for the student leaders will often determine the attitude, the atmosphere, and the level of achievement for the entire organization; they are the pace-setters for every member of the ensemble.

So many factors enter into this important choice. Are the candidates competent? Are they emotionally secure? Will they assume a leadership posture both in and out of the rehearsal environment? Can they handle stress and pressure? Are they willing to make decisions that are not self-serving but focused on their followers? Do they accept criticism and learn from their mistakes? Are they selfless rather than selfish? Ultimately, will they serve as positive role models for each and every band student? These are not easy questions to answer, but they are crucially important inquisitions, for it is unfair to everyone to assign leadership responsibilities to an individual who has not developed the level of maturity needed to assume the added responsibilities associated with productive leadership.

Over the years of teaching the skills and techniques of student leadership, I have observed so many students who are confident in their abilities and certain they can "do the job" and do it quite well; however, they have great difficulty turning hopes and visions into reality. The results are devastating to their followers, the program, and the perceived self-worth of the leader him/herself. In truth, everyone loses. How can we, as directors, avoid this dilemma?

In our urgency to have our students become more responsible and productive (perhaps these are one in the same), we are constantly looking for those opportunities of growth that will allow them to experience the pathway to success. After all, our fundamental mission as educators is to prepare students for the rigors of adulthood. It is exciting and personally gratifying when we see students rise to the occasion, but the penalty of failure has a high price tag in terms of the emotional damage to a student's self-concept. Unlike many other aspects of education, failure in student leadership means others are at the effect of the shortcoming. If a student leader does not accomplish the given task, it can (and often does) have a negative impact on all the followers, and the consequences can range from outward hostility to exclusion from the group. In extreme cases, the wounded student leaders will make a decision to never be put in a similar situation where they will be subject to such personal pain. They choose to sidestep any leadership responsibilities in the future.

Metaphorically, we do not pick a tomato from a garden until it is ripe, for it will be of no value to anyone. It is impossible to place the prematurely picked vegetable back on the mother-plant. Likewise, a student leader who is not ready (not ripe) will be incapable of surviving the pressure and stress of leadership if he/she has not grown to the necessary stage of leadership maturity. There is an art to the selection process, and veteran educators are careful to find the students who are:

- **Selfless** – Watch for the students who are always taking the time to help those around them. You can quickly identify this important trait—consideration for others—by simply observing their behavior before and after rehearsals.

- **Persistent** – Tenacity is an attribute necessary for attaining excellence at any discipline. Many people will begin a new endeavor with a sense of positive enthusiasm, but you are interested in the students who "complete" their assigned responsibilities. We are not measured by what we begin but by what we complete.

- **Consistent** – Most student leaders are at a time in their lives when they are establishing their personal habits and their life values; they are truly deciding "who they are." Dreams, goals, and desires can shift radically from one day to the next. Pinpoint the students who are predictable and demonstrate emotional stability; those who can "stay the course."

- **Affable** – It is often tempting to favor the student leader who is a gifted musician, and this is certainly an important aspect of his/her qualifications; however, it is vital for the student leader to have a healthy rapport with the other members of the organization. Popularity aside, the chosen student leader must be recognized and respected by the majority of the group.

- **Honest** – Slighting the truth is commonplace. The student who avoids the temptation to exaggerate or embellish the truth and is willing to accept the consequences that often accompany honesty is a rare commodity. Everyone will benefit from being in the presence of a person who demonstrates such personal integrity.

- **Faithful, Loyal** – "United we stand, divided we fall." This well-worn phrase is still classic advice for every leader. The students who are always tried-and-true loyalists are your best nominees for student leadership positions. At this stage of leadership, commitment to the group is mandatory, and any disagreements or issues should be dealt with behind closed doors and in strict confidentiality, but there must be a sense of unity in front of the ensemble members.

These six personality traits are only a starting point; however, they will establish a strong foundation for the selection/qualification of any student leader. We, as educators, must be sensitive to the overwhelming effects student leadership can have on the development of the individual. We are in a position to help our students create a sense of self-worth that will serve them throughout their lives. We can guide their efforts and energies to ensure a positive experience for all concerned. As their leaders, we have an immeasurable influence on their leadership for life.

A Paradigm Shift for Today's Leaders

The entire realm of leadership training has taken a dramatic shift over the last three decades. The strong-armed approach to leadership success has given way to the concept of allowing the follower to become an invested contributor to the overall mission. There is a greater emphasis on *intrinsic motivation* rather than using *extrinsic* rewards as a means to individual or group achievement.

The cornerstones of this paradigm shift emphasize a win-win concept embracing both the requirements of the project responsibilities and the welfare of the people involved. It diminishes the power struggle often associated with the traditional positioning, turf protection, rank-and-file status, etc. To find success in this modern-day blueprint of leadership style, these four laws of leadership must be understood and integrated into every decision made by the assigned leader; they serve as the foundation blocks of contemporary leadership.

People are more important than titles.

The focal point remains on the welfare of the people involved. The leader constantly monitors the overall attitude of the group, ensuring a sense of mutual understanding and synergistic effort based on individual and group commitment focused on the agreed objectives.

We can't lead others until we lead ourselves.

Role modeling plays a vital part in the leader's ongoing communication with the members of the organization. While delegation is still an important aspect of the process, the leader sets the pace by demonstrating the expectations and the standards desired to achieve positive results. The most effective form of leadership is positive role-modeling.

Leaders are measured by what they give.

Leadership is an opportunity "to give" to those who are part of the group, organization, ensemble. The position of leadership is a license to help all those who are part of the forum. If there is not a measured contribution to the forward progress of the group, the value of the leader is diminished to the point of being "merely a title carrier."

Leaders assume total responsibility.

When something goes awry, the leader immediately assumes the responsibility for the breakdown rather than pointing the finger of blame at anyone else. The welfare of the followers is primary in every facet of the leader's agenda.

Adapting this new leadership consciousness to any musical ensemble offers the individual players a greater opportunity to "own the group" and accept the responsibilities for the positive growth and development of the organization. Everyone wins.

The Personal Values of a Student Leader

When asked, "Who would like to serve in a leadership role as we continue to move forward with our band program?," do the students really comprehend the extended effort and energy required to fulfill the responsibility/agenda that lies ahead?

All too often an enthusiastic young want-to-be leader will eagerly assume the coveted title only to be quickly disillusioned following several unsuccessful attempts to garner group support while trying to accomplish the given project. Personal discouragement leads to "giving up," and (unfortunately) all future leadership opportunities are avoided based on past experiences of perceived failure.

Do we properly prepare our students for "what lies ahead" when they choose to become student leaders? Or do we simply (and randomly) pick this or that person to fill the given position? Are your leaders selected via a popularity vote, or are they chosen because of their abilities, skills, talents, and *intentions*?

Leadership is made up of two philosophical components:

> 1. Leadership is FOR GIVING.
> 2. Leadership is forgiving.

Many young people see a leadership position as the chance to be in charge, to tell others what to do, to delegate work, and to put themselves in a posture of authority. Nothing could be further from the truth. The essence of an effective leader lies in the student's ability to serve others, to create success for the people in the organization. It is the opportunity to give, to contribute, to roll up one's sleeves and begin moving in a positive forward direction. Whether it is straightening the chairs, putting the stands away, creating a colorful bulletin board, or working with someone on a musical passage, the leader is the person who does **what needs to be done, when it needs to be done, whether he/she wants to do it or not, without anybody asking.**

The second aspect of leadership centers on the concept of forgiving. When something goes awry (and it will), many young leaders want to react to the situation by reprimanding the followers for their inability to fulfill the leader's suggestions. However, the true leader will forgive the people involved and proactively refocus the energies to correct the problem and quickly get back on course. Psychologically (and intellectually) we know, "People do not get better by making them feel worse." All too often, there is a tendency for young leaders to chastise those who fall short of the given assignment; nothing could be more detrimental to the trust relationship necessary for future success in any leader/follower relationship. The solution is simple: forgive, correct, proceed forward.

When selecting those chosen students who will be working with their peers in a leadership capacity, look beyond their group popularity, their musical gifts, and even their academic standing; begin to observe how they interact with others, and pay special attention to those who always are considerate of their fellow students and willing to serve those by going above and beyond the call of duty. These are the candidates who are most likely to succeed as leaders; they "live" the values required of every contributing leader by *giving* and *forgiving*.

Choosing Leaders: Maturity Is the Key

- How do you choose your student leaders?
- Is there a specific criteria to use in the selection of these crucially important role models?
- Do you have a particular standard they must achieve before they are candidates?
- What are the expectations you have of these people?

After studying and working with countless student leaders over the years, it is clearly apparent: some students are ready for the extra responsibilities student leadership requires and many are not. What determines this crucial difference? It appears to lie in the area of individual maturity—not chronological age, but personal maturity. Some young folks easily assume (and consume) the added workload, while others may buckle under the pressure. As teachers, we have an obligation to be sensitive in our selection of student leaders, for we are asking these individuals to give up the privileges of their classmates and enter into a role that will demand their undivided attention if they are to succeed. As you can quickly see, being a student leader requires an individual to give up much of his/her freedom in return for the opportunity to dedicate more time and energy to the given goal.

While being a student leader is often misinterpreted as a status upgrade, it is, in truth, the acquisition of more responsibilities. It is all too easy for the aspiring student leader to be blinded by the enthusiasm of the moment and accept the charge before truly understanding what will be required of him/her. This is where we, as caring educators, must be cautious and realistic in our assessment of a student's "readiness." Once again, let us revisit the original questions pertaining to the selection process; it is imperative that we begin with this inquiry, "Is the student mature enough to emotionally embrace the

task(s) at hand in a fashion that will positively add to his/her personal growth and development?" Simply put, "Can the student handle what will be asked of him/her?" Although there is no definitive template to measure something as arbitrary as maturity, there are some general guidelines that can help you in identifying those students who are being considered for student leadership positions.

Levels of Maturity:

Level I: Selfish – Selfishness focuses on the pre-occupation with "self." A student might be a stellar musician, but he/she easily becomes upset unless everything support his/her personal welfare and opinion. Beware of the student who unconsciously, or by design, makes decisions that supports his/her self-promotion and/or personal agenda. Little will be gained if he/she is given the power to make decisions that will impact others. Inevitably, more time will be spent dealing with the problems caused by immature decision-making than will be spent enjoying the benefits of the young leader's efforts. We often rationalize the fact that these students might, in fact, prosper by putting them "up front" or giving them extra responsibilities. Alas, it is rare they will rise to the occasion. It would be a much kinder and more positive choice to allow them to spend extra time in the growth process before asking them to put others' considerations and personal welfare ahead of their own.

Level II: Independent – We often see "independence" as a reaction to the lack of results achieved with a "selfish" attitude. The human mind comes up with a logical reason why others do not respond to our wishes and concludes, "It is easier to just do it myself than to depend on others and be disappointed." Many people function at this level throughout life and are quite successful; however, they are unto themselves and perfectly satisfied to "do their own thing." In fact, they may be uncomfortable letting others get involved. Since they produce excellence in their area of interest, we are often deluded into thinking they will transfer a similar standard of achievement to their followers if they are given a leadership position; however, the "independent" may become frustrated when the followers do not immediately choose to replicate his/her personal habits and work patterns. These individuals have a tendency to give up in disgust when the going gets rough and revert to the "I'll just do it myself" habit that has served them so well in the past.

Level III: Cooperative – A student must be at Maturity Level 3 (Cooperative) before being considered for any kind of leadership position that involves dealing with other people. Cooperative personalities are aware that nothing will be gained without a sense of mutual understanding and that all this must be well fueled with a cooperative attitude. Then, and only then, I–me syndrome gives way to a genuine we–us approach to every situation.

Satisfying the ego will become secondary to the forward motion and the personal welfare of the group. This student leader understands the benefits of cooperative decision-making are far greater than self-serving independent choices. Granted, it takes a mature individual to see beyond the instant gratification derived from serving oneself before thinking of others. Level III, cooperative, is a transition to the final and most important perspective needed for effective leadership.

Level IV: Giving – We have many examples of "givers," and we all know those who will go the extra mile, but this level of "giving" does not require any kind of reciprocation. Those who operate from a posture of "giving" do so for the pleasure of the process. The payoff for this individual lies totally in the opportunity to serve. While thank you's are appreciated, they are not required. The payment lies in the process of the giving. So often student leaders will find themselves discouraged because nobody recognizes their dedicated efforts. It is true we all enjoy personal acknowledgement along the pathway of life, but a mature leader is clearly aware that the most important affirmation of his/her leadership success is often disguised in the extension of more work and extra responsibilities being added to the leadership agenda. In essence, "The reward for a job well done is the opportunity to do more." The student leader who is a genuine "giver" is a rare commodity; everyone in the group will gain by experiencing the magic created by a *giving* leader. It is his/her *presence* that makes the difference; what greater role model could there possibly be for the followers?

The student leader selection process is certain to affect every aspect of your program. All too often we make our choices based on everything from age, talent level, attendance, personal favors, etc. In all fairness to everyone, we must be honest in assessing the maturity of those students who want to be given the opportunity to serve others through various student leadership positions. Carefully seek the student who wants to improve the conditions for his/her compatriots by unselfishly contributing to the given goal. When you find this individual you have identified a student leader in action. Put this individual in charge; let this student take the lead.

Solution-Driven Leaders: The Ultimate Choice

How many times have we heard the haunting phrase, "You are either part of the problem or you are part of the solution,"? In choosing our student leaders, it is vitally important to select exemplary role models who are *solution-oriented*, rather than *problem-plagued.*

Students who wish to serve in a leadership capacity must first understand that true leadership requires an individual to do more than his/her counterparts; it is about serving others. Student leaders are the doers, they are the

people who roll up their sleeves and go to work.

Even after an extensive explanation of the personal and group expectations, I often wonder if the hopeful student leader really understands the level of commitment, dedication, patience, and personal sacrifice needed, required, even demanded. For those students who wish to take on the challenges of leadership, and for those directors who are looking for the student who has the right leadership qualifications, review the following thoughts, for these are the requisites in selecting and developing the solution-driven leader.

Focus on the solution, not the problem.

A gifted leader will seek an objective/solution and then begin to move in the direction of the given goal rather than dwelling on the current status and all the reasons the organization cannot reach the objective. This comes about by using a clear and concise blueprint of a *solution-driven* vs. a *problem-driven* plan of action.

The solution-driven leader (SDL) spotlights the strengths of the followers and emphasizes what is already working. Instead of quickly pointing out everything that is wrong, ineffective, inefficient, and preventing forward progress, the leader will first make a point to recognize the various aspects of the project (including the people) that give it credibility and make it worth the follower's investment of time and energy. The benefit package must be obvious, or there will be no ownership of responsibility by the followers and, thus, no group cooperation and lackluster participation.

The solution-driven leader sets a stage of open communication and personal involvement. Too often we look for those we can blame for the present predicaments; such behavior can garner initial agreement and emotional approval, but it has nothing to do with solving the problem. It is, at best, a momentary "feel good" and rarely serves the group or the leader. The SDL will create a safe, open forum of communication with everyone and begin to listen to any and all suggestions in an effort to attain a better outcome; in turn, everyone begins to become more involved in the implementation of a plan that reflects the group's thoughts and ideas.

The solution-driven leader keeps everyone focused on the goal. We often sabotage ourselves by dwelling on the opposite of what we want. Noted psychologist/philosopher, Abraham Maslow, said, "The mind will lead us in the direction of its dominant thought." If we spend our time thinking about why something will not work, we are leading ourselves to a predictable failure. A solution-driven leader will continue to communicate the desired goal to the members of the group; what the mind can conceive, the person can achieve. We must picture high-level achievement in our minds at all times and be realistic in the assessment of what it will take to reach the goal. This is one of

the fundamental responsibilities of every SDL; focus the energy of the followers on the anticipated results.

The solution-driven leader creates energy and enthusiasm. The best way a leader can create energy and enthusiasm for a group is to model positive energy and sincere enthusiasm. This does not necessarily mean assuming the role of a cheerleader or extending shallow, ingenuine compliments. It merely means demonstrating a genuine care for the people, the goal, and the welfare of everyone involved. A lethargic, negative leader will drain energy from any group, and he/she will amplify the problems facing the organization; on the other hand, an enthusiastic, positive leader will infuse the group with the needed energy to move forward and discover the endless possibilities available as a result of group cooperation. The SDL understands the secret to all leadership, the one aspect over which he/she has complete control in every situation: *the ability to choose one's attitude at every moment of every day.*

The solution-driven leader creates an atmosphere conducive to effective and efficient problem-solving while giving continuous renewal to everyone involved. Being a leader does not mean "having all the answers." Young leaders often think they are responsible for every solution, answer, and resolution; such logic can result in frustration, confusion, and even delusion. A perceptive and effective SDL will encourage an ongoing exchange of helpful ideas from those who are part of the group. Every suggestion will be met with genuine appreciation, and the communication will be used as an opportunity to confirm the value of the person involved. (If we inadvertently or purposefully reject someone's suggestions, we stifle his/her creativity and create a barrier for further communication.) Maintaining an open, honest, safe environment for group problem-solving is seen by many as the most important contribution of any solution-driven leader.

Young people are often enamored by the "idea" of leadership and the personal benefits they perceive to be a part of the leadership position. Choose those who can comprehend the "reality" of leadership, those who are willing to go the extra mile on behalf of their peers, those who understand that the key to quality is determined by the collective work ethic of their followers.

I Went on a Search to Become a Leader

I went on a search to become a leader. I searched high and low.
I spoke with authority; people listened. But alas, there was one who
was wiser than I, and they followed that individual.

I sought to inspire confidence, but the crowd responded, "Why
should I trust you?" I postured, and I assumed that look of leadership
with a countenance that flowed with confidence and pride, but many
passed me by and never noticed my air of elegance.

I ran ahead of the others, pointed the way to new heights. I demonstrated that I knew the route to greatness. And then I looked back, and I was alone.
"What shall I do?" I queried. "I've tried hard and used all that I know." And I sat down and pondered long.

And then, I listened to the voices around me. And I heard what the group was trying to accomplish. I rolled up my sleeves and joined in the work.
As we worked, I asked, "Are we all together in what we want to do and how to get the job done?" And we thought together, and we fought together, and we struggled towards our goal.

I found myself encouraging the fainthearted. I sought ideas of those too shy to speak out. I taught those who had little skill. I praised those who worked hard. When out task was completed, one of the group turned to me and said, "This would not have been done but for your leadership."

At first, I said, "I didn't lead. I just worked like the rest." And then I understood, leadership is not a goal. It's a way to reaching a goal.

I lead best when I help others to go where we've decided to go. I lead best when I help others to use themselves creatively. I lead best when I forget about myself as leader and focus on my group...their needs and their goals.

To lead is to serve...to give...to achieve together.

—Anonymous
(as it should be...)

PART II

THE BAND CONDUCTOR AS MUSIC TEACHER

Teacher Resource Guides

Grade Two

Teacher Resource Guide

A Ballad, Theme and Variations for Band

Vaclav Nelhybel
(1919–1996)

Unit 1: Composer

Vaclav Nelhybel was born in Polanka and Odrou, Czechoslovakia, on September 24, 1919. He studied musicology at Prague University and conducting and composition at the Prague Conservatory. In 1942, he continued his musical schooling at Fribourg University in Switzerland. Nelhybel then held conducting positions with Radio Prague and the Prague Stadttheater (1939–1942), and the Czech Philharmonic Orchestra (1945–1946). After World War II, he was named conductor and Composer-in-Residence at Swiss Radio and also served as a lecturer at Fribourg University (1946–1950). Nelhybel later served as music director of Radio Free Europe in Munich, Germany (1950–1957). In 1957, he emigrated to the United States of America, becoming an American citizen in 1962. Nelhybel taught at the University of Lowell, Massachusetts (1978–1979) and the University of Scranton, Pennsylvania, from 1994 until his death on March 22, 1996.

Nelhybel was an active composer, conductor, and clinician throughout the United States, Europe, and Australia. He was honored with four honorary doctoral degrees from American universities and co-founded the *World Premiere Composition Series*. Nelhybel's first published composition was String Quartet No. 1 (1950). His more than four hundred published works include compositions for band, orchestra, choir, chamber ensembles, and opera. His more popular band compositions include *Festivo, Trittico, Corsican Litany, Suite from Bohemia, High Plains March, Symphonic Movement, Suite Concertante,* and *Estampie*.

Unit 2: Composition

A Ballad, Theme and Variations for Band was published in 1976 by J. Christopher Music Company (JCMC of Illinois) as part of the *Music for Young Players and Singers, ABC Series, No. 1*. The publisher states:

> Compositions in this series were conceived with elementary and junior high students in mind. The difficulty level never exceeds grade three. *Ballad* is a set of variations on an archaic, choral-type theme. In the five variations, individual instrumental groups are featured in a great variety of contrasting moods.

The seven-section work opens with the main theme, is followed by five contrasting variations, and closes with a repeat of the main theme. Each of the contrasting sections/variations utilizes different instrumentation and evokes a different mood. The sections vary in length from forty-five seconds to one minute and forty seconds, with a total performance time between seven minutes and forty seconds and eight minutes and thirty seconds, depending on tempi and the amount of time taken between the seven sections. The composition requires a fairly complete instrumentation and musically independent students who are comfortable with transparent scoring and extended sections where they do not play (bass and alto clarinet are scored in only forty-nine of the work's 205 measures, while trumpets are scored in only sixty-four measures).

Unit 3: Historical Perspective

Much of Nelhybel's music is of a linear-modal orientation in which functional chordal tonality does not apply. It is often quite rhythmic in nature and makes use of a wide range of styles, dynamics, dissonances, and timbres. Thematic material is often borrowed from, or is reminiscent of, his Czech heritage of folk songs and plainchant. Other compositions with these characteristics include *Suite from Bohemia* and *Corsican Litany*. Nelhybel's music is often "conversational" in nature, pitting groups of instruments against each other in a sort of call-response or argument. Some of the music of W. Francis McBeth, such as *Canto, Chant and Jubilo, Kaddish,* and *Masque,* also embodies many of these characteristics.

Unit 4: Technical Considerations

The seven sections of *A Ballad* present the basic key centers of concert C minor, G minor, and D minor. Tempo varies from $\quartereq = 80$ to $\halfeq = 132$, and all sections are short (less than one minute and forty seconds). Most of the composition consists of quarter, half, dotted-half, and whole notes. The most difficult rhythm for the winds is eight pairs of eighth notes. Percussion is slightly more difficult with repeated patterns of eighth/two sixteenths and four sixteenths. Ranges are also reasonable with the possible exception of 1st clarinet, which goes up to a written C above the staff. Second clarinet stays below the break.

The score calls for a full instrumentation of flute, oboe, 1st/2nd clarinet, alto clarinet, bass clarinet, 1st/2nd alto saxophone, tenor saxophone, baritone saxophone, bassoon, 1st/2nd trumpet, horn, trombone, euphonium, and tuba. Percussion parts include timpani, bells, chimes, two triangles, snare drum, tenor drum, tom-tom, bass drum, and cymbals, with up to five parts at once. Much of the composition utilizes part doubling of flute and oboe in octaves. Of special note are the discrete, non-doubled parts for alto/bass clarinet (together), horn, euphonium, and tuba. Other discrete parts should not be problematic. While the opening theme (repeated to end the work) uses a full instrumentation, each of the five variations omits entire sections or instrument families for variety. Three of the composition's seven sections use no brass, two use no percussion, and one uses no woodwinds (please see the chart in Unit 7 for details).

Careful planning of rehearsal time will be required to avoid boredom and frustration for those students who are not playing for substantial lengths of time. An alternative method would be to approach the composition as a suite of five different chamber ensembles, beginning and ending with full band. This sort of "featured sections" approach would allow sections and individuals the opportunity to demonstrate a higher degree of musical independence than most works of similar technical difficulty.

Unit 5: Stylistic Considerations

A *Ballad* can be divided into two broad styles: *marcato* for the theme and variation III, and *espressivo*/slurred for variations I, II, IV, and V.

Rather than asking students to play a smooth *legato* style, Nelhybel has wisely made use of slurs to produce a sustained and connected sound. Slurs are much easier than articulated *legato* passages for young players.

There are few dynamic markings in the score. An effective performance should include dynamic nuance determined by the conductor. Special attention to dynamic phrase shaping (*crescendo–decrescendo*) in all of the expressive sections will also add to the value of this work.

Unit 6: Musical Elements

Familiarity with concert C minor, G minor, and D minor scales will be helpful. In several instances, students must play chromatic intervals in close proximity and should be familiar with fingerings and notation for concert F/F-sharp, B/B-flat, E/E-flat, and A/A-flat.

The theme and variations, while often falling in standard four- and eight-measure phrases, also include three- and five-measure phrases. Attention should be drawn to these differences during rehearsal.

Rather than *crescendos* when ascending and *decrescendos* when descending, a better choice would be to *crescendo* through these pickup notes toward their resolution, with short notes leading to long notes, often across bar lines. Careful attention should be paid to all notes that move while others are being held so the counterpoint and polyphony may be heard. Careful attention should also be given to the last note of every phrase in the *espressivo* sections. Young players will tend to abruptly chop these notes off. Variations I, II, IV, and V present wonderful opportunities for expressive musical playing using dynamics and *rubato*. Unfortunately, the specified instrumentation of these sections does not allow all instruments to participate.

The harmony of the composition is modal and chant-like. Many passages are simply in octaves. There are also sections that are essentially duet, trio, or quartet in approach. In this composition, a linear and balanced approach to the melodic content is more important than emphasis on harmony.

The rhythmic content of this composition should be easily accessible to all young players. The only difficulty lies in the variation in phrase lengths and the overlapping of phrase endings and beginnings. At times there are also canonic entrances.

As always, the production of the best possible characteristic tone is desired. In this work it is particularly important due to the lack of *tutti* scoring. For young players, this is best approached by first encouraging a big sound and then working to refine it rather than striving for a small, less offensive sound and hoping to build on it later.

Unit 7: Form and Structure

Theme Marcato f	C minor 4/4 at ♩ = 112 31 measures 1:10	All woodwinds	All brass	Timpani Snare drum Tenor drum Bass drum Cymbal
Variation I *Espressivo p*	C minor 3/4 at ♩ = 132 43 measures 1:00	1st/2nd B♭ clarinet 1st alto saxophone	No brass	No percussion
Variation II *Religioso p–f*	G minor 4/4 at ♩ = 80 32 measures 1:40	All woodwinds	No brass	Bells Chimes Triangles (2)

Variation III *Marcato f*	D minor 4/4 at ♩ = 138 24 measures 0:45	No woodwinds	All brass	Snare drum Tenor drum Bass drum
Variation IV *Cantabile p*	G minor 3/4 at ♩ = 100 30 measures 1:00	All clarinets All saxophones	Baritone Tuba	No percussion
Variation V *Misterioso pp–mf*	C minor 4/4 at ♩ = 80 24 measures 1:15	Flute 1st B-flat clarinet	No brass	Bells Triangle Tom-tom
Theme repeated *Marcato f*	C minor 4/4 at ♩ = 112 31 measures 1:10	All woodwinds	All brass	Timpani Snare drum Tenor drum Bass drum Cymbal

Unit 8: Suggested Listening

W. Francis McBeth:
   Canto
   Chant and Jubilo
Vaclav Nelhybel:
   Suite from Bohemia
   Estampie
   Corsican Litany

Recorded excerpts from many of Vaclav Nelhybel's compositions may be found at http://www.jwpepper.com

Unit 9: Additional References and Resources

"The Basic Band Curriculum: Grades I, II, III." *BD Guide* September/ October 1989, pp. 2–6.

Boonshaft, Peter L. "A Conversation with Vaclav Nelhybel." *The Instrumentalist*, May 1995, pp. 7–9.

Boonshaft, Peter L. "Discovering a Treasure of 160 Nelhybel Works." *The Instrumentalist*, January 1998, pp. 68–72.

Dvorak, Thomas L. *Best Music for Young Band.* Brooklyn, NY: Manhattan Beach Music, 1986.

Garofalo, Robert J. *Instructional Designs for Middle/Junior High School Band*. Fort Lauderdale, FL: Meredith Music Publications, 1995.

Kreines, Joseph. Music for Concert Band, *A Selective Annotated Guide to Band Literature*. Tampa, FL: Florida Music Service, 1989.

Laudermilch, Kenneth. *An Understandable Approach to Musical Expression*. Galesville, MD: Meredith Music Publications, 2000.

Lisk, Edward S. *Intangibles of Musical Performance*. Fort Lauderdale, FL: Meredith Music Publications, 1996.

McBeth, W. Francis. *Effective Performance of Band Music*. San Antonio, TX: Southern Music, 1972.

Rehrig, William H. *The Heritage Encyclopedia of Band Music*. Westerville, OH: Integrity Press, 1991.

Smith, Norman E. *Program Notes for Band*. Chicago, IL: GIA Publications, Inc, 2002.

VanderCook, H.A. *Expression in Music*. Miami, FL: Rubank, 1942.

Contributed by:
Wayne F. Dorothy
Director of Bands
Hardin-Simmons University
Abilene, Texas

Teacher Resource Guide

A Child's Embrace

Charles Rochester Young
(b. 1965)

Unit 1: Composer

Born in Belton, Texas, Charles Rochester Young completed high school in Fort Smith, Arkansas. Upon graduation, he returned to Texas, where he earned his Bachelor of Music Education degree at Baylor University. Young completed his Master's and his Doctor of Musical Arts in Saxophone Performance at the University of Michigan, where he was a teaching assistant for saxophonist Donald Sinta. His composition teachers in Ann Arbor included William Albright, Leslie Bassett, and George Wilson.

Young served on the faculty at the Interlochen Center for the Arts as Instructor of Music Theory and Composition, and was Director of Jazz Studies and Saxophone at Central Connecticut State University before joining the faculty at the University of Wisconsin–Stevens Point. Presently the Chair of Composition and Music Theory, he was named a Wisconsin Teaching Fellow in 1997. In 1999, he was recognized as the Wisconsin Professor of the Year by the Carnegie Foundation and the Council for the Advancement and Support of Education, and was nominated for a national award by those organizations in 2000. Young has been recognized internationally through major composition awards including the National Band Association/Merrill Jones Composition Competition for his work *Legends of the Northern Wind*. He has received commissions from members of the Boston Symphony, Detroit Symphony, and New York Philharmonic; from organizations such as the Green Bay Civic Symphony and the Big 12 Band Directors Association; and from soloists such as Keiko Abe and Donald Sinta.

Unit 2: Composition

A *Child's Embrace* was composed in honor of the birth of the composer's first child, Katherine Anne Young, who was born on January 18, 2000. The work was commissioned by the Traverse City East Junior High School Band and was first performed in Traverse City, Michigan, on March 16, 2000, under the direction of Peter Deneen. Southern Music Company in San Antonio, Texas, published *A Child's Embrace* in 2001. The work is five minutes long; supplemental European parts are available.

Unit 3: Historical Perspective

A *Child's Embrace* is reflective of a gentle lullaby or cradle song, a slow, *legato* melody used to lull a child to sleep. Famous lullaby melodies include Brahms's *Wiegenlied, Op. 49, No. 4*, and the French folk song *Fais do-do*. Works in a similar style often appear in instrumental works of the nineteenth and early twentieth centuries by composers such as Chopin, Schumann, Brahms, Liszt, Grieg, Debussy, and Ravel. An excellent example of a Romantic lullaby is Chopin's *Berceuse, Op. 57.*

Young composed his first work for wind band, *Tempered Steel*, in 1997 on a commission by the Big 12 Band Directors. Subsequent compositions include *Springtime Heralds* (commissioned by the Valley Southwoods High School Band in West Des Moines, Iowa) and *Legends of the Northern Wind* (commissioned by the Michigan School Band and Orchestra Association) that won the National Band Association Composers Competition in 2000.

It is significant that Young composed this beautiful lullaby for beginning band as a result of the birth of his first child, a monumental event in his personal life. He recognizes the impact of quality literature on young musicians: "We take children's writers such as Dr. Seuss very seriously. It is our responsibility to write equally rewarding repertoire for young bands; successful writers are being commissioned to write music for beginning ensembles, and this repertoire has an impact on far more musicians than a work for a college wind ensemble."

Unit 4: Technical Considerations

Woodwind writing does not employ extended ranges. In the brass, trumpets extend to high G while trombones reach to F above the staff, but most significantly, *A Child's Embrace* requires slow, controlled playing in 4/4 time. Percussion parts utilize mallet instruments and auxiliary percussion. Although the work is written in B-flat major, students must be comfortable reading accidentals, as the work extends to E-flat, A-flat, G-flat, and G major. The composer's use of both unison writing and chromatic harmonies demands that students work to develop their ability to detect discrepancies in balance and intonation.

The composer's program notes in the score suggest that if a vibraphone is not available for rehearsal and performance, bells can be substituted by playing the same written pitches with rubber mallets. Humming is incorporated in measures 3 through 20 and 51 through 60 to replicate the timbre of a children's chorus. Pitches are transposed to coincide with the players' instruments. Female voices are instructed to hum in the octave above middle C; male voices are encouraged to sing in the same octave or one octave lower.

Unit 5: Stylistic Considerations

In addition to *crescendos* and *decrescendos*, dynamics range from *pp* to *sfz*. Musical terminology includes *ritard.*, *a tempo*, *tenuto*, and accent markings. Students are required to play accents in a slow, *legato* style.

Expressive markings, slow tempo, and *legato* style encourage the development of a well-supported, open, and warm tone. The composer recommends the implementation of staggered breathing for the resolution of the work's climax in measures 47-50.

Unit 6: Musical Elements

Young presents four-measure phrase lengths, but extended phrases and transitions are also employed. Melodies begin on both the downbeat (e.g., measure 3) and the anacrusis (e.g., measure 20). Although the form is through-composed, formal compositional balance is created through the statement of the principal theme in the opening and closing of the work, in addition to the use of the vibraphone *ostinato* in its introduction and coda.

While Young uses familiar terms such as "calmly," "warmly," "innocently," "noble," and "reflectively" to communicate his message to younger players, other formal musical terms could be assigned to introduce musical terminology and characterize style and tone quality. For example, *maestoso* could be used to characterize the "noble" section at measure 32. The increase and decrease of musical textures are directly related to the formal structure of the work. It is appropriate to teach the full ensemble to play the melody when studying the piece to teach basic compositional concepts. Musical concepts such as homophony, unison, melody, countermelody, and accompaniment can easily be taught and modeled from this well-crafted work for young band.

Unit 7: Form and Structure

A Child's Embrace includes statements of a simple and beautiful melody that surround a tonally unstable center section. Young compares the center section at measure 20 to a snowball at the top of a hill that grows and morphs as it gains momentum.

The passage begins with a woodwind choir (twelve measures) that, through increased instrumentation, dynamics, texture, and harmonic interest, reaches a final climax (measure 46) with a delayed resolution.

MEASURE	EVENT AND SCORING
1–2	Introduction; vibraphone *ostinato* and chimes
3–10	Unison flute, clarinet, and voices introduce melody marked "calmly;" solo alto saxophone countermelody enters in m. 7, and bass voices enter in m. 9 to reinforce B-flat major authentic cadence (mm. 10–11)
11–19	"Warmly;" homophonic—melody with accompaniment; vibraphone *ostinato* ends in m. 16; 2/4 in m. 19 functions as an extension—an unwritten *fermata*; note chime entrance on beat 1
20–27	"Innocently;" tempo increases and humming stops; woodwind choir includes flute melody, clarinet and percussion accompaniment, and solo alto saxophone countermelody (section begins in E-flat major)
28–31	Texture increases; harmonically instability
32–45	"Noble"; full wind texture; similar melodic contours to principal theme, but more complex harmonic material; accents employed; 1st alto saxophone and horn countermelody; harmonic interest from G-flat to G major; F pedal established in m. 42; irregular phrase structure (4+4+6)
46–50	*Sfz* climax does not resolve immediately to B-flat major (augmented sixth chord with irregular resolution); dynamic energy decreases during transition before the return of the principal theme; vibraphone *ostinato* returns in m. 49
51–59	"Reflectively"; unison flute, clarinet, and voices with pedal tones in low woodwinds, and countermelody in alto saxophone; melodic augmentation in mm. 58–60
60–64	Coda; vibraphone *ostinato* continues (as in introduction); chime and triangle struck with vibraphone on the final downbeat

Unit 8: Suggested Listening
Johannes Brahms, *Wiegenlied, Op. 49, No. 4*
Frederic Chopin, *Berceuse, Op. 57*
Larry Daehn, *Song for Friends*
Frank Erickson, *Air for Band*
Charles Rochester Young:
   Concerto for Double Bass and Wind Ensemble
   Legends of the Northern Wind
   Northern Lights
   Springtime Heralds
   Tempered Steel

Unit 9: Additional References and Resources
Website: www.uwsp.edu/music/faculty/cyoung/cyoung.htm

Contributed by:
Wendy McCallum
Doctoral Conducting Associate
University of North Texas
Denton, Texas

Teacher Resource Guide

Aztec Dance

Michael Story
(b. 1956)

Unit 1: Composer

Composer and arranger Michael Story was born in Philadelphia, Pennsylvania, on April 27, 1956. He received Bachelor of Music and Master of Education degrees from the University of Houston, Texas. Story served as a teaching assistant, teaching band and music education classes at the University of Houston from 1979 to 1981. He then left teaching to devote his full time to arranging and composition. He has written extensively for school and college bands, and has served as arranger for the Houston Pops Orchestra. Story has published well over nine hundred arrangements and original compositions for concert band, jazz ensemble, marching band, and orchestra. Most of his works are published by CPP/Belwin, Warner Bros. (formerly Columbia Pictures Publications). He is also currently editor/producer of marching band publications for Warner Bros. Story states that he has learned a great deal from the music of "Holst, Grainger, Persichetti, Stravinsky, Ravel, and Bernstein as well as film writers such as John Williams, Tiompkin, and Rozsa." Story currently lives in Houston, Texas.

Unit 2: Composition

Aztec Dance, part of CPP/Belwin's *Beginning Band Series* for young bands, was published in 1997. It is an energetic, single-movement work beginning with a medium tempo introduction and followed by a fast dance. The composition contains fifty-one measures and is approximately one minute and forty seconds in length. The composition gains its exotic Aztec sound and mood through the use of a variety of minor modes and parallel fourths. Story states:

Although an original piece in a more contemporary setting than actual Aztec music would have sounded, *Aztec Dance* was written after experiencing works from composers from that part of the world, especially Revueltas and Chavez. It utilizes rhythms and melodies that are consistent with the musical style of the region.

Unit 3: Historical Perspective

As is the case in all American Indian cultures, music and dance were an important part of Aztec life. Music and dance were so closely linked to and integrated with religion that, in most cases, there was no word for music as a separate practice. The most common Aztec instruments were rattles, shakers, whistles, trumpets, flutes, drums, copper bells, and shells. Aztec children were taught to dance, sing, and play musical instruments between the ages of twelve and fifteen.

In addition to religious ceremonies, Aztec music and dance were often used to tell important stories. Indian cultures believed that music was a gift of the gods rather than being composed by man. Rhythm, call and response, and repetition are important aspects of American Indian music.

There is an excellent website, maintained by the teachers and students of *ThinkQuest*, on the art and history of the Aztec culture. This resource could be very helpful in generating ideas for cross-curricular lessons. The website is found at:

http://library.thinkquest.org/27981/index.html

Unit 4: Technical Considerations

The entire work has the key signature of concert E-flat, with tonality centered on G phrygian, F dorian, C minor, and ending in C major. Students should be familiar with fingerings and notation for concert pitches of B/B-flat, E/E-flat, A/A-flat, and D/D-flat. Orchestration consists of melody with accompaniment or melody harmonized, with accompaniment. The meter is 4/4 with a single measure of 2/4. Rhythms are simple, including quarter notes, half notes, dotted-half notes, whole notes, paired eighth notes, and dotted-quarter and eighth note patterns. Percussion parts are quite simple. There are no rolls, and the most difficult rhythm is paired eighth notes.

Ranges are easy in all instruments, with clarinets staying below the break. There is ample part doubling in this composition, allowing it to be performed with less than complete instrumentation. There are only two bass clef parts. Bass clarinet, baritone saxophone, and tuba are often doubled, and tenor saxophone, bassoon, trombone, and euphonium are often doubled. There is one clarinet part and one trumpet part. Horns are usually doubled by alto saxophone. Percussion instruments include bells, snare drum, bass drum, triangle, tambourine, and gong or crash cymbals.

Unit 5: Stylistic Considerations

While there are few style markings in the music, it will most likely be performed in either a *legato* or *marcato* style, or a combination of both. One pair of eighth notes is marked with *staccato* dots, and there are eleven accents (both > and roof-top). Most notes are articulated with only three pairs of slurred eighth notes. For contrast, the introduction could be performed in a more *legato/tenuto* style, with the dance being more *marcato* and march-like. Dynamic markings include *mp*, *mf*, and *f*. There are two written *crescendos* and one *decrescendo*. All of these demands should easily be within the capabilities of young bands, though attention should be paid so the piece does not become too choppy.

Unit 6: Musical Elements

The harmony of the composition is primarily minor and modal. Many passages are simply in octaves, while others are harmonized at the fourth. The work is largely homophonic and consonant. The main melody is mostly diatonic with no intervals larger than a fifth. There are several phrases that may require extra attention due to differing phrase lengths. As always, the production of the best possible characteristic tone is desired, even when there will be a tendency for young players to become overly aggressive rather than stylistically energetic.

Unit 7: Form and Structure

Section	Measure	Event and Scoring
Introduction – A	1–8	Moderately 4/4 (♩ = 100); G phrygian; call and response between most of the ensemble and unison alto saxophone/horn; uneven phrase lengths of ten, ten, and twelve beats; could be interpreted as *marcato* or *legato*; *ritard*.
Dance – B	9–18	Brightly (♩ = 126); F dorian; two-measure transition; melody seems to call for an energetic *marcato* style; main melody in unison clarinet accompanied by unison *ostinato* in tenor saxophone, bassoon, trombone, and euphonium; eight-measure phrase is truncated two beats with a single measure in 2/4

Section	Measure	Event and Scoring
B1	19–26	Melody repeated in upper woodwinds with harmony of fourths in alto saxophone and trumpet; other instruments provide accompanying *ostinato*
Development – A	27–36	C minor; development of intervallic material from the introduction; five-beat pattern superimposed through three measures; cadence on dominant setting return to C minor
Dance – B2	37–44	Melody repeated by unison alto saxophone and trumpet with new countermelody in upper woodwinds; simple accompaniment in low winds in octaves
Coda – b	45–51	C major; two-measure tutti transition followed by final statement of the main melody by flute and trumpet; *tutti* ending

Unit 8: Suggested Listening

James Barnes, *Trail of Tears*
Jay Chattaway, *Mazama*
William Hill, *Sioux Variants*
Quincy Hilliard, *Ghost Dance*
H. Owen Reed, *La Fiesta Mexicana*
Mark Williams, *Grant County Celebration*

Recorded excerpts from many of Michael Story's compositions and arrangements may be found at http://www.jwpepper.com

Unit 9: Additional References and Resources

"The Basic Band Curriculum: Grades I, II, III." *BD Guide,* September/
    October 1989, pp. 2–6.

Dvorak, Thomas L. *Best Music for Young Band.* Brooklyn, NY: Manhattan
    Beach Music, 1986.

Garofalo, Robert J. *Instructional Designs for Middle/Junior High School Band.*
    Fort Lauderdale, FL: Meredith Music Publications, 1995.

Kreines, Joseph. *Music for Concert Band, A Selective Annotated Guide to Band
    Literature.* Tampa, FL: Florida Music Service, 1989.

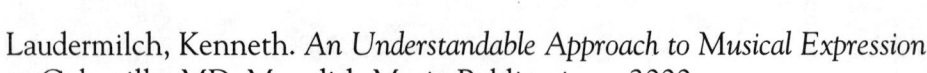

Laudermilch, Kenneth. *An Understandable Approach to Musical Expression*. Galesville, MD: Meredith Music Publications, 2000.

Lisk, Edward S. *Intangibles of Musical Performance*. Fort Lauderdale, FL: Meredith Music Publications, 1996.

McBeth, W. Francis. Effective Performance of Band Music. San Antonio, TX: Southern Music, 1972.

Rehrig, William H. *The Heritage Encyclopedia of Band Music*. Westerville, OH: Integrity Press, 1991.

Smith, Norman E. *Program Notes for Band*. Chicago, IL: GIA Publications, Inc., 2002.

VanderCook, H. A. *Expression in Music*. Miami, FL: Rubank, 1942.

Contributed by:
Wayne F. Dorothy
Director of Bands
Hardin-Simmons University
Abilene, Texas

Teacher Resource Guide

Bosnian Folk Songs
Fred J. Allen
(b. 1953)

Unit 1: Composer

Throughout his twenty-five year teaching career in Texas secondary schools and universities, Fred J. Allen (b. 1953, Longview, Texas) has remained very active as a composer. His published works for band (totaling eighteen at this writing) draw upon a wealth of experience as a professional educator. Chiefly, they provide vehicles for expressive playing within the range and technical considerations appropriate for developing instrumentalists. Like *Bosnian Folk Songs* (1997), many of his other works for band utilize existing folk melodies or hymn tunes, such as his *Fantasy on Barbara Allen* (1993), *They Led My Lord Away* (1990), and *Moravian Hymn Dance* (1994). Allen has been Director of Bands at Stephen F. Austin University (Nacogdoches, Texas) since the summer of 1994. In addition to his work with the university bands, he also teaches conducting and music education classes. His formal study includes degrees from Abiline Christian University (B.Mus.Ed.) and East Texas State University (M.M.).

Unit 2: Composition

Bosnian Folk Songs, composed in 1997, incorporates two folk melodies from a Yugoslavian region now known as the separate nation of Bosnia. Early in the twentieth century, Hungarian composer Bela Bartok (1881–1945) collected and documented these and many other folk melodies from Yugoslavia. Allen was commissioned by the West Ridge Middle School Band in Austin, Texas, to write a work in 1997 that would "draw attention to the suffering of young people in Bosnia." During that year, the unrest and atrocities in Eastern

Europe were widely reported and became much more a part of the world's collective awareness. The text of the first selected folk song is printed in the score:

> By Sarajevo there's a green garden.
> In that garden there's a well of cold water,
> By the well, a marble stone,
> On the stone, an aged vase,
> In the vase, three flowers bloomed.

Contrasting that serenity, the second folk song—while in a minor mode—has been characterized as a song of celebration. Indeed, the tempo and rhythmic vitality of the second section of this piece are that of a joyful dance. A return to the first tempo and the combination of the two folk melodies sparks a new emotional statement, one that could be described as pride or majesty. Consistent with those three musical expressions of *serenity*, *celebration*, and *majesty*, Allen included the following hopeful thought in the full score:

> Perhaps this music can remind us that even war cannot silence the joy that can be expressed in the simple folk songs of a nation....

Unit 3: Historical Perspective

The practice of integrating or setting folk songs within an instrumental work is something that can be traced back several centuries. Considering just this past century, a multitude of standard works in the wind band repertoire have folk song foundations. Ralph Vaughan Williams's *English Folk Song Suite* and Percy Grainger's *Lincolnshire Posy* are two shining examples. A short list of less difficult band works with folk song foundations are annotated in earlier volumes of this *Teaching Music through Performance in Band* series: *Cajun Folk Songs* by Frank Ticheli (Vol. 1, p. 166), *Deir in De* by Warren Barker (Vol. 3, p. 223), *Fantasy on "Sakura, Sakura"* by Ray E. Cramer (Vol. 2, p. 228), *Korean Folk Song Medley* by James Ployhar (Vol. 2, p. 137), *Llwyn Onn* by Brian Hogg (Vol. 1, p. 117), *Overture on a Shaker Tune* by John Higgins (Vol. 3, p. 182), *Three Hungarian Songs* by Bela Bartok/Gordon (Vol. 2, p. 177), and *Ye Banks and Braes o' Bonnie Doon* by Percy Grainger (Vol. 2, p. 280). A number of professional music educators this past century have also been active as composers, offering meaningful works with younger performers in mind. The firsthand insights of composer/educators have provided valuable contributions to the young band repertoire, as is the case with *Bosnian Folk Songs*.

Unit 4: Technical Considerations

Initially composed for a middle school ensemble, this work presents a healthy balance of comfortable playing demands along with more ground-breaking challenges for the second- or third-year student. The part divisions are common for younger bands: there is no piccolo part, and there are only single parts for oboe and bassoon. The horn and trombone sections have two parts each in the scoring. The individual pitch range and *tessitura* requirements of all solo and section lines is quite balanced. Similarly, there is decent democracy in the rhythmic challenges up and down the score. The coordination skills between "tongue and fingers" are age- and instrument-appropriate, with the upper woodwinds and mallets being challenged to be more facile than the rest of the band. The related keys of F major and F minor are the only two tonalities encountered. Perhaps one of the most demanding segments of the piece is the phrase referred to below as the "triumphal chorus" (beginning at measure 75). While this passage may appear quite simple, these *fortissimo* melodic augmentations will challenge the breath support and control of the wind section. Relatedly, throughout the piece the composer requests a full range of dynamic control, from *pianissimo* to *fortissimo*.

Unit 5: Stylistic Considerations

The first portion of this work requires the entire wind section to play in a lyrical manner, regardless of whether playing the main line or an accompaniment. Triangle and bell sounds should be resonant without a harsh beginning. As always, mallet selections and striking points should be carefully considered.

The contrasting second tempo brings a more vigorous articulation approach, both to the winds and the percussion. *Staccato* wind articulations should be air-filled rather than merely tongue-generated. The vibraphone mallets should be on the firmer end of the hardness spectrum.

The third section of the piece challenges the band to play with *broad* articulated sounds, a task which will likely require teacher assistance. Of further mention, the music of the introduction is nearly an exact duplicate of measures 87 through 90. Special attention should be given in measures 3 and 4 to maintain the full dynamic, unlike the later context of the same passage.

Unit 6: Musical Elements

MELODY:

The complete melodic scoring of *Bosnian Folk Songs* is annotated within Unit 7: Form and Structure. Having a folk song basis, this piece is quite melodically driven. Throughout the work, the primary melody is accompanied by one or more accompaniment strands that are also very melodious. This enriched accompaniment style requires focused attention to balances between all the lines ("strands") in the score. This can be achieved by isolating each part separately for the students to hear, presenting them in the order of importance (as determined from the conductor's interpretive score study). Notice the groupings of instruments in the first refrain at measure 15, for example. While all are marked with the identical dynamic marking, *mezzo forte*, it seems apparent from examining the score that the folk song melody should indeed still be the foreground sound. One interpretation, from most prominent to least prominent sound is:

1. Main melody (measures 15–18) – unison trumpet section with oboe
2. Bass line (measures 15–18) – tuba, low reeds, and timpani, then subordinate melodic strands (measures 15–18)
3. A tenor line – tenor saxophone, all horns, and euphonium
4. A soprano line – all flutes, all B-flat clarinets, and bells

Four measures later, a different configuration may be concluded:

1. Main melody (measures 19–22) – flute, oboe, 1st clarinet
2. A countermelody – 1st trumpet, 2nd/3rd clarinet
3. Bass line – tuba, baritone saxophone, timpani
4. Subordinate melodic strands as co-equals:
   - tenor line: euphonium, tenor saxophone, bassoon, bass clarinet
   - alto line: alto saxophone, 2nd/3rd trumpet

With many phrases consisting of a four- or five-strand texture, performers must maintain a keen attention to sound balances.

HARMONY:

Traditional harmonic progressions reinforce the tonality in both the major and minor key segments. Refreshingly, the score's straightforward harmonies are most often realized through contrapuntal movement. There are three places in the work, however, where a pure homophonic texture presents the harmony in stacked form. Significantly, each place is found where the idea of *serenity* is being projected: the opening of the first verse (measures 7 through 14), the winding down of the second song (measures 60 through 66), and during the coda of the work (measures 95 through 98).

RHYTHM:

The entire work is in common time, incorporating just two different tempi. Rhythmic interest is well maintained, however, through the independence of each accompanimental line. As indicated above (see MELODY), the work often incorporates four or five lines, each with separate rhythmic content. This challenges the performers to develop rhythmic independence as they play together. Most of the work's rhythm patterns are uncomplicated. There are some syncopated passages that will require special consideration. It may be useful to prepare a preliminary rhythm sheet for the entire ensemble to study and execute together. Such a sheet could display these related syncopations:

1. Song I verse: mm. 7–10   (repeated), clarinet melody
   same as: mm. 25–28   (repeated), low brass/reed
                                  melody

2. relate #1 to: mm. 1–4   (et al.), euphonium/bassoon line

3. relate #1 to: mm. 25–28   muted trumpet line

4. relate #1 to: mm. 56–59   flute/oboe, and 1st clarinet line

5. Song II: *   mm. 52–55   upper woodwinds and 1st trumpet

6. relate #5 to: mm. 42–45   trombone and baritone saxophone

7. relate #5 to: *   mm. 52–55   2nd/3rd clarinet and trumpet

8. relate #5 to: *   mm. 52–55   horn, trombone, and alto saxophone

9. relate #5 to: mm. 56–59   trombone, euphonium, tenor saxophone melody

* Identifying and learning a work's prominent rhythm patterns in unison is also an excellent way to teach balance ratios (or functional relationships) between simultaneous lines.

Timbre:

The orchestration of *Bosnian Folk Songs* is well-crafted, with frequent changes in tone color combinations. A quick scan reveals that about one-third of the piece employs all the winds (and most percussion) playing together, while the remaining two-thirds of the work presents a healthy mixture of varied timbres. There are six brief solo passages in the piece, each a different tone color. Solos are included for trumpet, alto saxophone, flute, clarinet, bassoon, and euphonium. Also, eight different percussion timbres are effectively employed, both as tone color enhancements and as rhythmic reinforcement.

Note: In measures 45 through 49, the tambourine rhythm is erroneously duplicated in the timpani part (in both the score and the part), when the timpani part should have rests instead.

Unit 7: Form and Structure

Lasting four minutes, the piece is in three primary sections, with the first folk song presented in F major (*moderato*), followed by a second folk melody in F minor (*allegro*), proceeding to a climactic F major combination (*moderato*) of these two melodic ideas in augmentation.

SECTION	SUBSECTION	MEASURE	EVENT AND SCORING
A Moderato	Introduction	1–6	*Tutti* ensemble; final phrase of the first folk song refrain (see mm. 87–90) followed by a two-measure lead-in

Section	Subsection	Measure	Event And Scoring
A	Song I, Verse I		"Serenity"
	a	7–10	Clarinet carries the melody; low brass and reeds on harmonic accompaniment
	a'	11–14	Same, with solo flute joining with a lyrical countermelody
	b (Refrain)	15–18	Trumpet and oboe take main melody; three strands of lyrical accompaniments
	b'	19–22	Flute, oboe, and 1st clarinet assume main melody; still three-strand accompaniment
	Link	23–24	Woodwinds, bells, and triangle lead in to Verse II
	Song I, Verse II		
	a	25–28	Low reeds, trombone, and euphonium on the folk song; 1st clarinet on bass line, muted trumpet, flute, and bells on other accompaniment strands
	a'	29–32	Tenor saxophone joins the melody; pedal point from tuba and bass clarinet; three additional accompaniment strands
	b	33–36	*Tutti fortissimo* refrain; 1st trumpet and 2nd/3rd clarinet on the folk tune; all others scored on four lyrical accompaniment lines
	Extension	37–41	Extension of the refrain, diminishing in volume and in scoring to unwind the first large segment of the work
B *Allegro*	Introduction	42–43	*Ostinato* patterns in low brass and reeds, vibraphone, and snare drum

SECTION	SUBSECTION	MEASURE	EVENT AND SCORING
	Song II		"Celebration"
	c	44–47	Four-measure trumpet solo accompanied by the continuing patterns from the brief introduction (joined by tambourine)
	c'	48–51	A slightly varied phrase of the same melodic idea—this time for solo alto saxophone; accompaniment group continues
	c''	52–55	A tutti celebration of the same basic theme, with soprano instruments on the tune along with four other spirited strands, including vital crash cymbals
	c'''	56–59	Main line continuing in trombone and tenor saxophone, with a countermelody in upper woodwinds derived from the first folk song (noe F minor)
	Extension	60–66	Passing around of second folk tune fragments (solo flute, then solo clarinet, then solo bassoon), ever slowing to a peaceful F major *fermata* chord
A' Moderato	Bridge	67–74	"Majesty" An eight-measure continuous build, incorporating first song material (mm. 67–70) and second song fragments (mm. 71–74)
	a and c (Triumphal chorus)	75–82	A recapitulation combining the first folk tune in the brass and low reeds with a second folk tune derivative in the upper woodwinds
	b (Refrain)	83–90	Continuation of the same spirit; *tutti* ensemble singing with full conviction—the dynamic climax of the work

SECTION	SUBSECTION	MEASURE	EVENT AND SCORING
	Extension	91–94	The volume and energy relax in this augmented repetition of the refrain's last phrase
	Coda	95–98	A final voicing of the first song's verse melody—euphonium solo or soli—with a tranquil harmonic accompaniment

Unit 8: Suggested Listening

Fred J. Allen:
> *Bosnian Folk Songs* (1997)
> *Celebration Hymn* (1995)
> *Chorale Prelude: Abide with Me* (1996)
> *Fantasy on Barbara Allen* (1993)
> *Moravian Hymn Dance* (1994)
> *Romanza Semplice* (1997)
> *Thanksgiving Hymn* (1998)
> *The Restful Journey* (1996)
> *They Led My Lord Away* (1990)
> *When the Stars Began to Fall* (1992)

—plus any of the folk-related works listed in Unit 3 of this Teacher Resource Guide

Unit 9: Additional References and Resources

Allen, Fred J. E-mail inquiry by Patrick Casey, 31 August 2001.

Bartok, Bela, and Albert B. Lord. *Yugoslav Folk Music*, Volumes 1–4. New York: State University of New York Press, 1978.

Miles, Richard, ed. *Teaching Music through Performance in Band*, Volume 1. Chicago: GIA Publications, Inc., 1997.

Miles, Richard, ed. *Teaching Music through Performance in Band*, Volume 2. Chicago: GIA Publications, Inc., 1998.

Miles, Richard, ed. *Teaching Music through Performance in Band*, Volume 3. Chicago: GIA Publications, Inc., 2000.

TRN Music Publishers, Ruidoso, NM.

"When the Stars Began to Fall: Fred J. Allen." *Teaching Music through Performance in Band*, Volume 3. Compiled and edited by Richard Miles. Chicago: GIA Publications, Inc. 2000.

Contributed by:

Patrick F. Casey
Director of Bands
Central Missouri State University
Warrensburg, Missouri

Teacher Resource Guide

British Isles Suite

Larry Daehn
(b. 1939)

Unit 1: Composer

Larry Daehn was born in 1939 in Rosedale, Wisconsin. He received his bachelor's degree from the University of Wisconsin–Oshkosh and earned a master's degree from the University of Wisconsin–Platteville. He taught vocal and instrumental music at the junior and high school levels for thirty-five years. Twenty-seven of those years were spent at New Glarus High School in New Glarus, Wisconsin.

Leaders of American Education honored Daehn in 1971, and he was acknowledged as Outstanding Bandmaster by Phi Beta Mu, Pi Chapter, in 1988. He is a member of several music organizations including MENC, Wisconsin Band Masters Association, ASBDA, Phi Beta Mu, and the Percy Grainger Society. As a Grainger scholar, Daehn maintains extensive research on the life and music of Percy Grainger. Since founding Daehn Publications in 1988, he has been responsible for the composing, arranging, and publishing of quality repertoire for wind band.

Unit 2: Composition

British Isles Suite was commissioned by the Wisconsin Youth Band Directors' Association and received its premiere performance on September 18, 1999, by the Wisconsin Youth Band Directors' Association Honor Band. It is a three-movement suite based entirely on folk music sources. Daehn's choice of folk songs provides continuity and contrast within each movement and to the overall structure of the work. "Marching Song" is a martial movement based on two Welsh folk songs: "Britons, Raise Your Banners High" and "March for the Men of Harlech." "Barbara Allen" is based on a traditional air of the same name. "Farewell, Dundee" combines the lilting, dance-like tune of "Adieu, Dundee" with the well-known ballad "Auld Lang Syne." The entire work is approximately six minutes and thirty seconds long.

Unit 3: Historical Perspective

There is a rich tradition of setting folk songs for wind band. The collection and research of folk song styles and materials have inspired many composers. *English Folk Song Suite* by Ralph Vaughan Williams and the *First* and *Second Suite* by Gustav Holst are some of the first works in the twentieth century's repertoire of compositions specifically composed for wind band. Percy Grainger's contributions to this medium are many, some of which include *Lincolnshire Posy, Ye Banks and Braes o' Bonnie Doon, Irish Tune from County Derry, Molly on the Shore,* and *Colonial Song.*

Nationalism was a strong influence during the years between the two World Wars. It was a movement characterized by an emphasis on national elements and resources of music. Composers expressed these national and ethnic traits by drawing upon folk melodies and dance rhythms, and choosing themes from their country's history and life.

British Isles Suite borrows folk songs from Wales, England, Ireland, and Scotland. "Marching Song" is based on two Welsh folk songs. "Britons Raise Your Banners High," also known as "The Departure of the King," is found in Alfred Moffat's 1906 *Minstrelsy of Wales.* The second tune, "March for the Men of Harlech," is more familiar and is also known as "Hark! I Hear the Foe Advancing!" This march was written to celebrate the Welsh defense of Harlech Castle during the War of the Roses in about 1468. Both songs are victorious and martial in nature.

"Barbara Allen" is a traditional air that is claimed by England, Ireland, and Scotland. There are many variations of this lovely tune and its lyrics. Both Scottish and English versions of the ballad appear in Grainger's 1765 *Reliques of Ancient English Poetry.* The ballad of "Cruel Barbara Allen" tells the story of a woman indifferent to the love of Johnny Grove, who dies of longing for her. She is then filled with remorse and dies herself. The number and diversity of variations of this song confirms its popularity and is emblematic of the song being handed down traditionally.

"Farewell, Dundee" is based on a lilting minstrel tune about the Scottish town of Dundee. This song was collected by Sir John Skene and reprinted in *Ancient Scottish Melodies from a Manuscript of the Reign of King James VI.* The second tune is the popular ballad "Auld Lang Syne." The familiar words by Robert Burns are set to an old Scottish strathspey dating back to 1711. A *strathspey* is a slow Scottish dance in quadruple meter with many dotted rhythms.

Texts are included below as they offer insight to the lyrical adaptation of these folk songs:

Britons Raise Your Banners High

>Britons raise your banners high,
>Gird your loins to meet the foe!
>Soldiers, smite them hip and thigh,
>In the dust we'll lay them low.
>Show your valour and your might
>In the thickest of the fight.
>Follow me! Follow me!
>Let the war cry be...
>Cambria ever shall be free,
>We will die for liberty.
>
>As the lion in his might
>Shakes the insects from his mane,
>Or the whirlwind in its flight,
>Furrows thro' the foaming main;
>So will we with deadly blows
>Scatter the usurping foes!
>Follow me! Follow me!
>Let the war cry be...
>Cambria ever shall be free,
>We will die for liberty.

March for the Men of Harlech

>Hark, I hear the foe advancing,
>barbed steeds are proudly prancing,
>helmets in the sunbeams glancing
>glitter through the trees.
>Men of Harlech, lie ye dreaming?
>See ye not their falchions gleaming?
>While their pennons gaily streaming
>flutter in the breeze.
>
>From the rocks rebounding,
>let the war cry sounding
>summon all at Cambria's call,
>the haughty foe surrounding.
>Men of Harlech, on to glory,
>See, your banner, famed in story
>waves these burning words before ye:
>"Britain scorns to yield!"

'Mid the fray, see dead and dying,
friend and foe together lying,
all around the arrows flying
scatter sudden death.
Frightened steeds are wildly neighing,
brazen trumpets hoarsely braying,
wounded men for mercy praying
with their parting breath!
See—they're in disorder!
Comrades, keep close order!
Ever they shall rule the day
they ventured o'er the border!
Now the Saxon flees before us,
victory's banner floateth o'er us,
raise the loud exulting chorus:
"Britain wins the field!"

Barbara Allen

In Scarlet town, where I was born,
there was a fair maid dwelling,
made ev'ry youth cry 'well-a-day;
her name was Barbara Allen.

All in the merry month of May
when green buds they were a swelling,
young Jemmy Grove on his deathbed lay
for love of Barbara Allen.

So slowly, slowly she came up,
and slowly she came nigh him,
and all she said when there she came:
"Young man , I think you're dying."

When he was dead and laid in grave,
her heart was struck with sorrow:
"Oh mother, mother, make my bed;
for I shall die tomorrow."

"Farewell," said she, "ye virgins all,
and shun the fault I fell in."
Henceforth take warning by the fall
of cruel Barbara Allen.

Adieu, Dundee

> Adieu, Dundee, from Mary parted,
> Here nae mair my lot may be.
> Wha can bear, when broken-hearted,
> Scenes that speak o' joys gone by.
> A'things ance were sweet and smiling
> In the light o' Mary's e'e,
> Fairest seemings maist beguiling
> Love, adieu! Adieu, Dundee.

> Like yon water softly gliding,
> When the winds are laid to sleep;
> Such my life, when I confiding
> Gave to her my heart to keep.
> Like yon water wildly rushing
> When the north wind stirs the sea,
> Such the change my heart now crushing,
> Love, adieu! Adieu, Dundee.

Auld Lang Syne

> Should auld acquaintance be forgot
> and never brought to min'?
> Should auld acquaintance be forgot,
> and auld lang syne?

> For auld lang syne, my dear,
> for auld lang syne.
> We'll take a cup of kindness yet
> for auld lang syne.

> And there's a hand, my trusty fiere*,
> and gie's a hand of' thine;
> we'll take a right gude-willy-waught*
> for auld lang syne.

> *Fiere = companion
> Gude-willy-waught = convivial drink

Unit 4: Technical Considerations

The scales of D aeolian (natural minor), B-flat major, E-flat major, and F major are required for the entire ensemble. Rhythms are straightforward, though subdivision of the pulse is essential in all movements. Standard concert band instrumentation is utilized, with limited divisi parts in 1st/2nd flute, 1st/2nd/3rd B-flat clarinet, 1st/2nd E-flat alto saxophone, 1st/2nd/3rd

B-flat trumpet, 1st/2nd French horn, and 1st/2nd trombone. Ranges are well within the ability of musicians in their second year of playing. Percussion requires one mallet player on bells and four players covering snare drum, bass drum, timpani, and cymbals. The accurate interpretation of each of these folk song settings is dependent on the execution of a variety of articulations. In "Marching Song," detached *tenuto*, *legato*, and *marcato* articulations are required. "Barbara Allen" requires a smooth *legato* and slurred articulations to support the sustained, lyrical lines. The final movement, "Farewell, Dundee," demands the use of a lightly detached articulation in the dance, and *legato* and slurs in the ballad.

Unit 5: Stylistic Considerations

Melodic lines are presented simply in various instruments and registers, with flowing countermelodies and harmonic accompaniment. Careful attention and support must be given to the melodic line at all times. Expressive characteristics are prominent, with many *crescendos* and *diminuendos*. Freedom of movement in the lyrical line is achieved by numerous *ritardando*, *rallentando*, *a tempo*, and *piu mosso* markings. Keep in mind the original form of these songs and encourage expressive playing in a singing style.

Unit 6: Musical Elements

MELODY:

The melodies of each movement are in folk song style using the concept of verse and refrain. Development and variation of the melodic line is achieved through modulation and changes in instrumentation and texture. Students need to be aware of the role they perform within the context of the overall work. Present each melody as it occurs in the score and have students label the voices that perform melodic functions in their parts. The concept of shaping the melodic line and phrasing should then be addressed. Have students transpose the melodies for their instrument and use this as a unison exercise to determine the peak and fall of phrases. This is also a good opportunity to discuss the supportive roles of countermelody and harmony. Regardless of melody or accompaniment, each instrument needs to develop an awareness of the expressive quality of its line and how it functions.

HARMONY:

The harmonic foundation of *British Isles Suite* is based on traditional progressions with tonal centers in D minor and F major, B-flat major, and E-flat major. Harmonies are triadic and diatonic. The homophonic texture utilizes shifting countermelodies and rhythmically active accompaniment figures.

RHYTHM:

Simple quadruple, triple, and compound duple meters are used in *British Isles Suite*. Discuss the basic differences between simple and compound meters using musical examples. Although rhythmically straightforward, subdivision of the pulse will ensure greater accuracy. Have percussion quietly subdivide the pulse while the ensemble claps/taps the rhythms. Due to the frequent tempo changes within phrases, "Barbara Allen" provides an excellent opportunity to sensitize young players to the conductor. Discuss and define the terms *andante espressivo*, *ritardando e diminuendo*, *a tempo*, *poco piu mosso*, *rallentando*, and *largo*. Ask students what effect these devices have on the music. Discuss the differences in interpretation between a soloist versus that of an ensemble. Have students hum the melody while you conduct. Emphasize the lyrical nature of this ballad with flowing, horizontal movements. Use "Barbara Allen" as a warm-up piece in rehearsal and change the way you conduct it each time, thus encouraging students to watch the conductor.

TIMBRE:

Daehn's writing effectively explores the unique timbres of the wind band and its choirs. There is interesting use of woodwind timbre in "Marching Song," where low woodwinds with piccolo and flute introduce the melody in measures 9 through 15. Percussion use is idiomatic and creates a military effect in the first and third movements. Bells and timpani are added for texture. In the second movement, percussion is employed for color purposes only. Brass writing is full, with a focus on the warmth of French horn and low brass sections. Contrast is achieved by scoring each repetition of the melody with a different instrumental family. By isolating melodic lines, this piece provides an excellent opportunity to define and discuss timbre.

Unit 7: Form and Structure

SECTION	MEASURE	TONALITY	EVENT AND SCORING
I: "Marching Song"			
A	1–8	D aeolian	Introduction percussion
	9–16		First statement of "Britons Raise Your Banners High"; low woodwinds with flute and piccolo
	17–24		Second statement of theme; trumpet with lightly textured accompaniment

Section	Measure	Tonality	Event and Scoring
	25–32		Third statement of theme; upper woodwinds and cornet with full accompaniment, followed by final statement by brass and saxophone
	32–35		Transition
B	36–43	B-flat	Legato treatment of "March for the Men of Harlech" melody in 1st clarinet, alto saxophone, and French horn; no percussion in verse
	44–51		Detached woodwind statement of refrain with marcato punctuation in brass; percussion is added
	52–55		Woodwind tutti and trumpet statement of refrain with march-like accompaniment
	56–63		Conclusion of refrain with melody in flute, 1st clarinet, 1st alto saxophone, 1st cornet; four-measure codetta

II: "Barbara Allen"

Section	Measure	Tonality	Event and Scoring
A	1–9	E-flat	Verse; clarinet and French horn with lightly textured accompaniment; percussion for color
	10–17		Verse; flute, oboe, clarinet, 1st cornet with minimal accompaniment
	18–25	B-flat	Verse; flute and cornet with rich, full-textured accompaniment

III: "Farewell, Dundee"

Section	Measure	Tonality	Event and Scoring
A	1–4	D aeolian	Introduction percussion
	5–8		First statement of "Adieu, Dundee"; flute soli
	9–16		Second statement; flute with sparse woodwind accompaniment

Section	Measure	Tonality	Event and Scoring
	17–25		Third statement; flute, clarinet, cornet with full accompaniment
	26–29		Chordal transition
	30–38		Fourth statement; initiated by clarinet/saxophone; addition of flute/cornet with chordal accompaniment
	39–47		Fifth statement in cornet with chordal and rhythmically active accompaniment
	48–51		Chordal transition
	52–69		Final statement returns to flute with sparse woodwind accompaniment
B	70–77	F	First phrase of "Auld Lang Syne" initiated in clarinet and alto saxophone; joined by flute and cornet with chordal accompaniment; color percussion only
	78–85		Second phrase; same treatment
	86–94		*Diminuendo* chords; addition of "military" percussion

Unit 8: Suggested Listening

William Byrd/Jacob, *William Byrd Suite*
Larry Daehn:
    As Summer Was Just Beginning
    Country Wildflowers
Percy Grainger:
    Irish Tune from County Derry
    Lincolnshire Posy
    Molly on the Shore
Brian Hogg, *Llwyn Onn*
David Holsinger:
    A Childhood Hymn
    On a Hymnsong of Philip Bliss

Gustav Holst:
First Suite in E-flat
Second Suite in F
Frank Ticheli:
Amazing Grace
Cajun Folk Songs
Shenandoah
Ralph Vaughan Williams:
English Folk Song Suite
Sea Songs

Unit 9: Additional References and Resources

Daehn Publications, New Glarus, WI.

Dvorak, Thomas L., and Richard Floyd. *Best Music for Beginning Band.* Edited by Bob Margolis. Brooklyn, NY: Manhattan Beach Music, 2000.

Gant, Andrew, ed. *Folk Songs of the British Isles.* Suffolk, UK: Kevin Mayhew, Ltd., 1997.

Garofalo, Robert J. *Instructional Designs for Middle/Junior High School Band.* Fort Lauderdale, FL: Meredith Music Publications, 1995.

Hopekirk, Helen, arr. *Seventy Scottish Songs.* New York: Dover Publications, Inc., 1992.

Kidson, Frank. *Traditional Tunes – A Collection of Ballad Airs.* Yorkshire, UK: S.R. Publishers Ltd., 1970.

Miles, Richard, ed. *Teaching Music through Performance in Band.* Chicago: GIA Publications, Inc., 1997.

Miles, Richard, ed. *Teaching Music through Performance in Band.* Chicago: GIA Publications, Inc., 1998.

Miles, Richard, and Thomas Dvorak, ed. *Teaching Music through Performance in Beginning Band.* Chicago: GIA Publications, Inc., 2001.

Moffat, Alfred. *The Minstrelsy of Wales.* London, UK: Augener Limited, 1906.

Palmer, Roy, ed. *Everyman's Book of Ballads.* London, UK: J.M. Dent and Sons, Ltd., 1980.

Randel, Don M., ed. *Harvard Concise Dictionary of Music.* Cambridge, MA: Belknap Press, 1978.

Contributed by:
Sheryl A. Bowhay
Director of Bands
Thornhill Secondary School
Markham, Ontario, Canada

Teacher Resource Guide

Caprice

William Himes
(b. 1949)

Unit 1: Composer

William Himes earned his Bachelor and Master of Music degrees from the University of Michigan. He has taught instrumental music in Flint, Michigan, as well as serving as adjunct lecturer in low brass at the University of Michigan-Flint. Himes has appeared as a guest euphonium soloist, composer, and conductor throughout the United States, Canada, England, Scotland, Norway, Sweden, and Australia. He serves as conductor of the Chicago Staff Band, an internationally recognized brass band, and as music director of the Salvation Army's Central Territory. Himes has numerous educational compositions to his credit, including *Creed, Medallion Overture, Cause for Celebration* and *Barbarosa*.

Unit 2: Composition

Caprice, composed in 1989, is part of the Neil Kjos *Best in Class Performance Selections* and is correlated directly to *Best in Class*, Book 2, page 12. It is ninety-two measures long, lasting approximately four minutes and thirty seconds. The work, classified by Kjos as grade two band literature, has gained general acceptance as a contest and festival piece, appearing on numerous state contest lists.

A *caprice* can be defined as a sudden, impulsive change of mind or emotion, a whim. In this work, the title can be related to the fanciful nature and the sudden contrasts between the driving, rhythmic A section and the lyrical B section.

Unit 3: Historical Perspective

A caprice is historically related to the *capriccio*, defined in the *New Harvard Dictionary of Music* as "a humorous, fanciful, or bizarre composition, often characterized by idiosyncratic departure from current stylistic norms." The musical form first appeared in sixteenth-century Italian baroque style and was a precursor to the fugue. Himes's *Caprice* relates most closely to the fanciful moods of caprices by Weber, Mendelssohn, and Brahms, with their *scherzo* style, fast-moving eighth notes.

Unit 4: Technical Considerations

As is the case with most compositions in this series, the publisher provides numerous "Learning Concepts" in both the score and parts that offer the conductor excellent devices for teaching scales, rhythm, melody, phrasing, intonation, and harmonic concepts contained within the piece. These offer both pre- and post-sight-reading warm-up exercises that aid the students' musical and technical development. The concert key of E-flat major is introduced within these concepts and used to assist with the rhythmic, melodic and phrasing, and tuning and harmonic skills activities.

The piece, in common time throughout, presents few rhythmic challenges as its lowest subdivision level is the eighth note. However, it does offer moderate use of syncopation within this framework. Wind players will need to be able to tongue repeated eighth notes at quarter note = 116+. Range requirements are moderate for most instruments with the exception of flute (written to F above the treble clef staff) and tuba (written to A-flat below the bass clef staff). Percussion requires eight performers, including xylophone, bells, tambourine, and triangle.

Conductors need to be aware that the piece makes brief forays into the concert keys of C minor (both the natural and harmonic forms) and E-flat minor (both forms), with the introduction of both D-flat and G-flat for all C instruments. These provide additional teaching opportunities about relative and parallel minor keys. Additionally, there is brief chromaticism present as well as the use of quartal and tertian harmonies.

Unit 5: Stylistic Considerations

The two primary stylistic considerations are *allegro leggiero* and *legato*. The *leggiero* (defined as "light and quick") needs to be performed with a separated, lifted tonguing style. There are a few *marcato* accents contained in the woodwind and percussion parts that should be treated carefully within the *leggiero* style. Attention should be given to balancing the melody and underlying rhythmic *ostinati* contained in the saxophone, brass, and percussion during the A section, as the initial melodic scoring is for flute, clarinet, and xylophone. The *legato* B section provides a connected contrast, essential for a successful performance. Students should be encouraged to perform as expressively as possible during this section, both in the melodic and accompaniment parts, with the development of phrasal contour being of primary concern. Likewise, the conductor should exercise restraint during the *forte*, *espressivo* section, placing emphasis on good tone production.

Unit 6: Musical Elements

MELODY:

According to the "Learning Concept Listening Chart" presented with the piece, there are three melodic ideas presented within *Caprice*. The first is presented in flute, B-flat clarinet, and xylophone beginning in measure 3. It is energetic and asymmetrical (four-measure antecedent: six-measure consequent). Melody two begins in measure 13. It is also asymmetrical (four-measure antecedent: three-measure consequent), continuing the character of the previous melodic idea. Melody three begins in measure 20 containing a four-measure antecedent and six-measure consequent in C minor. All melodies within the A section are performed in the *leggiero* style with energy. The B section melody is an augmentation of melody two and is performed in a *legato* style. The character is expressive and should maintain continued forward direction.

HARMONY:

The predominant key of the work is E-flat major. There are brief tonicizations of C minor (measure 20) and E-flat minor (measure 34) that need to be addressed. The harmony is predominantly tertian with brief quartal harmony appearing at measure 62.

RHYTHM:

Caprice contains whole notes, half notes, quarter notes, and eighth notes. The key element within the A section is the maintenance of an equal subdivision. This will help to keep the piece light and accurate.

TIMBRE:

Sensitivity to the issues of balance between melody and accompaniment figures is important throughout. Care should be taken with developing the proper tone color in the brass as they perform the light articulations needed in the A section. The sound should be full and not overblown during the *tutti espressivo* at measure 62. Consideration must be given to balance issues during this section so the upper woodwinds will be heard without having to force their sound.

Unit 7: Form and Structure

Caprice is composed in a ternary, ABA form. A complete breakdown of the work is contained in the score.

SECTION	MEASURE	EVENT AND SCORING
A	1–44	
	1	Introduction
	3	Statement of the first melody
	13	Statement of the second melody
	20 ·	Statement of a third melody
	30	Restatement of melody 2
	37	Transition to B section
B	45–79	
	45	B section; statement of melody 2 in augmentation
	62	B melody restated; reharmonized; full instrumentation
A'	80–92	
Da Capo	80	Coda
(mm. 1–27	89	*Allegro Vivo*
plus coda)		

Unit 8: Suggested Listening

James Curnow, *Rejouissance*
Chuck Elledge, *Esprit*
William Himes, *Creed*
Timothy Mahr, *Fantasia in G*
Bruce Pearson, *Jubilation*

Unit 9: Additional References and Resources

"The Basic Band Curriculum: Grades I, II, III." *BD Guide*, September/ October 1989, pp. 2–6.

Dvorak, Thomas L. *Best Music for Young Band*. Brooklyn, NY: Manhattan Beach Music, 1986.

Dorothy, Wayne F. "Creed: William Himes." *Teaching Music through Performance in Band*, Volume 3. Chicago: GIA Publications, Inc., 2000, pp. 138–41.

Garofalo, Robert J. *Instructional Designs for Middle/Junior High School Bands*. Fort Lauderdale, FL: Meredith Music Publications, 1995.

Contributed by:
Robert Meunier
Director of Bands
Drake University
Des Moines, Iowa

Teacher Resource Guide

Cumberland Cross
Carl Strommen
(b. 1940)

Unit 1: Composer

Composer, arranger, and music educator Carl Strommen received his B.A. in English Literature from Long Island University and his M.A. in Music from the City College of New York. He studied composition with Stephan Wolpe and arranging with Rayburn Wright and Manny Album. Equally skilled in the jazz ensemble, concert band, orchestral, and choral mediums, his many published compositions place him among the most performed composers in the United States.

For many years, Strommen was Director of Bands at Mamaroneck High School in Mamaroneck, New York. He is currently on the adjunct faculty at the C.W. Post campus of Long Island University, where he teaches arranging and orchestration. His music is published by Alfred Music, Warner Brothers, Carl Fischer, and Shawnee Press. He maintains an active schedule of composing, teaching, and serving as a guest clinician. He can be contacted by e-mail at cestrommen@aol.com.

Unit 2: Composition

This original composition for young band explores American folk style with the use of pentatonic melodies and traditional folk song harmonies. It is written in two sections with a short coda. The A section is a *largo* tempo chorale, and the B section is a lively dance reminiscent of Copland's *Hoedown*. The coda effectively ends the piece with a brief recapitulation of both themes. It is three minutes and fifteen seconds in length, and of medium difficulty level (grade two in the Texas UIL list).

Unit 3: Historical Perspective

Cumberland Cross is written in the American folk music style of such tunes as *Shenandoah, The Gift to Be Simple,* or *Hoedown.* The scoring, melodic and harmonic usage, and simple form of the piece recall such works as Aaron Copland's *Appalachian Spring* and *Rodeo.* Early in the twentieth century, Copland studied in Paris with Nadia Boulanger. She encouraged him to develop a style utilizing the unique folk music idioms of the Americas. The result was a return to the style known as nationalism, which has played a significant role in the composition of American music. Many composers of concert band music, including Roy Harris, Robert Russell Bennett, Clare Grundman, Frank Ticheli, and John Zdechlik have used folk, jazz, and popular American music sources in their compositions.

Unit 4: Technical Considerations

This work is wholly based on the B-flat pentatonic scale and accompanying diatonic chords, and is in the concert key of B-flat major throughout. The standard symphonic band instrumentation is appropriate for young (middle school-level) ensembles and includes piccolo, flute, oboe, 1st/2nd/3rd B-flat clarinet, alto clarinet, bass clarinet, bassoon, 1st/2nd alto saxophone, tenor saxophone, baritone saxophone, 1st/2nd/3rd trumpet, 1st/2nd/3rd/4th French horn, 1st/2nd/3rd trombone, baritone, tuba, and percussion (xylophone, bells, whip, tambourine, triangle, suspended and crash cymbals, and timpani). The piece is primarily in 4/4 with one 5/4 measure at the end of the A section, a 2/4 measure (twice used to close the b theme), and its repeat, in the *allegro*. The rhythmic values range from whole notes to various combinations of eighth and sixteenth notes, including the "scotch snap" eighth/sixteenth figure and eighth/quarter syncopated rhythms. Instrument ranges are not problematic, with the highest notes as follows: flute, c2; clarinet, A1; alto saxophone, b1; trumpet, g1; French horn, f1 (the high horn parts are doubled in alto saxophone), trombone, f; baritone, g; and tuba, e-flat (bass clef third space). The *allegro* section provides an opportunity to develop clarity and tonguing technique in rapid eighth and sixteenth note figuration, especially in the low brass melodic line at measure 45.

Unit 5: Stylistic Considerations

The A section opens with a broad melodic line that should be approached in a *legato*, chorale style with expressive markings that allow for liberties in tempo and dynamics. The repeat of the a theme utilizes woodwinds alone, followed by a *tutti* statement of the b theme, with the expectation that all parts will match in style and phrasing. The contrasting B section, in a lively dance style, requires light, separated articulations with special attention paid to the accented quarter note on beat 4 of each second measure. The last measure of the theme, with a stylized syncopation of eighth/quarter/quarter/ eighth/quarter, should be heavily accented to complete the phrase (and give the whole section a Copland-like "western hoedown" feel).

Unit 6 Musical Elements
MELODY:
Use of the pentatonic scale throughout the piece and limited melodic range make the two main themes in Sections A and B, very song-like and tuneful. Students will find it easy to sing the melodies and possibly improvise upon them, as is often done in the folk style. There is ample opportunity to teach *rubato* style and "elastic" phrasing in the first section, which could be included in a lesson on singing folk songs. The second section, a contrasting *allegro* dance style, gives each instrumental section an opportunity to play the melody. Each instrumental section might be asked to play the tune separately in a manner that matches the light, folk-dance style as the rest of the band listens and critiques the performance.

HARMONY:
The piece remains in B-flat throughout, with the exception of the b theme of Section A, which modulates to G minor. Diatonic chords, and plagal or V–I cadences, predominate in the A section. The B section makes liberal use of the flat seven to tonic chord progression, giving the dance section a modal harmonic feel. The lowered VII chord is generally placed on beat 4 and accompanied by a strong accent. Students might be encouraged to feel this beat more heavily and perhaps clap or stomp their feet if they are not playing at the moment.

RHYTHM:
The accents on beat 4, syncopated rhythms, and "scotch snap" sixteenth/eighth figuration all add rhythmic vitality to the dance section. The learning of these rhythms would be enhanced by isolating and clapping each rhythm separately and then in sequence. Divide the ensemble in two, and have one side clap the basic beat while the other side claps the rhythm. One unique, and perhaps challenging, rhythmic spot is the 2/4 at measure 40, and its repetition at measure 46. The whip is the only instrument to play on beat 2, followed by two sixteenth note pickups into the next measure in woodwinds and trumpet. For these measures to be effective, the downbeat must be released cleanly and the pickup sixteenths played together and in tempo. Again, clapping these measures before attempting to play them should make the passage easier to execute.

TIMBRE:
The piece offers many opportunities to highlight individual sections and encourage characteristic tone quality and careful listening. High woodwinds

are featured from measures 9 through 16. Clarinets alone play measures 23 and 24, followed after a pause by trumpet and horn introducing Section 2. From measures 33 to 36, while the high woodwinds repeat the melody, horn and trombone must play very delicate, harmonized eighth notes on each beat of the measure. A major challenge throughout the piece is the balance between accompaniment and melody. Each section must be aware of its function at the moment and be sensitive to its volume so the melodic line will predominate.

Unit 7: Form and Structure

The form of this piece is AB with a short coda that recapitulates the themes from both A and B.

SECTION	MEASURE	EVENT AND SCORING
A	1–24	*Largo* tempo; begins with an eight-measure melody (a) based on the B-flat pentatonic scale; full repeat of the eight-measure theme follows, this time played only by high woodwinds; the b theme, in G minor, an eight-measure variation of the a theme, concludes the A section, first as a lushly harmonized *tutti*, ending on a C major ninth chord, and finishing with unison clarinet playing a very soft echo of the last two measures of the a theme
B	25–58	*Allegro* tempo; three melodic ideas; may be diagrammed as aa–bb–c–(a variation of the A section, b theme)–aa–b
Transition	59–60	Two measures, using rhythmic syncopation
Coda	61–end	Recaps first the b melody from A (four measures), then the original opening melody with its original slow tempo (two measures), and finally the B section, c melody, at the *allegro* tempo for the final two measures

Unit 8: Suggested Listening

Robert Russell Bennett, *Suite of Old American Dances*
Aaron, Copland, *Appalachian Spring*
Aaron Copland/Patterson, *Down a Country Lane*

Clare Grundman, *American Folk Rhapsody Nos. 1–3*
Roy Harris, *Cimmeron*
Carl Strommen:
Ballymore Down (concert march)
Canterbury Walk
Harlequins Court March
Highlander
Frank Ticheli, *Shenandoah*
John Zdlechik, *Chorale and Shaker Dance*

Unit 9: Additional References and Resources

Alfred Publishing Company, Van Nuys, CA. www.alfredpub.com

Spotlight on Teaching Band. Music Educators National Conference, (2001).

Wind Ensemble and Symphonic Band Repertoire Database.
www.band-chat.org

Contributed by:

Philip G. Simon
Doctoral Conducting Associate
University of North Texas
Denton, Texas

Teacher Resource Guide

Flurry for Winds and Percussion
John Kinyon
(1918–2002)

Unit 1: Composer
John Kinyon earned degrees from Ithaca College and the Eastman School of Music, as well as an honorary doctorate from Limestone College. He served as an instrumental music director and music department head for several school districts, as educational director for Warner Brothers Music in New York, and as a professor of music education at the University of Miami, Florida. Kinyon published numerous original works in his lifetime, including marches, ballads, and overtures, through Alfred Publishing Company.

Unit 2: Composition
Flurry for Winds and Percussion, composed in 1983, was commissioned by and dedicated to the John M. Langston Junior High School Band in Danville, Virginia, with Robert R. Paquette directing. A *flurry* is defined as "a sudden blast or gust of wind." The composer intended to capture this with the fast-paced nature of the work. The form of this 68-measure work is ABA, with the tempo marked *Allegro e marcato*. The B section is a brief four-part canon based on the original A theme. The brass section is placed in opposition to the woodwinds and horns throughout much of the piece, with the percussion section reinforcing both choirs.

Unit 3: Historical Perspective
Flurry for Winds and Percussion is a contemporary educational composition. It offers the students opportunities to learn about ternary form and canon while presenting few real musical or technical difficulties. The work fits the style of

many educational pieces composed beginning in the 1950s, including *Overture for Winds* by Charles Carter, *Toccata for Band* by Frank Erickson and *Festivo* by Vaclav Nelhybel.

Unit 4: Technical Considerations

Flurry for Winds and Percussion focuses on the development of young players. As such, the work contains relatively simple harmonic and motivic ideas while presenting the developing player with reasonable technical and musical challenges. Range requirements for trumpet and horn are moderate, with only the 1st trumpet part extending outside of the staff (to G). Range requirements for all other instruments are also moderate, allowing all players to concentrate on good tone production and appropriate articulations. The piece has a key signature of two flats and works its way between C dorian, G-natural minor, and G dorian. The predominant time signature for the work is 4/4 with a meter change to 3/4 for four measures near the end. The smallest rhythmic value for the wind players is the eighth note, while snare drums perform some moderate sixteenth and sixteenth/eighth note combinations. Another rhythmic consideration is the use of quarter note triplets during two measures. Brief chromaticism is used in the B section, and chromatic alterations to move the harmonic structure between G-natural minor and dorian are also introduced. There is one brief, two-measure flute solo and a four-measure orchestra bell part.

Unit 5: Stylistic Considerations

The primary stylistic consideration is the use of *marcato*, with rare exception, throughout the piece. Students will need to be taught the art of properly separating notes to accomplish the overall style of the piece. The work also asks for five measures of *legato* playing at the cadential extension of the initial A section. Careful consideration should be given to the balance between woodwinds and percussion, especially during the A section and to the overall balance of the canon during the B section.

Unit 6: Musical Elements

MELODY:

The piece is deceptive in that the key signature of two flats sets up a certain expectation of key center that is not immediately apparent to the listener. The work actually begins in C dorian, as presented by the opening timpani/percussion *soli* (C and G timpani pitches) and the initial brass entrance beginning in measure 7. The key of G minor is established by the woodwinds beginning in measure 11 but moves to G dorian in measure 16. It is suggested that students become familiar with all three of these scales. Care should be taken to balance the brass choir to the woodwind choir as the piece moves back and forth between these entities during the A section. The phrasing during this section is often asymmetrical. A four-measure phrase is answered by a three-measure phrase, and a three-measure phrase is answered by a two-measure phrase.

Care must be taken to balance the four-part canon of the B section. The canonic subject is comprised of three three-measure phrases, the second of which uses chromatic motion. Each of the four entrances is staggered by three measures presenting unique balance issues, particularly between the brass and woodwind choirs. Of particular issue is the balance of the flute/oboe choir to the clarinet/alto saxophone and cornet choirs in measures 35 through 37. Likewise, the canonic entrance of the low voice choir in measure 38 may present difficulties with balance.

HARMONY:
The music of the A section is homophonic and homorhythmic within each choir. At times the choirs provide a singular chordal accompaniment for each other. This is in contrast to the polyphonic style of the canonic treatment used in the B section. Because of conservative instrumental ranges, all instruments do not play the entire subject of the canon.

RHYTHM:
The work offers few rhythmic challenges. The wind parts are written in whole note, half note, quarter note, and eighth note durations. The only exception is the use of quarter note triplets in measures 21 and 60. Care should be taken to teach this rhythm as it corresponds to eighth note triplet subdivision and not the often-used dotted-eighth/dotted-eighth/eighth substitute. The percussion parts use sixteenth notes and repeated patterns that offer little teaching or performance challenge.

TIMBRE:
It is important to strive for characteristic sounds from each choir throughout the work. Great care should be taken that the winds do not tongue too heavily and that they maintain a centered, focused sound within the *marcato* style.

Unit 7: Form and Structure
The structure of the work is as follows:

MEASURE	EVENT AND SCORING
1–6	Introduction
7–23 (beat 1)	A section
23 (beat 2)–28	A section cadential extension
29–45	B section (four-part canon)
46–62 (beat 1)	A section (exact repeat)
62 (beat 2)–68	Coda (use of 3/4 meter)

Unit 8: Suggested Listening

Charles Carter, *Overture for Winds*

Frank Erickson, *Toccata for Band*

Vaclav Nelhybel, *Festivo*

Unit 9: Additional References and Resources

"The Basic Band Curriculum: Grades I, II, III." *BD Guide*, September/ October 1989, pp. 2–6.

Dvorak, Thomas L. *Best Music for Young Band*. Brooklyn, NY: Manhattan Beach Music, 1986.

Dvorak, Thomas L., Robert Grechesky, and Gary Ciepluch. *Best Music for High School Bands*. Edited by Bob Margolis. Brooklyn, NY: Manhattan Beach Music, 1993.

Garofalo, Robert J. *Instructional Designs for Middle/Junior High School Bands*. Fort Lauderdale, FL: Meredith Music Publications, 1995.

Contributed by:

Robert Meunier

Director of Bands

Drake University

Des Moines, Iowa

Teacher Resource Guide

Harvest Hymn
Percy Grainger

(1882–1961)

arranged by Joseph Kreines

(b. 1936)

Unit 1: Composer

A noted pianist and accompanist, Joseph Kreines is also an accomplished conductor and clinician. He has served as the guest conductor for over three hundred bands, choirs, and orchestras throughout the state of Florida. Kreines has composed original works for all manner of ensembles. A prolific arranger and transcriber for concert band, he is best known for his editions of the works of Percy Grainger. In addition, he authored *Music for Concert Band*, an annotated guide to selected band literature that is graded by difficulty.

Kreines first moved to Florida from his native Chicago to serve as the associate conductor of the Florida Symphony Orchestra in Orlando. Later, he served as the conductor for the Brevard Symphony in Melbourne, Florida; associate conductor of the Florida Orchestra in Tampa; and musical director for numerous opera and musical theatre productions.

Unit 2: Composition

Harvest Hymn is similar in style, orchestration, and interpretive demand to other lyrical works by Grainger, such as *Ye Banks and Braes o' Bonnie Doon* and *Irish Tune from County Derry*. Awareness of the conventional interpretation of English band music in general and Grainger's music in particular is required to appropriately perform this work. Although the level of technical difficulty is generally low, the intonation, phrasing, and range demands are quite high.

Grainger sketched the first seventeen measures of *Harvest Hymn* in 1905 in London, under the title *Hymn Tune*. It took until 1932 while in Sweden to complete the composition. Although famous for the use of folk songs in his music, *Harvest Hymn* is based on an original melody. However, Kreines did not base this version of *Harvest Hymn* strictly on Grainger's original orchestral setting. Rather, he utilized a subsequent version arranged by Grainger for solo piano in 1936 while borrowing some scoring details from the original. *Harvest Hymn* takes approximately three minutes to perform.

Unit 3: Historical Perspective

As one of the few composers who wrote original works of substance for band in the early twentieth century, Grainger holds a position of great historical significance. Many of his works are considered among the gems of band literature, including *Lincolnshire Posy*, *Ye Banks and Braes o' Bonnie Doon*, *Irish Tune from County Derry*, *Shepherds Hey!* and *Molly on the Shore*, among others. Similar nationalistic flair can be heard in Ralph Vaughan Williams's *Folk Song Suite*, composed in 1924, and Gordon Jacobs's *An Original Suite*, composed in 1928.

Like all of the compositions mentioned above, a performance of *Harvest Hymn* requires great sensitivity to the traditional interpretation of English band music. The score provides a large amount of guidance in terms of dynamic contrasts, as well as stylistic and tempo information provided by Grainger's infamous quirky conjugations of the English language.

Unit 4: Technical Considerations

As is often the case in Grainger's music, the printed key signature (E-flat major) gives way to a large number of accidentals. Rhythmic demands are simple and largely confined to quarter notes and eighth notes, although flute, oboe, E-flat clarinet, and 1st clarinet have a double dotted-half note in measure 31 that might require some extra attention. *Harvest Hymn* will challenge the performers' ability to sustain a melodic line within a given instrumental voice, as well as the ability to sustain a melodic line passed between sections of the band. Despite limited technical challenges, the musical independence of each part, presence of accidentals, and unusual form should hold the interest of each player.

Kreines remains faithful to Grainger's tendencies regarding instrumentation. For instance, the treble clef baritone part is different from the bass clef euphonium part; two performers are required for these independent parts. Also, Kreines scores prominently for soprano saxophone, an instrumental preference Grainger acquired while a military musician.

Kreines utilizes four trumpet parts and makes substantial demands of the 1st trumpet player. For instance, in measure 28, the 1st trumpet part makes a solo entrance on a B-flat above the staff at a *forte* dynamic level after a twelve-measure rest. Cross-cues are provided in clarinet, but Kreines indicates a strong preference for the trumpet sonority. There are several other B-flats above the staff, as well as a sustained C above the staff. This requires a mature performer with precise upper register control for a successful performance. The 1st trombone part and treble clef baritone part require equivalent skill in the upper register.

Unit 5: Stylistic Considerations

Stylistic integrity is of primary importance in the performance of English band music. Kreines provides valuable information regarding expression and phrasing in the score by way of *crescendo/decrescendo* marks. Tempo indications and dynamic levels are frequently indicated as well. The conductor must be prepared to interpret Grainger's use of English terms to describe elements of performance rather than their Latin equivalents. For instance, Kreines (*ala* Grainger) uses "clingingly" rather than *sostenuto*, "slow off" rather than *ritardando*, "lingeringly" rather than *expressive* or *tenuto*.

The complexity of the chords and the constant presence of contrapuntal lines makes balance an item of concern when performing *Harvest Hymn*. Likewise, a rich, full tone color must be maintained throughout the ensemble, especially in the *tutti* sections, lest the brass overwhelm the sonority.

Unit 6: Musical Elements

MELODY:

As one might expect from Grainger, the initial melody is in a major key. Its lyrical character calls for a sustained performance and attention to the melodic contour. Long, connected phrases are required for an accurate performance. In measures 26 through 29, the phrase is passed between the woodwind and brass choirs in two-measure increments. Appropriate connection between these phrases requires great musical awareness. Kreines provides numerous guidelines for melodic interpretation via dynamic marks, tempo indications, and accents.

HARMONY:

Harvest Hymn contains the high degree of polyphonic movement often associated with Grainger's music. Maintaining musical balance between the contrasting melodic lines is crucial to an accurate performance of this composition. Chord construction begins within a relatively simple tonal framework but progresses to chromaticism and advanced harmonic motion by measure 30. The tonality returns firmly to E-flat major by the end of the piece.

RHYTHM:

Quarter notes and eighth notes, along with dotted-quarter notes and eighth notes, make up the bulk of the rhythmic demands of *Harvest Hymn*. Measure 31 calls for a double dotted-half note followed by an eighth note in the flute,

E-flat clarinet, and 1st clarinet parts. To facilitate an accurate performance of this rhythm, students should be instructed to focus on changing notes on the last eighth note of the measure. Treating this note as a pickup note to measure 32 will help ensure a continuous melodic line as well as simplify the rhythm. *Fermatas* are present in measures 33 and 48, although in his written preface to the score Kreines indicates that the *fermatas* should be interpreted as a rhythmic elongation rather than a break in the flow of the phrase. Conductors should note that the *fermata* in measure 48 does not appear in some of the brass parts in the score.

TIMBRE:

Instruments not always found in every band provide important tone colors in *Harvest Hymn*. Specifically, soprano saxophone, E-flat clarinet, and string bass play vital musical roles. Cross-cues are provided for these instruments in most cases but only at a loss of the unique tone colors that constitute the charm of Grainger's music.

The first parts for both trumpet and trombone, as well as for treble clef baritone, are demanding in terms of *tessitura*. Exquisite control of intonation, volume, articulation, and tone color in the upper register are required to adequately perform this work. Merely reaching the highest notes will not suffice; the players assigned the parts described above must be able to blend with each other, match woodwind voices for pitch, and maintain the stylistic integrity of the performance.

Due to the finesse and musical maturity required within the upper register, *Harvest Hymn* would be best performed by college level or advanced high school ensembles.

Unit 7: Form and Structure

SECTION	MEASURE	EVENT AND SCORING
A	1–4	Melody in 1st clarinet and soprano saxophone; tonal center in E-flat; texture limited to woodwinds and string bass
A'	5–8	Flute and oboe join 1st clarinet and soprano saxophone on melody
B	9–12	Texture expands to full ensemble; melody in flute, oboe, E-flat clarinet, 1st clarinet, soprano saxophone, and 1st trumpet
C	13–16	Melodic scoring same as B

SECTION	MEASURE	EVENT AND SCORING
	17–20	Melodic variation based on dotted-quarter note/eighth note rhythmic motif from A; texture changes to low clarinet and saxophone choir; chromaticism and passing tones incorporated into harmonic structure
	21–25	Similar melodic content scored for oboe, clarinet, alto clarinet, and bass clarinet
	26–31	Three two-measure phrases: the first stated by woodwinds, the second by brass, and the third by all winds
	32–33	Rhythmic motif returns; scored for flute, oboe, E-flat clarinet, and B-flat clarinet; supported by baritone, euphonium, and all trombones; fermata in m. 33
	34–39	Melodic variation continues using rhythmic motif; motif appears in different voices, switching almost by measure between woodwinds and brass
	41–44	A returns in oboe, E-flat clarinet, 1st clarinet, and 1st trumpet
	45–48	B; scored in 1st alto saxophone, tenor saxophone, 1st/3rd horn, baritone, and for one measure 3rd/4th trumpet
	49–52	Rhythmic motif and scalar decoration culminating in cadential gesture from C

Unit 8: Suggested Listening

Percy Grainger:
    Children's March
    Colonial Song
    Hillsong #1 and #2
    Irish Tune from County Derry
    Lincolnshire Posy
    Marching Song of Democracy
    Molly on the Shore
Gordon Jacob, *An Original Suite*
Ralph Vaughan Williams, *Folk Song Suite*

Unit 9: Additional References and Resources

Bird, John. *Percy Grainger*. London: Faber and Faber, 1976.

Dreyfus, Kay. *The Farthest North of Humanness: Letter of Percy Grainger 1901–1914*. Saint Louis, MO: MMB Music, 1985.

Fennell, Frederick. "Molly on the Shore, An Interpretive Analysis." *The Instrumentalist*, October 1983.

Fennell, Frederick. "Ye Banks and Braes o' Bonnie Doon." *The Instrumentalist*, September 1981, pp. 29–32.

Lewis, Thomas P. *A Source Guide to the Music of Percy Grainger*. White Plains, NY: Pro/Am Music Resources, 1991.

Miles, Richard, ed. *Teaching Music through Performance in Band*, Volume 3. Chicago: GIA Publications, Inc., 1997.

Mellers, Wilfrid. *Percy Grainger*. New York: Oxford University Press, 1992.

Sadie, Stanley, ed. *The New Grove Dictionary of Music and Musicians*. London: Macmillan Inc., 1980.

Slattery, Thomas. "Percy Grainger: The Inveterate Innovator." *The Instrumentalist*, 1974.

Slonimsky, Nicolas, ed. *Baker's Biographical Dictionary of Musicians*. New York: Macmillan Inc., 1992.

Smith, Norman, and Albert Stoutamire. *Band Music Notes*. Lake Charles, LA: Program Note Press, 1989.

Contributed by:

Thomas Bough
Southern Illinois University
Carbondale, Illinois

Teacher Resource Guide

Kachina: Chant and Spirit Dance
Ann McGinty
(b. 1945)

Unit 1: Composer

Anne McGinty has over 150 published compositions and arrangements for concert band. This makes her one of the most prolific women composers in the field of concert band literature. She has written and arranged compositions for band at all levels of performance ability from elementary school through college. More than thirty of her works were commissioned by bands in the United States, and she is the first women composer to be commissioned to write an original work for the United States Army Band.

McGinty started her formal education at The Ohio State University, where she studied with Donald McGinnis. She left The Ohio State University to pursue a career in flute performance, and played principal flute in the Tucson Symphony Orchestra in Tucson, Arizona. She returned to college at Duquesne University, where she received her Bachelor of Music degree and Master of Music degree in Flute Performance, Theory, and Composition. While at Duquesne University, she studied flute with Bernard Goldberg and composition with Joseph Willcox Jenkins.

Unit 2: Composition

Kachina: Chant and Spirit Dance is a work that celebrates a portion of the rich Pueblo Indian culture. This programmatic work depicts the Kachina, a supernatural being that is associated with ancestral spirits, animal spirits, and natural forces such as thunder, wind, clouds, and rain. Kachinas are represented in two ways: by carved figures (called *kachina dolls*) and by elaborately costumed, masked male members of the tribe impersonating spirits in sacred ceremonial dances. The kachinas (the men dancing at ceremonies) act as a link between gods and mortals for entertainment so their beauty will bring joy to others.

Unit 3: Historical Perspective

Kachinas are part of the traditional religion of the Hopi who lived on the American continent in the areas now known as Arizona and New Mexico. The name *Hopi* translates roughly as meaning "good, peaceful, or wise." These people followed a tranquil way of life, raising crops in the arid climate of the Southwest.

Growing crops and farming always was precarious in the arid climate of the Southwest. Annual kachina ceremonies emphasize fertility, germination, growth, and maturity of Hopi crops. They focus on the elements of nature to ensure a fruitful outcome of their crops and peace and joy in life. More than two hundred kachina spirits are each distinguished by personality, costume, and body posture. This piece is a musical representation of the character and spirit of the kachina.

Unit 4: Technical Considerations

This composition can serve as a vehicle to enhance and develop artistic use of percussion instruments in a young band. The prominent use of percussion throughout this piece makes it ideal for developing percussionists to improve in the areas of touch, good section balance, and technique on keyboard percussion and several types of drums. In the *allegro* section, the phrases are irregular in that they are not the typical four-measure groupings. This will require careful counting for all players. In measures 20 through 21 and 48 through 49, the flute and 1st clarinet are scored for relatively weak registers. Therefore, good wind support is needed on these instruments so their melodic material can be heard in good balance.

Unit 5: Stylistic Considerations

To achieve the plaintive chant style in the opening section of this piece, wind players will need to spin the air through the instruments continuously with lots of energy and be careful not to tongue heavily. Careful attention must be given to the ends of phrases to ensure that sustained notes are held full value so holes do not occur between statements of the chant and imitative material. It will also be important to observe the *decrescendo* at the end of each statement of the chant or melodic material as indicated in the parts. This will allow the next statement of the chant or melodic motif to be heard without being covered by the sustained notes.

Dynamics and articulations have been carefully indicated in a manner that enhances the imitative style of this piece and brings out the musical connection to a style of Native American drumming. Care needs to be taken to ensure an equal and even balance of sound between all sections in the ensemble (woodwinds, brass, and percussion).

Unit 6: Musical Elements

This piece is built on two primary musical elements. First, the percussion instruments are used as a prominent element in establishing the musical character. They present a portion of the musical materials and the tonal center on which the chant and the spirit dance are based. The second musical element that is used to develop this piece is an imitative chant/plain-song style that is imitative in a statement-and-response format. When presenting statements of main melodic material, individual sections of instruments (such as clarinet or trumpet) and larger groups of instruments (such as woodwinds, low brass and low woodwinds, or percussion) are used. The tonal center for this work is G minor.

Unit 7: Form and Structure

MEASURE	EVENT AND SCORING
1–2	Chant (slow section); percussion; statement of rhythmic material and establishment of the tonal center by bells
3	Clarinet; chant motive I
4	1st cornet/trumpet; chant motive II (response/echo statement)
5	2nd cornet/trumpet; chant motive II (response/echo statement)
6	Flute and oboe, chant motive III; low brass and low woodwinds, chant motive IV
7	Alto saxophone, chant motive II statement
10	Clarinet, chant motive I
11	Horn, cornet/trumpet, tenor saxophone, chant motive II (response/echo statement); flute and oboe, chant motive III
12	Clarinet, chant motive III; cornet/trumpet, horn, tenor saxophone, chant motive II; low brass and low woodwinds, chant motive IV
16	*Allegro* (spirit dance section); percussion; rhythmic statement of melodic motive I

MEASURE	EVENT AND SCORING
17	Cornet/trumpet, horn, tenor saxophone, statement of melodic motive I
20	Woodwinds, bells, statement of melodic motive II
23	Low brass and low woodwinds, statement of melodic motive III
25–44	Development section
45	Cornet/trumpet, horn, tenor saxophone, percussion; return statement of melodic motive I
48	Flute, oboe, clarinet, alto saxophone; return statement of melodic motive II
51	Low brass and low woodwinds; return statement of melodic motive III
53	Transition to closing section
55	Closing section based on all three motives and the percussion rhythmic/harmonic material from the opening slow chant section; materials are presented imitatively as follows: clarinet, motive I; cornet/trumpet, motive II (response/echo statement); alto saxophone, tenor saxophone, and horn, motive II; flute and oboe, motive III; low brass and low woodwinds, motive IV
63–64	*Tutti*; closing statement based on motive I from *Allegro* (spirit dance) section

Unit 8: Suggested Listening

John Barnes Chance, *Incantation and Dance*
W. Francis McBeth, *Chant and Jubilo*
Michael Sweeney, *Lament and Tribal Dances*
John Zdechlik, *Chorale and Shaker Dance*

Unit 9: Additional References and Resources

Anderson, William, and Joy Lawrence. *Integrating Music into the Classroom.* Second edition. Belmont, CA: Wadsworth Publishing Company, 1985.

Dvorak, Thomas L. *Best Music for Young Bands*. Brooklyn, NY: Manhattan Beach Music, 1986.

Mark, Michael L. *Contemporary Music Education*. Second edition. New York: Macmillan, Inc., 1973.

May, Elizabeth, ed. *Music of Many Cultures: An Introduction*. Berkeley, CA: University of California Press, 1980.

Contributed by:

Marcellus Brown
Boise State University
Boise, Idaho

Teacher Resource Guide

Lion of Lucerne

James Curnow
(b. 1943)

Unit 1: Composer

James Curnow was born on April 17, 1943, in Huron, Michigan. He received his formal training at Wayne State University in Detroit and at Michigan State University in East Lansing. At Michigan State University, he was a euphonium student of Leonard Falcone and a conducting student of Dr. Harry Begian, two of the most prominent collegiate music educators of the twentieth century. He has taught in all areas of instrumental music, both at the public school and college and university levels. He is a member of such noted organizations as ABA, CBDNA, NBA, WASBE, and ASCAP. In 1980, Curnow received the National Band Association's Citation of Excellence. A prolific writer, he has well over 250 compositions and arrangements to his credit, as well as numerous awards for band compositions. He currently lives in Nicholasville, Kentucky, where he is president, composer, and educational consultant for Curnow Music Press, Inc. He also serves as Composer-in-Residence on the faculty of Asbury College in Wilmore, Kentucky.

Unit 2: Composition

Lion of Lucerne was written by James Curnow and published in 1986. It was inspired when the composer viewed the magnificent sculpture by the same name carved into the face of a rock in Lucerne, Switzerland. The carving commemorates a contingent of Swiss guards who died in Paris defending the palace of the King on August 10, 1792, during the French Revolution. The approximately six-minute work is built upon three main themes: "Majesty – The Sculpture" (*Maestoso*), "Spirit of the Swiss Guard" (*Allegro con spirito*), and "Unser Leben" or "Life's Journey" (*Andante cantabile*). The work bears Curnow's stamp of solid instrumental doubling and compositional devices typical of the band overtures genre.

Unit 3: Historical Perspective

As a relatively recent composition, *Lion of Lucerne* reflects the conventions of modern band scoring. Dynamic changes are meticulously marked in each part, as are phrase marks and tempo changes. Adherence to the printed page will ensure a musically effective performance.

Unit 4: Technical Considerations

The scales of F, B-flat, and E-flat concert are required for the full ensemble. Portions of an A-flat scale, created by accidentals, are required for most of the ensemble as well. Piccolo, flute, clarinet, oboe, alto and tenor saxophone, 1st/2nd trumpet, horn, euphonium, vibraphone, and bells must play four-note scale fragments at 76 beats per minute in the keys described above. Low brass and low reeds must be familiar with the individual notes of C-flat and F-flat. The rhythmic demands are basic, primarily combinations of quarter and eighth notes. When syncopation is present, it usually occurs as a background figure scored for many voices within the ensemble. Range demands are within the grasp of most high school bands.

Unit 5: Stylistic Considerations

Curnow has provided a great deal of stylistic information in the score. *Staccato*, *legato*, slurs, and other articulations are clearly marked, as are breath marks for the full ensemble. Dynamic contrasts are enhanced by Curnow's scoring of *soli* and solo passages, logical use of background verses foreground instruments, and combinations of voices within the ensemble texture as well as plentiful dynamic markings. Numerous tempo changes are present, including several *rallentandi*, plus the tempo contrasts inherent between the three sections of the composition.

The opening *Maestoso* must be performed with accurate subdivision and great rhythmic clarity, supported by *tenuto* performance of the quarter note figures in the low brass and low reeds.

The central *Allegro con spirito* section requires the performers to execute repeated eighth notes with an unobtrusive volume and a subtle degree of articulation. The melody scored above these *ostinato* figures includes a dotted-half note in the second measure that sounds best when energized by a slight *crescendo* to propel the listener into the third measure.

If the published phrase marks are observed in the final *Andante cantabile* section, the appropriate singing style will be achieved. Depending upon the size of each section and the strength of the players, better balance may be achieved in measures 81 through 88 by utilizing either the 1st or 2nd trumpet parts rather than both as marked.

Unit 6: Musical Elements

MELODY:

Theme 1 is based on a motif of four sixteenth notes. Although the moderate tempo of 76 beats per minute should pose no significant technical difficulties, students often compress sixteenth note patterns, playing them faster than necessary. Subdivision within the minds and fingers of the students will help ensure an accurate performance, especially at this tempo. In Theme 2, energize the dotted-half notes in the melody with a slight *crescendo* to enhance the melodic contour. Clarinet and alto saxophone have this figure at measures 36 and 40, while piccolo, flute, oboe, clarinet, and trumpet have this figure at measures 44 and 48.

HARMONY:

The scale passages utilized in Theme 1 reinforce the printed key signature of E-flat major. However, the first sixteen measures of Theme 1 are harmonized using chords borrowed from the key of C-flat major. The large number of accidentals used to create these harmonies may pose problems for students. The director may elect to rehearse only the quarter notes that form these chords in measures 3, 6, 11, 12, and 15 to allow the students time to internalize the tonality. Even though most of the chords are major, the students may need time to assimilate the context in which these chords occur.

Curnow utilizes a number of chords that extend beyond the limits of common practice tertian harmony. That is, rather than creating chords using only the root, third, fifth, and seventh, he often adds the ninth degree of the chord as well. As a result, students will be challenged to tune notes within chords that sound dissonant. In some cases, the orchestration of such chords results in the interval of a whole step being created within differing parts of the same instrument—for example, between 2nd and 3rd trumpet in measures 2 and 3, 1st and 2nd clarinet in measure 33, as well as 1st and 2nd horn and 1st and 2nd flute. There are also frequent instances of whole step dissonances created by passing tones.

From measures 52 through 58, Curnow creates a sequence of suspensions within the clarinet parts. The musical tension created by this use of dissonance should be made clear to the listener within the context of the prevailing soft dynamic levels. The presence of these relatively advanced harmonic concepts does not detract from the accessibility of this composition. Rather, the concepts blend into the polyphonic whole to enhance the interest of both the listener and the player.

RHYTHM:

Virtually all of *Lion of Lucerne* is in common time. There are a number of tempo changes between sections of the piece, especially from the final chorale to the end. Rhythmic precision plays an important role in each section of this composition. Theme 1 requires accurate subdivision of the four sixteenth notes motif, accompanied by syncopated figures thickly scored in the low brass and low reeds. Within Theme 2, from measures 60 through 63, the whole ensemble has a syncopated figure that combines eighth notes into groups of 3+3+2. Students can be shown a graphic representation of these groupings by drawing a triangle over each group of three notes followed by a slash over the group of two notes. The chorale from Theme 3 poses no rhythmic complexity other than requiring independence between voices.

TIMBRE:

The trumpets begin this composition accompanied only by vibraphone and suspended cymbal. Although marked at a *fortissimo* dynamic, the trumpets must take care to retain a characteristic sound rather than distort the tone. An appropriate trumpet sound can be described as resonant, pure, clear, or ringing, and should be demonstrated to the students via a recording (or better yet a professional trumpet player). From measures 28 through 43, all trumpets are scored with a straight mute. The use of a straight mute will raise the pitch of each instrument—that is, make the trumpet section sharp. A tuner should be used to determine exactly how far each trumpet player must pull out the main tuning slide to compensate for the pitch alteration created by the mute. The director needs to monitor and reinforce the adjustment of the tuning slides until this behavior is firmly established. When the mutes are removed, the students must push their slides back in to their original position. Experienced players often write cues to themselves in their parts reminding them to adjust their slides after a mute change: such written cues would benefit students as well.

If possible, students should all play the same make and model of straight mute. At the very least, the director should verify that all students are in fact using a straight mute (as opposed to no mute at all or whatever mute they happen to own), especially since other types of mutes affect intonation in different ways.

Curnow calls for specific mallet selections in the percussion section to create certain timbres. These mallet specifications can be interpreted and adjusted according to the preferences of the director. For instance, the opening suspended cymbal roll calls for plastic mallets. If one does not appreciate the sound produced by those mallets, perhaps hard yarn mallets would create a timbre more likely to blend with the trumpets. Likewise, Curnow specifies that the vibraphone be played with bell mallets. Some percussionists warn of damage to the relatively soft bars of the vibraphone if anything harder than cord-wound yarn mallets are used.

By combining winds and percussion, Curnow achieves unique timbral effects. In measures 101 through 104, the bells and chimes reinforce the 1st and 2nd clarinet parts. At measures 107 through 109, the xylophone reinforces the flute and piccolo, while at measures 77 and 78, the chimes are combined with muted 1st and 2nd trumpet.

Unit 7: Form and Structure

SECTION	MEASURE	EVENT AND SCORING
Theme 1	1–7	Theme divided between trumpet and piccolo, flute, oboe, and clarinet; five-note melodic fragment used to embellish and accompany melody; melody in E-flat major but harmonized in C-flat
Transition	8–18	Fragments of Theme 1 presented by flute and oboe, harmonized by clarinet; solo trumpet foreshadows Theme 2 melody via fragmentation and repetition
Theme 1	19–25	Theme stated by piccolo, flute, clarinet, and 1st/2nd trumpet, with mallet percussion; syncopated background figures played by rest of ensemble
Theme 2	36–43	Theme 2 melody scored for clarinet and alto saxophone in E-flat major; ensemble plays repeated eighth note *ostinato* with *staccato* bass pattern under melody
Theme 2 (repeated)	44–51	Theme played by piccolo, flute, oboe, clarinet, trumpet, and mallet percussion; countermelody played by alto saxophone and horn
Theme 2 (repeated)	69–75	Theme played by piccolo, flute, oboe, 1st clarinet, trumpet, and bells; countermelody played by 2nd/3rd clarinet, alto saxophone, and tenor saxophone; end of this melody statement altered and extended to create a transition into the next section

SECTION	MEASURE	EVENT AND SCORING
Theme 2	81–88	Sostenuto, four-voice chorale played by 1st/2nd trumpet, horn, trombone, and euphonium; optional cues provided in saxophone choir and bass clarinet, but brass ensemble preferred
Theme 3 (repeated)	93–100	Chorale re-orchestrated for full band; countermelody added, played by alto and tenor saxophone and 2nd trumpet
Theme 1	114–120	Harmonized version of Theme 1 presented in F major
Theme 2	121–128	Theme 2 played by piccolo, flute, oboe, 1st clarinet, 1st trumpet, euphonium, and mallet percussion in the key of B-flat major
Coda	131–137	Re-orchestration of first measure followed by transitional material and a two-measure reprise of Theme 3 chorale leading to a final cadence in B-flat major

Unit 8: Suggested Listening
James Barnes, *Westridge Overture*
James Curnow, *Superstition Mountain Overture*
Ed Huckeby, *Declaration, Ballade and Finale*

Unit 9: Additional References and Resources
Cook, Gary. *Teaching Percussion*. Second edition. New York: Schirmer Books, 1997.

McBeth, Francis W. *Effective Performance of Band Music*. San Antonio, TX: Southern Music Company, 1972.

Whitener, Scott. *A Complete Guide to Brass*. Second edition. New York: Schirmer Books, 1997.

Contributed by:
Thomas Bough
Southern Illinois University
Carbondale, Illinois

Teacher Resource Guide

Old Churches
Michael Colgrass
(b. 1932)

Unit 1: Composer

Michael Colgrass was born on April 22, 1932, in Chicago, Illinois. Raised in the small town of Brookfield, Illinois, movies were his initial window into culture. At age ten, he saw drummer Ray Bauduc in "Big Noise from Winnetka," and from then until age nineteen, jazz was his only ambition. Colgrass was a jazz drummer in the Chicago area from 1944 to 1954, and in 1954, he graduated from the University of Illinois in music performance and composition. While at university, Colgrass studied percussion with Paul Price who, after hearing Michael's critique of a percussion ensemble concert, challenged Colgrass to write music himself. "Three Brothers" (for nine percussionists) was the result and has gone on to become a percussion classic. Colgrass studied composition at the University of Illinois with Eugene Weigel, at Aspen with Darius Milhaud, and at Tanglewood with Lukas Foss.

After spending just less than two years in Stuttgart, Germany, as a timpanist in the Seventh Army Symphony Orchestra, Colgrass went to New York, where he worked as a top freelance percussionist from 1956 to 1967. During this time, he continued to study composition with Wallingford Riegger (1958) and Ben Weber (1958–1960), and he performed with groups such as the New York Philharmonic, Dizzy Gillespie, the original *West Side Story* orchestra on Broadway, the Columbia Recording Orchestra's *Stravinsky Conducts Stravinsky* series, and numerous ballet, opera, and jazz ensembles.

In 1967, Colgrass began to study theater directing, mime, fencing, voice, ballet, and modern dance. The Rockefeller Foundation gave him a grant to pursue these studies in Europe, studying with the Tomeshevsky Mime

Company, clown training with commedia del arte actors from Milan, and Grotowski physical training. After these experiences, Colgrass began to offer workshops for performers, which have grown to include people of all professions. He has written about these workshops in his book called *My Lessons with Kumi – How I Learned to Perform with Confidence in Life and Work*.

For the past twenty-five years, Colgrass has been giving workshops in performing excellence combining Grotowski physical training, mime, dance, and neuro-linguistic programming. As a percussion soloist, he has premiered a number of his own works and has been commissioned to write works for many of the world's most prestigious orchestras. His works have been played by all the major symphony orchestras in North America and many throughout Europe, Great Britain, and Japan. Numerous recordings have been made of his works.

In 1978, Colgrass won the Pulitzer Prize for Music for *Déjà Vu*, which has been rescored for wind ensemble. In 1982, he was awarded an Emmy for the PBS documentary "Soundings: The Music of Michael Colgrass." Other prizes include two Guggenheim Fellowships, a Rockefeller grant, a Fromm Award and Ford Foundation Award, First Prize in the Barlow and Sudler International Wind Ensemble Competitions, and the 1988 Jules Leger Prize for New Chamber Music.

Colgrass lives with his wife in Toronto, Ontario, Canada, writing music and giving workshops on an international scale.

Unit 2: Composition

Old Churches was commissioned by The American Composers Forum as part of their *BandQuest* series, which states as its mission to take "young bands out of the rehearsal room and immerse them in the works of world-class composers." Through the project, composers were asked to work with middle-school band programs to "create original pieces of music that would inspire, challenge, and educate" (*BandQuest* pamphlet). Colgrass worked in partnership with Winona Drive Public School of Toronto, Ontario, Canada. As the title suggests, *Old Churches* is a musical tour of ancient places of worship. In the words of the composer, "The piece is based on Gregorian chant and replicates the feeling and sound of monks singing and praying in ancient churches."

The piece offers middle-school bands an opportunity to work with special effect techniques of aleatoric music, such as murmuring, free rhythm improvisation, and open bar techniques that allow for musical decisions to be made by the ensemble and conductor, unique to each performance of the work. Imaginative percussion sounds, so integral to much of Colgrass's music, call for aluminum bowls typically found in kitchens to imitate the distant sound of church bells. A single-movement work of only fifty-three measures at quarter note = 60 beats per minute, the piece is approximately five minutes and twenty seconds in length. This length will vary with the open measures according to the decisions made with each performance.

Unit 3: Historical Perspective

Old Churches is a meeting of old and new, Gregorian chant, and aleatoric techniques. In early polyphony, c. 850 to 1200 A.D., parallel organum began with simple octave doubling, the result of combining men's and boys voices. *Scholia enchiriadis*, a contemporary commentary on *Musica enchiriadis*, the first treatise to clearly describe music in more than one voice, moves beyond this first step to organum at the fifth or fourth. A plainsong melody was sung in the *vox principalis* and was duplicated a fifth or a fourth below in the *vox organalis*. Throughout *Old Churches*, the interval of a fifth or fourth runs underneath the chant melody, and the note against note movement of these lyrical lines is highly reminiscent of this early organum. Measure 29 makes use of a diminished fifth, an interval avoided in early polyphony as the *diabolus in musica*, the devil in music. This is a point of tension that adds to the haunting quality of the piece.

Drawing special effects from the twentieth century, Colgrass has incorporated elements of aleatoric music by providing sections within the piece that leave choice open to the conductor and the musicians. Each effect has clear instructions, which are then interpreted by the player. In this way, each performance of *Old Churches* will be unique within specific compositional guidelines.

Unit 4: Technical Considerations

In the words of the composer, "*Old Churches* is modal, with some feeling of atonality at times, a mysterious atmosphere." Primarily centered on the A aeolian mode, throughout the piece the intervals of open fifths and fourths are predominant. The transparent nature of the piece requires particular attention to tuning these open intervals. There is minimal chromaticism but frequent dissonance as lines move away from one another in the early polyphonic style mentioned in Unit 3. This style also requires independence between divisi parts. While the lyrical lines are primarily in rhythmic unison, individual lines diverge and converge with one another.

Instrumental ranges are within the grasp of middle school players. Clarinets play above the break, and 1st trumpet reaches a written G above the staff. In measures 1 through 6, 1st/2nd flutes should have at least three players on each part to cover all of the pitches, and 3rd flute should have a minimum of two players. In the notes to the director, Colgrass recognizes the possibility of limited instrumentation and has "over-orchestrated" some of the sections (like measures 33 through 41). Directors are free to thin out instrumentation as needed. Bassoon is often doubled in either horn or tenor saxophone.

Special effects, such as the long/short-note effect and "murmuring," are explained fully in the notes at the front of the score. Mention is also made to have the trumpets and trombones muted throughout. If mutes are not available, trumpets and trombones will need to be reduced in volume. If mutes are used, intonation may require attention.

The percussion for *Old Churches* is played entirely on mounted aluminum kitchen bowls ranging in diameter from 8 to 16 inches. These should be mounted on cloth so they resonate when struck with pieces of wood (drumsticks may be too harsh). The number of players and bowls may vary.

Unit 5: Stylistic Considerations

The notes for the band director state "...that the overall style of the playing is *molto legato*, resembling the vocal style of monks singing Gregorian chant. Phrases should start and end smoothly and without noticeable attack. Even the *forte* sections should be played with some restraint, strong but not blasting. The overall effect should be that of long, smoothly connected vocal lines, always lyric. The character should be that of mystery, almost like spirits from the past singing to us."

Stylistic considerations require musicians to be comfortable with sustained *legato* playing and *tenuto* articulation. Players should use a "du" or "lu" articulation where needed, always with good air support to make the back of one note touch the front of the next without sagging in pitch or tone quality.

Unit 6: Musical Elements

As part of the American Composers Forum *BandQuest* series of commissions, an accompanying interdisciplinary CD-ROM curriculum has been developed, which complements and enriches each piece. "Designed to help you teach the music through a range of interdisciplinary materials, each interactive CD-ROM is informed by the National Standards for Arts Education. Throughout the course of the learning process, the *BandQuest* series promotes a deeper appreciation for how music relates to other aspects of life and learning." (*BandQuest* pamphlet)

In considering melody, harmony, and timbre, Colgrass states that *Old Churches* is "very melodic, in fact vocal in nature. The harmony is modal, textures are full and rich and strongly doubled to give kids a feeling of security when playing with their peers."

Unit 7: Form and Structure

Colgrass describes the form and structure of the piece as "simple development of a theme through different instrumental groupings, song-like."

SECTION	MEASURE	EVENT AND SCORING
Introduction	1–5	Free rhythm, bowls in percussion, flute tone cluster freely alternating long/short notes; 1st/2nd clarinet, 3rd flute divisi, open fifths, A aeolian mode; *p* dynamic marking
Chant melody	6–8	1st clarinet *legato* lyrical chant (*soli*) melody; m. 8, bass clarinet, bassoon, alto saxophone murmuring ad-lib; *p* dynamic marking
Chant melody (choir)	9–11	Bassoon, tenor saxophone, 1st/2nd trumpet, horn, and baritone with *legato* chant melody; trombone and tuba with sustained open fourths; A aeolian mode; *p* dynamic marking
	11–12	Free rhythm, bowls; clarinet alternates long/short freely; *mf* dynamic marking
Woodwind chant	13–18	Flute and oboe lyrical chant melody; m. 17, 1st clarinet, alto saxophone *legato* chant melody; 2nd/3rd clarinet, bass clarinet, bassoon, horn, and 1st/2nd trombone *tenuto* open fifths; A aeolian mode; *mf, crescendo*
Brass chant	19–21	Baritone saxophone, 1st trombone melody, baritone, tuba *legato* chant melody; bass clarinet, bassoon, tenor saxophone, horn, 3rd trombone *tenuto* open fourths; A aeolian mode; *f* dynamic marking
	22–23	Free rhythm, bowls; flute and clarinet murmuring effect; *mf*
Chant melody (soprano)	24–25	Flute, 1st/2nd trumpet chant melody; oboe, alto saxophone, tenor saxophone, 3rd trumpet, and horn *tenuto* open fifths; A aeolian mode; *mf* dynamic marking

SECTION	MEASURE	EVENT AND SCORING
Chant melody	26–28	Bassoon, tenor saxophone, horn, 1st/2nd (bass) trombone, baritone, tuba *legato* chant melody
Harmonic excursion	29–31	Flute chant melody in A harmonic minor using a tritone; clarinet, alto saxophone, tone cluster harmony, unison rhythm with flute; *mf* dynamic marking
	31–32	Bowls, freely; *mf*
Chant melody	33–38	Woodwinds, trumpet chant melody; woodwinds/trumpet with underlying open fourths in A aeolian; mm. 36–38 harmonic excursion ends with sustained open fourths A–E 2/4 measure; *f* dynamic marking
Chant melody	39–41	Bass clarinet, bassoon, saxophone, low woodwinds/brass, chant melody in A melodic; brass minor; *f* dynamic marking
	41–42	Free rhythm, bowls in percussion; flute tone cluster freely alternating long/short notes
	43–45	Clarinet and oboe unison chant melody; *mp* dynamic marking
Harmonic excursion	46–48	Sustained open fifths in alto and tenor saxophone, horn, trombone, and tuba in A aeolian mode; 1st flute A harmonic minor melody over oboe and clarinet harmonic major arpeggiated accompaniment; *mp* dynamic marking
	49–50	Free rhythm in bowls; aleatoric upper woodwinds; tone cluster free articulation increasing in speed at m. 49, decreasing in speed at m. 50

SECTION	MEASURE	EVENT AND SCORING
Open bars	51–53	Low woodwind and low brass pickup into A aeolian open bar holding open fifths under flute free ad-lib; *p* dynamic marking; repeat in m. 53, add bowls; indeterminate ending, fade out one by one to *pp*

Unit 8: Suggested Listening
Michael Colgrass:
    Arctic Dreams
    Déjà Vu
    Urban Requiem
    Winds of Nagual
Ron Nelson, *Medieval Suite*
Gregorian chant
Early music of Palestrina, Machaut, Josquin, Monteverdi

Unit 9: Additional References and Resources
American Composers Forum. *Let's hit the musical highway with BandQuest* [pamphlet]. Hal Leonard, 2002.

Colgrass, Michael. Interview by author, 30 March 2002, Saskatoon. E-mail.

Colgrass, Michael. *Michael Colgrass, Composer, Writer and NLP Teacher.* Available from http://michaelcolgrass.com; accessed 24 March 2002.

Davison, Archibald, and Willi Appel. *Historical Anthology of Music.* Cambridge, MA: Harvard University Press, 1977.

Grout, Donald J., and Claude V. Palisca. *A History of Western Music.* Fourth edition. New York: W. W. Norton & Company, Inc., 1988.

Contributed by:
Jennifer McAllister
University of Saskatchewan
Saskatoon, Saskatchewan, Canada

Teacher Resource Guide

Overture on a Minstrel Tune
Pierre La Plante
(b. 1934)

Unit 1: Composer

Pierre La Plante was born in Milwaukee of French Canadian descent. He grew up in Sturgeon Bay, Wisconsin, and received Bachelor of Music and Master of Music degrees from the University of Wisconsin at Madison. He spent thirty-two years teaching classroom, vocal, and K–12 instrumental music at all levels. Most recently, he retired from the Pecatonica Area School District.

As a bassoonist, La Plante has performed with the Dubuque Symphony, the Unitarian Society Orchestra, the Madison Theatre Guild Orchestra, and the Beloit-Janesville Symphony. Currently, he resides in the Madison, Wisconsin area, where he continues to compose and play bassoon in the Madison Wind Ensemble.

Unit 2: Composition

This overture is based on "De Boatmen's Dance," a minstrel tune from the nineteenth century composed by Daniel Decatur Emmett. It is a single-movement work with three distinct sections. Standard band scoring is utilized with only three horn parts. Percussion includes tambourine and triangle in addition to standard instruments. Published in 1979 by the Bourne Company, this piece is approximately three minutes and forty seconds in duration.

Unit 3: Historical Perspective

Minstrel groups were very popular theatrical and entertainment groups during the second half of the nineteenth century. One of the earliest groups in the United States was the Virginia Minstrels, whose banjo player was Daniel

Emmett. Written for the Virginia Minstrels in 1843, "De Boatmen's Dance" became a huge success. While not as well known today as his contemporary, Stephen Foster, Emmett composed many other songs that eventually became very popular, such as "Dixie," "Blue-Tailed Fly," and "Old Dan Tucker." The Virginia Minstrels are known to have worked primarily on the East Coast, but they also performed in Britain.

Unit 4: Technical Considerations

Articulation and style are the most challenging technical issues. To accurately represent the style of the minstrel band unquestionably using fewer players than today's ensembles, it is necessary for performers to place both dynamics and sound quality in context. A more transparent texture can be achieved by limiting the number of players at different times, using all players in the *tutti* sections. Articulation must be refined and crisp, with precision as the primary goal. Technical demands on the performers are not great; however, to play the correct style presents the more serious challenge. The only solo is for 1st cornet.

Unit 5: Stylistic Considerations

Separation is a very important stylistic concern throughout the first and third sections, especially regarding the dotted-eighth/sixteenth note figure each time it occurs. Unanimity of articulation style is of great importance. Players must use a very light, crisp, *staccato* articulation. Ensemble consistency must be developed through listening exercises and matching articulations from instrumental group to instrumental group. Rhythmic precision is often difficult to achieve, especially with younger groups. Those players with offbeat rhythms must actively stay involved with the strong beats against which they are playing. First clarinets are asked to play the first statement of the melodic material "quasi banjo." A dry, crisp articulation with little resonance will produce the requisite percussive effect.

Unit 6: Musical Elements

MELODY:

Much of the writing is of a tuneful nature with simple harmonic support. Repetitive melodic and accompaniment patterns abound. It is important to make sure the sixteenth note pickup (melody section A) is clearly heard as a part of the melody. Often a *legato* tongue on the second note of a slur, as in this case, may help the definition of this important note. As the melodic figures repeat, increasing agogic stress should be placed on each subsequent figure to provide forward motion. The *espressivo* required in the supporting half note chords in the opening of the second section of the piece is best achieved by leaning on the first half note of each pair, providing a feeling of tension and release.

HARMONY:

This piece uses a very simple harmonic structure based upon that of the original tune. The outer sections are in the key of E-flat, and the middle section is more lyrical and in the key of A-flat. There are no harmonic surprises as the work progresses. La Plante retains the simple harmonic flavor of "De Boatmen's Dance" and achieves variety and contrast through the use of different orchestrations.

RHYTHM:

This piece contains several characteristic rhythms, which gives forward impulse to the music and helps to create the flavor of the authentic style. The popular music of the nineteenth century usually required strong pulses, each often followed by a short note of lesser emphasis. This type of "boom-chick" sound is most obvious in percussion, using tambourine rather than cymbals, and the tuba/low woodwind combination with horn or *tutti* eighth notes. Other characteristic rhythms include a quarter note followed by a dotted-eighth/sixteenth note figure, which typifies this type of folk song material. The return of the original material in Section III eliminates several beats at the resolution of the phrase, resulting in the use of 3/4 measures (measures 110 and 114). This mixed meter creates an impetuous forward motion to the phrase.

TIMBRE:

As mentioned earlier, the indication in measure 5 for the clarinets to play "quasi banjo" presents a challenge. The sound should be very short and sharply articulated. This sound should be used throughout Sections I and III. The brass sound should be light, even at *fortissimo*. Emphasis must be on aggressive air pulses to create the effect of energy without too much volume. This will also assist in correct stylistic performance. The tambourine is a very effective tone color and adds much to the stylistic flavor. Warmth of sound in the lyrical section of the piece is very important. Softer phrases will present a challenge to maintain a rich, resonant sound. Open mouth cavities assist in achieving this resonance, as will a clear understanding of air support and flow.

Unit 7: Form and Structure

SECTION	MEASURE	EVENT AND SCORING
Introduction	1–4	Quiet and lyrical, 4/4 time; woodwinds and low brass
Section I	5–12	Quick 2/4 at approximately quarter note = 120–126; rhythmic set-up; clarinet asked to create banjo sound

SECTION	MEASURE	EVENT AND SCORING
	13–24	1st cornet solo statement of melody A section
	25–35	Statement of melody B section by trombone and saxophone
	36–43	Melody A section stated again by upper woodwinds followed by alto or tenor instruments in a canonic fashion
	44–57	Melody B section played in augmentation by the low brass and low woodwinds, with highly rhythmic figures in upper woodwinds
	58–75	Transition; sustained quiet sounds with quarter and dotted-eighth/sixteenth figure traded from horn to cornet to low instruments
Section II	76–84	Melody A section first presented in a lyrical espressivo style by flute with very thin clarinet and alto saxophone texture, later completed by horn with brass and low woodwind texture, still quiet
	85–92	Melody B section stated in augmentation by solo cornet accompanied by a countermelody in trombone and bassoon using the melodic fragment presented in the transition section
	93–102	Transition fragment reappears here setting up the return of the original material and style
Section III	103–114	Return of the material from Section I; last note of each phrase shortened by three beats, requiring a 3/4 measure; texture is cornet with only baritone saxophone and baritone

SECTION	MEASURE	EVENT AND SCORING
	115–122	*Tutti;* rhythmic elements of the melody A section used with embellishment; *marcato* style with heavily syncopated figures in the accompanying instruments
	123–136	Melody B section returns once again in augmentation stated by flute, alto saxophone, 1st cornet, and baritone accompanied by aggressively accented moving eighth notes in low woodwinds and low brass
	137–142	Rhythmic figure first stated in transition section appears with indications to broaden the style and tempo; this declamatory style ends with a loud trill in the upper woodwinds and triangle, which sets up the coda
Coda	143–151	*Tutti* finale with trills in the upper woodwinds, quarter and dotted-eighth/ sixteenth rhythms in upper brass; full percussion

Unit 8: Suggested Listening

Pierre La Plante:
  American Riversongs
  Prairie Songs (Wisconsin Landscapes)
  The Red River Valley
  Western Portrait

Unit 9: Additional References and Resources

Battisti, Frank. *The Twentieth Century American Wind Band/Ensemble: History, Development and Literature.* Fort Lauderdale, FL: Meredith Music Publications, 1995.

Band Music Guide. 1983 edition. Evanston, IL: The Instrumentalist Company, 1983.

Dvorak, Thomas L., Robert Grechesky, and Gary M. Ciepluch. *Best Music for High School Band.* Edited by Bob Margolis. Brooklyn, NY: Manhattan Beach Music, 1993.

La Plante, Pierre. Telephone interview by Sean Flanigan, 1 August 2000.

Nettle, Bruno. *Folk Music in the United States: An Introduction.* Third edition. Detroit, MI: Wayne State University Press, 1976.

Rehrig, William H. *The Heritage Encyclopedia of Band Music.* Edited by Paul E. Bierley. Westerville, OH: Integrity Press, 1991.

Sadie, Stanley, ed. *The New Grove Dictionary of Music and Musicians.* London: Macmillan Publishers Limited, 1980.

Slonimsky, Nicolas. *Baker's Biographical Dictionary of Musicians.* Eighth edition. New York: Schirmer Books, 1992.

Contributed by:
Sean Flanigan
Assistant Director of Bands
Drake University
Des Moines, Iowa

Teacher Resource Guide

Russian Folk Fantasy

James Curnow
(b. 1943)

Unit 1: Composer

James Curnow was born in Port Huron, Michigan, and was raised in Royal Oak, Michigan. He received his formal education at Wayne State University in Detroit and at Michigan State University in East Lansing. While at Michigan State University, Curnow was a euphonium student of Leonard Falcone and a conducting student of Harry Begian. He studied composition and arranging with F. Maxwell Wood, James Gibb, Jere Hutchingson, and Irwin Fischer.

Curnow is currently serving as president, composer, and educational consultant for Curnow Music Press of Lexington, Kentucky. He is also Composer-in-Residence on the faculty of Ashbury College in Wilmore, Kentucky, and serves as editor of all music publications for The Salvation Army in Atlanta, Georgia. He has also taught instrumental music in the public schools and at the college and university levels.

Curnow has been commissioned to write over two hundred works for concert band, brass band, orchestra, choir, and various vocal and instrumental chamber ensembles. He has over four hundred published works, which include commissions from the Tokyo Symphony Orchestra for *Concerto for Euphonium and Orchestra*; the U.S. Army Band, Washington, DC, for *Lochnivar* (Symphonic Poem for Winds and Percussion); *The Olympic Fanfare and Theme for the Olympic Flag*, Atlantic Committee for the Olympic Games, 1996; the Kentucky Music Teachers Association for *On Poems of John Keats for String Quartet*; and the U.S. Navy Band for *Turning Point*. Curnow has received numerous awards for his work as an educator and composer, including the ASBDA/Volkwein Composition Award (1977), the National Band Association's Citation of Excellence (1980), the ABA/Ostwald Award (1980 and 1984), the Sixth International Competition of Original Compositions for Band (1985), the Coup de Vents Composition Competition of Le Havre, France (1994), Composer of the Year by the Kentucky Music Teachers Association (1997), and Who's Who in America.

Unit 2: Composition

This composition is a setting of three Russian folk songs that can be found translated in the text *Russian Folk Songs*, edited by Rose Rubin and Michael Stillman, and published by Random House. "The Slender Mountain Ash" is a love song about a thin ash tree that feels lonely and sad because she sees a big strong oak tree across the river that she would like to whisper to and whose branches she would like to touch. The slender ash would also like to be close to the oak tree for protection from the wind breaking her branches. However, the fate of the slender ash is forever to be on the other side of the river longing to be with the oak.

The "Troika Rushing" is a story about a man riding in a traditional three-horse drawn carriage traveling to see his true love. The song describes the running horses, the dust under their hooves, and the laughing, crying, and ringing of the bells that are on the running horses. Questions are asked in the song: "who is the rider, from where is the rider coming, and where is the rider going?" The song ends without one knowing whether the rider ever reaches his final destination to see his true love.

"No Sounds from the City Are Heard" is a reflective song about the tragedy of a man who has to be in prison for the rest of his life. The song starts with a verse that describes the peaceful city under the full moon as the wind dances and blows through the leaves and blossoms of the trees. At this most peaceful and quiet time, the prisoner starts his song. In his song, he says goodbye to his home, his family, his father, his bride, and his wedding ring, knowing that he will be in prison forever. He knows that he will never become a husband or a father, and in the quiet of the night in his prison, the song is completed by the whispering wind.

Unit 3: Historical Perspective

Folk music is the musical repertory and traditions of communities. Folk music exists in almost every part of the world, and by far the largest part of this tradition has been handed down through the oral tradition of singing and, thus, is known as folk songs. Folk songs of a nation have certain characteristic features that at times can be difficult to describe and are clearly felt to represent the national traits of the people. The impact of folk songs on Russian composers has been enormous. The folk music of Russia, with its originality of harmony, rhythm, and melody, has been skillfully borrowed and used by major Russian composers since Mikhail Ivanovich Glinka. The list of composers includes Mili Balakirev, Alexander Borodin, César Cui, Modest Moussorgsky, Nicolai Rimsky-Korsakov, Peter Ilyich Tchaikovsky, Alexander Scriaban, Sergei Rachmaninov, Dmitri Shostakovich, and Igor Stravinsky.

Unit 4: Technical Considerations

Only a few demanding technical sections are found in this piece. A sixteenth note passage occurs in the trumpet part in measure 59; the flute and oboe parts in measure 67 could be considered challenging. In measures 102 and 110, a two-beat sixteenth note passage for piccolo, flute, clarinet, 1st alto saxophone, and trumpet will require good facility. In the melodic line of "No Sounds from the City Are Heard," there are interval skips of fifths and sixths. The challenge here would be to make the melody smooth and song-like.

Unit 5: Stylistic Considerations

The opening and introductory material of *Russian Folk Fantasy* should be played in a majestic, heroic style, with sustained note lengths that should be firmly articulated. The introduction contrasts the *legato* style, quiet, to which "The Slender Mountain Ash" should be performed. "Troika Rushing" should be played in a lively dance style, with more weight and accents on dotted-eighths and quarter notes. "No Sounds from the City Are Heard" should be performed like a ballad, with close attention given to the dynamics and the rise and fall of the musical line of the melody. The closing material is from "Troika Rushing" and should be performed in a march style, with detached eighth and quarter notes. Care should be taken not to clip notes too short when they are marked with accents or indicated to be played *staccato* or *marcato*.

Unit 6: Musical Elements

The tonality of the introduction and the first two folk songs are in D minor with the use of a picardy third in the final cadence of the first folk song ("The Slender Mountain Ash") in measure 55. Transition to B-flat major occurs in measure 92. This is the tonality for the final folk song and closing material.

Unit 7: Form and Structure

MEASURE	EVENT AND SCORING
1	Introduction; high woodwinds, high brass, keyboard percussion, and triangle
11	Introduction continued; *tutti*
21	Transition/introduction for "The Slender Mountain Ash"; low woodwinds, low brass, and percussion

MEASURE	EVENT AND SCORING
25	Folk song statement ("The Slender Mountain Ash"); flute and muted 1st trumpet
27	Countermelody; alto saxophone and horn
49	Transition to "Troika Rushing"; low woodwinds, low brass, and timpani
56	Folk song statement ("Troika Rushing"); bassoon, tenor saxophone, baritone saxophone, trombone, euphonium, and tambourine
60	Continuation; statement of "Troika Rushing"; tenor saxophone, trumpet
64	Continuation; statement of "Troika Rushing"; addition of piccolo, flute, and oboe
92	Transition to "No Sounds from the City Are Heard"; clarinet and low woodwinds, horn, and low brass
99	Folk song statement ("No Sounds from the City Are Heard"); solo trumpet
103	Continuation; statement of "No Sounds from the City Are Heard"; *tutti*
107	Second statement of folk song ("No Sounds from the City Are Heard"); solo flute
111	Continuation; statement of "No Sounds from the City Are Heard"; *tutti*
114	Closing material from "Troika Rushing"; *tutti*
132	Timpani solo

Unit 8: Suggested Listening

James Curnow, *Korean Folk Rhapsody*
Antonín Dvorak: *Slavonic Rhapsody, Slavonic Dance*
Nicolai Rimsky-Korsakov, *Overture on Russian Folk Themes*
Dmitri Shostakovich, *Overture on Russian and Kirghiz Folksongs* (folk themes)

Unit 9: Additional References and Resources

Anderson, William, and Joy Lawrence. *Integrating Music into the Classroom.* Second edition. Belmont, CA: Wadsworth Publishing Company, 1985.

Dvorak, Thomas L. *Best Music for Young Bands.* Brooklyn, NY: Manhattan Beach Music, 1986.

Mark, Michael L. *Contemporary Music Education.* Second edition. New York: Macmillan, Inc., 1973.

May, Elizabeth, ed. *Music of Many Cultures: An Introduction.* Berkeley, CA: University of California Press, 1980.

Seaman, Gerald R. *History of Russian Music.* New York: Frederick A. Praeger Publishers, 1967.

Swan, Alfred J. *Russian Music and Its Sources in Chant and Folk-Song.* New York: W. W. Norton & Company, 1973.

Contributed by:

Marcellus Brown
Boise State University
Boise, Idaho

Teacher Resource Guide

Songs of the Whalemen
Elliot Del Borgo
(b. 1938)

Unit 1: Composer

Elliot Del Borgo was born in Chester, New York, on October 27, 1938. He received his B.S. from the State University of New York and his Ed.M. from Temple University. While completing his M.M. degree at the Philadelphia Conservatory of Music, Del Borgo studied theory and composition with Vincent Persichetti and trumpet with Gilbert Johnson. In 1973, he was granted doctoral equivalency by SUNY and was elected to membership in the American Bandmasters Association in 1993.

Early in his career, Del Borgo taught instrumental music in the Philadelphia school system before taking a position as Professor of Music at the Crane School of Music of the State University of New York in Potsdam, a position he held from 1966 through 1995. Since retiring from the Crane School of Music, Del Borgo has focused full-time energy on his work as a composer and conductor. He is an internationally known conductor of bands and orchestras, and is in demand as a clinician, lecturer, and adjudicator in the United States and abroad. An award-winning ASCAP composer, Del Borgo's music was used in celebration of the 1980 Olympic Games in Lake Placid, New York. To his credit are nearly five hundred compositions, over three hundred of which are written for concert band.

Unit 2: Composition

Songs of the Whalemen is a single-movement work comprised of two distinct contrasting sections (slow/fast) based on material from two traditional sea songs of the British Isles: "Adieu to Erin" and "Blow Ye Winds." The first section is marked "Cantabile" and is in ABAB form before a short transition into "Blow Ye Winds," which is a lively contrasting sea chanty in ABA' form. Del Borgo's composition is true to a twentieth century aesthetic in its use of a vigorous harmonic and rhythmic style, especially in the syncopated rhythms of the second section. Published in 1995, Hal Leonard attaches a grade two rating to this approximately seven-minute piece.

Unit 3: Historical Perspective

This piece was written during a period of time when Del Borgo was using folk music as raw material. These two authentic folk melodies are treated in a symphonic manner through written transitions and the development of a polyphonic texture, which utilizes some chromaticism. Transitions connect the two contrasting folk tunes and also serve to expand the development section of "Blow Ye Winds." Both original melodies are from anonymous sources, the first being lyrical in style and the second dance-like in character. The first melody, "Adieu to Erin," is a traditional whalemen's song whose first line, "Oh when I breathed a last Adieu…," lends insight into the spirit behind the melody. "Blow Ye Winds," ca. 1830, is also a traditional whalemen's song in the spirited style of a sea chanty. Though based on folk songs from the long ago past, Del Borgo treats the melodic material with a thoroughly modern approach.

Unit 4: Technical Considerations

Songs of the Whalemen was written specifically for traditional band instrumentation at the grade two level. Flute, alto saxophone, trumpet, and horn are split into first and second parts (although 1st flute and 1st trumpet have divisi sections), and clarinet is written in three parts. It should be noted that 2nd/3rd clarinet do not go across the break, and trumpet goes no higher than a concert D at the top of the staff. A convertible bass line doubles the tuba, one octave higher.

The first section, in 4/4, is centered in D minor, and the second section, in 2/4, is primarily in F major. Chromaticism appears in both sections, and players should be familiar with scales up to four flats to encompass these alterations. Flute, oboe, 1st clarinet, and alto saxophone have a technical barrier of playing the aforementioned scales in sixteenth notes at quarter note = 132 for best execution of technical passages. Flute and 1st clarinet have exposed melodic lines, particularly in "Blow Ye Winds." Syncopation is used across the ensemble to create rhythmic energy, and some attention will need to be paid to note length and rhythmic security. The idiomatic dotted-eighth/sixteenth rhythm, inherent to sea songs, is a primary rhythmic motive for the work and will be discussed specifically in later units.

The second section begins with a percussion *soli* featuring a snare drum solo over a sustained timpani roll. The wood block is then added with a syncopated rhythm. Timpani uses C, D, and F, with one change from D to C. The composer noted that all effort should be made to use the best equipment possible, especially in the percussion section, which is used as a "source of color and texture" and is deserving of due attention.

Unit 5: Stylistic Considerations

Del Borgo's symphonic approach to this folk material creates a polyphonic texture, often contrapuntal in nature, which requires the treatment of each voice as integral in importance to the composition as a whole. Not only are elements of melodic material passed throughout the ensemble giving all sections the focus at some point, but harmonic lines have linear purpose as well. The composer noted that this linear motion is important in every part. As the contrapuntal texture thickens, care must be taken to balance the moving lines with the melody.

"Adieu to Erin" is marked "Cantabile" at quarter note = 72. The opening motive in 2nd/3rd clarinet is marked with a two slurred/two slurred articulation, which immediately establishes the lilting style of a sea song. The rearticulation is clear and slightly lifted without clipping the end of the eighth note, and is followed by two full quarter notes. Articulation will be discussed further in Unit 6.

The lyrical style of the opening changes abruptly in measure 40 with a tempo change to quarter note = 132 and the introduction to "Blow Ye Winds" in the snare drum. The idiomatic dotted rhythm returns in a dotted-eighth/sixteenth figure, which stylistically is light and crisp, lifted with a slight space before the sixteenth. Balance issues arise with each new entrance, and to remain true to the composer's polyphonic intent, care must be taken in this area, especially in divisi parts. The stylistic and dynamic markings included by Del Borgo are specific and often address this balance issue; as such, they must be adhered to. In *marcato* and accented sections, agreement must be made on note length across the ensemble, and clear articulations with a strong start and good support will help these stylistic elements come to the forefront. This will also provide greater contrast with the *cantabile* sections. In measure 84, the syncopated rhythmic motive begins. The *marcato* style requires clear articulation, agreement on the release of notes for note length, and slight separation between the consecutive quarter notes. The rhythmic energy created by this line drives the piece forward. The last five measures also require attention to note length. The accented quarter note chords in measures 207 through 210 should be full length, releasing on count two. The final accented note in the last measure should be shorter, but long enough for the quality of the open fifth F–C to ring, well balance and in tune, and should be released with an open release.

Unit 6: Musical Elements

Several composers and publishers have begun to include specific conceptual information to build skills across the ensemble that relate specifically to the composition at hand. With this in mind, suggestions for ensemble skill building specific to *Songs of the Whalemen* follow.

MELODY:

A unison arrangement of the original folk material is a beneficial exercise for all members of the ensemble. This material can be located in the following measures:

"Adieu to Erin"   Flute part   measures 3–18 (16 measures total)
> Concepts that may be addressed:
> - *Legato* articulation using "tu" or "du."
> - *Cantabile* lyrical style throughout the melody by not clipping the ends of notes. Lyrical, linear phrases with direction of the air shaping the phrase.
> - The question-and-answer nature of antecedent (mm. 3–6) and consequent (mm. 7–9) phrasal structure.
> - Breathing and phrasing for four- and eight-measure phrases. Avoid breathing in the middle of the phrase.

"Blow Ye Winds"   Flute part   pickup to mm. 48–63 (16 measures total)
> Concepts that may be addressed:
> - The primary focus of greatest stylistic benefit comes by working on the dotted-eighth/sixteenth note rhythmic figure. Articulation in a light, lifted style (which can translate well into the *marcato* elements of the work), with a lift between the dotted-eighth and the sixteenth.
> - Technical fluency in general.
> - Four-measure phrasing.

RHYTHM:

Consider isolating the rhythmic motive of measures 56 and 57 on a single pitch and work for separation between the dotted-eighth and the sixteenth, a light lifted style on the eighth notes, and full, slightly separated quarter notes. This rhythmic motive permeates the work and is idiomatic of sea songs in general. Working to isolate it initially will establish style for the rest of the piece.

Del Borgo's symphonic treatment of the material uses a vigorous syncopated rhythmic energy. A unison or major chord arrangement of the rhythm, which occurs in the trombone and baritone part in measures 84 through 91, provides all the elements that reappear in measures 100 through 103 and measures 176 through 183 in various combinations across the ensemble from the flutes down to the wood block. A steady pulse and clear articulation using "ta" or "da" provide clarity and security.

HARMONY:

The composer cites thirty years of experience teaching counterpoint as a major influence on his approach to writing in a symphonic manner. Stress should be placed on each individual player having a linear approach to the part, whether it be melody or a line with slower harmonic function. Discuss where an individual line is going and how the air moves in that direction. This linear approach is what creates the polyphonic, contrapuntal style of this work.

Unit 7: Form and Structure

SECTION	MEASURE	EVENT AND SCORING
"Adieu to Erin"		
Introduction	1–2	*mp*; D sustained in timpani, open fifth D–A in low brass, low woodwinds, 2nd/3rd clarinet accompaniment eighth note figure
A		
Antecedent	3–6	Flute and 1st clarinet enter with melody
Consequent	7–10	Bells added to melody; flute 8va.; 1st clarinet begins countermelody; horn joins harmonic line
B		
Antecedent	11–14	Upper woodwinds only; flute and 1st clarinet divisi melody/countermelody over alto saxophone descending whole note line; triangle
Consequent	15–18	Upper woodwinds continue melody; countermelody; alto saxophone and trumpet divisi *cantabile* linear line adds to polyphonic texture
A'		
Antecedent	19–22	Melody in bassoon, 2nd/3rd clarinet, tenor saxophone, trombone, baritone; 1st clarinet, flute, and bells exchange rising eighth note figure; section finishes with a p suspended cymbal roll

SECTION	MEASURE	EVENT AND SCORING
Consequent	23–26	Countermelody added in trumpet; *mf cantabile* bass line in low brass and low woodwinds not involved in melody
B' Antecedent	27–30	Melody in divisi trumpet; ensemble *crescendo* to *f*
Consequent	31–32	*mp*; trumpet continues melody to the *fermata*
Transition	33–39	Woodwinds pass melodic motive based on consequent phrase material from flute down to alto saxophone with low woodwind, low brass chords; finish section on a D major chord with *fermata*
"Blow Ye Winds" Introduction	40–47	Open fifth F–C in low brass and low woodwinds; p timpani roll; snare drum solo; wood block added in m. 44 with syncopated rhythmic motive
A Antecedent	48–56	Melody in F major flute *soli* divisi
Consequent	56–63	Divisi clarinet sustained open fifths
Antecedent	64–71	Melody in 1st clarinet; alto saxophone joins melody at m. 68; flute, oboe syncopated countermelody; 2nd/3rd clarinet linear half note line; triangle
Consequent	72–79	Tenor saxophone, horn, trombone join 2nd/3rd clarinet linear line at *mf*; ensemble *crescendo* at mm. 77–79
Transition	80–83	*F*; *marcato* quarter notes on A-flat major chord in brass and low woodwinds; alternate measures with upper woodwinds, flute, oboe, 1st clarinet ascending eighth note line; repeated on a G major chord

Section	Measure	Event and Scoring
	84–87	Snare enters; bassoon, 2nd/3rd clarinet, alto and tenor saxophone, horn, trombone, baritone with *marcato* syncopated rhythmic motive
Antecedent	88–95	Melody *marcato* in trumpet; syncopated accompaniment continues
Consequent'	96–102	Melody reinforced in bassoon, 2nd/3rd clarinet, alto and tenor saxophone, horn, trombone, baritone; flute, oboe, 1st clarinet ascending sixteenth note figure
Transition	103–107	Increased chromaticism, descending line; *fp* C–G open fifth sustained chord in mm. 106–107; accented quarter notes in trumpet
Development B		
Antecedent'	108–111	Trumpet marcato at mm. 108–109, then flute, oboe, 1st clarinet, bells complete phrase at mm. 110–111; melodic material based on A melody
Consequent'	112–115	2nd/3rd clarinet, alto and tenor saxophone, low brass, and low woodwinds at *f*; *marcato* descending eighth note line under variation on consequent phrase divided between trumpet and upper woodwinds
Antecedent'	116–119	Opening "Blow Ye Winds" dotted rhythmic motive in bassoon, trumpet, horn, trombone, baritone at *ff*; followed by upper woodwinds sixteenth note ascending, scalar flourish; suspended cymbal
Consequent'	120–123	Melody in trumpet, horn, low brass, and low woodwind descending eighth note line

Section	Measure	Event and Scoring
Transition	124–127	Upper woodwinds and trumpet syncopated melodic line
	128–131	Opening dotted rhythmic motive in bassoon, tenor saxophone, trumpet, horn, trombone, baritone, followed by upper woodwinds sixteenth note ascending, scalar flourish
	132–135	Opening dotted rhythmic motive in bassoon, 2nd/3rd clarinet, tenor saxophone, trumpet, horn, trombone, baritone, under upper woodwind ascending line; low brass and low woodwinds descending eighth note line
	136–143	C minor; *fp* sustained C–G; flute, 1st clarinet, alto saxophone C minor arpeggiated descending line; wood block enters with syncopated line
	144–159	*mf*; cantabile flute and clarinet divisi antecedent folk material in augmentation; polyphonic texture created by contrapuntal line in alto saxophone then in bassoon, tenor saxophone, trombone, baritone
	160–163	Snare solo *mp*; timpani, 2nd/3rd clarinet, low brass, and low woodwind sustained *p*; concert F
	164–167	*mp*; alto saxophone, horn, trombone with opening dotted-eighth/sixteenth motive; flute, oboe, 1st clarinet answer with folk-like material
	168–171	Alto saxophone, trumpet, horn with opening dotted-eight/sixteenth motive; flute, oboe, 1st clarinet answer with folk-like material varied from previous phrase

SECTION	MEASURE	EVENT AND SCORING
	172–175	Alto saxophone, trumpet, horn with opening dotted-eighth/sixteenth motive; *crescendo* to *ff*; flute, oboe, 1st clarinet, tom-toms, bass drum, suspended cymbal increase rhythmic motion
	176–179	*ff*; trumpet added with syncopated rhythmic line
A' Antecedent	180–183	Melody returns in low brass and low woodwinds;
Consequent	184–187	*ff*; in dense, full ensemble polyphonic texture
Antecedent'	188–191	Upper woodwinds and trumpet *marcato* melody over half-note harmonic texture
Consequent	192–194	Melody in bassoon, tenor saxophone, trombone, baritone; 2nd/3rd clarinet, alto saxophone, trumpet, horn syncopated line; flute, oboe, 1st clarinet flourish
Coda	195–198	*ff* accented; terraced entrances building an F chord; upper woodwinds with repeating eighth note figure
	199–202	Bassoon, 2nd/3rd clarinet, alto saxophone, trumpet, horn, trombone, baritone, snare drum, accent dotted-eighth/sixteenth rhythmic motive; flute, oboe, 1st clarinet ascending E-flat major run; suspended cymbal *crescendo* roll
	203–211	Arrival; flute, oboe, 1st clarinet, trumpet, horn, bells on F major chord; descending quarter note line in all other parts to accented, open fifths on F–C exclamations over active percussion *soli*

Unit 8: Suggested Listening

Elliot Del Borgo:
   Sailing Songs
   Two British Folksongs
   Two Welsh Folksongs
Percy Grainger, *Lincolnshire Posy*
Gustav Holst:
   First Suite in E-flat
   Second Suite in F
W. Francis McBeth, *Of Sailors and Whales*
Ralph Vaughan Williams, *Sea Songs*

Unit 9: Additional References and Resources

Del Borgo, Elliot. Saskatoon, Saskatchewan, Canada. Interview with the composer, November 2001.

F. J. H. Music Company, Inc. *FJH Composers and Writers*. Available from http://www.fjhmusic.com/composer/edelborgo.html. Accessed 9 August 2001.

Havlice, Patricia. *Popular Song Index*. Metuchen, NJ: Scarecrow Press, Inc., 1975.

Huntington, Gale. *Songs the Whalemen Sang*. Barre, MA: Barre, 1964.

Lax, Roger, and Frederic Smith. *The Great Song Thesaurus*. New York: Oxford University Press, 1989.

Sadie, Stanley, ed. *The New Grove Dictionary of Music and Musicians*. Volume 7. London: Macmillan, 1980.

Contributed by:

Jennifer McAllister
University of Saskatchewan
Saskatoon, Saskatchewan, Canada

Teacher Resource Guide

Three Chinese Miniatures

Robert Jager
(b. 1939)

Unit 1: Composer

Robert Jager was born in Binghamton, New York in 1939. He is a graduate of the University of Michigan. For four years, while a member of the United States Navy, he served as the staff arranger at the Armed Forces School of Music. He is now retired and is Professor Emeritus at Tennessee Technological University in Cookeville, Tennessee.

Jager is a widely commissioned and performed composer with some 115 published works to his credit, including compositions for band, chorus, orchestra, and various chamber ensembles. He has received commissions from some of the finest performing organizations in the world, including the Tokyo Kosei Wind Orchestra, the Republic of China Band Association, all of the Washington-based service bands, bands and/or alumni groups from the universities of Michigan, Illinois, Nebraska, Arkansas, Nebraska Wesleyan, Purdue, and Butler. In addition, he has received grants from Meet the Composer and the Tennessee Arts Commission. He has conducted and lectured throughout the United States, Canada, Europe, Japan, and the Republic of China. In addition, his music has been performed by the National Symphony Orchestra, the Nashville Symphony, the Charlotte Symphony, the Virginia Symphony, the Bryan Symphony Orchestra of Tennessee, the Minot (ND) Symphony, the Greater Lansing Symphony Orchestra, and the Omsk Philharmonic in Russia.

Jager has won a number of awards for his music, including being the only three-time winner of the American Bandmasters Association's Ostwald Award. He is two-time winner of the National School Orchestra Association's

Roth Award, and also received the Kappa Kappa Psi's Distinguished Service to Music Medal in Composition (1973), the 1975 Friends of Harvey Gaul bicentennial competition, the 1976 American School Band Director's Association's Volkwein Award, the National Band Association's Citation of Excellence (1978), the Orpheus Award from Phi Mu Alpha Sinfonia (1980), and the Citation with Distinction from the University of Michigan Band Alumni Association in 1985. In 1986, he received a MacDowell Colony Fellowship to compose at the Colony in Peterborough, New Hampshire. He received the Individual Artist Fellowship in Composition from the Tennessee Arts Commission in 1996, and in 1998 was selected to receive Tennessee Tech University's highest faculty award, the Caplenor Faculty Research Award. Jager is the first faculty member in the arts to receive this annual award.

Most recently, Jager won the 2000 Delius Composition Contest, sponsored by the Delius Association of Florida and Jacksonville University, in the keyboard category, for his *Dialogues for Two Pianos*. He is a member of the American Society of Composers, Authors, and Publishers (ASCAP); the American Bandmasters Association; Phi Mu Alpha Sinfonia; Kappa Kappa Psi; and an honorary member of the Women Band Director's National Association.

Some of Jager's works for band include:

A Cockney Rhapsody (Columbia Pictures Publishing, 1983)
Apocalypse for wind ensemble (Edward Marks Music, 1978)
Carpathian Sketches (Edward B. Marks Music, 1979)
Cliff Island Suite (Kjos Music Co., 1980)
Esprit de Corps (Edward Marks Music, 1985)
Heroic Saga (Columbia Pictures Publications, 1987)
Japanese Prints (Edward B. Marks Music, 1979)
Jubilate (Southern Music Company, 1978)
March Dramatic (Southern Music Company, 1967)
Old Time Spirit (Kjos Music)
Pastorale and Country Dance (Kjos Music Company, 1979)
Prelude on an Old Southern Hymn (Kjos Music Co., 1984)
Sinfonia Noblissima (Elkan-Vogel Co., 1965)
Symphony (No.1) for Band (Volkwein Bros., Inc., 1965)
Symphony No. 2 for Wind Orchestra (Kjos Music Co., 1978)
Testament (Kjos Music Company, 1989)
Third Suite for Band (Volkwein Bros., Inc., 1966)
Variations on a Theme of Robert Schumann (Volkwein Bros., Inc., 1968)

Unit 2: Composition

Commissioned in 1991 for the Seventh Asian-Pacific Band Convention and published in 1995, *Three Chinese Miniatures* is a multi-movement work that captures the soul of three authentic Chinese folk songs. It was commissioned in 1991 by the Asia-Pacific Band Directors Association for their seventh convention held in Taiwan. The premiere was conducted in 1992 by David Chen, the music director of the Taiwan Symphony Orchestra.

In his program notes, Jager states that Movement I, "The Wind," "begins solemnly and builds like the wind." Jager cleverly uses attainable stylistic elements to achieve a wind-like effect. Players will experience gradual change in density and texture, a tempo shift, modulations, and tidal dynamics (< >) to represent swirling and swooshing. The whole movement could be thought of as a great peaking and subsiding as it builds towards the midsection and concludes with sparse instrumentation as in the beginning.

Movement II, "Sen Jin De Ma (A Maiden)," begins benignly and sweetly, again with sparse instrumentation and open voicing. The introduction leads to melodic material stated by solo trumpet and answered by flute. A similar pattern continues with the upper voices and trumpets engaging in a call/response segment, and finally a solo oboe emerges as the voice of the main theme with light accompaniment in the upper woodwinds and bells. The trumpets return in answer and the section concludes quietly.

Movement III, "A Love Song of the Kang Tang City," is energetic, confident, and bustling. The use of echoing as a compositional technique creates a thicker texture, and later in the work the melodic line taken over by low winds punctuated on offbeats in the accompanying lines contributes to the forward drive. The movement builds in momentum and comes to a definitive conclusion.

Duration of the entire work is approximately six minutes and forty-one seconds.

Unit 3: Historical Perspective

This work is a setting of three Chinese folk songs set in a Western style. When teaching the piece, it would be helpful to devote time to teaching a few basic compositional elements sometimes heard in Chinese music. Of course, the most obvious element would be the pentatonic scale that is utilized in this piece. The pentatonic scale uses five tones and is often heard in older Chinese music. Another scale used in music of this culture is the heptatonic (seven-tone) scale, which is sometimes thought of as an expanded pentatonic. This scale is often found in folk music of Northern China.

This work is Jager's third venture into music of another culture. The two works that precede *Three Chinese Miniatures* are *Carpathian Sketches* and *Japanese Prints*, both of which can be used to reinforce the focus on music from

another culture. *Sinfonia Hungarica*, a work that is primarily an introduction to the music of Bartok, is Jager's most recent work in this realm.

Unit 4: Technical Considerations

In the first movement, the use of articulation to emphasize style will be noticed immediately. Wind players in particular will need good instruction in creating clear differences between *tenuto* and *staccato* tonguing. Of equal importance to these different attacks and durations are subtleties in releases in accompanying voices, generally stated in low winds. These players must carefully observe eighth rests following sustained notes. The spirited tempo suggested by Jager should be observed. In doing so, directors might also note that the otherwise uncomplicated eighth note melodic material becomes more challenging and will require practice. The tempo assists student musicians in feeling the syncopation more naturally. An appealing trait in this movement is the asymmetric shape of the phrasing. As this technique provides an interesting listening experience, it may be an unusual experience for students. Directors will need to focus attention on logical places for wind players to breathe. Wind parts are somewhat athletic, often moving leapwise. Attention to embouchure and air stream will be key. Key changes and changing meter occurring at the climax of the movement requires students to stay attuned to accidentals and shifting temporal emphasis.

Movement II opens with several measures of changing meter at a slow tempo. The flute soloist is asked to perform grace notes to embellish the line. Again, attention to accidentals will be important in all performing voices. Crisp execution of dotted-eighth/sixteenth rhythms are critical, as they are complementary to the dotted-quarter/eighth rhythms. As in the first movement, Jager relies on color and articulation for contrast. These elements should not be overlooked. This movement calls for talented flute, trumpet, and oboe soloists. As is true with all wind parts, there are no obvious range challenges.

The final movement is the most demanding in terms of technique. Even though the tempo is swift and there are plenty of notes to perform, there is also enough repetition to instill some practice time right into the rehearsal. Additionally, most of the wind lines lie neatly under the fingers. After a few times through the opening section, there should be no problem with execution. There will be a tendency for the ensemble to rush at measure 23. An echo feature between upper woodwinds and first trumpets will need accurate counting, listening, and watching. Piccolo, tenor saxophone, and baritone horn have an important function at measure 55 as they maintain a steady *staccato* eighth texture under the melodic line; this part should be brought out. Several instances of unison and octave playing in this movement will necessitate a keen focus on intonation. In this movement as in the first two, percussion work is relatively straightforward, with the keyboards having the most challenging lines.

Unit 5: Stylistic Considerations

Since the first movement of this work is said to represent the wind, the music should be examined for elements that would suggest wind-like features. These can be found in the addition and elimination of voices, a move that affects texture and dynamics. Additionally, the director will need to take notice of the changes in dynamics that the composer adds purposefully. For this and the other two movements, accurate articulation will be critical to an exacting performance of the work.

Several tempo changes in the opening measures give the work a feeling of anticipation. It provides a good opportunity for the director to work on ensemble listening, watching the conductor, and performing together. At measure 55, the melodic line is heard in augmentation in the low winds with light accompaniment on top. The melody should not become too cumbersome and the accompaniment too overbearing. The echo becomes a factor at the first key change, and its polyphonic impact is enhanced with the key change and increased dynamic level. *Tutti* playing is heard here, adding to the enlarged sound. At measure 76, a significant change in style is noted in the articulation. The work moves from pointed *staccato* and detached to a smoother *legato* style that is underscored with the tidal or swell dynamics previously referred to in Unit 2. This texture is heard primarily in the woodwinds. Later, the brass and percussion enter with a contrasting line with heavily accented articulation. This section finally resolves to light *tutti* eighths followed by heavy quarter accents at the midpoint and end of the phrase. The work begins to calm and finishes with sparse texture, light articulation, and soft dynamics as in the beginning, thus completing the arch form.

As the title of the second movement ("A Maiden") suggests, the stylistic focus of this section is contemplative and quiet. Jager has said that the elements of mood and instrumental color are principal factors. This is seen immediately in the use of contrasting *glissandi* in the bells, open fourths in the horns with contrasting dissonant key levels between 1st and 2nd, and 3rd and 4th horns, and a similar sound in the clarinets. All of this is carpeting for a plaintive flute solo above. Trumpet and flute solo interplay characterize the next segment, and this idea is expanded to include a full trumpet section and most of the upper woodwinds. This dialogue gives way to a graceful oboe solo with lilting accompaniment, and finally the movement comes to a serene conclusion.

Program notes for the third movement indicate this movement is a tribute to the city, boisterous and full of musical surprises. It begins with a fanfarish proclamation that announces the statement of the main theme. The thematic material is supported with insistent eighths in snare drum, horn, and saxophone, an idea that is then handed to trombone. The drive of this simplistic accompanying material becomes the heartbeat of the city. In the next section, the accompaniment becomes more adamant as it moves from repeated eighths to punctuated quarters. This line not only serves to propel the melody but also acts as a metronome to help the ensemble maintain steady beat. Later, the accompanying line, played on the offbeats, takes on a more brazen feel as it supports the melodic material. The director will find that the music moves back and forth between outright bold and impishly holding back. It will be important that elements of dynamics, technique, articulation, and balance are addressed fully.

Unit 6: Musical Elements

MELODY:

Three Chinese Miniatures utilizes the pentatonic scale as a basis for its melodic material. It is a good work for reinforcing the concept of the pentatonic scale and how it compares to other scales. The word *pentatonic* is derived from *penta* meaning *five* and *tonic* meaning *tone*. A pentatonic scale is a five-tone scale. In jazz, the minor pentatonic is often used as the basis of the blues scale. Innovative directors might provide students with combinations of half and whole steps needed to build different scales (major, minor, pentatonic) and allow them to try their hand at composing or improvisation using any or all of these scale structures.

The melody of the first movement is presented in its entirety following a brief introduction in which melodic material has been heard. It is given a C minor tonal center and has an asymmetric shape. The sixteen-measure phrase is built as a combination of seven- and nine-measure subphrases. The second statement of the melody is heard in 1st trumpet with a countermelodic line played above it in flute and piccolo. Following is the first subphrase of the melody performed in augmentation by horn, trombone, and baritone. The change is not strict augmentation of each rhythmic unit, but the values do elongate and the rhythmic units lose the dotted features. This elongation is echoed in measure 58 by alto clarinet, bass clarinet, bassoon, baritone saxophone, and tuba. The second subphrase marks a departure from the augmentation back to familiar rhythmic units. This change is fortified with a key change. At measure 69, the entrance of the second subphrase appearing first in oboe, 1st clarinet, and alto saxophone. A beat later it is heard in trumpet, another beat later in 2nd and 3rd clarinet, tenor saxophone, horn, and baritone, and finally another beat later in piccolo, flute, and xylophone. A brief "windy" interlude follows at measure 76, where undulating textural material portrays the wind. Material reminiscent of the melody is now performed in low brass and timpani. This leads the work into measure 92, where the first part of the phrase is performed twice in a recognizable form. In the next section, the melody begins to fragment as the movement heads toward conclusion.

The melody of the second movement is foreshadowed by the solo flute and stated in full at measure 9 by solo trumpet. In this manner, Jager used colors reminiscent of the first movement. In contrast with the first movement, the harmonic support of the pentatonic melody is decidedly major and centers on E-flat. The melodic rhythm utilizes dotted rhythms to a greater extent compared to the first movement. Following the beginning of the movement, Jager makes use of many different instruments that are used to state all or parts of the theme, creating a nice palette of color. The oboe solo is cued in 1st alto saxophone.

Melodic fragments comprise the introductory eleven measures of the third movement, and the theme is first heard at measure 12. The pentatonic scale is retained with the tonal focus centering on F minor. The melody of this movement requires far more technical agility of all players in comparison to the other movements. Coordination of fingers, breath, and articulation will be a key issue in teaching the work. In a style similar to the first movement, the melody is offset against itself by one beat at measure 23 when it is first performed in piccolo, flute, oboe, and 1st clarinet. This is echoed one beat later by the rest of the clarinets and 1st trumpet. The result is a thicker texture. It will require a great deal of listening and accurate counting. Set in binary form, the energetic, symmetric eight-measure initial phrase yields at measure 34 to a more romantic, asymmetrical melodic phrase. This is followed by a heroic rendering of the original initial melody in the low winds at measure 47. The offsetting of the melody is once again used as the work pushes to the end. At measure 94, the upper woodwinds and xylophone state the theme while the trumpets echo a full measure later. The whole ensemble performs the last part of the phrase to bring the work to a conclusion.

HARMONY:

All three movements make use of the pentatonic scale as a principal compositional tool. The supporting harmonic structures give each movement a different flavor. A C minor tonal center in addition to the prominence of the descending and ascending minor third in accompaniment voices give an earthy quality to the melodic material of the first movement. Students will move through several key changes that will move them from this foreboding minor quality to major, returning again to minor. Directors should be attentive to the dissonances found in the trombone voices and rehearse these sections so the sound is confident and in tune.

Dissonant clusters heard in the sustaining voices at the opening of the s econd movement are derived from tones of the pentatonic scale. This blocking and the subsequent downward movement of the clusters through three key levels provide a very ethereal quality, before finally centering on

E-flat major. Throughout much of this movement, harmonic accompaniment is slowly moving and uncomplicated. Bring out inner voices in the few instances where they maintain a moving line that passes through non-chord tones.

With F minor as the harmonic foundation, Jager uses a similar pentatonic clustering technique in the repeated eighth note accompaniment figures in the initial portion of the third movement. The countermelody at measure 55 not only provides some contrapuntal interest but also helps to reinforce the harmonic movement. The descending motion of the harmonic accompaniment at measure 65 gives the music a slight character change to almost a modern urban feel, which then returns to the original nature.

The inclusion of an imploded rehearsal piano part at the bottom of the score will assist the director in a quick understanding of the harmonic movement of the work.

RHYTHM:

Although few of the rhythmic units in this work should present a challenge to most students capable of performing grade three literature, there are some instances that require some attention.

In Movement I, the asymmetrical nature of the phrase shape will call for keen counting among musicians and good cues from the conductor. There are some occurrences of syncopation that, after sight-reading, should feel quite natural to the students. Reinforcement of counting the syncopation and understanding of beat emphasis should be addressed. As important is a lift-off of the dotted-quarter notes at measure 19. Wind players must be reminded to create some space between the dotted-quarter notes (emphasized rhythmically with an eighth rest) and not linger over into the rest. Changing meter beginning at measure 79 will need attention, particularly as these changes affect placement of articulations.

In Movement II, brief moments of changing meter in the beginning of this movement are easily attainable for most. Scoring is sparse here, and emphasis will be placed on good entrances in the accompaniment voices with accurate counting in the solo flute. The addition of grace notes in the solo line should not deter from following a well-defined meter beat. Dotted rhythms in this movement (dotted-quarter/eighth and dotted-sixteenth/eighth) will require contrast.

Movement III, being the most technically challenging is also the most rhythmically challenging. Even though the other movements contain similar rhythmic units, this movement moves more swiftly and there are more notes to perform in a shorter amount of time. The opening rhythm (two sixteenths/eighth) is likely to evoke some articulation laziness from players. All three notes should be heard equally. As previously mentioned, dotted rhythms should be performed crisply. Offbeat accompaniment figures are not likely to be problematic because of the heavy nature of this accompaniment figure and the number of players responsible for this part. Repetition of rhythmic units over the course of the work will help to reinforce concepts and allow for repeated practice.

TIMBRE:

Jager uses color combinations in this work to elicit certain images (wind in the first movement) or feelings (gentility in the second movement). There is a predominant reliance on solo flute and trumpet voices to present themes and ideas. Percussion is used tastefully to support but is not the primary focus of the work. The use of metallic percussion such as gong, triangle, and bells in addition to the use of xylophone and temple blocks add to the Asian quality of the work. The composition generally keeps instrument families together. Weaving back and forth between sparse and thick scoring creates textural interest throughout.

Unit 7. Form and Structure

SECTION	MEASURE	EVENT AND SCORING
Movement I: Introduction	1–18	Alto saxophone and muted trumpet perform melodic material; sustained, sparse scoring in accompaniment; deliberate pauses between phrase segments
	19–22	Brief introduction to melody at m. 23; addition of triangle suggests color change, which is expanded upon at m. 23
A theme	23–40	Melody in 1st flute and 1st clarinet; bells are added, increasing color sphere; follows a quarter note pattern that reinforces the first and third eighth performed in the melodic line; accompaniment voices generally sustain with dotted-quarter movement in trombones; asymmetrical phrase shapes
Variation I	41–55	Melodic line repeated in 1st trumpet, now playing open; countermelody is added in piccolo and flute; addition of snare line and punctuated accompaniment voices alter style

Section	Measure	Event and Scoring
	55–56	Brief transition heralding new accompaniment material
Variation II	57–68	Melody performed in augmentation (although not strict) in horn, trombone, and baritone; an echo beginning at m. 58 is heard in low woodwinds and tuba; eighth note figures in upper woodwinds and bells serve as textural accompaniment; segment comprised of the first subphrase of the main theme
Variation III	69–75	A continuation of the variation on the main theme with the second subphrase; key change and the addition of accidentals in several parts; echoing feature is prominent; dynamic level at *ff* in full ensemble
B	76–91	Wind finally blows full force in this section with undulating eight note patterns in most of the woodwind voices; dynamic swells add support to the undulation as well as sustained rolls in percussion; full brass perform heavily accented melodic material; changing meter provides asymmetry
A, Variation IV	92–98	Measures repeat; key change; melody in alto saxophone and trumpet; eighth note insistence is maintained but the articulation is now pointed rather than slurred as in the B section
Variation V	99–111	Melodic fragments characterize this section, which is very transitory in nature; key change
Conclusion	112–130	After the key changes one final time, the piece concludes in a similar style in which it began

SECTION	MEASURE	EVENT AND SCORING
Movement II: Introduction	1–8	Marked with deliberate pauses midphrase, flute opens the movement with a plaintive, lyrical solo and sparse accompaniment
A	9–33	Melodic material is shared between solo trumpet and flute; sustained, sparse accompaniment; dynamic level builds into m. 26; sharing of melody continues at m. 26 with fuller orchestration; inner voices acquire greater movement; tidal dynamics dominate
B	34–49	*Staccato* accompaniment in upper woodwinds and bells, with timbre reinforced by triangle and suspended cymbal; oboe solo presents melodic material; texture thickens at m. 42 as other voices take over melodic responsibilities; sections slows and softens toward measure m. 50
Conclusion	50–55	The work concludes as it began, with melodic fragments performed by solo trumpet and flute, using the same accompanying material
Movement III: Introduction	1–11	Aggressive sixteenth note patterns mark the opening of this movement; dialogue ensues between Group I (piccolo, flute, oboe, 1st clarinet, 1st trumpet, xylophone) and Group II (alto and tenor saxophone, 2nd and 3rd trumpet, horn, and snare drum) with punctuation in alto and bass clarinet, bassoon, baritone saxophone, trombone, baritone, tuba, timpani, and bass drum; *ff* dynamics *decrescendo* into m. 12

SECTION	MEASURE	EVENT AND SCORING
A	12–22	Theme stated in upper woodwinds with repeated eighth note accompaniment in alto and tenor saxophone, horn, and snare drum; transition from m. 20 to m. 22 includes shifting of eighth accompaniment to trombone with punctuated dialogue in low woodwinds (m. 20) followed by a trumpet response (m. 21)
A'	23–33	Thematic material is here stated in piccolo, flute, oboe, and 1st clarinet; melody follows in imitation one beat after the upper woodwinds and is heard in 2nd and 3rd clarinet, and 1st trumpet; upper woodwind line is punctuated by bells; *staccato* accompaniment prevails; *decrescendo* at m. 32
B	34–46	A change in melody stated by trumpet; eighth accompaniment in woodwinds and snare drum; on second statement of the B theme, first few notes are echoed in flute, oboe, and xylophone; mm. 45 and 46 give transition into m. 47, with first three notes of the main theme heralded by alto and tenor saxophone, 3rd trumpet, and horn
A	47–54	A raucous rendering of the main theme with lower voices while upper voices and percussion add emphasis on offbeats
A'	55–64	With only slight variation, trumpet takes over the melody while accompaniment is divided into voices performing *staccato* quarters and moving *staccato* eighths in piccolo and baritone (an interesting and effective color combination); brief two-measure transition into m. 65 is characterized with some syncopation and *decrescendo*

SECTION	MEASURE	EVENT AND SCORING
B	65–82	A return to the alternate melodic material is stated here in 1st clarinet and 1st trumpet; echo is offset by a full measure in tenor saxophone and baritone; sparse *staccato* accompaniment is present, with Jager again using interesting color combinations of flute, bass clarinet, horn, and tuba; triangle adds brilliance in this section; material reminiscent of earlier moments appears in mm. 73–78; a long sustained *decrescendo* ushers in m. 83
Transition	83–93	Beginning softly, this section builds in texture and dynamics to lead towards the final phrase
Conclusion	94–106	Melody is once again heard in imitation as it is stated first by upper woodwinds, alto saxophone, and xylophone and echoed a full measure later by trumpet; accompaniment remains detached and incessant; at m. 100, the work winds up to a furious conclusion.

Unit 8: Suggested Listening

Toshio Akiyama, *Japanese Songs for Band*
Warren Barker, *Chinese Folk Suite*
Richard Brown:
    Chinese Folk Rhapsody
    Little Chinese Suite
John Barnes Chance, *Variations on a Korean Folk Song*
Ray Cramer, *Fantasy on Sakura, Sakura*
James Curnow, *Korean Folk Rhapsody*
Robert Garofalo, *Chinese Folk Song Medley*
Clare Grundman, *Japanese Rhapsody*
Paul Hindemith, *Symphonic Metamorphosis*
Robert Jager, *Japanese Prints*
Lawrence Moss, *Chinese Lullaby*
James Ployhar, *Korean Folk Song Medley*

Unit 9: Additional References and Resources

Jones, Stephen. *Folk Music of China: Living Instrumental Traditions*. New York: Oxford University Press, 1998.

Lai, T. C., and Robert Mok. Jade. *Flute: The Story of Chinese Music*. New York: Schocken Books, 1985.

Lee, Yuan-Yuan, and Sin-Yan Shen. *Chinese Musical Instruments*. Woodridge, IL: Chinese Music Society of North America, 1999.

Lenzini, Catherine S. "A Conversation with Robert Jager." *The Instrumentalist*, December 1998.

Malm, William P. *Music Cultures of the Pacific, the Near East, and Asia*. Upper Saddle River, NJ: Prentice Hall, 1996.

Contributed by:

Deborah A. Sheldon
Esther Boyer College of Music
Temple University
Philadelphia, Pennsylvania

Teacher Resource Guide

Toledo

Bruce Carlson
(b. 1944)

Unit 1: Composer

Bruce Carlson was born in Toronto, Ontario, in 1944. He was educated at the University of Waterloo (Waterloo, Ontario), the University of Toronto, and the University of Manitoba (Winnipeg, Manitoba). While studying at the University of Manitoba, his primary composition teacher was Dr. Robert Turner, one of Canada's best-known composers.

Carlson is a founding member of the Manitoba Composers Association and an associate member of the Canadian Music Centre. He currently holds the position of supervisor of the Eckhart-Gramatte Music Library in the School of Music at University of Manitoba. He also owns *DOX*, the publishing company through which he publishes his band and choral music.

The recipient of more than thirty commissions from professional and educational performing organizations such as the Winnipeg Symphony, the Purcell String Quartet, the Manitoba Chamber Orchestra, the Winnipeg Singers, and numerous high school and university bands, Carlson's works have been aired nationally and locally on radio and television networks of the Canadian Broadcasting Corporation. His band works have been performed throughout Canada and in Hong Kong, Germany, and many parts of the United States.

Carlson's band works include *Three Canticles, Atlantis, Operation Noah, Breugel's Icarus, Tower of Babel Revisited,* and *Stability in Turmoil,* as well as two works for chorus and winds, *Fanfare and Hymns,* and *Toledo II.*

Unit 2: Composition

Toledo was written in 1992 on a commission from the John Henderson Junior High Wind Ensemble, conducted by Jeff Kula. It was the first school band work to be supported by a grant from the Manitoba Arts Council. In the years since its premiere, it has been performed by high school, university, and professional bands in Canada, the United States, Germany, and Hong Kong.

This composition was inspired by three related sources: the famous painting *View of Toledo* by El Greco; the *Spiritual Canticle* by St. John of the Cross; and the ruminations on both of the above by the twentieth century Christian monk, Thomas Merton. El Greco was a resident of Toledo, Spain, from 1577 until his death in 1614. *View of Toledo* was painted sometime in the later years of the sixteenth century. At the same time that El Greco was painting in Toledo, St. John of the Cross was imprisoned in the city because of his support for the Carmelite reforms initiated by St. Teresa of Avila, which were vehemently opposed by the senior members of the Order. He was held in a tiny cell, which he called "the belly of the whale," that was completely dark except for one small, high window. When he escaped, apparently assisted by the Blessed Virgin herself (Bruno 1949, 5), he had written his *Spiritual Canticle*, a poem that is widely accepted as superior to all others in the Spanish language.

Merton appears to have been the first scholar to note the connection between these two great artists by remarking that "the belly of the whale" must lie somewhere in the middle of El Greco's painting. He was also intrigued by the contrast between the two artistic works, which both aspire to God but in very different ways. According to Merton, El Greco's painting "is very dramatic...full of spiritual implications.... The dark city surges with life, coordinated by some mysterious, providential upheaval which drives all these masses of stone upward toward heaven, in the clouds of a blue disaster that foreshadows the end of the world...the movement is a blind upheaval in which earth and sky run off the top of the canvas." By contrast, St. John's creation is the result of silence and patience, waiting quietly "for the divine answer that would end this dark night of his soul.... The movement is centripetal [tending toward the centre]. There is tremendous stability, not merely in the soul immobilized, entombed in a burning stone wall, but in the depths of that soul purified by a purgatory...[and] emerging into the Centre of all centers, the Love which moves the heavens and the stars, the Living God." Of the *Spiritual Canticle* itself, Merton wrote:

> The joy of this emptiness, this weird neutrality of spirit which leaves the soul detached from the things of the earth and not yet in possession of those of heaven, suddenly blossoms out into a pure paradise of liberty, of which the saint sings in his *Spiritual Canticle*: it is a solitude full of wild birds and strange trees, rocks, rivers, and

desert islands, lions and leaping does. These creatures are images of the joys of the spirit, aspects of interior solitude, fires that flash in the abyss of the pure heart whose loneliness becomes alive with the deep lightnings of God."
(McDonnell, 1974, pp. 285–7, 291)

Carlson was profoundly moved by the painting, the poem, and Merton's insight into both. His *Toledo* is "an attempt to reflect musically various glimpses of the *View of Toledo*, both as a whole and in its various parts, including that part near the middle of the canvas, a building containing the ten-foot by six-foot dungeon, where the *Spiritual Canticle* by St. John of the Cross, miraculously bloomed." The composer has also indicated that the following words from the *Spiritual Canticle* were especially influential:

My Beloved is like the mountains.
Like the lonely valleys full of woods
The strange islands
The rivers with their sound
The whisper of the lovely air!

The night, appeased and hushed
About the rising of the dawn,
The music stilled
The sounding solitude
The supper that rebuilds my life
And brings me love.

Our bed of flowers
Surrounded by the lions' dens
Makes us a purple tent,
Is built of peace.
Our bed is crowned with a thousand shields of gold!

Fast-flying birds
Lions, harts, and leaping does
Mountains, banks, and vales
Streams, breezes, heats of day
And terrors watching in the night:

By the sweet lyres and by the siren's song
I conjure you: let angers end!
And do not touch the wall
But let the bride be safe: let her sleep on!
(McDonnell 1974, p. 287)

Carlson prefers that a slide of *View of Toledo* be displayed above the band while the work is being performed. At one point in the piece, the band members verbally discuss the painting, and a few measures later they comment musically on it through improvisation. However, the composer has also provided the option of not displaying the image and leaving out the verbal discussion.

The work is sectionalized, essentially alternating sections addressing the dramatic, stormy painting and sections concerned with the serene words of the poem. In several cases, sections are named in the score, making it easy to follow the alternation between the two external sources.

Toledo is scored for standard band instrumentation with a large percussion section that requires piano, celesta, vibraphone, marimba, crotales, chimes, two sizes of triangle, three sizes of suspended cymbal, three sets of wind chimes (glass, wood, metal), timpani, and crash cymbals. Several instruments have important symbolic roles. The high, clear ring of the triangles represents the emergence of the *Spiritual Canticle* out of the darkness of the dungeon where St. John of the Cross was imprisoned. The piano provides a low-register *ostinato*, consisting of a tritone, throughout the several sections that address the same idea. Musically this passage contributes rhythmic energy and forward momentum to these sections, but it seems also to represent the pulse of creative life, inextinguishable even in a desperate situation.

Toledo is approximately ten minutes long.

Unit 3: Historical Perspective

In *Toledo*, Carlson drew on many of the compositional techniques associated with the late twentieth century: improvisation, time controlled in seconds rather than by strict rhythm, and a stanch reliance on timbre and texture, especially percussion sounds.

Harmonically, the work draws on pitch set theory. Carlson designed a chord, which he designated the "Toledo chord," consisting of alternating tritons and perfect fourths (spelled upwards from the bass: F, B, E, B-flat, E-flat, A). The notes of this chord form a pitch set that provides most of the harmony and much of the melodic material in the work. Such limited pitch use recalls Schoenberg's principle of the "integration of musical space," and similar pitch sets employed both harmonically and melodically appear regularly in the music of Stravinsky. However, the most obvious historical association is with Scriabin. The quartal structure of Carlson's chord and its persistent occurrence throughout the work evokes Scriabin's "mystic chord" and its pervasive use in *Prometheus*.

Toledo is remarkable in the young band repertoire. Not only does it grow out of the rich history of musical development in the twentieth century, but it also attempts to deal with profound spiritual concerns. Few works at this level can make such a claim. Because of its superior musical quality, it has attracted the attention of bands at all levels of accomplishment.

Unit 4: Technical Considerations

Since the work was written for a junior high band, the demands in terms of range and technique are moderate for the most part. Certain exceptions are notable. First clarinets are required to reach D above the treble staff. First alto saxophones stretch to high E-flat, and most surprisingly, the 1st oboes double 1st flutes up to E-flat above their treble staff. Rhythmically, this music rarely exceeds eighth notes at a moderate tempo, although meter changes occur frequently and some of the meter signatures (6/4, 7/4, 9/4) may not be familiar to young players.

The biggest challenge to performing this work is improvisation and the interpretation of contemporary notation. From the initial measures, all members of the band are required to hold short or long notes through time sequences measured in seconds. Players must attend carefully to the conductor's cues. At the same time, the percussionists are asked to improvise "sparingly" in "short subtle outbursts of predominantly upward sounds." At other points, the percussionists are assigned specific notes but in free rhythm. Everyone must interpret graphic notation at several points in the score.

A unique element of this piece is the verbal discussion and musical interpretation through improvisation of the El Greco painting. Students must be carefully led through the imagery of the painting so they understand what effect they are trying to achieve. Carlson has made this process easier by providing suggestions, such as "swirling sounds," but students are unlikely to understand these nuances unless it is made clear to them that such ideas are drawn directly from the structure of the painting. At one point in the piece, Carlson has extracted the actual line that represents the ground contour in the painting and interpolated it into the score as a "ground bass" that controls the registral profile of the improvisation. Students also need to be encouraged to control their individual volume even at the loudest points in order to hear each other and to imitate ideas offered by someone else. The main climax of the piece is prepared by a long *crescendo*, especially in the percussion. This gradual build-up must be carefully measured so correct balance can be achieved.

Another challenging aspect of this music is its reliance on solo performers. Clarinet, celesta, vibraphone, marimba, and triangle all have exposed solo passages.

Unit 5: Stylistic Considerations

Since this work dates from the last decade of the twentieth century, the precise interpretation of non-traditional notation is a crucial aspect of its style. Merton's words and those of the *Spiritual Canticle* may help to comprehend the meaning and, thus, the interpretation of the graphically notated sections.

Articulations are varied, and many of them have an important musical, even programmatic, role. The low-register piano *ostinati* are marked *staccato*, and a separated style is necessary to communicate the momentum and energy contributed by these passages. All of the loud sections are notated with accents. These sections represent bell sounds, and while the notation implies a certain amount of decay, this might be somewhat exaggerated to emphasize the programmatic image. At the other end of the articulation scale, certain passages require a very sustained and lyrical approach. Measures 22 through 31 are virtually pointillistic in texture. All notes need to be held for their full value in order that the melodic ideas (a kind of contrapuntal *Klangfarbenmelodie*) are perceivable. The section that follows (measures 32 through 46) is among the most lyrical in the entire composition. All of the instruments playing during this section are percussion instruments, which require an especially gentle attack to preserve the lyrical style.

Unit 6: Musical Elements

MELODY:

This work employs motives rather than melodies. The first melodic idea to appear (around measure 2) is a three-note "chant fragment" that is the first reference to the *Spiritual Canticle*. This motive is developed in a fragmentary way for the next few measures. It is replaced by a clarinet solo (measures 7 through 12) that is a horizontalization of the "Toledo chord" and encompasses a considerable range. The chant fragment is then harmonized with a three-note segment from the "Toledo chord," essentially integrating the initial two melodic ideas. Carlson also creates a motive in whole tones that appears in the loud sections of the piece and produces very effective bell sounds. As noted earlier, the section beginning at measure 22 fragments the melodic motives among the various instrumental groups. Careful attention to line is essential. Measures 32 through 46 present the only actual melody in the work. This idea is a development of the chant fragment and comprises three phrases, divided 4 measures + 5 measures + 6 measures. Additionally, the directions provided by the composer give many of the improvised sections a compelling melodic element. Directions include the general profile of individual improvisations ("predominantly upward sounds") and their overall character ("swirling sounds").

HARMONY:

Virtually all of the harmony is drawn from the "Toledo chord," which appears in every section of the work, either complete or in three- or four-note segments. This sonority and the tritone interval drawn from it are major unifying elements in *Toledo*. A remarkable deviation from the above can be seen at measures 53 through 56, where the whole-tone motive mentioned above is harmonized by a series of major chords. This unusual harmonic occurrence, appearing at the beginning of the work's primary climax, produces a captivating impression of a multitude of pealing bells.

RHYTHM:

The rhythm of the traditionally notated sections is straightforward, although marked by numerous simple meter changes. In the *senza misura* sections, the rhythmic context is considerably more complex. Improvisation produces multiple layers of disjunct rhythm that is controlled by clock time, requiring careful attention to the conductor. These sections also demand substantial creative input by the performers, who must both match and deviate from the efforts of their colleagues to generate the rhythmic independence implied by the notation.

TIMBRE:

The tone color is highly varied, with dramatic changes of scoring between formal sections. Graphic notation at various points in the score produces a soundscape unique to this work. Percussion is especially important in the creation of this individual timbre, and percussion sounds often have a symbolic role. For example, the two triangles are associated with the emergence of the *Spiritual Canticle* out of the darkness of the Saint's prison cell. Mallet percussion (including celesta and piano) and solo or *soli* passages contribute significantly to the delicate textures of much of the piece. By contrast, the full band sections are scored for maximum resonance and are very powerful.

TEACHING CONCEPTS AND STRATEGIES:

Performers will have difficulty understanding this work unless they are first introduced to the *View of Toledo* and the *Spiritual Canticle*. Initial rehearsals should begin by displaying a slide of the painting and by reading excerpts from the *Spiritual Canticle*. Younger students will need to be guided through these great works of art to understand that the imagery presented is highly symbolic. For example, the storm that towers over Toledo in El Greco's painting is not a simple summer storm but is, as Merton indicates, a symbol of the end of the world, and this great city with its castles, cathedrals, and rugged stone walls is completely at its mercy. The people in the painting are minute and seem oblivious to the "blue disaster" spread out above them, implying perhaps that humankind is never prepared for the end of the world. The grand scale of the painting, incorporating earth and heaven, makes the serene words of St. John of the Cross, rising from somewhere in the midst of these massive stone buildings, all the more poignant and remarkable.

On a practical level, students will need to be taught to improvise. This is best done over some considerable time by introducing short improvisational sessions into the warm-up period. Ideas for such sessions can be drawn from books like Sidney Hodkinson's *Contemporary Primer*. Students, however, need to understand that improvising does not mean playing anything at all. They need to listen just as carefully for balance, blend, and dynamics as they would in traditionally notated music. They should also be encouraged to listen to other students' efforts and to imitate or develop melodic or rhythmic fragments that they hear.

Ultimately, students will need to be drawn to the painting itself as a basis for improvisational ideas. Carlson has helped this process by making some suggestions. "Swirling sounds" might represent the wind-blown trees in the foreground or the angry clouds. "Predominantly upward sounds" are suggested because all the lines of the painting draw the eyes upward—to God's majesty displayed in the sky. Teachers/directors, however, need to be careful not to dictate interpretations. Part of the success of this work lies in the individual thoughts that performers bring to it. Some of these ideas might be brought out by carefully designed, "unanswerable" questions such as: What sounds describe the greens in the painting? How might you play the white spots in the sky? Reading the painting from left to right or bottom to top, how might you distinguish musically between the curved lines of the natural landscape and the straight lines of the man-made objects? What sounds describe anger? fear? etc.

Preparing and performing this work provides an excellent opportunity to illustrate the contrasted means by which the arts of painting, literature, and music express similar and profound ideas.

Unit 7: Form and Structure

Toledo is divided into easily recognizable sections but adheres to no specific formal pattern. No sections are repeated, but the work is tightly integrated through the use of musical material, especially the "Toledo chord" or derivatives of it, which appear in virtually every section.

SECTION	MEASURE	EVENT AND SCORING
Introduction	1	One long measure (ca. 90 sec); *senza misura*, time measured in seconds; chime stroke at beginning establishes mood, introduces musical elements especially "Toledo chord"; timpani solo later; chant fragment forms elision to next section

SECTION	MEASURE	EVENT AND SCORING
A	2–12	"Spiritual Canticle emerging"; measured time, shifting meter, chant fragment developed; sparse percussion accompaniment mm. 7–12 clarinet solo melodic idea from the "Toledo chord"; same measures piano low-register *ostinato* on a tritone interval—creative energy in the darkness of a dungeon; piano solo connects this section to the next
B	13–21	"Belly of the whale"; full band, dense texture, bell sounds; chant fragment in high voices harmonized by a trichord drawn from the "Toledo chord"; whole-tone motive at mm. 19–20 leads to free section in which percussion improvises on the chant fragment; piano *ostinato* returns and wind instruments use air only, perhaps an evocation of the line " The whisper of the lovely air" from the *Spiritual Canticle*
C	22–31	Segmented "Toledo chord" spread through the instruments in a type of contrapuntal Klangfarbenmelodie; gradually increasing tempo; two-measure phrases; piano *ostinato*, perhaps a representation of the process of creative thought—the *Spiritual Canticle* gradually taking shape
D	32–46	Lyrical; faster tempo; all high percussion sounds except for piano *ostinato*, three phrases (4+5+6 measures); presence of triangle suggests the realization of at least part of the *Spiritual Canticle*
E	47–59	Musical realization of *View of Toledo*; verbal discussion followed by musical impression through improvisation of

SECTION	MEASURE	EVENT AND SCORING
		the painting; leads to work's primary climax; full band; whole tone motive over major chords and percussion improvisation; pealing of many bells; m. 59 is free, improvisation (everyone) to follow the "ground bass"—a line representing the ground contour in the painting, all upward lines representing Merton's words "earth and sky run off the top of the canvas"
F	60–67	"Blooming of the *Spiritual Canticle*"; gentle mood; whole-tone motive in canon played by mallet percussion; triangle representing the completion of the poem; seems to stand still like St. John of the Cross in his tiny cell; see Merton, "the movement is centripetal" and "suddenly blossoms out into a paradise of liberty of which the saint sings in his *Spiritual Canticle*"
Coda	67–74	All conflicts ended, perhaps a reference to the phrase "let angers end!" from the *Spiritual Canticle*; final chord is E-flat major; final sounds are marimba, vibraphone, crotales, and triangle providing a distant echo of the chime stroke that opened the piece

Unit 8: Suggested Listening

Alan Bell, *From Chaos to the Birth of a Dancing Star*
Daniel Bukvich, *Symphony No. 1: In Memoriam Dresden*
Ron Nelson, *Medieval Suite: Homage to Leonin*
Gunther Schuller, *Seven Studies on Themes by Paul Klee*
Alexander Scriabin, *Prometheus* (excerpts)

Unit 9: Additional References and Resources

Bronstein, Leo. *El Greco*. New York and Toronto: Harry N. Abrams Publishers and Thomas Allen Ltd., 1950. (This book has an especially good image of View of Toledo.)

Brown, Jonathan, William Jordan, Richard Kagen, and Alfonso Pérez Sánchez. *El Greco of Toledo*. Boston: Little, Brown and Co., 1982.

Bruno de J. M., Father, ed. *Three Mystics: El Greco, St. John of the Cross, St Teresa of Avila*. New York: Sheed & Ward, 1949.

Canadian Music Centre, website: www.musiccentre.ca/CMC/dac_rca/eng/a_/Carlson_Bruce.html

McDonnell, Thomas P., ed. *A Thomas Merton Reader*. Revised edition. New York: Image Books, 1974.

St. John of the Cross. *A Spiritual Canticle of the Soul and the Bridegroom Christ*. Translated by David Lewis. Edited by Benedict Zimmerman, O.C.D. London: Thomas Baker, 1919. (This book, while rather old, contains a concise biographical sketch of St. John of the Cross, a translation of the entire Spiritual Canticle, and a wonderful stanza-by-stanza commentary.)

Watkins, Glenn. *Soundings: Music in the Twentieth Century*. New York and London: Schirmer Books, 1988.

Contributed by:
Keith Kinder
McMaster University
Hamilton, Ontario
Canada

Teacher Resource Guide

Tricycle

Andrew Boysen, Jr.
(b. 1968)

Unit 1: Composer

Andrew Boysen, Jr. is presently an assistant professor in the music department at the University of New Hampshire, where he conducts the wind symphony and teaches conducting, composition, and orchestration. Previously, Boysen served as an assistant professor at Indiana State University, director of bands at Cary-Grove (Illinois) High School, and music director and conductor of the Deerfield Community Concert Band. He remains active as a guest conductor and clinician, appearing with high school, university, and festival ensembles across the United States and Great Britain.

Boysen earned his Doctor of Musical Arts degree in wind conducting in 1998 at the Eastman School of Music, where he served as conductor of the Eastman Wind Orchestra and assistant conductor of the Eastman Wind Ensemble. He received his Master of Music degree in wind conducting from Northwestern University in 1993 and his Bachelor of Music degree in Music Education and Music Composition from the University of Iowa in 1991.

Boysen won the International Horn Society Composition Contest in 2000, the University of Iowa Honors Composition Prize in 1991, and has twice won the Claude T. Smith Memorial Band Composition Contest (in 1991 for *I Am* and in 1994 for *Ovations*). Boysen has several published works with the Neil A. Kjos Music Company, Wingert-Jones Music, and Ludwig Music, including pieces for band, orchestra, clarinet and piano, and brass choir. Recordings of his music appear on the Sony, R-Kal, Mark, St. Olaf, and Elf labels. Other works for band include *Conversations with the Night, I Am, Urban Scenes, Song of the Sea Maidens, John Henry, Simple Song,* and *Kirkpatrick Fanfare.*

Unit 2: Composition

Tricycle was commissioned by the Northshore Schools, District 112 (Illinois) for the inaugural All-City Band Festival. Directors of the participating schools were Mike Brehmer, Jason Meltzer, Dennis Runyon, Steve Zachar, and Glenn Williams. The title of the work refers to both the structure of the piece and the event for which it was commissioned. The All-City Band Festival involves three schools performing and working together as one, much as all three wheels of a tricycle must work together to move forward. The music reflects this idea by having three separate themes introduced on their own before finally being combined to work together as one musical entity. The title is even more appropriate considering the playful and innocent qualities of the piece as a whole. *Tricycle* is a piece that is meant to be light, fun, and happy.

 Tricycle is in one movement and is approximately four minutes in length. Although it is a grade three work, there are significant rhythmic challenges. The piece includes the use of singing and examples of hemiola and *ostinato*. It is quite fast (quarter note = 208) and is in 5/4 for much of the time.

Unit 3: Historical Perspective

Tricycle was composed in 1994 and published in 1997. The main rhythmic motive of the work is similar to the underlying rhythmic pattern that dominates the second movement of Frank Ticheli's *Cajun Folk Songs*. A study of this piece could demonstrate how composers create completely different works from similar materials.

Unit 4: Technical Considerations

Although *Tricycle* does not have a key signature in any of the transposed parts, most of the piece is centered around C major. Exercises and scales in this key will be of benefit in preparing to play the work.

 Range is not an issue, as the 1st trumpet part only ascends to D4 and the 1st trombone reaches E3. The most unusual demands are found in the percussion. Most of the standard percussion instruments are used (minus timpani), but there are also parts for sandpaper blocks, guiro, brushes on a suspended cymbal, as well as the use of hand dampening in the triangle part.

 The major demand of the piece, and the greatest opportunity for teaching, is in its rhythmic aspects. A good portion of *Tricycle* is in a fast 5/4 meter, with a constant underlying rhythm of quarter/eighth/quarter/eighth/quarter/quarter. This rhythm could be written out for all students and then used as the basis for a C major scale and other related exercises. At measure 52, the meter switches to 4/4, and in measure 56, the underlying rhythm is changed to quarter/eighth/quarter/eighth/quarter (with the last quarter note of the original rhythmic pattern omitted). A simple exercise might involve alternating bars of 5/4 and 4/4 using these rhythms.

The piece also includes three instances of hemiola (measures 12 through 13, 52 through 55, 141 through 142), substantial use of syncopation, rhythmic augmentation of the main *ostinato* (suspended cymbal in measures 145 through 146), and many entrances on beats other than one. Various counting exercises in 5/4 might be written out and sung by the students in preparation for different sections of the piece.

Since the tempo is so fast, the conductor may want to initially conduct the piece in five at a slower tempo and then move to a two pattern (3+2 grouping) as the students become more comfortable with the fast tempo. Some conductors may also choose to conduct the underlying rhythmic motive by using a four pattern with unequal beat lengths (dotted-quarter/dotted-quarter/quarter/quarter).

Unit 5: Stylistic Considerations

The overall approach to *Tricycle* needs to be light and playful. Nothing in the work is big or heavy. Light separation is appropriate between notes of the first theme and notes of the rhythmic *ostinato*. The slower moving chords (such as measures 5 through 6, 8 through 9, 10 through 11, etc., and the second and third themes) should be more connected.

Most of the piece is quite soft and should have a sense of waiting for the "big moment." That moment occurs between measures 106 and 130, when the dynamic level reaches *forte* and then finally *fortissimo*.

Unit 6: Musical Elements

MELODY:

The melody of the first theme is in C major. The primary challenge with this melody is to play the detached notes with matching length and a sense of direction. Try having the melody group sing their parts and listen to each other to match the lengths of their notes. The underlying countermelody (in bass clarinet, bassoon, tenor saxophone, horn, and euphonium at measure 17) should be played with connected notes in contrast to the main melodic idea.

The second theme (initially presented by the trumpet) and the third theme (initially presented by low woodwinds and low brass) should be played in a more connected manner, again in contrast to the separated nature of the first theme.

HARMONY:

The harmony throughout the work is triadic and tonal. There are brief moments of dissonance, such as in measures 19 and 20 when the countermelody briefly moves out of C major and contrasts with the melody in the upper voices. Since many of the chords are major triads, there is a good opportunity to teach the concept of tuning the third of a major chord. For example, measure 126 (or measure 130) has all members of the ensemble involved in a C major chord. Begin by tuning the Cs, then adding the Gs, then adding the Es.

RHYTHM:

The most difficult aspects of *Tricycle* are found in its rhythmic demands. The underlying rhythm of quarter/eighth/quarter/eighth/quarter/quarter should be rehearsed separately by the whole ensemble. Sing the rhythm as a group and practice playing it by using the rhythm on each note of a C major scale.

TIMBRE:

In general, *Tricycle* uses the contrast between high and low groupings of instruments rather than scoring by choir (woodwinds, brass, percussion). However, the sections from measures 39 through 52 and 96 through 106 provide good examples of alternating choirs. The percussion is used both to highlight certain moments and as an integral part of the structure of the piece.

Again, the climactic chords at measures 126 through 134 provide an opportunity to work on balance and blend by starting with the low instruments and attempting to create a solid foundation for the upper instruments.

Unit 7: Form and Structure

SECTION	MEASURE	EVENT AND SCORING
Introduction	1	Initial presentation of *ostinato* with alternating chords in woodwinds and trombone; in 5/4
Theme 1	17	Melody in upper woodwinds and 1st trumpet; C major
Transition	25	Low woodwinds and brass play transitional melody; end on V
Theme 1 (restated)	31	*Ostinato* now in trumpet instead of trombone; still C major
Development of Theme 1	39	Alternating presentations of the first measure of the melody in F major and B-flat major; eventually returns to C major
Transition	52	Change to 4/4
Theme 2	60	Solo trumpet with group singing a pedal C

Section	Measure	Event and Scoring
Theme 3	82	Theme in low woodwinds and brass
Development of Themes 3 and 1 (retransition)	89	Alternating statements of altered form of Theme 1 with bass line continuing; B-flat major to D-flat major to V of C major
All three themes	106	Return to 5/4 and C major; themes presented in succession (first theme, then third theme, then second theme); climax of piece at m. 126
Coda	134	Return of introductory material

Unit 8: Suggested Listening
Andrew Boysen, Jr.:
   Kirkpatrick Fanfare
   Simple Song
   Urban Scenes
Frank Ticheli, *Cajun Folk Songs*

Unit 9: Additional References and Resources
Miles, Richard, ed. *Teaching Music through Performance in Band*, Volume 1. Chicago: GIA Publications, Inc., 1997, pp. 166–9.

Rehrig, William H. *The Heritage Encyclopedia of Band Music, Supplement*, Volume 3. Westerville, OH: Integrity Press, 1996, pp. 108–9.

Smith, Norman E. *Program Notes for Band*. Chicago, IL: GIA Publications, Inc., 2002, pp. 82–3.

Contributed by:
Andrew Boysen, Jr.
Director of Bands
University of New Hampshire
Durham, New Hampshire

Teacher Resource Guide

Two Hebrew Folk Songs
(Songs for Chanukah)

arranged by Norman Ward
(b. 1927)

Unit 1: Composer

Norman Ward graduated from the Juilliard School of Music in 1952 and received his master's degree from Columbia University in 1953. He has taught in the Long Island School System and has over one hundred pieces published by Kendor, Belwin, Studio P.R., and Shawnee Press. He has also started his own music publishing company, Hollow Hills Press, which publishes band, orchestra, and choral music for schools, as well as method books and other related items. In addition to his ongoing commitment to music education, Ward has composed two musical shows for children, served as arranger/director and accompanist for numerous commercial productions, and authored the book *How to Submit Manuscripts to Publishers*. Examples of Ward's diverse output include *Lost City*, *Sight Reader for Young Bands*, and *Andy Griffith Theme*.

Unit 2: Composition

Published in 1965, *Two Hebrew Folk Songs* arranges two famous Hebrew songs that are often sung for Chanukah. The composer states that the piece "was written in the days when the publishers were only publishing Christmas music and there was, here in New York, a real need for Chanukah music for the winter concerts." The work is in two distinct, short movements. The first movement, "Al Hanisim," is based on a liturgical song with the following text in Hebrew and English:

238

Al hanisim v'al hapurkan v'al hag'vurot
V'al hat'shuot v'al hamilchamot
Sheasita lavotenu bayamim hahem
Baz'man haze

We thank you for the miracles, for the redemption,
for the mighty deeds and triumphs, and for the
battles which you performed for our fathers in those
days, at this season.

It is in ABA form with a short two-measure coda at the end of the movement. There are short flute, oboe, and clarinet solos at the opening.

The lively second movement, "S'vivon," is more difficult than the first and features a driving theme at a quick tempo. "S'vivon" is a children's song dealing with the joy of the celebration of Chanukah. It is sung to the following text in Hebrew and English:

S'vivon sov sov sov Chanukah hu chag tov
Chanukah hu chag tov s'vivon sov sov sov
Chag simcha hu laam nes gadol haya sham
Nes gadol haya sham chag simcha hu laam

Little dreydl, spin, spin, spin. Chanukah is a day of joy.
Great was the miracle that happened there. Spin little
dreydl spin, spin, spin.

The entire piece is approximately three minutes in length and effectively portrays two distinct styles of Hebrew folk music.

Unit 3: Historical Perspective

Folk music can be defined as the musical traditions of a community that generally develop anonymously and are passed from generation to generation aurally. Some form of folk music is found in virtually every culture and usually holds great significance for the people of that culture. Hebrew folk music is no exception and can be either liturgically influenced (sacred) or secular in nature. The setting of folk songs to music for orchestra and band is a very common practice and has been done by such composers as Percy Aldridge Grainger, Ralph Vaughan Williams, Bela Bartok, and Peter Ilyich Tchaikovsky, to name a few. More recent pieces for wind band based on Hebrew folk music include *Yiddish Dances* by Adam Gorb, *Rikudim* by Jan Van der Roost, and *Hatikvah* arranged by Elliot Del Borgo.

Unit 4: Technical Considerations

Two Hebrew Folk Songs is essentially in F minor with a pentatonic melody in each movement. The piece opens with a sensitive *ostinato* in the percussion that requires tambourine to be played with the fingertips. The first movement is in a slow cut time and is fairly chromatic. Furthermore, the articulations are varied and require light and fairly quick tonguing in brass as well as smooth *legato* technique in woodwinds for the short eighth note runs. Coordinating the three *ritardandos* in the movement also might be challenging. Range is not a problem throughout the piece, with trumpets never playing above the staff.

The second movement is in quick 2/4 time and requires the musicians to place the accent on the second beat of the measure. Although there are eighth and sixteenth notes at quarter note = 138, they are all short, scalar passages. There is an exposed flute solo at rehearsal C, but most of the writing is very full in texture. There are some easy syncopated passages in the music that add to the excitement of the theme, but the music has steady four-measure phrasing throughout most of the piece.

Unit 5: Stylistic Considerations

Due to the subject matter of the first movement, the mood should be one of great seriousness and passion. The *legato* articulations should be very smooth and connected, leading to the top of each four-measure phrase. Chromatically altered notes in the melodic line should be given a slight agogic accent to emphasize the use of the altered dorian mode. The accompaniment must stay secondary to the flowing melodic line, especially in the percussion.

The second movement is in complete contrast to the first, with a celebratory and joyful feel being appropriate. Eighth notes should be slightly spaced and light, while quarter notes should be given weight and extended to lead to the downbeat of the next measure. The ensemble sound could even become somewhat raucous to capture the spirit of the movement.

Unit 6: Musical Elements

MELODY:

The melody of the first movement is based on the altered dorian scale. The dorian scale consists of a series of notes in the following pattern of half and whole steps.

Dorian:

Whole–Half–Whole–Whole–Whole–Half–Whole

Example: B-flat–C–D-flat–E-flat–F–G–A-flat–B-flat

It is typical of Hebrew folk music to use the altered dorian scale, which raises the fourth degree of the scale to create an augmented second between the third and fourth scale degrees. The first movement uses the following pattern and notes to create its melody.

Altered Dorian:
Whole–Half–Augmented second–Half–Whole–Half–Whole
Example: B-flat–C–D-flat–E–F–G–A-flat–B-flat

The second movement utilizes a pentatonic scale for its melody (F–G–A-flat–B-flat–C). A pentatonic scale can be any scale that uses five notes. The scale used in the second movement happens to be based on the first five notes of the F minor scale.

HARMONY:

This piece uses traditional harmony throughout and is homophonic. The accompaniment in the first movement often uses open fifths to support the melody. An open fifth (e.g., C–G) does not provide a major or minor tonality since it is missing the third of the chord.

RHYTHM:

The first movement is in cut time, with half note = 66. It might be a good idea to rehearse the piece in common time so the players understand the concept of subdividing in cut time. The feel of the rhythm and meter is in two, but it should be counted in four.

TIMBRE:

Tone color is essential in making the appropriate contrast between the first and second movements. Strive for a dark, somber, and controlled sound in the first movement. Meanwhile, in the second movement try to achieve a bright sound portraying the frivolous joy of the music. You might listen to a recording of a klezmer band to hear an example of Jewish music played in a characteristic style and tone.

Unit 7: Form and Structure

SECTION	MEASURE	EVENT AND SCORING
Movement 1: "Al Hanisim" Form: ABA'		
A	Open–A	Opening percussion *ostinato*; Theme A in solo winds
	A–B	Theme A in clarinet
	B–C	Countermelody in trumpet; theme in woodwinds
B	C–E	Theme B in flute, oboe, clarinet, and trumpet
A'	E–Close	Two-measure coda

SECTION	MEASURE	EVENT AND SCORING
Movement 2: "S'vivon" Form: arch		
	Open–A	Introduction
	A–B	Theme in woodwinds
	B–C	Theme in upper winds; accompaniment more sparse
	C–D	Theme in solo flute
	D–E	Repeat of B–C
	E–F	Repeat of A–B (add cornet)
	F–Close	Coda

Unit 8: Suggested Listening

Milton Barnes, *Chanukah Suite No. 1 for Chamber Orchestra*
Elliot Del Borgo, *Hatikvah*,
Adam Gorb, *Yiddish Dances*
Jan Van der Roost, *Rikudim*
Ralph Vaughan Williams, *English Folk Song Suite*

Unit 9: Additional References and Resources

Apel, Willi, ed. *Harvard Dictionary of Music*. Second edition. Cambridge, MA: Belknap Press, 1970.

Pasternak, Velvel, ed. *Jewish Holidays in Song*. Tara Publications, 1985.

Sadie, Stanley, ed. *The New Grove Dictionary of Music and Musicians*, Volume 13. Second edition. London: Macmillan Publishers Limited, 2001.

Slobin, Mark, ed. *Old Jewish Folk Music; The Collections and Writings of Moshe Beregowski*. Philadelphia, PA: University of Pennsylvania Press, 1982.

Additional notes provided by Norman Ward.

Contributed by:
Michael Alexander
Conductor
Waukesha Area Symphonic Band
Waukesha, Wisconsin

Teacher Resource Guide

Variation Overture

Clifton Williams
(1923–1976)

Unit 1: Composer

James Clifton Williams was born in Traskwood, Arkansas. His early musical experience included playing French horn in school band and orchestra in Malvern and Little Rock, Arkansas. His interest in composing began while still in high school.

After serving as a bandsman during World War II in the United States Army Air Corps, Williams attended Louisiana State University, where he studied composition with Helen Gunderson. In 1949, he earned his Master of Music degree at the Eastman School of Music. While at Eastman, Williams studied composition with Bernard Rogers and horn with Arkady Yegudkin. He joined the faculty at the University of Texas in Austin in 1949, and continued to play horn in the San Antonio Symphony and the Austin Symphony. He was an articulate spokesperson and interpreter of contemporary music. As a teacher and friend, Williams influenced many talented young composers, including Francis McBeth, Lawrence Weiner, and John Barnes Chance. In 1966, he accepted a position as Chairman of the Department of Theory and Composition at the University of Miami, where he remained until his death in 1976.

During his professional career, Williams won numerous awards and honors for his compositions and contributions to the profession. Twenty-eight of his thirty-one published compositions are listed in the *1982 Band Music Guide*. Notable works by Williams include *Dedicatory Overture, Dramatic Essay for Trumpet and Band, Fanfare and Allegro, Festival, The Sinfonians,* and *Symphonic Suite.* Williams is regarded as a composer of serious concert music for wind band. His widely performed works continue to influence the standards of literature for school, college, and military concert bands.

Unit 2: Composition

Variation Overture is dedicated to the American School Band Directors' Association and received its world premiere performance at the American School Band Directors' Association Convention at Cleveland, Ohio, in December 1961. It is a concert overture that utilizes the structure of theme and variations. The simple, diatonic theme is presented in four distinct settings: march, waltz, lyric, and fanfare. Williams's contemporary harmonies and romantic melodic style are prevalent in this work for young band. *Variation Overture* is 184 measures long and is approximately six minutes in duration.

Unit 3: Historical Perspective

Variation Overture was composed and first performed in 1961. It was somewhat unusual at that time for a composer of major stature to write music for young instrumental ensembles that employed sophisticated compositional techniques within a simple framework. It is a contemporary work in the style of the American romanticists. Characteristics of this compositional style are variation in tempi, dynamic range, special effects and devices, and the use of contemporary harmonies with traditional voice leading. Of particular value to the study and approach of this work is the music of Howard Hanson. His lush romantic style provides an excellent model for the attitudes, styles, and markings of this school of composition. Compositions by Hindemith, Mennin, Persichetti, Schuman, Clifton Williams, and others of the same period began to add strength and depth to the repertoire for wind band.

Unit 4: Technical Considerations

The theme and each variation are presented in a different tonality. The scales of C major, F major, B-flat major, and E-flat major are required for the entire ensemble. Accidentals appear in parts due to the use of chromaticism and modal techniques. It is rhythmically straightforward with minimal use of syncopation. Ranges are well within the ability of young musicians. Extended ranges occur in first parts only briefly and are doubled. Standard concert band instrumentation is utilized, with independent writing in all sections. Percussion writing is idiomatic and requires snare drum, bass drum, cymbals, and timpani. The use of mallet percussion is limited. The greatest challenges will be achieving a sustained, lyrical line in the waltz and lyric variations, and executing precise and rapid articulations in the fanfare.

Unit 5: Stylistic Considerations

An awareness of the five-note theme is extremely important to the interpretation of *Variation Overture*. Each setting of this theme requires careful attention to phrasing, articulation, and dynamics. The first variation is in the style of a march. The melody occurs in four-measure motives with a detached, chordal accompaniment. Uniform articulation and precise note lengths are vital to the clarity of texture. Variation two is a melancholy waltz that requires *legato* playing. The lyric variation is even more demanding due to a slower tempo, soft dynamics, and sustained lines. The final setting is a brilliant fanfare in which the brass play a series of rapidly tongued eighth note and sixteenth note motives over woodwind chords and trills. Precise articulations and attention to ensemble entrances and releases are essential.

Block dynamics are present throughout the work. However, there is contrast within each variation and theme. The use of *crescendo* and *decrescendo* markings support inflection in phrases and transitions. Attention to balance between melody and accompaniment are important. There is much variation in tempi as is typical of music in the romantic style. Tempo markings include *Majestically, With dignity, Moderate Waltz, slowing down, Slowly, In singing style, Fast and bold, getting slower and louder, Vigorously, Broadening to the end.* Williams is specific and accompanies these descriptors with metronome markings. Numerous tempo changes provide a challenge, as the ensemble must be sensitive to the conductor at all times.

Unit 6: Musical Elements

MELODY:

Exploration of the simple, diatonic theme will assist students in gaining a greater understanding of compositional techniques and the theme and variation form. Referencing the score and parts, have students play the first four measures as written. Then isolate the intervals diatonically in unison F–G–A, then A–B–C, and F–G–A–B-flat–C, as well as F–G–A–B–C. Explore the melodic intervals of a major third, perfect fifth, and minor third, and point out the raised fourth. One can incorporate these intervals and patterns into ear training exercises.

Following this introduction, point out the structure of the theme as it appears in each variation. The A motive utilizes the diatonic intervals of the major third and perfect fifth prominently, whereas the A1 motive is initiated with the diatonic minor third. In the march variation, have the upper woodwinds and brass play measures 11 through 14 and 15 through 18. Both motives are identical. This four-measure motive is the first representation of the five-note theme. Next, have the cornets play measures 19 through 22. This four-measure motive contains elements of the first phrase and is, thus, referred to as A1. Note the melodic line moves up one step, and the melodic motion of the second measure imitates that of the fourth and final measures in the previous phrase. Referencing each of these motives in the remaining variations allows students to make observations of the melodic design and how it is being manipulated.

The phrase structure follows period form. The march consists of a sixteen-measure sentence with two eight-measure phrases classified as the antecedent phrase and the consequent phrase. Period construction displays a similarity between the antecedent and consequent phrases. Sometimes the phrases appear to be identical, differing in harmony or cadence only, or the resemblance may be a similarity in the opening notes or sequence of each phrase. Take time to point out the use of significant compositional techniques. Inversion occurs in the accompaniment to the A1 theme at measures 81 through 89. Augmentation of the melody occurs in the lyric variation, and diminution occurs in the fanfare in measures 131 through 146.

HARMONY:

Williams extends the boundaries of diatonic tonality with the use of harmonic and melodic material from other modes with the same tonic. Tonal notes that are shared in these harmonies are the tonic, subdominant, and dominant. The introduction of "flattened" notes or modes produces an increased warmth and, thus, a more lush and romantic quality. These techniques are prominent throughout *Variation Overture*.

The introduction of the theme and transition to the march variation appears to be in C major; however, the use of chromaticism and the C pedal implies a modal variation on the dominant going to the tonic in F major. The chord structure in the march is triadic, with alternating F major and D-flat major chords. A triadic relationship exists between these chords, as D-flat is a major third below F. This same treatment can be seen in the B-flat and G-flat chords in measures 129 through 147 and 155 through 160. In the waltz variation, the use of the lydian mode is implied with the appearance of E-natural, a raised fourth, in the melody. This is derived directly from the theme in measure 3. The return to E-flat in the following measure serves to introduce the tonality of B-flat major. The use of a modal cadence, the F minor seven chord in measure 43, acts as a pivot chord. The root movement then sets up an implied transition to E-flat major at measure 45. This technique is utilized again at the end of the variation in measures 71 through 73.

The lyric variation is in E-flat major and uses the same technique of the dominant pedal as seen in the introduction.

The introduction to the fanfare variation borrows both harmonic and melodic material from measures 1 through 10. Note the descending chromatic lines below the elongated five-note theme in measures 101 through 114, and the syncopated pedal in measures 123 through 129. Triadic harmonies are present throughout the fanfare. The tonality of B-flat major is hinted at through root movement and finally comes to rest in the final four measures.

Traditional harmonic movement is employed throughout *Variation Overture*. However, the use of modal techniques brings about increased expression and a more contemporary sound.

RHYTHM:

Rhythm and meter play a significant role in the modification of the five-note theme. Simple duple, triple, and quadruple meters are present. Draw out the differences between each of the variations. Point out how rhythm helps create the lilting feel in the waltz variation. Augmentation and diminution are present in the melodies of the lyric and fanfare variations. Note the use of rhythmic diminution in the syncopated rhythms of the fanfare (measures 123 through 129) as compared to the introduction (measures 5 through 10). The rhythmic motive of eighth note/two sixteenths is introduced in measure 100 and provides a unifying element in the final variation.

TIMBRE:

The overall tone color of this composition is lush and warm due to the vertical sonorities. The wind and brass writing is very idiomatic, with emphasis on full section playing with few solo requirements. Most instruments perform melodic functions at some point, and there is much blending of woodwind and brass choirs. The initial phrase of both the waltz and lyric variations feature small chamber-like ensembles before returning to the *tutti* texture. This provides an excellent opportunity to isolate and transfer the concepts of blend and balance.

Unit 7: Form and Structure

Variation Overture provides an excellent teaching tool for the introduction of theme and variation form. Variation form involves the statement of an idea or theme, which is then modified and altered while still retaining one or more essential features of the original. Such compositions appear as independent works and also exist within the structure of larger works as a single movement in an instrumental suite, sonata, or symphony. The basic thematic material of *Variation Overture* is the first five notes of the major scale, with a raised fourth. The diatonic intervals of a major third, perfect fifth, and minor third are skillfully woven into the entire composition. *Variation Overture* is sectional in nature as there is usually a pause or caesura at the end of the theme and each variation. Williams maintains the melodic content of the original theme and manipulates each setting to represent a different musical genre. Musical elements that provide contrast are rhythm and tempo, texture, instrumentation, tonality, and dynamics.

SECTION	MEASURE	EVENT AND SCORING
Introduction (majestically)		F major
	1–9	Five-note theme/transition
Variation I (with dignity)		F major
A	10	Introduction
A	11–14	Upper woodwinds/brass
A	15–18	Upper woodwinds/brass
A'	19–22	Solo cornet, woodwinds
A	23–26	Brass
Variation II (moderate waltz)		B-flat major
A	27–44	Woodwinds, baritone
A1	45–62	1st clarinet, saxophone, flute
A	63–72	Flute, clarinet, cornet, baritone
Variation III (slowly, in a singing style) E-flat major		
A	73–80	Solo cornet, 1st clarinet
A1	81–88	1st flute, oboe, 1st clarinet, 1st cornet
A	89–100	Clarinet, 1st cornet
Variation IV (fast and bold)		B-flat major
A	101–108	Brass rhythmic motive
A1	109–116	Brass motive/woodwind chords
	117–128	Brass motive/woodwind chords and trills
(vigorously)	129–130	Introduction
A	131–146	Clarinet, 1st cornet, 1st trombone, baritone
A1	147–154	Low woodwinds/brass
A	155–162	Clarinet, 1st cornet, 1st trombone, baritone
	163–170	Transitional material
	171–184	Coda

Unit 8: Suggested Listening

William Byrd/Jacob, *William Byrd Suite*
   (Movement 3, "John Come Kiss Me Now")
John Barnes Chance, *Variations on a Korean Folk Song*
Norman Dello Joio, *Variations on a Medieval Tune*
Howard Hanson:
   Chorale and Alleluia
   Dies Natalis
   Laude

Franz Joseph Haydn:
   Emperor Quartet, Op. 76, No. 3 (Movement II)
   Surprise Symphony (Movement II)
Charles Ives, *Variations on "America"*
William Schuman, *Chester Overture for Band*

Unit 9: Additional References and Resources

Battisti, Frank. The *Twentieth Century American Wind Band Ensemble: History, Development, and Literature*. Fort Lauderdale, FL: Meredith Music Publications, 1995.

Delamont, Gordon. *Modern Melodic Technique*. Delevan, NY: Kendor Music, Inc., 1976.

Dvorak, Thomas L., Gary M. Ciepluch, and Robert Grechesky. *Best Music for High School Band*. Edited by Bob Margolis. Brooklyn, NY: Manhattan Beach Music, 1993.

Dvorak, Thomas L., Cynthia Crump Taggart, and Peter Schmaltz. *Best Music for Young Band*. Edited by Bob Margolis. Brooklyn, NY: Manhattan Music, 1986.

McBeth, W. Francis. *Effective Performance of Band Music*. San Antonio, TX: Southern Music, 1972.

Miles, Richard, ed. *Teaching Music through Performance in Band*, Volume 3. Chicago: GIA Publications, Inc., 2000.

Smith, Norman E. *Program Notes for Band*. Chicago, IL: GIA Publications, Inc, 2002.

Randall, Don M., ed. *Harvard Concise Dictionary of Music*. Cambridge, MA: Belknap Press, 1978.

Contributed by:
Sheryl A. Bowhay
Director of Bands
Thornhill Secondary School
Markham, Ontario, Canada

Grade Three

Teacher Resource Guide

Angel Band

Walter S. Hartley
(b. 1927)

Unit 1: Composer

Walter Hartley has composed twenty-three original works for band, including *Symphony Nos. 1, 2, 4, and 5, Sinfonia Nos. 1, 4, 5, and 9*, and *Sinfonietta*. His other band works include *Rondo for Winds and Percussion, Southern Tier Suite, Coast Guard Suite, Essay for Band: Triads and Trichords, Hallelujah Suite, and Angel Band Suite*. He has written thirteen concerti for solo instrument(s) with wind ensemble/band and five arrangements for band.

Hartley attended the Eastman School of Music in Rochester, New York, where he studied with Howard Hanson, Bernard Rogers, Burrill Phillips, Thomas Canning, Herbert Elwell, and Dante Fiorillo. He has taught at the Interlochen Arts Camp, Davis and Elkins College, and SUNY Fredonia, where he is currently Professor Emeritus of Music and Composer-in-Residence.

Unit 2: Composition

Angel Band is a three-movement suite based on eighteenth and nineteenth century American hymn tunes: Timothy Swan's *Rainbow* (Movement 1), William Billings's *Africa* (Movement 2), and William Bradbury's *Angel Band* (Movement 3). These hymns are located in various editions of *The Christian Harmony* and *The Sacred Harp*, anthologies of American hymn music. *Angel Band* combines material borrowed from the three hymn tunes with the composer's own harmonic and melodic material. The work is approximately six minutes in length.

Unit 3: Historical Perspective

The hymn tune was an important part of musical culture in America in the eighteenth and nineteenth centuries. Most hymns sung in America during this time were of European origin (mainly German chorales and English psalms and anthems), with the first American contributions to the hymn repertoire appearing at the end of the eighteenth century. Hymnody in America became quite diverse during the nineteenth century. In addition to the singing-school hymns that originated in the Northeast late in the eighteenth century, folk hymns composed by European-American and African-American composers in the South and frontier states flourished in the early decades of the nineteenth century. These folk hymns became the foundation of the spiritual tradition. Additionally, Lowell Mason and other prominent musicians in the Northeast developed a style of hymnody more closely allied to European models in the mid-nineteenth century.

The three composers from whom Hartley borrows material for the *Angel Band* suite played a prominent role in early American hymnody. Timothy Swan (1758–1842) published *The Songster's Assistant* and *The Songster's Museum* in the early years of the nineteenth century. William Bradbury (1816–1868) composed hymns, was an early advocate of music in the New York City public schools, and wrote *The Jubilee*, a widely used singing method in the mid-nineteenth century. William Billings (1746–1800) is best known as the composer of *Chester*; he also wrote several songbooks, including *The New England Psalm Singer* and *The Continental Harmony*.

Unit 4: Technical Considerations

"Rainbow" and "Finale" are primarily in the key of B-flat major, and "Africa" is mainly in the key of E-flat major. "Africa" also uses the keys of E-flat minor and F dorian, and "Finale" contains episodes in the keys of A-flat major, D-flat major, C major, and F major. The first movement is in 2/2 (half note = 96), the second movement is in 3/4 (quarter note = 76), and the third movement is in 6/8 (dotted-quarter note = 120–126). Rhythm patterns consist primarily of simple divisions of the beat (quarter notes in the first movement and eighth notes in the second and third movements).

Instrumental ranges are conservative with the following exceptions: tuba goes to F one octave below the bass staff in the second movement, 1st trombone goes to B-flat one octave above the bass staff in the closing measures of the third movement, 4th horn has repeated written F's below the treble staff in the third movement, 1st trumpet goes to written C above the staff at the conclusion of the third movement, and 1st clarinet goes to written G one octave above the treble staff in the third movement. There are no solo passages.

The most demanding technical passages are in the third movement, where nearly every section has scalar eighth-note passages at some point. The percussion section includes timpani, triangle, snare drum, bass drum, and suspended cymbal. *Angel Band* contains no unusually demanding articulations or extended techniques, and the overall writing is quite idiomatic.

Unit 5: Stylistic Considerations

The primary stylistic challenge of *Angel Band* will be to effectively represent the style and sprit of the hymn tunes in the instrumental setting. To this end, the conductor is strongly encouraged to study the original versions of the hymns, familiarizing himself/herself with the text of each hymn and discovering how Hartley has used the original material in his setting. Ideally the conductor should make the original versions readily available to students so they, too, can become familiar with the original source material. Additionally, students should have the opportunity to hear performances of hymns (several hymn recordings are included in Unit 8). The overall style of each movement will be determined by the content of the text. "Rainbow" celebrates the power and goodness of God and should be performed in a straightforward, energetic style. "Africa" deals with the idea of God as a source of comfort and mercy, and should be played reflectively and with great feeling. "Finale" describes a soul who joyfully anticipates being escorted to its immortal home by a company of angels, calling for a jubilantly brisk approach. Additionally, the conductor should discuss the texts of each hymn tune with students, asking for verbal and/or written responses on how the overall style and meaning of each hymn is represented in Hartley's setting.

Having the students sing the original hymns would be highly beneficial in developing an appropriate conception of balance and style. The ranges of the original hymn parts rarely exceed a sixth and contain much scalar and triadic motion, so students should be able to perform them with reasonable success. While proper balance and the projection of primary melodic material are major objectives in any composition, they are especially important issues in a piece rooted in vocal music. Because the composer freely borrows material from all parts of the original four-part settings, the conductor should make a thorough comparison of the original hymns with the instrumental setting, identifying borrowed material and determining from which vocal part it came. Material from the tenor (melody) line will take precedence over material borrowed from other parts of the original version. Singing the original hymns will also help students develop an appropriately lyrical approach to the instrumental setting.

Angel Band has an extremely wide dynamic range, from *ppp* to *fff*. Students will need to be reminded to play with good characteristic sounds at extremely loud and soft dynamic levels. The dynamic range of "Africa" spans from *ppp* to *p*, and the idea of playing an entire movement in such a soft dynamic range may be a difficult concept for students to grasp. The conductor may wish to demonstrate the powerful expressive possibilities of extremely soft playing through recordings. Works such as Samuel Barber's *Adagio*, Aaron Copland's *Appalachian Spring*, and Leonard Bernstein's *West Side Story* have appropriately soft passages to demonstrate this concept.

Finally, playing each movement at the proper tempo will be a crucial factor in achieving a truly convincing performance. This is especially so in "Africa," which will sound like a dirge if performed at a tempo slower than quarter note = 76, as indicated by Hartley.

Unit 6: Musical Elements

Angel Band provides many opportunities to expand students' knowledge of the fundamental elements of music and how they are used by a composer in creating a musical work. The presentation of these concepts within the context of a piece that is being prepared for performance should result in an enhanced knowledge of the primary elements of music and a more insightful performance. The conductor is encouraged to develop a comprehensive instructional approach emphasizing (1) the development of aural, conceptual, and analytical skills in conjunction with the sheer executive skills required to play a wind or percussion instrument and (2) the ability of each student to synthesize these skills in making informed, meaningful contributions to rehearsals and performances. A teaching/rehearsal plan that examines the fundamental elements of music (literally the "tools" of musical composition) and the way in which a composer uses these tools will foster an increased awareness and appreciation of the creative process, helping students to become better-informed music makers. The conductor may wish to incorporate the following suggestions in developing an instructional plan for *Angel Band*.

MELODY:

Begin rehearsal plans for *Angel Band* by introducing the scale materials used in the score. Students should be proficient in the concert keys of B-flat, E-flat, A-flat, D-flat, C, and F. Review the interval patterns for the major scale. Spell each major scale found in the score at concert pitch while students write the appropriate transposition for their instrument on staff paper. Hartley also writes passages in E-flat natural minor and F dorian in "Africa." Play the E-flat major scale followed by the E-flat natural minor scale, asking the students to aurally compare and contrast the two. Direct the students to listen to the difference between the major third and minor third, as well as the difference between the half step relationship between leading tone and tonic in major versus the whole step relationship between the subtonic and tonic in natural minor. Discuss the interval pattern of the natural minor scale, spelling the E-flat natural minor scale while students again write out the appropriate transposition for their instrument. Use the same procedure to present the dorian mode.

The melodic material of *Angel Band* provides a wealth of opportunities to develop skills in musicianship. The *legato*, cantabile melody of "Africa" would be an ideal example with which to begin teaching concepts in melodic playing and phrasing. This melody is presented at concert pitch in Example 1.

Example 1:

Demonstrate appropriate phrasing by playing or singing this melody, then have the students sing or play the melody in unison, paying attention to uniform observance of melodic contour, articulation, and breath points. Repeat the same procedure with the primary melodic material of "Rainbow" (Example 2) and "Finale" (Example 3). Both examples appear at concert pitch.

Example 2:

Example 3:

Ask the students to compare and contrast the phrase structure of the primary melodies. "Rainbow" (two six-measure phrases) and "Africa" (two seven-measure phrases) are somewhat unconventional, while "Finale" has a more predictable structure (three four-measure phrases). The first two measures of the second phrase of "Rainbow" are frequently presented as a motive in imitative texture, providing an opportunity to discuss imitation as a compositional device.

HARMONY:

Rehearsal plans should include discussions of harmonic progression, cadences, and modulation. *Angel Band* is based primarily on diatonic harmony, so begin by asking students to spell triads on each scale degree in B-flat major and E-flat major, the primary keys of the work. Play the diatonic triads at the keyboard and ask students to aurally identify the difference between the types of triads they hear (major, minor, diminished). Discuss the interval patterns of the triads, involving students in further triad spelling exercises. Referring back to the diatonic triads in B-flat major and E-flat major, introduce the appropriate Roman numeral symbols for each triad and explain that many pieces revolve around the primary triads (I, IV, V) in any key. Have the ensemble play the I, IV, and V triads in the key of B-flat major, then play the first six measures of "Rainbow" (which consists almost exclusively of those triads) to illustrate the primary chords in context.

It will also be necessary to discuss borrowed/altered chords. Example 4 is a reduction of measures 59 through 66 of "Rainbow," which makes extensive use of such chords.

Example 4:

Introduce Example 4 at the keyboard, asking students to aurally identify the difference between this progression and what they heard in the opening measures of "Rainbow." Provide a printed version of Example 4 and the diatonic triads in B-flat major for the students, discussing the differences between the two. Students should observe that Example 5 uses triads that are clearly outside the scope of ordinary diatonic triads in B-flat major. Discuss the use of altered chords as a means of achieving harmonic variety. Rehearse measures 59 through 66 slowly so students are able to establish an aural connection between the reduction and the "live" version.

Rehearsal plans should include an introduction to cadences and an examination of their function in *Angel Band*. Demonstrate the function of cadences as musical points of arrival, playing several types of cadences (authentic, half, plagal, deceptive) at the keyboard or having the ensemble play isolated cadences from warm-up chorales or actual pieces. Discuss the similarities between language and music, especially the parallel relationship between the sentence in language and the phrase in music. Explain that cadences are the punctuation marks of musical syntax, functioning like periods, commas, exclamation points, and question marks in language. Just as punctuation marks define sentences, cadences define musical phrases. Replay the cadences demonstrated previously, asking students to associate a punctuation mark with each cadence. If the students have trouble with this concept, guide them to the conclusion that authentic and plagal cadences generally sound like periods as they serve to close phrases, half cadences tend to sound like commas because they give the impression of being in mid-thought, and the unexpected resolution of deceptive cadences can sound like a question mark. Supply the Roman numeral formulas for each type of cadence, and explain that *Angel Band* has many authentic and half cadences. Note that "Africa" contains several plagal cadences; explain to students that this type of cadence is frequently used in hymn settings.

Rehearsal plans should also include an examination of modulation as a general concept and its practical application in *Angel Band*. Explain that modulation is one of a composer's primary tools in achieving variety and interest in a piece of music. Illustrate the concept by having the ensemble play measures 70 through 82 in "Finale." This is a sequence of three four-measure phrases in three different keys (F major, D-flat major, and C major). Ask the students if the passage would be as interesting if it were in only one key. Lead the students through a brief analysis of the various keys used in *Angel Band*, explaining that cadences and keys serve to define phrases and provide shape to the overall structure of any piece of music. "Rainbow" is primarily in B-flat major with a brief deviation to E-flat major in the middle of the movement. "Africa" begins in E-flat major, changing to E-flat minor and F dorian before returning to E-flat major. "Finale" has the most harmonic variety of the three movements, moving from its home key of B-flat major to episodes in A-flat major, F major, B-flat major, D-flat major, C major, and F major before returning to B-flat major.

RHYTHM:
Because the rhythms of *Angel Band* are well within the grasp of young players, the conductor should place special emphasis on perfecting the most fundamental rhythm issues: the maintenance of steady tempo and consistently accurate performance of recurring rhythm patterns within any piece. Since the rhythm patterns rarely exceed simple division of the beat ("Rainbow" and "Africa" each contain one pattern involving subdivision), begin by establishing a counting syllable system for the meter of each movement and

having the students count both the beat, division, and subdivision (for "Rainbow" and "Africa") of the beat to establish a consistent tempo concept for each movement. Point out that "Rainbow" and "Africa" are examples of simple meter (dividing the beat into two equal parts) while "Finale" is an example of compound meter (dividing the beat into three equal parts). Examples 5 ("Rainbow"), 6 ("Africa"), and 7 ("Finale") show counting syllables for the meter of each movement.

Example 5:

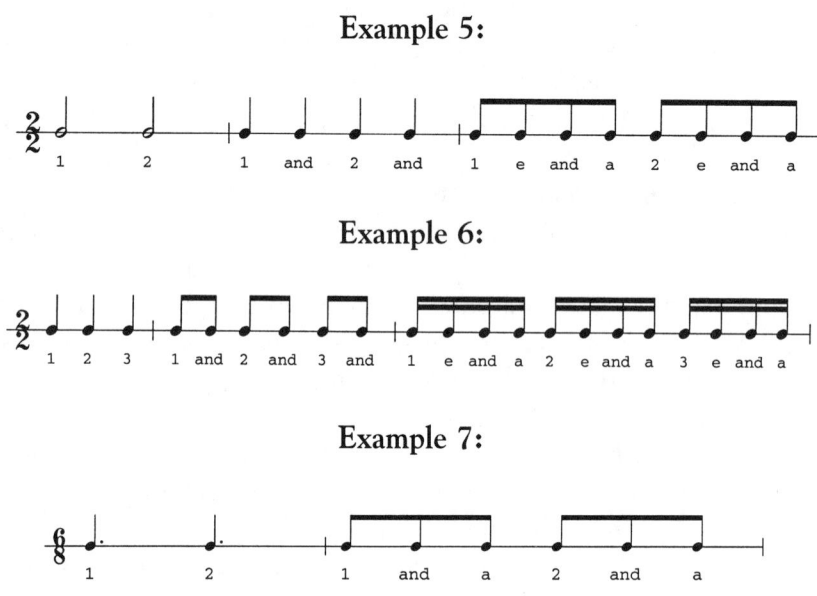

Obviously, exercises like Examples 5 through 7 can be performed in a variety of ways. The use of a metronome and sound system can be helpful in achieving consistent tempo, and assigning the beat to one group of students and the division to another can help to develop rhythmic independence. Clapping might serve as an additional reinforcement. Present the primary rhythm patterns of *Angel Band*, asking students to count these patterns based on the rhythm syllables introduced previously. The primary rhythm patterns are shown in Examples 8 and 8a ("Rainbow"), 9 ("Africa"), and 10 ("Finale").

Example 8:

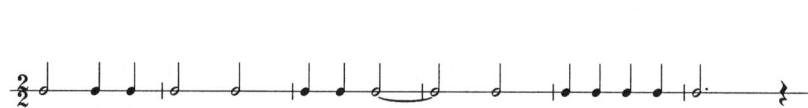

Example 8a:

Example 9:

Example 10:

TIMBRE

Rehearsal plans should emphasize the development of aural skills as they relate to balance, blend, and intonation. To fully realize the timbres intended by the composer, lead students in developing a large scale diagram of each movement that identifies (1) where thematic and accompanying lines occur and (2) which instruments or groups of instruments play them. After specific doublings have been identified, encourage students to blend individual sounds within their own section as well as other sections with which they share primary melodies or accompanying figures. The development of blending skills should eliminate many balance and intonation problems. Since "Africa" is the most transparently scored movement in *Angel Band*, introduce the idea of blending sounds by rehearsing any or all of the following passages:

Measures 3–9	hymn tune in 1st horn, 3rd clarinet 3
Measures 16–33	hymn tune in tuba, euphonium
Measures 37–44	hymn tune variant in bass reeds
Measures 45–51	hymn tune variant in piccolo, 1st flute, 1st clarinet
Measures 52–57	hymn tune variant in saxophone, bassoon, alto and bass clarinet

Work to achieve a blended sound within the individual sections in each passage before rehearsing multiple sections together.

Clearly the development of beautiful, characteristic wind and percussion sounds extends far beyond rehearsal plans for *Angel Band*. Students should have the opportunity to hear artist-level players as soloists, chamber musicians, and large ensemble members. The conductor is strongly encouraged to provide students with as many models as possible, either through live performances or recordings.

Unit 7: Form and Structure

MEASURE   EVENT AND SCORING

Movement 1: "Rainbow"

1–21	Initial presentation of hymn tune by trumpet, horn, upper woodwinds (Example 3); B-flat major established as tonal center
22–36	Second phrase of hymn tune presented in imitative texture by various sections; modulation to E-flat major
37–41	New melodic fragment in E-flat major presented by upper woodwinds
42–50	Second phrase of hymn tune presented in imitative texture by various sections
51–58	Fragment of first phrase of hymn tune presented by brass; second phrase of hymn tune in woodwinds; retransition to B-flat major
59–65	First phrase of hymn tune in brass (altered chord progression shown in Example 5), return of B-flat major as tonal center
66–83	Closing section; second phrase of hymn tune presented in imitative texture by various sections; movement concludes in B-flat major

Movement 2: "Africa"

1–2	Introductory chord establishes E-flat major as tonal center
3–9	First phrase of hymn tune (Example 2) presented in E-flat major by 1st/2nd horn and 3rd clarinet; countermelody in euphonium, bassoon, and alto clarinet
10–16	Phrase 2 of hymn tune presented in E-flat major by 1st clarinet

Measure	Event and Scoring
17–25	Phrase 1 variant presented in E-flat major by tuba, euphonium, and 1st trumpet
26–33	Phrase 2 divided between upper woodwinds and 1st trumpet; countermelody in euphonium and tuba; phrase concludes with plagal cadence in E-flat major
34–37	Phrase 1 presented in E-flat minor by 1st flute; countermelodies in 1st/2nd clarinet
38–44	Phrase 1 variant presented in E-flat minor by tuba and bass reeds; countermelody in 1st alto saxophone and oboe
45–51	Phrase 1 variant in E-flat major presented by piccolo, 1st flute, 1st clarinet; countermelody in 1st trumpet
52–57	Phrase 1 variant in F dorian presented by saxophone, bassoon, bass and alto clarinet
57–63	Retransition to E-flat major; phrase 1 variant presented by piccolo, flute, oboe, 1st clarinet, trumpet; movement concludes in E-flat major

Movement 3: "Finale"

Measure	Event and Scoring
1–10	Introductory section; establishes B-flat major as tonal center
11–21	Primary melodic material (Example 4) by 1st trumpet in B-flat major
22–37	Fragments of primary melodic material presented by various sections in B-flat major
38–51	New material introduced by trumpet and trombone, restated by horn; transition to new section
52–69	Variant of primary melodic material in A-flat major presented by trumpet, restated by upper woodwinds
70–77	Two sequential four-measure phrases in B-flat major and D-flat major, variant of primary melodic material in trumpet answered by quote of primary melodic material in low brass
78–81	New material in trumpet and upper woodwinds in C major
82–87	Retransition to B-flat major, scalar passages for woodwinds alone

MEASURE	EVENT AND SCORING
88–95	Variant of primary melodic material presented by 1st trumpet in B-flat major
96–107	Primary melodic material presented in original form by trumpet and trombone in B-flat major
108–115	Closing section in B-flat major

Unit 8: Suggested Listening

William Billings:
> *Africa, Chester,* and other hymns – The William Appling Singers, William Appling, conductor: New World Records NW80539

Walter Hartley:
> *Centennial Symphony* – Tokyo Kosei Wind Orchestra, Frederick Fennell, conductor: Kosei Publishing Company KOCD-3569
> *Concerto for 23 Winds* – Tokyo Kosei Wind Orchestra, Frederick Fennell, conductor: Brain Company Ltd. BOCD-7506
> *Hallelujah Fantasy* – ACC Heritage of America Band, Lowell Graham, conductor: USAF compact disc
> *Psalm for Strings* – Slovak Radio Symphony, Robert Black, conductor: MMC Recordings MMC 2002
> *Sinfonia No. 4* – Tokyo Kosei Wind Orchestra, Frederick Fennell, conductor: Kosei Publishing Company KOCD-3569

David Holsinger:
> *A Childhood Hymn*
> *On a Hymnsong of Lowell Mason*
> *On a Hymnsong of Philip Bliss*
> *On a Hymnsong of Robert Lowry*
> *On a Southern Hymnsong*
> *On an American Spiritual*
> Concordia University Wind Symphony and Kapelle Choir, Richard Fischer, conductor: Mark Recordings 1862-MCD

William Schuman:
> *Chester*
> *New England Triptych* (Be Glad Then, America, When Jesus Wept) Dallas Symphony Orchestra, Andrew Litton, conductor: Dorian Records DO 90224

Timothy Swan:
> *Rainbow* and other hymns – His Majestie's Clerkes, Paul Hillier, conductor: Harmonia Mundi HMV 907128
> *Balloon* and other hymns – The Boston Camerata, Joel Cohen, conductor: Erato #12711

Unit 9: Additional References and Resources

Dvorak, Thomas, Gary Ciepluch, and Robert Greschesky. *Best Music for High School Band: a selective repertoire guide for high school bands and wind ensembles*. Brooklyn, NY: Manhattan Beach Music, 1993.

eConcertBand.com website (Walter Hartley link): http://www.econcertband.com/band/hartley.html

Frederiksen, Brian. *Arnold Jacobs: Wind and Song*. Edited by John Taylor. Gurnee, IL: WindSong Press Limited, 1996.

Green, Elizabeth A. H. *The Conductor and His Score*. Englewood Cliffs, NJ: Prentice-Hall, 1975.

_____. *The Dynamic Orchestra: principles of orchestral performance for instrumentalists, conductors, and audiences*. Englewood Cliffs, NJ: Prentice-Hall, 1987.

Hartley, Walter, website: http://www.mindspring.com/~c_hartley

McGraw, Hugh, ed. *The Sacred Harp*. Bremen, GA: Sacred Harp Publishing Company, 1991.

Miles, Richard, ed. *Teaching Music through Performance in Band*, Volume 2. Chicago, IL: GIA Publications, 1998.

Sadie, Stanley, ed. *The New Grove Dictionary of Music and Musicians*. New York: Grove's Dictionaries, Inc., 2001.

Sindberg, Laura Kautz. "Concerts that Teach". *Teaching Music* 5, June 1998, p. 36.

Sigma Alpha Iota website (Walter Hartley link): http://www.sainational.org/phil/composers/whartley

Walker, William, ed. *The Christian Harmony*. Philadelphia, PA: Miller's Bible and Publishing House, 1873.

Musical examples used by permission of Southern Music Company, San Antonio, TX

Contributed by:

John Bleuel
Assistant Professor of Music
State University of West Georgia
Carrollton, Georgia

Musical examples generated by:

Thomas George Caracas Garcia
Assistant Professor of Music
State University of West Georgia
Carrollton, Georgia

Teacher Resource Guide

Black Canyon of the Gunnison
Frank Erickson
(1923–1996)

Unit 1: Composer

Frank Erickson was one of the best-known and respected professionals in the educational music industry because of the quality of his compositions for school bands. Erickson was born in Spokane, Washington, on September 1, 1923, and he began his studies of piano and trumpet while in elementary school. His first composition for band, *The Fall of Evening*, was composed during his final year in high school.

During World War II, Erickson served in the Army Air Corps as a weather forecaster, and he also arranged music for several Army bands. After the war, he worked for two years as a dance band arranger and then began his studies at the University of Southern California in 1948, where he studied with Mario Castelnuovo-Tedesco and Halsey Stevens. After earning his bachelor's and master's degrees, he taught at the University of California at Los Angeles and San Jose State College. Erickson also had a successful career as music editor for several publishers, including Bourne, Belwin, and G. Schirmer. In 1970, he organized Summit Publications and, in 1995, Frank Erickson Publications.

Erickson earned high regard for his compositions beginning in the 1950s with publication of his *Toccata for Band, Air for Band, Balladair,* and *Black Canyon of the Gunnison*. At the time of his death on October 21, 1996, he had more than five hundred publications, including three hundred original works for band. He was a member of the American Bandmasters Association; the American Society of Composers, Authors and Publishers; and the Academy of Wind and Percussion Arts. He was honored with a Life Membership in the

National Band Association and was the recipient of many awards, including the A. Austin Harding Award from the American School Band Directors Association.

Unit 2: Composition

Black Canyon of the Gunnison was written in 1954. This original composition is a musical portrait of the Gunnison River and its Black Canyon in Colorado. Erickson displays a very economical use of material in this work, as most of the melodic elements are found in the first few measures of the piece. His use of thick chords moving in parallel motion produces an expansive sound meant to describe the canyon. The use of chromaticism and whole-tone movement effectively convey the movement of the river. Erickson scored many open fifths, including a ten-measure section with an open fifth drone or pedal in the lower voices, which seems to be a reference to the open spaces of the Black Canyon. The principal tonalities are E-flat and B-flat major, but the use of mixolydian inflections is an important melodic and harmonic tool.

This piece, lasting six minutes and thirty seconds, is in three main sections and is 112 measures long. The technical demands of the piece would seem to indicate a grade three piece; however, the shifting tonalities and the resulting abundance of accidentals, do increase its level of difficulty somewhat.

Unit 3: Historical Perspective

Programmatic music has long enjoyed the favor of composers and audiences. This effective programmatic work gives us a musical picture of a unique and rugged area in western Colorado about 250 miles southwest of Denver. The Gunnison River rushes through the twelve miles of the Black Canyon, dropping quickly in a series of churning rapids. Within the Black Canyon, the Gunnison River drops an average of ninety-five feet per mile, which is one of the greatest rates of fall for any river in North America. The Black Canyon has dramatic sheer sides rising two thousand feet above the river, giving a spectacular view to park visitors.

The area known as the Black Canyon of the Gunnison became a National Monument on March 2, 1933, and a National Park on October 21, 1999.

Unit 4: Technical Considerations

The piece is scored for full concert band, but for only one part on flute, oboe, bassoon, alto saxophone, and horn. Percussion writing is quite sparse (only timpani, suspended cymbal, triangle, crash cymbal, and snare drum are required), and the parts require only moderate technical skill. It seems unusual that more extensive use of percussion was not made in this descriptive piece to help paint an aural image.

Solos are written for trumpet (highest note is written C on the staff) and trombone (highest written note is F above the staff). Ranges for all instruments are moderate: flute to G-sharp an octave above the staff, clarinet to D above the staff, oboe to C above the staff, trumpet to G-sharp just above the staff (briefly), and trombone to G above the staff.

While written primarily in E-flat major and B-flat major, the piece includes mixolydian inflections and occasional whole-tone allusions. Frequent use of accidentals and enharmonic writing are found throughout the piece, as well as basic syncopation. There are isolated instances of single 2/4 or 3/4 measures in the middle of large 4/4 sections. Erickson's jazz background clearly seems to have influenced this composition.

Unit 5: Stylistic Considerations

The music calls for accented, *legato*, and *staccato* styles of playing, which students should be able to define as well as perform. Requested styles and phrasing are carefully and clearly marked. The dynamic and stylistic changes indicated are essential for this programmatic piece.

Suggested educational strategies include teaching students the mixolydian scales used in the piece (C, A, and G) and pointing out their occurrence in the piece. Students will also find it helpful to know, and be able to identify (by ear and sight), whole-tone scales and scale fragments.

Unit 6: Musical Elements

MELODY:

Black Canyon of the Gunnison makes economic use of melodic material. The two principal themes and much of the transition material contain melodic elements found in the first few measures of the piece. After an introductory section, the first theme is presented by trumpet beginning in measure 21. The second theme is also presented by 1st trumpet beginning in measure 48.

HARMONY:

This piece makes use of major (E-flat and B-flat), mixolydian (C, A, and G), and lydian inflection at the end. Erickson uses some very interesting and unexpected chord movement in this programmatic piece. One interesting example is the last four measures, which move—as expected—from E-flat to A-flat, B-flat, A-flat, and then to B and A before arriving back at E-flat. The progression to the B major chord is not surprising because the chord is the enharmonic (C-flat) flat-sixth scale degree, a typical chromatic third relationship. However, the A major triad forms a tritone relationship with the impending tonic, a chord that represents the most remote relationship to E-flat major, and provides an interesting and unexpected ending.

RHYTHM:

This piece is not rhythmically complex. Using only 4/4, 3/4, and 2/4 meters, Erickson writes basic rhythmic patterns using whole notes to sixteenth notes. The primary syncopated figure is a basic eighth rest/quarter note/eighth note figure. Usually, that figure is fully articulated with a long and accented quarter note and a *staccato* eighth note.

TIMBRE:

Erickson uses all instruments in a variety of interesting and effective groupings. Musically depicting the changes in the river as it progresses through the Black Canyon, he alternates small groups with the full ensemble at a variety of dynamic levels.

Unit 7: Form and Structure

SECTION	MEASURE	EVENT AND SCORING
A		(in 4/4, with three isolated measures of 3/4)
	1–20	Slowly; introduction
	21–39	*Allegro*; first theme (based on the opening trumpet line) is presented and developed; section ends with a descent to B-flat through a succession of chords whose roots form a descending whole-tone scale
B		(in 4/4, with a single 2/4 measure)
	40–47	Slower; transition using references to the first theme and a hint of the second theme; presented over open fifths (B-flat and F) in lower voices
	48–59	*Allegro*; Theme 2 is presented by 1st trumpet, then used with the first theme
	60–91	*Allegro*; syncopated section using references to Theme 1
A		(in 4/4, with single 2/4 and 3/4 measures)
	92–116	Slowly; return to the first theme
	117–122	Slowly; coda

Unit 8: Suggested Listening
Samuel Adler, *Southwestern Sketches*
Timothy Broege, *Train Heading West and Other Outdoor Scenes*
Frank Erickson, *Sinfonia for Winds*
Ferde Grofe/Leidzen, "On the Trail" from *Grand Canyon Suite*
David Holsinger, *On the Grand Prairie Texas*

Unit 9: Additional References and Resources
Dvorak, Thomas L., Cynthia Crump Taggart, and Peter Schmaltz. *Best Music for Young Band*. Edited by Bob Margolis. Brooklyn, NY: Manhattan Beach Music, 1986.

Dvorak, Thomas L., Robert Grechesky, and Gary Ciepluch. *Best Music for High School Band*. Edited by Bob Margolis. Brooklyn, NY: Manhattan Beach Music, 1993.

Kreines, Joseph. *Music for Concert Band*. Tampa, FL: Florida Music Service, 1989.

National Band Association Selective Music List for Bands. Fourth edition. Nashville, TN: National Band Association, 1997.

Contributed by:
Lynn G. Cooper
Director of Bands
Asbury College
Wilmore, Kentucky

Teacher Resource Guide

Bouquets, Op. 87

Martin Mailman
(1932–2000)

Unit 1: Composer

Martin S. Mailman served on the College of Music faculty at the University of North Texas in Denton, Texas, for thirty-four years as Coordinator of Composition, Regents Professor of Music, and Composer-in-Residence. He served for two years in the United States Navy, was a Ford Foundation composer in Jacksonville, Florida, and was the first Composer-in-Residence at East Carolina University in Greenville, North Carolina. A composition student of Louis Mennini, Wayne Barlow, Bernard Rogers, and Howard Hanson, he earned his B.M., M.M., and Ph.D. degrees from the Eastman School of Music in Rochester, New York.

Mailman received numerous awards and grants for composition, which included two American Bandmasters Association/Ostwald prizes for composition (*Exaltations* in 1983 and *For Precious Friends Hid in Death's Dateless Night* in 1989), the National Band Association/Band Mans Company prize for composition (*For Precious Friends Hid in Death's Dateless Night* in 1989), and the Edward Benjamin Award (*Autumn Landscape* in 1955), a National Endowment for the Arts Composers Grant (1982), Composer of the Year (named by the Texas Music Educators Association in 1989), and the 1982 Queen Marie-Jose Prize for composition (*Concerto for Violin and Orchestra* in 1982). His more than one hundred works include chamber music, band, choral, and orchestral music, film scores, television music, an opera, and a requiem for chorus, orchestra, and soloists. He was a member and active supporter of ASCAP, MENC, Phi Mu Alpha Sinfonia, Pi Kappa Lambda, the American Bandmasters Association, and Sigma Alpha Iota.

A frequently sought-after clinician and teacher, Mailman served as guest conductor-composer at more than ninety colleges and universities across the United States and Europe. The impact of his music, teaching, and career is immeasurable. He was a leader in promoting comprehensive musicianship programs through MENC throughout his career and gave presentations at conventions and schools across the country. He passed away at his home in Denton, Texas, on Tuesday, April 18, 2000, at the age of sixty-seven. His last work, *Vocalise, Op. 99*, was premiered posthumously at the Sigma Alpha Iota National Convention in Dallas, Texas, on August 5, 2000.

Some of his other works for band include *Geometrics 1 for Band, Op. 22; Concertino for Trumpet and Band, Op. 31; Liturgical Music for Band, Op. 33; Geometrics 3 for Band, Op. 37; Geometrics 4 for Band, Op. 43; Association No. 1 for Band, Op. 45; Shouts, Hymns, and Praises, Op. 52; A Simple Ceremony: In Memoriam John Barnes Chance, Op. 53; Decorations for Band, Op. 54; Let Us Now Praise Famous Men, Op. 56; Geometrics 5 for Band, Op. 58; Night Vigil, Op. 66; Exaltations, Op. 67; The Jewel in the Crown, Op. 78; For Precious Friends Hid in Death's Dateless Night, Op. 80; Toward the Second Century, Op. 82; Concertino for Clarinet and Band, Op. 83; Concerto for Wind Orchestra (Variations), Op. 89; Secular Litanies, Op. 90;* and *Pledges, Op. 98*. Information on his extensive catalog, including publishers and availabilities, is handled by his son, Matthew.

Unit 2: Composition

Bouquets was composed in October 1991 in Denton, Texas. It was "Commissioned by and dedicated to The Colony High School Wind Symphony 1991–1992, Richard Clardy, director" and was premiered by them with the composer conducting on February 4, 1992, at The Colony High School in The Colony, Texas. The Colony High School Wind Symphony performed the work again at the 1994 Midwest Band and Orchestra Clinic in Chicago. The piece is a grade four+ difficulty (although listed here in Volume 4 as Grade three), lasts approximately eight minutes, and is published by Carl Fischer, Inc. (J734).

About his music, the composer wrote:

> While I do not mind making appropriate verbal remarks to perform-
> ers during a rehearsal of my music, I do find myself loathe to write or
> speak comments under other circumstances. I feel that if I have done
> my work as a composer properly, the music will not benefit from my
> words.
>
> I am reminded of the time when I was being interviewed by a
> reporter after the premiere of my *Concerto for Violin and Orchestra* in
> Geneva. She began the interview by telling me a wonderful story of
> her impression of my piece, then asking me if this was indeed my cre-

ative motivation for the work. It was not, but had I written whatever my thoughts about the work may have been, she would have never had the freedom to create her own rich imagery.

The work is not programmatic; rather, it is inspired by the word "bouquet." *Bouquets* sets a mood and deals with emotions and feelings that leave the power and impact in the *music* and not the referential external. Another example of a work for band of this ilk might be *Emblems* by Aaron Copland.

A "bouquet" [French, from Middle French, thicket, from Old North French *bosquet*, from Old French *bosc* forest – first appeared circa 1716] is defined as "a bunch of flowers fastened together in a bunch, a compliment, a distinctive and characteristic fragrance (as of wine), a subtle aroma or quality (as of an artistic performance or a piece of writing), or a medley of songs." Although there is no specific program, the title reflects the colorful collection of sounds that present a musical "bouquet." *It should be noted that on direct questioning on more than one occasion, Mailman refused to admit which definition of "bouquet" represented this piece but rather acknowledged that "bouquet" had several definitions!* Listed below are definitions of the word:

> bou•quet (noun)
> [French, from Middle French, thicket, from Old North French
> *bosquet*, from Old French *bosc* forest—more at BOSCAGE] –
> first appeared circa 1716]
>> 1 a : flowers picked and fastened together in a bunch : NOSEGAY
>> b : MEDLEY <~ of songs>
>> 2 : COMPLIMENT
>> 3 a : a distinctive and characteristic fragrance (as of wine)
>> b : a subtle aroma or quality (as of an artistic performance or a
>>   piece of writing)

> Synonyms:
>> bunch (n): bunch, nosegay, posy, garland, wreath, spray
>> scent (n): scent, fragrance, aroma, odor, smell

Unit 3: Historical Perspective

Mailman belongs to a generation of late twentieth century composers that includes Ron Nelson, John Barnes Chance, and Fisher Tull. He was one of the composers selected to participate in the Ford Foundation Contemporary Music Project, which was an important educational vehicle for several aspiring musicians. He was constantly in demand as composer, conductor, and clinician, and his works are highly respected (as is evidenced by his masterwork *For Precious Friends Hid in Death's Dateless Night* being the first composition to be awarded both the National Band Association/Band Mans Company Prize for Composition in December 1988, and the American

Bandmasters Association/Ostwald Prize for Composition in January 1989). Mailman was particularly intrigued by the compositional process and the concept of music as "organized sound with intent over time." *Bouquets* is one of Mailman's later band works.

Unit 4: Technical Considerations

While most of the parts are not technically difficult, the ensemble precision required makes this a challenging work for any level group. All instruments are required to play independently, and specific sections are frequently featured and exposed. The piece has no key signatures, so accidentals abound; however, the tonality seems to gravitate towards A-flat major. There are articulations of every kind. Contrasts and repetitions are vitally important, and the conductor must insist that they be played as written.

All instruments are essential; the work is scored for standard symphonic band instrumentation plus double bass (which is its own separate part—*not* a tuba doubling—and must be covered). Five percussionists are required, and the instruments used are timpani, glockenspiel, xylophone, marimba, vibraphone, triangle, bass drum, temple blocks, suspended cymbal, deep tom-tom, and gong.

When asked about the tempo, the composer answered, "Take it as slow as your ensemble can play it." The tempo, marked quarter note = 58, should be slow throughout, meaning the ensemble must maintain a consistent sense of purpose, line, and breath support for the entire piece, which can be a challenge for less-experienced groups. There are *fermatas* and *ritardandos*, as well as phrase build-ups, so there are opportunities to take liberties with the tempo and to create genuine interpretations. Because of the slow tempo, great patience on the part of both the conductor and the ensemble members is required for performance. Playing the piece too fast or in a hurried fashion utterly destroys the effect of the music.

The conductor and ensemble must have a clear conceptualization of the piece and its presentation to successfully perform the work since the piece does not "play itself"; however, good high school ensembles up to advanced ensembles will find this work accessible and rewarding.

Unit 5: Stylistic Considerations

Articulations should be as accurate as possible (see above). All markings in the score support this. The intensity and movement of the music should be equal to the phrasing, articulation, rhythms, and principles of the line. This is a twentieth century work with twentieth century sounds and also romantic impressions; it should be approached with an open-minded, omniscient, aesthetic interpretation.

The following instructions from the composer are included in the score:

The work will be most successfully performed with considerable freedom of tempo and real dynamic awareness, particularly in achieving and expressive soft dynamic level. The change of intent in measure 28 relies heavily on the fourth beat being a real contrast to the second beat separated by the *fermata*. Delayed downbeats in measures 35, 42, and 80 will be effective. Care to keep everything soft and clear from measure 70 with a gradual *crescendo* to the climax at measure 87 is most important.

Maintaining the *ff* volume level established at the beginning (and in other spots in the piece) is crucial. The dynamics must be maintained for several measures at a time. It can also be *very* difficult for younger groups to sustain a controlled *ff* with intensity and good sound for extended periods.

There are combinations of *legato* lines played against *staccato* accompaniments throughout the piece, so great effort to maintain the contrasting horizontal/vertical elements of the parts must be made. This is perhaps the greatest challenge in approaching this work.

Unit 6: Musical Elements

MELODY:

The opening features an extended *soli* with trumpet and trombone dramatically presenting the main theme. Adding the following lifts to trumpet and trombone can greatly improve ensemble precision: measure 5 after the first eighth note; measure 6 after beat 4; measure 8 after the half note; measure 10 after beat 4. The addition of ensemble lifts/breaths in sections similar to this one greatly enhances the vertical sense of the line; the composer not only approved of this but recommended it as well.

The second section of the piece features an extended poignant alto saxophone solo, which should be played as lyrically/horizontally as possible— a challenge given the very vertical accompaniment that should contrast the solo. The soloist absolutely must phrase the lines dynamically. The piccolo also has a substantial solo.

HARMONY:

The tonality seems to gravitate towards A-flat major. The harmony in general would be considered by most listeners to be "tonal." Triadic harmony exists throughout, although there are examples of tonal clusters (e.g., measures 17 through 22 in trumpet). The homophonic sections (measures 17 through 22, 91 through 93) must be performed with exact ensemble precision of articulation, note lengths, and balance. Lifts must be absolutely clean; isolating and repeatedly rehearsing these sections would be important.

RHYTHM:

There are six changes of meter, all either 3/4 or 4/4. Rhythms are not difficult in general. There are sections where tied notes must be carefully counted. Attention must be given to these spots (e.g., opening trumpet and trombone). All grace notes are to be performed on the beat.

TIMBRE:

There are many different colors presented in *Bouquets*, from upper woodwinds and percussion to the low instruments of the band. Identifying all of the colors required is essential for any conductor approaching this work. All colors are idiomatic for the instruments (bright flutes, "thuddy" tubas, etc.), so having the students play the instruments with the best quality and sound production, as well as replicating the composer's intent within specific sections, should also be stressed. The bright high sounds of the opening measures introduce the main thematic material and return at the climax near the end of the piece. Between these statements are lyrical lines that are contrasted with dry, rhythmic figures in the low instruments. *Bouquets* contains sections of fanfare-like depth, crystalline purity, and dream-like warmth, all of which drive towards a powerful conclusion. Conductors should endeavor to make students aware of the importance of all of these timbral qualities.

Unit 7: Form and Structure

SECTION	MEASURE	EVENT AND SCORING
A	1–3	Opening
	4–11	Theme 1 statement
	12–16	Opening motive
	17–22	Theme A variation with B section accompaniment
	23–28	Closing
B	29–34	Theme 2, statement 1; alto saxophone solo
	35–41	Theme 2, statement 2 (extended); alto saxophone solo
	42–54	Theme 2, statement 3; clarinet
	55–58	Climax and falling
	59–69	Brass chorale (homophonic)
	70–79	Gradual build; part 1 (use of points of imitation)
	80–86	Gradual build; part 2

Section	Measure	Event and Scoring
A	87–90	Climax; Theme 1 fragment
	91–93	Brass and low reeds chorale based on Theme 1 fragment and B section accompaniment
	94–96	Climax

Unit 8: Suggested Listening

Martin Mailman:

    A Simple Ceremony: In Memoriam John Barnes Chance, Op. 53

    Alarums for Band, Op. 27

    Association No. 1 for Band, Op. 45

    Concertino for Clarinet and Band, Op. 83

    Concertino for Trumpet and Band, Op. 31

    Concerto for Wind Orchestra (Variations), Op. 89

    Decorations for Band, Op. 54

    Exaltations, Op. 67

    For Precious Friends Hid in Death's Dateless Night, Op. 80

    Geometrics 1 for Band, Op. 22

    Geometrics 3 for Band, Op. 37

    Geometrics 4 for Band, Op. 43

    Geometrics 5 for Band, Op. 58

    Let Us Now Praise Famous Men, Op. 56

    Liturgical Music for Band, Op. 33

    Night Vigil, Op. 66

    Pledges, Op. 98

    Secular Litanies, Op. 90

    Shouts, Hymns, and Praises, Op. 52

    The Jewel in the Crown, Op. 78

    Toward the Second Century, Op. 82

Unit 9: Additional References and Resources

Baker, Theodore. "Mailman, Martin," *Baker's Biographical Dictionary of Musicians*. Sixth edition. Revised by Nicolas Slonimsky. New York: Schirmer Books, 1984.

Boonshaft, Peter Loel. "Band and Wind Ensemble Review – *Bouquets*." *The School Music News*, October 1995, p. 43.

Ewen, David. *A Comprehensive Biographical Dictionary of American Composers*. New York: G. P. Putnam & Sons, 1982.

Mailman, Martin. *Bouquets*, Op. 87 (score and parts). New York: Carl Fischer Music (J734), 1994.

Mailman, Martin. *Bouquets, Op. 87*. Dick Clardy and the Colony High School Wind Symphony. Compact disc "1994 Midwest Band and Orchestra Clinic Concert," Mark Custom Recordings MW94MCD-10, 1994.

Mailman, Martin. *Bouquets, Op. 87*. Joseph W. Herman and the Tennessee Technological University Symphony Band. Compact disc "1998 Carl Fischer Concert Band Sampler," CN-98085, 1998.

Mailman, Martin. *Bouquets, Op. 87*. Matthew Mailman and the Central Oklahoma Directors Association High School All-Region Honor Band. Compact disc "1997-1998 All Region Honor Bands," 1998.

Mailman, Martin. *Bouquets, Op. 87*. Matthew Mailman and the Oklahoma City University Symphonic Band. Compact disc "Memorials" (available through Matthew Mailman), 2000.

Mailman, Martin. *Bouquets, Op. 87*. Matthew Mailman and the Oklahoma City University Symphonic Band. Compact disc "Music of Martin Mailman, Volume 6: Late Band Works" (available through Matthew Mailman), 2000.

Mailman, Martin. *Bouquets, Op. 87*. Daniel Schmidt and the Mars Hill College Wind Symphony. Compact disc "Power & Glory," 1998.

Mailman, Martin. *Concertino for Clarinet and Band, Op. 83*. Matthew Mailman and the Oklahoma City University Symphonic Band, Patricia Card, clarinet. Compact disc "Martin Mailman – Concertino for Clarinet and Band, Op. 83" (available through Carl Fischer), 1997.

Mailman, Martin. *For Precious Friends Hid in Death's Dateless Night, Op. 80*. Eugene Corporon and the University of North Texas Wind Symphony. Compact disc "Dialogues and Entertainments," KCD-11083, 1997.

Mailman, Martin. *Geometrics No. 4, Op. 43*. Compact disc "Warner Brothers Music for Concert Band Symphonic Band Series," CATCD95-4, 1998.

Mailman, Martin. Interview by Matthew Mailman, 18 January 1999.

Mailman, Martin. *Liturgical Music, Op. 33*. Jack Stamp and the Indiana University of Pennsylvania Symphony Band. Compact disc "IUP Concert Bands of 1998," 1998.

Mailman, Martin. *Secular Litanies, Op. 90*. Jack Stamp and the Indiana University of Pennsylvania Wind Ensemble. Compact disc "IUP Concert Bands – 1996," 1996.

Mailman, Matthew. Unpublished personal files. Oklahoma City, OK.

Miles, Richard, ed. "Martin Mailman – *Exaltations, Op. 67.*" *Teaching Music through Performance in Band*, Volume 2. Chicago: GIA Publications, Inc., 1997, pp. 442–6.

Miles, Richard, ed. "Martin Mailman – *For Precious Friends Hid in Death's Dateless Night, Op. 80.*" *Teaching Music through Performance in Band*, Volume 3. Chicago: GIA Publications, Inc., 2000, pp. 259–62.

Miles, Richard, ed. "Martin Mailman – *Liturgical Music, Op. 33.*" *Teaching Music through Performance in Band*, Volume 1. Chicago: GIA Publications, Inc., 1997, pp. 259–262.

Miles, Richard, ed. "Martin Mailman – *Secular Litanies, Op. 90.*" *Teaching Music through Performance in Band*, Volume 3. Chicago: GIA Publications, Inc., 2000, pp. 413–8.

National Band Association Selective Music List for Bands.

Rehrig, William H. *The Heritage Encyclopedia of Band Music*. Westerville, OH: Integrity Press, 1991.

Speck, Frederick. "Analysis: Martin Mailman's *For Precious Friends Hid in Death's Dateless Night.*" Journal of Band Research. Volume 26/I/Fall 1990, pp. 14–29.

Contributed by:
Matthew Mailman
Director of Bands and Associate Professor of Music
Oklahoma City University
Oklahoma City, Oklahoma

Teacher Resource Guide

Candide Suite
Leonard Bernstein

(1918–1990)

adapted by Clare Grundman

(1913–1996)

Unit 1: Composer

Leonard Bernstein is arguably one of the most famous American composers of the twentieth century. While probably most widely known for his score to *West Side Story*, his contributions to music and music education are many and varied. He is recognized as a composer, conductor, pianist, and music educator.

A significant segment of Bernstein's compositional output is dramatic or theatrical, beginning with incidental music for Aristophanes' play "The Birds" in 1938. The ballet *Fancy Free* (1944); the musicals *On the Town* (1944), *Wonderful Town* (1953), and *West Side Story* (1957); the film score *On the Waterfront* (1954); and the comic operetta *Candide* (1956) all speak to his success with an affinity for dramatic works. Most of Bernstein's compositions have a vocal or dramatic basis.

Bernstein was born in Lawrence, Massachusetts on August 25, 1918, to Russian immigrants. Although not a rabbi, his father was a practicing Jew from a long line of rabbis, which may provide the basis for Bernstein's natural affinity for teaching. Bernstein began his formal musical training through piano lessons at the age of ten. He later studied with Walter Piston at Harvard and with Randall Thompson and Fritz Reiner at the Curtis Institute. In 1942, he was assistant conductor to Serge Koussevitsky at Tanglewood and in 1943 was made assistant conductor to Artur Rodzinski, the music director of the New York Philharmonic Orchestra. Bernstein became the first American-born music director of the New York Philharmonic in 1958, a post he held until 1969 when he decided to concentrate on composing, lecturing, and guest conducting.

As a pianist, Bernstein was a dynamic performer. However, his composition and conducting overshadow this area. In addition, he used the piano as an important tool in every aspect of his musical life, including his work as an educator. While this was not surprising or particularly innovative, his use of television as a medium was. He produced programs that provided insight into music while remaining accessible to children and adults alike. Probably the most famous and controversial presentations were the Charles Eliot Norton Lectures at Harvard (1973–1974), during which he advocated tonality over the twelve-tone method.

In the later part of his life, Bernstein suffered from progressive emphysema and chronic pleurisy. He died of a heart attack in New York City on October 14, 1990.

Unit 2: Composition

Clare Grundman includes the following in the full score of *Candide Suite*:

> This Suite for concert band is made up of five numbers from the musical *Candide*, which premiered on Broadway in 1956. The satiric novella Candide by Voltaire was the basis for a political and musical satire, with a libretto by Lillian Hellman and music by Leonard Bernstein. *Candide* as a musical has since had many reincarnations, but the sections of this *Suite* utilize musical numbers that have remained virtually unchanged from the original Broadway production.

1. "The Best of All Possible Worlds"
   Doctor Pangloss, Voltaire's satirical portrait of the philosopher Gottfried von Leibnitz, tutors his Westphalian pupils (Candide and Cunegonde among them) in the finer points of optimism, refined by a classical education. The music alternately enjoins the pupil's responses with Pangloss's pedantic, free-associative explanations that the ills of this world are somehow all for the best. The refrain is, of course, that this is the best of all possible worlds.

2. "Westphalia Chorale and Battle Scene"
   The devout Westphalians sing a chorale praising the integrity of their homeland, after which they are massacred by the invading Bulgarian army. The "Battle Scene" adroitly juxtaposes major and minor modes of material familiar from the *Overture*.

3. "Auto-da-fe" (What a Day)
   Candide and Doctor Pangloss find themselves in Lisbon where, being free thinkers (and optimists), they are prosecuted as heretics by the

Spanish Inquisition. The handling of heretics was meant to prevent earthquakes, and the joyous music depicts the happy crowd celebrating their deliverance. However, the earthquake happens anyway, and Candide and Doctor Pangloss escape.

4. "Glitter and Be Gay"
Cunegonde, Candide's true love, has become the reigning madam in Paris, France. In a parody of "Jewel Songs" (such as that in Gounod's *Faust*), she sings of how she endeavors to maintain a brilliant, carefree exterior, while she may (or may not) be tortured inwardly by self-doubt.

5. "Make Our Garden Grow"
At the conclusion of the musical, and of Voltaire's novella, Candide realizes that the only purpose of living is to cultivate the earth and to create a garden. He enjoins the others to assist him in bringing things to life, and even Cunegonde proposes to bake a loaf of daily bread. Optimism is transformed into practical necessity, and the entire cast of characters join in a hymn full of hope.

Unit 3: Historical Perspective

Candide was composed and first produced in 1956. It had a relatively short initial run on Broadway followed by similarly short and monetarily unsuccessful runs in Boston and London (1957). The production was revived in the early 1970s with limited success.

Candide was billed as a "comic operetta" in a time when the Broadway musical was flourishing. Jerome Kern's classic *Show Boat*, originally produced in 1927, was revived by the New York City Opera in 1954. Rogers and Hammerstein were busy producing memorable shows, including *South Pacific* (1949), *The King and I* (1951), and *The Sound of Music* (1959). In addition, *My Fair Lady* by Lerner and Loewe, based on George Bernard Shaw's *Pygmalion,* had an unprecedented first run of 2,717 performances in 1956.

In an age of light-hearted musical comedy, *Candide* was anything but light-hearted. Lillian Hellman, Bernstein's collaborator, had adapted Voltaire's original work with a particular slant that reflected her experience with the McCarthy anti-Communism campaign of the early 1950s. However, somewhat paradoxically, Bernstein's music is viewed as more reflective of Voltaire's original concept with more of a "best of all possible worlds" feel.

This suite was adapted for concert band by Grundman in 1993 from Bernstein's original score. There are also two orchestra suites (*Suite for Orchestra from Candide* arranged by Charlie Harmon, 1998, and *Candide Suite* arranged by John Mauceri, 1973), but they are related to Grundman's adaptation only in that they use the same original material by Bernstein. In addition, two arrangements of the *Overture to Candide* are available for concert band, one by Walter Beeler (1962) and the other by Clare Grundman (1986).

Unit 4: Technical Considerations

The major technical demands in *Candide Suite* fall in the categories of articulation, rhythm, and independence of line. Rapid, articulated passages form the basis for much of the energy and forward motion in this suite, particularly "Auto-Da-Fe." Much of the rhythmic content is based on the half note as the pulse. Changing meter, while not particularly difficult due to the nature of the melodies, which flow easily through the meter changes, could prove problematic for less-experienced ensembles. Solos and lines requiring independence are prominent and important in this piece. In the final movement, "Make Our Garden Grow," the melody is presented by solo English horn, and while the part is cued in the oboe and piccolo lines, English horn is preferable to any substitution. In addition, the "Battle Scene" ends with a very exposed, soloistic section in the woodwinds, and "Auto-Da-Fe" includes rhythmic complexities (see Figure 7) that require independence. Similar to the changing meter issue, the key relationships could be problematic for less-experienced ensembles, but they should not be a problem for more advanced ensembles.

Unit 5: Stylistic Considerations

The most important thing to keep in mind when preparing this work is that it is based upon themes that reflect text and action in a comic operetta. The theatrical nature of the material must be obvious to the listener. The energy and forward motion of the fast movements, especially "Battle Scene," "Auto-Da-Fe," and "Glitter and Be Gay," should be in stark contrast to the reflective "Westphalia Chorale" and "Make Our Garden Grow." The feeling of optimism inherent in the text of "The Best of All Possible Worlds" and "Glitter and Be Gay" must be strong in spite of the lack of text in this setting. The tempo indications, articulations, and phrasing both indicate and support the composer's desires for the original theatrical production. A rather flamboyant interpretation and performance is appropriate. The "Westphalia Chorale" is the only place where there is some possibility of ambiguity. The use of minimal stylistic indicators demonstrates an expectation that the ensemble will interpret this section in traditional chorale style.

Unit 6: Musical Elements

MELODY:

The most familiar melodies in this suite are those that are also found in the popular *Overture to Candide*, including thematic material found in Figures 1, 4, 5, and 9. The trills in Figure 1 must begin with a solid accent as indicated, and the *marcato* accents in Figure 4 must occur on the beat and not on the grace note. Similarly, in Figure 9, the accent in the third measure is important as it reinforces the composer's desire that the final eighth note be tongued and, thereby, highlight the syncopation.

In the early thematic material in the "Battle Scene" (Figure 3), there must be obvious space between the *staccato* notes, but they must not be so short as to lose pitch. In addition, the accents (measure 5) are highlighted with *sfz*, which must be very strong. In contrast, the horn melody in Figure 5 must be more tuneful yet strong and *crescendo* through the repeated figure in the last three measures.

The melodies that reflect the optimistic nature of the characters are found in "The Best of All Possible Worlds" and "Glitter and Be Gay." In each of the examples (Figures 2 and 8, respectively), the thematic material consists of *staccato* segments with longer notes interspersed to provide a dance-like feel. These melodies must be performed with a light tongue and a slight bounce. They should not be straight and machine-like. "Auto-Da-Fe" has a segment (Figure 6) that should be performed in a similar manner but with greater intensity.

The most tuneful melody in the suite is found in the final movement, "Make Our Garden Grow" (Figure 10). The English horn soloist must feel free to be expressive, and the ensemble must carry through with that same expressiveness as the performers enter with the melody or supporting material.

Harmony:

The harmonic language is interesting but not experimental or unusual, especially for the period in which the original work was written. Experimentation with new sounds and new approaches was common, but Bernstein chose to espouse tonality. The places of primary concern harmonically are the noted key changes at measures 10 and 29 in the "Westphalia Chorale and Battle Scene," measure 60 in "Auto-Da-Fe," measures 20 and 28 in "Glitter and Be Gay," and measures 6, 27, and 46 in "Make Our Garden Grow." The transitions at these points must be given appropriate attention by both performer and conductor. The key relationships are all logical, but some of the keys are not typical "band" keys (e.g., E-flat minor, A major, and E major). Work with scales in these "unusual" keys and attention to key signatures (i.e., observing and verbalizing the names of the sharps or flats in the key signature) may be necessary with less-experienced ensembles.

Rhythm:

The rhythmic content is based primarily on the half note as the pulse. Performers must be capable of playing a true cut-time feel and not merely a fast four. Changing meter, while not particularly difficult due to the nature of the melodies that flow easily through the meter changes, could prove problematic for less-experienced ensembles. All performers, especially those who do not have the melody, must concentrate on the shape and content of the melody rather than the meter; otherwise, the flow and forward motion could be compromised.

The most difficult rhythmic content occurs in "Auto-Da-Fe" at measure 27 (Figure 7). The triplet must be strong and accurate. It is likely that less-experienced performers will rush the triplet. Clapping exercises can be helpful here. For example, while maintaining a metronome click for the downbeat of each measure, performers might first clap a steady two beat, stop, initiate a three beat, stop, return to the two beat, and segue into the three beat. Once the ability to change has been perfected, it is important to monitor the opposing rhythms that are performed simultaneously (e.g., upper woodwinds on the top line of Figure 7 versus lower woodwinds and brass on the bottom line). One may try to follow the other. It is important that both groups focus on the conductor and maintain their own subdivision.

TIMBRE:

Bernstein uses timbre masterfully, and Grundman is true to Bernstein's original intent in his adaptation. He never allows the ear to become bored. The suite opens with the same fanfare that opens the familiar *Overture to Candide*, which is primarily brass versus woodwinds. This is followed with a statement of the melody by muted solo trumpet and muted solo trombone. The woodwinds then take the second portion of the theme (indicated as "Theme B" below), which is followed by the return of introductory material. This kind of constant timbral evolution is typical of the entire suite. While all of the movements are beautifully orchestrated to take advantage of the variety of colors available in the ensemble, "Make Our Garden Grow" has the most striking timbral elements with the opening melodic statement performed by solo English horn, which is blended with solo flute for the second statement and then gives way to clarinet and piccolo. Performers must not be timid. Often changes in timbre are drastic and quick. This is intentional and desirable.

Figure 1: The Best of All Possible Worlds

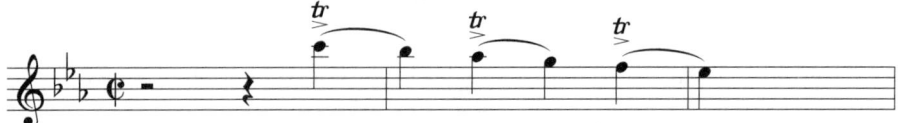

Figure 2: The Best of All Possible Worlds

Figure 3: Battle Scene

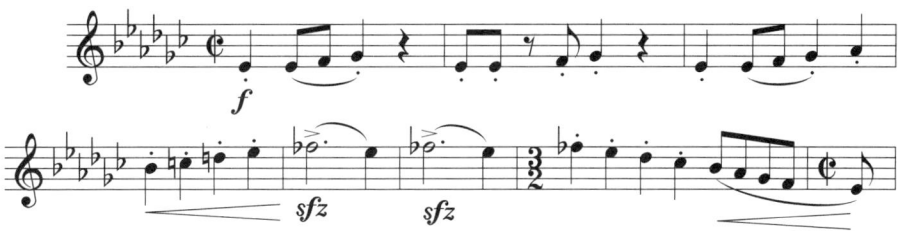

Figure 4: Battle Scene

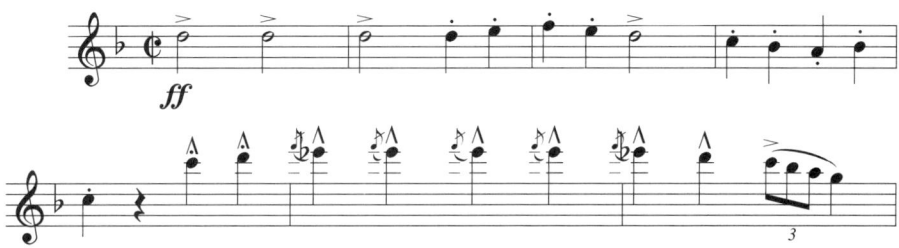

Figure 5: Battle Scene

Figure 6: Auto-Da-Fe (What a Day)

Figure 7: Auto-Da-Fe (What a Day)

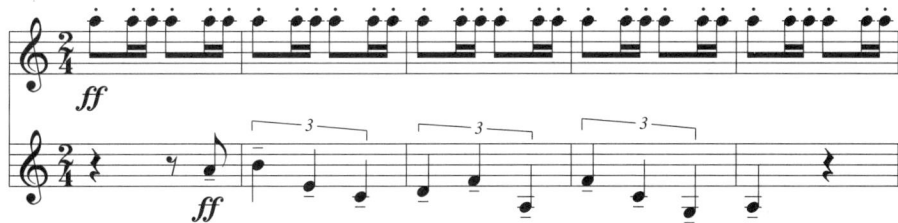

Figure 8: Glitter and Be Gay

Figure 9: Glitter and Be Gay

Figure 10: Make Our Garden Grow

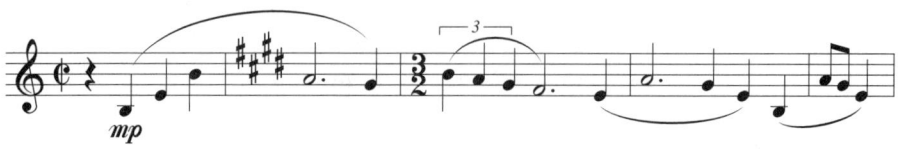

Unit 7: Form and Structure

The form of nearly all of these movements and the thematic structures are based on or are the result of vocal texts.

SECTION	MEASURE	EVENT AND SCORING
"The Best of All Possible Worlds" (E-flat major) Opening/		
introductory material	1–7	Full ensemble
	1–4	Brass fanfare
	5	Woodwind cascade (Figure 1)
	6–7	Vamp
Theme	8–31	
Theme A (Figure 2)	8–15	Trumpet and trombone
Theme B	16–23	Woodwinds
Opening/		
introductory material	32–38	Full ensemble
	32–35	Brass fanfare
	36	Woodwind cascade (Figure 1)
	37–38	Vamp
Theme	39–54	
Theme A (Figure 2)	39–46	Clarinet and trombone
Theme B	47–54	Piccolo, flute, and trumpet
Opening/		
introductory material	55–60	Full ensemble
	55–58	Brass fanfare
	59	Woodwind cascade (Figure 1)

SECTION	MEASURE	EVENT AND SCORING
	59–60	Vamp
Transition	61–70	Clarinet with bassoon
	71	Woodwind cascade (Figure 1)
	72–73	Vamp
Theme	74–89	
Theme A (Figure 2)	74–81	Clarinet, trumpet, and trombone
Theme B	82–89	Flute, oboe, and trumpet
	90–102	Development of woodwind cascade
	103–110	Climax; full ensemble
	111	Woodwind cascade (Figure 1)
Coda	112–119	Full ensemble

"Westphalia Chorale and Battle Scene" Chorale
(B-flat major)

	1–9	Four two-measure statements alternating woodwind/brass /woodwind/brass with a culminating full ensemble statement

Battle Scene
(E-flat minor/D minor)   10–75

Transition	10–11	Full ensemble
A (Figure 3)	12–18	Clarinet, saxophone, and trumpet
A (Figure 3), extended	19–28	Clarinet, saxophone, and trumpet
Transition	29–32	Full ensemble
B (Figure 4)	33–44	Brass/upper woodwinds
B (Figure 4)	45–50	Brass/upper woodwinds
C (Figure 5, begins at m. 53)	51–57	Horn
Coda	58–75	Woodwinds (soli/solo)

"Auto-Da-Fe" (What a Day)
(A minor/A major)

A	1–6	Bassoon, trumpet, and trombone
B (Figure 6)	7–13	Flute and clarinet
A	14–19	Clarinet, saxophone, bassoon, trumpet, and trombone
B (Figure 6)	20–26	Horn and trombone

SECTION	MEASURE	EVENT AND SCORING
C (Figure 7)	27–35	Horn with bassoon and saxophone
Transition	36–41	Woodwinds/brass/ woodwinds/brass/full ensemble
D	60–69	Solo cornet
D	70–77	Trumpet, saxophone, and trombone
Coda	78–89	Trumpet and baritone

"Glitter and Be Gay"
(C minor/C major/A-flat major)

Introduction	1–4	English horn solo
	5–19	English horn and flute/oboe duet
A (Figure 8)	20–28	Trumpet
Transition	29–35	Upper woodwinds/trumpet
B (Figure 9)	36–45	Flute and oboe
B (Figure 9)	46–53	Flute and oboe in canon with trumpet
B (Figure 9)	54–60	Flute and clarinet in canon with saxophone and horn/ baritone
C	61–68	Trumpet, horn, flute, and bassoon
C	69–76	Trumpet, horn, baritone, flute, bassoon, English horn, and clarinet
C	77–84	Trumpet, horn, baritone, flute, bassoon, English horn, clarinet, oboe
Transition	85–92	Woodwinds vs. brass
Development of B (Figure 9)	93–114	Woodwinds with horn and baritone
Coda	115–127	Full ensemble

"Make Our Garden Grow"
(E major/A-flat major/C major)

Introduction	1–5	Flute, clarinet, bassoon, harp
Theme (Figure 10)	5–16	English horn
Transition – theme with introductory material	17–26	English horn with flute
Theme (Figure 10)	26–38	Clarinet and piccolo

SECTION	MEASURE	EVENT AND SCORING
Coda based on theme (Figure 10)	39–57	Full ensemble; shortened version of the theme is employed to blend with the text, and the suite ends exactly as the operetta does

Unit 8: Suggested Listening

Leonard Bernstein:
> *Candide* (comic operetta, 1956, or final revised version, 1989)
> *Candide Suite* (band, adapted by Grundman, 1993)
> *Candide Suite* (orchestral, arr. by Mauceri, 1977)
> *On the Town* (musical, 1944)
> *Overture to Candide* (band, arr. by Beeler, 1962)
> *Overture to Candide* (band, arr. by Grundman, 1986)
> *Overture to Candide* (orchestral)
> *Suite for Orchestra from Candide* (arr. by Harmon, 1998)
> *West Side Story* (musical, 1957)
> *West Side Story: Symphonic Dance Music* (band, arr. by Polster, 1980)

George Gershwin, *Porgy and Bess* (opera/musical, 1935)

Unit 9: Additional References and Resources

Baker, Theodore. *Baker's Biographical Dictionary of Musicians*. Eighth edition. Revised by Nicolas Slonimsky. New York: Schirmer Books, 1992.

Bernstein, Leonard. *Candide: A Comic Operetta in Two Acts*, full score. New York: Jalni Publications, 1994.

Bernstein, Leonard. *Candide: A Comic Operetta Based on Voltaire's Satire*, vocal score. New York: Amberson Enterprises, Inc., 1958.

Bernstein, Leonard. *Candide Suite*, adapted by Clare Grundman, full band score. New York: Leonard Bernstein Music Publishing Company LLC, 1993.

Bernstein, Leonard. *Findings*. New York: Simon and Schuster, 1982.

Burton, Humphrey. *Leonard Bernstein*. New York: Doubleday, 1994.

Chase, Gilbert. *America's Music: From the Pilgrims to the Present*. Revised third edition. Chicago: University of Illinois Press, 1992.

Miles, Richard, ed. *Teaching Music through Performance in Band*, Volume 1. Chicago: GIA Publications, Inc., 1997, pp. 341–4.

Myers, Paul. *Leonard Bernstein*. London: Phaidon Press Limited, 1998.

Peyser, Joan. *Bernstein: A Biography-Revised & Updated.* New York: Billboard Books, 1998.

Rehrig, William. *The Heritage Encyclopedia of Band Music.* Edited by Paul E. Bierley. Westerville, OH: Integrity Press, 1991, 1996.

Sadie, Stanley, ed. *The New Grove Dictionary of Music and Musicians.* London: Macmillan, 2001.

Contributed by:
John A. Lychner
Western Michigan University
Kalamazoo, Michigan

Teacher Resource Guide

Concord

Clare Grundman
(1913–1996)

Unit 1: Composer

Clare Ewing Grundman was born on May 11, 1913, in Cleveland, Ohio. He received a Bachelor of Science in Education from The Ohio State University in 1934 and returned for his Master of Arts degree in 1937. During the interim three years, Grundman served as an instrumental music teacher at public schools in Kentucky and Ohio. He received his master's degree from The Ohio State University in 1939 and continued there as an instructor of orchestration, bands, and woodwinds until 1941 when he left to study with Paul Hindemith. Grundman credited Manley R. Whitcomb, Director of Bands at The Ohio State University at the time, with first encouraging him to write for bands. It was Hindemith, at the Berkshire Music Centery in New Lenox, Massachusetts, who provided Grundman with the practical techniques for composition. During World War II, he served as chief musician in the U.S. Coast Guard. After the war, Grundman began to achieve recognition for his compositions. He wrote scores and arrangements for all of the major radio and television networks, motion pictures, ballet, and Broadway musicals. The Edwin Franco Goldman Memorial Citation, the Academy of Wind and Percussion Arts Award, and the Midwest International Band and Orchestra Clinic Medal of Honor were among his many awards, along with awards from the American Bandmasters Association and the National Band Association.

Grundman wrote over seventy compositions for student ensembles that serve as excellent teaching pieces. These works are notable among his band compositions, as he drew on folk and popular melodies for their inspiration. In addition to his many works for band suitable for inexperienced instrumentalists, Grundman also composed, orchestrated, or arranged works that demand the technical and musical maturity of professional performers.

Unit 2: Composition

Concord, composed in 1987, was the result of a commission by the United States Marine Band, conducted by Colonel John Bourgeois. The piece, dedicated to Bourgeois and the Marine Band, received its first performance on July 21, 1987, at the Third Conference of the World Association of Symphonic Bands and Ensembles in Boston, Massachusetts. The work, approximately five minutes in length, includes "three traditional tunes from old New England: *The White Cockade*, William Billings's *America*, and *Yankee Doodle*," according to Grundman's program notes. Each part of the medley has a unique character, while the overall work is organized in the fast–slow–fast manner. As in his four-part *American Folk Rhapsodies*, Grundman provides fresh and interesting treatments to familiar melodies that are an integral part of American history and have continued to be performed to this day. Interdisciplinary opportunities that enhance this work are combining with geography and social studies. Grundman was a master at orchestration, and *Concord* is no exception. The tessituras are more demanding than *American Folk Rhapsodies* and *Kentucky 1800*, but extensive doubling allows this piece to work for most grade three ensembles. What the conductor should particularly consider is the ability of the ensemble's piccolo to perform an extended solo (although not necessarily difficult), exposed field drum work, bassoon and oboe solos, and a baritone part that reaches B-flat4 (which is doubled by the horns).

Unit 3: Historical Perspective

Each of the tunes in the *Concord* medley provide historical departures that allow students insight into music in the early United States and the roots of American folk tunes. *The White Cockade* was quite popular during the American Revolution, and the term "white cockade" allows for several related, non-musical references. Along with the term "blue blood," "white cockade" is traced to the Middle Ages, with the color white being associated with purity. Cockade came from the Old French word for vain or cocky, "coquarde." The word "cocky" applies nicely to the piccolo solo in *Concord*. During the Jacobite rebellion in Scotland, just prior to the American Revolution, supporters of Bonnie Prince Charlie wore a white cockade to identify themselves. Later, France divided into the red cockades camp and the white cockades camp, with the latter group supporting the French monarchy. The tune *The White Cockade* is found as an old Celtic jig that, during the American Revolution, was an oft-performed fife-and-drum marching song.

Grundman's identification and use of William Billings also lend insight into his approach to the center section of *Concord* and musical forms adopted for the entire piece. Billings, who was one of the first American composers to emphasize a creative independence, published *The New England Psalm-Singer*. He established a distinctive religious music, termed "Yankee hymnody," identified by angular melodies and open fifths that were uncommon in the current, European tradition. Grundman constructs the middle section of *Concord* similar to a favorite Billings's form, the fuguing tune, which is a four-part piece that began like a hymn and ended like a round.

The final part of the medley, *Yankee Doodle*, is another old fife-and-drum tune that was a favorite during the Revolution. An English Army surgeon, Dr. Richard Schuckburgh, wrote the words to the American version during the French and Indian War in 1755 to ridicule untrained American troops. The tune was often sung by American troops when going into battle, and it was performed as the British left after Yorktown. Grundman uses the melody of the tune as motive material for thematic development.

Unit 4: Technical Considerations

Concord is programmable for a very good grade three ensemble. The key signatures are not an issue, as the work begins in the key of C major and continues through the first complete statement of "The White Cockade." The full ensemble moves into B-flat major with a return to C major when returning to the piccolo solo. The lyrical middle section continues around the C key signature. In the final section, Grundman moves to E-flat concert when he works around the bridge, so the pedal is on A-flat. Accidental recognition in the transition to B-flat is particularly important. Accidentals provide the harmonic contrast for motives in the final section, although the key signature and resolution is in B-flat. Grundman uses open fifth and fourth intervals a great deal and exploits tetrachords moving from the fifth and fourth for motivic material.

The instrumentation is traditional, requiring no special instruments outside of the normal symphonic band. While there are parts for string bass and E-flat clarinet, those parts double others throughout the piece. In terms of range, Grundman pushes the grade three envelopes on several instruments, which will have to be addressed. Range and instrumentation considerations include flutes to B-flat6 and oboes to C6, 1st clarinet to G6 and 2nd clarinet to C6, 1st cornet /1st trumpet to C5, 2nd cornet to C5, horn in F to F5, trombone to F4, and baritone to B-flat4. The section that has the baritone going to B-flat4 is a unison double of the entire horn section. Two possible solutions are rewriting the baritone down an octave or having the baritone double the third trombone part in that section. A prominent percussion section makes *Concord* work well for larger ensembles and uses bells, triangle, snare drum, field drum, bass drum, xylophone, chimes, and cymbals.

Tempo markings include *Alla marcia, Moderato, Broadly, Vigorously and very rhythmic, Poco meno mosso, ma marcato,* and *Tempo di prima.* Time signatures include 2/4, 3/4, and 7/8. The work in the 7/8 sections is made easier through rhythmic motifs reinforced throughout the ensemble. Once patterns are established, students find fitting parts in to be relatively simple. However, the countermelody at measure 201 in horn and baritone will require a good amount of counting independence since Grundman disguises both the strong pulses and style. Another rhythmic concern presents itself in the introduction as entrances occur on the second part of the pulse. This is also accented to line up with sixteenth/dotted-eighth note figures. Working on the sixteenth note subdivision is important for this reason in addition to dotted-eighth/sixteenth note figures.

Unit 5: Stylistic Considerations

Tempi for *Concord* should reflect the martial/dance-like heritage of the tunes. Care should be taken not to rush the outer sections, while the middle section tempo sometimes will drag. Articulations are a major part of this piece, and Grundman employs *staccato*, *legato*, and accents. The approach to the "The White Cockade" articulations may be different to those employed in "Yankee Doodle," as the style changes from that of traditional military to dance. A slight separation in the final section allows for a *marcato* feel. The *forte/piano* attack with *crescendo* occurs several times, so balance will be of concern. Dynamics range from *pianissimo* to *fortissimo*, and there are plenty of opportunities for discussion of reinforcing the contour of both the melodic line and the harmonic figures. The harmonic motion is quite homophonic, and Grundman created a great deal of interest with the countermelodies.

Unit 6: Musical Elements

MELODY:

"The White Cockade" melody, introduced by piccolo in measure 19, primarily centers around the first, third, and fifth scale degrees of C major. The downward tetrachord from the four is the primary scale pattern. By placing a little weight at the beginning of each slurred figure, musicians create a "cocky" lilt. The ensemble performs in the same manner as the soloist when restating the melody in the key of B-flat.

The "America" section is not what most students will recognize as the familiar *America* based upon *God Save the Queen*. It is important for the ensemble to 'follow the line' as lines move in and out of the texture. Measures 110 and 111 provide an opportunity to introduce dynamic contrast during a sequence for woodwinds, as does measure 107 for horn and baritone. Consider playing the compact disc *Early American Choral Music*, Volume. 1, by His Majestie's Clerkes, Paul Hiller, conductor, as a means of providing the students with a concept of the "singing school" approach to lines.

"Yankee Doodle" moves from the traditional treatment in two to the contemporary 7/8. Grundman returns to 2/4 at the bridge but continues to truncate the melody. Since students know the traditional melody well, they will enjoy identifying the pieces of melody and exaggerating the differences. Of interest to the students will be the variation of the "America" first strain found in the horn and baritone countermelody at measure 201.

HARMONY:

The harmonies are simply orchestrated, and the open fifths and octaves allow for work on tuning issues. Grundman introduces the added ninth in the second measure that, through the scoring, provides a hint of merriment. Scalar motion often creates harmonic interest, and this is initially introduced in measure 8. Choirs approach the root from the fourth and fifth scale degree with tetrachord in opposite directions. This reinforcement of the major second interval makes the interval more acceptable when scored vertically as the added ninth. Demonstrate how the scoring allows the interval to sound as a major second or minor seventh. This would be a good time to talk of tuning tendencies by scale degree. Each section cadences with V–I, so having students recognize this through singing also helps with tuning issues at the end of phrases. Measures 159 through 163 present an ideal opportunity to demonstrate taking the tetrachord through a chromatic sequence to modulate from E-flat to B-flat, as the entire ensemble performs either one of the two tetrachords or the V–I cadence. This reoccurs in measure 195 but in the form of question and answer between the brass and woodwind choirs.

RHYTHM:

Measures 159 through 163 are significant from the standpoint of manipulating meter. While notated in 2/4, the feel is actually 5/8. Students will want to rush this section, but the 5/8 naturally creates the impetus from 2/4 back to 7/8. The separation at measure 195 between choirs often leads to one group waiting on the other, so understanding the subdivision is important. In the "Yankee Doodle" section, students (and conductor) must work on keeping the eighth note consistent. Throughout the 7/8 section, the conducted pulse is short–short–long. Students should count and clap rhythms to work on ensemble subdivision. This will be helpful at measure 201 when horn and baritone must fit the lyrical countermelody into the rhythmic *ostinato* figures.

Two opportunities exist to discuss diminution and augmentation of rhythm. Measure 8 is measure 7 in diminution, and augmentation of the melody occurs in the piccolo and bassoon solos in measures 87 through 94.

TIMBRE:

The scoring of muted trombones at measure 27 with the accompanying woodwinds provides a unique look at how timbre can be affected through both the scoring and devices. The muted trumpet also enhances the woodwind sound in measures 63 through 78 as it doubles the melody.

Grundman also doubles the cadence points in this section in flute and clarinet to provide a definite cadential timbre. Grundman uses the saxophone choir as a bridge between the woodwind choir and brass choir in measures 102 through 117. This is a study in the changing blend concepts throughout the center section. At measure 135, it is a good idea to point out the use of the pedal point scored in the xylophone as opposed to a traditional bass voice—and again at measure 180.

Unit 7: Form and Structure

Concord is a medley of three tunes, *The White Cockade*, William Billings's *America*, and *Yankee Doodle*.

Section	Measure	Event and Scoring
Introduction	1–10	Fanfare establishing C major
	11–18	Field drum solo
I	19–50	Piccolo introduces the initial "The White Cockade" tune in C major
	51–55	Interlude to second statement with restatement of the cadence in the woodwind choir; down a step to B-flat major followed by percussion break
	56–78	Upper woodwinds perform the second statement of the tune in B-flat major with brass and percussion accompaniment
Bridge	79–97	Transition to next section featuring piccolo, bassoon, horn, and field drum back in C major
Introduction	98–101	Oboe solo
II	102–109	Brass choir presents first strain of the "America" tune in C major; saxophone choir enters with a pickup into m. 106
	109–112	Woodwind choir introduces the second strain
	113–117	Saxophone continues into a brass choir
	118–131	Ensemble repeats scoring presentation sequence to complete hymn

SECTION	MEASURE	EVENT AND SCORING
Bridge	132–134	Transition to next section featuring low and middle brass with woodwind descending pyramid
Introduction	135–140	Rhythmic vamp establishing 7/8 feel in clarinet choir and horn over xylophone pedal
III	141–144	Flute, piccolo, E-flat clarinet, and muted trumpet introduce the contemporary "Yankee Doodle" motive in C major
	145–148	Builds through the addition of the other brass accompanying the melody
	149–158	Trumpet performs the first portion of the bridge melody in 2/4 time moving into treble woodwinds, middle and low winds, to full ensemble in E-flat major
	159–163	Full ensemble performs chromatic modulation from E-flat to B-flat major
	164–177	Two restatements of contemporary "Yankee Doodle" in B-flat with the third pulse varied in the second statement
Bridge	180–199	Transition to coda featuring 2/4 traditional first part of "Yankee Doodle" through chromatic and orchestration build
Coda	200–213	Two-measure statement of contemporary "Yankee Doodle" theme over horn and baritone countermelody based upon the middle section's "America" tune

Unit 8: Suggested Listening

Bela Bartok, *Three Hungarian Songs*

Frank Erickson, *Two Norwegian Folk Dances*

Morton Gould, *Yankee Doodle* (setting for band)

Clare Grundman:
> *American Folk Rhapsody 1–4*
> *An Irish Rhapsody*
> *Kentucky 1800*

Pierre La Plante, *American Riversongs*

Vaclav Nelhybel, *Suite from Bohemia*

William Rhodes, *Three Russian Cameos*

Unit 9: References and Resources

"The Basic Band Curriculum: Grades I, II, III." *BD Guide*, September/October 1989, pp. 2–6.

Billings, William. *Early American Choral Music*, Volume 1. His Majestie's Clerkes, Paul Hiller, conductor. Audio compact disc, Harmonia Mundi, France, 2001.

Grundman, Clare. *Concord*, score. New York: Boosey & Hawkes, Inc, 1988.

Garofalo, Robert J. *Instructional Designs for Middle/Junior High School Band*. Fort Lauderdale, FL, 1995.

Kvet, Edward, ed. *Instructional Literature for Middle-Level Band*. Reston, VA: Music Educators National Conference, 1996.

McKay, D. P., and William Billings. *The New Grove Dictionary of Music and Musicians*. Edited by Stanley Sadie. New York: MacMillan Publishers, Ltd., 1980, pp. 703–5.

Music Educators National Conference, Committee on Performance Standards. *Performance Standards for Music*. Reston, VA: Music Educators National Conference, 1996.

Silverman, K. *A Cultural History of the American Revolution*. New York: Columbia University Press, 1987.

Contributed by:

Rod M. Chesnutt

Director of Symphonic/Marching Bands

University of Northern Iowa

Cedar Falls, Iowa

Teacher Resource Guide

Crystals

Thomas C. Duffy
(b. 1955)

Unit 1: Composer

Thomas C. Duffy was born in Brooklyn, New York. He began formal accordion lessons at age seven. Throughout the rock-and-roll days of the late 1960s and 1970s, he taught himself piano and guitar, and wrote his first arrangements for his high school rock and jazz bands and musical pit orchestras. After a high school sports injury left him with no feeling in two fingers, he adopted the saxophone as his major instrument. Duffy earned a Bachelor of Science in Education (magna cum laude) and the first Master of Musical Arts in Composition from the University of Connecticut, where he was a student of Charles Whittenberg, Hale Smith, and James Eversole. At the University of Connecticut, he served as assistant director of the marching band for one year and started the jazz program, which is flourishing today. After one year as chairman of the Theory Division at the Hartford Conservatory of Dance and Music, he entered Cornell University, where he earned his Doctor of Musical Arts in Composition, studying with Karel Husa and Steven Stucky. At Cornell, he worked with the jazz, marching, and concert bands while studying conducting and theory in addition to his composition major.

In 1982, Duffy accepted the position of Director of Bands at Yale University, where he works today. He is Professor (adj.) of Music and Deputy Dean of the Yale School of Music. He has taught music courses at the Hartford Conservatory of Dance and Music, University of Connecticut, Auburn (New York) Maximum Security Correctional Facility, Cornell University, and Yale University. He has served as president of the New England College Band

Association, College Band Directors National Association–Eastern Division, and Connecticut Composers, Inc. He has served as editor of the CBDNA Journal and chairman of CBDNA's Commissioning and Gender/Ethnic Committees, the World Association of Symphonic Bands and Ensembles Publicity Committee, and Connecticut Music Educators Association Professional Affairs and Government Relations Committees. He is a member of the American Composers Alliance, BMI, and the American Bandmasters Association. In 1996, Duffy was selected as Outstanding Music Educator of the Year by the Connecticut Music Educators Association.

In addition to *Crystals*, Duffy has written forty-nine wind band compositions, which are published by Ludwig Music Publishing Company, Bourne Company Music Publishers, the American Composers Alliance, Neil A. Kjos Music Company, Hal Leonard, and his own publishing company, Plankton Press. He maintains a website with program notes for all of his music: www.duffymusic.com.

Duffy's first serious musical influence was Charles Whittenberg, whose music was cited in *The New Grove Dictionary of Music and Musicians* as "coupling of constant activity with constant change, rapidly shifting, timbrally defined blocks and sharp, angularly contoured lines are woven together, interspersed, superimposed and always 'on the go.'" While studying with Whittenberg, Duffy worked in depth with serialism and the ordering of all parameters of music. He was attracted to the music of his teacher, Karel Husa, for its unique combination of the art of musical composition with themes of contemporary importance. Duffy first came into contact with Husa's quarter tones and proportional notation as a saxophonist in the Wind Ensemble at the University of Connecticut. While at Cornell, he also studied with Steven Stucky, from whom he inherited an interest in the music of Dallapiccola, Ligeti, Reich, Glass, Xenakis, and Lutoslawski.

Unit 2: Composition

Crystals was commissioned and premiered in 1985 by the Killingly (Connecticut) High School Band, John Kusinski, director. It is a one-movement tone poem divided into four sections. In each section, the music explores the sounds that might be associated with four different crystals (ice, jewels, cyanide, limestone).

The score carries the following program note:

Crystals is a one-movement tone poem divided into four sections. Each section musically represents a type of crystal. Thus, each section is a vignette with its own title and style, as follows. The first, "Dark Ice," combines water sounds with quartal harmonies and a modal melody to suggest the mystery and terrible majesty of glaciers, icebergs, and things in and under them. The second, "Underwater

Rubies," again uses water sounds to suggest beams of sunlight ricocheting off gems spilling from a sunken treasure chest. The third section, "Cyanide," is of a violent and percussive spirit which, by its brevity, mimics the horrible potency of its namesake. Finally, "Monolith" aspires to images of huge piles of stone and granite, either natural promontories or manmade, such as perhaps Stonehenge or Big Ben's tower. Though impressionistically blurred and buried, throughout this section one can hear the chiming of Big Ben's hourly bells sounding from the granite tower high above London.

The piece was written to fulfill the following commission goals, all of which were determined in advance by the composer in collaboration with the commissioning body: a piece of music that,

1. like the finest orchestral music embodied a wide range of tempi, styles, and meters within one formal unit;
2. was constructed of separate sections, each of which could be rehearsed fully in one short rehearsal period;
3. allowed musicians to make some of their own choices about and contributions to the overall tapestry of sound;
4. introduced students to aleatoric techniques;
5. offered the percussion section both the more traditional accompanimental role and a part equal in presence, color, and technique to that of the other instruments in the ensemble; and
6. could be assimilated rather quickly by an audience of dilettantes.

The composer originally conceived of *Crystals* as one movement of a three-movement suite, entitled *The Crystal Suite*. Each of the three pieces in the suite includes significant parts for tuned crystal glasses. The other two movements were to be based on *The Song of Hiawatha* (Ludwig, 1987) and *Prehistoric Promenade* (Plankton Press, 1989). When all was done, the three pieces did not necessarily fit together as a suite, crystal glasses notwithstanding.

The *Pennsylvania Music Educators Association News* (1990) says of Crystals:

Grade IV. This is a one-movement tone poem which is divided into four short sections... Within its 5:35 duration, much happens: water sounds, quartal harmonies, half-valve murmurs, whistlers, hummers, water gongers, mixed meters, and some traditional splashes of colors and motifs. A good work, a fun work, a great change of pace without painstaking rehearsal.

Unit 3: Historical Perspective

In 1985, the high school band music repertoire did not include many pieces that employed the full range of twentieth century compositional techniques. The professional and college-level wind repertoire included the works of Joseph Schwantner, Donald Erb, David Borden, Karel Husa, and others who regularly and skillfully wove aleatory and extended performance techniques into their compositions. *Crystals* was designed to serve as a technical primer for the more difficult works of these great composers (and specifically Joseph Schwantner's *and the mountains rising nowhere*).

The music of the first section of *Crystals*, "Dark Ice," reflects both the sparkle and purity of ice crystals and the more ominous and potentially dangerous collections of ice (icebergs, glaciers, avalanches). The sparkle of the metal percussion instruments in combination with the pentatonic murmur of woodwinds serves as background to an austere brass fanfare. This fanfare is constructed of perfect intervals (as was the woodwind figure in measure 3), and progresses with parallel motion, all reminiscent of the sounds of the late Middle Ages. (Listen to Guillaume Dufay, *Missa L'Homme Armé*; Claude Debussy, *La cathédrale engloutie*.)

The second section, "Underwater Rubies," begins with a short two-phrase homophonic statement and ends with a series of sonic events that are both aleatoric and "measured." The aleatoric elements require musicians to match given pitches by singing and whistling, percussion to play the Lion's Roar and produce tam-tam *glissandi*, and saxophones to play tuned crystal glasses. This second section reflects the techniques and sounds most affiliated with twentieth century compositional schools. (Listen to Jacques Castérède, *Divertissement d' Été*; Joseph Schwantner, *and the mountains rising nowhere*.)

Of the four, the third section, "Cyanide," is the most conservative with respect to traditional band scoring; it features a "chic-boom" percussion accompaniment with a jazzy walking bass *ostinato*. (Listen to Leonard Bernstein, "Three Dance Episodes" from *On the Town*.)

The final section, "Monolith," is based on the melody of London's most famous clock, Big Ben. The four-note motive of Big Ben's tolling chimes is blurred slightly, in the fashion of the nineteenth century Impressionist school of composition. (Listen to Claude Debussy, *La Cathédrale engloutie, La Mer*.)

Thus, this one-movement, four-section composition, itself a twentieth century artifact, is comprised of sections that reflect elements of musical styles from the Middle Ages to the present.

Unit 4: Technical Considerations

The aleatoric sections encompass the following:

1. Temporal notation (i.e., musical events measured in seconds rather than metric beats)

2. The repetition of short motives that "repeat over and over," "afap" (as fast as possible) – The repeated motives are constructed from segments of a pentatonic scale, based on C (C–D–E–G–A).

3. Trills between pitches of varying intervals

4. Brass half-valve "murmurs"

5. "Water" gong *glissandi* (small tam-tam lowered into water while being struck to lower the pitch)

6. Saxophonists playing tuned crystal glasses (a pentatonic scale: A–B–C–E–F-sharp) at measures 23 through 32 and 81 through 84

7. Upper woodwind players whistling (measures 25 through 30) pitches given by the glockenspiel

8. Brass players singing "ahhhh" (measures 29 through 31), given by the clarinets (measure 28).

The non-aleatoric sections encompass the following:

1. Second and third clarinet, glockenspiel, and oboe playing sixteenth note figures against eighth note triplets in 1st clarinet (measures 9–10)

2. Musicians trilling between pitches of varying intervals

3. Sixth percussion playing the Lion's Roar

4. Flute and oboe "sharing" a single line of sixteenth note sextuplets (measures 60–66), scored so 1st flute contributes an eighth note and a sixteenth note triplet, while 2nd flute and oboe contribute the corresponding sixteenth note triplet and an eighth note – The overall effect should be one line of unbroken sixteenth note sextuplets. The clarinets "share" a single line of sixteenth notes scored so that, in each measure, each part contributes one beat of sixteenth notes and two beats of eighth notes. Initially, piccolo tops off the seven-measure phrase with two measures of *legato* and then non-*legato* sixteenth notes. The overall rhythmic effect should be that of running sixteenth notes in piccolo and clarinet, which combine with the flute/oboe part to produce a two-against-three background counterpoint. (Notice that the rhythmic roles reverse for a moment in measures 64 and 65.) The section winds down as the rhythmic juxtaposition moves from two-against-three to three-against-four in measure 67. Musicians must maintain the rhythmic independence of their own parts, even while fitting them into the greater pattern.

5. The first three sections of the piece are written without key signature but do have tonal centers. "Dark Ice" sits on or around C (pentatonic)

and uses, harmonically and melodically, pentatonic scales based on C (C–D–E–G–A) and its relative minor, A (A–B–C/C-sharp–E–F-sharp).

"Underwater Rubies" begins with a repeated two-chord figure, the first of which is a perfect fourth dyad (IC 5–E, A), the second a triad of perfect fifths (PC 0, 2, 7–C, G, D). Over this harmony, the piccolo/flute melody is drawn from the A and C pentatonic scales from the first section. Pitches for the aleatoric measures are all drawn from the A pentatonic scale.

"Cyanide" is in, on, or around the pitch A and its relative major, C. Upper woodwinds move in parallel augmented triads, low brass and woodwinds spit out aggressive little half-step clusters, and the section ends with a jazzy *ostinato* in A-natural minor.

"Monolith" begins in A minor and moves to the key of B-flat by measure 59. The key area then moves by descending half steps (through a series of augmented sixth chords) from B-flat to G (measures 69 through 76). The final aleatoric section is based on pitches from the G pentatonic scale (G–A–B–D–E), set over the crystal glass pedal of A pentatonic pitches.

6. The individual rhythm patterns throughout Crystals include motives to be played as fast as possible and repeated over and over, eighth note and sixteenth note triplets, dotted-eighth/sixteenth patterns, dotted-eighth/two thirty-second note patterns, offbeat eighth notes, and simple syncopation. Collective rhythms generate patterns of three-against-four and two-against-three, and several sections place a metered melody over an aleatoric harmonic background. Meters include common time, three-quarter time, and *senza misura* (free time).

Unit 5: Stylistic Considerations

Crystals is a tone poem set in contrasting styles. The first and second sections are impressionistic and require careful adherence to the written dynamics. As every ensemble is different, the conductor should adjust balances so as to distinguish musical figures that are melodic and meant to occupy the foreground from those that are accompanimental and meant to occupy the background. Several of the melodies have "shadows" (simultaneous statements of the melody at a reduced dynamic level) or "smears" (rhythmic extensions of the melodic pitches by instruments other than those playing the melody, as in the fuguing of a melody at pitch at the rhythmic interval of one eighth note or quarter note), for which the main melody clearly needs to be the most clear:

mm. 16–23   piccolo – melody; 1st/2nd flute – shadow

m. 28   1st clarinet – melody; 2nd clarinet – smear

mm. 52–58	trumpets have "carillon-like" phrase; each of four trumpet parts must contribute articulations of equal presence, resulting in a smeared, chime-like descending pattern, with "chimes" on each eighth note
mm. 67–76	upper woodwinds and 1st/2nd trumpet – melody; 3rd/4th trumpet – smear

The third and fourth sections should be approached with the arsenal of performance techniques associated with the romantic style. These sections (aside from the final aleatoric coda in measures 77 through 84) are best served by a great dynamic range, aggressive interpretation of accents, slight space between dotted notes and their shorter partners, melody lines that sing out above the complicated background harmonies (measures 64 through 67), and the emphasis on the pitches in the augmented sixth chords that cause the harmony to move down by half steps (measures 69 through 76).

Durations (in seconds) for measures in the aleatoric sections (measures 1 through 5; measures 24 through 31; measures 77 through 84) can be adjusted with regard to the reverberation time in the performance space. Allow enough time for each section's events to be introduced and established before moving on to the next.

Unit 6 Musical Elements
MELODY:

While there are traditional melodies in *Crystals*, most of the melodic lines are smeared. The smearing (or blurring) reflects programmatic concepts involving water or fog, or reverberation.

Melody becomes increasingly more blurred throughout the first two sections. There are clear unblurred melodic statements at measure 3, measures 6 through 11, measures 16 through 23, measures 33 through 36, and measures 64 through 66.

Piccolo and flute first present melody that is slightly blurred (measures 16 through 23). Flute plays the piccolo's exact pitches (but two octaves lower), trilling slowly throughout. This produces a "liquid-sounding" shadow.

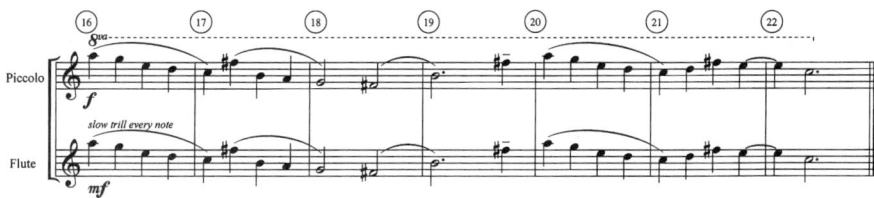

Example 6.1. Mm. 16–22. Piccolo and Flute "shadow."

Flute should have no problem remaining subservient to piccolo. Throughout this section, the harmony and rhythm parts should be well in the background (*p* or *pp*), flute should fill the middle ground, and piccolo alone should occupy the foreground.

The first actual melodic smear occurs in measure 28 between 1st and 2nd solo clarinets. Here, 2nd clarinet answers 1st clarinet one eighth note later.

Example 6.2. Mm. 28. Clarinet smear.

Whatever there is of melody in the four-measure phrase from measures 33 through 36 is contained in eighth note triplets. Woodwinds and upper brass split the melodic line (which requires an even balance between the two groups).

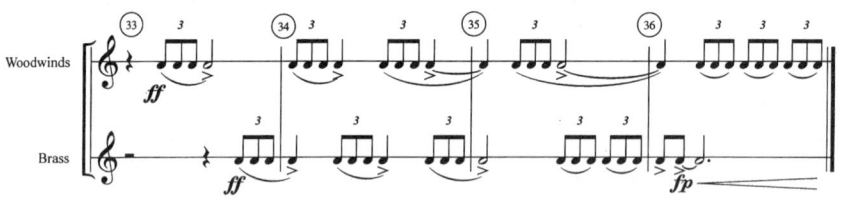

Example 6.3. Mm. 33–36. "Shared" triplet melody.

Alto saxophone and clarinet carry the melody in quarter notes in measures 37 through 40. Each quarter note is "modified" by a woodwind eighth note triplet on the same beat. Carefully balance the melody note and its modifiers.

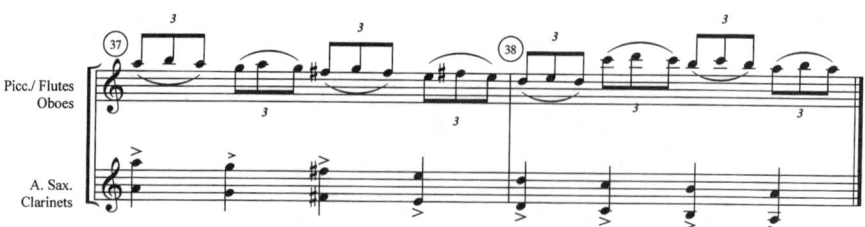

Example 6.4. Mm. 37–38. "Modified" melody.

The melody from measures 52 through 58 is a descending quarter note figure split between the four trumpets. (See comments under "Timbre.")

Section four, "Monolith," begins with a fanfare (measures 59 through 68). All of the instruments that begin the fanfare with a dotted-eighth note should play with space between all dotted-rhythm notes and their partners. First balance the upper voice of the fanfare (bass clarinet, bassoon, saxophone, horn, trumpet, and 1st/2nd trombone) with the bass line (3rd trombone, euphonium, and tuba). Then add the upper woodwind counterpoint, keeping it equal to but no greater than the fanfare's presence.

The four-pitch melody from measures 69 through 76 is the famous Big Ben motive, heard in piccolo, 1st flute, tenor saxophone, and 1st/2nd trumpet. In each of the four two-measure "phrases," the melody is both harmonized and smeared. (See more under "Harmony" and "Timbre.")

Example 6.5. Mm. 69–76. "Big Ben" melody.

HARMONY:

The first melodic snippet (measure 3) is a six-note motive, harmonized at IC 5 (perfect fourth and its transposition).

Example 6.6. Mm. 3. Harmonized melody.

The second melodic section (measures 6 through 11) contains two phrases: measures 6 through 7 and 8 through 11. The first measure of each phrase contains melody harmonized with IC 5 (perfect fourths and fifths); the second part of each phrase contains melody with triadic harmonization.

Example 6.6a. Mm. 6–7. Harmonized melodies.

The simple two-chord harmony from measures 14 through 22 must be balanced and very quiet. Often the ensemble is reduced to one player per part in this section. The two-chord figure is constructed of perfect intervals: the first is a perfect fourth dyad (IC 5–E,A), the second a triad of perfect fifths (PC 0, 2, 7–C, G, D).

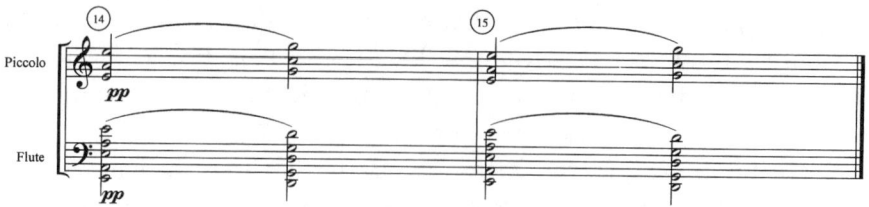

Example 6.7. Mm. 14–22. Two-chord harmonic background.

Big Ben's clock-chime motive comes in two varieties, a six-pitch motive (measures 49 through 50) and a four-pitch motive (measures 69 through 76). The motive moves in parallel motion from pitch to pitch and is harmonized as a major (or minor) triad plus sixth chord in first inversion (PC 0, 3, 5, 8 or 0, 4, 5, 8). This places the tonic of the chord in the melody as the primary pitch.

Example 6.8. Mm. 49–52. "Big Ben" with harmony.

The fanfare section from measures 59 through 68 is set in the key of B-flat. The section from measures 69 through 76 moves chromatically from B-flat to G, using German augmented sixth chords to lower the key center by one half step every two measures.

Example 6.9. Mm. 69–76. Augmented 6th chord hormonic motion.

RHYTHM:

The most complicated rhythms in this piece are the frequent pairings of independent parts so as to place a triple pulse against a duple pulse. Musicians might find it helpful to practice clapping their rhythms both alone and with their partners. For example, in measures 6 and 7, oboes could clap sixteenth notes, 1st clarinets eighth note triplets, and 2nd and 3rd clarinets two patterns of eighth and sixteenth notes.

Example 6.10. Mm. 6–7. Duple and triple rhythms.

Other areas that feature this triple/duple pairing are measures 33 through 40 and measures 60 through 67.

All of the AFAP (as fast as possible) aleatoric motives must be played rapidly. However, speed is less important than overall blend. Some tempo-ambitious players may have to slow down to better play *pp* and blend with the other musicians.

TIMBRE:

Here are three exercises designed to produce the best aleatoric "murmurs" from the ensemble.

1. Measures 3 through 4, brass half-valve murmur – Brass must play the murmur so that no individual instruments can be heard but, rather, only the writhing "wall of sound." This must be *pp*.

2. Measure 4, AFAP woodwinds – Play AFAP motives so that no individual instruments can be heard but, rather, only the babbling "wall of sound." If the "wall" is too loud, it might be helpful to ask musicians to slow down, sacrificing speed in favor of blend.

3. Measure 5, upper woodwind AFAP parts – Play AFAP motives so that no individual instruments can be heard but, rather, only the sparkling "wall of sound." This "wall" must be forceful and aggressive, and should begin exactly on the conductor's downbeat.

Smears and blurred melodies must be played so the main melody is clearly in the foreground. Four trumpets "smear" a melody in measures 52 through 58. When played effectively, the melody is heard as bell-like eighth notes, ringing out through a pentatonic haze.

Other areas that have smeared melodies are measure 4, 1st/2nd clarinet; measures 25 through 27, whistlers; measures 69 through 76, 1st/2nd trumpet (and harmonized woodwinds) and 3rd/4th trumpets.

Whistlers must listen carefully for the beginning of the water gong's glissando in measure 30. The whistlers must execute a whistled glissando that parallels the rate of change of pitch in the water gong. Singers must do the same in measure 31.

In the aleatoric sections, each measure has its own distinct ensemble timbre, a collection of "walls of sound." Each "wall of sound" must begin exactly together and should sustain without wobbling until it is time to cut off or move on. In the final section from measures 77 through 81, each subsequent "wall" is added on to pre-existing sounds, all of which is swept clean by the percussion "thump" in measure 81.

Unit 7: Form and Structure

Here is the overall form for each of the four sections of *Crystals*.

Measure	Tonal Area	Motive ID	Event and Scoring
"Dark Ice"			
1–2	C	a	Octave Cs/metal sounds
3	C pentatonic	X	First melody fragment
4	C pentatonic	b	Harmonic murmur (water sounds)
5	A pentatonic	c	Bright sparkle murmur (ice)
6–13	A minor	Y	Ominous fanfare
6–7			Antecedent fanfare
8–9			Consequent fanfare + four-measure extension
"Underwater Rubies"			
14–15	Quartal on C	X	Chordal introduction
16–24	C and A pentatonic		Two-part, eight-measure phrase
16–19			Antecedent
20–22			Consequent
24			Percussion extension
25–27	A pentatonic	c	Whistle triad begins
28–29	A pentatonic	Z	Smeared melody fragment plus one-measure extension to voices
30		Transition	Cadence for whistle triad
31		Transition	Cadence for voice pedal pitch
"Cyanide"			
32		Introduction	One-measure percussion introduction
33–40			Two four-measure phrases

MEASURE	TONAL AREA	MOTIVE ID	EVENT AND SCORING
33–36		W	Aggressive cluster chords
37–40	A dorian	Z	Ostinato jazzy bass line pentatonic melody
33–40			Repeated
41–48	A pentatonic	Y	Eight-measure phrase
41–42			"boom-chic" transition
43–44			Horn/euphonium "fanfare" antecedent
45–46			Trumpet and tutti consequent
47–48	A and E (fifth)		Cadence

"Monolith"

MEASURE	TONAL AREA	MOTIVE ID	EVENT AND SCORING
49–51	A minor	BB	Big Ben motive
52–58	A minor	Z	Smeared "carillon" melody
59	B-flat	Introduction	Fanfare introduction
60–68	B-flat	AA	Two phrases
60–63			Antecedent phrase
64–68			Consequent phrase
69–76		BB	Big Ben motive
67–70	B-flat		Smeared Big Ben motive
71–72	A		Smeared Big Ben motive
73–74	A-flat		Smeared Big Ben motive
75–76	G		Smeared Big Ben motive
77–84			Coda
77	G	x'	Dyad (perfect fifth)
78–79	G pentatonic	y'	Harmonic murmur (water sounds)
80	G pentatonic	z'	Bright sparkle murmur (ice)
81	a pentatonic		Cadence; water gong
82–84	a pentatonic		Final cadence

A form chart like this is most useful when viewed with a graph of other musical phenomena. These graphs of dynamics, maximum number of separate articulations per measure (whole note = 1, two half notes = 2, 12 eighth note triplets over 8 eighth notes = 16, etc.), and maximum number of instruments playing per measure outline the very structure that is most evident when actually hearing the music.

The most musical "action" can be heard in those areas where articulations, dynamics, and number of instruments are simultaneously high. The composite graph shows peaks in the areas around measures 36 through 41 and measure 65. *Crystals* is approximately five minutes and thirty-five seconds in duration; the positive Golden Section point falls roughly at or around measure 41.

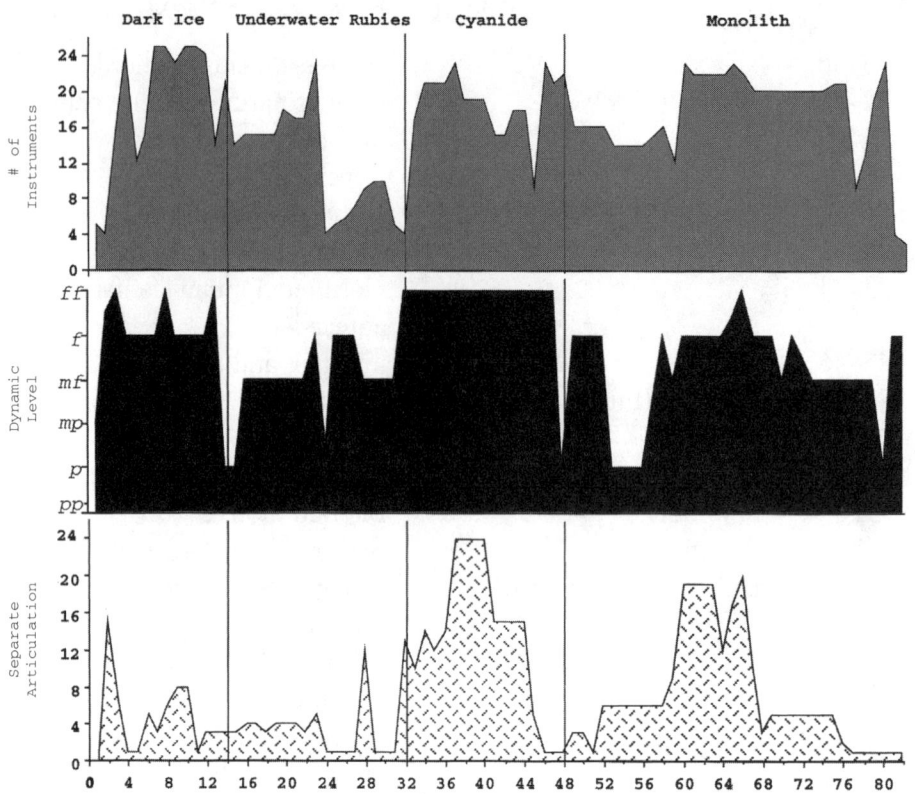

These are graphs of phenomena in *Crystals*. The top graph depicts the total number of instruments playing in each measure. The middle graph depicts the maximum dynamic level in each measure ($pp = 1$, $p = 5$, $mp = 10$, $mf = 15$, $f = 20$, $ff = 25$). The bottom graph depicts the total number of separate articulations (attacks) in each measure (for example, an eighth note triplet played over two eighth notes generates four separate attacks, given that they share the downbeat). Vertical lines separate the piece into its four components sections: "Dark Ice," "Underwater Rubies," "Cyanide," and "Monolith."

Unit 8: Suggested Listening

David Borden, *In That Jingle Jangle Morning…*
Daniel Bukvich, *Symphony No. 1*
Claude Debussy:
    La Cathédrale engloutie
    La Mer
Guillaume Dufay, *Missa L'Homme Armé*
Thomas C. Duffy:
    Crystals (CD Denon 32CG 1877)
    Pilgrims Progress

Snakes!
Zephyrs
Donald Erb, *Stargazing*
Alan Hovhaness, *Fantasy on Japanese Wood Prints*
Karel Husa:
 Music for Prague
 Concerto for Wind Ensemble
John Paulson, *Epinicion*
John Pennington, *Apollo*
Joseph Schwantner:
 and the mountains rising nowhere
 From a Dark Millennium
 In Evening's Stillness
 Music of Amber

Unit 9: Additional References and Resources

Program notes, timings, availability, and commission and premiere histories
 for all of Thomas C. Duffy's music are listed at www.duffymusic.com.

Fibonacci numbers and Golden Section proportions
 are discussed in great and interesting detail at
 www.mcs.surrey.ac.uk/Personal/R.Knott/Fibonacci/fib.html.

Contributed by:

Thomas C. Duffy
Director of Bands and Deputy Dean, School of Music
Yale University
New Haven, Connecticut

Teacher Resource Guide

Giles Farnaby Suite

freely transcribed by Gordon Jacob

(1895–1984)

after Giles Farnaby

(1563–1640)

Unit 1: Composers

Known for his interest in wind instruments, Gordon Jacob was one of Great Britain's important musical voices of the twentieth century. Educated at Dulwich College and the Royal College of Music, Jacob studied with Charles Villiers Stanford (1852–1924), Herbert Howells (1892–1983), Ralph Vaughan Williams (1872–1958), and Sir Adrian Boult (1889–1983). As a member of the faculty at the Royal College of Music from 1926 through 1966, Jacob taught theory, orchestration, and composition. His textbook, *Orchestral Technique* (1931), remains a valuable resource for students of orchestration. His music possesses a polished level of craftsmanship along with an immediacy and accessibility for the listener. Of his more than seven hundred compositions, a number of them are significant works for band. These include *An Original Suite*, *William Byrd Suite*, *Music for a Festival*, *Symphony AD 78*, and *Flag of Stars*.

Giles Farnaby, while not of the stature of the more prominent Elizabethan composers like William Byrd (1543–1623), John Bull (1562–1628), and Orlando Gibbons (1583–1625), nonetheless contributed compositions that demonstrate an infectiously attractive musical instinct. A key feature is the chromaticism that results from modal mixture. This is derived from the relationship between the melodic content and his pitch preferences in the contrapuntal embroidery. Although he wrote psalms, motets, and canzonets, Farnaby has been most recognized for his fantasias and miniatures for the virginal. Though none of his virginal music was published during his lifetime, fifty-two of these compositions were later printed in the *Fitzwilliam Virginal Book*.

Unit 2: Composition

Giles Farnaby Suite is a selective compilation of eleven of Farnaby's pieces for virginal. A few of them, *Giles Farnaby Suite*, *A Toye*, *Loth to Depart*, and *Tower Hill*, are among his best-known works. When considered as a whole, the entire suite has a duration of approximately nineteen minutes. Each short piece shows both Farnaby's talent for weaving attractive accompaniment and Jacob's skillful ability as an orchestrator for the wind band. Depending on the complexity of the counterpoint, the movements vary in orchestrational treatments. Jacob's settings range from sparse textures that reveal the woodwinds and brass independently to full-bodied *tutti* orchestrations in the songs that are less contrapuntally complex.

Unit 3: Historical Perspective

As a genre of keyboard composition, Elizabethan virginal music defines a fundamentally English characteristic of Renaissance expression. (Though the term "virginal" has been casually applied to all instruments of the harpsichord family, its earliest application described a small, portable instrument with a horizontal string configuration. Such an instrument could even be situated on the performer's lap.)

Roughly paralleling the time during which William Shakespeare (1564–1616) was active as a poet and playwright, this musical style relied on a peculiar mixture of melodic and harmonic simplicity combined with decorative and sometimes complex contrapuntal accompaniment. The melodies themselves were most often drawn from folk tunes or dances, serving as the basis for variation. While the music relies on the direct strength of consonant triads for its harmonic basis, it simultaneously incorporates a high degree of contrapuntal complexity and chromatic inflection. In fact, it is often more chromatic than the keyboard music written later by J. S. Bach.

Though history views the technical achievements of Giles Farnaby as secondary in comparison to those of Byrd, Bull, and Gibbons, he is still known for having contributed an individual voice to the categories of the fantasia and the miniature. In fact, his best efforts were found in the small frameworks of the miniatures referred to as *fancies*. Examples of both the fantasia and his eccentrically titled miniatures are found in this suite.

Noting the essentially English character of the virginal music genre, it is not surprising that Jacob was drawn to set this music for wind band. Aside from its nationalist dimension, the contrapuntal nature of the music is quite sympathetic with the orchestrational clarity possible by employing the instruments of the wind band.

Unit 4: Technical Considerations

Range demands are moderate, but the ensemble will be challenged to achieve mature tone production and good intonation due to the exposure created during sections of sparse scoring. The meters of 4/2 and 6/4 are encountered in addition to the more usual meters of 3/4, 4/4, and 2/2. Although the rhythmic sophistication of individual parts is not severe, challenges will be found in the relationships created because of the counterpoint. Whereas key signatures present no unusual challenges to the players, the Renaissance modalities, sequential transpositions resulting from imitation, and unusual chord relationships that predate common practice harmonic function will add more challenges in becoming comfortable with the work. Nearly every piece is also marked by the demand for confident, independent musicianship—these demands being most apparent in No. 7 ("Tell Mee, Daphne") and No. 8 ("Rosasolis"). In addition, there are several passages throughout, during which bassoon, alto clarinet, and bass clarinet have essential and exposed contrapuntal activity. The absence of these instruments (or adequate performers) may necessitate writing cues for coverage in other instruments.

Unit 5: Stylistic Considerations

One should consider that during the period when these pieces were written, wind instruments tended to have a lighter, more compact sound than their modern counterparts. Though Jacob conceived the transcription for modern instruments, the performance character might be enhanced by achieving a lighter-than-usual approach to the sonority. Dynamics in general should be handled in an elegant manner, creating an unforced, somewhat restrained character to the *forte* playing. In addition, the conductor may wish to experiment with one on a part playing in certain passages or even complete pieces (e.g., No. 5, "His Rest"). This may be relevant especially where the texture invites a chamber music treatment. Care should also be taken so imitative gestures are given the same nuance when passed between instruments.

Unit 6: Musical Elements

MELODY:

The melodic material for each piece is succinct and direct, though at times phrase lengths may seem unusual to student performers. For example, in No. 1 ("Fantasia"), cadences are heard in the third measure of the phrase, while in No. 3 ("Giles Farnaby's Dreame"), the phrase extends gracefully through its fourth measure creating an arch that feels more nearly unified as eight measures. In yet another situation, No. 8 ("Rosasolis"), a basic two-measure group is presented with varying degrees of ornamentation, sometimes to the extent that only a couple of the important structural pitches and the general shape of the figure are maintained. All of these irregularities present teaching opportunities, as students may be led to compare and contrast the elements found in these melodies and their variations. In addition, while studying the idiosyncratic natures of these melodies, students might reinforce their understanding by writing and performing some similar melodies of their own, or even improvising in the style.

HARMONY:

Among the Elizabethan composers of virginal music, Farnaby is said to have had the greatest affinity for the tonic and dominant. Still, there are attributes of the harmonic language that may seem unusual to the performer. One example of a somewhat unusual harmonic device is found at the end of No. 7 ("Tell Mee, Daphne"). After a convincing final phrase has begun in the last four measures, the projected G minor cadence is averted, with the progression instead arriving at a G major chord. This device, foreshadowing the picardy third, results in an element of harmonic surprise. Furthermore, the cadence is achieved in a weak metric placement (the third beat of the third measure of the phrase) only to gain agogic reinforcement through repetition in the final measure of the piece.

Another unusual harmonic occurrence is found in No. 10 ("Loth to Depart"), where the initial harmonic statement moves from a C major chord to an A-flat major chord. Though the direction of this harmonic statement becomes more clear a few measures later as the F minor chord is heard as a point of arrival, the initial sound of successive major chords with roots related by third may be disorienting. Students need to understand that this uniqueness is responsible for the inherent beauty of the sound. Exercises with the voices (half of the ensemble performing the passage on instruments while stand partners sing) might help students become accustomed to the sensation of this type of chord succession.

These, and other harmonic elements such as the modal mixture and abrupt tonal shift appearing in No. 3 ("Giles Farnaby's Dreame"), are characteristic of Farnaby's writing and will easily convince the performer that the music is derived from another time and culture. Becoming accustomed to the harmonic vocabulary is analogous with learning the inflections of a dialect of a spoken language.

RHYTHM:

At the surface, there are no rhythmic complexities that stretch beyond the division of the beat into eighth and sixteenth notes. However, ensemble challenges of the rhythmic figures of the work reside in their contrapuntal relationships. Perhaps the suite's finest example of contrapuntal elaboration exists in No. 7 ("Tell Mee, Daphne"), where the initial tune dissolves into delicious swirls of polyphonic figuration. This, of course, brings with it a challenge to the performer to develop a confident sense of ensemble pulse and finessed timing as related to performing individual layers of the texture.

TIMBRE:

While it was Farnaby who contributed the elements of melody, harmony, and rhythm, the element of timbre belonged to Jacob. A primary characteristic of the work is Jacob's alternation of the woodwind and brass choirs. In fact, Jacob further subdivides the choirs, featuring the even smaller consorts of the clarinet choir, the saxophone ensemble, and the cylindrical brass contrasted with the conical brass. A percussion complement including timpani, glockenspiel, xylophone, crash cymbal, triangle, snare drum, tambourine, and bass drum is used for delicate ornamentation, occasional melodic coloration, and tasteful reinforcement of climactic moments.

Unit 7: Form and Structure

In the general organization of the suite, Jacob has given attention to the alternation of movements in a way that allows contrasting expressions of the richness of full textures with the clarity and lightness of textures that more truly embody chamber music. The tonal centers of each movement are either related by perfect fifth or remain the same. While the tonics of C and G are heard, the prevailing center of the work is F. Of the eleven pieces, ten are transposed down a major second from the keyboard source material, with only No. 2 ("The Old Spagnoletta") remaining on its original tonic.

NO. 1: "FANTASIA"

As an example of the Elizabethan fugue, Farnaby's offering is attractive but not architecturally rigorous. Lasting thirty-three measures, it constitutes a sort of introduction to the compound meter Lavolta (a quick Galliard in 6/4) that follows.

NO. 2: "THE OLD SPAGNOLETTA"

A "spagnoletta" is a triple meter dance (written in 6/4 in this case). As a dance form, it had origins in Spain; however, it also propagated an English country dance cousin. After a simple rhythmic pattern of dotted-quarter note/eighth note/quarter note defines the rhythmic motive, elaboration through the development of continuous cascades of eighth notes creates an ongoing sense of motion.

NO. 3: "GILES FARNABY'S DREAME"

In the music of this period, the title *Dreame* was commonly used as a fanciful representation for a simple piece of tranquil character. Musically, the intrigue of this piece is in the modal mixture. In this example, an arching phrase expands a melody that begins with mixolydian inflection but cadences with the sound of a major tonic on C. At the point of the second phrase, which has a similar arch contour, there is an abrupt shift to center on E-flat major—such a shift without modulation being common to Farnaby's harmonic language. Just as the opening period drew poetic tension from the balance between mixolydian and major, the third and final period utilizes harmonic deception by wavering from E-flat major toward a C minor melodic target, this target only to be colored by the deceptive harmonization of an A-flat major chord. Finally, after reminiscing the mixolydian to major relationship of the first period, the melody descends to achieve a final cadence at a C major chord.

No. 4: "Farnaby's Conceit"

This piece is sprightly, direct, and compact. While contrapuntal lines serve to enhance the forward motion, there is no florid embellishment. The opening four-measure phrase and its repetition are comfortably settled in F major. This is contrasted by greater tension in an eight-measure period that follows. Musical intrigue is created as the fourth measure cadences on a G major chord prior to returning to the stability of F major. After this entire period is restated in a version orchestrated for the full ensemble, the entire piece is repeated.

No. 5: "His Rest"

A small, quiet piece of only thirty-three measures in length, "His Rest" is beautiful in its simplicity. Set in 3/4 meter, a dotted-quarter note followed by an eighth and a quarter stands as the primary rhythmic motive. Scored at *piano* and *pianissimo* dynamic levels throughout, Jacob first presents the melody and its reserved contrapuntal accompaniment in a small brass ensemble of three cornets, trombone, and tuba. The second phrase is then stated in the woodwinds before a third and final phrase (which is repeated) joins the brass and woodwind choirs together.

No. 6: "His Humor"

In character, this piece resembles a march, using the woodwinds to present the primary melodic material in the opening eight measures, with the brass reserved to create structural emphasis and reinforcement. Following the exposition of thematic material, the piece continues, being extended through imitative counterpoint. This contrapuntal section is itself twice the length of the opening statement, even when considering the opening repeat. The close of this imitative section culminates with a thickened ensemble texture that is built by means of a *stretto*, which has a subject that is formed from a motive that is derived from an inversion of the opening melody of the piece.

No.7: "Tell Mee, Daphne"

Jacob has used the delicate and sensitive lines of this piece to produce a beautiful chamber music setting. Another miniature of only twenty-five measures, this piece begins with the elaborated setting of the melody as set in the woodwinds, only to close with a restrained and less complex brass choir version.

No. 8: "Rosasolis"

"Rosasolis" offers a curious example of Farnaby's inventive spirit, embroidering strands of variation on a musical fabric of the smallest conceivable means. All of the material for the piece is derived from a four-measure phrase. This phrase, stated nine times to comprise the piece, alternates a two-measure antecedent that undergoes embellishment each time it is stated with a two-measure consequent that, with minor exceptions, remains fixed. In the area of orchestration, Jacob took advantage of the compact nature of the phrase, contrasting the brass and woodwind choirs in varying degrees of textural density.

No. 9: "A Toye"

In Elizabethan musical terminology, the title *toye* was attached to pieces that were simple, perhaps trifling in character. Though Farnaby's *toye* is simple and brief, it is not a trifle in terms of the beauty of its musical expression. The first statement of the four-measure melody, along with its contrapuntal accompaniment, is made in the saxophone choir alone. (Although there is a part for bass saxophone, it is cued in the bassoon part.) Subsequently, the clarinet choir is engaged but never the brass or percussion. Beginning in G minor, the piece ultimately shifts its mode to major in the measures preceding the ending.

No. 10: "Loth to Depart"

Just as a single phrase provided the foundation of "Rosasolis," again Farnaby bases an entire piece on repetition and embellishment. In "Loth to Depart," a period eight measures in length is stated six consecutive times. As in previous pieces of this suite, it is not phrase contrast, but rather variation, that creates musical interest. In this piece, Jacob highlights both the woodwind and brass choirs separately in addition to joining them together for the sake of creating a sense of weight and emphasis.

No. 11: "Tower Hill"

As the final piece in the suite, "Tower Hill" exhibits the strength of the full ensemble. A direct, two-note, echo figure of a major third is used in imitation whenever the primary phrase is heard. One of Farnaby's most notable pieces, the title refers to the infamous London prison where Anne Boleyn (1507–1536), who was herself a virginalist and composer, was held for treason and ultimately beheaded.

Unit 8: Suggested Listening

William Byrd, transcribed by Gordon Jacob, *William Byrd Suite,* performed by the Tokyo Kosei Wind Orchestra, KOCD-3563.

William Byrd, Giles Farnaby, John Munday, and Peter Philips, *The Fitzwilliam Virginal Book,* performed by Martin Souter, CCL-CD006.

Unit 9: Additional References and Resources

Atlas, Alan W. *Renaissance Music*. New York: W. W. Norton and Company, 1998.

Baker, Theodore. *Baker's Biographical Dictionary of Music and Musicians*. Eighth edition. Revised by Nicolas Slonimsky. New York: Schirmer Books, 1992.

Bruce, Marie Louise. *Anne Boleyn*. New York: Coward, McCann and Geoghagen, Inc., 1972.

Fuller, J. A., and W. Barclay Squire, eds. *The Fitzwilliam Virginal Book*. Volume 2. New York: Dover Publications, Inc., 1979.

Glyn, Margaret H. About Elizabethan *Virginal Music and Its Composers*. London, UK: William Reeves Bookseller Ltd., 1924.

Grout, Donald Jay, and Claude V. Palisca. *A History of Western Music*. Fifth edition. New York: W. W. Norton and Company, 1996.

Miles, Richard, ed. *Teaching Music through Performance in Band*. Chicago: GIA Publications, 1997.

Rouse, A. L., ed. *Shakespeare's Sonnets*. New York: Harper and Row, 1964.

Contributed by:

Frederick Speck
Director of Bands
University of Louisville
Louisville, Kentucky

Teacher Resource Guide

If Thou Be Near
(Bist du bei mir)
Johann Sebastian Bach

(1685–1750)

attributed to Gottfried Heinrich Stölzel

(1690–1749)

arranged by Alfred Reed

(b. 1921)

Unit 1: Composer

As one of the giants of Western music, Johann Sebastian Bach's reputation and biographical background are well documented. As was common in the pre-industrialized world, Bach was from a lineage of two hundred musical ancestors who worked in both sacred (church) and secular (courtly) positions. Left as an orphan at the age of ten, his early training came from his older brother and organist Johann Christian Bach. As a singer at St. Michael's Church, he learned to be proficient at both violin and keyboard. In 1707, at the age of eighteen, he assumed the position of organist at Arnstadt. This was the first among many posts he held within the limited geographic area of around 250 miles. His other posts included working as an organist at Mühlhausen (1707–1708), as the court organist and eventually concertmaster for the chapel of the Duke of Weimer (1708–1717), as the court music director for a prince in Cöthen (1717–1723), and until his death in 1750 in one of the preeminent musical positions of the Lutheran world, as cantor of

St. Thomas School and music director in Leipzig. While it is an error to suggest that Bach's music was forgotten after his death in 1750, it might be correct to say that it was neglected. His nearly unsurpassable organ works continued to be revered; however, some critics found much of the other works confusing and overly elaborated. They preferred the newer and more tuneful homophonic styles. It is also well known that Haydn owned a copy of *Mass in B Minor* and Mozart knew *The Art of Fugue* and studied motets on a visit to Leipzig in 1789. It wasn't, however, until the nineteenth century that Bach's genius was fully recognized. A biography on J. S. Bach, published in 1802 by J. N. Forkel, and a performance in 1829 of *St. Matthew Passion* under the baton of Felix Mendelssohn established Bach as one of the greatest musical minds in the history of Western civilization.

As nearly an exact contemporary of J. S. Bach, the life of Gottfried Heinrich Stölzel is known only in broader, more general terms. He was born on January 13, 1690, in Gründstädtel, about nineteen miles southeast of Zwickau, and died November 27, 1749, in Gotha. Between 1707 and 1710, he studied at Leipzig University where he was a member of the Collegium Musicum. Before Stölzel's arrival, Telemann had led the organization. He was known to have traveled extensively for the next ten years to locations that included Halle, Venice (where he is thought to have met Vivaldi), Rome, Florence, Prague, and Beyreuth. During that time he studied, composed, and taught students. He married in 1719 and was appointed as Kapellmeister in Gotha (Saxe-Gotha) in 1720, where he remained until his death in 1749. It is notable that in 1739 he became a member of Correspondirenden Societät der Musicalischen Wissenschaften, of which Bach later on also became a member.

Unit 2: Composition

The song *Bist du bei mir (If Thou Be Near)* is adapted from the second of two notebooks that were compiled in 1725 by Bach for his young wife, Anna Magdelena. One of Bach's most tender and best-loved songs, it may have been transcribed and set by Bach as a solo aria appropriate for his wife's voice. In its original version, it was simply configured as a texted melody with a non-figured bass line. In his arrangement published in 1984, Reed maintains the simple dignity and *cantabile* quality of the original setting in his realization for the symphonic band. Though the original score omitted figuration, Reed has created an appropriate and logical harmonic realization of the work as well as the original Bach/Magdelena notebook key of E-flat major. Only fifty-five measures in length, the work lasts approximately three minutes.

Unit 3: Historical Perspective

In general, the solo song in Johann Sebastian Bach's era did not hold a high place of importance; that was for the latter decades of the eighteenth century. The continued use of continuo was problematic for the development of an independent accompaniment. It was, therefore, Bach's interest in his young wife's continuing musical education that gave rise to the work. The daughter of a court trumpeter of Weissenfels and considered to be a fine singer, Anna Magdelana Wülken in 1721 became Johann Sebastian Bach's second wife. Together they created her notebooks, the source of *If Thou Be Near*.

It is here that the ambiguity of the actual composer of the melody comes into play. Many scholars attribute the actual melody to Bach's contemporary, Gottfried Heinrich Stölzel. It is not so unusual in the baroque era for such ambiguities to occur. As was the case with many composers in the baroque era, the practice of collecting and copying music without the proper citation or attribution was commonplace. It is unclear as to the intentions of Bach. It seems clear, however, that Bach had great respect for Stölzel, a noted composer in every genre of the musical baroque. It may have been an innocent omission or carelessness on his part, or perhaps a flagrant theft. Again, this is not unprecedented, as George Frederic Handel was also suspected to have been a noted borrower of contemporary melodies.

Identifying the poet of the text for *Bist du bei mir* is even a greater challenge. The poet that inspired Stölzel to create the melody, and subsequently Bach to create a solo song for his young wife, may remain unknown. Not a religious text, the poem is tender, reflective, and of a conjugal affection. Nevertheless, the joy and fidelity of love in the face of death implies the piety of the Lutheran Christian tradition of the era.

Text in the original German and English translation:

Bist du bei mir, geh' ich mit Freuden
Zum Sterben und zu meiner Ruh'.
Ach, wie vergnügt wär'so mein Ende,
Es drückten deine lieben Hände
Mir die getreuen Augen zu!

Be thou with me, and I'll go with joy
To death and to my repose.
Ah, how my end would bring contentment,
If, your beloved hands close
My faithful eyes.

Unit 4: Technical Considerations

The work is written in the key of E-flat major with some derivations into C minor, the relative minor key. The meter is 3/4 and the tempo indication is quarter note = c. 52. The melodic line is centered primarily in the upper woodwinds. Clarinets often cross the "break" of their instruments while maintaining slurred eighth note passagework. The very slow tempo offers the challenge of maintaining the *sostenuto* line without rushing the tempo. The mid-registration of the melodic line in the upper woodwinds requires a sensitive balancing of the supporting lower woodwind sustained lines so as not to cover the melody. With the last three measures marked "*poco allargando*," the conductor will need to explain the necessity of subdividing the pulse to the sixteenth note. This is a result of the gradual slowing of the dotted-eighth/sixteenth rhythms. The greatest difficulties in this work do not lie with excessive technical demands but with the subtleties of passing harmonies, consistent and refined articulations, and the continuity of the melodic line in relationship to subordinate parts.

Unit 5: Stylistic Considerations

While many compositions attributed to Johann Sebastian Bach are very elaborate and contrapuntally complex, *If Thou Be Near* was conceived as a simple song and, thus, should always keep its *cantabile* character. Appropriately, Reed requires the woodwind instruments to simulate the lyrical quality of the soprano voice. The woodwind choirs should predominate throughout the work, even in the final measures where cornets reinforce the melody. The musicians will need to focus their attention on a long, sustained, and well-supported line. Because of the slow tempo, maintaining the musical direction of the melodic line may be challenging for younger players but may also serve as an excellent tool for teaching phrasing and musicality.

Unit 6: Musical Elements

The conductor should clearly understand the text-driven nature of the song as it defines the overall form of the work. Lyrical four-measure phrases are followed by five more disjunct but lyrical eighth note phrases, which often coordinate with the original text and its repetitions. The arranger suggests that careful attention be paid to creating a *sostenuto* style. An emphasis upon blend, balance, and beauty of sound will lead to the most sonorous and satisfying performances.

MELODY:

The melodic line presented by the woodwinds should try to mimic the solo soprano voice. The players, especially clarinets, will need to compensate for the registration of the melody in the middle ranges of their instruments.

HARMONY:

While the harmonies of J. S. Bach are, as expected, traditional and diatonic, emphasis or slightly added weight should be given to passing tones and accidentals played within the inner voices, such as 2nd and 3rd clarinet.

RHYTHM:

Even though the slow tempo of the work might tempt the conductor to conduct in subdivision, it would be best, at least in performance, to conduct the longer duration of the quarter. It may prove useful in rehearsals to play it through a time or two using the eighth note as the subdivision. This is especially important during the final three *poco allargando* measures. The players, while maintaining the song-like quality in three, should never lose sight of feeling the underlying eighth. The subdivision should be divided to the sixteenth in the final three measures. Careful attention should be paid to matching the note lengths of the dotted-eighth/sixteenth rhythms. A slight lift or separation should, uniformly, come between them.

TIMBRE:
Overall, the work focuses upon the woodwind choir with passing phrases and harmonic support provided by horn, euphonium, and tuba. Most of the clarinet lines are located in the lower clarion and throat tone registers of the instrument. Alternate fingerings to create resonance in the throat tones will be necessary to create a richer and fuller sound. According to the arranger, while trumpet and trombone enter for only the final eleven measures, it will be important not to allow them to dominate the woodwind color of the work.

Unit 7: Form and Structure
The work is in a simple three-part song form with voice exchanges to create interest in repeated sections. The overall form follows:

SECTION	MEASURE	EVENT AND SCORING
A	1–4	Song-like phrase in 1st clarinet; 2nd/3rd clarinet, bass clarinet, baritone saxophone, baritone provide a realized figured bass
	5–9	B section of phrase with moving eighths in E-flat soprano and 1st clarinet; falling eighth note transition to m. 10
	10–18	Repetition of first nine measures, with added instrumentation of piccolo, flute, English horn, saxophone, horn, and tuba
B	19–22	Lyrical melody in 1st oboe; resembles A melody in inversion
	23–27	Eighth note phrase using oboe, English horn, E-flat soprano clarinet, and 1st horn

SECTION	MEASURE	EVENT AND SCORING
	28–36	Repetition of section with modulatory progression to C minor
A	37–45	Primary song melody restated by 1st clarinet, with addition of 1st/2nd cornet
	56–52	Full band; *molto sonore* final statement of song material
	53–55	Full band; *poco allargando* conclusion

Unit 8: Suggested Listening

J. S. Bach:
  Air on the G String
  Chorale Preludes (organ recordings)
  Orchestral Suites
  Schafe können sicher weiden (solo song for soprano with instruments)
J.S. Bach/Reed:
  My Heart Is Filled with Longing
  My Jesus! Oh, What Anguish
  Thus Do You Fare
  My Jesus

Unit 9: Additional References and Resources

"Bist du bei mir." Available from
    http://classicalmus.hispeed.com/articles/bachl.html; Internet consulted,
    17 September 2001.

Dvorak, Thomas L., Robert Grechesky, and Gary Ciepluch. *Best Music for High School Band*. Brooklyn, NY: Manhattan Beach Music, 1993.

Marshall, Robert L. *The Music of Johann Sebastian Bach*. New York: Schirmer Books, 1989.

Whitwell, David. "Bach–Wind Music." *The Instrumentalist*, XXI, November 1966, p. 39.

Contributed by:

Douglas A. Peterson
Music Program Manager
Daytona Beach Community College
Daytona Beach, Florida

Teacher Resource Guide

In the Forest of the King
Pierre La Plante
(b. 1934)

Unit 1: Composer

Pierre La Plante was born in Milwaukee, Wisconsin, on September 25, 1934. He received his Bachelor and Master of Music degrees from the University of Wisconsin at Madison, where he was a composition student of Jim Christensen. His desire to compose was fueled by the realization that limited repertoire was available for young band.

La Plante, of French-Canadian descent, plays bassoon with the Beloit-Janesville Symphony Orchestra. He recently retired after teaching general music and beginning band at Pecatonica Elementary School in Blanchardsville, Wisconsin, for twenty-five years. His other works for band include *Overture on a Minstrel Tune* (1978), *Prospect* (1983), *Lakeland Portrait* (1987), *A Little French Suite* (1987), *A March on the King's Highway* (1988), *All the Young Sailors* (1988), *American Riversongs* (1990), *Nordic Sketches* (1994), and *Come to the Fair* (1995).

Unit 2: Composition

In the Forest of the King, subtitled "A Suite of Old French Folksongs," was almost entitled *Trois Chansons Populaires,* or "popular songs." The three contrasting movements are based on traditional French folk songs. Originally scored for woodwind quintet, they were expanded by La Plante for full band on commission by Richard Sanger, conductor of the Thoreau Middle School Symphonic Band of Vienna, Virginia. The first movement, "Le Furet (The Ferret)," is an old children's song. The second folk song is the slow and wistful "The Laurel Grove," an eighteenth century tune popular at the Court of Versailles. The final movement, "King Dagobert," pokes a bit of fun at the king, who is about to go hunting but has put his trousers on backwards. The work is approximately eight minutes and forty-five seconds in length, and the composer provides program notes and performance suggestions in the conductor's score, including the original lyrics to each of the three folk songs.

Unit 3: Historical Perspective

The suite form originated in the baroque period and usually was comprised principally of dance movements. Each movement in this suite is a French folk song that has existed for centuries. The first, "Le Furet," can be sung in a circle game, with the tempo of the song determining the pace of the game. The imagery in the second, "The Laurel Grove," is both pastoral and festive, recalling a time in the innocence of early childhood that can never be regained. The third evokes King Dagobert's (a monarch in seventh century France) hunt on horseback, complete with hunting horns and drums. Folk song collections that depict the rich traditions and culture of the country they represent are a staple of band literature. Collections by Percy Grainger (*Lincolnshire Posy*), Gustav Holst (*Suite in E-flat, Suite in F*), Gordon Jacob (*William Byrd Suite*), Darius Milhaud (*Suite Francaise*), and Ralph Vaughan Williams (*Folk Song Suite*), all of whom devoted a significant portion of their skills to the preservation of folk songs, are part of the core repertoire for modern winds.

Unit 4: Technical Considerations

The ensemble should be familiar with the scales of B-flat major, E-flat major, and F major. Accidentals are not prevalent, and ensemble rhythms are basic. All dotted-eighth/sixteenth figures should be performed cleanly, and woodwinds should not rush sixteenth note runs. Trumpet parts require straight mutes.

The first movement is very quick (quarter note = 162–172), much like the movements of a lively ferret.

The second movement begins *legato* at a moderate tempo, and changes key, tempo, and style midway through. The conductor should point out the D.S. al Coda in measure 84 before rehearsing the movement or the ensemble may continue playing directly into the coda.

The final movement is the most technically challenging. The 6/8 meter is marked *Allegro ma non troppo,* and at measure 17 should not be performed faster than dotted-quarter note = 126. The opening drum roll may be performed with snares off. To maintain clarity and precision, the *accelerando* beginning at measure 99 should not exceed dotted-quarter note = 136.

Unit 5: Stylistic Considerations

In the Forest of the King provides an excellent opportunity to perform both in a light, buoyant manner and in a singing, *cantabile* style. Dynamic contrast is essential in each movement, and La Plante provides a full dynamic palette from *piano* to *fortissimo*.

Movement I requires quickness, so the eighth notes must be light and separated throughout.

Movement II begins in *legato* style and requires special attention to longer phrases. The ensuing *allegretto* section in Movement II should be happy and buoyant, and the hemiola from measures 55 through 66 should not rush.

In Movement III, the quarter notes should be detached but not *staccato* to capture the festive mood of the hunt. Because of its light and transparent texture, the entire suite may be performed with wind ensemble instrumentation rather than full band.

Unit 6: Musical Elements

In the Forest of the King has three tonal centers: the first and third movements are entirely in B-flat, while the second begins in E-flat, modulates to F, and returns to E-flat. Melodies are lyrical and singable, generally in four-measure phrases. Harmonies are triadic throughout with some seventh chords at cadence points.

The introduction to the first movement calls for grace notes; the band should rehearse the introduction first without the grace notes, and then add the grace notes while keeping the primary note on the beat. Dynamic contrast is important, so the band must observe the *decrescendo* in measure 44 and the *crescendo* back up to *forte* in measure 55. Measure 87 includes the direction "en pressant," meaning to press forward. As the first movement ends, the band should not play louder than its best, most balanced sound.

In the second movement, the ensemble should strive for longer lines in that many folk songs are written in four-measure phrases. The tone color in the slow section of this movement should be rich and resonant with *legato* articulation, in contrast to the 2/4 section, which calls for a lighter and brighter style to depict children at play. The hemiola-like figure between measures 53 and 67 provides an excellent opportunity to explain the concept of two against three.

The third movement opens with a fanfare announcing the king and his hunting party. The drums should not overpower trumpet, and horn and saxophone should play in equal balance. All eighth notes not under a slur should be separated to maintain a festive character. The ensemble should understand and perform "*leggiero, non legato*" at measure 54 and keep their articulation light even in the louder passages. In the *accelerando* from measures 99 through 112 and on to the end, it is important to play with proper balance and resonant sound, regardless of the *fortissimo* markings.

Unit 7: Form and Structure

SECTION	MEASURE	EVENT AND SCORING
Movement I: "Le Furet"		
Introduction	1–6	Motive in upper woodwinds and 1st trumpet; B-flat major; *allegro molto*; in 2/4 time
Theme 1	7–15	Melody in upper woodwinds
Theme 2	15–23	Melody in alto saxophone; joined by clarinet and oboe in m. 19
Theme 1	23–31	Flute melody; taken over by bassoon, tenor saxophone, and euphonium at m. 27
Transition	31–46	Fragments of Theme 1 begins in oboe and continues through horn and woodwinds, flute, and piccolo
Theme 2	46–54	Motive in call and response between muted trumpet and flute
Theme 1	54–62	Upper woodwinds, alto and tenor saxophone, and euphonium
Variation on Theme 1	62–78	Motive in alto saxophone at m. 62; picked up by piccolo, oboe, muted trumpet, and xylophone at m. 71; 3/4 measure provides rhythmic interest at m. 77
Theme 1	78–107	Four statements of the theme, each with thicker texture and faster tempo
Coda	108–112	Lower brass and woodwind descending line leads to fragment of Theme 1
Movement II: "The Laurel Grove"		
Section A		
Theme 1	1–4	Motive in alto saxophone; E-flat major; *poco moderato* in 4/4
Theme 2	5–9	Melody in flute and trumpet; 2/4 measure at m. 9
Theme 1	9–14	Slight variation of the theme

SECTION	MEASURE	EVENT AND SCORING
Theme 2	14–17	Flute and clarinet carry the motive
Codetta	18–21	Trumpet in call and response; using fragment of Theme 2
Transition	21–26	Tonal center of B-flat major; *poco piu mosso*
Section B Theme 1	27–36	Original Theme 1 in diminution; F major in 2/4; *allegretto e scherzando*
Theme 2	37–52	Original Theme 2 in diminution
Variation on Theme 1	53–67	Upper woodwinds in hemiola against trumpet
Theme 2	68–79	Theme 2 rescored and slightly varied
Transition	80–84	Fragment of Theme 2 slightly varied; leads to D.S. and E-flat major
Coda	85–90	Uses fragments of both themes and trumpet in call and response, as at m. 18
Movement III: "King Dagobert" Introduction	1–24	Fanfare in trumpet and horn; motive with saxophone will recur; B-flat major; *allegro ma non troppo* in 6/8
Theme 1	25–32	Hunting motive in upper woodwinds
Theme 2	33–36	Horn motive with tenor saxophone and euphonium
Theme 1	37–44	Thicker texture with countermelody in tenor saxophone
Theme 3	44–53	Saxophone and horn
Theme 4	54–78	All sections play in fugue style
Transition	79–87	Horn motive from introduction
Theme 1	88–95	Upper woodwinds similar to m. 25 with countermelody in trombone and euphonium

SECTION	MEASURE	EVENT AND SCORING
Coda	96–112	Fragments of trumpet fanfare, horn motive, and Theme 1 combine and accelerate
	112–124	*Tempo giusto* to end

Unit 8: Suggested Listening
Percy Grainger, *Lincolnshire Posy*
Robert Hanson, *Four French Songs*
Robert Jager, *Colonial Airs and Dances*
Pierre La Plante:
    A Little French Suite
    American Riversongs
Darius Milhaud, *Suite Francaise*
Frank Ticheli, *Cajun Folk Songs*
Ralph Vaughan Williams, *English Folk Song Suite*

Unit 9: Additional References and Resources
Battisti, Frank, and Robert Garofalo. *Guide to Score Study*. Ft. Lauderdale, FL: Meredith Music Publications, 1990.

Dvorak, Thomas L., Cynthia Crump Taggart, and Peter Schmaltz. *Best Music for Young Band*. Brooklyn, NY: Manhattan Beach Music, 1986.

Garofalo, Robert J. *Instructional Designs for Middle/Junior High School Band*. Fort Lauderdale, FL: Meredith Music Publications, 1995.

Grout, Donald Jay, and Claude V. Palisca, ed. *A History of Western Music*. Sixth edition. New York: W. W. Norton & Co., 2001.

Randel, Don Michael. *The New Harvard Dictionary of Music*. Cambridge, MA: Harvard University, 1986.

Sadie, Stanley, ed. *The New Grove Dictionary of Music and Musicians*. Second edition. London: Macmillan, 2001.

Smith, Norman, and Albert Stoutamire. *Program Notes for Band*. Chicago, IL. GIA Publications, Inc., 2001.

Contributed by:
Michael Burch-Pesses
Director of Bands
Pacific University
Forest Grove, Oregon

Teacher Resource Guide

Military Symphony in F
Francois Joseph Gossec

(1734–1829)

edited by Richard Franko Goldman

and Robert L. Leist

Unit 1: Composer

Francois Joseph Gossec[1] was born in Vergnies, Belgium, on January 17, 1734, and died in Passy, near Paris, France, on February 16, 1829. He was a prolific composer of over fifty published symphonies, as well as chamber works, sacred vocal music, music for the stage, and a large variety of works for the French Revolution.[2] Gossec was one of those who would adapt to conform to what was popular. He began his career as a performer and composer for the established society. When the revolution came, he was a revolutionist. After the revolution, he was a professor of composition.

In 1751, Gossec went to Paris, where he met Jean-Philippe Rameau (1683–1764) and Johann Stamitz (1717–1757). He was active as a performer (on violin and bass) with the private ensemble of La Poupeliniere. He also published a number of symphonies, *opèra comique*, and *tradègie lyrique*. In 1773, he became the director of the *Concert spiritual*, and in 1775, he was also *maitre de musique* at the Opera. He became one of most established composers in France.

---

1 Randel, Don Michael. *The Harvard Dictionary of Music*. Cambridge, MA, and London, England: The Belknap Press of Harvard University Press, 1996, p. 324.

2 Whitwell, David. *A Concise History of the Wind Band*. Northridge, CA: Published by Winds, 1985, p. 147.

Gossec was the leading composer for the French Revolution (1789–1799). He actually composed more band music for the revolution than any other composer. On July 14, 1790, Gossec's *Te Deum* was the principal musical portion of the great Festival of the Federation. The large number of musicians at this performance foreshadows the mass bands assembled by Patrick Gilmore for the Grand National Concert in New Orleans in 1864, the National Peace Jubilee in Boston in 1869, and the World Peace Jubilee in Boston in 1869.[3]

After 1799, Gossec was a professor of composition at the conservatory, and he was made Chavalier of the Legion d' Honor in 1804. In 1816, Louis XVIII closed the Conservatory, and Gossec was left without means of support. Gossec was impecunious when he died in 1829.

Unit 2: Composition

Gossec's works were the central musical contribution for many of the ceremonies held for the French Revolution.[4] *The Military Symphony in F* was most likely composed for the Feydeau Street Concert of May 30, 1794.

The revolutionists favored music with broad appeal. They rejected the values of the aristocracy, and wanted music that was intentionally popular. The goal of the composer was to stir the patriotic emotions of the listener. This is not so different from patriotic music throughout history. Beethoven's *Wellington's Victory* is an important example of this type of music. Socialist realists of the Soviet Union in the 1930s[5] also had similar goals. Powerful writing for the brass and percussion, and memorable song-like melodies are characteristics of this style. The effective dynamic contrast between loud and soft between the various instruments of the ensemble is one of several techniques the composer uses to engage the attention and interest of the listener.

Movement

3 Schwartz, H. W. *Bands of America*. New York: Da Capo Press, 1975, p. 50.

4 Whitwell, David. *Band Music of the French Revolution*. Tutzing, Germany, Hans Schneider.

5 Morgan, Robert P. *Twentieth Century Music*. New York, London: W. W. Norton & Company, 1991, p. 243.

Unit 3: Historical Perspective

The Band of the Paris National is of importance in the history of modern wind band. It set a number of precedents that would be followed by bands to the present day. It had forty-five or more members at a time when most wind bands consisted of approximately twelve. The clarinet replaced the oboe as the fundamental melodic vehicle. Related to this was the use of repeated doubling of the clarinet parts, much as string instruments are doubled in an orchestra. The band was born with the French Revolution. The sound was distinctly different from Louis XVI's *Les Grands Hautbois*. The *Les Grands Hautbois* provided background music for the king. "They were themselves a symbol of the king."[6]

ORIGINAL INSTRUMENTATION[7]:
T small flues, oboes, two clarinets (in C), two trumpets (in F), two horns (in F), two bassoons, serpent or string bass, timpani, bass drum.

INSTRUMENTATION FOR THE MODERN EDITION:
Piccolo (in C), piccolo (in D-flat), flute, oboe, solo clarinet, 1st/2nd/3rd B-flat clarinet, E-flat alto clarinet, B-flat bass clarinet, 1st/2nd alto saxophone, B-flat tenor saxophone, 1st/2nd B-flat cornet, 1st/2nd B-flat trumpet, 1st/2nd/3rd/4th horn (in E-flat or B-flat), 1st/2nd/3rd trombone, B-flat baritone (treble clef), euphonium (bass clef), basses, string bass, percussion, timpani.

Unit 4: Technical Considerations

The technical demands of this piece are modest, appropriate for a good high school band. The work stays in or around the keys of F and C major. Even in the development sections, the piece never goes to remote tonal areas. The work has no rapid scalar passages. Several trills are called for in flute and clarinet. The brass parts will not be taxing for players of average endurance, as there are rests in every part. The range demands are modest for a high school trumpeter. The highest written notes in the 1st trumpet part are two Bs in the last phrase of the first movement. The trumpet parts are simpler than the cornet parts and consist mostly of fanfare-type material, reflecting the practice of the time.

Unit 5: Stylistic Considerations

Symphony in F holds a place that is significant in the history of the wind band. It was featured in one of the major festivals of the French Revolution. Care should be taken in the preparation of this piece to ensure that intonation, tone, and dynamic shading work together to make it meaningful for listeners and performers.

---

6 Whitwell, David. *A Concise History of the Wind Band.* Northridge, CA: Published by Winds, 1985, p. 185.

7 Whitwell, David. *Band Music of the French Revolution.* Tutzing, Germany, Hans Schneider, p. 148.

Dynamic contrast must be clear and striking but should not become exaggerated, which could lead to a caricature of the style. Younger players will tend to play this music too loud for their skill because the *forte* and *fortissimo* markings are used freely. Dynamic markings are always relative to the context. Great care should be taken in getting the proper sound from the percussion. The loud dynamics must not become distorted and harsh.

In music that is essentially diatonic in nature, accurate intonation is essential. This work can be used to train the band to play in tune. Perfect intervals (fourths, fifths, and octaves) played at a moderate dynamic produce "resultant tones." When the interval is in tune, the players can learn to hear these tones and so learn how to be in tune. This has the distinct advantage of being an aural method of tuning, done by the students, rather than a visual response to an electric tuner.

There is much doubling in the score. The conductor may wish to thin this out for clarity and contrast. It might be effective to thin the parts out the first time and bring in the full ensemble on the repeats.

Unit 6: Musical Elements

MELODY:
The melodic materials used by Gossec are diatonic and simple. This is the nature of revolutionary and patriotic music. Most of the themes move by step, with only occasional leaps.

HARMONY:
The harmonic syntax of the symphony is conservative. Only basic harmonies of the tonic, subdominant, and dominant are used. The development of the first movement uses only a slightly more complicated harmony, having a single diminished chord (C-sharpDim7th).

The third movement is in C major. The first half concludes on the dominant. The second half starts on the dominant of D minor and then goes to a dominant chord of the tonic key (A7– Dm7–G7–C)—a series of ii–V harmonies in C.

RHYTHM:
Most of the rhythmic figures in this work are simple. There are several sixteenth figures, but they are of brief duration, move stepwise, and are in a comfortable register and key.

TIMBRE:
The tone color of *Military Symphony in F* is determined by its instrumentation and orchestration. There is little solo writing, but much doubling. This arises most likely from the fact that it was written for outdoor performance for massive crowds. Subtle effects of shading would have not been heard by the crowd and would have likely detracted from the musical impact of the work.

Unit 7: Form and Structure

Military Symphony in F is in three movements, each consisting of two repeated sections.

Movement I – *Allegro Maestoso*

The symphony opens with a melody constructed from a thickly harmonized descending F major triad. The rhythm is stately, almost courtly in character. It brings to mind the principle theme from Wagner's *Overture to Die Meistersinger.*

The first movement is a sonata form, with both the exposition and the development–recapitulation repeated. The tonality of the movement is F major.

MEASURE	EVENT AND SCORING
1–27	Exposition
	Repeat
28–39	Development
40–end	Recapitulation
	Repeat

The development section lasts for only twelve measures; it opens in the brass with an inversion of the opening arpeggio, but in C major. After four measures, the woodwinds join the brass at a moderate dynamic. After some suspensions, the music returns to C major for the recapitulation.

The recapitulation is straightforward and brief, lasting only twenty measures. The movement closes with *tutti* playing syncopated fanfare material against eighth notes, concluding with three *fortissimo* quarter notes. No *ritard.* is indicated in the score. The entire second section is repeated.

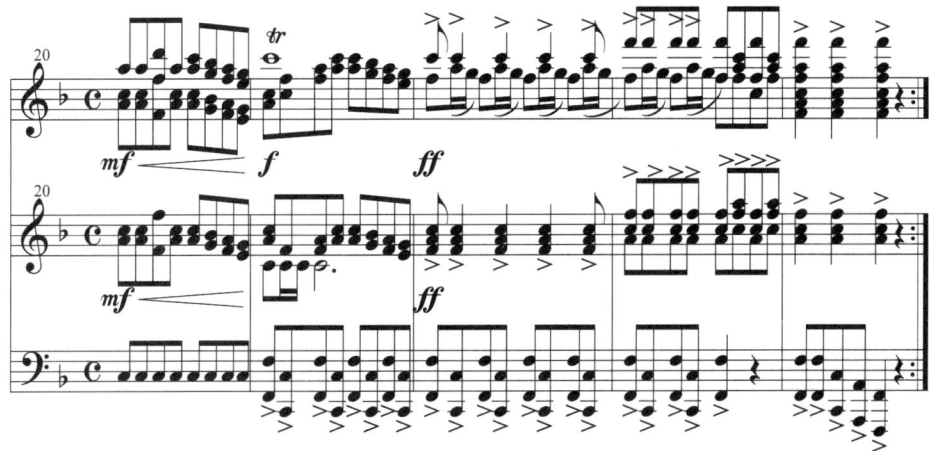

Movement II – *Larghetto*

The second movement is a rounded binary form | |:A | |:B A1 | | in F major. The meter is 6/8.

The tempo of the second movement is *Larghetto*, and it is characterized with dynamic contrast. The *forte* figures last for three beats, and the overall character of the first half of the movement is quiet. Only four chords are used.

The second section of the movement begins with a similar melodic figure and uses the same dynamic alternations as the first, but the dynamic builds to *fortissimo*. A pedal point on C is used to usher in the final chord.

Movement III – *Allegro*

The third movement, in C major, consists of two repeated sections. In the beginning, after four measures of C major and G7 chords at a *fortissimo* dynamic, the woodwinds play a simple theme in stepwise motion, decorated with a trill.

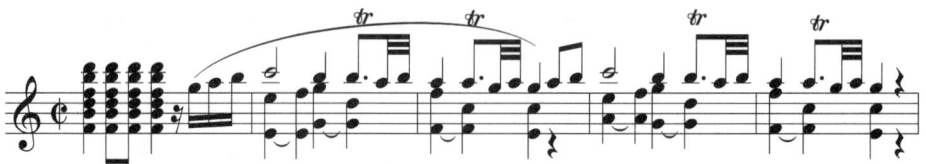

This is followed by an oboe duet at the same dynamic level. The band enters suddenly with a *fortissimo* C major descending quarter note arpeggio.

The second section starts with a minor seventh G in oboe against an A in brass at a moderate dynamic level. The second measure completes the A7 chord implied by the first measure, and oboe continues with a simple duet. Clarinet joins oboe in the third measure, still at a moderate dynamic. In the next measure, the entire band comes in with a *forte* C major scale.

The symphony remains in C major to the end and closes with the full ensemble playing over pedal point G quarter notes, leading to a C major chord, repeated three times. The first and final movements conclude with the same three-note hammer strokes.

Unit 8: Suggested Listening

Ludwig Van Beethoven:
  Symphony No. 3 in E-flat
  Wellington's Victory
Hector Berlioz, *Symphonie funèbre et triomphale*, Op. 15
Richard Strauss, *Festmusik der Stadt Wien*

Unit 9: Additional References and Resources

Whitwell, David. *A Concise History of the Wind Band*. Northridge, CA: Winds, 1985.

Whitwell, David. *Band Music of the French Revolution*. Copyright by Hans Schneider, 1979.

Schwartz, H. W. *Bands of America*. New York: Da Capo Press, 1975.

Contributed by:

James L. Klages
School of Music
University of Central Oklahoma
Edmond, Oklahoma

Teacher Resource Guide

On a Southern Hymnsong

David R. Holsinger
(b. 1945)

Unit 1: Composer

David Holsinger was born in Hardin, Missouri, on December 26, 1945. He received his Bachelor of Music degree from Central Methodist College in Fayette, Missouri, and his Master of Music degree from Central Missouri State University in Warrensburg. He did further post-graduate study at the University of Kansas, where he served as staff arranger for the university bands and director of the swing choir.

Holsinger's original compositions for winds and percussion have been programmed by countless military, university, high school, and middle school bands. Holsinger has twice been the recipient of the prestigious Ostwald Award, sponsored by the American Bandmasters' Association, for *The Armies of the Omnipresent Otserf* and *In the Spring, at the Time When Kings Go Off to War*. Of his band compositions, some of his most notable include *Havendance*, *On a Hymnsong of Philip Bliss*, *On Ancient Hymns and Festal Dances*, and *To Tame the Perilous Skies*. After serving for sixteen years as Composer-in-Residence at Shady Grove Church in Grand Prairie, Texas, Holsinger now resides in Cleveland, Tennessee, where he serves as director of the Lee University Wind Ensemble.

Unit 2: Composition

On a Southern Hymnsong was commissioned by Betty Bates, director of the Scottsboro High School Symphonic Band in Scottsboro, Alabama. The work joins a series of hymnsong compositions based on traditional hymns indigenous to America. Previous works in Holsinger's hymnsong series have

344

included treatments of *It Is Well with My Soul (On a Hymnsong of Philip Bliss)*, *My Faith Looks Up to Thee (On a Hymnsong of Lowell Mason)*, *Were You There When They Crucified My Lord (On an American Spiritual)*, *Jesus Loves Me (A Childhood Hymn)*, and *Nothing But the Blood of Jesus (On a Hymnsong of Robert Lowry)*. *On a Southern Hymnsong* is ninety-one measures, and is approximately four minutes and forty seconds in length.

Unit 3: Historical Perspective

On a Southern Hymnsong is based on the spiritual entitled *There is a Balm in Gilead*, found in many denomination hymnals throughout the United States. Holsinger, in investigating the history of this particular spiritual, found that the hymn's origin was a bit more cloudy than would be presumed. Although White spirituals would be published in shaped-note tunebooks two decades before Negro spirituals began to appear in print, both bodies of congregational folk song existed side by side in the pre-Civil War period. It is clear that these bodies of song intermingled and influenced each other, but the evidence is insufficient for either tradition to claim priority to several of the more familiar spirituals, *Gilead* included. Regardless of their label, spirituals have become a deeply meaningful expression of a common faith for many American congregations.

Considered a spiritual of hope and healing, the words are as follows:

There is a Balm in Gilead,
To make the wounded whole,
There is a Balm in Gilead,
To heal the sin-sick soul.

Sometimes I feel discouraged,
And think my work's in vain,
But then the Holy Spirit,
Revives my soul again.

There is a Balm in Gilead,
To make the wounded whole,
There is a Balm in Gilead,
To heal the sin-sick soul.[1]

Unit 4: Technical Considerations

On a Southern Hymnsong was written for full band instrumentation. Required percussion includes orchestral bells, timpani, bar chimes, triangle, tambourine, snare drum, suspended and crash cymbals, temple blocks, and

---

1   Arthur C. Jones. *Wade in the Water: The Wisdom of the Spirituals*. Maryknoll, New York: Orbis Books, 1993, p. 121.

bass drum. Percussion parts are appropriate for this level and can be covered by six players (one timpani, one bells, four battery). The timpanist, however, must be skilled in re-tuning, as some tuning changes occur rather quickly.

Many parallel key relationships and stylistic changes are employed throughout the composition to maintain interest and add variety to the strophic nature of the piece. As such, musicians must have confidence in moving quickly through many musical styles (e.g., *legato*, *cantabile*, light *staccato*, playful, etc.) and tonal centers, which include D minor, D major, B-flat major, C major, and C minor. As much band literature of this level employs flat keys, *On a Southern Hymnsong* provides opportunities for students to master the technical proficiencies required to perform competently in sharp keys. Particularly the key of D major, which involves four sharps and five sharps, respectively, will challenge B-flat and E-flat transposing instruments.

With minor exceptions, *tessitura* for woodwinds and brass is reasonable for this level. First flute will need to have a range to B-flat3; 1st clarinet to written C3 (concert B-flat); 1st trumpet to written A2 (concert G); horn to written G2 (concert C); baritone to E-flat1; and 1st trombone to G1. (Middle C is considered C1.) Technical demands are also reasonable, with most passages being relatively scalewise. The greatest challenge awaiting students will be to perform in a *cantabile* style that expresses the hymnsong's character. Students will be expected to play long, sustained passages in moderate to extreme ranges at times. Moreover, alto saxophone, tenor saxophone, and horn often have contrapuntal lines that require rhythmic independence.

Although the piece is written in simple meter throughout, students must be able to move between duple and triple subdivisions easily, as quarter note and eighth note triplets are approached by eighth notes and sixteenth notes in various locations throughout the piece. Sextuplets and quintuplets do occur, but they usually appear in scalar flourishes in the woodwinds.

Unit 5: Stylistic Considerations

Careful attention to proper balancing, projection of melodic and countermelodic line, dynamic contrast, stylistic contrast, and *rubato* are paramount to the success of *On a Southern Hymnsong*. *Legato* lines must be sustained, supported, and performed *cantabile* to portray the hymnsong in its proper style. Additionally, all melodic passages must be performed with a rich, beautiful tone quality that is full but not strained.

Performers are also required to transition between several subtle styles during the piece. The work begins "gently" (circa 72 beats per minute) with the theme being presented in D minor, thus creating a dark and mysterious character. The first transition (measure 24) is marked by a modulation to the parallel major and an increase in tempo (circa 96). These two alternations combined with light *staccato* playing in trombone and offbeats in baritone saxophone and bassoon give the hymn an accompaniment that is light and playful in nature. The piece alters style again at measure 31 (marked "with strength...") by modulating back to the original key of D minor and increasing tempo (circa 126). Here, the urgent character is portrayed by a rhythmically vital *ostinato* in upper woodwinds and baritone that accompanies a powerful statement of the theme (slightly varied) begun by trombone and horn and later joined by trumpet and tuba. Modulating to B-flat major, the work changes character again at measure 53. Tempo is also slowed (circa 112–116) to present a glorious return to the statement of the theme in major mode. To increase the drama, the next full statement of the theme modulates up a whole step (C major) and is marked slightly slower. By modulating to the parallel minor (C minor) and returning to the original tempo, the final transition (measure 78)00 briefly restates the mysterious, gentle character that begun the work before concluding, peacefully, in the relative major (E-flat major).

Unit 6: Musical Elements

Melody:

As *On a Southern Hymnsong* is composed by using D minor (some allusions to F major), D major, B-flat major, C major, C minor, and E-flat major, warm-up material should be based on these scales. Students should not only be able to perform these scales but should also be able to discriminate aurally between them. Students should understand the theoretical relationship between these key centers and be able to identify and define parallel and relative scale relationships. Young players familiar only with major keys can be eased into learning minor scales by using the relative major scale as a starting point. By beginning with a scale that is already familiar (e.g., E-flat major) and "walking down" to its sixth degree (concert C), students can be asked to perform a scale from concert C to concert C with the same key signature as E-flat major. After this is done, students might be asked to comment on the different sonorities heard. The concept of minor mode and relative major can then be introduced. After students have mastered relative major and minor key relationships, parallel major and minor relationships can be introduced and contrasted with the previously learned concept.

The hymnsong theme and its fragments provide an excellent opportunity for students to play expressively. Expressive playing can be addressed outside of the piece in group warm-ups that utilize scales and arpeggios as vehicles for exploring various ways of expressing the same material. Addressing this concept outside of the piece with memorized material will allow students to concentrate their efforts on listening to various ways expression can be achieved. Returning to the hymnsong, students can be shown how the music contains areas of repose and unrest that are created by antecedent and consequent phrases, harmony, harmonic rhythm, rhythm, and timbre, and how these moments can be accentuated through expressive performance. Students might be asked to identify where they think the areas of rest and unrest are within the composition and how they might highlight these areas. Students can also be encouraged as individuals to perform their "personalized" interpretations of scales, thematic material from *On a Southern Hymnsong*, or originally composed/improvised work.

Additionally, the melodic material contained in the piece can be compared to teach students how a composer can maintain interest in a work by using different modalities, augmentation, diminution, and fragmentation. This can be related to in- and out-of-class listening assignments to familiarize students with this concept further.

HARMONY:

Harmonic interest is generated through the various key relationships Holsinger employs throughout the work. By comparing and contrasting each presentation of the hymnsong theme combined with its harmonic accompaniment, students will have ample opportunity to understand how a composer uses harmony to maintain and magnify interest in a composition. Students should understand the strophic form of the composition and how this form presents a challenge to composers, particularly in maintaining variety and interest in a composition. Each section can be analyzed both vertically and harmonically to reveal the compositional devices employed by Holsinger. Once students begin to understand the devices employed, students may be asked to comment on where they believe the climactic moments of the piece occur and to give harmonic evidence supporting their decisions.

Furthermore, students should be cognizant of countermelodic lines that appear throughout the work. These lines should be isolated in rehearsal so each student can identify these lines when they appear in context. Vocalizing (i.e., singing) these lines both in and out of context will assist students in identifying these countermelodies.

A potential assignment for students to demonstrate their mastery of these compositional techniques might be to take a familiar piece of music that is simple in nature and compose variations on the piece using the same compositional devices Holsinger employs. The project could begin with the manipulation of melody lines only and eventually progress to more advanced techniques of harmonization and contrapuntal writing.

RHYTHM:

The greatest challenge in *On a Southern Hymnsong* is for students to move from duple to triple subdivisions evenly. Students should be encouraged to subdivide upcoming rhythmic events through longer note values when possible. Students must also subdivide eighth note triplets through quarter note triplets to ensure that these figures are performed accurately. Complex rhythms should be isolated and performed on warm-up passages to assist students' aural representation of the rhythm. Additionally, students should vocalize or clap difficult rhythms out of context before applying the rhythm in context. One strategy for getting students to move between duple and triple subdivisions is to set a metronome to quarter notes (or have a snare drummer tap quarter notes) while students alternate counting or singing one measure of eighth/sixteenth notes with one measure of triplets. Alternating between duple and triple subdivisions should be reduced gradually until students can alternate between one beat of triplets and one beat of eighths/sixteenths. Drilling this skill daily is essential to improving the rhythmic accuracy and independence of the group.

TIMBRE:

The aspect of timbre can be presented to students in an effort to demonstrate how a composer uses the various colors of an ensemble to convey the character of the music. For example, the character of the introduction is gentle and transparent. Consequently, the composer chooses to orchestrate this by using a small number of instruments in some of their less powerful registers (e.g., throat register of B-flat clarinet). In more powerful sections (e.g., measure 33), Holsinger places the melody in low brass instruments and creates a sense of urgency by composing a rhythmically vital *ostinato* and scoring it in the more extreme ranges of flute, oboe, and clarinet. By analyzing each section in this manner, students will begin to understand how a composer uses timbre to convey character and mood.

Unit 7: Form and Structure

SECTION	MEASURE	EVENT AND SCORING
1	1–8	Gentle opening; 1st clarinet and 1st alto saxophones have melody; 2nd clarinet and 2nd saxophone create texture with *ostinato*
	9–12	Flute and oboe enter with statement of the hymnsong theme in minor mode; *ostinato* in clarinet and alto saxophone becomes contrapuntal; 1st clarinet timbre is added to theme (mm. 10–12)
	12–15	Trumpet takes over hymnsong theme alluding to relative major (F major), but concludes on tonic of D minor; horn and alto saxophone harmonize theme (mm. 14–15); flute, oboe, and clarinet provide counterpoint; baritone enters for first time (m. 15)

Section	Measure	Event and Scoring
	16–23	Repeat of opening eight measures; flute added in m. 20 to begin transition to next section
2	24–30	Key modulates to parallel major (D major); tempo increases (circa 96); flute and 1st clarinet state theme in its major form; oboe harmonizes theme; horn (cued in alto saxophone) has countermelody; 1st bassoon and baritone saxophone have offbeats to bass clarinet, tenor saxophone, trombone, and tuba downbeats; temple blocks add to light, playful character
	31–32	Modulation back to parallel minor (D minor); transition to Section 3
3	33–41	Modulation to D minor finalized; tempo increases (circa 126); "urgent" *ostinato* in upper woodwinds; baritone has syncopated *ostinato*; march-like snare drum drives music; variation of theme appears in powerful statement by tenor saxophone, trombone, and horn; trumpet and tuba are added to theme in m. 39
	42–52	Transitional section moving away from minor tonality; tenor saxophone and horn have important melodic line that must project; tempo begins to gradually slow (mm. 48–52) for dramatic return to statement of the theme in major mode that is approaching
	53–60	Modulation to B-flat major is finalized; trumpet, baritone, tenor saxophone, and 1st trombone have hymnsong theme; two counterlines are present: one in flute, oboe, and clarinet, and the second in alto saxophone and horn

SECTION	MEASURE	EVENT AND SCORING
	61	Modulatory measure leading to C major
4	62–73	Hymnsong theme stated in C major; orchestration similar to Section 3 with the exception of baritone, which is removed from the theme; last statement of theme is augmented (mm. 68–70) and appended (mm. 71–73) for concluding and transitional purposes
	74–77	Transition back to gentle character/ minor tonality; flute and oboe hint at playful character of Section 2
Coda	78–81	Restatement of Section 1 in C minor
	82–85	Trumpet enters stating hymnsong theme alluding to relative major (E-flat major); unlike Section 1, theme augmented and concludes in relative major
	86–91	Flute presents fragmented hymnsong theme in E-flat major; piece concludes on tonic triad of E-flat major

Unit 8: Suggested Listening

David Holsinger:
    A Childhood Hymn
    On a Hymnsong of Philip Bliss
    On a Hymnsong of Robert Lowry
    On an America Spiritual
William Schuman, *When Jesus Wept*
Frank Ticheli, *Amazing Grace*

Unit 9: Additional References and Resources

Apel, Willi, ed. *Harvard Dictionary of Music*. Second edition. Cambridge, MA: Belknap Press, 1970.

Cone, James H. *The Spirituals and the Blues: An Interpretation*. Westport, CT: Greenwood Press Publishers, 1972.

Jackson, George P. *White and Negro Spirituals: Their Life and Kinship*. New York: J. J. Augustin Publisher, 1943.

Jones, Arthur C. *Wade in the Water: The Wisdom of the Spirituals*. Maryknoll, NY: Orbis Books, 1993.

Lisk, Edward S. *The Creative Director: Alternative Rehearsal Techniques*. Third edition. Fort Lauderdale, FL: Meredith Music Publications, 1991.

Lisk, Edward S. *The Creative Director: Intangibles of Musical Performance*. Fort Lauderdale, FL: Meredith Music Publications, 1996.

Randel, Don Michael. *The New Harvard Dictionary of Music*. Cambridge, MA: The Belknap Press of Harvard University Press, 1986.

Contributed by:
Daryl W. Kinney
Assistant Professor of Music Education
Kent State University
Kent, Ohio

Teacher Resource Guide

Portraits

Jim Colonna
(b. 1970)

Unit 1: Composer

Jim Colonna was born on May 2, 1970. He is an instrumental music instructor at Laramie County Community College in Cheyenne, Wyoming. He conducts the wind symphony and the jazz ensemble, and teaches theory, music history, and composition. He is also the assistant conductor of the Cheyenne Symphony Orchestra.

Prior to his appointment at LCCC, Colonna served as a graduate teaching assistant at the University of North Texas, under Eugene Corporon, where he earned his Master of Music in Conducting and Composition. He also taught music in grades seven through twelve in the public schools of Pennsylvania, where he conducted concert band, marching band, and chorus, and he started a local *Meet the Composer* for middle school children that included work with Michael Colgrass, David Diamond, and John Corigliano, to name a few.

Colonna studied composition with Jack Stamp for five years and Cindy McTee for two years. He has had numerous commissions from public schools and colleges, and has been published since 1996 with Larry Daehn Music Publishers and C-Alan Publications. Many of Colonna's works have been recorded on compact disc, including *The Soaring Eagle*, *Fanfare on "Adeste Fidelis,"* *Grantham Fanfare*, and *Portraits*.

Unit 2: Composition

Portraits was commissioned by Annette Cooper and the Granger Middle School Wind Ensemble in 1998. The work, originally titled *Three Miniatures*, had its premiere in March 1999. The composition is comprised of three

353

small musical portraits of favorite composers and their contribution to American music. The music is intended to imitate the composer's sound and to maximize the ability of talented middle school students. The work uses many traditional American twentieth century techniques, such as polytonality, quartal/quintal harmony, bleed through harmony, and complex rhythm. There are three movements: Movement I, "Fanfare," a musical portrait of Colonna's teacher, Jack Stamp; Movement II, "Song," a lyrical movement that is strongly influenced by Morton Gould and Aaron Copland; and Movement III, "Burlesque (Homage to Lenny)," a tribute to the overall greatest American musician of our century, Leonard Bernstein.

Unit 3: Historical Perspective

Many works for band have been set in three sections. *Portraits*, unlike many other band works set in three sections, is able to stand alone; however, due to the length of the sections, this practice is not advised. Colonna's early compositional style is greatly influenced by the traditional American sound set out by Aaron Copland, William Schuman, and Leonard Bernstein.

In recent years, there has been a great deal of interest in fanfares for full band rather than brass alone. Jack Stamp has written many fanfares for band. These fanfares serve more as a prelude incorporating fugues (usually at the fourth rather than the Bach fifth, a unifying motive, and a lyrical setting of the fanfare themes, then a return through the unifying motive and a brief coda). *Portraits* is influenced by the historical American music sounds of spacial chords using fifths and fourths, and rhythmic influences of jazz syncopation and mixed meters. The following selections are good examples of these sounds and influences: Jack Stamp's *Cheers!*, Aaron Copland's *Lincoln Portrait*, Bernstein's *Slava!*, and Morton Gould's *Ballad for Band*. They give a full sense of the historical sounds *Portraits* draws its influence from.

Unit 4: Technical Considerations

Although *Portraits* was commissioned by a middle school band, it contains some interesting technical demands. The work is scored heavily for trombone. The "Fanfare" requires a good sense of balance after each entrance of the melody. The first statement is a bit tough to play exactly in tune due to its scoring and timbral combinations of trombone, horn, and tenor saxophone. Like any fugue, the countersubject must be a dynamic level lower than the subject. Although this is the case in this fanfare, many times a motivic variation on the subject is played, and these small fragments are meant to be heard as such. The timpanist must use hard mallets in this movement for the solos. In the *legato* statement of the melody, the polychordal movement of the accompaniment must seem fully connected. The melody is harmonized by "wrong note bass lines." This *legato* section should feel in two, using the large beat in 4/4 of beat 1 and beat 3. The closing should take full advantage of the accents and non-accented works for the return to be effective.

The "Song" has some quirky *ostinati* in flute and clarinet. There are divisions in four and divisions of three against each other: these should not be noticed or accented, but rather imitate a screen of sound. The brass chorale in the second part should be faster, more *rubato*. Here, the low trumpets pose definite intonation problems, but this should sound effortless and resonant. The closing canon is a simple two-part canon, and both voices should be equal in strength. The inner voice movement in trumpet must be heard as an equal voice as well. The cup mutes in the final measures must be tight cups, and the sound must be strong. The trumpets split into six parts, so it is important that they do not lose strength, even at the soft dynamic.

The "Burlesque" movement is definitely the most challenging in terms of activity and range. Here, the skips of a fifth and a ninth in the first theme in the trumpet solo and section are problematic. The changing simple meters in the full band can pose rhythmic delays. This movement contains the only solos. These short solos for oboe, bassoon, clarinet, flute, and tuba can pose time delays between the sections. Many younger bands will have trouble initially maintaining the tempo of the first section with the 7/8 motor. Here, the melody is presented as an alto saxophone solo and four different canons at different pitch levels. The canon voices must be equal, and it is within this canon that French horn extends to a high A, which is also doubled by trumpet to firm up the sound of beginning horn players. The bell tones in the final eight measures must begin the note with verve and decal until one measure before the 7/8, where everyone should *crescendo* to the end.

Unit 5: Stylistic Considerations

In the first section, "Fanfare," the challenge will be for the band to play the subject with high energy, receding a slight bit at the countersubject without getting faster. The *legato* section must also not slow down; it must only change character.

The opening of "Song," the second section, is marked "dreamlike," which will be difficult to maintain for the entire section. It should be ethereal and transparent. The bleed through harmonies should be magical, just filling in the sound rather than making the new pitch sound strongly. The balance of tune with the bass line is difficult, with harmonic voices popping out. Even though marked with accents in the canon, the melody must always be *sostenutto*—not bell tone-like—throughout. It is also necessary that all six trumpets have the same cup mute so there are no variations in the sound.

In the final section, "Burlesque," the style is whimsical and bright. It is important that the melodies and harmony match style, making sure all of the articulations are as written. The 7/8 meter must keep moving forward and remain light. The key to this movement is light articulation to maintain the tempo.

Unit 6: Musical Elements

"FANFARE":

The subject is presented at the fourth measure, beginning in F and then traveling by fourths as follows: F–B-flat–E-flat–A-flat–D-flat (These are not keys, but rather pitch centers.) The countersubject is in agreement with the new voice entrance and its pitch center. The "wrong note harmony" (a harmony that is not key centered but based on pitches of the melody) and polychordal harmonies in the *legato* section are wandering harmonies searching for a key right up to the recapitulation.

"SONG":

The opening cascading, bleed through harmonies are based on the first themes pitches: E–D–C–G, E–D–C–A, E–D–C–G–F). The harmonies in the theme are diatonic to the key of C major or A minor, depending on which phrase is being played. The brass chorale is polychordal at measure 13 and should be played freely and a little faster than the opening statement. The retransition begins in measure 27, pushing forward to the climax in measure 32. Measure 32 is a canon of the theme in high then low voices, with an inner voice movement in 2nd/3rd trumpet. The closing bleed through harmonies in six trumpets and piano are the same as the opening in the woodwinds.

"BURLESQUE":

This movement is based largely on Stephen Foster's *Camptown Races*. It should be fast at a tempo of quarter note = 152, although a range as low as 140 will also work. The language is simple melody over a harmonic bass line. The introduction is quirky, with very tight minor seconds and major sevenths that create a humorous sound. The percussion is crucial to the overall humor of this movement. The theme is stated by 1st trumpet in measure 9 and should be multiple tongued at faster tempi. Later at measure 22, the full band announces the theme and presents a false canon in the lower woodwinds and brass. Section one (measures 1 through 33) is primarily in C major and is based on the *Camptown Races* fragment. Section two, beginning in measure 34, is set in E-flat–B-flat–F–C–D at each statement of the melody. The most important element is the 7/8 meter. This should be very light and consistent in articulation. (Try to teach the 7/8 by having a drumset player hit the bass drum on 1–2–1++ and then have the band clap 12–12–123, making sure the last three eighth notes are even and not triplets.) Measure 70 is an interruption of the introduction, only to return to the second theme in measure 75. The movement closes with a recapitulation of the first theme and ends with a phrase from the second.

Unit 7: Form and Structure

Section	Measure	Event and Scoring

"Fanfare" – percussion introduces each statement of the theme

Section	Measure	Event and Scoring
A	1	Tonal center around F
	6	Tonal center around B-flat
	10	Tonal center around E-flat
	14	Tonal center around D-flat
	16–21	Unifying element and bridge
B	22	Homophonic statement of the theme
	39–40	Unifying element
	41	Closure

"Song"

	1–4	Introduction
	5–12	First full statement of the theme in B-flat
	13–20	Second theme based on the rhythm of the first theme
	21–25	Theme 1
	26–31	Retransition
	32–42	Canon of the melody in 3/4; B-flat
	43–47	Recap of Introduction as a coda

"Burlesque"

	1–8	Introduction
	9–16	Theme A
	17–21	Transition based on Introduction
	22–29	Theme A in C with false canon
	30–33	Transition based on Theme A
	34–43	Theme B in E-flat
	44–50	Theme B in F
	51–59	Theme B in B-flat canon
	60–69	Theme B in C canon
	70–73	Reintroduces Introduction
	74–82	Theme B in G
	83–88	Theme B in D
	89–91	Recap of Theme A over D pedal point
	92	Interruption in C
	94–97	Theme A in G
	98–104	Coda

Unit 8: Suggested Listening

Leonard Bernstein:
> *On the Town Dances*
> *Slava!*

Aaron Copland, *Lincoln Portrait*

Morton Gould, *Ballad for Band*

Jack Stamp:
> *Centotaph*
> *Cheers!*

Contributed by:

Jim Colonna
Laramie County Community College
Cheyenne, Wyoming

Teacher Resource Guide

Prairie Songs
Pierre La Plante
(b. 1934)

Unit 1: Composer

Pierre La Plante was born in Milwaukee, Wisconsin, in 1934 of French Canadian descent. He received both B.M.E. and M.M. degrees from the University of Wisconsin at Madison. While an undergraduate, he studied arranging with Jim Christensen, a prominent commercial arranger, composer, conductor, and music educator. La Plante has taught classroom, vocal, and instrumental music at the elementary, secondary, and college levels. He retired in May of 2001 after thirty-two years of teaching in Oregon, Wisconsin. A bassoonist, he currently performs with the Beloit-Janesville Symphony. Among his compositions are works for band, orchestra, choir, solo literature, and chamber music.

Unit 2: Composition

Prairie Songs was commissioned by the Central Middle School Band of Waukesha, Wisconsin, Laura Kautz Sindberg, conductor. La Plante published *Prairie Songs* in 1998 as part of the sesquicentennial (150-year) celebration for the state of Wisconsin. This composition utilizes contrasting melodies from two Wisconsin folk songs, *The Pinery Boy* and *The Turkey Song*. "The Pinery Boy" tells of the heartbreak of a young woman who learns that her lover drowned while working on the river. It is set to a somber melody, notable for the dramatic upward leap of a minor sixth in the first measure. The text of "The Turkey Song" is much less serious. The musical character is much faster and lighter, and brings to mind lively folk-like music played for dancing.

Other compositions by La Plante include *Come to the Fair, Red River Valley, In the Forest of the King,* and *Serenade and Jig on English Folksongs.*

Unit 3: Historical Perspective

Prairie Songs was composed for the modern concert band by an experienced public school music educator. Therefore, the scoring practices represent skillful use of each instrumental voice within conventional roles and ranges. The percussion parts are integral to the success of the piece due to their use as carriers of the melody. Stylistically, the challenge lies in an accurate execution of the articulations, accents, and slurs present in Theme 2 to achieve the appropriate style. *Prairie Songs* is similar in style to *Kentucky 1800* by Clare Grundman and *Rodeo* by Aaron Copland.

Unit 4: Technical Considerations

Fluency in the scales of B-flat and F major is required to perform *Prairie Songs.* Occasionally, chromatic passing tones are required as well. Rhythmic demands include a mastery of syncopation, dotted-eighth and sixteenth notes, and eighth notes grouped across the bar line. La Plante consistently scores each instrument within its traditional ranges and roles, which should help any ensemble achieve a characteristic sound. His use of the percussion section adds a vibrant tone color to the band, for instance, the use of timpani as a melodic voice in measures 66 and 77.

Unit 5: Stylistic Considerations

An accurate performance of *Prairie Songs* will require students to contrast the *legato* slurred articulation of Theme 1 with the combination of *staccato*, accents, and short slurs of Theme 2. While Theme 1 should be interpreted in a lyrical, connected, *cantabile* style, the articulations marked in Theme 2 invite comparisons to fiddle music played at a country dance in a folk music style. The contrasts of tongued and slurred, long and short, and frequent accents are meticulously marked throughout Theme 2. Likewise, a number of dramatic dynamic contrasts are included in the score; if observed, they clarify the start of each theme as well as the melodic gestures in the coda.

Phrase endings are an important element in the introduction since the first four phrases are each only two measures long. Precise, resonant releases by the ensemble are required to perform this section correctly. As an interpretive device, the conductor may intentionally extend the duration of these short phrases, thus distorting the rhythmic pulse but increasing the musical clarity.

Unit 6: Musical Elements

MELODY:

Most of *Prairie Songs* has a concert key signature of one flat. However, Theme 1 is in F major, while Theme 2 is in D minor. This duality provides a wonderful opportunity to talk about major keys and their parallel minor key. Motific repetition is also present, and should be pointed out to the students. For instance, the melodic figure of dotted-eighth/sixteenth note from measure 17 reappears as the transitional material in measures 32 through 37. Not only does this gesture return in measures 105 through 108, but it serves the same function (i.e., to introduce Theme 2).

Most of Theme 1 of *Prairie Songs* is polyphonic (i.e., a linear melody is harmonized by musical lines moving around it). Careful dynamic balance must be sought to allow the melody to be heard while maintaining the sonic presence and harmonic contribution of the other lines. Identifying which instruments perform the same musical line is critical to adjusting the volume levels required to achieve this balance. La Plante utilizes suspended chords in measures 20 through 22; students should be taught to emphasize the suspended note by playing as much as one dynamic level louder then marked for only the duration of that note.

The numerous imitative sections in *Prairie Songs* require students to consider the need to project a new entrance of a given theme without altering the style and overall dynamic level of the theme statements that preceded it.

RHYTHM:

The only time signature shifts in *Prairie Songs* are from common time to 2/4 time. A relatively high degree of syncopation is present due to the folk-like character of the second theme. The second theme also frequently utilizes a dotted-eighth/sixteenth note figure as well as an eighth/ two sixteenth note figure. In measures 151 through 156, the ensemble plays accent patterns formed by eighth notes grouped in three note patterns. This pattern of syncopation distorts the bar line and could create performance problems for students. Rehearse this section by first pairing the snare drum, flute, oboe, clarinet, and alto saxophone. Clarify to the rest of the band the connection between their rhythms (dotted notes and tied notes) and the accents of the group described above. Or, to make the same point in a different manner, the low brass and low reeds may profit from a reminder that within their dotted-quarter note/quarter tied to eighth note figure, an interior pulse (subdivision) of three eighth notes must be felt.

TIMBRE:

La Plante utilizes a wide degree of the timbral palette. For instance, at measures 9 through 12, he scores the chorale for woodwind choir plus horn. At measures 40 through 47, he scores the melody for low reeds joined by flute and piccolo. Percussion instruments are used to provide frequent flashes of color, for instance, the keyboards in measure 47, the rattle in measure 65, or the woodblock in measure 109. They are also used as independent carriers of the melody, for instance, the timpani in measures 77 through 83 or the bells in measures 105 through 107.

Twice the trumpet section is scored as a dramatic *soli*, from measures 48 through 55 and from measures 76 through 83. In such passages, young players are often tempted to blow too hard and play too loud, distorting balance, tone color, and intonation. At measure 48, encourage students to blend their sounds while trying to find a single sound for the entire section that imitates the resonance and pure tone achieved by professional players.

La Plante scores the trumpet section with straight mutes from measures 76 through 84, which presents a number of challenges. The use of a straight mute will raise the pitch of each instrument. A tuner should be used to determine exactly how far each individual must pull out his or her main tuning slide to compensate for the pitch alteration created by the mute. The director needs to monitor and reinforce the adjustment of the tuning slides until this behavior is firmly established. When the mutes come out, the students must push their slides back in to their original position. Experienced players often write cues to themselves in their parts to remind them to make the appropriate tuning adjustments; such written cues would benefit students as well. If possible, students should all play the same make and model of straight mute. At the very least, the director should verify that all students are in fact using a straight mute as opposed to no mute at all or whatever mute they happen to own.

Unit 7: Form and Structure

SECTION	MEASURE	EVENT AND SCORING
Opening	1–8	Eight-measure introduction broken into four two-measure phrases
Theme 1	9–14	Begins at m. 9; key of F major; melody in 1st clarinet; based on the Wisconsin folk song *The Pinery Boy*, which utilizes the relatively wide melodic scope of an octave plus three notes; tenor saxophone and 3rd clarinet double in octaves at mm. 13–14
Transition	19–24	Repeat introductory material with added quarter note suspensions in mm. 20 and 22 in both 2nd clarinet and 2nd trumpet

SECTION	MEASURE	EVENT AND SCORING
Theme 2 (repeated)	24–32	Melody voiced in alto and tenor saxophone plus euphonium at m. 24; surrounded by rich counterpoint
Transition	32–37	Time signature changes to 2/4 in m. 34; fragmentation and repetition of melody leads to second theme at m. 40; preceded by a two-measure introduction in the new *allegro* tempo at m. 38
Theme 2	40–48	Occurs at m. 40; in the key of D minor; melody based on The Turkey Song, a lively, playful folk-like melody that demands careful attention to slurs, accents, *staccato*, and articulation; second eight measures of melody presented by trumpet in m. 48
Transition	63–75	Melodic repetition, variation, and chromatic harmonization of first half section of Theme 2
Theme 2		Second half of Theme 2 presented by muted trumpet
Canonic/ transitional section	84–109	Key change to B-flat major at m. 109; section continues until m. 138
Themes combined	139–147	*Maestoso*; key signature returns to F major/D minor; Theme 1 played by flute, oboe, 1st clarinet, and 1st trumpet; Theme 2 played by 3rd clarinet, alto saxophone, horn, 1st trombone, and bells
Ending	147–156	At m. 147, melodic fragment of Theme 2 returns, as does *allegro* tempo; use of ties, dotted notes, and eighth notes grouped in threes serve to obscure the bar line in mm. 151–156; rapid tempo changes; *sfp* effects and rapid dynamic swells create a dramatic ending

Unit 8: Suggested Listening
Aaron Copland, *Rodeo*
Clare Grundman, Kentucky 1800
Barry Kopetz, *Americana Folk Suite*
Pierre La Plante, *American River Songs*

Unit 9: Additional References and Resources
McBeth, Francis W. *Effective Performance of Band Music*. San Antonio, TX: Southern Music Company, 1972.

Whitener, Scott. *A Complete Guide to Brass*. Second edition. New York: Schirmer Books, 1997.

Contributed by:
Thomas Bough
Southern Illinois University
Carbondale, Illinois

Teacher Resource Guide

Prelude in the Dorian Mode
Antonio de Cabézon

(1510–1566)

scored for wind band by Percy Grainger

(1882–1961)

edited by Keith Brion and Michael Brand

Unit 1: Composer

Antonio de Cabézon, born of Spanish nobility in 1510, was blind since birth. He received most of his musical training in Palencia. In 1526, he became organist in the chapel of Queen Isabella. He later served Philip II, often traveling abroad with him, and he was instrumental in Philip's marriage to Queen Mary of England. During his lifetime, de Cabézon became one of the greatest organ and clavichord performers and composers of the sixteenth century.

Percy Aldridge Grainger was born in Melbourne, Australia, on July 8, 1882. He was the first significant twentieth century composer, who wrote his finest music for the wind band. His individualistic understanding of and scoring for winds and percussion was innovative for the then-young concert band medium, and his prolific output for "wind groups" made him one of the most significant figures in band history. He was a staunch supporter of the efforts of Edwin Franko Goldman in building a repertory of original band works, and continued his support through public concert appearances and teaching, among those his work at the Interlochen Arts Festival, from which this work is a result.

Unit 2: Composition

Prelude in the Dorian Mode was one of Grainger's "chosen gems" for band or wind groups (one of the many irregular terms employed by Grainger, particularly from the 1920s on in a form he called "blue-eyed English"), composed for Joseph Maddy and the Interlochen Arts Festival. The *Prelude* is a wind band scoring of de Cabézon's *Tiènto del Segundo Tono*, a richly polyphonic keyboard work. de Cabézon composed a number of polyphonic sacred works, versillos, diferencias, and twenty-nine tientos, of which this one "on the second tone" was one. Grainger collected and set twenty-three "chosen gems," historic music he deeply valued. As quoted by Richard Franko Goldman, "The 500 years of decipherable music that precedes Bach is at least as lovely and important as all post-Bach music." Grainger set *Prelude in the Dorian Mode* in his concept of elastic scoring, with linear "tone strands" that may be performed by various combinations of instruments. These polyphonic works among the "chosen gems" were ideal for such settings.

Unit 3: Historical Perspective

Grainger was perhaps at the height of his popularity among the band world when he created these "chosen gems" for Maddy and Interlochen. Though he was also becoming more eccentric, and battling his personal demons of hearing loss and illness, he increasingly expressed his pleasure at the acceptance of his music by band leaders during this time in his life. In one of his Round Letters (a general letter that he circulated to friends and relatives) dated June 7, 1949, Grainger stated: "Now the whole thing is just-right: They are doing me a kindness, in forth-playing my wretched tone-works...Between March 17 and June 15 I will have heard...CHOSEN GEMS for bands or wind groups (13th year–hundred English, 15th y–h Burgundian, 16th y–h Spanish, 17th y–h English, and so on) once or more."

Conductors in choosing historic works for their programming needs can set *Prelude in the Dorian Mode* as an authentic example of polyphonic music for winds. Grainger expounded on this in a 1948 letter as he wrote, "The fact that church choirs in the Middle Ages were equipped with portative and positive organs...shows that wind color, as much as string color, was considered a normal tonal background to vocal music." An additional historic place for this tiento could be in its connection to music of the time of Christopher Columbus and the courts of Queen Isabella and Philip II.

Unit 4: Technical Considerations

The polyphonic writing, relatively easy key, and tempo of half note = 63 relegate *Prelude in the Dorian Mode* to a difficulty rating of III in considering this work for performance. The ranges are not extreme, and the florid middle section of mostly diatonic eighth notes is well within the capabilities of a good high school band. The only mildly problematic consideration inherent in this, as with most polyphonic music, is rhythmic accuracy of the lines following notes tied across to strong beats within the pulse.

A unique aspect of Brion and Brand's edition is the understandable conveying of Grainger's elastic scoring. The full score notes the Graingeresque "tone strands" by the letters A, B, C, and D to the left of the instrumentation column, and the top four staves can serve as a condensed score of the four-part writing. Using this indication, one can choose to perform this work in the full band setting, with homogeneous or mixed quartets, or balanced-per-part chamber groups, using the printed parts from this fine edition. The "tone strand" and part are as follows:

Tone Strand A – Flute I and II, Oboe I, Soprano Saxophone, Alto
  Saxophone I, Cornet I
Tone Strand B – Oboe II, English Horn, Alto Saxophone II, Horn I
Tone Strand C – Bassoon I, Tenor Saxophone, Baritone (Euphonium)
Tone Strand D – Bassoon II, Contrabassoon, Baritone Saxophone, Tuba

Unit 5: Stylistic Considerations

The opening style indication of Grainger, "Flowingly," aptly describes the performance style, regardless of the varying ensembles one chooses to use in playing *Prelude in the Dorian Mode*. Each line is well marked in this edition to lead the players to perform their individual linear voice authentically, and the score is similarly well marked to aid in the best teaching of this fine work. For the full band, the dynamics indications are exact and will lead to a performance in the true Grainger sense of tone color. In performing this tiento with chamber players, the teacher should use the full score as a guide to the weight of each voice among the four plus, with regard to the varying strengths of the performers involved, to achieve stylistic balance. Regardless of the ensemble used, this work provides an excellent opportunity to teach polyphonic style in an artistic and historic setting.

Unit 6: Musical Elements
MELODY:

The flowing, graceful melody, mostly diatonic with a few interval leaps of a fifth, is quite accessible to moderately technical players. The Dorian mode allows for teaching the theoretic (and possibly the historic) concepts of scales. The equality of parts of polyphonic playing, yet entering at differing pitches, also allows for teaching equal preparation responsibility and the imitative style concept from player to player.

HARMONY:

Again, as a teaching concept inherent in polyphony, the harmony in this sixteenth century counterpoint is a controlled result of the linear line. To reinforce theory instruction (or to introduce a bit of theory), the conductor may during rehearsals add *fermatas*, encourage listening, and also point out linear cadences that later led to our now-common tonic–dominant–tonic harmonic movement in homophonic music.

RHYTHM:
There are no difficult rhythmic patterns within *Prelude in the Dorian Mode* and, with attention to the technical consideration noted in Unit 4, correct rhythmic performance should be easy.

TIMBRE:
This work allows for student exposure to the Graingeresque wind band tone color in a moderately easy technical setting. This provides a great performance opportunity for several instruments usually relegated to background or foundational scoring. In smaller chamber settings of the work, performers can learn the task of matching and/or establishing a characteristic tone color of small ensemble playing.

Unit 7: Form and Structure
Prelude in the Dorian Mode is in a common A–B–A polyphonic architecture, opening with a *legato* subject and adding texture with the subject's imitative entrances. The middle section is more florid, mostly diatonic polyphony, and the return is the antecedent opening polyphonic line with the consequent phrase of the opening subject also imitated in somewhat the form of a double fugue.

Unit 8: Suggested Listening
As of the publication of this text, there were no known recordings of *Prelude in the Dorian Mode*. For the purpose of teaching polyphonic style performance, the conductor may choose from the myriad examples of Bach, particularly in regard to some of the saxophone quartet performances or of the numerous brass quartet recordings of fugues available.

Unit 9: Additional References and Resources
The inside first two pages of the score to *Prelude in the Dorian Mode* contain more detailed notes regarding this fine work and some additional quotes that will be of interest to all conductors. The 1994 Clarendon Press–Oxford publication, *The All-Round Man, Selected Letters of Percy Grainger, 1914-1961*, edited by Malcolm Gillies and David Pear, provided additional data for this chapter and is a source of a great deal of insight into Grainger. Additional information may be found on the various Grainger websites and composers' websites for Antonio de Cabézon.

Contributed by:
Robert Belser
Associate Professor of Music and Director of Bands
University of Wyoming
Laramie, Wyoming

Teacher Resource Guide

Salvation Is Created
Pavel Tschesnokoff

(1877–1944)

arranged by Bruce Houseknecht

Unit 1: Composer

Pavel Tschesnokoff was one of Russia's most prolific composers of Russian Orthodox church music. He was born in 1877 near Moscow and remained there throughout his lifetime. Because instruments were forbidden in the church, all of his sacred music was written for unaccompanied choir. At the age of seven, Tschesnokoff began extensive musical training at the Moscow Synodal School, a renowned school for church musicians. He took courses including nine years of solfege; seven years of score reading at the keyboard; four years of harmony, counterpoint, and form; seven years of piano, seven years of violin; and four years of string ensemble playing and conducting. At Synodal, he was a pupil of Stephan Vasil'evic Smolenskij.

After graduating in 1895, Tschesnokoff studied with the prominent composer Sergei Taneyev, an expert in polyphonic choral compositions and the director of the Moscow Conservatory. While at the conservatory, Tschesnokoff also studied with Mikhail Ippolitov-Ivanov.

During his studies, Tschesnokoff worked as a choirmaster in many elementary and secondary schools. At an early age, he gained a reputation as a great conductor, leading many groups including the Russian Choral Society Choir. He founded a program of choral conducting at the Moscow Conservatory and taught there from 1920 until his death.

The revolution of 1917 stopped Tschesnokoff from composing or directing any sacred music. All of the approximated four hundred sacred works written by Tschesnokoff were completed by the age of thirty. After that time, he composed over one hundred secular and stage works, and conducted only secular choirs, including the Moscow Academy Choir and the Bol'shoy Theatre Choir.

The rule under Stalin was hard for many Russian Orthodox people. Tschesnokoff was the last choirmaster of Christ the Savior Cathedral in Moscow. This cathedral was destroyed during Stalin's anti-religious purge, which bothered Tschesnokoff so much that he stopped writing music. As a composer, Tschesnokoff died with the cathedral.

Unit 2: Composition

Arranged by Bruce Houseknecht in 1957, *Salvation Is Created* has become a standard in wind literature. It is a Russian Orthodox Communion hymn based on a simple chant melody and Psalm 74. Since the fall of the Soviet Union, *Salvation Is Created* has become a favorite in the Russian Orthodox church. This wind band version is published by Neil A. Kjos Music Co. The original Russian text is as follows:

> *Spaseniye Sodelal Yesi Posrede Zemli Bozhe. Alliluiya.*
> *(Salvation is created in the midst of the earth, O God. Alleluia.)*

This arrangement may be performed separately as a composition for band or used as an accompaniment to the octavo choral arrangement by Matterling (Kjos 7038). If this arrangement is used in joint performance of band and chorus, the first four measures serve as the introduction, and the players should be told to repeat the first four measures in every part.

Unit 3: Historical Perspective

Beginning in the seventeenth century, Russian church music was primarily polyphonic. Tschesnokoff studied with Sergei Taneyev, a renowned composer of polyphony. With the publication of Tchaikovsky's *The Divine Liturgy of St. John Chrysostom* in 1878, there was enormous interest in Russian church music that lasted until the Revolution in 1917. During these twenty-nine years, many composers wrote thousands of polyphonic choral works of Russian Orthodox text.

An important landmark in the choral studies is Tschesnokoff's book, *The Choir and How to Direct It*, which he considered his most important work. The book is divided into two sections about leading and organizing a choir, and choral conducting. The book was completed in 1930 but was not published until 1940. Tschesnokoff wrote to Rachmaninoff, who was residing in America, and asked for his help in publishing the book. Rachmaninoff replied that there was a depression in the arts and America was focusing mostly on dance music. When the book was finally published in Russia, its popularity was so great that it sold out and was reprinted in two later editions. This book is important to conductors of Tschesnokoff's music because he makes references to interpretation, the use of staggered breathing, and nuances of phrasing.

Because of its popularity, *Salvation Is Created* has been written in many different versions. Other editions include TTBB and SATTBB in both Russian and English, six-part brass ensemble (two horns, euphonium, three tubas), and eight horns. This wind band arrangement is very close to the original composition except for the addition of timpani, chimes, and crash cymbal.

Unit 4: Technical Considerations
The scale of C minor and E-flat major are required of the entire ensemble. The sustained, vocal-like quality of the melodic line and harmonies places great demands on the breath control of wind performers. While technicality and range are not a problem, tone control and intonation are large challenges in this piece. The E-flat contra-alto clarinet and string bass are doubled by the tuba part.

Unit 5: Stylistic Considerations
Most importantly, the phrasing must have direction, including the sustained chords. Overlapping phrases of the A theme allow for smooth movement. Staggered breathing should be practiced throughout with the exception of the beat before the B and B1 theme. Special attention should be given to the difference of dynamics in measures 9 and 30, where wind players *decrescendo* while the timpani *crescendos*. Do not be too large at measure 10. Save the largest growth to begin at measure 31.

Unit 6: Musical Elements
The challenge is to vary the melody each time it appears. Houseknecht helps by changing the instrumentation. Explore the different shapes of the phrases. According to Tschesnokoff, even if there are dynamic markings and clear cadences, the conductor must put his/her own nuances into the music.

The moving quarter and eighth notes are always the most important notes. Be sure to balance the chords under the moving notes. Propel the phrase forward and pull it back when appropriate.

Unit 7: Form and Structure

MEASURE   EVENT AND SCORING

1–10   A theme in C minor; begins with choir of clarinet, bassoon,
                 string bass, E-flat contra-alto clarinet, solo horn, and two
                 tubas followed by a color change in m. 5 of the same theme
                 with flute, one oboe, alto saxophone, cornet, 1st/2nd horn,
                 bassoon, and timpani

10–19   B theme in E-flat major; full band with *forte* and *crescendo*;
                 cymbal crash sets up the arrival at m. 10 and chimes enter;
                 add contrabassoon to the bassoon line but down an octave;
                 entire group *decrescendos* to *p*

19–21   Transition leading to C minor; fragmented B theme in solo
                 horn

22–31   A1 theme in C minor; low brass plays the theme; in m. 26,
                 the theme is restated by flute, clarinet, bassoon, alto
                 saxophone, and cornet; timpani leads into m. 31

31–39   B1 theme in E-flat major; main arrival; add contrabassoon
                 to the bassoon line but down an octave; entire group plays a
                 weighted accent of *forte*, softening to *mp* by m. 38

40–42   Coda in E-flat major; fragmented B theme in flute,
                 1st clarinet, and 1st horn

Unit 8: Suggested Listening

Johannes Brahms/Buehlman, *Blessed Are They* (from "A German Requiem")
J. S. Bach/Reed:
   Come Sweet Death
   My Jesus! Oh, What Anguish

Unit 9: Additional References and Resources

Elzinga, Harry. "The Sacred Choral Compositions of Pavel Grigor'evich
   Chesnokov (1877–1944)." Ph.D. diss., Indiana University, 1970.

Leonard, Richard Anthony. *A History of Russian Music*. New York: The
   Macmillan Company, 1957.

Rommereim, John Christian. "The Choir and How to Direct It: Pavel
   Chesnokov's Magnum Opus." *Choral Journal* 38, n7, February 1998, pp.
   29–42.

Swan, Alfred J. *Russian Music and Its Sources in Chant and Folk-Song*. New
   York: W. W. Norton & Company, Inc., 1973.

Velimirovic, Milos M. *Christianity and the Arts in Russia*. New York: Cambridge University Press, 1991.

Contributed by:
Joan deAlbuquerque
Doctoral Conducting Associate
University of North Texas
Denton, Texas

Teacher Resource Guide

Serenade, Op. 22c
Derek Bourgeois
(b. 1941)

Unit 1: Composer

British native Derek Bourgeois was born in the town of Kingston on Thames in 1941. He graduated with honors in music from Cambridge and later earned his doctorate there. Further study at the Royal Academy of Music included composition with Herbert Howells and conducting with Sir Adrian Boult. He has worked as lecturer in music at Bristol University, director of the National Youth Orchestra of Great Britain, and founder of the National Youth Chamber Orchestra. Currently, he is Director of Music at the St. Paul's Girl's School in London, a post he has held since 1993.

A prolific and often-commissioned composer, Bourgeois has worked across many genres, writing nine symphonies (including two for wind band), eight concertos (including a popular concerto for trombone and band), a full opera, and numerous chamber, vocal, and instrumental works. He is also a very popular composer in the highly competitive field of brass band. Though perhaps not as familiar an artist to American audiences, he is well known in European circles for his craftsmanship and melodic creativity, as well as his approachable sense of harmony and structure.

Unit 2: Composition

The composer writes, "I wrote all the music for my own wedding—the *Serenade* was the closing movement as we processed out and was originally entitled *Wedding March* (the publishers changed the title). I had strict instructions from my bride-to-be. The piece was to be jolly so that no one would feel like bursting into tears as they so often do in weddings. Also it was to be in an irregular meter so that the guests would be unable to march out of the church in step."

The *Serenade* was originally written for solo organ in 1965 as Op. 22 and was premiered at the composer's own wedding. It was arranged by the composer for concert band in 1980 and dubbed Op. 22c. (Op. 22b is an arrangement of the same piece for brass band.) While lasting only three minutes, the piece is a marvelous example of craft in service of melody, a miniature gem of flowing grace. Its unpretentious surface style hides a subtle, unbalanced rhythmic feel and uneven meter, giving the piece a character and personality all its own.

Unit 3: Historical Perspective

With its gracious and easygoing airs, this piece falls firmly into the long-established British tradition of what is often referred to as "light concert music" for large ensembles. Many British composers have served this tradition in the past, with Elgar, Holst, Vaughan Williams, and Walton all having contributed stellar examples. And the audience for such compositions in Europe continues to be strong both in the brass band and concert band fields. The tradition of amateur wind or brass groups formed from either community members and/or the employees of an industrial concern survives to a much greater extent in Europe than in America. The easily grasped style and form of *Serenade* is exemplary of the audience-pleasing number that is a staple of many amateur (and professional) band concerts.

Unit 4: Technical Considerations

The main challenge to many younger musicians will be the uneven meter and asymmetrical division of the piece. A large portion is in 11/8 meter (divided 3+3+2+3) or 13/8 meter (divided 3+3+2+2+3), with several short side steps into other uneven divisions. Before tackling the piece proper, conductors should spend time rehearsing scalar/unison patterns on uneven division of measures and also make sure they are comfortable conducting the patterns required in a relaxed style. Taking rhythmic patterns out of the piece and applying them to scales or triads will save rehearsal time in the long run.

The woodwinds have several measures calling for repeated runs and trills, which may look intimidating on the page but are not so difficult at the required tempo. Slow practice and repetition will win the day. The score calls for three cornet and two trumpet parts, but the piece can be performed with just the cornet parts. In one measure only, the 1st cornet part goes to B-flat above the staff and the 1st trumpet to D-flat above the staff. Percussion requirements are slim, mostly serving as color effects, such as tambourine and maracas.

Solos for piccolo, alto clarinet, and E-flat clarinet are cued in the flute and B-flat clarinet parts, respectively.

Unit 5: Stylistic Considerations

Most importantly, the rather devious nature of the meter should be concealed with a light, effortless style. At all times, this piece needs to sound as simple as breathing or blinking. Woodwinds carry the weight of the melody in the first half and should play with relaxation and delicate articulation, never forcing the occasional *staccato* notes and always flowing through to the end of each phrase.

The clever melody always needs a feeling of movement to its end, a particular challenge when the low brass and woodwinds briefly take over the tune in the second half. There is a need for subtle shaping of the melody as well, rising and falling in a natural style as the director sees fit.

The bass line accompaniment is in detached quarter notes for the most part and could be thought of as resembling the sound of a *pizzicato* string bass, with just enough resonance to not sound choppy.

Unit 6: Musical Considerations

Melody:

As the title implies, this piece is all about the melody, which should clearly float over the accompaniment figures. For the most part, the themes are in four-measure units and are fairly wide in their range, from lowest note to highest (an interval of a ninth figures prominently in the first theme). Players should direct and shape the flow of the themes all the way to the end of each phrase, performing the complete phrase as a unit and not just as individual measures or fragmentary figures of the melody. Directors should give special attention to the accompaniment figures and their balance, keeping them unobtrusive and out of the way—supporting the melody, not fighting it.

Harmony:

The harmonic structure of *Serenade* is uniformly tonal and unambiguous, with the occasional dashes of Bolero-like parallel chordal movement. One can hear charming echoes of Ravel and the Impressionists, particularly in the most dramatic section of the work at rehearsal no. 8. The piece begins in B-flat major and modulates to G major in the second section before returning to B-flat for the final third.

Rhythm:

Beyond the looping, graceful melody, what gives this piece its character is the uneven metrical division. Like the melodies, it brings to mind a pleasant but slightly eccentric individual who goes his own way, a wanderer who always finds his way back home. The accompanying *ostinato* figure resides primarily in the low voices and middle brass, where it should be played with a delicate touch—not abrasive or clipped, but light and energetic. The ending of the piece calls for special attention as it winds down with several duplets of rather exposed nature traded between tuba and clarinet.

TIMBRE:

As would be expected, scoring is light for the most part, with the woodwind voices carrying the melodic weight for the first two-thirds and trumpet scoring kept to a minimum. The sparse percussion is used to maximum effect, with maracas and tambourine adding delightful color to the *ostinato* figure. Again, the ending is exposed and delicate, with tuba and clarinet trading notes in a charming, brief conversation.

Unit 7: Form and Structure

The *Serenade* falls into a solid arch form: A section up to rehearsal no. 4, B section up to rehearsal no. 6, a return to the A theme with slight variations up to rehearsal no. 9, and a brief coda. The A section is in the key of B-flat major, and the B section resides in G major. Changes from section to section are also heralded by changes in the metrical feel (a different division of 11/8 leading into the B section, an unexpected measure of 7/8 leading back into the A section).

Unit 8: Suggested Listening

Derek Bourgeois, *Concerto for Trombone and Band*
Maurice Ravel, *Bolero*
William Walton, "Popular Song" from *Facade*
Recordings of *Serenade, Op. 22c*, have been made by the following groups: The Band of H.M. Royal Marines, the Royal Artillery Band, the City of London Wind Ensemble, the Ad Hoc Wind Orchestra, and the Mid-West Parkway Wind Ensemble

Unit 9: Additional References and Resources

Holland, Hughina, Clark Rundell, and Timothy Reynish, comp. *British Wind Music of Four Decades* (1951–1991). Manchester, England: Royal Northern College of Music, 1991.

Sadie, Stanley, ed. *Norton/Grove Concise Encyclopedia of Music*. New York: W. W. Norton & Co., 1988.

Derek Bourgeois's website: www.tramuntana.demon.co.uk

Other websites of interest:
www.warwickmusic.com/mall/bourgeois.asp
www.britishacademy.com/members/bourgeois

Contributed by:

Doug Norton
Director of Bands
Batesville Community Schools
Batesville, Indiana

Teacher Resource Guide

Shenandoah

Frank Ticheli
(b. 1958)

Unit 1: Composer

Frank Paul Ticheli was born in Monroe, Louisiana, on January 21, 1958. He began his musical career by learning the trumpet at age nine. In 1971, he and his family moved to Richardson, Texas, where he stayed through high school and college. After graduating from Southern Methodist University in 1980, Ticheli attended the University of Michigan and received his M.M. in 1983 and his D.M.A. in 1987. He has studied under Donald Erb, William Albright, Leslie Bassett, Wilham Bolcom, and George Wilson.

After high school and university teaching in Texas, Ticheli moved to Pasadena, California, where he became Composer-in-Residence of the Pacific Symphony Orchestra from 1991 to 1998 and served as Associate Professor of Composition at the University of Southern California.

Ticheli's compositions span several genres including band, orchestra, and chamber music. He has received numerous honors for these compositions. His awards include the Charles Ives Scholarship and Goddard Lieberson Fellowship from the American Academy and Institute of Arts and Letters, First Prize in the Texas Sesquicentennial Orchestral Composition Competition, the Frances and William Schuman Fellowship from the MacDowell Colony, and the Ross Lee Finney Award. The Pacific Symphony Orchestra's recording, which features Ticheli's *Radiant Voices* and *Postcard*, received an honorable mention from the National Association of Independent Record Distributors in 1994. His numerous compositions for wind ensemble and concert band have been performed throughout the world and have been awarded several prizes, including the 1989 Walter Beeler Price and First Prize in the eleventh annual "Symposium for New Music" held in Virginia.

Unit 2: Composition

Shenandoah was commissioned by the Hill Country Middle School Symphonic Band and dedicated to a horn player who passed away in 1997. The title of the work is in reference to the Shenandoah River located in Virginia. The composition uses the popular folk song entitled *Shenandoah*. The origin of this folk song is unclear. It has been attributed to various sources. Some believe that it derived from a Pennsylvania coal miner, others believe it came from a young student of Stephen Foster, and still others believe it originates from a Kentucky housewife. Many variations of the melody and text have been handed down as well. It is most commonly believed to be the tale of a love between a Native American woman and an early settler. This folk song serves as the basis for Ticheli's composition. In the words of the composer:

> In my setting of *Shenandoah,* I was inspired by the freedom and
> beauty of the folk melody and by the natural images evoked by
> the words, especially the image of a river.

This composition is listed as a grade three by Manhattan Beach Music and is approximately six minutes and thirty seconds in length.

Unit 3: Historical Perspective

The setting of a familiar tune in a new setting is a compositional technique almost as old as polyphony itself. A great deal of sacred and secular music throughout history was derived by creating new settings of familiar tunes. In the baroque period, for example, Bach mastered the genre of the chorale prelude, which put new settings to well-known hymns and chorales. Settings of American folk songs can be traced through such major composers as Charles Ives and Aaron Copland. This compositional technique was also popular in early wind band music as well. Gustav Holst and Ralph Vaughan Williams used a great deal of British folk songs in their early band compositions.

Unit 4: Technical Considerations

In this lush setting of the popular tune, there is not a great deal of dexterity required for a successful performance. However, there are several important technical factors needed for a meaningful performance. The work stays in the key of E-flat major throughout. Moving through the development section, Ticheli shifts the tonal center to B-flat major as well as a brief section of G-flat major. Aside from these tonal centers, there is very little chromaticism used. Ranges for particular instruments are not excessive. Trumpets do not ascend above the staff; however, the horns do start the piece on an exposed F below the staff. Solos or "one on a part" sections include euphonium, trumpet, and flute trio.

Unit 5: Stylistic Considerations

From the opening *legato* line of euphonium and French horn, the piece flows along in a beautiful chorale style. This composition gives directors an opportunity to either introduce or reinforce the concepts of the chorale style. Articulations throughout the piece should be *legato* and well connected. The interpretation of all accents should be done by thinking of a fuller sound with more weight rather than a heavy tongue articulation. The composer also specifies on a few occasions that the pitches marked *"ten"* (*tenuto*) should be played slightly longer, as if it had a very slight *fermata*. This serves to heighten the drama.

The tempo and phrasing are also important considerations. Although Ticheli gives the conductor some degree of freedom to fluctuate from the tempo provided, he warns us not to overdramatize them. This freedom gives the ensemble many opportunities for expression while at the same time forcing the ensemble to watch its conductor. In order for a chorale to be effective, excellent breath support and phrase resolution must be achieved. The phrases are quite clear in the composition, frequently being indicated with dynamic shadings. The dynamic range in the composition goes from *fortissimo* to *"n"* or *niente* (meaning *nothing* in Italian). This is a very dramatic effect when done well. Fading a *decrescendo* to silence is a technique that will take some practice, but at the same time, it gives the director an opportunity to reinforce the importance of a strong embouchure and breath support.

Another important chorale concept tied to dynamics is ensemble balance and overall mood of the work. The composer asks for a singing melody at all times. The conductor must always make sure the melodic phrases and fragments are being heard over its harmonic support. The mood of the work evolves throughout the piece as it enters new sections through the use of different tonal areas and dynamic levels. In Ticheli's words:

> Sometimes the accompaniment flows quietly under the melody; other times it breathes alongside it. The work's mood ranges from quiet reflection, through growing optimism, to profound exaltation.

Unit 6: Musical Elements

MELODY:
Since the piece is predominantly in the key of E-flat, a good warm-up to playing this work would be scales, arpeggios, chorales, and etudes in this key.

There are two primary themes presented throughout the work. To play these themes effectively, the students must understand how to play a full phrase. For example, the opening of the piece provides the first statement of the main theme.

This eleven-measure theme must sound like one musical sentence. The long notes must not only be held to their full value but should have dynamic shaping to them as well. A very *legato* tongue and good breath support should also be taught. The line needs to be as linear and seamless as possible. The dynamic subtleties of the line can be left to the director, but Ticheli does want the peak of the line to be in measure 8. The most efficient way to rehearse this melody would be for the director to have the whole ensemble play the melody in unison and strive for a uniformity in phrasing.

The second melodic theme appears in solo flute and alto saxophone at measure 23. The same concepts of *legato* tonguing and uniform, linear phrasing apply. This theme is later fragmented in the development section.

HARMONY:
The composition as a whole is a tonal setting of the folk tune. Cadences are clear, while the use of suspensions create some very musical moments. In addition to these standard chorale components, there are a few interesting harmonic elements.

During the second theme at measure 23, the only harmonic background is 1st and 2nd clarinet moving in parallel motion. This line must sound seamless to achieve the desired color and texture. All breathing in this section must be staggered. The end of this section (measures 31 through 34) moves briefly to the tonal area of G-flat, giving a transition to the key of B-flat for the upcoming development section.

Beginning in measure 35, pulsating quarter note chords alternating between B-flat major and C minor in wide scoring provides a harmonic theme, which recurs frequently throughout the piece. These chords, in the composer's words, "Gives the effect of a solemn church organ. These chords represent life—they breathe, they have a heartbeat." These chords should be kept at a *piano* dynamic with a slight emphasis on beats 1 and 3. A retransition at measure 52 again leads through the key of G-flat to the home key of E-flat. At measure 56, the composer gives the final statement of the main tune doubled at the octave with a countermelody and the pulsating chords. A beautiful coda section winds down to the final chord of E-flat major.

RHYTHM:

Written completely in 4/4 meter, there are few rhythmical challenges in this work. The smallest subdivision of the beat in the composition is an occasional dotted-eighth/sixteenth or sixteenth/dotted-eighth. The most rhythmically challenging section of the piece comes in measure 41, where a flute trio states the main theme in canon. The three statements are only one beat apart. In addition to these three statements, 1st clarinet plays the melody in augmentation.

This presents a very ethereal effect. A canon is a rhythmically based compositional technique that students need to understand. This section provides a good teaching opportunity to explain what a canon and augmentation is. If time allows, having the whole ensemble play these statements at different rhythmic intervals would help reinforce the concept.

TIMBRE:

Ticheli uses many color combinations throughout the work, which gives interest to his setting. The progression of colors that he applies to the melody throughout are very well thought out and effective.

He begins by setting the opening theme in horn and euphonium, with lower voices providing harmonic support. This produces a very dark and warm timbre. In the second statement, Ticheli brightens the timbre slightly by setting the melody in horn, trumpet, and alto saxophone. Flute and oboe enter with a light echo figure. The second theme is lighter still, voiced in octaves between flute and alto saxophone solos. The only harmonic support here is in the parallel clarinet lines. After moving through a transition to the development section, we arrive at the flute canon. The texture thins out greatly here, leaving us with the lightest timbre of the whole work. This completes a climb in the *tessitura* of the melody from the beginning. The flute trio is instructed to play with very little vibrato to help enhance the ethereal quality.

The 1st trombone and 1st trumpet join the foreground, giving more thickness and depth to the texture. The composer continues to add more voices to strengthen and darken the ensemble timbre, which culminates in the final statement (measure 56). Although this is the most powerful section, the tone color should remain dark and full. This last statement fades into a *mezzo piano* brass chorale that grows to *forte* before having an echo in the woodwinds. The final cadence is set in the low woodwinds and low brass, fading out at different times. This beautiful effect is only achieved if the two groups can fade out at the appropriate times. Low brass and bassoon must fade to *niente*, leaving the clarinet choir to finish the composition by fading the final chord.

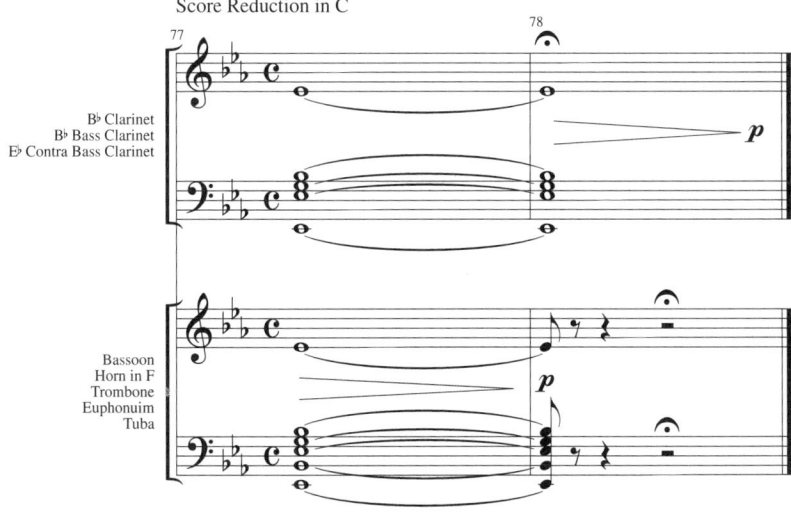

Score Reduction in C

Unit 7: Form and Structure
A basic outline of the formal structure is provided by the composer in the program notes.

SECTION	MEASURE	EVENT AND SCORING
Exposition	1–11	E-flat; first statement (low register)
	12–22	E-flat; second statement (full texture)
	23–30	E-flat; new theme (Theme B); derived from main melody
	31–34	G-flat to B-flat; transition to Development section
Development	35–40	B-flat; "pulsating" chords; variant of Theme B
	41–51	B-flat; main melody in three-part canon (flute)
	52–55	G-flat; retransition to final statement
Recapitulation	56–68	E-flat; final statement (climax)
	69–end	E-flat, coda (brass chorale)

Unit 8: Suggested Listening
Frank Ticheli:
   Amazing Grace
   An American Elegy

Other settings of *Shenandoah*:
Warren Benson, *Daughter of the Stars*
James Curnow, *Shenandoah*
Pierre La Plante, *American Riversongs*
James D. Ployhar, *Shenandoah*
Claude T. Smith, *Shenandoah*
John Tatgenhorst, *Shenandoah*

Unit 9: Additional References and Resources
Manhattan Beach Music. Manhattan Beach Music, 10 August 2001. http://members.aol.com/mbmband/

Miles, Richard, ed. Teaching Music through Performance in Band, Volume 3. Chicago: GIA Publications, 2000.

Smith, Norman E. *Program Notes for Band*. Chicago, IL: GIA Publications, Inc., 2001.

Ticheli, Frank. European American Music Distributors LLC, 10 August 2001. http://www.eamdc.com/ticheli.html

Ticheli, Frank. *Shenandoah*. Brooklyn, NY: Manhattan Beach Music, 1999.

Contributed by:

Paul Nickolas
Director of Bands
Sam Barlow High School
Gresham, Oregon

Teacher Resource Guide

Sussex Mummer's Christmas Carol
Percy Grainger

(1882–1961)

arranged by Richard Franko Goldman

(1910–1980)

Unit 1: Composer

Percy Grainger, a composer and pianist, was born in Australia in 1882. His first musical experiences came from his mother, who taught him piano. At age ten, he performed his first recital, and his recognizable talent earned him the opportunity to study in Europe. By age eighteen, he had performed on three continents of the Eastern Hemisphere and was a recognized authority on the interpretation of Bach. During his travels, he became friends with Edvard Grieg, and the two promoted each other's music before Grieg's death in 1907. His interpretation of Grieg's Concerto earned him great acclaim. During these years, Grainger became an expert in the collection of folk songs in the British Isles. He began experiments in random music, electronics, and irregular meter long before Cage, Varese, and Bartok. After a stint as an army bandsman (where his love for the soprano saxophone was established), Grainger moved to America where he became famous in spite of his extremely eccentric behavior and reputation as a (mere) folk song collector and arranger. It is only in recent years that his foresight as an avant-garde composer and troubled genius has been recognized.

Unit 2: Historical Perspective

The *Carol* is a tune transcribed by Lucy Broadwood in 1880 and set for piano by Grainger in 1905. The *Carol* was a series of folk music settings written in memory of Edvard Grieg, who died after the *Carol* was composed. Toward the end of his life, Grainger began a wind band version of the *Carol*, which was finished by Richard Franko Goldman and published in 1965.

Unit 3: Composition

The *Carol* was originally composed for piano and later transcribed for wind band. The composition itself is very Grainger-like, utilizing the many colors of the wind band, crafty modulations, homophonic harmonies, and an ionian opening melody. The relatively short piece, at two minutes and eight seconds, is set in two simple verses.

Unit 4: Technical Considerations

The piece is a very lyrical and flowing line in common time. Its rather slow tempo (eighth note = 84–100) provides the challenge of forward motion and control of tone and pitch qualities. The tonal center of D-flat and G-flat provides a challenge for the young to intermediate player. Rhythm patterns of eighth notes, dotted-eighths, and triplet eighths offer a variety of rhythmic challenges. Articulations include *legato*, slurred and detached patterns, and long, sustained lines. Ranges are in the comfortable area with the exception of the bass clef baritone, which reaches D-flat above the staff.

Unit 5: Stylistic Considerations

The primary style consideration is a long, flowing, and well-supported musical line. Attention to the moving line to be heard over the longer tones' harmonic structure is of prime importance. There are many dynamic shifts in the typical Grainger style offering a wide array of tone colors throughout. Breath marks and phrasing issues abound to allow for flexibility in interpretation of the musical line. There are a few subtle tempo adjustments and dynamic contrasts, also typical of the elastic Grainger melody. Balance within the brass and woodwind choirs is essential to offer clarity and representation of all voices.

Unit 6: Musical Elements

The melodic line is the focus of the *Carol*. The line works its way through the instrumentation of the ensemble in a typical Grainger fashion, requiring a mature level of phrasing, shaping, blend, and balance. The theme is stated at the beginning, again at measure 23 with a rhythmic variation using triplets at the A tempo (measure 12), and again at measure 25. Harmonies and rhythms are consistently Grainger-like, requiring special attention to the "color" chords used in low brass and reeds. There is no use of percussion in the *Carol*.

MELODY:

The main musical element of the *Carol* is the melody. Incorporating the *Carol* into warm-ups through the use of long tones, shaping, and phrasing will assist the flow of the on line throughout. Ed Lisk's *Circle of Fourths* is a great place to start utilizing the G-flat and D-flat key signatures.

HARMONY:

Harmony aspects can be addressed by isolating sections of the piece and omitting the melody, allowing the ensemble to hear, sing, and tune the harmony. Steve Melillo's *Function Chorales* will work well.

RHYTHM:

The rhythmic component of the *Carol* is basic and simple. The incorporation of dotted rhythms and eighth notes into the warm-up could encourage sustained, rhythmic playing.

TIMBRE:

The Grainger sound dictates a mixture of pitch, style, and timbre. Special emphasis should be placed on achieving characteristic tone colors from all instruments.

Unit 7: Form and Structure

This beautiful ballad is only thirty-three measures in length, requiring great attention to the passing melodic line.

MEASURE	EVENT AND SCORING
1–8	D-flat; theme in flute, oboe, tenor saxophone, horn, baritone
9–11	D-flat; transition to repeat of theme (clarinet, cornet, alto saxophone)
12–20	G-flat; theme once again stated in upper woodwinds; counterline in horn
20–22	G-flat; transition back to D-flat
23–27	D-flat; theme in low voices with harmony and counterlines provided by cornet, clarinet, and tenor saxophone
27–30	D-flat; *tutti* statement of theme and countermelody
31–33	D-flat; theme stated in flute, oboe, alto saxophone, and baritone; texture things to final chord

Unit 8: Suggested Listening
Percy Grainger:
    Colonial Song
    Harvest Hymn
    Irish Tune from County Derry
Leslie Howard, *Sussex Mummer's Christmas Carol* (Piano Music, Volume II)

Unit 9: Additional References and Resources

Mellers, Wilfrid. *Percy Grainger*. London: Oxford University Press, 1992.

Slattery, Thomas C. *Percy Grainger, The Inveterate Innovator*. Northfield, IL: The Instrumentalist Company, 1974.

Bird, John. *Percy Grainger*. London: Faber and Faber, 1982.

Contributed by:
Frank C. Tracz
Director of Bands
Kansas State University
Manhattan, Kansas

Teacher Resource Guide

Ukrainian Folksongs
Halsey Stevens

(1908–1989)

arranged by William A. Schaefer

(b. 1918)

Unit 1: Composer

Halsey Stevens, born in Scott, New York, in 1908, is recognized as an important American composer, teacher, and writer on the subject of music. He studied at Syracuse University and received a Bachelor of Music degree in 1931 and a master's degree in music in 1937. He continued his studies at the University of California and studied with the famous composer Ernst Bloch in 1944. In 1946, he joined the faculty of the University of Southern California in Los Angeles. As a faculty member at USC, he taught a variety of courses and subjects. He also was a visiting professor at various universities and colleges throughout the United States during his thirty-year tenure at the USC.

Stevens was a prolific composer who wrote numerous orchestral, chamber, and instrumental solo works, as well as a number of vocal pieces, but he wrote no music for the theater or ballet. Stevens was particularly interested in the music of Bartok and Hungarian folk songs, and he mastered the Hungarian language so he could travel to Hungary and assemble materials on Bartok's life. This resulted in a biography that is a standard on the life and music of Bela Bartok.

During his lifetime, Stevens received numerous grants and honors, including two Guggenheim fellowships, a grant from the National Endowment for the Arts, and the Abraham Lincoln Award from the

American Hungarian Foundation in 1978. Of his music, Nicolas Slonimsky, the famous chronicler of biographies, states:

> His music is, above all, a monument of sonorous equilibrium. Melodies and rhythms are coordinated in fine mellow rhythmic polyphony. Dissonances are emancipated and become natural consorts of triadic harmony. Tonality remains paramount, while a stream of coloristic passages contributes to the brilliance of the instrumental texture.[1]

Ukrainian Folk Songs was arranged for band by William A. Schaefer. Schaefer was born in 1918. He received a Bachelor of Music degree in 1939 from the University of Miami-Ohio, taught briefly in the public schools, and was then called to serve in the Army during World War II in the Pacific theater. Following World War II, he was given charge of an occupation force Army band in Japan. He then attended Juilliard School of Music and the University of Michigan. He taught for five years at Carnegie Mellon University beginning in 1948, and in 1953, he was hired at the University of Southern California for a variety of duties, including directing the USC Wind Symphony. Additionally, Schaefer was music appreciation teacher on an early CBS television program.

With an active interest in arranging, Schaefer wrote a major arrangement or transcription for every concert he conducted with the USC Wind Orchestra. Among his favorite arrangements is a setting of three movements of Shostakovich's *Ninth Symphony*, which Shostakovich heard when he visited the USC campus in the late 1960s. Shostakovich was so pleased with the arrangement that he asked for a copy of the score, and it was one of the few transcriptions he had in his library upon his death.

Schaefer continues to be active as an arranger to this day and has recently arranged the music of Tippet, Handel, Weber, Schumann, and Elgar for publication in England. He currently resides in Cambridge, England.

Unit 2: Historical Perspective

The Ukraine is in Eastern Europe, located on the north edge of the Baltic Sea in a region known as the Steppes, which is in the southern part of the central Russian upland. Because of its location, the Ukraine has not enjoyed an extended independent existence from other countries. At times the Russians and the Poles have controlled it, and it was once part of the Austro-Hungarian empire. As might be expected, the music of the Ukraine has been highly influenced by the cultures that governed the country at various times. Ukrainian music exhibits a wide variety of forms and textures. It includes a

1 Slonimsky, Nicolas. "Halsey Stevens" in *Baker's Biographical Dictionary of Musicians*. Centennial Edition. New York: Schirmer Books, 2001.

number of common traditional instruments, such as flute, trumpet, bagpipes, and drums. Although one can find influences in the music from countries in west Asia, the music of the Ukraine has been most strongly influenced by the Western major/minor diatonic system. Like Western music, their folk music can be divided into three main categories: 1) around the calendar year, 2) ritual, and 3) celebratory pieces that include texts dealing with agriculture and domestic life.

Unit 3: Composition

Ukrainian Folk Songs was first published in 1956 as a collection of piano pieces. According to Schaefer, it was originally written as teaching pieces for Halsey Stevens's children.[2] The composition was first performed by the University of Southern California Wind Orchestra under the direction of William Schaefer. Each of the eleven folk songs is set so as to reflect the character inherent in each piece. Schaefer skillfully arranges the pieces, using only the instruments and textures he needs to create a sonority unique to each work. Each one of the movements is less than a minute in length, and the overall piece is eleven minutes and thirty seconds long. The movements include:

Family Gathering
Repentant Wife
Easter Song
Under the Cherry Tree
The Sun Has Set
Mother's Concern
Trouble with Hemp
A Merry Widow
Love Song
Why Do You Pout, Dear?
Wife Who Beat Her Husband

Unit 4: Technical Considerations

Although originally intended to be performed as a single composition, one could certainly create one's own suite from the eleven folk songs presented in *Ukrainian Folk Songs*. One of the major challenges for the conductor will be the variability of the instrumentation in each movement. One of the beautiful aspects of this arrangement is that it is not over-scored. Only Movements 2 and 7 utilize all players of the ensemble. One possible rehearsal strategy would be to rehearse the movements in order of diminishing forces. This would allow the director to dismiss the players who would be idle while movements were rehearsed. There are several solo passages in the piece for

2 Telephone conversation with William A. Schaefer, Tuesday, 30 October 2001.

flute, oboe, bassoon, alto saxophone, and horn. There is also an English horn solo. Many of the solos are cross-cued (the English horn, for example, is cued in the clarinet and alto saxophone parts). Brass ranges are not extreme; however, both 1st and 2nd trumpet play above the staff, and 1st trombone and euphonium play into the treble clef staff.

Harmonically, the piece is classified as a twentieth century setting of nineteenth century folk material. Stevens is very sensitive in his application of twentieth century harmonic language in the writing of this piece which, like Grainger's *Lincolnshire Posy*, enhances these folk melodies. The combination of modern tonal language and transparent scoring will present an immediate challenge in the first rehearsals. In addition to the melodic and harmonic considerations, *Ukrainian Folk Songs* presents a variety of keys, including C major, C minor, E-flat major, E minor, F major, G major, G minor, A-flat major, and B-flat major.

There is a variety of time signatures as well, including 3/8, 3/2, 5/4, and 7/4. Aside from the use of these less-common time signatures, the piece is uncomplicated rhythmically and should not present great difficulty. Tempo varies greatly, and the challenge will be to properly sustain the movements in the slower tempi.

Unit 5: Stylistic Considerations

Each of the pieces is a setting of folk song music, and yet each is scored in its own idiomatic way. The style is a modern setting of folk material. Throughout the piece there is a variety of articulations: *staccato*, accents, and *tenuto* marks. Six of the movements use phrase lines and expression marks, but no articulations are given. There is also a variety of dynamic markings, from *pianissimo* to *fortissimo*.

The real challenge is to make meaningful music by attending to balance in the light scoring, with phrase shaping that reflects the folk-like quality of the music. Attention to the character of the tune will, in turn, dictate the character of the accompaniment. *Staccato* notes, for example, should be light and detached, but not too short.

Unit 6: Musical Elements

Each of the eleven movements is based on a folk melody. The melody constructions are simple song forms. For example, the melody for the first movement, "Family Gathering," contains two phrase elements:

The A phrase consists of two two-measure units that are almost identical. The B phrase contains one measure of a new idea (measure 5) that is repeated and a repetition of the material from the A phrase. This is also referred to as rounded binary structure. Two-part folk songs are used in Movements 3, 5, 8, 9, 10, and 11. In Movement 5, the B section is more varied on the repetitions of the melody. In Movements 2 and 4, the B phrase is recapitulated, creating an A–B–B melodic scheme.

The remaining two movements are in another song form construction. This is the theme from Movement 6, titled "Mother's Concern":

There are three phrases in the melody. Note that each of the measures is completely different, with a two-measure sequence occurring in measures 6 and 7. Movement 7 is similarly constructed.

Each movement embraces conventional diatonic tonality with the use of two important twentieth century harmonic techniques. The first of these techniques is pandiatonicism. The term implies the use of tonality without the traditional harmonic functions. Many of the major twentieth century composers have used this technique, particularly Stravinsky. In *Ukrainian Folk Songs*, the presence of pandiatonicism is subtle. In Movement 1, for example, the 3rd trombone, acting as a filler voice between the *ostinato* bass figure and the melody, provides an occasional tonal blur. Even earlier in the movement (measures 3 and 4), the interior parts move in thirds, creating some tonal obfuscation.

A second technique is another form of pandiatonicism. The most common form is called the *major/minor conflict*. This occurs when there is interplay between the third scale degree of both the major and minor scales. In the Movement 3, a conflict between the two forms of the minor scale is established. In the natural minor scale, the seventh degree is lowered. The harmonic minor scale has a raised seventh degree. Between measures 95 and 104, the conflict plays out between elements in accompaniment.

Although the rhythmic element is not as complex as the harmonic language, it is an important element to consider in preparing this piece. As mentioned earlier, there are several time signatures employed in this work. Some are asymmetrical (5/4, 7/4), but most are simple meters. Only Movement 3 is conceived in a linear (polyphonic) style. The melodies are constructed of basic rhythmic patterns, typical of most folk music. There are no triplets or complicated polyrhythms.

Ukrainian Folk Songs is an excellent study in wind tone color, texture, and timbre. Schaefer is judicious in his use of the full band sonority. In fact, he uses the concert as a sonority resource rather than a sonority source. The solo passages for flute, oboe, English horn, bassoon, alto saxophone, and horn are accompanied in such a way that problems of balance and blend are minimalized. Generally speaking, the texture of the music is homophonic, with some exceptional passages (like Movement 2, measures 66 through 69, and Movement 3, measures 95 through 104).

Ukrainian Folk Songs provides a wealth of opportunities to create concepts for presenting and teaching the musical materials. The following ideas will serve as suggestions, but one should feel free to try new approaches. As with all music teaching, the suggestions flow from the music itself. The focus of the first rehearsals will undoubtedly center on pitch and rhythm. Because some time signatures (such as 3/8, 5/4, 7/8, and 3/2) may be new to students, it is suggested that rhythm sheets be produced for each meter. These rhythm sheets should include a line that consists of just the beats (eighth notes for 3/8, quarter notes for 5/4 and 7/4, half notes for 3/2) and a line devoted to the underlying metrical feel (sixteenth notes in 3/8, eighth notes in 5/4 and 7/4, and quarter notes in 3/2). The subsequent lines can be common patterns of rhythm for the particular meter and patterns of rhythm for the melodies.

Developing melodic awareness for each movement would be beneficial in creating a meaningful interpretation. Writing the tunes out for the ensemble to perform in unison is one activity. Identifying the melody by having the students stand when they play the melody is another. Creating a simple diagram of each of the melodies, like those in this resource guide, is another way of understanding the melodic structure.

There are several approaches to developing scale fluency, from the use of supplementary warm-up materials to employment of specific methodologies, such as Edward Lisk's *Alternative Rehearsal Techniques*.

As rehearsals progress, the focus should shift from the technical to the musical aspects. Once again, score knowledge is key to achieving musical understanding. Directors are encouraged to study the chapters presented in the other volumes of *Teaching Music through Performance in Band* as well. Of particular interest is Eugene Corporon's presentation titled "The Quantum Conductor" in Volume 1, Edward Lisk's "The Rehearsal-Mastery of Music Fundamentals" in Volume 2, Richard Miles's "Teaching Music with Emphasis on Form and Structure" in Volume 3, and Corporon's "Fervor, Focus, Flow and Feeling: Making the Emotional Connection," also in Volume 3. These articles will undoubtedly provide you with additional ideas for finding the meaning in the music.

Unit 7: Form and Structure

The following is a brief synopsis of each of the eleven movements of *Ukrainian Folk Songs*.

MOVEMENT 1: "FAMILY GATHERING"
Length: 28 measures
Tempo marking: *Andante*
Key: F major
Time signature: 4/4
Melodic structure: Continuous rounded binary form (AB)
Movement structure: Three statements of the melody; scored for all winds and timpani (no percussion)

MOVEMENT 2: "REPENTANT WIFE"
Length: 55 measures
Tempo marking: *Allegro vivace*
Key: B-flat major
Time signature: 2/4
Melodic structure: Sectional binary form (ABB)
Movement structure: Four statements of the melody with an extended closing phrase; scored for full ensemble, with solo for flute

MOVEMENT 3: "EASTER SONG"
Length: 30 measures
Tempo marking: *Moderato*
Key: G minor
Time signature: 3/8
Melodic structure: Simple binary form (AB)
Movement structure: Two statements of melody with a two-measure introduction to the second statement; scored for woodwinds, horn, tuba, and percussion, with English horn and alto saxophone solo passages

MOVEMENT 4: "UNDER THE CHERRY TREE"
Length: 26 measures
Tempo marking: *Andante*
Key: G major
Time signature: 2/4
Melodic structure: Sectional binary form (ABB)
Movement structure: Two statements of melody with a two-measure closing phrase; scored for woodwinds, partial brass, and no percussion with solos for flute, oboe, and bassoon

MOVEMENT 5: "THE SUN HAS SET"

Length:	16 measures
Tempo marking:	*Lento moderato*
Key:	E minor
Time signature:	7/4 (also 3/4 and 5/4)
Melodic structure:	Rounded binary (AB) modified in subsequent repetitions
Movement structure:	Three statements of the melody; scored for brass section

MOVEMENT 6: "MOTHER'S CONCERN"

Length:	39 measures
Tempo marking:	*Allegretto*
Key:	E-flat major
Time signature:	3/8
Melodic structure:	Three phrases (ABC)
Movement structure:	Three repetitions of the melody with an additional closing phrase; scored for woodwind section, two horns, and bells

MOVEMENT 7: "TROUBLE WITH HEMP"

Length:	46 measures
Tempo marking:	*Pesante*
Key:	C minor
Time signature:	2/4
Melodic structure:	Three phrases (ABC)
Movement structure:	Three statements of the melody with introduction; scored for full band

MOVEMENT 8: "A MERRY WIDOW"

Length:	12 measures
Tempo marking:	*Lento*
Key:	G minor
Time signature:	5/4
Melodic structure:	Sectional binary form (AB)
Movement structure:	Two repetitions of the melody; scored for small group of woodwinds, brass, and percussion with solos for oboe, horn, and English horn

MOVEMENT 9: "LOVE SONG"

Length:	19 measures
Tempo marking:	*Andante con moto*
Key:	E-flat major
Time signature:	3/2 (also 2/2)
Melodic structure:	Sectional binary (AB)

| Movement structure: | Three repetitions of the melody with an additional closing phrase; scored for full band and timpani (minus percussion) |

MOVEMENT 10: "WHY DO YOU POUT, DEAR?"

Length:	39 measures
Tempo marking:	*Allegretto*
Key:	A-flat–C–A-flat
Time signature:	2/4
Melodic structure:	Continuous rounded binary (AB)
Movement structure:	Four repetitions of the melody; scored for full band and timpani (minus percussion)

MOVEMENT 11: "THE WIFE WHO BEAT HER HUSBAND"

Length:	34 measures
Tempo marking:	*Allegro moderato*
Key:	F major
Time signature:	2/4
Melodic structure:	Sectional binary (AB)
Movement structure:	Two repetitions of the melody; scored for full band minus timpani

Unit 8: Suggested Listening

The following is a short list of compositions that utilize folk music:

Percy Grainger, *Lincolnshire Posy*
Clare Grundman, *Little English Suite*
Barry Kopetz, *Americana Folk Suite*
Pierre La Plante, *American River Songs*
Anton Liadov/ Goldman, *Eight Russian Folk Songs*
Darius Milhaud, *Suite Française*
William Grant Still, *Folk Suite*
Frank Ticheli, *Cajun Folk Songs*
Jan Van der Roost, *Suite Provençale*
Ralph Vaughan Williams, *English Folk Song Suite*

Unit 9: Additional References and Resources

The New Encyclopedia Britannica, 2002 edition. "Ukraine," by Lubomyr A. Hajda.

Miles, Richard, ed. *Teaching Music through Performance in Band.* Volumes 1–3. Chicago: GIA Publications, 1997–2000.

Murphy, Howard. *Form and Music for the Listener.* Camden, NJ; Radio Corporation of America, 1945.

Sadie, Stanley, ed. *New Grove Dictionary of Music and Musicians*. Second edition. New York: MacMillan, 2001.

Slonimsky, Nicolas. *Baker's Biographical Dictionary of Musicians*. Centennial Edition, New York; Schirmer Books, 2001. "Halsey Stevens," by Nicolas Slonimsky.

Contributed by:
Jay W. Gilbert
Doane College
Crete, Nebraska

Teacher Resource Guide

Walls of Zion
Greg Danner
(b. 1958)

Unit 1: Composer

Greg Danner is Professor and Coordinator of Academic Studies in Music at Tennessee Technological University. Born in St. Louis, Missouri, he received his B.A. from Southeast Missouri State University, his M.M. from the Eastman School of Music, and his Ph.D. from Washington University. His awards include the College Band Directors National Association Music for Young Band prize, vocal category and grand prize in the Delius Society Composition Contest, first prize in the Taghkanic Chorale Composers Competition, and the Louisiana Music Teachers Association Composer Commission Award. He has also received annual ASCAP awards for composition since 1989. Danner has participated as a resident composer at the Charles Ives Center for American Music and has been an associate in the Kennedy Center for the Performing Arts "Performing Arts Centers and Schools" program.

Unit 2: Composition

Walls of Zion was written to be appropriate yet challenging for a typical high school band. Though not a commissioned work, it was written with the composer's daughter's high school band (Cookeville High School, Tennessee) in mind, and solo passages were written for the students in that band. Though premiered by the Tennessee Tech Symphony Band, it was performed by the Cookeville High School Band the following year. *Walls of Zion* was the winner of the 1999 CBDNA Young Band Composition Contest and is dedicated to the composer's daughter, "whose love of melody suggested the composition."

Unit 3: Historical Perspective

During the nineteenth century, a body of rural American hymnody was developed using "shaped-note" notation, where the shape of each note corresponded to a solfege syllable. This technique was developed to aid congregational singers with little or no musical training in reading music without having to read conventional notation. Benjamin Franklin White and E. J. King published one collection of this genre, *The Sacred Harp*, in 1844. King went on to become an active proponent of what came to be known as "sacred harp singing" through his work on subsequent editions of the collection and his establishment of the Southern Musical Convention, which helped to spread the use of the volume throughout the American South. Books of shaped-note hymnody were often oblong in shape and contained extensive prefatory comments to aid the singer in understanding the notation. These books were non-denominational in character and served as the basis for shaped-note singings, gatherings that were as much social as religious in nature.

An equally strong tradition of spiritual singing using conventional notation developed alongside shaped-note singing, primarily in the northern states. The musical style and religious zeal was comparable to that of shaped-note singing, and many melodies were shared between the two traditions. This sharing was so prevalent, in fact, that a single melody would often have several sets of texts, though sometimes with slight alterations of the pitch or rhythmic content.

"Zion's Walls" appears in an 1853 book titled *The Sacred Harp* and is attributed to Reverend John G. McCurry. It is also found in a 1953 volume titled *Down-East Spirituals and Others*, edited by George Pullen Jackson. Jackson noted that he changed the flawed rhythmic notation of the earlier version while leaving the pitch unchanged. Related tunes include "Christian Warfare," "Louisiana," and "Judgement Day." Most of Jackson's collection is derived from the Baptist and Methodist traditions of the northeast, with a particular focus on New England spirituals.

Unit 4: Technical Considerations

The main tonal centers of the piece are F and B-flat major. While the primary thematic material is presented in these keys, the accompaniment and transition areas frequently contain accidentals, which suggest lydian and other modes requiring special attention.

Meters utilized include 2/4, 3/4, 4/4, 6/8, and 9/8. While none of these present major difficulties in isolation, the frequency of meter changes and the transitions between simple and compound patterns may challenge some performers. Twenty-five meter changes are found in the piece, four of them occurring between simple and compound patterns. Aside from these issues, the only rhythmic challenge for players at this level may be differentiating the iambic and trochaic rhythmic material. This may be aided by isolating these rhythmic patterns and having the full group play them either in unison, as chords, or in a scalar passage:

Tempo is slow, ranging from 60 to 72 beats per minute. Four changes occur throughout the piece and are intended as subtle intensifications or relaxations rather than abrupt shifts of tempo.

Technical demands are isolated to brief sixteenth note passages for flute, oboe, 1st clarinet, and alto saxophone in the opening and a middle transition period of the piece. The slow tempi and the scalar nature of the runs alleviate any difficulties, though the above-mentioned accidentals may need attention.

While most of the technical aspects of individual parts are not excessively demanding, the rapid canonical entrances (often at the eighth note or quarter note level) may challenge ensemble clarity. Scale or unison exercises with canonical entrances at a full or half beat would be helpful in improving this precision.

Ranges should not present a problem for the band at this level. First trumpet and horn parts go to written G on top of the staff, while 1st trombone parts reach F above the staff. However, in all cases, these notes are used sparingly and are usually approached by a scalar passage. There are solos in the oboe (cued for alto saxophone), trumpet, horn, and clarinet parts that are exposed but not technically difficult. While there are four percussion parts plus timpani, the parts are not difficult, do not call for any exotic instruments, and are very tastefully written. Percussion instruments required for this piece include timpani (four drums are necessary and there is one pitch change involving two of the four drums,) suspended cymbal, triangle, crash cymbals, wood block, snare drum, bass drum, bells, and chimes.

Unit 5: Stylistic Considerations

As this work is based on a vocal hymn, it would be extremely helpful to share the words of the original with students:

> Come fathers and mothers, come
> Sisters and brothers, come
> Join us in singing the praises of Zion.
>
> O, fathers, don't you feel determined
> To meet within the walls of Zion
> We'll shout and go round the walls of Zion.

Copland's version repeats:

> Come fathers and mothers
> Come sisters and brothers
> Come join us in singing the praises of Zion.

The subtle change from the first to last verse in Copland's setting involves the placement of the word "come," which may have important ramifications for phrasing.

Even though Danner avoided direct references to any other setting of this hymn, it would certainly be valuable for both conductor and players to spend time listening to Copland's (or any other vocal version) to get a sense of how the words impact the phrasing.

As would be expected from a vocally derived piece, the style is broad, connected, and lyrical. With the exception of accents in the four measures at the climax of the piece, the only articulations indicated are *legato* and *marcato*. Dynamics at the *forte* level or louder are used very sparingly; only twenty of the work's 131 measures are marked at this level. Close attention to a soft but supported and blended sound will be both the challenge and the reward of this piece.

Unit 6: Musical Elements

As is often the case with pieces of this style, it would be very helpful to transcribe the main melody for the entire band to play so everyone gets a chance to hear it and play it. Even though the melodic material is liberally spread throughout many sections of the ensemble, no single section or solo instrument has a complete statement of it. The challenge of connecting the various phrases together with a consistent approach and style will be aided by having everyone (even those who never play it!) become familiar with a consistent interpretive approach.

Since the melody is based on a pentatonic scale, it would be helpful to have the ensemble play this in unison to get accustomed to the sound. While no awkward intervals are used, it is different enough from the more familiar major and minor tonalities to warrant extra attention:

♪♪♪|♪♪ versus ♩ ♪|♪♪♪

The melody is extremely accessible, and as it is the unifying feature of the piece, it becomes particularly important to achieve a uniform interpretation. A slight emphasis on each downbeat will help reinforce a dance-like character of the music. Care needs to be taken in the canonical sections that each separate line does not get too bloated and interfere with the simple character of the music.

In keeping with the original character of the music, the harmonic structure is not complicated. One of the biggest challenges of the harmony is acclimating the ear to the lack of dominant-tonic movement. Much harmonic movement is by seconds and thirds instead of the more common fourths and fifths. This is another reflection of the nineteenth century Americana from which the melody is derived.

A significant part of the piece features woodwind and brass choirs in contrast or opposition. Exceptions to this occur when the saxophone and clarinet sections are opposed to the low brass and low woodwinds, but here the colors of each timbral group still must be maintained. As the climax of the piece is approached, it becomes important to subdue the accompanimental upper woodwinds and sustained parts so the melodic development in the bassoon, trombone, and euphonium can be heard without being forced. Overall a warm, rich, and relaxed sound in all parts will bring out the desired sound.

Unit 7: Form and Structure

SECTION	MEASURE	EVENT AND SCORING
Introduction	1–14	Establishment of F and B-flat tonal centers with lydian runs in upper woodwinds on both tonics; mood is pensive and spacious with a growing intensification; key center of primarily F
	15–27	Brass chorale section; harmonic movement is based on thirds (E-flat to C), and the melody in 1st trumpet hints at the style but not melody of the main theme; chorale ends on a unison F, but upper woodwinds and percussion add a three-measure extension, creating tonal ambiguity
Main theme	28–48	"Zion's Walls" stated in a series of four-measure phrases featuring oboe (cued in alto saxophone,) flute, trumpet, and flute/clarinet, respectively; final phrase is five measures and acts as a transition into the interlude; primary key area still F even though the final cadence contains a pedal G to create ambiguity in the harmony

SECTION	MEASURE	EVENT AND SCORING
Interlude I	49–54	Upper woodwinds have sixteenth note runs that mix F major and lydian tonalities; canonical entrances that occur one half beat from preceding entrances supply additional instability
Main theme	55–76	Main theme returns, this time in B-flat and always in unison/octave canon at one beat; as in the first statement, each four-measure phrase features a different combination of instruments; first three phrases rise orchestrationally from low brass/low winds to flute/oboe/piccolo/clarinet, only to return to low brass for the final statement; final phrase again followed by a five-measure transition
Interlude II	76–86	Woodwind chorale similar to brass chorale in m. 15, though here the minor third relationship is between B-flat and G in mm. 76–79 then E-flat and C in mm. 80–83; solo trumpet added as a descant
	86–93	This section continues the primarily woodwind texture of the previous chorale, though here using non-thematic transition material; secundal harmonic movement dominates this section as opposed to the minor thirds of before; four measures each of C and D prepare for the E-flat of the next section
Intensification	94–101	New material is heard in bassoon, trombone, and euphonium; isolated to this section, it can be heard as derived from the intervallic structure of the theme
	102–105	Using the same instrumentation as before but adding trumpet; short four-measure statement of the theme is heard, building towards m. 106

SECTION	MEASURE	EVENT AND SCORING
Climax	106–115	A fanfare figure in A-flat is heard with the first and only *fortissimo* of the piece; gradually decays both dynamically and orchestrationally to the coda while moving to F major
Coda	116–122	Piece starts to unwind as clarinet and oboe trade one-measure solos derived from motivic material; tempo slows to 66 from the previous 72 bpm
	123–126	This section is nearly identical to the chorale at m. 15, though with added voices in woodwinds
	127–131	These last four measures are very similar to the beginning, though much less dense and active; piece closes with an F major triad in the low brass and bass clarinet, decaying with a coin-scraped suspended cymbal

Unit 8: Suggested Listening

Aaron Copland:
> *Old American Songs*
> *Second Set*
> *The Tender Land Suite*

James Curnow, *Rhapsody on American Shaped Note Melodies*
Donald Grantham, *Southern Harmony*
Walter Hartley, *Angel Band*
Randall Thompson, *Peaceable Kingdom*
Dan Welcher, *Zion*

Unit 9: Additional References and Resources

Crawford, Richard. *America's Musical Life*. New York: W. W. Norton and Company, 2001.

Jackson, George Pullen, ed. *Down-East Spirituals and Others*. New York: J. J. Augustin Publisher, 1953.

Sadie, Stanley, ed. "Shaped-note hymnody," *New Grove Dictionary of Music and Musicians*. 29 Volumes. London: MacMillan, 2001.

Contributed by:
Andrew Mast
Director of Bands and Music Department Chair
St. Ambrose University
Davenport, Iowa

Grade Four

Teacher Resource Guide

A Festival Prelude

Alfred Reed
(b. 1921)

Unit 1: Composer

Alfred Reed was born in Manhattan, New York, on January 25, 1921. He began his musical training on trumpet by the age of ten and became interested in theory and composition in high school, where he began his formal training with John Sacco and Paul Yartin. At the age of seventeen, he began working at the National Youth Administration Radio Workshop in New York as staff composer, arranger, and assistant conductor.

In 1942, Reed enlisted in the Army during World War II, where he served in the 529th Army Air Force Band. During his tenure as associate conductor and staff arranger, Reed produced nearly 150 compositions and arrangements. Among these works was his first public success, *Russian Christmas Music*, which premiered December 12, 1944, but remained unpublished until 1968. After his discharge from the Army in 1946, Reed attended the Juilliard School, where he studied composition with Vittorio Giannini. In 1948, he accepted a position as staff composer and arranger for the National Broadcasting Corporation and held a similar post at the American Broadcasting Corporation in 1949.

Reed was appointed conductor of the Baylor University Symphony Orchestra in 1953. While at Baylor, he continued his formal education and received his Bachelor and Master of Music degrees in 1955 and 1956, respectively. Reed joined Hansen Publications as an instrumental editor in 1955, and he continued to contribute a variety of original compositions to the wind band repertoire. His association with the University of Miami began in 1966 with an appointment to teach composition and music theory. During his tenure, he also taught courses in music education, music marketing, and conducting, and served as the wind ensemble conductor from 1980 to 1987 following the retirement of Frederick Fennell.

Reed continues an active career as a guest conductor and lecturer throughout the world and remains one of the most prolific composers of our time with more than 250 works for band, orchestra, chorus, and chamber ensemble to his credit. Some of Reed's more familiar works for band include *Chorale Prelude in E Minor* (1953), *Lumberjack Overture* (1954), *Ballade* for saxophone and band (1956), *Ode* for trumpet and band (1956), *Serenade* for clarinet and band (1957), *Might and Majesty* (1958), *Greensleeves* (1961), *A Sacred Suite* (1962), *Seascape* for baritone and band (1962), *Symphonic Prelude* (1963), *A Festive Overture* (1964), *Passacaglia* (1967), *The Music-Makers* (1968), *Wapawekka* (1968), *A Jubilant Overture* (1970), *A Ceremonial Fanfare* (1971), *Imperatrix* (1972), *In Memoriam* (1972), *Alleluia! Laudamus Te* (1973), *Armenian Dances I–II* (1974, 1978), *Othello* (1977), *Second Symphony* (1979), *Second Suite for Band* (1980), *The Enchanted Island* (1980), *The Hounds of Spring* (1981), *The Garden of Prosperpine* (1982), *Viva Musica!* (1984), *3 Revelations from the Lotus Sutra* (1985), *Centennial* (1986), *El Camino Real* (1986), *Praise Jerusalem!* (1988), *Symphony No. 3* (1988), *A Springtime Celebration* (1991), *Hymn Variants* (1992), *Concertino* for marimba and winds (1993), *Fourth Symphony* (1993), *The Ramparts of Courage* (1995), *Fifth Symphony* (1995), *Divertimento* for flute and winds (1997), and *The Golden Year* (1998).

Unit 2: Composition

A *Festival Prelude* was written in 1957 to commemorate the twenty-fifth anniversary of the Tri-State Music Festival, held in Enid, Oklahoma. The Music Department of Phillips University sponsored the annual event where the work was premiered by the Phillips University Concert Band, under the direction of the composer.

The inspiration for the work came after Reed's first visit to the festival the previous year. He noted that the Tri-State Festival was one of the largest and most impressive events of its kind. Reed suggested that the event was "so large and important an occasion (that it) might be served by a special introductory piece."[1] Reed continued:

> The work was conceived specifically in terms of its title: as an "opening" kind of piece, whether for an actual festival, concert, or similar musical (or even extra-musical) event. The music was to establish and maintain a bright and brilliant mood throughout, with no other connotation in mind.[2]

---

1 Alfred Reed to Richard Lundahl, 1 July 2001, correspondence in the hand of Richard Lundahl.

2 Alfred Reed, "Works: A Festival Prelude." *The School Musician* 39, No. 8, 1968, p. 62.

Reed's association with Hansen Publishing Company in 1957 did not hasten the publication of A *Festival Prelude*. The work was deemed too difficult for junior high level band, in which the Hansen Company specialized. After the initial performance, the work was held in manuscript for four years because of the technical demands, though it gained wide acclaim and a number of performances throughout the United States. It was finally published in 1961 by Edward B. Marks Music Corporation. The piece is five minutes in duration.

Unit 3: Historical Perspective

Descriptive and "occasion" music have long held a position of prominence in Western culture. This music has marked openings, celebrations, and other historically significant events. Yet without the event or program, some suggest this music may lack the ability to stand on its own. Well-crafted music needs no event or introduction to flourish successfully. Musical interest remains over time while the memory of the event may often fade.

Reed's inspirational pretext for A *Festival Prelude* was a specific event, as are many of today's brief works for the wind band. Many of those pieces will fade without much consequence while the well-crafted will remain. Reed's work continues to withstand the test of time while the initial "occasion" has faded over nearly forty-five years. The work is performed around the world in its original version as well as an orchestral version (1968), a young band version (arranged by James Curnow, 1991), and a marching band version (1984).

Unit 4: Technical Considerations

A *Festival Prelude* is written for large symphonic band instrumentation with very few solo requirements. Reed's generous *tutti* writing brings to rehearsal a relative ease of this sonorous work. Interest is developed by the use of full woodwind and brass textures contrasting with one another. Technical demands begin with a rhythmic *ostinato* of triplets presented by trumpet and later echoed by baritone. An ability to triple-tongue by brass will help clarify the rhythmic declarations throughout the work.

As with other Reed works, there are five separate trumpet parts: two cornet and three trumpet. Other instrumentation requirements include piccolo, two flutes, E-flat clarinet, three B-flat clarinets, bass clarinet, B-flat contrabass clarinet, two bassoons, four saxophones, four horns, baritone, three trombones, tuba, string bass, timpani, and percussion requiring at least three additional performers.

A demanding first trumpet range extends to C above the staff, while all four horns must play fifth-line F. The woodwind technical demands are limited to sixteenth note runs written in related scale patterns.

Unit 5: Stylistic Considerations

The title inspires an announcement of a grand event while the music serves as a brilliant introduction to a concert or a special occasion. *A Festival Prelude* provides the rich contrast of sonorous woodwinds versus heralding brass. Reed chooses choirs of instruments in various combinations as the underlying texture of the work. A full range of carefully inserted dynamics creates contrasts that complement the musical phrase.

The articulation required is generally *legato*, with a few declamatory brass statements requiring accents and the use of triple-tongue technique. Tempo varies from *Broadly* (quarter note = 72) to *Allegro ma non troppo* (quarter note = 132).

Unit 6: Musical Elements

MELODY:

The melodic content of *A Festival Prelude* is introduced with the outline of the B-flat triad, first presented by trumpet. The introduction gives way to a hint of the main theme found in woodwinds, cornet, and baritone. The first motive presented and later developed centers around four pitches: F, G, D, and C. These tones become the melodic contour of the work. The second, fanfare-like motive is the repeated triplet figure found in the brass. This motive is used to create tension beneath the development and as transitional material.

HARMONY:

Traditional harmonic treatments are used throughout the work. The tonal center begins in the key of B-flat major, moving to D minor, and then back to B-flat major for the work's conclusion. Reed uses three motives, heard singularly or in various harmonic combinations. The opening motive, built upon the first three tones of a B-flat major triad, is later harmonized with seventh, ninth, and eleventh chords. Reed also adds a contrapuntal bass line that generates its own harmonies throughout the work. Parallel harmonies, unison melodic lines, block triads, and pure triads in first inversion in the style of *faux Bourdon* (false bass) provide a rich and contrasting harmonic vocabulary upon which the composer draws.

RHYTHM:

The rhythmic complexities are minimal in this work. The score is primarily in common time with changes only to complete the melodic phrase. Sixteenth note subdivision and proper release of ties will contribute to a successful performance. The triplet motive provides some challenge for inexperienced performers as they assimilate three versus two. The sixteenth note triplet may provide a challenge to brass players who have not yet mastered a triple-tongue technique.

TIMBRE:

Reed uses varying compositional techniques throughout his works that demonstrate the palette of colors available from the wind band. His crafted scoring underlies the rich sonorities that are present in all of his works. A *Festival Prelude* is a true example of contrasts. At times, the woodwind writing is warm and gentle while the brass writing is bright and declamatory. His use of muted trumpet in the second section provides a stark and cold contrast to the warmth of the full band *tutti* found immediately prior.

Unit 7: Form and Structure

In a discussion about the work, Reed suggested that *A Festival Prelude* appears to have three parts for the listener: a beginning section in B-flat major, a middle section centered around D minor, and a return to B-flat major. Yet Reed recalls his own feelings about the apparent tertiary form of this work:

> I think it only fair to say that the perception of this three-part form by the listener or student may be mainly as a result of the inevitable return to the original key center toward the end, and not because the work was planned as a three-part form originally. I realize here that although I myself thought of this music as a series of sectional variations on three basic motives (only one of which I would call a "theme" in the true sense of the word) with constant shifting of tonal centers, the listener or analytical student may feel differently. I would be inclined to respect his belief because of my firm conviction that the response to the formal structure of a piece of music is as personal as the purely emotional response.[3]

SECTION	MEASURE	EVENT AND SCORING
Introduction	1–10	Opening motive; B-flat triad in the key center of B-flat major
A	11–18	Four-note motivic statement of main theme
	19–23	Second triplet motive
	24–27	Four-note motivic statement of main theme by brass and saxophone
	28–39	Rhythmic variation of theme by full band

---

3 Ibid

Section	Measure	Event and Scoring
B	40–47	Main theme utilizing the four-note motivic statement in the key center of F major
	48–51	Interlude with second triplet motive by brass in the key center of D minor
	52–56	Interlude with second triplet motive by woodwind
	57–66	Main theme returns by full band in D major
	67–79	Second triplet motive slightly varied, serving as a transition
C	80–95	Main theme returns in augmented form with countermelody in horn and cornet while the key center of B-flat major returns
	96–102	Second triplet motive used as transition
Coda	103–108	Four-note motivic statement of Main theme by brass, punctuated by percussion and woodwinds

Unit 8: Suggested Listening

Aaron Copland, *Fanfare for the Common Man*
James Curnow, *Fanfare and Flourishes for a Festive Occasion*
Karel Husa, *Smetana Fanfare*
Alfred Reed, *Russian Christmas Music*
Fisher Tull, *Fanfare for Band and Antiphonal Brass*
Ralph Vaughan Williams, *Flourish for Wind Band*
John Williams, *Olympic Fanfare*

Unit 9: Additional References and Resources

Battisti, Frank. *The Twentieth Century American Wind Band/Ensemble*. Fort Lauderdale, FL: Meredith Music Publications, 1995.

Chronological Listing of Published Works by Alfred Reed. website address: http://www.lackland.af.mil/box/Reedworks2.html, accessed 15 May 2001.

DeCarbo, Nicholas J. "Alfred Reed: Composer of Our Time." *The Instrumentalist* 40, No. 3, 1985, pp. 20–2.

Dunnigan, Patrick. "Reverse Transcriptions, From Bands to Orchestras." *The Instrumentalist* 51, No. 7, 1997, pp. 22–6.

Dvorak, Thomas L., Robert Grechesky, and Gary Ciepluch. *Best Music for High School Band*. Brooklyn, NY: Manhattan Beach Music, 1993.

Groeling, Charles. "Band Classics Revisited." *The Instrumentalist* 45, No. 9, 1991, p. 73.

Jordan, Douglas M. *Alfred Reed: a bio-bibliography*. Westport, CT: Greenwood Press, 1999.

Jordan, Douglas M. "The Russian Christmas That Took 24 Years to Arrive." *The Instrumentalist* 50, No. 3, 1995, pp. 26–7.

Macy, Laura, ed. *The New Grove Dictionary of Music and Musicians*, Volume II, electronic version, website address: http://www.grovemusic.com, accessed on 15 June 2001. "Alfred Reed," by Raoul F. Camus.

Marcus, Rachel. "Professor/Composer Teaches Realities of the Changing Music Industry." *Veritas* 31, No. 5, 1990, p. 3.

Moss, Lee. "Composer Alfred Reed's Thoughts on Creativity." *The Instrumentalist* 32, No. 8, 1978, pp. 34–5.

Murakami, Y. *The World of Alfred Reed: All About the Composer and His 77 Compositions*. Tokyo: Kosei Publishing Company, 1997.

Reed, Alfred. "Composer – Performer – Publisher – Audience: A Quadraphonic Relationship." *The Instrumentalist* 41, No. 12, 1987a, pp. 22–4.

_____. "Works: A Festival Prelude." *The School Musician* 39, No. 8, 1968, pp. 62–4.

_____, to Richard Lundahl, 1 July 2001. Correspondence in the hand of Richard Lundahl.

Stagg, David L. "A Comprehensive Performance Project in Band Conducting with a Catalogue of Original Works for Wind Ensemble or Concert Band by Alfred Reed from 1953 to 1983 with Performance Comments on Selected Works." DMA dissertation, University of Iowa, 1985.

Strange, Richard. "The New Music of Alfred Reed." *Bandworld* 2, No. 5, 1987, pp. 18, 33, 40.

Contributed by:
Richard Lundahl
Assistant Director of Bands
University of Wisconsin–Milwaukee
Milwaukee, Wisconsin

Teacher Resource Guide

A Moorside Suite
Gustav Holst

(1874–1934)

transcribed by Glenn Dennis Wright

Unit 1: Composer

Gustav Holst was born in Cheltenham, England, on September 21, 1874, and died in London on May 25, 1934. He was born to a family that was of Swedish ancestry, having settled in England in the early 1800s after living in Russia for a brief period. His birth name was Gustavus Theodore von Holst, which he changed to Gustav Holst at the outbreak of World War I.

Holst entered London's Royal College of Music (R.C.M.) in 1893, where he studied composition, piano, organ, and trombone. It was during his student years at R.C.M. that he befriended Ralph Vaughan Williams. After graduating from R.C.M., he earned a living as a professional trombonist. It was his experience as a trombonist that made him aware of the expressive qualities of the brass choir and potential of the military band as serious musical medium.

In 1903, Holst began a career of composing and teaching, and taught at a number of schools including Morley College, R.C.M., and St. Paul's Girls School in London. As a composer, Holst was strongly influenced by English folk song. Other important influences upon his music were his study of Eastern philosophy, Sanskirt, and astrology.

Holst is one of England's most respected composers. His compositional output includes opera, ballet, chamber music, solo songs, and choral works. His band works, *First Suite in E-flat* (1909) and *Second Suite in F* (1911) are universally acknowledged as the foundation of the serious band repertoire. These works, coupled with his *Hammersmith, Prelude and Scherzo* (1930), are considered among the band's standard repertoire.

Unit 2: Composition

Holst originally wrote *A Moorside Suite* for brass band. Historically, concert bands and brass bands had their beginnings, in part, with the fifes, drums, and trumpets associated with European courts and armies. Early military music generally fell into one of two categories: cavalry music or infantry music. Trumpets and kettledrums were associated with the cavalry music, while bagpipes and fifes were associated with the infantry. The brass band is considered a descendant of the cavalry band.

Brass bands began to appear in England around 1833. British brass bands flourished as organizations that provided wholesome recreation for factory and mine workers. The popularity of those early British brass bands continues today in Britain, as witnessed by the large number of amateur British brass bands associated with industrial enterprises and collieries (i.e., coal mines). In Britain, a sizable body of brass band repertoire has been developed, including original compositions by leading British composers such as Sir Edward Elgar, John Ireland, Ralph Vaughan Williams, and Gustav Holst. Brass band festival and contests are regular events in Britain.

In 1928, Holst was commissioned by the organizers of the National Brass Band Festival to compose a work for their annual championship contest. While Holst had never written for brass band, as a former trombonist he was comfortable composing for this medium. He preferred the brass band to the military band because of its more homogeneous tonal blend. He found enjoyment in the challenge of composing for the brass band with its inherent technical problems and in writing music interesting for the players and aesthetically satisfying to the listeners. The commissioned work he wrote was the three movement (Scherzo, Nocturne, and March) *Moorside Suite.*

In 1932, Holst made an arrangement of *A Moorside Suite* for strings. He also began scoring the suite for full band, completing only "Scherzo" and the first thirty-eight measures of "Nocturne." Holst's unpublished and incomplete full band version resides in the British Library. Subsequent scorings of *A Moorside Suite* for full band include versions by Gordon Jacob (published in two sections: "March," 1960; and "Scherzo and Nocturne," 1970), and Denis Wright. Holst saw and approved of the Wright version.

Unit 3: Historical Perspective

As members of the Folk Song Society, Holst, Vaughan Williams, and Grainger are considered three of the most important and influential composers for band of the twentieth century. At a time when few composers were writing for band, they established the traditions of British band literature through composition of original works. Holst, Vaughan Williams, and Grainger all had a strong interest in British folk songs, and their compositions were greatly influenced by folk songs.

Holst wrote *A Moorside Suite* six years prior to his death. Like his *Hammersmith, Prelude and Scherzo*, it is a product of his mature compositional period. The suite embodies a synthesis of Holst's creative compositional talents coupled with strong folk song influences.

The title itself, "Moorside," seems to imply a country setting and the use of English folk song. The term "moor" refers to an expanse of open rolling land dominated by wild grasses and sedges. The influence of folk song in *A Moorside Suite* is unmistakable. It is evident in the use of modal writing and harmonies, delicate solo lines, counterpoint, the skipping 6/8 of the "Scherzo," the sweeping and arching lyrical lines of the "Nocturne," and the vivacity of the final "March."

All of the melodies in the suite are Holst originals—he used no existing folk song melodies. Imogen Holst, Gustav Holst's daughter, wrote:

> Although the *Moorside Suite* for brass band seems to be looking back reminiscently to the folk song settings of twenty years ago, the music has vitality, and it looks forward as well as back. There is a rare tenderness in the opening of the Nocturne...recalling the poignancy of *I Love My Love*...[and] instinctively turning towards the *Lyric Movement* of five years later. The last movement of the suite is like a mature comment on the early *Marching Song* of 1908; it is a fitting acknowledgement of twenty years' debt of gratitude for the solid and companionable help that folk songs had brought him. They had been a refuge on so many occasions. But in 1928 he could afford to do without their help, for he had already found his own secure refuge in the empty solitude of *Egdon Heath*.

Unit 4: Technical Considerations

A Moorside Suite is scored for a musically mature ensemble. As a contest piece for the 1928 British Band Festival Championship, Holst resisted the temptation to write difficult brass virtuoso technical passages laced with double and triple tonguing. Instead, he challenged the musicality of each band and its players by writing parts requiring mature tone, a highly developed sense of nuance of phrasing, and superior control and mastery of *legato* playing. In both the horn and trumpet parts, Holst uses ledger lines above the staff sparingly. The brass parts are interesting, melodic, practical, and allow time for breathing.

The Wright scoring requires piccolo, 1st/2nd flute, oboe, 1st/2nd bassoon, E-flat soprano clarinet, 1st/2nd/3rd B-flat soprano clarinet, alto clarinet, bass clarinet, 1st/2nd alto saxophone, tenor saxophone, baritone saxophone,

1st/2nd/3rd/4th F horn, 1st/2nd/3rd cornet, 1st/2nd trumpet, 1st/2nd/3rd trombone, baritone, tuba, string bass, orchestra bells, timpani, snare drum, bass drum, and cymbals.

The wind parts require technically proficient players. The ensemble must be able to perform comfortably an array of articulations, styles, tempi, and dynamics. Chorale-like sections of the work require maturity of tone, tonal blend and balance, tonal control, and subtlety of phrasing. Articulated contrapuntal passages require precision and balance to achieve transparency and clarity of intertwining lines and vertical sonorities. An innate sense of rhythmic pulse and precision are essential to the performance of the work.

Unit 5: Stylistic Considerations

For the 1928 National Brass Band Championship of Great Britain, Holst chose to write a contest piece in the form of a suite, that is, a group of three short, contrasting movements. Utilizing this form, each movement challenged each band and its ability to perform various styles, tempi, articulations, and dynamics. *A Moorside Suite* embodies Holst's mature composition style.

MOVEMENT I: "SCHERZO"

Scherzo is defined literally as a sprightly and humorous instrumental composition in triple time. Holst's "Scherzo" movement requires transparency of parts resulting in light articulations and clarity from the players. Tonal control and maturity is required throughout this movement, as there are few *forte* and *fortissimo* passages. The driving rhythmic force is the compound duple meter of 6/8 with the requisite lilting pulse. The trio section with its arched lines requires a *cantabile* (singing) style.

MOVEMENT II: "NOCTURNE"

Nocturne is defined literally as a dreamy or pensive romantic character piece dealing with the evening or night. A nocturne is typically written in a somewhat melancholy or languid style with an expressive melody. Holst's "Nocturne" movement requires soloists capable of playing in an expressive lyric and "*molto legato*" style. The soloists must be capable of projecting and blending their individual lines in numerous overlapping phrases with subtlety of nuance and careful dynamic balance while maintaining tonal control at very soft volume levels. The ensemble must be able to perform in a *legato* style with a full-bodied tone at a *pianissimo* (*ppp*) volume level.

MOVEMENT III: "MARCH"

A march is defined literally as a composition usually in duple meter with a strongly accentuated beat. A march is typically designed or suitable to accompany the marching of groups of people or soldiers. Holst's "March" movement requires from the players an energetic playing style with clarity and uniformity of matching *marcato* spaced and weighted articulations. Essential to the march style in this movement is the need of exact vertical alignment and vertical sonority of musical figures and lines. Holst's use of the term *staccato* (separated style of articulation) in this movement refers to an articulated style that is *leggerio* (light and nimble).

Holst attended the 1928 National Brass Band Festival to hear bands perform his *Moorside Suite* contest piece. Concerning those performances, he commented that he was impressed by the flexibility of rhythm of the best bands but was somewhat disappointed that some cornet and euphonium soloists indulged in vibrato when the music called for a calm, smooth *cantabile* style. Holst indicates *senza vibrato*, without vibrato, in measure 22 of the "Nocturne." He also commented that there was a tendency for some soloists to turn equal quavers (eight notes) into dotted notes in slow passages.

Unit 6: Musical Elements

Throughout his career, Holst used the "Scherzo" more as a method of artistic presentation than as a strict formal structure. A scherzo, often identified as the third movement of a symphony, is used in *A Moorside Suite* as the opening movement portraying light-heartedness and humor.

A characteristic music element of Holst is the use of repetitive bass line scales as counterpoint to upper voices. Rising and falling scales are used in the "Nocturne" (measures 27 through 43 and 59 through 76).

Holst's mature compositional style encompasses the entire chromatic spectrum. Holst often wrote modal harmonies and melodies. The use of modal writing is evident throughout the entire *Moorside Suite*. He also used the entire chromatic spectrum as a musical element available for instantaneous modulation. Such modulations will occur often without transition and preparation. An example of this type of modulation can be found in the "Nocturne" (measures 22 through 23), where the unprepared move from F minor/aeolian to C major has little feeling of a tonic-dominant relationship and sounds more like a shift to a new and fresh key.

Holst used the expressive interval of the falling sixth throughout his "Nocturne." This sweeping, emotive melodic interval is a pervasive musical element of his compositional style and can be found in the slow movement of his *Second Suite in F*, "I Love My Love."

Holst often used a combination of rhythmic displacement and syncopation as a compositional musical element. The use of this rhythmic device creates interest for players and listeners. An example of this rhythmic element can be found in the "March" (measures 148 through 155).

Holst also often used rhythmic diminution to bring a melodic phrase to termination, as evidenced in the "March" (measures 4 through 9).

The interval of a perfect fourth, a predominate characteristic of the "March," is also a characteristic musical element of Holst's compositional style.

Unit 7: Form and Structure

SECTION	MEASURE	TONAL CENTER	EVENT AND SCORING

Movement I: "Scherzo"

A scherzo is literally a joke or jest. It is an instrumental piece of a light, piquant, humorous character; a vivacious movement with strongly marked rhythm and sharp and unexpected contrasts in rhythm and harmony; usually in triple meter and quick.

A – Theme 1 area

SECTION	MEASURE	TONAL CENTER	EVENT AND SCORING
	1–10	B-flat dorian	Presentation of Theme 1 (m. 1 material used as Motive 1 and m. 9 material used as Motive 2)
	‖: 11–22	B-flat dorian	Use of Motive 1 in imitation with use of Theme 1 in *stretto* (overlapping of phrases)
	23–33	B-flat dorian	Theme in *tutti* presentation
	34–41 :‖	B-flat dorian at m. 31moving to B-flat aeolian at m. 38	Use of Motive 2 in imitation as a transition to B section
B – Trio: Theme 2 area			
	42–59	B-flat major with B-flat/F pedal in bass	Motive 1 imitation with presentation of Theme 2 in upper woodwinds
	‖: 60–78	B-flat major with melody transposed down a perfect fifth with B-flat/ F pedal in upper brass; mm. 66–70 F major/ mm. 71–78 B-flat major	Motive 1 in imitation with Theme 2 in low reeds and low brass
	79–86	B-flat major	Motive 1 in imitation with Theme 2 in upper woodwinds
	87–91 :‖	B-flat major	Closing section with use of Motive 1 as closing material
	92–93	B-flat major	Use of Motive 1 as closing and transition to A section
A	D.C. al Fine		Repeat of A section mm. 1–41

Section	Measure	Tonal Center	Event and Scoring

Movement II: "Nocturne"

A nocturne is literally a night piece or serenade. It is a composition of dreamily romantic or sentimental character without a fixed form.

A – Theme 1 area

	1–9	F aeolian	Theme 1 presented in oboe; Motive 1 in mm. 1–4 and Motive 2 in mm. 2–9
	10–13	F aeolian	Motive I in flute and alto saxophone with presentation of countermelody in clarinet, low reeds, and low brass
	14–17	F aeolian	Motive 2 in oboe with countermelody in euphonium
	18–22	Aeolian moving at mm. 20–22 (dominate V chord in second inversion) to C major at m. 23	Closing section on permutations of Motive 2, Motive 1, and countermelody
Transition	23–26	C major/ C mixolydian	Permutation of Motive 1

B – Theme 2 area

	27–36	C major	Choral melody/phrase A presentation with rising and falling scale passages in low reeds and brass
	37–43	C major	Choral melody/phrase B presentation with rising and falling scale passages in low reeds and brass
Transition	44–46	D dorian	Permutation of Motive 1
A'	47–53	F aeolian moving to B-flat aeolian at m. 50	Permutation of Motive 1 and Motive 2 presented by oboe
	54–58	B-flat aeolian at m. 50; phrygian cadence at m. 58	Permutation of countermelody

Section	Measure	Tonal Center	Event and Scoring
B'	59–68	F major	Choral melody/phrase A presentation with rising and falling scale passages in low reeds and brass
	69–75	F major	Choral melody/phrase B presentation with rising and falling scale passages in low reeds and brass
Coda	76–86	G dorian at mm. 76–79, D lydian at mm. 81–82, F mixolydian at mm. 83–85, F major at m. 86	Closing section with permutation and elongation of Theme 1, Motive 1

Movement III: "March"

A march is literally a work written for a parade or procession. It is usually in duple meter with regular phrases and strongly marked rhythmic figures.

Introduction	1–3	B-flat aeolian	Fanfare motive
A – Theme 1 area			
	4–9	B-flat aeolian	Motive 1
	10–15	B-flat aeolian	Motive 1 with rhythmic derivation on fanfare motive
	16–21	B-flat aeolian moving to B-flat minor at m. 21	Motive 1
	22–27	B-flat minor moving to D-flat major at m. 27	Transition on Motive 1
	28–35	D-flat major with plagal cadence (IV–I) at mm. 34–35	Motive 2
	36–43	D-flat minor moving to B-flat minor at m. 43	Motive 2
	44–49	B-flat minor	Motive 1

Section	Measure	Tonal Center	Event and Scoring
B – Theme 2 area			

(legato tune reminiscent of the "land of hope and glory" or "Britain Forever")

Section	Measure	Tonal Center	Event and Scoring
	50–65	B-flat major	Motive 3a
	66–75	B-flat major	Motive 3b
	76–91	B-flat major	Motive 3a
	92–97	B-flat major	Motive 3b'
	98–114	B-flat major moving to F dominant pedal at m. 114	Motive 3a'
Transition	115–129	F dominant pedal at m. 115; A dominant pedal in D minor at m. 119; B-flat dominant pedal in E-flat minor at m. 125	Augmentation and *stretto* on fanfare motive with scale passages
	130–137	F dominant pedal in B-flat minor	Fanfare motive *stretto* with scale passages
	138–148	B-flat minor with F dominant prolongation in rhythmic figures	Fanfare motive rhythmic derivation
	149–154	B-flat phrygian scale passage moving to B-flat minor	Fragment of Motive 1 prolongation
A'	155–160	B-flat minor	Motive 1
	161–166	B-flat minor	Motive 1 with rhythmic derivation on fanfare motive
	167–172	B-flat minor moving to D-flat major	Motive 1
	173–180	D-flat major w with plagal cadence at mm. 179–180	Motive 2

SECTION	MEASURE	TONAL CENTER	EVENT AND SCORING
	181–188	D-flat major moving to B-flat minor half cadence at mm. 186–188	Motive 2
Transition	189–194	B-flat minor	Motive 3a
	195–204	B-flat minor	Fanfare motive rhythmic derivation
	205–211	B-flat phrygian	Fanfare motive rhythmic derivation
	212–217	Phrygian scale moving to B-flat major	Fragment of Motive 1 prolongation
B"	218–233	B-flat major	Motive 3a
	234–236	B-flat major	Closing

Unit 8: Suggested Listening

Gustav Holst:

> A Moorside Suite (Dennis Wright edition)
> A Moorside Suite (original brass band version)
> Egdon Heath
> First Suite in E-flat for Military Band
> Lyric Movement for Viola
> Marching Song
> Planets
> Second Suite in F for Military Band

Unit 9: Additional References

Apel, Willi. *Harvard Dictionary of Music*. Second edition. Cambridge, MA: The Balkan Press of Harvard University Press, 1970.

Fennell, Frederick. "Gustav Holst: 'A Moorside Suite.'" *The Band's Music*. Edited by Kenneth L. Neidig. Traverse City, MI: Village Press Publications, 1992.

Holst, Imogen. *The Music of Gustav Holst*. Second edition. London: Oxford University Press, 1968.

Mitchell, Jon C., "Sketches for Holst's 'A Moorside Suite.'" *Journal of Band Research*, Volume 22, No. 2, Spring 1987. Troy, AL: Troy State University Press.

Short, Michael. *Gustav Holst, The Man and His Music*. London: Oxford University Press, 1990.

Rehrig, William H. *The Heritage Encyclopedia of Band Music*. Edited by Paul Bierley. Westerville, OH: Integrity Press, 1991.

Contributed by:

Victor A. Markovich, Ph.D.
Professor of Music and Director of Bands and Winds/Percussion Studies
School of Music
Wichita State University
Wichita, Kansas

Teacher Resource Guide

After a Gentle Rain

Anthony Iannaccone
(b. 1943)

Unit 1: Composer

Anthony Iannaccone holds degrees from the Manhattan School of Music and the Eastman School of Music. A native of New York City, he performed as a professional violinist there prior to his appointment as Professor of Composition at Eastern Michigan University in 1971. He has published numerous compositions, including works for orchestra, wind ensemble, and chamber ensemble. His teachers include Samuel Adler, Aaron Copland, David Diamond, and Vittorio Giannini.

A critically acclaimed composer, Iannaccone is a two-time Ostwald winner (*Psalms for a Great Country* in 1996, and *Sea Drift* in 1995), and in 1988 he won the National Band Association's Annual Composition Contest with *Apparitions*.

Unit 2: Composition

After a Gentle Rain is a two-movement composition, approximately seven minutes in length. It is perhaps Iannaccone's most well-known wind composition, having been performed in excess of one thousand times. It was commissioned and premiered in 1979 by the Eastern Michigan Symphonic Band, Max Plank, conductor.

The first movement, entitled "The Dark Green Glistens with Old Reflections," begins with a series of two triads in secession: B-flat major and C major. Iannaccone refers to this as "superimposed major triads." The composer notes in the score that this opening *arpeggio* is the "main harmonic and melodic idea of the entire piece"—and indeed it is. Throughout the first movement, the superimposed triads appear in several keys and are played by numerous instruments. Marked "Warmly" at quarter note = 54, this movement contains several subtle, but clearly marked tempo changes, and as the title of the movement suggests, it is the more introverted of the two movements. The tempo changes allow the conductor to push and pull the tempo, creating orchestrated tension and release.

The second movement, "Sparkling Air Bursts with Dancing Sunlight," is the more lively of the two movements and is marked "With spirit." It begins in a dance-like 6/8 at dotted-quarter note = 104–108. Divided into three sections by tempo changes, this movement is full of hemiola and, following a sparsely orchestrated slower center section, ends strongly with a lively *piu mosso*.

Unit 3: Historical Perspective

As the title of the composition and the title of both movements suggest, *After a Gentle Rain* is to a certain degree both quasi-programmatic and quasi-impressionistic. Programmatic in nature due to the composer's comments in the score, referring to "...old memories in a quiet, meditative context" from the first movement and "...the joy and freshness that seems to fill the air after a gentle rain" from the second movement. Both of these comments refer to events, and should the listener choose to reflect on these comments, it is easy to tie them (along with the titles of the movements) to the music.

Impressionistic elements include harmonic content (specifically the use of the superimposed major triads in the first movement), orchestration (specifically the combination of instruments to create numerous unique sounds within the ensemble), and a reference made by the composer as to the influence of Debussy's *Les collines d'Anacapri*, from *Preludes*, Book 1, on *After a Gentle Rain*.

From an historical prospective, the ability to reference nineteenth century programmatic music and twentieth century impressionism should make *After a Gentle Rain* a very good piece to help introduce both students and audience alike to music from these eras.

Unit 4: Technical Considerations

The most challenging aspect of *After a Gentle Rain* will likely prove to be rhythm. The first movement, although slow, contains sextuplet sixteenth notes outlining the superimposed major triads. This motive is performed by numerous instruments throughout the movement. Accompanying parts are eighth notes, but the challenge is to make the sextuplets fit rhythmically with the accompaniment. Additional technical challenges in this movement include the subtle tempo changes indicated in the score. While not technically challenging at these places, listening and watching the conductor closely are skills that will need to be developed to navigate through the tempo changes.

The second movement has a considerable amount of hemiola throughout. Written in a dance-like 6/8, the hemiola is beamed by the composer to indicate the desired rhythmic emphasis. Careful attention should be paid to tempo throughout these sections, as it is easy to lose momentum as the rhythmic emphasis shifts back and forth. The slower center section of this movement is more chamber oriented than any other section in the entire piece, requiring only five soloists. Great care will need to be taken to ensure this section becomes chamber music.

Unit 5: Stylistic Considerations

As the composer indicates in the score, the first movement is "...quiet, meditative, and introverted," while the second movement is "...sparkling, dance-like, and extroverted." The players must approach each movement from opposite ends of the stylistic spectrum. The style of the first movement, while certainly more subtle in nature, requires the performers to respond to the many tempo changes, thus giving ebb and flow to the music. The ability to let the music breathe in this manner is important to the style of the movement; it should not be metronymic in nature. The conductor should have the ability to make the music slightly different each time through, giving life to the music as a result of the tempo changes.

In contrast, the second movement should be strictly metronymic in nature. Variation in tempo during the sections where hemiola plays a role will simply sound like the performers are playing with poor time. Articulation in this movement must also be much more energetic in nature, as indicated by the composer. It is, after all, a lively dance-like movement, so the performers must play with a great deal more vigor in contrast to the first movement.

Unit 6: Musical Elements

MELODY:

Throughout the composition, one consistent six-note melody is present. It first appears in measure 9 of the first movement in the piccolo, flute, and oboe parts. It is only one and one-half beats long, but its presence is unmistakable throughout the work. Iannaccone transforms this simple melody several times, augmenting the duration of the melody, changing orchestration of the melody, and even changing the timbre of a particular instrument performing the melody (e.g., in the second movement, the trumpet plays this melody slowly with harmon mute, no stem). It is this melody that helps give the two movements continuity despite their completely different styles.

Having students identify this melody at various places in the composition will help develop both listening and performance skills, as one of the first rules of performance is to always listen for the melody. In this case, the melody is very short and often presented in a subtle way, requiring attentive performers throughout the ensemble.

HARMONY:

After a Gentle Rain contains mainly major and minor triads, both melodically and harmonically. However, it is the manner in which Iannaccone combines these simple chord structures into more complex sounds through both his choice of harmony and orchestration. For example, the opening superimposed major triad is a common chord heard in jazz (a thirteenth chord), with the exception of one characteristic: there is no seventh (major or dominant) in the chord. Added to the opening superimposed major triads is tremolo in clarinet, outlining the first of the two chords (B-flat major). This use of both harmony and orchestration creates a very unique sound, pointing to the composer's understanding of both.

The use of these simple chords in more complex ways gives the listener and performer alike new sounds to digest. Students will likely be familiar with the sound of major chords, but not two different ones at the same time. Identifying this sound and then breaking down what notes are being played should enhance the harmonic knowledge of the players.

RHYTHM:

In the second movement, hemiola and syncopation present ample opportunity for development of rhythmic skills and subdividing. The hemiola is in the form of three quarter notes in a 6/8 time signature. Usually, this type of hemiola is three quarter note triplets in 2/4, with no clear subdivision of the quarter note. But in 6/8, there is a basic subdivision for the quarter notes made by the eighth notes. This is helpful in defining how long each quarter note should be by simply thinking about where the emphasis should fall, with the emphasis being on the first, third and fifth eighth note instead of on the first and third. Iannaccone takes groups of six eighth notes and groups them in two ways: 3+3 and 2+2+2. He indicates in the score where the emphasis should be through changes in how he beams the eighth notes.

While the hemiola gives performers a way of easily defining the underlying subdivision, the syncopation used in the second movement is something altogether different. It is much more challenging than standard syncopation found in duple meters, where the syncopation is on offbeats. In 6/8, there are two options for syncopation—the second or third eighth note—and both are found in the second movement. The syncopation happens fast, and considering the tempo, the players must possess advanced subdivision skills to accurately perform these rhythms.

TIMBRE:

Through his use of harmony and orchestration, Iannaccone has created a composition that paints two different aural pictures. In the score, he describes the first movement as being meditative and introverted while the second movement is sparkling and extroverted. Certainly in describing the timbre of these two movements, one could easily use these very words even without having access to the composer's written thoughts. Of particular interest is the use of piano, not as a solo instrument but rather as a color instrument. In the first movement, the piano doubles the upper woodwind and mallet percussion parts. Added to that particular combination of instruments is a soft tremolo in the clarinet and saxophone parts.

In the second movement, the piano is used with the same instruments but with a completely different result. The lively, bright timbre of this movement is also a result of the rhythmic accents provided by hemiola and syncopation. The result is a dramatic departure from the mood of the first movement.

Another point of interest is the markings for muted trumpet. Iannaccone uses straight mute, Harmon mute (both with stem in and stem out), and cup mute. Each mute change points to the composer's desire for small timbre changes from the same instrument.

To perform each movement accurately requires both conductor and ensemble to understand the completely opposite timbre of each movement and how these differences should relate to performance. There are also numerous dynamic changes and different articulations. Each performer must take great care to perform all the markings within the score.

Unit 7: Form and Structure

The first movement is divided into six basic sections. Each section is delineated by a tempo change and changes in orchestration. The first two sections present and develop the superimposed major triads and the six-note melody found throughout the composition. The movement reaches its climax in the third section (measures 45 through 54), culminating with a strong *fortissimo*. The following sections wind down into a recap of the opening section. The last section (measures 73 through 86) concludes the movement in much the same way it began, with the *pianissimo* superimposed major triads and the six-note melody once again.

The second movement begins with a long, dance-like section. The opening six-note melody is developed into a stronger statement in this section. Many spirited rhythms using syncopation, hemiola, and hocket are present. This long section leads into a shorter, slower section where only five players are required. This short section is slightly reminiscent of the first movement in that it is more relaxed in nature and far less spirited than the opening section. The last section of the movement is only twenty-one measures long and returns to the spirited rhythms of the first section. The movement concludes with a flurry on a B-flat major chord, the same chord as the opening three notes of the superimposed major triads.

Unit 8: Suggested Listening
Anthony Iannaccone:
> *Antiphonies*
> *Apparitions*
> *Images of Song and Dance, No. 1: Orpheus*
> *Images of Song and Dance, No. 2: Terpsichore*
> *Interlude*
> *Of Fire and Ice*
> *Plymouth Trilogy*
> *Scherzo*
> *Sea Drift*
> *Suite for Orchestra*
> *Toccata Fanfare*

Claude Debussy, *Les collines d'Anacapri*, from Preludes, Book 1

Unit 9: Additional References and Resources
Clarion Wind Symphony, Max Plank, conductor: Wind Music of Anthony
    Iannaccone, Troy 280. CD recording.

Websites:
> http://www.sai-national.org/phil/composers/aiannocc.html
> http://utopia.knoware.nl/~jsmeets/cgi-bin/ccd.cgi?comp=iannaccone
> http://www.lib.umd.edu/MUSIC/ABA/Ostwald/iannacco.html

Contributed by:
John M. Laverty
Director of Bands
Syracuse University
Syracuse, New York

Teacher Resource Guide

American Overture for Band
Joseph Willcox Jenkins
(b. 1928)

Unit 1: Composer

Pennsylvania native Joseph Willcox Jenkins decided upon a career in music after receiving a pre-law degree from St. Joseph's College. His compositions number over two hundred, including works for orchestra, choir, organ, bagpipe, and concert band. Jenkins studied composition with Vincent Persichetti at the Philadelphia Conservatory of Music and with Thomas Canning and Howard Hanson at the Eastman School of Music. He received his Bachelor of Music and Master of Music degrees from Eastman before earning his Ph.D. at the Catholic University of America.

Jenkins currently resides in Pittsburgh, where he serves as an adjunct Professor of Theory and Composition at Duquesne University, having formerly served as chairman of the theory and composition department and conductor of the Duquesne orchestra and choir. He has received the ASCAP Serious Music Award annually since 1964, and he continues to maintain an active composing and conducting schedule. Jenkins works for wind band include *American Overture for Band*; *Charles County Overture*; *Christmas Festival Overture*; *Cumberland Gap*; *Cuernavaca*; *In Traskwood Country*; *Pieces of Eight, Op. 8*; *Symphonic Jubilee*; *Three Images*; and *Toccata for Winds, Op. 104*.

Unit 2: Composition

American Overture for Band was written for the United States Army Field Band in 1955 and dedicated to its conductor, Chester E. Whiting. Its driving rhythms, sweeping melodies, strong accents, and virtuosic demands characterize the work. The initial declaration in unison horn is among the most recognized in the repertoire. In a 1983 report compiled by Robert Hornyak, entitled *The Repertoire of the College and University Band: 1975–1982*, Jenkin's *American Overture for Band* was listed as being among the twenty-four most-performed works of the period.

Unit 3: Historical Perspective

The mid-1940s and entire decade of the 1950s represent a period of considerable growth and maturity for the wind band and its literature. Encouraged in part by the College Band Director's National Association (CBDNA), the number of original works for the medium grew in quality and quantity, resulting in an impressive listing of pieces that have entered the band's repertoire.

American Overture for Band by Joseph Willcox Jenkins (1955)
Canzona by Peter Mennin (1951)
Chester Overture by William Schuman (1957)
Chorale and Alleluia by Howard Hanson (1954)
Divertimento by Vincent Persichetti (1950)
Fanfare and Allegro by Clifton Williams (1956)
George Washington Bridge by William Schuman (1951)
La Fiesta Mexicana by H. Owen Reed (1949)
Suite Française, Op. 248, by Darius Milhaud (1945)
Suite of Old American Dances by Robert Russell Bennett (1950)
Symphony for Band by Morton Gould (1952)
Symphony in B-flat by Paul Hindemith (1951)
Symphony No. 6, Op. 69, by Vincent Persichetti (1956)
Tunbridge Fair by Walter Piston (1950)

Unit 4: Technical Considerations

Two significant technical challenges are present when approaching *American Overture for Band*: (1) deciding upon a tempo that allows for clarity of line while realizing the inherent momentum that propels the work toward a thrilling finish, and (2) the necessity for every musician to possess or acquire technical proficiency of rapid tonguing. The initial tempo, *allegro molto*, requires the conductor to choose and maintain a consistent pulse that most closely realizes the energetic rhythmic drive crafted into the work. A tempo between quarter note = 144 and 160 seems appropriate, with clarity of line and accuracy of tonguing dictating the decision.

A fine line exists between a reckless single tongue and an intelligible double tongue, and every player is called upon to present clarity in rapidly articulated figures. A tempo of quarter note = ca.152 may give a slight edge to the performance while allowing the ensemble to achieve clarity of line. The pulse must be maintained from measures 1 through 138, even in the more *legato* passages. The final *accelerando* should be dramatic but not frantic, allowing the triplet figures to create much of the driving momentum to the *presto*. A final tempo between quarter note = 162 and 174 may be appropriate, with the ensemble's ability to perform the music with definition and clarity influencing the conductor's decision.

American Overture for Band has been published with only a condensed score available since 1956.

Unit 5: Stylistic Considerations

Few works in the wind band literature require the refined nuance of rapid tonguing technique—required from every musician—as found in *American Overture for Band*. A slight *crescendo* should be added for each repeated note pattern to add clarity and direction to the line. The work is relentlessly driven by rhythm, and achieving a tempo that allows for rhythmic integrity and clarity of articulation will make the work seem even faster and more difficult than it is. Approaching a work as "fast for the sake of fast" is rarely successful, and *American Overture for Band* must settle into a well-controlled but forward-moving momentum.

Motifs derived from each principal theme recur throughout *American Overture for Band*, serving to unify the work and challenge the listener's ear. Locating these musical nuances and bringing them to the front of the musical texture is an important element in accurately representing the composer's craft and intent.

Horn is a key instrument in this piece, but musicians in this section must not think of *American Overture for Band* as a concerto grosso—or of horn vs. ensemble. From the first measure, the sweeping melodies should be presented with vigor and enthusiasm but without overpowering or overbalancing the ensemble. The first measure is often presented as forced and overblown, creating an unfortunate mindset from the start. Approaching the piece with controlled excitement, created through a combination of tempo and wide dynamic contrast, is a recommended path to fully experiencing this musically worthy composition.

Unit 6: Musical Elements

There are numerous examples of music teaching tools found within *American Overture for Band*. The concept of the overture may be addressed, including its traditional or logical placement within an overall concert program. Musicians might be encouraged to consider the essence of programming itself, as well as briefly studying the history of the overture. The role of horn in music can be visited (with references to Richard Strauss, Johannes Brahms, Wolfgang Mozart, and Richard Wagner), the crook and development of the valve, the natural horn, the single and double horn, use of the word "French" and the horn, and contemporary performers (including Barry Tuckwell, Philip Farkas, Dennis Brain, and Dale Clevenger), fostering discussion and discovery.

The form of *American Overture for Band* is reminiscent of the sonata form, allowing the conductor-educator to discuss concepts of musical form, the history and structure of sonata form (most notably its utilization in the classical period), and champions of its development (Haydn, Mozart, and Beethoven, among many). Jenkin's use of neomodal style, including both the lydian and mixolydian modes, can lead to a discussion of mode and key. Motifs derived from the primary themes of the work appear frequently and can be used to discuss concepts of unity, representation and symbolism, motives in sonata form development sections, or perhaps the Leitmotif.

Articulation—most notably full ensemble unison passages and double tonguing—is a central musical concept to teaching *American Overture for Band*. Demonstrating like and dissimilar approaches to a rhythm or tonguing pattern can serve to heighten aural skills and reinforce positive rehearsal listening.

Unit 7: Form and Structure

American Overture for Band is crafted in a free adaptation of sonata form. Thematic motifs are used throughout to unify and connect phrases and sections of the work.

SECTION	MEASURE	EVENT AND SCORING
Introduction	1	Horns
Allegro molto	2–3	Full ensemble *crescendo*
Exposition	4–22	Themes 1 and 2 call and response; highly accented with rapidly articulated figures
	23–40	Bridge; alternating rhythmic patterns and *legato* material; unison rhythms and fragments developed from Themes 1 and 2
	41–59	Theme 3; horn with sweeping melody; offbeats in low brass; cornet melody
	60–72	Bridge; segmented material based on Theme 3; rhythmic statements passed between registers
Development	73–83	Reduced dynamics; exploration of motifs leading to four-measure modulatory bridge

SECTION	MEASURE	EVENT AND SCORING
	84–94	Development of Theme 3 material; bassoon and timpani *ostinato*
	95–99	Chromatic, bold, widely accented passage with highly articulated figures and Theme 3 motifs
	100–109	Unison rhythmic statements and punctuated figures; motif from Theme 1 leading to recapitulation
Recapitulation	110–120	Themes 1 and 2; horn and trumpet melody; less dense scoring than in exposition
	121–139	Motifs from exposition building in dynamic and texture
Coda	140–154	*Accelerando* to *presto*; widely unison rhythms

Unit 8: Suggested Listening

Leonard Bernstein, *Overture to "Candide"*
Paul Creston, *Celebration Overture*
Morton Gould, *American Salute*
Ron Nelson, *Rocky Point Holiday*
Dmitri Shostakovich/Hunsberger, *Festive Overture*, Op. 96
Clifton Williams, *Fanfare and Allegro*
John Williams/Curnow, *The Cowboys*

Unit 9: Additional References and Resources

Battisti, Frank. *The Twentieth Century American Wind Band/Ensemble: History, Development and Literature*. Ft. Lauderdale, FL: Meredith, 1995.

Jenkins, Joseph Willcox. *American Overture for Band*. Bryn Mawr, PA: Theodore Presser, 1956.

Music for Winds and Percussion, Volume IV. Northern Illinois University Wind Ensemble, Stephen Squires, conductor.

Pageant. Keystone Wind Ensemble, Jack Stamp, conductor.

Smith, Norman, and Albert Stoutamire. *Program Notes for Band*. Chicago, IL: GIA Publications, Inc., 2002.

Contributed by:
Glen J. Hemberger
Director of Bands
Southeastern Louisiana University
Hammond, Louisiana

Teacher Resource Guide

An American Elegy
Frank Ticheli
(b. 1958)

Unit 1: Composer

The music of Louisiana-born composer Frank Ticheli has garnered numerous awards and prizes, resulting in his standing among the most-prolific and most-performed champions of late twentieth century wind band literature. In the years from 1987 to 2000, Ticheli's contributions to the wind band literature gained widespread acclaim and acceptance: *Amazing Grace, An American Elegy, Blue Shades, Cajun Folk Songs, Cajun Folk Songs II, Concertino for Trombone and Band, Fortress, Gaian Visions, Music for Winds and Percussion, Pacific Fanfare, Portrait of a Clown, Postcard, Shenandoah, Sun Dance,* and *Vesuvius.*

Ticheli's honors include the 1989 Walter Beeler Prize, the Charles Ives Scholarship and Goddard Lieberson Fellowship from the American Academy and Institute of Arts and Letters, the Frances and William Schuman Fellowship from the MacDowell Colony, the Ross Lee Finney Award, and commissions from organizations such as the Indiana Bandmasters Association, The American Music Center, the Adrian Symphony, and Chamber Music America.

Ticheli received his Bachelor of Music in Composition from Southern Methodist University, where he studied with Donald Erb. He also earned doctoral and master's degrees in composition from the University of Michigan, where he studied with William Albright, George B. Wilson, and Pulitzer Prize winners Leslie Bassett and William Bolcom. After serving on the faculty at Trinity University in San Antonio, Texas, Ticheli currently lives in Los Angeles, where he is an associate professor of theory and composition at the

University of Southern California. From 1991 to 1998, he was Composer-in-Residence with the Pacific Symphony Orchestra in Orange County, California.

Unit 2: Composition

An American Elegy was commissioned by the Columbine Commissioning Fund, a consortium founded by the Alpha Iota Chapter of Kappa Kappa Psi at the University of Colorado. The project centered on the creation of a musical work on behalf of the Columbine High School Band of Littleton, Colorado, in remembrance of the shooting tragedy that befell the school in 1999. Contributors included local, national, and alumni members of Kappa Kappa Psi and Tau Beta Sigma—National Honorary Band Fraternity and Sorority—and friends close to the project.

The work received its premiere by the Columbine High School Wind Symphony on Easter Sunday, April 23, 2000, in Macky Auditorium Concert Hall on the University of Colorado–Boulder campus, with the composer conducting. The concert, inspired by children and innocence, featured *An American Elegy* as its cornerstone and included nearly 140 musicians from the University of Colorado's Wind Symphony and Symphonic Band, and Columbine High School. Also on the program were "Children's Gallery" from *Scenes from the Louvre* by Norman Dello Joio, *Children's March* by Percy Grainger, *An American Pageant* by Thomas Knox, and a setting of *Amazing Grace* by the University of Colorado Alum Andy Tisdale.

Ticheli writes of the commission:

> An American Elegy is, above all, an expression of hope. It was composed in memory of those who lost their lives at Columbine High School on April 20, 1999, and to honor the survivors. It is offered as a tribute to their greatest strength and courage in the face of a terrible tragedy. I hope the work can also serve as one reminder of how fragile and precious life is and how intimately connected we all are as human beings.
>
> I was moved and honored by this commission invitation and deeply inspired by the circumstances surrounding it. Rarely has a work revealed itself to me with such powerful speed and clarity. The first eight bars of the main melody came to me fully formed in a dream. Virtually every element of the work was discovered within the span of about two weeks. The remainder of my time was spent refining, developing, and orchestrating.

The national office of Kappa Kappa Psi presented Ticheli with its highest award, the Distinguished Service to Music Medal, for *An American Elegy*.

Unit 3: Historical Perspective

Musical works written in memoriam—in memory, remembrance, tribute, or commemoration—can be found throughout history. *An American Elegy* joins a growing and distinguished list of works for wind band composed to commemorate a person, place, or historical event. An abridged listing of representative works includes:

A Light Unto the Darkness by David Gillingham (1997)
A Movement for Rosa by Mark Camphouse (1992)
And Can It Be? by David Gillingham (2000)
Chaconne (In Memoriam...) by Ron Nelson (1994)
Commemoration Symphony by Anton Reicha (1815)
Elegy for a Young American by Ronald LoPresti (1964)
For Precious Friends Hid in Death's Dateless Night by Martin Mailman (1988)
For the Unfortunate by H. Owen Reed (1975)
Heroes, Lost and Fallen by David Gillingham (1989)
I Am by Andrew Boysen, Jr. (1990)
In Memoriam: Kristina by Bruce Yurko (1995)
In Memoriam Vincent Persichetti by Jacob Druckman (1987)
J. F. K.: In Memoriam by James Curnow (1995)
Kaddish by W. Francis McBeth (1977)
Music for Prague 1968 by Karel Husa (1968)
Postcard by Frank Ticheli (1991)
Symphonie Funèbre et Triomphale by Hector Berlioz (1840)
The Leaves Are Falling by Warren Benson (1964)
The Passing Bell by Warren Benson (1974)
Trauersinfonie by Richard Wagner (1884)
Watchman, Tell Us of the Night by Mark Camphouse (1995)
With Quiet Courage by Larry Daehn (1995)

Unit 4: Technical Considerations

Ticheli's work is scored for symphonic wind band and off-stage trumpet soloist. The score includes twenty-nine distinct parts, and the rich sonorities and strong dynamic passages strongly suggest utilization of a large ensemble. Important to an effective performance of *An American Elegy* are two sensitive yet powerful horn parts. First horn extends from written c' to g", and 2nd horn from c' to f", with both parts serving in primary melodic roles. Two solo oboe passages (measures 71 through 78 and 128 through 131) are cross-cued in flute and saxophone, respectively, but best reflect the serenity and reflection of the work when performed on the intended instrument. The off-stage trumpet part may be actualized by an ensemble member moving to position during the piece but is most effective when the audience is unaware of the origin of the sound. The desired "quite distant and ethereal, even other-worldly" effect of the trumpet solo is best achieved by dedicating a musician only to this task, placing the musician well out of view. Time spent investigating various remote locations for the soloist is critical, with a carefully balanced blend of trumpet and ensemble resulting in a celestial moment of musical realization.

Unit 5: Stylistic Considerations

An American Elegy requires a refined balance of extreme musical styles for its performance: tension and release; *tutti* and solo; *cantabile* and *maestoso*; *rigorosamente* and *rubato grazioso*; *fortissimo* and *pianissimo*. Much of the work demands a focused and unforced tone with richly balanced harmonies underlying sweeping lyrical melodies. Ticheli's desire for "subtle elasticity, free and fluid, but not too disruptive" is essential, as an over-romanticized approach can result in a labored and ineffective presentation.

Ticheli writes:

> The work begins at the bottom of the ensemble's register and ascends gradually to a heartfelt cry of hope. The main theme that follows, stated by the horns, reveals a more lyrical, serene side of the piece. A second theme, based on a simple repeated harmonic pattern, suggests yet another, more poignant mood. These three moods—hope, serenity, and sadness—become intertwined throughout the work, defining its complex expressive character. A four-part canon builds to a climactic quotation of the Columbine Alma Mater. The music recedes, and an offstage trumpeter is heard, suggesting a celestial voice—a heavenly message. The full ensemble returns with a final, exalted statement of the main theme.

While researching and contemplating the grievous circumstance that resulted in the work's commission, Ticheli sought inspiration from Columbine's own musical history. "After learning that Columbine High School did not have a school song," wrote Ticheli, "I composed one for them, and they adopted it as their official *Alma Mater*." The *Columbine Alma Mater* is majestically incorporated into the wind band setting, serving as one of the most poignant and reflective musical moments of the work. Its words, written by Ticheli, reflect the unity, simplicity, and emotion that permeate the work:

Mountains rising to the sun,
   tow'ring o'er the plains.
Heads held high we stand as one,
   And proudly we proclaim:
We are Columbine! We all are Columbine!
Let the world be told,
   Blue and silver we uphold—Forever.

Unit 6: Musical Elements

Opportunities to explore several musical concepts exist in teaching *An American Elegy*. The work begins with delicate and exposed moments of challenging tuning and balance issues, progressing through fourteen measures of additive construction and dynamic growth. Concepts of line shaping and *cantabile* style abound in the long, sweeping melodies and counterlines. Discussions of imagery and emotion in music present themselves throughout the work. The six-measure dreamlike section (measures 91 through 96) presents trios of woodwind tone color and issues of chordal balance alternating in short dynamic swells. A four-part canon (measures 97 through 110) affords discussion of imitation and balance. The resulting climactic peak (measures 111 through 113) is a quotation of the *Columbine Alma Mater*, and sharing words and music to the nine-measure song can be insightful and revealing to the performers. The final section (measures 132 through 152) presents rising suspensions and fourteen measures of carefully measured *crescendo* resulting in a resounding peak and subsequent evenly gauged *diminuendo* into the coda. The final five measures are highlighted by a reflective horn passage, softly fading chords requiring cautious balance and tuning, and two final statements of a motif based on the "Columbine" theme. Focusing attention on the unifying minor second interval, and its relationship to the entire work, may result in heightened awareness of the compositional craft that underlies *An American Elegy*.

Unit 7: Form and Structure

A framework for the piece is supplied by the composer:

SECTION	MEASURE	EVENT AND SCORING
Introduction	1–14	B-flat
Main theme	15–30	B-flat
Episode	31–46	B-flat
Main theme	47–62	B-flat
Second theme	63–96	B-flat/D-flat
Four-part canon	97–110	F
Climax	111–113	F; excerpt from *Columbine Alma Mater*
Bridge	114–117	F; based on second theme
Second theme (variation)	118–127	B-flat; offstage trumpet solo
Bridge	128–131	B-flat
Main theme	132–end	B-flat; final statement

Unit 8: Suggested Listening

Warren Benson, *The Leaves Are Falling* – Benson, Brant, Hanson, Eastman Wind Ensemble, Donald Hunsberger, conductor

Andrew Boysen, Jr., *I Am* – *Teaching Music through Performance in Band*, Volume 2, North Texas Wind Symphony, Eugene Migliaro Corporon, conductor: GIA CD–446

David Gillingham, *A Light Unto the Darkness*

Ronald LoPresti, *Elegy for a Young American* – *Symphonic Songs for Band*, Tokyo Kosei Wind Orchestra, Frederick Fennell, conductor

Ron Nelson, Chaconne (In Memoriam…) – *Holidays and Epiphanies*, Dallas Wind Symphony, Jerry Junkin, conductor: reference recordings RR76CD

Frank Ticheli, *Amazing Grace* – *American Variations*, Cincinnati Wind Symphony, Eugene Migliaro Corporon, conductor: Klavier KCD11060

_____, *Postcard* – *Postcards*, Cincinnati Wind Symphony, Eugene Migliaro Corporon, conductor: Klavier KCD11058

_____, *Shenandoah* – *Equus!*, University of North Carolina–Greensboro Wind Ensemble, John R. Locke, conductor

Bruce Yurko, *In Memoriam: Kristina* – *Teaching Music through Performance in Band*, Volume 2, North Texas Wind Symphony, Eugene Migliaro Corporon, conductor: GIA CD-446

Unit 9: Additional References and Resources

Ticheli, Frank. *An American Elegy*. Brooklyn, NY: Manhattan Beach Music, 2000.

Contributed by:

Glen J. Hemberger
Director of Bands
Southeastern Louisiana University
Hammond, Louisiana

Teacher Resource Guide

Be Thou My Vision
David Gillingham
(b. 1947)

Unit 1: Composer

David Gillingham was born on October 20, 1947, in Waukesha, Wisconsin. One notable influence in his early childhood was his aunt, an organist for a Methodist church who lived in the upstairs portion of the Gillingham house and often practiced hymns. David Gillingham received his piano training from her and was a church organist for many years. "I could actually quote the hymn tunes better than I could the actual text of the pieces. But I've become more interested in the text as I continue to compose."[1] Much of Gillingham's music is programmatic using liturgical themes. He is also an excellent euphonium player.

Gillingham earned his bachelor's and master's degrees in music education from the University of Wisconsin–Oshkosh in 1969 and 1977, respectively, and he earned his Ph.D. in Music Theory and Composition from Michigan State University in 1980. His principal composition teachers were Roger Dennis, Jere Hutcheson, James Niblock, and H. Owen Reed. Gillingham is a professor of music composition and theory at Central Michigan University. His national reputation as a composer of quality wind and percussion music has precipitated commissions dating into 2005.

Gillingham is the recipient of numerous awards and honors, including First Prize in the International Barlow Composition Contest in 1990 (*Heroes, Lost and Fallen*), 1990 National Association of Wind and Percussion

---

1 Bradley, Raydell Cecil. "A Study of the Use of Programmatic and Liturgical Themes in Selected Wind Ensemble Compositions of David Gillingham." D.M.A. dissertation, University of Washington, 2000, p. 6.

Instructors Composition Award (*Serenade, Songs of the Night*), a Summer Fellowship, a Research Professorship (Central Michigan University), and Composer-in-Residence at several Midwest universities and colleges. His most recent work, *Interplay for Piano Four-Hands and Orchestra* was performed and recorded on compact disc by the Czech Radio Symphony conducted by Vladimir Valek, with soloists Daniel Koppelman and Ruth Neville. His compositions have been performed throughout the United States, Europe, and Japan, and his works are published by Carl Fischer, Music for Percussion, C. Alan, Hal Leonard, MMB, Moon of Hope, Southern Music, I.T.A. Press, and the T.U.B.A. Press. Gillingham is a member of ASCAP and the Society of Composers, Inc.

Unit 2: Composition

Be Thou My Vision (1998) was composed for Ray and Molly Cramer in honor of their parents, Harold and Ora Murphy and Harold and Gladys Cramer, in appreciation for their Christian guidance and positive influence on their lives. It was premiered by the Indiana University Wind Ensemble under the direction of Ray Cramer. *Be Thou My Vision* happened to be a favorite hymn of both mothers. Gillingham states:

> The work is heartfelt, expressive, and hopefully inspiring. The hymn tune, Slane, is one of my favorites and inspired me to compose a countermelody which is likened to an old Irish ballad. Since Slane is, in fact, an old Irish ballad, the two tunes share this unique camaraderie. The work is a sort of "fantasy" on the hymn tune and presents it on two levels: one mysterious and the other dramatic. The piece opens with a medieval-like flavor of reverence leading to the first presentation of Slane. This is followed by the newly composed Irish ballad, which is "sung" by the flute. This leads to a dramatic statement of *Be Thou My Vision*. The work is interrupted by a prayerful interlude. Following is the marriage of the two Irish tunes that grows to a glorious climax and then subsides. An ascent into heaven closes the work.[2]

Unit 3: Historical Perspective

The words of the first verse of *Be Thou My Vision* are as follows:

Be thou my vision, oh Lord of my heart;
   naught be all else to me save that thou art.
Thou my best thought, by day or by night,
   waking or sleeping, thy presence my light.

---

2 E-mail from Gillingham.

This verse is from an eighth century anonymous Irish poem. It has been associated with the hymn tune *Slane* since 1919. Slane is a hill ten miles from Tara in County Meath, where St. Patrick is said to have challenged King Loegaire and the Druid priest by lighting the Pascal fire on Easter eve.

Unit 4: Technical Considerations

There are many tempo changes and many different meters in this piece, including 4/4, 3/4, 6/4, 9/8, and 12/8. Some of the 6/4 measures may be done in 3/2.

There are significant solos for euphonium and flute, and short solos for alto and tenor saxophone. The most technically challenging sections in this piece are the sixteenth note flourishes. Measures 54 through 62 pose a challenge to keep the sixteenth note voices together. It is best for players to think of the subdivided beat to play these flourishes accurately and together. In measures 77 through 92, the flourishes must also be subdivided. Throughout this section, the flourishes are often broken up among the instruments and must be very rhythmically precise to be handed off between the instruments.

There are four keys that are used, including D minor, F major, A major, and D-flat major. Horn range extends to A-flat, clarinet to F-sharp, and trumpet to G-sharp. Percussion parts are almost all mallet parts, with the marimba being the most difficult. Although there are four horn parts, there are only two different parts throughout, with the exception of measures 4 and 5 splitting into four parts and measures 61 through 64 splitting into three parts.

Unit 5: Stylistic Considerations

Style is very important in relating a mood. Gillingham had the following to say regarding his music:

> The mood is very important to me, you see. I want to capture both the mood and the listener's attention. I want to draw people into a story that I'm telling. I want them to come into the music some-how...the more serious the emotional content of the program, the deeper into the music the audience and performers seem to go."[3]

Since this piece is based on a hymn tune and an Irish ballad, the instrumental solos are the voices that should "sing" the melody.

Gillingham was working on this piece while on Beaver Island, Michigan, during the summer of 1999. He says that the surf of Lake Michigan directly influenced the accompaniment in measures 33 through 50. He describes measures 68 through 71 as "sort of rays of sunlight from Heaven."

---

3 Batcheller, James Christopher. "Waking Angels, A Light Unto Darkness, and A Crescent Still Abides: The Elegiac Music of David R. Gillingham." University of Oklahoma, 2000, p. 4.

Gillingham gives specific directions on how each section should be played (i.e., With quiet reverence; with dramatic dignity), and these words must be considered in the style.

Unit 6: Musical Elements

To assist the players in rehearsal and/or performance, conductors should consider subdividing during some difficult technical passages and *ritardandos*. Bring the horns to the fore in beats 2 and 3 of measure 64. Equally balance both melodies, the hymn tune and the Irish ballad, in measures 78 through 95.

Ray Cramer also added some elements approved by Gillingham. He believes these elements really help to evoke more emotion from the piece: Add mordents and grace notes to the flute solo at measure 33 for authenticity of Irish flavor; a *subito piano* (*sp*) at measure 61 and then *crescendo* to measure 62 works extremely well.

Unit 7: Form and Structure

SECTION	MEASURE	EVENT AND SCORING
Introduction (fragments of Theme A)	1–15	Slow and mysterious, alluding to motives of the hymn; key of D minor
Theme A	16–32	Mysterious presentation of the hymn; somber and chant-like solo in euphonium of the hymn tune in augmentation accompanied by flute and clarinet eighths, which are rhythmically displaced
Theme B	33–50	Newly composed Irish ballad; flute solo over cascading sixteenths in 1st clarinet, bass clarinet, and marimba; key of F major
Transition	51–53	Transition
Theme A	54–67	Hymn tune in dramatic style; key of A major
Interlude	68–71	Interlude interrupting the hymn before the last phrase
(fragment of Theme A)	72–75	Last phrase of hymn; alto saxophone solo
Transition	76–77	Brief transition to D-flat major
Themes A and B	78–95	"Marriage" of the hymn tune and the Irish ballad

SECTION	MEASURE	EVENT AND SCORING
Coda	96–108	"Ascent into heaven"
Errata:		
	12	2nd clarinet add a slur from beat 1 to beat 2
	39	1st clarinet should have a slur over the entire measure
	42	Marimba beat 2 should be E–G–F–D (not F–G–F–D)
	58	Baritone saxophone should be concert C-sharp (not A)
	61	3rd trombone and euphonium should have a dotted-quarter on beat 7
	84	Piccolo and oboe: a sixteenth note rest is missing
	85	Oboe should have slurs over the thirty-second notes
	91	Horn should have a slur from beat 1 to beat 2

Unit 8: Suggested Listening

David Holsinger, *On a Hymnsong of Philip Bliss*
Jack Stamp, *Chorale Prelude: Be Thou My Vision*
Frank Ticheli, *Amazing Grace*

Unit 9: Additional References and Resources

Gillingham's website:
    http://web.mus.cmich.edu/gillingham/

Contributed by:

Joan deAlbuquerque
Doctoral Conducting Associate
University of North Texas
Denton, Texas

Teacher Resource Guide

Blue Lake Overture
John Barnes Chance
(1932–1972)

Unit 1: Composer

John Barnes Chance was a native Texan, born and raised in Beaumont. His musical career began at the early age of nine with piano lessons. By age twelve, he was playing timpani in the Beaumont High School Orchestra. He began studying composition at the age of fifteen, with several of his compositions receiving performances while he was still in high school. He continued his education at the University of Texas, earning his bachelor's and master's degrees in composition while studying with the likes of Kent Kennan, Clifton Williams, and Paul Pisk. In 1956, Chance was awarded the Carl Owens Award for best composition by a student. Upon completing his degrees at the University of Texas, he spent time with the Fourth and Eighth United States Army Bands as staff arranger.

In 1960, the Ford Foundation Young Composers Project selected Chance to participate in their program. They placed him as Composer-in-Residence at Greensboro Senior High School in North Carolina, where Herbert Hazelman was Director of Bands. During his stay in Greensboro, he composed seven different pieces for student ensembles, one being his first piece for wind band, *Incantation and Dance*. In 1966, Chance joined the faculty at the University of Kentucky, teaching theory and composition until his untimely death in 1972 from electrocution while working in his back yard.

Chance composed for band, chorus, orchestra, solo instruments, and chamber groups. He has several published works for band, including *Incantation and Dance, Introduction and Capriccio, Symphony No. 2 for Winds and Percussion, Elegy,* and *Variations on a Korean Folk Song,* which won the American Bandmasters Association Ostwald Award in 1966.

Unit 2: Composition

Blue Lake Overture was published in 1971 by Boosey & Hawkes Company and was dedicated to the Blue Lake Fine Arts Camp of Twin Lakes, Michigan. This overture for band displays the composer's ability to develop thematic material in many ways. The entire piece is developed out of the initial horn statement presented in measure 1. Next, Chance develops a woodwind fugue at rehearsal no. 45, which gives way to a brass fugue of like material at rehearsal no. 57. The composer then creates a middle section with the opening theme repeated and presented in a waltz. The main thematic material returns and, through thematic development, guides the piece to the *sostenuto ma marcato*, which brings a return of the *legato* theme from rehearsal no. 26. This *legato* theme is accompanied by an *ostinato* woodwind figure based on the thematic material from the beginning of the piece. *Blue Lake Overture* is 182 measures in length and has a performance time of approximately five minutes.

Unit 3: Historical Perspective

This composition was written within the concert overture genre. This nineteenth century genre was an independent orchestral composition written within the same guidelines as the operatic overture but was contained in one movement. Many other overtures of this kind were written to be performed as an introduction for spoken plays and are frequently performed as concert pieces. Two such pieces falling within this particular genre are Beethoven's overture to Goethe's *Egmont* and Mendelssohn's Overture to *A Midsummer Night's Dream*. *Blue Lake Overture* was intended to be performed as an independent piece much like the aforementioned overtures. The composer uses much thematic development, which was also very predominate in the romantic period. His waltz-like statement of the theme in the middle section brings to mind the great waltzes of Johann and Richard Strauss.

Unit 4: Technical Considerations

Every piece contains certain obstacles to overcome to ensure a great performance. This piece is no exception. Although the technical considerations dealing with keys and brass ranges are almost nonexistent, the counting and rhythmical challenges provide the conductor and performers alike with ample opportunities to better themselves as musicians.

For example, syncopation is very predominate within this piece. The composition begins with the initial statement of the main theme beginning on the and-of-one and is repeated by the woodwinds with syncopation existing throughout the second half of the measure. This syncopation dominates the piece through measure 26, when a *legato* theme is presented for the first time. The *legato* theme is accompanied by an *ostinato* based on the opening thematic statement. This leads us into the next section of the piece where, regrouping and rebarring will help the ensemble more precisely perform the rhythms.

Rehearsal no. 45 is a fugue that begins in the low reeds. If the conductor stays within a traditional 4/4 pattern, the players' rhythmic patterns do not line up with the conductor's beats. If the conductor regroups the notes and conducts the measure as if it were in 8/8, grouped 3–2–3, it is more beneficial to the players playing those figures. This regrouping should continue to measure 64, where the conductor may decide to rebar the next eight measures. This rebarring constitutes moving the bar lines to line the rhythmic activity up on the big beats of a 9/8 pattern. As the waltz begins in measure 72, everything should be back to the original grouping and bars. In measure 163, the conductor may decide to again regroup, but it is not as imperative as it is earlier in the piece. This composition will better the whole ensemble both in counting and playing syncopated figures.

Unit 5: Stylistic Considerations

The style of this overture mirrors the style of overtures written during the romantic period. For example, Chance used sudden dynamic contrasts throughout the piece. A statement may build to a *fortissimo* and then immediately drop with a *subito piano*. The conductor must emphasize the contrasts as much as possible. The dramatic intentions of this writing depend solely on the ability of the ensemble to bring as much contrast as possible to these sections.

In addition, strict attention should be paid to the articulation throughout the piece. Chance was very meticulous in notating both accents and articulations. The articulations and accents should be addressed in such a way that the players understand the significance and the differences between accents and non- accented notes as well as the differences between *staccato* notes and those that are not *staccato*. By paying close attention to all articulations and accents, the players will be able to play the rhythms more precisely.

Also, there are several places within this composition where the composer has contrasting styles taking place simultaneously. In measure 26, the accompaniment is very articulate and rhythmic while the melody is very *legato* and flowing. The conductor needs to make sure the two do not start sounding alike.

Unit 6: Musical Elements

MELODY:

Blue Lake Overture is primarily developed out of the initial horn statement in measure 1. The only motif that is not a derivative from the horn statement is the *legato* theme presented in measure 29. Chance used much imitation throughout the piece as he developed the initial thematic statement. The imitation is used with different key centers and also stated in its inversion. As the piece progresses, the imitation is extended and eventually develops an *ostinato* pattern that is used throughout the piece. Chance then used the theme from the beginning to create a fugue that is presented in the woodwinds and then answered in the brass. The initial theme is again altered and set into a waltz-like feel.

This piece lends itself to teaching all about thematic development. The entire piece uses the initial thematic statement of the horns. Teaching this to the ensemble could be done by having the horns play the initial theme in measure 1 and then having the ensemble find places in their parts where they have a part that is like or similar to the initial statement.

HARMONY:

The harmonic structure of this piece shifts around as much as the thematic material shifts. The individual parts do not have a beginning key signature because the composer writes the key within the parts as accidentals. Because the piece shifts key centers as much as it does, the composer probably found it easier to write the accidentals in the parts instead of writing key signatures for all of the changes.

The harmonic structure lends itself to helping an ensemble better themselves at reading accidentals. The conductor can also use this piece to train the ensemble at identifying keys in individual parts. This is a skill that will aid students in reading and performing music in the future.

RHYTHM:

Of the musical elements, rhythm predominates this piece more than any of the other elements. The combination of offbeat playing and accents being placed on weak beats and "ands" of beats creates moments when the players do not feel comfortable playing. With the piece being written in common time, the conductor can be of little help to the musicians because the conductor's common time pattern does not line up with the rhythmic figures of the players. Through the section at measure 28t, the conductor needs to teach the ensemble to look for the sections where the conducting pattern and rhythmic figures line up. At measure 28, that would be beats 1 and 4. Conductors can teach their ensemble to use those beats as benchmarks for the *ostinato* pattern that exists through that section of the piece.

The fugue section at measure 45 is yet another opportunity for the conductor and the musician to work out a system of benchmarks. Regrouping is the best way for the conductor and players to make it through this section. The conductor can regroup each bar so that it lines up with the figures the player is reading. This piece will force the group to become comfortable with syncopation and irregular note groupings within common time.

TIMBRE:

Chance used several combinations of textures within the piece. The first twenty-five measures place woodwinds and brass in a call-and-response setting, with the main theme being altered from statement to statement. In measure 26, the woodwinds play accompaniment in an *ostinato* pattern while oboe and horn present the *legato* theme for the first time in measure 29. Chance then created two fugues, the first being scored in the woodwinds and the second scored in the brass. The woodwinds join the brass fugue, which culminates in the waltz-like middle section of the overture. Again, Chance opened with the woodwinds and then followed with the brass on the second statement. The final statement has the woodwinds playing the *ostinato* figure while the brass return with the *legato* theme leading the piece into its short coda.

The ensemble will work primarily with balance within the woodwind and brass statements, individually and then within them as a whole. The *ostinato* must not cover the new material; moreover, it is vital not to allow the long notes to cover the rhythmic activity. This delicate balance is imperative to a successful performance of this piece.

Unit 7: Form and Structure

MEASURE	EVENT AND SCORING
1–12	Introduction starts with a horn motif and a response in upper woodwinds; trumpet and trombone take over the theme followed by yet another response in woodwinds; this foreshadows the *ostinato* that is used later in the piece as well as the thematic development that is to follow
13–25	Repeat of the first section in a different key and with slightly different orchestration between the repeated sections
26–35	Flute and upper woodwind *ostinato* from the initial horn statement being played as accompaniment; *legato* B theme is stated in solo oboe and horn; solo oboe takes over the *ostinato* accompaniment, which signals the next section
45–56	A masterfully composed woodwind fugue starting with the statement in low reeds followed by upper clarinet and then eventually all upper woodwinds presenting the initial fugal statement

MEASURE	EVENT AND SCORING
57–71	Brass take over the fugue starting with low brass, which gives way to horn and then to trumpet; woodwinds enter near the end of the fugal section along with the percussion to bring this section to a close
72–80	Woodwinds play initial statement of the waltz based on the main theme from m. 1
81–88	Horn takes over the waltz melody while low brass accompany with woodwinds playing a countermelody
89–99	Full band transition into a return of the countermelody from the waltz section
100–119	Countermelody of the waltz scored in woodwinds while the main motif is scored in trumpet and trombone
120–137	Woodwinds finish this section with flute playing the theme from the beginning of the waltz; segment ends with a flute and clarinet quartet stating the countermelody of the waltz
138–162	Repeat of all thematic material from the beginning returns throughout this section;. all of the material segmented and scored for full ensemble; composer uses a call-and-response setting as they venture through the thematic material
163–176	Woodwinds return to the ostinato from the beginning as the full brass section plays a harmonized version of the *legato* or B theme
177–end	A short coda scored for full band as brass and woodwinds perform a call and response of the main theme from m. 1

Unit 8: Suggested Listening

Ludwig van Beethoven, *Egmont Overture*
Hector Berlioz, *Le Carnaval Romain*
Johannes Brahms, *Akademische Festouverture*
John Barnes Chance:
    Incantation and Dance
    Introduction and Capriccio
Felix Mendelssohn, *Overture to A Midsummer Night's Dream*

Unit 9: Additional References and Resources

Anthony, D. A. *The Published Band Works of John Barnes Chance.* Ann Arbor, MI: UMI Company 1981.

Apel, Willi, ed. *The Harvard Dictionary of Music*. Cambridge, MA: The Belknap Press of Harvard University, 1972.

Chance, John Barnes. *Blue Lake Overture*. New York: Boosey and Hawkes, 1971.

Creasap, Susan, and Rodney C. Schueller. "Incantation and Dance: John Barnes Chance." *Teaching Music through Performance in Band*, Volume 2. Compiled and edited by Richard Miles. Chicago: GIA Publications, Inc., 1998.

Smith, Norman, and Albert Stoutamire. *Band Music Notes*. Lake Charles, LA: Program Note Press, 1989.

Tower, Ibrook. "Elegy: John Barnes Chance." *Teaching Music through Performance in Band*, Volume 3. Compiled and edited by Richard Miles. Chicago: GIA Publications, Inc., 2000.

Contributed by:

Bradley Genevro
Associate Director of Bands
Oklahoma State University
Stillwater, Oklahoma

Teacher Resource Guide

Elsa's Procession to the Cathedral from Lohengrin Richard Wagner

(1813–1883)

transcribed by Glenn Lucien Cailliet

(1891–1985)

Unit 1: Composer

Richard Wagner was born in Leipzig, Germany, on May 22, 1813. His father died shortly after his birth, and his mother remarried Ludwig Geyer, an actor and theatrical figure based in Dresden. Wagner's genius was recognized at an early age, and he seemed destined for a career as philologist. However, he turned his efforts to more artistic modes of expression—first to poetry, then to drama, then to music. He was primarily a self-taught composer, training himself through hours of study of Beethoven and von Weber. His early compositional output includes several short pieces for piano, two symphonies, and his first opera, *Die Feen*, completed in 1833.

The following years were spent in various cities throughout Germany working as an orchestra leader. During this time, Wagner composed two symphonic overtures and a second opera, *Das Liebesverbot* (1836). His first major recognition came with the operas *Rienzi* (1838) and *The Flying Dutchman* (1842). The success of these two works earned him the conducting position at the Dresden Opera in 1843. Other operas completed during this time included *Tannhauser* (1845) and *Lohengrin* (completed in 1846).

Under the threat of arrest and imprisonment for involvement in political demonstrations, Wagner fled Germany and moved to Zurich, Switzerland, in 1849. In 1850, he published a book outlining his philosophy of music drama and the use of the *leitmotiv* as a compositional device. He then set out to display the tenets of his book in a massive four-part operatic cycle, *Der Ring des Nibelungen* (*Das Rheingold*, 1869; *Die Walkure*, 1870; *Siegfried*, 1876; *Die Gotterdammerung*, 1876). The creative process for this cycle occupied Wagner for the better part of fifteen years. Each of these four works is over four hours in length, requiring large orchestral forces and specially trained singers who can handle the extreme physical demands of the vocal parts.

To provide financial resources to support him while working on the *Ring*, Wagner produced two operas: *Tristan und Isolde* (1865) and *Der Meistersinger von Nurnberg* (1868). *Tristan und Isolde* is perhaps his most complex work, and for many scholars marks the beginning of twentieth century harmonic practice. Following completion of the *Ring*, ill health slowed his compositional output a great deal. *Parsifal* (1882) was the only opera he composed after 1876. In 1882, he founded the opera house in Bayreuth, which was designed specifically for performances of his works and is still in use today. Although turmoil and upheaval marked the early part of his life, Wagner spent his later years in peace and tranquility. He died in Vienna in 1883.

Lucien Cailliet enjoyed a long and productive career as composer, arranger, teacher, and performer. He received his early training in France and came to America in 1920. He played clarinet and bass clarinet in the Philadelphia Orchestra until 1938, when he moved to Los Angeles to accept a position teaching orchestration, counterpoint, and conducting at the University of Southern California. He produced over one hundred original compositions, numerous transcriptions of orchestral works for band, and twenty-five film scores. He served as musical and educational director for the G. LeBlanc Corporation for several years. He died in 1985 at the age of ninety-three.

Unit 2: Composition

Lohengrin received its first performance in Weimar on August 28, 1850, under the baton of Franz Liszt. The libretto, written by Wagner himself, was based on a lengthy medieval poem entitled *Wartburgkrieg*. Wagner's exile from Germany for his radical political beliefs combined with conflicts over the appropriate language for the opera resulted in its production being delayed for over four years. When it was finally premiered, a grossly undermanned orchestra (thirty-eight pieces total, including eleven violins) and unprepared singers produced a disastrous failure. After several revisions, the opera was restaged and has since become standard repertoire in many countries. A brief synopsis of the plot is as follows:

> Elsa, a young, beautiful heiress, dreams of an unknown knight who claims he will come to her in a time of need. After the disappearance

of her younger brother, Elsa stands accused of the boy's murder. The unknown knight appears in a boat drawn by a swan and fights for Elsa, winning her freedom from her accusers. The knight asks two things of Elsa: her hand in marriage and that she never ask him to reveal his name. Elsa agrees and the two are married despite many attempts from patrons at the wedding to learn the knight's identity.

On the night of the wedding, two conspirators against Elsa pour poison in her ear in an effort to make her question her new husband. This she does, and the mystery is revealed. The knight's name is Lohengrin, and he is the son of Percival, one of the Knights of the Round Table and guardian of the Holy Grail. The price of Elsa's curiosity is a heavy one, for Lohengrin must now return to his homeland. As his boat appears, the swan suddenly transforms into Elsa's missing brother. Lohengrin departs (this time his boat pulled by doves descended from Heaven), and Elsa's grief at the loss of her true love consumes her—she dies of a broken heart.

Elsa's Procession to the Cathedral appears towards the beginning of Act II as she and her bridal party enter the cathedral for her marriage to Lohengrin. Cailliet's transcription was published in 1938 and is approximately six minutes in duration. Instrumentation is for standard concert band; percussion requirements include timpani, bass drum, snare drum, crash cymbals, and suspended cymbal.

There are extensive cues and doubling among instrumental parts, allowing a band of limited instrumentation access to the work. However, large numbers of players are necessary as many of the individual sections are divided into multiple parts, including three flute parts, four clarinet parts, three trombone parts, and four horn parts. There is a part for harp that is absolutely necessary (especially between rehearsal numbers 6 and 7). If no harp is available, an electronic keyboard with a harp patch could serve as an acceptable substitute.

Unit 3: Historical Perspective

When viewed in the overall progression of Western art music during the course of the nineteenth century, Wagner's music represents the pinnacle of the romantic tradition. His concept of the *leitmotiv* can be seen as directly influenced by Berlioz, as were his techniques on orchestration. The influence of Beethoven and Liszt can be felt in Wagner's grandiose conception of form and thick orchestral textures. His flair for drama and overall effect of music, poetry, and scenery can be attributed to the influence of von Weber, whom he greatly admired and respected.

Wagner and his contemporaries, such as Brahms and Bruckner, expanded the concept of harmony by obscuring traditional tonal progressions through the use of extended chords and delayed resolutions of tonic triads. In many of his works, it is not at all uncommon for the final cadence to be the first and only cadence in the tonal center indicated by the key signature. Later composers such as Straus and Mahler continued this chromatic expansion until Schoenberg brought the development to its inevitable conclusion—atonality. According to Eric Salzman, Wagner's influence is also felt in non-German composers such as Debussy, Ravel, Stravinsky, and Dvorak.

Lohengrin is Wagner's fourth major work; therefore, many of the characteristics of later works are either underdeveloped or non-existent. The chromatic expansion in *Elsa's Procession* is evident but usually occurs within standard four- and eight-measure phrases. Although the topic is somewhat under debate, most Wagnerian scholars do not recognize the use of *leitmotiv* in the score of *Lohengrin*.

Unit 4: Technical Considerations

In terms of notes and rhythms the technical demands of this piece are not extreme. There are some instances of rhythmic notation that are not common in modern practice, such as double dotted-quarter notes, but these are infrequent and should not present major problems. There is limited use of syncopation that is usually presented in the following pattern:

B-flat clarinet II, mm. 33–35

There is some use of extended ranges in the woodwinds, especially in bass clarinet, bassoon, and 1st clarinet parts. First and 3rd horns are extended to written A above the staff, and 1st trumpets are extended to written C above the staff. Apart from that, other ranges in the brass are very manageable.

The technical difficulties in playing this music lie in production of consistent tone and pitch in a wide range of *tessituras* and dynamics. One possible approach to teaching these skills in a full ensemble setting is through the use of a typical four-part harmonized chorale, such as the Bach chorales transcribed for band by Mayhew Lake. In each individual part, certain phrases or measures could be displaced by octaves into uncomfortable registers. The director could then isolate or combine various sections or individual players in different places within the same chorale. For example, flute and clarinet could be asked to play the first phrase up one octave while the rest of the ensemble plays it as written. After the first *fermata* or natural break in the music, the director could then instruct saxophone to play the next phrase up one octave, everybody else as written, and so on throughout the chorale. This approach might prove useful if only for the fact that it lifts the stigma of "drill and practice" from skill development and roots it firmly in the context of musical expression. Students performing the phrases in the displaced registers must make their part fit and sound correct within the context of an overall musical structure; students performing parts as written can be given specific locations to "tune their ears" (e.g., "Listen for the trombones in the high register") for critical evaluation.

Unit 5: Stylistic Considerations

Full *legato* style dominates throughout the duration of this work. There are a few instances of *staccato* note markings (see example below); however, in the context of this piece, it clearly indicates a slight lift and separation between each note rather than the clipped, brisk style one would associate with a march.

Horn I & II, mm. 17–18

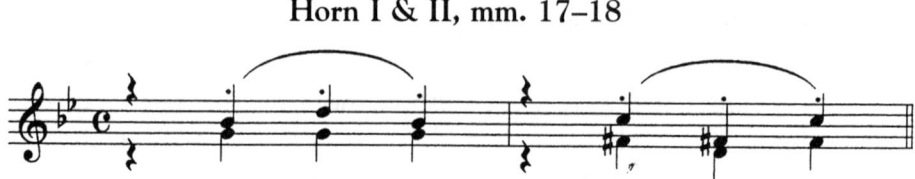

There is limited use of accented notes (both traditional and rooftop types) in the closing sections. These should be held for their full rhythmic value, the accent being achieved through clean articulation and emphasis of air at the beginning of each note.

Balance between instrumental parts deserves special attention. It is something that must be considered within short formal sections as melodic material is passed between varying instruments, and over the entire duration as the brass gradually overtake the woodwinds and assume a dominant role in the closing measures. It also involves the interaction of each individual part within the overall musical texture. Accompanying material is tightly interwoven with primary melodic material, as evidenced in the following excerpt.

Alto Sax I & II; Horn I & II, mm. 33–36

When asked about interpretation of his scores, Wagner remarked "The big notes will take care of themselves; the little notes…are the things to watch." While it may not be entirely practical to let big notes "take care of themselves," it is clear that detail was important to Wagner, and attention to that detail should be reflected in an effective performance of his music. It is essential that students and director make informed musical decisions with regards to which lines are brought out and when, and those decisions must be executed in a proficient and convincing manner.

A method that may be of aid in making these decisions is the development of a "single-line score." The process is demonstrated using the following example from the flute and bassoon parts from the original score.

Flute I & Bassoon I, mm. 9–16

Important events and musical ideas are then condensed into a single line that can be reproduced (sung or played) by one person.

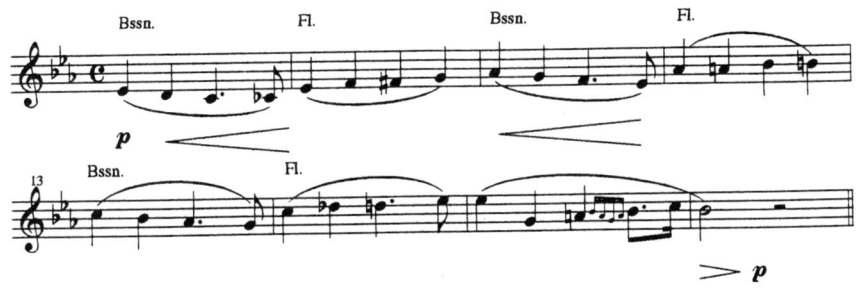

It is possible for the director to use a single-line score for the purposes of assessing student knowledge and performance of musical principles. For a detailed description of how this can be accomplished in a full ensemble setting, James Byo's recent article "Developing Substantive Playing Tests – A Model" is recommended (see Unit 9).

Unit 6: Musical Elements

Melody in this piece is predominantly diatonic, though the contour and tessitura of the melody is wide and varying. Accompanying material contains accidentals and non-harmonic tones, which help create the effect of an obscured tonic triad. For this reason, all players should be comfortable with the chromatic scale in most every register and should be proficient with enharmonic spellings and uncommon accidentals, such as C-flat.

As mentioned earlier, the final cadence in E-flat major is one of only a few cadences in this tonal center, even though the key signature of E-flat major is printed for most of the piece. The dominant tonal center is B-flat major throughout much of the work, which contributes to the effect of a delayed and obscured tonic. Measures 33 through 42 are written in the key signature of E major; however, the key of B major is tonicized. This is important to consider given that B major is the farthest removed key from E-flat major (the final tonic).

Rhythmically, the work is not overly difficult. There is some use of ornamental turns in the melodic lines, but as most are written out, the primary issue becomes rhythmic placement. There are some uncommon notations, such as double dotted notes, but these are few. In terms of timbre, the piece is scored predominantly in choirs. The woodwind choir dominates the first half, but over the course of the work the brass choir sound gradually emerges and takes over in the final measures. There are measures at the beginning of the piece where texture is thin in terms of number of parts or players, yet the scoring of these parts is very dense. This type of scoring underscores the issues of balance discussed in Unit 4.

Unit 7: Form and Structure

SECTION	MEASURE	EVENT AND SCORING
a	1–8	B-flat major
b	9–16	B-flat major
c	17–24	F major
Transition	25–32	Key change to E major
c	33–42	E major (B major implied)
Transition	42–46	Key change to E-flat major (B-flat major implied)
d	47–54	B-flat major
a	55–62	B-flat major
b'	63–75	B-flat major
Coda	75–85	E-flat major

Unit 8: Suggested Listening

Richard Wagner:
> "Entry of the Gods into Valhalla" from *Das Rheingold*
> Overture to *Die Meistersingers von Nurnburg*
> Overture to *The Flying Dutchman*
> Prelude to Act III of *Lohengrin*
> *Trauersinfonie*

Unit 9: Additional References and Resources

Amis, John, and Michael Rose. *Words about Music: A Treasury of Writings*. New York: Marlowe and Company, 1989.

Byo, James L. "Designing Substantive Playing Tests – A Model." *Music Educators Journal* 88, September 2001, pp. 39–44.

Landormy, Paul. "Richard Wagner." *The Music Lover's Handbook*. Edited by Elie Siegmeister. New York: William Morrow and Company, 1943.

McBeth, W. Francis. "The Score – Mechanics of Study." *The Instrumentalist*, May, 1990, pp. 8–11.

Rehrig, William H. *The Heritage Encyclopedia of Band Music*. Edited by Paul E. Bierley. Westerville, OH: Integrity Press, 1991.

Salzman, Eric. *Twentieth-Century Music: An Introduction*. Third edition. Englewood Cliffs, NJ: Prentice Hall, 1988.

Simon, Henry W. *100 Great Operas and their Stories*. New York: Doubleday, 1960.

Smith, Norman, and Albert Stoutamire. *Band Music Notes*. Lake Charles, LA: Program Note Press, 1989.

Thompson, Oscar, and Nicolas Slonimsky, eds. *The International Encyclopedia of Music and Musicians*. Fourth edition. New York: Dodd, Mead & Co., 1946.

Upton, George P., and Felix Browski. *The Standard Opera and Concert Guide*. Revised and enlarged edition. New York: Halcyon House, 1928.

Contributed by:
Jeremy S. Lane
Doctoral Graduate Assistant, Music Education
Louisiana State University
Baton Rouge, Louisiana

Teacher Resource Guide

Epinicion

John Paulson
(b. 1948)

Unit 1: Composer
John Paulson was born on March 6, 1948, in Minneapolis, Minnesota. He received his music degrees from the University of Minnesota and the Eastman School of Music. He conducted high school bands for nine years while teaching classes in music theory, music history, twentieth century music, chamber music, jazz, and electronic music. He is currently president of Coda Music Technology in Eden Prairie, Minnesota, where he provided the infrastructure for the development of the *Vivace* accompaniment hardware and software, as well as the creation of the state-of-the-art music notation software *Finale* for music publishing. Paulson remains active as a composer, clinician, and guest conductor.

Unit 2: Composition
An epinicion (epp-ih-NIH-shun) is an ancient song of victory sung at the conclusion of a triumphant battle. The Greeks would sing it as they walked through the battlefield sorting the wounded from the dead. Written in 1972, *Epinicion* is the composer's personal abstraction of war in general and the Vietnam War in particular. The approximate length of this work is six minutes. *Epinicion* is published by Neil A. Kjos Music Company.

Unit 3: Historical Perspective
The epinicion originated as a choral ode honoring a victor in the Hellenic games, which was performed as part of the improvised celebration the champion received upon his return to his home city. One of the earliest examples

of epinicia still in existence is that of *Simonides of Ceos*, an ode for Olympic victory in 520 B.C. The epinicion ode did not use traditional lines or stanzas. The meter was formed for each poem and was never used again in exactly the same form. The strophes, either single or in systems of three, were repeated through the poem. Its performance required a trained choir and musicians skilled in the lute and lyre. It was the Persian invasion of Greece in 500 B.C. that influenced Simonides to write poems of rejoicing at Greece's victories and of mourning for its glorious dead.

Epinicion was written during the final days of the Vietnam War. Through the use of air blown through instruments, dense tone clusters, unmetered cadenzas, and a long aleatoric tone row section, Paulson attempts to portray the inevitable insanity, despair, and absolute horror of war.

Unit 4: Technical Considerations

The augmented symphonic band instrumentation calls for one piccolo, four flutes, alto flute (cued in the clarinet part), two oboes, two bassoons, E-flat clarinet, six B-flat clarinets, E-flat alto clarinet, B-flat bass clarinet, two E-flat alto saxophones, B-flat tenor saxophone, E-flat baritone saxophone, three B-flat cornets, two B-flat trumpets, four F horns, three trombones, euphonium (treble clef part included), and two tubas. Percussion parts require a minimum of six players. The percussion instrumentation includes large and small cymbals, tam-tam, bells, chimes, vibraphone, xylophone, timbales, temple blocks, snare drum, bass drum, and timpani.

Ranges are appropriate for this grade four piece, although some of the repeated aleatoric rhythmic patterns may present a challenge initially. A full range of dynamics, from *pp* to *fff*, is utilized in this work.

Various meters—6/8, 12/8, 3/4, 4/4—are used in addition to measures time-framed in seconds. Suggested metronome markings for the aleatoric patterns are clearly indicated throughout the work.

There is no printed key signature, as this work utilizes twelve-tone techniques. Symbols used for the various aleatoric effects are clearly described in the printed rehearsal notes on the score but not in the parts.

Unit 5: Stylistic Considerations

The theme is always presented in a *legato*, recitative style. With each presentation of the theme, the volume and tension builds. In contrast, many of the aleatoric figures require a light articulation at a soft dynamic level.

In keeping with aleatoric techniques, players must be able to independently perform short patterns in contrasting tempi and rhythms. Care must also be given by the individual players to maintain the continuity of the aleatoric patterns from section to section.

Unit 6: Musical Elements

The players will immediately notice the aleatoric symbols on their music. The interpretation of these symbols should be discussed and demonstrated prior to the first reading of the work. To be sure each pitch is covered, players will need to be assigned individual notes to perform in the tone clusters.

Paulson uses the following tone row for his theme:

The lyrical nature of the theme provides an excellent opportunity to review and apply proper breath control techniques. The conductor must clearly indicate the phrasing of the theme, which is indicated in both the score and the parts. Since the theme is frequently presented in unisons and octaves, intonation will need to be addressed.

Players may need to be reminded to avoid sacrificing characteristic tone quality when performing at the loud dynamic levels required at the end of *Epinicion*.

Unit 7: Form and Structure

MEASURE	EVENT AND SCORING
1	Air blown through instruments; random cymbal/tam-tam rolls, 6"– 10"
2–7	First presentation of theme by unison cornet/trumpet
8–14	Theme performed by solo flute
15	Accented tone cluster in flute
16–17	Theme presented in fragmentation by piccolo, alto saxophone, clarinet, and bassoon
19-23	Variation of theme presented by cornet, trumpet, piccolo, E-flat clarinet, and alto saxophone
24	Presentation of theme in chimes; individual aleatoric effects begin in upper woodwinds and horn
25	Presentation of theme in tuba; aleatoric effects continue in woodwinds and percussion
26	Presentation of theme in muted cornet/trumpet; aleatoric effects continue
27	Presentation of theme (f) in low woodwinds, saxophone, and horn

MEASURE	EVENT AND SCORING
28	Presentation of theme (ff) in low brass
29	Final presentation of theme (fff) in cornet/trumpet
30–37	Aleatoric and dynamic effects at Vivace tempo
38–39	Percussion cadenza (fff) with impact cluster in winds
40	Slurred aleatoric fragments in piccolo, solo flute, and alto flute

Unit 8: Suggested Listening

Daniel Bukvich, *Symphony No. 1, In Memoriam, Dresden, Germany, 1945*
David R. Gillingham, *Heroes, Lost and Fallen*
David R. Holsinger, *In the Spring, at the Time When Kings Go Off to War*
Karel Husa, *Music for Prague 1968*
Ron Nelson, *Morning Alleluias for the Winter Solstice*

Unit 9: Additional References and Resources

"The Basic Band Curriculum: Grades IV, V, VI." *BD Guide*,
   September/October 1987, p. 12.

Weisberg, Arthur. *Performing Twentieth-Century Music: A Handbook for
   Conductors and Instrumentalists*. New Haven and London: Yale University
   Press, 1993.

Contributed by:

L. Kevin Kastens
Associate Director of Bands
University of Iowa
Iowa City, Iowa

Teacher Resource Guide

Five Miniatures

Joaquin Turina
(1882–1949)

Unit 1: Composer

Joaquin Turina was a native of Spain. He was born in Seville on December 9, 1882. Much of his early life and study took place in Madrid. During his early study, he became acquainted with Manuel de Falla. Turina's involvement with de Falla greatly influenced his writing style, and he adopted many of the strong trends toward nationalism and the nationalistic writing techniques that were gaining popularity in the late nineteenth century and early twentieth century.

During the early 1900s, Turina extended his musical study to Paris, where he resided for approximately ten years. During this period, he studied at the Schola Cantorum. While studying in Paris, he was influenced by master composers such as D'Indy, Debussy, and Ravel. These composers had a profound impact on the impressionistic tendencies that are evident in Turina's compositions.

Turina returned to Spain in 1914. From that time on he continued to develop his interests in the nationalistic music of Spain. Although many of his countrymen experienced difficulty gaining significant recognition, Turina was able to develop a substantial following and a noteworthy reputation for his work.

Turina died in Madrid, Spain, on January 14, 1949. By our modern standards, he has become recognized as one of the most prolific of the noteworthy Andalusian composers.

Unit 2: Composition

Turina is recognized for his writings of orchestral works, chamber music, piano solos, vocal music, and guitar solos. Arguably his most famous orchestral work is his symphonic poem *La Procession du Rocio*, written in 1913. This work remains in the popular repertoire of many of the world's major symphonies and is presented regularly by many second- and third-level orchestras as well.

The chamber works of Turina are most strongly represented by *The Toreador's Prayer*. This is a work that is frequently performed by string quartets and by small chamber orchestras. Additionally, he is recognized for a significant body of works that display his nationalistic allegiances. These tendencies are reflected in titles such as *Memories of Ancient Spain* and other similar selections.

His works for piano represent a similar significant body of literature. *Eight Miniatures*, a work that presents several short vignettes depicting life in Spain, is the original material from which John Krance transcribed *Five Miniatures*, the selection that represents the work being studied in this guide. Turina's nationalistic influence is well represented in this work and also in several other examples, including his *Through the Streets of Seville*, written in 1943.

The vocal works created by Turina are also nationalistic in character. *Poems in the Form of Songs* along with several suites and song sets help to define his Andalusian heritage. Through his songs, he attempts "to evoke a romantic picture of the Spain of memories long past."

Turina further defines his nationalistic tendencies through his compositions for guitar, an instrument that is recognized for creating and defining essentially a Spanish sound. His works such as *Sevillana*, *Fandanguillo*, *Rafaga*, and *Homenaje a Tarrega* have served as a means for defining the literature for this ethnically associated instrument.

Unit 3: Historical Perspective

Five Miniatures was transcribed and arranged for symphonic band by John Krance in 1959. The original work was written for piano. The copyright date is 1930, and there was an additional copyright in 1958. This five-movement suite was extracted from Turina's setting of *Eight Miniatures for Piano*.

The United States Army Field Band from Washington, DC, commissioned Krance to write this work, and as such, the selection is dedicated to this outstanding symphonic ensemble and Major Chester E. Whiting. Major Whiting was serving as the commander and conductor of the ensemble at that time.

Five Miniatures is an excellent example of Turina's nationalistic style. The five movements are titled "Dawn," "The Sleeping Village," "Promenade," "The Approaching Army," and "Fiesta." The style within each movement is somewhat impressionistic, with traditional Spanish characteristics masterfully integrated into the sonorities and textures of each vignette.

Unit 4: Technical Considerations

The first two movements present minimal technical challenges. The difficulty in these movements is to deal with the harmonic and chordal effects Turina created through the use of pentatonic passages, planing, chromatic harmony, and non-functional chord tones. Additional complexity is derived from the transparency and independence of each voicing. All parts are soloistic in nature, and exposures require competent performances on all parts. Although some of the solo lines are cross-cued, an accurate performance would require an English horn, a trumpet, a flute, a clarinet, and a harp soloist. These solos are not technically demanding but will require a mature sense of time, lyricism, and expression.

The third movement shifts to the use of modalism. There remains a regular integration of non-functional chord tones and development that is often chromatic in nature. The style is somewhat march-like. The same solo voicings utilized in the previous movements are required. Wider dynamic ranges are explored, but the transparency and independence of parts and voices remain consistent with the earlier movements.

The fourth movement is a march. Polytonality, quartalism, and non-functional harmonies are included in some of the compositional devices used. The percussion section plays a much more significant role and serves as a featured element through large segments of the movement. The wind parts remain disjunct and frequently present a juxtaposed melodic and harmonic framework that develops to *tutti* climax points.

The final movement, "Fiesta," returns to the use of modalism and planing. Non-functional harmony continues to be used and creates a sense of uniformity and cohesiveness for the entire work. Voicings are much more densely combined for longer segments. Solos are required for clarinet, celesta, and harp. The overall technical demands remain at a moderate level, but again the musical demands seem far more extreme. Although there is more *tutti* playing, the stylistic and articulation concerns will require more attention.

Unit 5: Stylistic Considerations

Each of these five movements possesses unique characteristics. Both nationalistic and impressionistic characteristics are evident throughout. Movement 1 is very light and transparent at the introduction. From the beginning throughout the movement, there is a constant *crescendo* and increase in density as the music develops toward the concluding E major climax.

Movement 2 has a tempo marking of *Lento*. The lines are very lyric and soloistic. Turina's impressionist characteristics are clearly demonstrated throughout this movement. The textures utilized in this movement are more representative of chamber ensemble literature. There are only four measures where the *tutti* ensemble is presented.

Movement 3 is titled "Promenade" and is stylistically presented with detached articulations. The tempo is suggested as *Andantino*. Percussion writing is rudimental in style and reinforces the somewhat march-like character. The overall dynamic shape of this movement is a bell curve that begins softly, builds to a *fortissimo* climax, and then gradually resolves back to the *pianissimo* level.

Movement 4 is a march. The editor's tempo marking is stated as *Allegro alla Marcia*. The regimental percussion scoring assists in establishing and maintaining the style throughout. *Tutti* ensemble textures and passages are utilized in a limited capacity.

The final movement is a dance in 6/8 time. The tempo marking is *Allegro vivo*. Much of the movement is presented by contrasting a somewhat lyric phrase with more rhythmically active material. Harp is used to present some solo runs and regularly presents the melodic material in conjunction with a variety of other voicings. These harp passages are not cross-cued. This movement concludes with a rhythmically active passage progressing to a *tutti* chord, with percussion providing the rhythmic motivation that propels the work to its conclusion.

Unit 6: Musical Elements

This work serves as an example of some of the early wind ensemble literature that has been transcribed from original piano compositions. The instrumentation is typical of the modern wind ensemble, and it has been expanded to include parts for cello, string bass, and contrabassoon. The percussion demands are traditional, but harp and celesta are utilized liberally throughout several movements.

The nationalistic and impressionistic characteristics and tendencies of the composer are evident in the writing style and textures that the arranger has artfully maintained. Krance has done a masterful job of orchestrating and arranging the various sounds while maintaining the transparency that is evident in the original piano score. Stylistic characteristics, ensemble densities, and harmonic colorings have been preserved throughout. The five vignettes selected produce a pleasantly paced suite that serves as a worthy introduction to the music of Turina.

Unit 7: Form and Structure

MEASURE	KEY	EVENT AND SCORING
Movement 1: "Dawn"		
1–4	E-flat	Introduction; English horn and clarinet melody
5–6	F	Chordal transition

MEASURE	KEY	EVENT AND SCORING
7–12	A-flat	Theme 1 presented in flute and horn
13–16	C-sharp minor	Theme 2 presented in upper woodwinds and trumpet
17–18	A-flat	Transitional material
19–22	E	Theme 2 brass statement and *tutti* repeat
23–24		Chordal suspension with clarinet pentatonic runs
25–end		Conclusion of movement embellished by an extreme dynamic impact and a *molto allargando*

Movement 2: "The Sleeping Village"

1–5	C minor	Introduction and presentation of Theme 1 in flute and English horn
6–8	B-flat	Trumpet solo using Theme 1 material
9–11	E-flat	Meter change to 3/4; brass add chordal accompaniment to trumpet solo
12–16	B-flat	New rhythmic motives introduced in low brass and strings
17–19	F	Rhythmic motives developed as introduction to Theme 2
20–26	B-flat minor	Theme 2 presented in upper woodwinds
27–28	F Flute cadenza	
29–33	C minor	Recap of Theme 1 with more active keyboard and harp accompaniment
34–end	F	Augmentation of rhythmic motives from mm. 17–19 leading to final resolution

Movement 3: "Promenade"

1–4	E minor	Introduction: low brass and strings predominant parts
5–8	C	Piccolo, trumpet, clarinet, and harp present introductory material
9–14	A minor	Theme 1 presented in upper woodwinds
15–18		Brass and regimental percussion present Theme 2
19–24	C	Introduction of dotted-eighth/sixteenth motive, which is passed from alto to soprano and then to tenor voicings

MEASURE	KEY	EVENT AND SCORING
25–30	A-flat	Upper winds rhythmically active in counterpoint to middle low wind chordal passage
31–34	E minor	Restatement of first four measures
35–40	A minor	Restatement of Theme 1 in original form
41–end		Coda leading to the conclusion

Movement 4: "The Approaching Army"

1–8	C minor	Percussion introduction
9–20		Percussion continues; ostinato figure introduced in bassoons; short motivic ideas presented in trumpet and woodwinds
21–28	C	Trumpet, xylophone, and clarinet present Theme 1 with light accompaniment
29–32		Theme 2 presented; change of style required
33–37	A	Merge of earlier rhythmic motives with Theme 1 to create Theme 3
38–45	C	Diatonic quarter note developmental passage integrating previously stated rhythmic motives in trumpet and clarinet
46–49	E	Upper woodwinds state Theme 1
50–53	B	Clarinets restate Theme 1
54–58	A	Restatement of Theme 3
59		Grand pause
60–67	C	Concluding material based on fanfare motives

Movement 5: "Fiesta"

1–10	E	Introduction
11–14	A	Transitional interlude
15–18	E minor	Upper woodwinds and harp present contrasting lines
19–22	A	Interlude restated
23–28	E minor	Clarinet and celesta soli Theme 1
29–34	C	Low winds present theme with upper winds rhythmic accompaniment
35–44	E-flat	Upper woodwinds present Theme 2

MEASURE	KEY	EVENT AND SCORING
45–46	A	Chordal variation of interlude material
47–50	E minor	Piccolo, oboe, and bells restate Theme 1
51–54		Diatonic transitional passage
55–60	A	Arpeggios in a pyramid starting in the low winds and progressing by voicings through piccolo
61		Final resolution with tutti percussion providing rhythmic reinforcement

Unit 8: Suggested Listening

Lewis Buckley, *Bright-Colored Dances*
Norman Dello Joio:
   Satiric Dances
   Scenes from "The Louvre"
Martin Ellerby, *Paris Sketches*
Vincent Persichetti, *Divertimento*
Joaquin Turina, *La Procession du Rocio*

Unit 9: Additional References and Resources

Sadie, Stanley, ed. *New Grove Dictionary of Music and Musicians*. London: Macmillan Publishers Unlimited, 1980.

Salter, Lionel. Record jacket notes. New York: Associated Music Publishers, 1957.

Smith, Norman, and Albert Stoutamire. *Band Music Notes*. Lake Charles, LA: Program Note Press, 1989.

Smith, Norman (2000). *Program Notes for Band*. Chicago, IL: GIA Publications, Inc., 2002, p. 596.

Electronic reference retrieved 4 April 2001, from
   http: //www.hnh.com/composer/turina.htm

Electronic reference retrieved 5 July 2001, from
   http://source.unco.edu/search/w/ Turina

Electronic reference retrieved 23 April 2001, from
   http://dbx.icorp.net/ss/dir/t/turina.htm

Electronic reference retrieved 23 April 2001, from
   http;//music.netstoreusa.com/504/HL50481571.shtml

Contributed by:

Paul R. Hinman
Director of Bands
Leander High Schools
Leander, Texas

Special thanks to Dr. David Champouillon, Instructor of Trumpet at East Tennessee State University, for his assistance with the harmonic analysis of this selection.

Teacher Resource Guide

Folk Dances
Dmitri Shostakovich

(1906–1975)

arranged by M. Vakhutinskii

edited by H. Robert Reynolds

Unit 1: Composer

Dmitri Shostakovich, the son of an engineer, was born on September 25, 1906, in St. Petersburg (Leningrad), Russia. In 1919, he enrolled at the Petrograd Conservatory, where he studied piano with Leonid Nikolayev and composition with both Alesandr Glazunov and Maksimilian Steinberg. Though he was a renowned pianist (even entering the Chopin International Competition for Pianists in 1927, at which he was awarded Honorable Mention), Shostakovich had far greater success as a composer, particularly after his *First Symphony* (1925), which earned him immediate worldwide notoriety. The composer's early works exhibit his free experimentation with a variety of forms, but Joseph Stalin's First Five-Year Plan in 1928, which banned avant-garde and jazz music, severely restricted Shostakovich's creativity. The dictatorial demands on the style of music creativity initiated by Stalin, causing some noted condemnations of the composer, have elevated Shostakovich to an almost folk-hero status as a composer. In reality, he was a gregarious, sincere person deeply devoted and loyal to the roots of his country, which is very evident in his *Folk Dances*. This set of Russian folk music emerged from the 1940s, during which he wrote some of his best music. After Stalin's death in 1952, Shostakovich was less restricted in his creative endeavors, traveled extensively in Europe and to the United States (in 1949), and was awarded several prestigious prizes and honorary doctorates. The composer died in Moscow on August 9, 1975.

Not a great deal of information is available regarding the primary arranger of *Folk Dances*, M. Vakhutinskii, other than as an arranger of music for Russian bands and as a musicologist with deep interest in Russian folk music. He was a co-author of the 1991 Russian text, *Practical Course of Playing Russian Folk Wind and Percussion Instruments*, and was part of a Melodiia recording of folk wind band music entitled *Chudesnyi rozhok* ("The Wonderful Rozhok").

H. Robert Reynolds is one of the most-esteemed conductor/educators in the band world. Conductor emeritus of the renowned University of Michigan bands and founder of the Detroit Chamber Winds, he is equally important for his writings and teaching on wind band education and his careful editing of important masterworks for bands. As editor of *Folk Dances*, Reynolds took Vakhutinskii's orchestration for Euro-Russian bands and authentically scored it for American bands; it was published by Carl Fischer, Inc., in 1979. Also published the same year by Belwin Mills, a similar and fractionally easier edition of *Folk Dances* was scored by Frank Erickson.

Unit 2: Composition

Folk Dances was originally the third movement of a suite for orchestra entitled *Native Leningrad*, Op. 63, first published in 1942 and reissued in 1970 as *Suite, My Native Country*. This suite was assimilated from the incidental music to a theatrical production of the same opus entitled *Motherland*. Shostakovich collected several native Russian dance tunes and carefully tied them together into this single composition. In the theatrical production, this set was called *Youth Dance* or *Dance of the Sailors*—a name, though not specifically noted, that held over to the orchestral suite. Vakhutinskii arranged this suite for Russian band instrumentation (a greater percentage of brass parts than American instrumentation) in 1952. When the work became available in the United States in 1979, both Reynolds and Erickson scored their versions available for American bands. Its diatonic technical lines are similar to the principal themes of the composer's *Festive Overture*, but it is dissimilar to Shostakovich's original band work from the same era (but without an assigned opus number), *Solemn March for Military Band*, written in 1941. The difficulty range is between grades four and five, but as in any consideration of technical difficulty perusal of the score is critical and individual performance potential should be based upon the conductor's assessment of strong to less-strong sections within the band.

Unit 3: Historical Perspective

Shostakovich wrote the music that became *Folk Dances* between his *Leningrad (Seventh) Symphony*, Op. 60 (1941) and his *Symphony No. 8*, Op. 65 (1943). The socio-political environment for the composer during this time is striking both from the difficulties he encountered with Stalin and from his emotions at seeing his hometown under siege by the Nazis. Shostakovich musically expressed his feelings, though, in dramatically opposing means ranging from the power of his *Seventh Symphony* (regarding which in testimony stated was "not about Leningrad under siege [but] about the Leningrad that Stalin destroyed and Hitler merely finished off") to the lightheartedness of the music that became *Folk Dances,* to which the dedication reads "Written as a tribute to the courage of the citizens of Leningrad."

Unit 4: Technical Considerations

In considering this work for performance, bands with a solid foundation in scales, arpeggios, and maintaining a solid pulse without rushing should find *Folk Dances* a straightforward work: a bit challenging but not too difficult. The "fun in playing" aspect will lead most performers to solve on their own their individual technical deficiencies. The most demanding and critical technical considerations will be the style of the various articulations and avoiding the tendency to play all notes too short. Of course, the conductor must determine note length issues with careful regard to ensemble clarity in individual performance venues.

Unit 5: Stylistic Considerations

Though a twentieth century composition, *Folk Dances* is more characteristic of late romantic style period nationalism, with its harmonically simple base and direct incorporation of native dance tunes. Marked "*Moderato* (quarter note = 116)" at the beginning, and from rehearsal no. 6 accelerating to "*Allegro molto* (quarter note = 144)" at rehearsal no. 7, the work can validly be performed at those indicated tempi. Another possibility, and equally valid with respect to the form of eastern European folk dances, would be to begin a bit slower (quarter note = 108), accelerate as indicated at rehearsal no. 6 toward rehearsal no. 7, but at measure 132 holding that tempo until a slight acceleration to measure 144 at rehearsal no. 8, then at rehearsal no. 12 beginning an *accelerando poco a poco al fine* to tempi within the technical confines of the band.

Unit 6: Musical Elements
MELODY:
The melodies are simple, from the opening trumpet "come join the dance" fanfare (which reappears slightly altered at rehearsal no. 9), through the mostly diatonic woodwind, to the "Russian sounding" lower-voiced lines that drive the pulse forward. With almost every section repeating, teaching the varying melodies is easily successful if the approach is in teaching proficiency of each short motivic line.

HARMONY:

The central tonalities are based around G minor, with typical sections in G major, B-flat, and D. The G-flat and D-flat section at rehearsal no. 11, particularly at the tempo marked and the articulation, will need some attention to tuning. The D major arpeggiated section at rehearsal no. 15 can be a "knuckle buster" for the woodwinds, but it gives the conductor an opportunity to incorporate focused warm-ups with the band on the musical element contained in the performance music (i.e., the scales and arpeggios contained within that chosen music).

RHYTHM:

Throughout, the rhythmic motive of quarter/eighth/eighth and its reverse are as important as the pitches in the melody. The simple "boom-chick, boom-chick" background, if played without rushing, leads to great success in performance—particularly if those players perform confidently enough to follow the pulse in acceleration of the conductor and maintain good ensemble.

TIMBRE:

The "Russian" sound of *Folk Dances* is maintained by performing the work with a dark, rich tone. It is easy for players to make these melodies and the background bright, so the conductor needs to strive for each individual player creating his/her darkest tone from the onset of teaching the work, particularly with younger bands. Shorter, less resonant articulations can also lead to bright playing; therefore, the conductor is also encouraged to promote slightly longer, yet separated when indicated, note lengths.

Unit 7: Form and Structure

Folk Dances is in a single rhapsodic movement that can be performed "excitedly" in approximately four minutes yet be just as "audience pleasing" and musically valid in approximately four minutes and twenty seconds. The construction is a series of similar two-step dance tunes, beginning comfortably and ending in a flourish.

Unit 8: Suggested Listening

Folk Dances – North Texas Wind Symphony, Eugene Corporon, conducting: Klavier K11077

Unit 9: Additional References and Resources

Many texts regarding the composer are available at most libraries, and an extensive reference on the music is available at the Ithaca College School of Music. Numerous websites regarding many non-music aspects of Shostakovich provide interesting insight into his life, works, and "mystic."

Contributed by:
Robert Belser
Associate Professor of Music
University of Wyoming
Laramie, Wyoming

Teacher Resource Guide

Handel in the Strand

Percy Grainger
(1982–1961)

Unit 1: Composer

Born in Melbourne, Australia, Percy Grainger was the son of John Harry and Rose Aldridge Grainger. John, an architect, and Rose, the daughter of a London hotelier, both dabbled in the arts and music. Percy's father was mostly absent, being dedicated to wine and women, while Rose's constant doting over him reached heights of obsession. Rose took Percy away from state schools early in childhood to tutor him herself. The ultimate obsessive act may have been her suicide in 1922, an event that had a lasting effect on Percy.

Grainger holds two positions in music history. He is well known as both a concert pianist and a composer. By the age of twelve, he had studied piano with both his mother and Louis Pabst, who was a renowned teacher in Melbourne. His debut recital was in the Masonic Hall of Melbourne in 1894. His formal study of music was in Frankfurt, Germany, where he stayed until 1901. With his student days over, both he and Rose moved to London, where he began his career as a concert pianist.

As a pianist, Grainger became well known. He performed Bach and Schumann while enjoying modern composers like Debussy and Ravel. Through an acquaintance, Grainger began a close relationship with Grieg between 1905 and 1908. Their friendship and musical collaboration resulted in Grainger's premiere of Grieg's A minor concerto. Grieg was to have conducted the premiere, but his untimely death did not permit it. Grainger's performance was a huge success.

Grieg's influence on Grainger's musical life was also felt when he encouraged Grainger to explore the use of folk songs in his performances and compositions. Thus began Grainger's pursuit of collecting folk songs sung by local singers around the world and recording them on the wax cylinder phonograph.

Due to the outbreak of the war, the impact it might have on Grainger's career, and Rose's failing health, the two moved to New York in September of 1914. His concert piano career quickly bloomed while his compositions were being performed by various orchestras. Both contributions to the New York music scene were widely accepted by critics.

When the involvement of the United States in the war had escalated, Grainger enlisted as a bandsman in the Army and was assigned to the 15th Band of the Coast Artillery Corps in 1917. He was not a successful soprano saxophonist, but he did gain enough proficiency on the oboe to be promoted to Bandsman 2nd Class. It is in this environment that Grainger flourished as a composer and arranger of music for band.

In 1921, Grainger and his mother moved to White Plains, New York. He married Ella Viola Strom-Bandelius in 1928 and continued world tours as pianist and composer until his death of abdominal cancer in 1961.

Unit 2: Composition

Handel in the Strand was dedicated to William Gair Rathbone, a banker friend who not only served Grainger in "fatherly" ways but also encouraged his musical growth by introducing him to the latest music of French composers. The title suggests Grainger's bridge between aristocratic art and proletarian entertainment. The "Strand" in the title points to the Edwardian Music Hall of London, while the reference to Handel indicates the influence of Handel's *Harmonious Blacksmith Variations*. Grainger referred to *Handel in the Strand* as a "clog dance" and preferred that people dance to it, clogs and all.

Lasting three minutes and thirty seconds, this work of light music of a dance nature is much like a significant portion of Grainger's music in the way it parallels the music of Bach. Although not nearly as substantive, Mellers believes Grainger's attraction to "Bach-like continuity of beat, consistency of figuration, and interdependence between horizontal and vertical harmony" is apparent.

The tempo is marked at quarter note = 120–132, "fast and merry." The composition incorporates the use of *ostinato*, light articulation, lyricism, wide dynamic range (*pp* to *fff*), intricate rhythms, mixed meters, countermelody, ornamentation, various weighted accents, extended but predictable harmonies, dense polyphony, and active parts for the players to enjoy.

The Brion/Schissel arrangement used in this resource guide employs a significant use of soprano saxophone and utilizes independent trumpet, cornet, and flugel horn parts. It is written in comfortable tessitura for most players. However, the cornet and euphonium solos tend to remain in the upper register. This arrangement adheres to Merz's use of color choices, applies shortened note values in the accompaniment figures, and encourages lightened articulations. Although it is scored heavier than the Goldman setting, it allows for more easily achieved balances. Alto saxophone and 4th clarinet parts are provided in case a soprano saxophone or E-flat alto clarinet is not available.

Unit 3: Historical Perspective

Grainger has not always enjoyed deep respect as a composer. Having been omitted from many popular music history books, his large musical output has only recently come to be seen as significant and colorful. During his career, he was viewed as a serious musician by Delius (who was a good friend), Britten, Busoni, Stokowski, Cowell, and many other noted composers.

Grainger is also known as an innovator. His fresh contributions include free music, wide use of the saxophone family in his orchestrations, expanded use of keyboard percussion, and elastic scoring.

Handel in the Strand was composed in 1911 and first published by Schott & Co. in 1912. This original composition was first written for violin, cello, and piano. Later, Grainger changed the medium and wrote arrangements for strings and piano in 1912, orchestra in 1949, piano in 1930, and two pianos in 1947. He also allowed the famous band of John Phillip Sousa to arrange and perform this and other works. Goldman's arrangement in 1962 has served the band literature well, having been performed often and by a variety of wind ensembles. The arrangement used for this study of *Handel in the Strand* was released in September 2001 by the C.L. Barnhouse Co. in collaboration with Willow Blossom Music. Noted Sousa experts Keith Brion & Loras Schissel reworked the arrangement Otto Merz wrote for the Sousa band to make it even more adaptable for modern bands.

Much of Grainger's research papers, manuscripts, and other memorabilia can be found in the University of Melbourne's Grainger Museum. Other materials are housed in the Library of Congress in Washington, DC, and the Grainger Library in White Plains, New York, where he lived for twenty-one years.

Unit 4: Technical Considerations

The first order of business with regard to technical skill development is that of articulation. As noted in Unit 5, the style is light and separated. Students must be able to physically separate notes while thinking long, musical lines. To accomplish this,

1. Have the students sustain a pitch that does not waiver.
2. Then have the tongue move quickly to touch the air at quarter note = 72. The air stream must stay sustained between notes that are articulated.

3. Then subdivide in eighth notes with the tongue while sustaining the air.
4. Finally, have the tongue separate the notes while maintaining a sustained air stream and thought.

Continue working with this style on a single pitch while increasing the tempo until students can perform the notes lightly and separated.

Repeating several scales at various tempi and styles will aid in the students' technical development. Most of the melodic material centers around F major. Chromaticism is found in the *ostinato* figure and other polyphonic lines. The students will need to be familiar with F minor for the transition material from measures 41 through 47. Following are a few ways to keep the boredom out of practicing scales:

1. Play slowly and in a swing style.
2. Divide the band in half. Half the band plays long tones; the other half plays a rhythm from the work on a single note.
3. Perform the scale in this fashion: 1, 1–2, 1–2–3, 1–2–3–4, 1–2–3–4–5, 1–2–3–4–5–6, 1–2–3–4–5–6–7, 1–2–3–4–5–6–7–8…then descending.
4. Do chromatic scales as in 3) above.
5. Divide the band in half. Have one group perform F major while the other group performs F minor. Students can begin to identify inappropriate sounds in major or minor.

The rapid tempo combined with the high quantity of notes requires patience to achieve the highest rate of part acquisition. Rehearsing at a slow tempo will be helpful. While the tempo is slow, the director should encourage good listening and understanding of the harmonic structure as it moves through a series of logical progressions. When errors in notes occur, ask the students if they hear the difference in harmony with correct notes versus the unwritten ones. Because much of the music is detached, it is sometimes more effective to rehearse in a slow chorale style to allow better listening opportunities.

This piece remains in the upper-middle register throughout. There are a few places where performers are asked to play in uncomfortably high registers for a short time (for example, flutes play high A, cornets high B, solo euphonium G above the staff). In combination, these registers can cause the tone to become bright and brittle. Have students perform expanding scales while encouraging them to remain open and resonant. One might consider having a good vocalist come to class and speak about the issue of ascending without changing beauty of tone.

Unit 5: Stylistic Considerations

The overall style of the work combines the density of late baroque with the light articulation and lyrical qualities of the classical period. Students should have the opportunity to listen to the music of Bach, Handel, and Mozart to begin to understand the characteristics involved in the performance of this piece. Students might benefit from listening to opera arias to hear the potential for expanding the expressiveness of a long, lyrical line.

The articulation required for the *ostinato* figure is light and delicate. Students should be asked to tap their left arm with their right index finger lightly to feel the delicacy. The director could also have a string player come to class to model *pizzicato* for the students to emulate.

The wide range of dynamics requires several skills for the students to master. The quieter dynamics employed (*pp*, *p*, *mp*) are often difficult to control with regard to tone and articulation. This is generally due to the misconception of students that the energy required to perform at these dynamics is less than stronger dynamics. For the students to feel the energy required to produce quiet sounds that project, have the students, one at a time, move to the back of the room and whisper something to the front of the room. The voice must project in an energetic way for all to hear but remain a whisper. Do not allow students to perform at the upper end of the dynamic level until they are able to produce a clear, resonant tone at *mezzoforte*, *piano*, and *pianissimo*. Then expand the volume without changing the tone.

Students should be able to perform music with varying degrees of weight applied to the articulation. There are extensive expressive markings in this score. Allow students to experience different weighted articulations in this piece by pointing out the many opportunities for variety. For example, as the music grows and expands in volume, students often perform heavier. Practice different weights away from the music by having students punch the air, tap a friend's shoulder, brush lint away from cloth, catch a fly, jump rope, etc. The idea is to not allow a different style to enter the music just because the weights change. With diligent work, the students should begin to feel, hear, and perform the subtle differences in weight.

The mood of the work is lighthearted. Ask the students to give this music their own title based on what they hear. Then attempt to portray that title through their performance. The atmosphere is busy, conversational, productive, hopeful, and just to the point of bursting with energy.

Unit 6: Musical Elements

MELODY:

Grainger's polyphonic style allows students greater opportunity to experience linear direction of musical line and study relationships of notes in terms of harmonic direction. This arrangement employs a wide use of expressive markings for *crescendos* and *diminuendos*, sometimes to a fault. For example, the euphonium solo in measure 9 includes a long tone on C that drops to the leading tone for a half beat before resolving back to C. The dynamic is marked *piano* with a *crescendo* and then a slight *diminuendo* at the resolution. Students should be taught to hear and feel that notes are either pushing toward a tendency or pulling from one. Often students are taught to *crescendo* through long notes, creating music that sounds forced and insincere. When students are able to hear that music moves toward or pulls away from a point of harmonic logic, there is greater opportunity for expressiveness. Students can also benefit from being given opportunities to listen to professional vocalists perform. Students will likely hear movement from note to note that is shapely (like a geometric figure) rather than mathematical (like a written *crescendo* appears).

One way for students to feel the pushing and pulling sensations involved in harmonic movement is by following this strategy:

1. Have students pair up into A and B partners.
2. Person A grasps the palm of person B.
3. In eight counts, have Person A gently push the palm of Person B, who is providing minimal resistance. Feel free to change the number of counts depending on the pace of the harmonic movement.
4. After eight counts, Person A then gently pulls Person B for eight counts back to the starting position while Person B provides minimal resistance.
5. All movements should be done in a controlled manner.
6. Then have the students apply this sensation while performing concert F.
7. Hopefully, the sound will have a movement of greater or lesser intensity depending on the push or pull.

The application of listening for and physically feeling the movement toward or away from harmonic logic can aid students in their understanding of relationships of notes.

The rhythmic *ostinato* can also be observed melodically by listening to the movement toward harmonic cadences. For example, in the first measure, 1st clarinet and tuba create logical flow by beginning on F (the tonal center for the work), first moving away from and then toward F on the third beat, and then repeating that activity to the downbeat of the second measure. The second measure moves further away from F by including a secondary dominant that correctly and quickly resolves, pulling the music back to F on the downbeat of measure 3. Creating movement through rapid harmonic changes allows the music to flow.

HARMONY:

Handel in the Strand does not present major obstacles in terms of harmonic complexity. As previously stated, the music centers around F major, with occasional chromaticism appearing that helps create tension and drama. The harmony is generally clear throughout the homophonic *ostinato* and melody. When more lines are added creating a dense polyphony, the harmony remains apparent with the exception of one area. Measure 41 opens with a strong and surprising cadence on F minor, beginning a wandering of tonal centers. The following two measures take the listener through a harmonic progression that cadences on D-flat major in measure 43. The music quickly departs D-flat major and moves toward F minor, with a strong cadence in measure 45. The following chord progression, heard in measures 45 through 47, leads the listener to a comfortable place of C major at measure 48, which is the dominant of F:

Measure 45: F minor – G7 with raised 4 – F minor
Measure 46: D-flat7 – B-flat7 – F with raised 5
Measure 47: B-flat7 – G7 with raised 5
Measure 48: C major

Measures 48 through 56 shift cadences from C to F, finally landing solidly at measure 57 with a strong cadence in F major.

Measures 42 through 47 lend themselves to in-depth study of progressive movement through sounds to logical conclusions. Because the harmony shifts on every eighth note, it is a good idea to slow the music to give the students an opportunity to hear these sophisticated chords. The director might be advised to transcribe the chords in an arrangement for full band in a Bach chorale style to be performed at the beginning of rehearsal as an "ear" warm-up. Encourage the students to listen for movement tendencies. These chords might also lend themselves to an introduction to or reinforcement of jazz sounds.

RHYTHM:

Due to the frenetic nature of the piece and the high degree of activity in the individual parts, the first order of business as it pertains to rhythm is teaching the students to find and maintain a steady pulse. The strategy outlined below may help students recognize that they are capable of keeping a steady internal pulse that is not related to watching the conductor for the beat:

1. Clear the band room of equipment or go to the gymnasium or marching field.
2. Have the students stand in a circle or circles.
3. Set the tempo with the metronome (or establish it some other way) at quarter note = 120.
4. Have the students clap their hands in small circles to the pulse.
5. Next have them clap every two beats, continuing the circular motion between claps. The circular clapping will enlarge.
6. Then have them clap every four beats, continuing the circular motion. The circular clapping will enlarge.

7. Now change the metronome to quarter note = 30 and clap on each beat, maintaining a steady pulse through the silence. Remember to keep the hands moving around in a circle between claps. This begins to develop a sense of movement to a point.

8. This exercise can also be done by walking instead of clapping. In addition to the goal of maintaining a steady pulse, students learn to move their bodies through space. This is another way students can become "connected" to the sense of physical movement and its relationship to musical movement.

As is typical of Grainger's music, there are "tricky" rhythms that are difficult to count but, when performed correctly, add a wonderful dance flavor to the music. Rhythmic figures like syncopation, Scottish snaps, dotted-eighth/sixteenths, sixteenth note triplets, and sextuplets are all used to keep the listener off balance. Mixed meter and the use of the constant eighth note help add to this effect.

Creating a counting system that helps students understand rhythms is not always the most effective means, particularly with some of Grainger's figures. For example, measures 57 through 58 show flute and trumpet with a rhythm that might be more easily performed if it were not counted. One way to allow the students to think about only the rhythm is to extract the difficult figures from the music and create a rhythm chart with the difficult figures. Students can then clap, perform on one note, tap, or in any other way hear and feel the rhythm. When students are physically connected to the rhythm, they might have a better chance to remember and perform expressively.

Measure 58 has an intricate rhythm, found in trombone. The syncopation after the tied eighth note is often difficult to feel. Ask the students to remove the tie for a few rehearsals.

The only mixed meter section is from measures 42 through 47. The meters are 5/8, 3/4, 2/4, 3/8, and 2/4. The eighth note, as indicated in the score, "is always at original speed." Have the students perform the number of eighth notes from measures 42 through 47 on a scale. Change notes at the beginning of each measure, accenting the downbeat. This will give the students an opportunity to feel the steadiness of the eighth note and the actual meter changes.

TIMBRE:

The various ways in which the arrangers present the melodic and harmonic materials create intriguing shifts in tone colors. The first theme begins in measure 9 with solo euphonium. The solo voice is then joined by cornet and flugel horn, creating a warm timbre with a hint of brightness. The opening figure has a unique combination of winds and percussion, particularly for an *ostinato*. The use of clarinet, bassoon, muted horn, tuba, and marimba reminds us of Grainger's unique orchestration of the first movement of *Lincolnshire Posy* where muted trumpet, bassoon, and muted horn begin the work. Teaching students to achieve and maintain a characteristic tone while blending with other voices is a difficult task. Allowing students to study works of art that use different colors to create an image is sometimes helpful.

Grainger repeats one of the main themes five times in its entirety. The arrangers change the orchestration each time, creating interest through variety. It is also common for this theme to begin in one voice and be joined by another, as in the opening theme. For example, the main theme appears in measure 33 with flute, soprano saxophone, cornet, and euphonium. The 3rd trombone joins them while flute changes to other material to help complete the line for measures 35 and 36. To help students understand the impact of adding colors to a line, have one student with a low voice begin speaking a sentence of any content. Then have another student with a high-pitched voice join the other student speaking the same sentence.

Unit 7: Form and Structure

MEASURE	EVENT AND SCORING

(A–B–C–C–Transition–C–C–A–B–Transition–C–C)

1–8	Introduction using rhythmic *ostinato*; F major tonal center
4–8	Theme I; consequent phrase; euphonium solo
9–16	Theme I; euphonium, cornet, and flugel horn; rhythmic *ostinato* continues
17–24	Theme II begins in tenor saxophone and euphonium to be picked up by soprano saxophone and 1st cornet; euphonium continues with countermelody; alto saxophone and 2nd cornet begin yet another countermelody; rhythmic *ostinato* continues
25–32	Theme III appears in upper woodwinds; new countermelody arrives in the alto saxophone, euphonium, 1st cornet, and flugel horn; trombone introduces a fanfare-like figure
33–40	Theme III appears again with the antecedent being played in cornet, euphonium, soprano saxophone, flute, and tenor saxophone; clarinet supplies the countermelody from mm. 25–32; horn projects the fanfare motif
37	Consequent of theme III provided with the addition of trombone; clarinet quietly states the fanfare motif

MEASURE   EVENT AND SCORING

40–50   Begins transition measures with a cadence in F minor; series
                 of harmonic movements through F minor and D-flat major
                 with measures in mixed meter takes the tonal center to C
                 major

50–61   Strong cadence on F major begins a section that uses part of
                 Theme II (mm. 50–54) as an antecedent and part of Theme
                 III (mm. 57–61) as the consequent; two measures of
                 transition material separate the two; hints of the *ostinato*
                 reappear in flute, horn, and bassoon

62–69   Theme III is stated in its entirety beginning with oboe,
                 soprano saxophone, and clarinet for the first four measures;
                 m. 66 sees oboe and soprano saxophone finishing the
                 melody, with 2nd oboe and alto saxophone providing
                 countermelody; clarinet interjects the fanfare motif

70–77   Fourth statement of Theme III appears; fanfare motives are
                 heard in oboe, trumpet, bassoon, and flute

78–85   Theme I with *ostinato* figure is stated as a replica of mm.
                 9–16

86–91   Theme II is heard with countermelodies from mm. 17–24;
                 cadence, however, in m. 92 is C major

92–100   Transition material, *ostinato*, and parts of Theme II are all
                 used to set up a false ending; two *fermatas* hold a IV–V7
                 cadence that does not end the piece

101–112   Theme III is heard for the fifth and final time;
                 countermelody that has accompanied this theme is also
                 orchestrated; trombone gives the fanfare motif for the last
                 time; transition material found in the upper woodwinds and
                 horn accompanies the last two measures of the theme; final
                 two measures outline F major with ascending and
                 descending lines that bring the work to an exuberant close

Unit 8: Suggested Listening

Percy Grainger, *Handel in the Strand*
    Eddie Green, University of Houston Wind Ensemble,
        Mark Custom Records
    Frederick Fennel, Eastman Rochester "Pops" Orchestra, Mercury
    Richard Hickox, City of London Sinfonia and Joyful Company of
        Singers, Chandos – Volume 3 of *The Grainger Edition*

Edward Peterson, Washington Winds, Walking Frog Records
    Academy of St. Martins in the Fields Chamber Ensemble, Chandos
Percy Grainger:
    Lincolnshire Posy (Movements I and II)
    Mock *Morris*
George Frederic Handel, *Harmonious Blacksmith Variations*
Johann Sebastian Bach, *English Suites*
Edvard Grieg, *Piano Concerto in A Minor*

Unit 9: Additional References and Resources

Bird, John. *Percy Grainger*. New York: Oxford University Press, Inc., 1999.

Gillies, M. *The All-Around Man, Selected Letters of Percy Granger 1914–1961*. Edited by D. Pear. New York: Oxford University Press, Inc., 1994.

Grainger, Percy. *Handel in the Strand*. Preface to the score by Keith Brion and Loren Schissel. Oskaloosa, IA: C.L. Barnhouse Co., 2001.

Mellers, Wilfrid. *Percy Grainger*. New York: Oxford University Press, Inc. 1992.

Slattery, Thomas C. Percy Grainger, *The Inveterate Innovator*. Evanston, IL: The Instrumentalist Co., 1974.

For a more extensive listing of references, including books, articles, dissertations, and discography, refer to John Bird's book titled *Percy Grainger*, published in 1999 by Oxford University Press.

Contributed by:
Richard A. Greenwood
Director of Bands
University of Central Florida
Orlando, Florida

Teacher Resource Guide

Lullaby for Kirsten

Leslie Bassett
(b. 1923)

Unit 1: Composer

Leslie Bassett is Professor Emeritus at the University of Michigan, where he holds the Albert A. Stanley Professorship in Composition. His teachers include Homer Keller, Ross Lee Finney, Arthur Honegger, Nadia Boulanger, and Roberto Gerhard.

During World War II, Bassett was a trombonist with the Army Band. Once his tour of duty ended, he continued his interrupted musical education at California State University–Fresno and then later moved to the University of Michigan. Upon completion of his master's degree at the University of Michigan, he studied at the *Ecole Normale de Musique* in France. Bassett then joined the University of Michigan faculty in 1952.

Bassett's numerous awards for composition include The Society for the Publication of American Music in 1959, The *Prix de Rome* in 1961, a citation from The National Institute of Arts and Letters in 1964, and the Pulitzer Prize in 1966.

Unit 2: Composition

Composed in 1985, *Lullaby for Kirsten* was commissioned by the student members of the University of Michigan Band to celebrate the birth of the youngest daughter of former Director of Bands H. Robert Reynolds. Recorded by the North Texas Wind Symphony on their *Dream Catchers* compact disc (KCD11089) in 1998, Bassett is quoted in the liner notes as believing that the *Lullaby* "...may possibly be the only lullaby ever specifically written for, and commissioned by, a band." The premiere took place in Ann Arbor, Michigan, on October 4, 1985, performed by the University of Michigan Band under the direction of H. Robert Reynolds, Kirsten's father. The program note in the score states that she was present and "seemed to approve." *Lullaby for Kirsten* is available through C. F. Peters Publishing.

Unit 3: Historical Perspective

Lullabies have been a part of the fabric of every society since parents began singing their children to sleep. One can only speculate when that began. There is a long tradition of setting these primarily vocal melodies for instrumental ensembles. Often, composers have taken the properties of a vocal lullaby and created an original instrumental work in this style. *Lullaby for Kirsten* is strophic, like a simple song, and the melody is lyrical and beautiful. What makes it unique, aside from the composer's assertion that it might be the first lullaby written for a band, is that it uses Bassett's non-serialized, atonal harmonic language. The popular school of thought on atonal music is that it is not lyrical, and many would argue against its ability to be beautiful. Bassett clearly contradicts this thought process by creating a lovely lyrical, colorful yet atonal work.

Unit 4: Technical Considerations

The technical demands of this work are minimal if one only considers manual technique. The only passages that may pose a challenge include the whole-tone scale harmonized in thirds in measure 9 for flute and the *accelerando/rallentando* at measures 29 through 33 for woodwinds.

The primary difficulty in this work is feeling the proper subdivision at a slow tempo. It often requires the musicians to feel a shift from duple to triple subdivisions and back again. There are multiple places where the melody is broken and chords build by adding instruments almost every half beat. This creates colorful sonorities but could be difficult if the group is not subdividing well.

The range required in some instruments might cause a few problems. The bassoons are a perfect example of this, as they are required to play from low D below the staff to third ledger line A-flat above the staff in the first measure alone.

Unit 5: Stylistic Considerations

Smoothness and seamless execution of lines are essential to achieve the proper musical effect. When building the chordal pyramids, the musicians may have to place a little more front on the note in order for the color shift to be heard. Given that, they need to adjust their dynamics once the note is established to clear the way for the next entrance. Each phrase is introduced by a three-note anacrusis or pickup that is either marked by a series of *fermatas* or *tenutos*. There should be growth through each of these notes into the fourth to provide tension and direction. Pay careful attention to execute the dynamic indications; they are painstakingly marked and are often accompanied by *crescendos* and *diminuendos*.

Unit 6: Musical Elements

As stated before, the harmonic language is freely atonal. There are whole tone-based arpeggios and scales. Pay particular attention to the accompaniment during each repetition of the melody since this is what changes musically.

The meter is essentially in four, although the introduction is in three and measure 21 is in 9/8. The 9/8 measure should be conducted in four, with beat 4 having an added eighth note. The musical effect is that of a metric *rallentando*.

The melody repeats three times. Each repetition is scored differently to create a panorama of colors. The first statement features woodwinds with trumpet in cup mute. The second statement features oboe and open trumpet. The third statement utilizes horn, trombone, and euphonium as the main melodic voices. The general effect is a gradual darkening of color—a fade to black, so to speak, akin to the gradual process of falling asleep.

Unit 7: Form and Structure

The form of *Lullaby for Kirsten* is really quite simple. There is a short introduction, three repetitions of the melody, and a short codetta. The measure scheme is as follows:

MEASURE	EVENT AND SCORING
1–5	Introduction
6–13	First melodic statement
14–23	Second melodic statement
24–33	Third melodic statement
34–end	Codetta

In looking at the third melodic statement, it is interesting to note that the melody is interrupted by the *accelerando/rallentando* before it ends. The actual ending of the third melodic statement occurs in the codetta.

One other point of interest is at the very end in measure 38. Flute and glockenspiel sound the pitches of C and E-flat. This minor third is very reminiscent of the opening of another famous lullaby by Johannes Brahms.

Unit 8: Suggested Listening

Leslie Bassett:
>*Colors and Contours*
>*Designs, Images, and Textures*
>*Five Pieces for String Quartet*
>*Lullaby for Kirsten*
>*Sounds, Shapes, Symbols*
>*Variations for Orchestra*

Ross Lee Finney, *Skating on the Sheyenne*

Arthur Honegger, *Pacific 231*

Unit 9: Additional References and Resources

Bassett, Leslie. *Lullaby for Kirsten*. Glendale, NK: C. F. Peters Corp., 1991.

Corporon, Eugene Migliaro. *Dream Catchers*. Klavier Records (KCD11089), 1998.

LaRue, Jan. *Guidelines for Style Analysis*. New York: W. W. Norton & Co., 1970.

McKoin, Sarah. "Colors and Contours" in *Teaching Music through Performance in Band*, Volume 3. Chicago: GIA Publications, 2000, pp. 310–5.

Contributed by:

Edwin C. Powell
Director of Bands
McLennan Community College
Waco, Texas

Teacher Resource Guide

Morning Alleluias for the Winter Solstice

Ron Nelson
(b. 1929)

Unit 1: Composer

Ron Nelson, a native of Joliet, Illinois, was born on December 19, 1929. He began piano lessons at the age of six and composed his first work, *The Sailboat*, at that same tender age. As you might expect from a young boy, he found it "more fun to improvise than to practice." By age thirteen, he was working as a church organist, a job that prepared him well for future endeavors: "...they [organ lessons] revealed the basic principles of orchestration." Nelson began to develop his compositional skills as a student at Joliet Township High School. He also taught himself to play string bass in order to play in the high school band. With the support of his high school band director, Bruce Houseknecht (an Eastman alumnus), Nelson was given the opportunity to conduct and arrange, and he wrote his first major work, a 22-minute concerto for piano and symphonic band. As a seventeen-year-old, he played the first and last performance of the concerto with his high school band.

Nelson attended the Eastman School of Music at the University of Rochester, where he received his Bachelor of Music (1952), Master of Music (1953), and Doctor of Musical Arts (1956). His teachers included Howard Hanson and Bernard Rogers. The recipient of a 1954–1955 Fullbright Award, Nelson studied in Paris at the *Ecole Normale de Musique* and the Paris Conservatory with Tony Aubin. On his return to Eastman, he became involved with film music, preparing for two careers: "one in film scoring and one in academia, as a backstop. Later, I reversed the order and put academia first."

Upon his graduation from Eastman in 1956, Nelson joined the Brown University faculty as an assistant professor, attaining the rank of associate professor in 1960 and full professor in 1968. He served as Chairman of the Department of Music from 1963 to 1973 and finally retired as Professor Emeritus in 1993.

His numerous awards and honors include a Fullbright Award (1954–1955), a Ford Foundation Fellowship (1963), a Benjamin Award (1964), a Howard Foundation Grant for World Tour (1965–1966), National Education Association grants (1973, 1976, 1979), and several ASCAP (American Society of Composers, Authors, and Publishers) Awards (1962–present). Nelson is the first musician to be awarded the Acuff Chair of Excellence in the Creative Arts (1991). At the time of this writing, he is the only composer to win all three major band composition contests in the same time period, 1993–1994 (including the National Band Association William D. Revelli Memorial Band Composition Contest, the American Bandmasters Association Ostwald Band Composition Contest, and the Louis and Virginia Sudler International Wind Band Composition Contest), with the same work, *Passacaglia (Homage on B-A-C-H)*. Commissioning organizations include the National Symphony Orchestra, Rochester Philharmonic, Aspen Music Festival, Brevard Music Center, United States Air Force Band, and numerous universities and choral groups.

Nelson's compositional output includes two operas, one mass, one cantata, one oratorio, ninety choral works, and over forty instrumental works, half of which have been composed for band. His writing encompasses the television and film industry, including a number of film scores for Eastman Kodak, Columbia Pictures, and NBC. Boosey and Hawkes, Carl Fischer, Elkan-Vogel, and Ludwig Music have published almost one hundred of his works for orchestra, chorus, and band. Recordings of his music can be found under several labels.

Some of Nelson's other works for band include *Aspen Jubilee, Chaconne (In Memoriam…), Courtly Airs and Dances, Danza Capriccio, Epiphanies (Fanfares and Chorales), Fanfare for a Celebration, Fanfare for the Hour of Sunrise, Lauds (Praise High Day), Mayflower Overture, Medieval Suite (Homage to Leonin, Homage to Perotin, Homage to Machaut), Passacaglia (Homage on B-A-C-H), Resonances I, Rocky Point Holiday, Savannah River Holiday, Sonoran Desert Holiday*, and *To the Airborne*.

Where many composers are known for a particular "sound" or style, Nelson's compositions encompass such a variety of style and form that his writing is difficult to channel into one single category. When asked about Nelson's music, conductor Leonard Slatkin had the following to say:

Nelson is the quintessential American composer. He has the ability to move between conservative and newer styles with ease. The fact that he's a little hard to categorize is what makes him interesting."[1]

Ron Nelson resides in Scottsdale, Arizona.

Unit 2: Composition

Contemporary in overall style, *Morning Alleluias for the Winter Solstice* is a blend of new and old. The rhythmic vitality and pulse of minimalism, coupled with non-pulsed "special" notation and improvisatory *ostinati*, are set against musical effects (gliding tones) indigenous to Asian music for over one thousand years. These "gliding tones" (slow *glissandos*) are inspired by the ancient classical music of Japan, China, and Korea. The total effect of the musical elements is a combined mixture of somber reflection, joyous celebration, and final declaration. Outside of the actual musical elements, there are important historical and cultural events that give relevance to the work. They include the destruction of Hiroshima, Japan, at the end of World War II, the poetry of Alfred Lord Tennyson, and the Winter Solstice.

Morning Alleluias for the Winter Solstice was composed at the request of Frederick Fennell. A single-movement work, the score bears the inscription, "Commissioned by Frederick Fennell—for the People of Hiroshima, Japan." At the time of the commission, Fennell served as principal conductor of the Tokyo Kosei Wind Orchestra. Fennell writes,

> *Morning Alleluias for the Winter Solstice* probably became the spirit as well as the title which Ron Nelson chose for this music when I told him of my personal experience in awakening one morning in a Hiroshima hotel room that was ablaze with brilliant morning sunlight. As I lay in bed with so many dark thoughts also crowding in on that morning's bright expectancies for the living day ahead, I knew that these moments could only be celebrated as the triumph of the people of Hiroshima through the creation of a musical expression. The Hiroshima morning was in late November. Ron accepted my commission a few days later in Chicago. Other work was put aside so Ron could produce the score, which he signed on March 1, 1989. The Tokyo Kosei Wind Orchestra and I concluded our spring tour in Hiroshima on Sunday afternoon May 14, 1989, with the first performance of Ron's *Morning Alleluias for the Winter Solstice*.[2]

---

1 Conversation with composer. Quote taken from a West Coast newspaper.
2 Inscription in score.

Nelson recalls that "the deadline for completing *Morning Alleluias for a Winter Solstice* was very short." He recalls a conversation during the Midwest Clinic in 1988:

> Fred and I were standing at the elevator, and he told me he needed a work for a performance in May. When he described to me his personal experience on that morning in Hiroshima, it triggered the ideas necessary to get me started."[3]

The second part of the work's title...*for the Winter Solstice*, has virtually nothing to do with Fennell's description of a bright sunny Japanese morning. This half of the title is derived from Nelson's own spiritual connection with the Winter Solstice. Each year, for many years, Nelson would make a ritual of writing music for the Winter Solstice. These works include a variety of music from solos to this large-scale instrumental work. *Morning Alleluias for the Winter Solstice* was Nelson's solstice composition for 1998. Nelson admits the majority of the compositions he has written for this special season are not published.

Many of Nelson's band compositions show evidence of his strong choral background. *Morning Alleluias for the Winter Solstice* not only incorporates elements of singing, but the second half is based, almost literally, on one of Nelson's choral works, "Ring Out, Wild Bells" from *Three Pieces after Tennyson*. "I often ask players to 'sing' their parts, and sometimes literally to sing."[4] Nelson's *Ring Out, Wild Bells* was originally commissioned for men's chorus, piano four-hands, and instruments.

The opening forty-four measures of *Morning Alleluias for the Winter Solstice* are "reflective and poignant, and focus on what you would expect"[5] when thinking about a country that has survived a nuclear bomb. Through his music, Nelson is able to evoke a musical illustration, which begins very free sounding—almost ethereal and timeless in character. The music soon shifts to joyous affirmation. Regarding the opening tempo of this work, Nelson says, "I never heard a rehearsal of it or anything before it went into print. The first time I heard it played, I thought it was too fast. Normally I don't fool around with my tempos, but with this piece, when I conducted it, I wanted it slower."[6] He recommends 58 to 60 beats per minute for the quarter note.

Beginning at measure 45, Nelson suggests a tempo marking of quarter note = 126 (instead of the written quarter note = 132). He recommends beginning a "good *poco ritardando*" in measures 124 through 126 rather than where it appears in the score (measure 129). He suggests 72 to 76 beats per minute for

3 Conversation with composer.
4 Ibid.
5 Ibid.
6 Ibid.

the quarter note on the last two measures, and he suggests the last chord be held out—"add a *tenuto* marking to the last note." "The last three chords," Nelson remarks, "were an affirmation...like three pounds of a fist on the table."[7]

Morning Alleluias for the Winter Solstice is 138 measures long and is approximately five minutes and thirty seconds in duration. It is published by Ludwig Music.

Unit 3: Historical Perspective

In twentieth century art, *minimalism* is defined as a movement and/or style that stresses the idea of reducing a work of art to its basic or minimum number of shapes, colors, values, and/or textures. In late twentieth century music, minimalism is defined as a compositional style characterized by short melodic and rhythmic figures combined with a steady pulsing beat. Minimalistic music employs a large amount of repetition, sometimes with variations that are barely perceptible. Compositions of this nature tend to emphasize simplicity in melodic line and harmony. It is also termed "process music." Nelson remarks, "All that remains identifiable with minimalism in my music is my use of *ostinati*."[8]

Ever since a visit to the Orient in the 1960s, Nelson has been enchanted and influenced by the distinctive music of its culture. "The gliding tones seen in the beginning of the composition (trombone and vocal "slow *glissando*") came directly from music I heard in Japan, called Gagaku. The Japanese use a lot of those gliding tones in their music."[9] Although sometimes heard at Shinto-shrines or Japanese-style wedding ceremonies, Gagaku is a form of Japanese classical music that has been performed at the Japanese Imperial Court for over a millennium. Rooted in the musical styles of ancient China and Korea, Gagaku was first performed by nobles and professional musicians who belonged to hereditary guilds in the eighth century. Although it is presumed that the music, as well as its style of performance, has been subjected to natural change over the one thousand years it has been practiced in Japan, it is one of the strongest surviving music traditions in Asia. The musicians of the Japanese Imperial Palace Music Department serve as teachers of this ancient tradition. They are, for the most part, descendents of members of the original hereditary guilds.

Thrust into the atomic age at the end of World War II, Hiroshima, Japan, and the rest of the world were to witness the horror and utter destruction of life and landscape on August 6, 1945. The atomic bomb, "Little Boy," was dropped on Hiroshima by the Enola Gay, a Boeing B-29 bomber, at 8:15 in the morning on that fateful day. Japan surrendered soon thereafter.

7 Ibid.
8 Ibid.
9 Ibid.

Born in Somersby, Lincolnshire, England, in 1809, Alfred Tennyson had established himself as the most popular poet of the Victorian era by age forty-one. The money from his poetry (sometimes exceeding 10,000 pounds per year) allowed him to write in relative seclusion. In 1884, he accepted a peerage, becoming Alfred Lord Tennyson. He died in 1892 at age eighty-three, and was buried in Westminster Abbey—the famous London historical site where kings and queens, statesmen, warriors, scientists, musicians, and poets have been buried through the ages.

Nelson borrowed the first four and eighth stanzas from the "Ring Out, Wild Bells" section of Tennyson's poem *In Memoriam, A.H.H.*, for text in his choral work, *Ring Out, Wild Bells*. The five (of eight total) stanzas used from Section CVI are quoted almost word for word; the stanzas do not appear in the same order. Nelson substitutes the word "world" for "Christ" in the last line.

In Memoriam, A.H.H., begun in 1833 and published in 1850, is considered one of Alfred Lord Tennyson's major poetic achievements. All of the 131 sections are separate poems, and together serve as an elegy mourning the unexpected death of his friend and poet, Arthur Henry Hallam. Hallam was engaged to marry Tennyson's sister Emily when he died suddenly of a stroke in Vienna on September 15, 1833, at the age of twenty-two. In literary circles, *In Memoriam, A.H.H.* is often used as an example of an elegy—a melancholy poem lamenting its subject's death but ending in consolation. In poetry, the "In Memoriam" stanza is a quatrain (rhyming four-line stanza) with a rhyme scheme of "a–b–b–a." This rhyme scheme is sometimes termed "envelope" or "enclosed." Written in iambic tetrameter, it is named after Alfred Lord Tennyson's poem of the same name.

Below are the stanzas Nelson borrowed from *In Memoriam, A.H.H.*, for his choral work "Ring Out, Wild Bells" from *Three Pieces after Tennyson*.

Ring out, wild bells, to the wild sky,
The flying cloud, the frosty light;
The year is dying in the night;
Ring out, wild bells, and let him die.
Ring out the old, ring in the new,
Ring, happy bells, across the snow:
The year is going, let him go;
Ring out the false, ring in the true.

Ring out the grief that saps the mind,
For those that here we see no more,
Ring out the feud of rich and poor,
Ring in redress to all mankind.

Ring out a slowly dying cause,
And ancient forms of party strife;
Ring in the nobler modes of life,
With sweeter manners, purer laws.

Ring in the valiant man and free,
The larger heart, the kindlier hand;
Ring out the darkness of the land,
Ring in the World (Christ) that is to be.

The Winter Solstice marks the shortest day and the longest night of the year. The sun appears at its lowest point in the sky, and its noontime elevation appears to be the same for several days before and after the solstice. The origin of the word "solstice" is derived from the Latin word "solstitium," which translates to "sol" (sun) and "stitium" (to cause to stand still). Following the Winter Solstice, the days grow longer and the nights shorter. In the Northern Hemisphere, the Winter Solstice occurs around December 21 or 22, when the sun shines directly over the Tropic of Capricorn. The Summer Solstice (longest day and shortest night) occurs around June 21 or 22, when the sun shines directly over the Tropic of Cancer. In the Southern Hemisphere, the winter and summer solstices are reversed.

Many cultures have celebrated the middle of winter for centuries, especially the northern latitudes. The importance of agriculture in early societies made the seasons very important to their celebrations. Spring and summer were times of new growth and life, and fall was the time of the harvest. Winter, generally a cold and dark time of year, was a time of little sunlight. With the approach of the Winter Solstice, and the time of year when light returns, celebrations and traditions of all kinds materialized to honor the sun back to its full strength. The importance of the lights of Hanukkah and Christmas can be said to have Solstice origins. In Europe, the tradition of the Yule log is celebrated on Winter Solstice. A special log is brought in and placed on the hearth where it glows for the twelve nights of the holiday season. The Christmas tree also dates from old European or pagan rituals. It was the time to celebrate the renewal of the earth, and greens (trees) were used as its symbol. Red candles were used to symbolize the fire and heat of the returning sun as the days begin to lengthen. The ancient Romans celebrated Saturnalia, an event honoring Saturn, the god of agriculture. This special celebration was a time of feasting, gift giving, and visiting friends. Evergreen trees were covered with fruit and other decorations, and candles became popular gifts to give.

Unit 4: Technical Considerations

Morning Alleluias for the Winter Solstice was written for the Tokyo Kosei Wind Orchestra and uses the following instrumentation: piccolo, three flutes, two oboes, English horn, two bassoons, contrabassoon, E-flat soprano clarinet (part does not appear in score—doubles the piccolo), four B-flat soprano clarinets, two E-flat alto saxophones, B-flat tenor saxophone, E-flat baritone saxophone, four B-flat trumpets, four horns, four trombones, tuba, and string bass (cued in other instruments). There is no euphonium part. Other color instruments include four-hand piano (one piano—two players) and celesta (written in the 2nd piano part). Percussion requirements are somewhat extensive: timpani, glockenspiel, crotales, vibraphone, marimba, sleigh bells, triangle, crash cymbals, bell tree, bell chimes (wind chimes), bass drum, attached cymbal, and gong. Outside of the piano parts, the actual percussion parts can be covered with six players. The vibraphone part requires two players in the initial forty-four measures.

Upon first review, the work appears to be relatively straightforward and technically accessible by good high school bands and second bands at the university level. Further study will reveal exposed solos in oboe, English horn, and French horn; the need to read tenor clef (1st/2nd trombone and bassoon); and upper range requirements for 1st trumpet (E-flat above the staff), 2nd trumpet (A above the staff), 3rd trumpet (B above the staff), 1st horn (B above the staff), and 1st trombone (F-sharp above the staff). Although there is no key signature, some players experience up to seven sharps in selected passages (alto saxophones). Clarinets will need to use cross fingerings to maneuver smoothly between B-natural and C-sharp above the break. The 3rd and 4th horn parts are written in bass clef for two measures.

On most all of the parts, there are modest singing requirements in the opening forty-four measures. Players are asked to sing or vocalize long, held-out tones on the syllable "Lu." These vocal passages, all unison, are written in concert pitch no matter on what part they appear. This can be confusing to players if not explained ahead of time. (It is recommended that the conductor study the individual parts.) This integral vocal line should be heard clearly at all times. For large ensembles with many players per part, cutting down to one/two players per part will help balance this line. With different voice types singing the same note, octaves will most likely sound displaced rather than a unison pitch. "While octave displacement is okay," Nelson advises that "care should be taken to maintain the source."[10] When sliding from one pitch to another, be sure to define the exact placement of the new sound. The 1st or 2nd trombone part (muted) is almost always playing with the vocal line.

---

10 Ibid.

An experienced percussion section is needed for the marimba, xylophone, vibraphone, and bell parts, even though many of the technical passages are repeated patterns. Percussionists should know how to "pull" sound from a vibraphone bar using a string bow. (Note: Start moving the bow before the sound is to be heard so it will sound in time.) Nelson also recommends that conductors adapt the work for the instruments available in their bands, especially in the area of percussion. "If you don't have enough bodies, adapt it for the people you do have...and for their technique. That's what I call creative adaptation."[11]

In the opening twenty-three measures, an illusion of timelessness is created with overlapping *ostinato* patterns in the percussion section and the use of spacial notation in trumpet, bass clarinet, English horn, and oboe. In spacial notation, noteheads are clustered at various distances from one another. This distance is relative to the placement of the sound. The further apart the noteheads appear, the more time is taken between the articulated sounds. The closer the noteheads, the faster the sounds are articulated. Because this technique fosters an absence of time, players easily can lose sense of where they are in the measure or phrase if not observant. Nelson describes this type of notation as "free form notes." "The absence of pulse that is created with this effect formulates a motive that I associate with eternity or timelessness."[12] Originally written for one to a part, these passages should be articulated with clarity and brought out of the underlying texture, especially the initial sounds of each entrance.

For young flute players, playing lyrical passages at a soft dynamic in the upper register can be quite challenging. If using multiple players per part, the conductor may want to reduce to one on a part in the opening section to help balance and bring out the shifting tonal colors.

The second half of the work is joyous and "alleluia-like" in nature, and it has a rhythmic structure that is essentially grouped in simple repeated combinations of accented quarter, eighth, and sixteenth notes. Precise placement of each eighth note will ensure rhythmic and melodic transparency.

Unit 5: Stylistic Considerations

There's no doubt that Nelson's studies at Eastman had a profound influence on his writing for band. "In my writing now, you might find an avoidance of the 'typical band sound.' At Joliet I was part of a large, Revelli-style band program—you know, a lot of people with a 'sea' of clarinets in the band. I had that sound in my ear when I composed my first work for band and piano at age seventeen."[13]

---

11 Ibid.
12 Ibid.
13 Ibid.

At Eastman, Nelson was exposed to a new transparent, yet compact sound in the form of the Eastman Wind Ensemble (under Frederick Fennell). This new sound was soon to become infused into Nelson's musical consciousness. "The old Revelli-style sound did not appeal to me anymore. It wasn't transparent enough."[14]

There are no heavy textures or thick sonorities in *Morning Alleluias for the Winter Solstice*. Even with the underlying *ostinato* patterns, clarity and simplicity of line are very evident in the opening passages. To ensure an effective performance, care should be taken to keep everything within the noted dynamic context. In the lyrical *legato* passages, students should be encouraged to play in a connected style as if they were indeed singing the passage (both primary and secondary material). Tonguing should be accomplished in a light manner using a "du" or "da" tongue stroke. Tubas can use "doe."

With the establishment of the new tempo at measure 45, lightness of articulation and unison/octave blending is imperative. There is a great deal of doubling between the woodwinds and keyboard instruments. Articulating tongued passages in a light, detached manner will help reinforce clarity. Ideally, you want to mimic the lightness of the mallets striking the keyboards. It is recommended that the conductor define the types of accents, styles markings, and lengths of all notes within individual passages. Accented notes should be approached in a separated, "lifted" manner. Nelson notes, "It's okay to think of the text from *Ring Out, Wild Bells* at Rehearsal 56. The rhythm of the work is generated by the words. It makes a nice springboard into the instrumental sound. 'Ring out wild bells, ring out wild bells.'"[15]

Unit 6: Musical Elements

MELODY:

Phrase lengths in *Morning Alleluias for the Winter Solstice* are generally four to eight measures. For young players, the challenge in the opening section will be to sustain and express melodic and non-melodic material at the various *piano* dynamic levels. Mature ensembles will accomplish long, quiet, sustained passages with a well-developed approach to breathing and tonal support as well. Conductor and students should have an understanding of the hierarchy of balance so that secondary material is always subordinate to the melody. This is especially true when secondary material is in the same register as the melody. The initial lyrical solo lines may need to be adjusted "up" one dynamic level in the beginning, notably the French horn in measure 7, and English horn in measure 15, especially if the other wind parts are doubled.

Expressive music is characterized by its ability to communicate through nuances of phrasing, tempo, articulation, dynamics, style, and sound. The

---

14 Ibid.
15 Ibid.

"ebb and flow" of the phrasing is critical to the understanding of expression. One way Nelson has approached this is through the consistent and thoughtful use of dynamic markings. He is very specific in his use of *crescendo* and *diminuendo* markings to aid in the contour or shape of the musical line. Because composers leave many interpretive decisions up to conductors, there are a few basic rules of musical expression that can be followed. Repeated notes should *crescendo* or *decrescendo*, all phrases should have some type of dynamic contour, and long notes should sound into rests or the next sound. In slow music, mature players will let the last note "sound" while taking a breath. Students should be discouraged from breathing collectively at the ends of measures, or bar lines, unless at the end of a phrase. "Stagger breathing" should be encouraged whenever possible, especially in the opening forty-four measures. Nelson marks this in the score and on most parts as well. This is critical for both melodic and supportive material in slow tempi. In slow music, bar lines tend to act as visual barriers for students. For *crescendos* occurring across a bar line, ask students to pretend they are "pushing the bar line over with their air stream, as if it were a gate, so it falls to the right."

Once the tempo picks up, many layers of musical material are presented at one time. The conductor should isolate and rehearse each musical idea separately. When a slur connects a series of eighth or sixteenth notes in fast passages (e.g., measures 52 through 63, piccolo and clarinets), students should be encouraged to "lift," lighten, or shorten the last note in the grouping. This, along with a light separated tonguing style, will help establish an overall sense of lightness.

HARMONY:

Morning Alleluias for the Winter Solstice is both homophonic (one melodic line over chords or secondary material) and polyphonic (two or more significant melodic lines appearing together). Texturally, musical lines and ideas are generally grouped together within "families" of instruments. There is an absence of "first parts only" playing the same melodic line. Nelson remarks, "I realized the sound of the band has such beautiful potential with all the available colors of each of the instruments. It's hard to imagine the potential of the band without having a choice of those sonorities."[16]

Harmonically, the composition is centered around certain notes or "centricities," which sometimes hint to key centers or modes. "I never embraced twelve-tone techniques. And, any serial techniques that I have used are not really all that dissonant. I love melodies and the wonderful play of harmony when you make nice chords connect nice chords to nice chords."[17]

For centuries, much of Western music has been based on church modes, which are directly related to what we refer to as scales. Three of the seven

---

16 Ibid.
17 Ibid.

basic church modes correspond to major scales, and four correspond to minor scales. Two of the seven basic modes are identical to our descriptions of the major scale (ionian) and the natural minor scale (aeolian). Modes can begin on any pitch and are defined by the sequence of their individual whole- and half-step patterns.

Using only the white keys on the piano as an example, the seven basic modes and their whole and half-step sequences would appear as follows:

C–C = Ionian

(whole step, whole step, half step, whole step, whole step, whole step, half step)

D–D = Dorian

(whole step, half step, whole step, whole step, whole step, half step, whole step)

E–E = Phrygian

(half step, whole step, whole step, whole step, half step, whole step, whole step)

F–F = Lydian

(whole step, whole step, whole step, half step, whole step, whole step, half step)

G–G = Mixolydian

(whole step, whole step, half step, whole step, whole step, half step, whole step)

A–A = Aeolian

(whole step, half step, whole step, whole step, half step, whole step, whole step)

B–B = Locrian

(half step, whole step, whole step, half step, whole step, whole step, whole step)

The mixolydian, dorian, ionian, and aeolian modes are the most common. Modes are determined by their linear structure (melodic material) more so than their vertical structure (harmony).

Much of the material for *Morning Alleluias for the Winter Solstice* is constructed using the E mixolydian, E ionian, G mixolydian, and G aeolian modes.

For an example, consider the E mixolydian mode. The E mixolydian mode contains half steps that occur between the third and fourth scale degrees (3–4) and the sixth and seventh scale degrees (6–7). The mixolydian mode corresponds to the scale constructed from the fifth degree of any major scale. For example, if you take the A major scale (three sharps: F-sharp, C-sharp, G-sharp) and find the fifth scale degree (E), you can build the mixolydian mode using the next seven tones in that key (e.g., E, F-sharp, G-sharp, A, B, C-sharp, D, E). The half steps occur between the G-sharp and A (3–4) and the C-sharp and D (6–7).

Teaching Strategy – Distribute staff paper to students. Using a chalkboard or dry-erase board, draw four staffs. You will also need a large picture of a piano keyboard. Discuss the relationship of the white and black keys on the piano (half steps and whole steps). Next, have students write their respective clefs on their staff paper for four separate lines/staffs. On the first staff, have students build an A major scale (A ionian) one octave up and down in half notes, starting on A above middle C and repeating the upper note (A, B, C-sharp, D, E, F-sharp, G-sharp, A, A, G-sharp, F-sharp, E, D, C-sharp, B, A). Tell students to mark the pitches where the half steps occur (3–4, 7–8, 8–7, 4–3). Then have students transpose the mode for their instrument on the second staff.

On the third staff, have students build an E mixolydian scale (one octave up and down in half notes, again starting on above C, and repeating the upper note (E, F-sharp, G-sharp, A, B, C-sharp, D, E, E, D, C-sharp, B, A, G-sharp, F-sharp, E). Tell students to mark the pitches where the half steps occur (3–4, 6–7, and 2–3, 5–6). Have students transpose the mode for their instrument on the fourth staff.

Once this is done, you can play and sing each scale/mode. Divide the band into sections and have half play and half sing. Discuss the relationship of modes and tonal centers. How are they different and similar?

RHYTHM:

In the opening forty-four measures of the composition, the meter changes often, though the quarter note pulse remains constant. For those students playing the opening "free form note" passages, a sense of independence coupled with an overall sense of time and phrasing is needed. A stand partner can help keep track of "time" or pulse. Students can practice independence of playing outside of class on their own with a metronome and tape recorder. Record the precise number of quarter notes for each phrase. Improvise by playing the "free form notes" over this pulse.

Because the second half of the work is extremely rhythmic and pulse-oriented, students are encouraged to practice using a metronome set at a slower tempo in the early learning stages. Encourage students to work for rhythmic subdivision and alignment. In fast tempi, tied note passages can be problematic. Young players may have a tendency to "cheat" the rhythm. To help combat this, disregard the tie and tongue all the notes until the students are able to achieve good subdivision and clarity. Add the tie back in when appropriate. A common rule used with ties in fast music is to stop the sound, or create a small break, when you reach the note connected by the tie. This is the opposite of slow music; in slow music, the sounds should meld into one another. Once students have established a good sense of internal pulse, disregard the metronome. Encourage students to listen for lines different from their own. The wind players should listen back to the percussion section in this work. Mature players make a point to know where the melody is located and how their part fits into the total structure. In time, this makes for a more challenging and rewarding performance atmosphere.

Teaching Strategy – Notation is one way of structuring music so multiple players or singers can perform the same or like material at the same time, every single time. Not all cultures use the same notation styles. Improvisation demonstrates how every performance can be slightly different. "Spatial notation" is a way to include improvisatory skills within a loose notated structure.

> Activity #1: Have one student draw an abstract picture of lines, colors, curves, dots, etc., on a piece of paper. Draw from the left side of the paper to the right. Next, have another student "interpret" the drawing musically using voice or instrument. Have another student interpret the drawing through dance or physical movement.

> Activity #2: Play a piece of music and have the students "notate" it using lines, colors, curves, objects, etc. Explore the relationship between our surroundings and music. Discuss the relationship between objects, emotions, and sounds. What would represent the ocean? A blue sky? Rain? Anger? Sadness?

TIMBRE:

In those bands we recognize as "superior," students have acquired a basic understanding of quality tone production. In addition, they perceive the mechanics of pitch matching (a continual decision-making process), and they know how to blend or fuse sounds together when required. These skills require students to be discriminating listeners: to themselves, to those close at hand, and to those across the ensemble.

Teaching Strategy – Developing an excellent characteristic sound in all dynamic levels and tempi should be a priority. Over the years, long-tone studies have been used to foster good breath support, a requisite for good tone. Here is another exercise that allows the teacher to check breath support (i.e., air speed) and articulation at the same time.

1. Select or write an exercise that has unison rhythmic complexities. This material can include leaps, or notes that cross the break (clarinet).

2. Have students stand and then sit down in their chairs with both feet on the floor. Their torso should still be "standing up."

3. Have students play the desired passage. Do not try to correct anything.

4. Next, have the students "play" it again by only blowing air through their horns while they articulate. Tell them to tongue the passage as if

they were producing a sound, but no buzzing or tones should be produced. Amazingly, you will be able to tell if their air stream is full and supported (steady, warm rush) or weak (barely audible). It is difficult to support a good tone, play over the clarinet break, or slur intervals on brass instruments with a weak air stream. Fast, warm air is needed. With just air passing through the instruments, it also becomes easier to hear how the students are tonguing or articulating the passages. If there is no clarity, then the air stream is weak.

5. Repeat the air-only exercise, and tell the students to push the air with energy while they tongue. This will also send the air through the horn faster. You should be able to hear the tongued articulations as audible interruptions in the air stream.

6. Once you achieve the desired air stream strength and articulation, have the students repeat the exercise, this time with tone production. More often than not, you will be amazed at how much their sound and technique improves.

Unit 7: Form and Structure

MEASURE   EVENT AND SCORING

MM = 69 (Nelson recommends MM = 58–60)

1–6	*Ostinato* (D–E); singing parts (B–E); centricity is E; "free form" notes move to and away from E; *p, pp, ppp*
7–11	French horn solo (melody A part 1) centers around C centricity; horn begins move to C lydian over E pedal; oboe solo (melody A, part 2) in m. 9 centers around G centricity; *mf, p, pp*
12–20	C lydian established by m. 12 in woodwind chords and brass *ostinati*; *mf, p, pp, ppp*
21–43	Melody A continues in French horn; woodwind lyrical motive grouped: clarinet/flute–oboe; settling of opening material; percussion ostinati continues; *ppp, pp, p, mf, f*
44 C	major triad with added ninth completes slow section and foreshadows end of work; *pp*

MM = 132 (Nelson recommends MM = 126)

MEASURE	EVENT AND SCORING
45–51	Pitches A and E are sustained to set new tonal area; *p, pp, ppp*
52–55	Motor rhythm begins in woodwinds, keyboard percussion, and piano; first hint of E mixolydian, dynamic change in m. 54 with low brass/low woodwind accent; *f, sffz*
56–63	Two additional melodic rhythmic figures enter—brass: 1st through 4th trumpet, 1st through 4th horn, 1st and 2nd trombone; and saxophones: 1st and 2nd alto, tenor, baritone; main melody in brass (Ring Out, Wild Bells); *f, fp*
64–73	Texture thins; shift to E ionian; new woodwind melody (melody D) supported by sustained E in 3rd French horn; *pp, p, mf, f*
72–81	Material from mm. 56–64 repeated almost verbatim; some differences appear in low brass/low woodwinds; back to E mixolydian; *mf, fp, f*
82–92	Reduction in texture; shift to G mixolydian; melody in upper woodwinds; absence of percussion; *pp, mf, f*
93–95	Shift to E mixolydian; first ending; motor rhythms reappear; *f, ff, fff*; repeat back to m. 56
96–97	A major triad with added B and F-sharp pitches in trombone (second ending)
98–99	Shift to C and G centricities
100–107	Five rhythm groups; similar material to phrases seen in mm. 56 and 72; piccolo line is new; shift to G mixolydian; *mf, f, ff, sffz*
108–115	Two rhythm groups; woodwinds and percussion, with intermittent trumpet; shift to G aeolian; *mp, f, mf*
116–123	Five rhythm groups; similar material to phrases at mm. 56 and 72; shift to G mixolydian; *f, ff, fff*
124–127	Sustained chords; motor rhythm; shifting to C ionian; *ff, fff*
128–133	C ionian established; hint of F ionian, back to C ionian; motor rhythms in woodwinds, keyboard percussion, and piano; diffuse to long quarter and eighth notes; *fff*

(Note: Correct the 1st trumpet C-flat to C-natural.)

Errata:

Conductors score, m. 17:   Change the treble clef to bass clef in the timpani part.

Percussion 2 part: Add "gong" and "triangle" to the list of instruments needed.

Alto saxophone part, m. 68:   Add a sharp to the C-natural.

Unit 8: Suggested Listening

Works for band:

Yasuhide Ito, *Gloriosa*

David Maslanka, *Golden Light*

Ron Nelson:

> *Aspen Jubilee*
>
> *Chaconne (In Memoriam…)*
>
> *Courtly Airs and Dances*
>
> *Epiphanies (Fanfares and Chorales)*
>
> *Holiday and Epiphanies – The Music of Ron Nelson*
>> Dallas Wind Symphony, Jerry Junkin and Ron Nelson, conductors (RR-76CD)
>
> *Lauds (Praise High Day)*
>
> *Morning Alleluias for the Winter Solstice – Piece of Mind*: Tokyo Kosei Wind Orchestra, Frederick Fennell, conductor (KOCD-3569)
>
> *Passacaglia (Homage to B-A-C-H)*
>
> *Rocky Point Holiday*
>
> *Sonoran Desert Holiday*

Bernard Rogers, *Three Japanese Dances*

Works for choir:

Ron Nelson:

> *Processional and Prayer of Emperor of China on the Altar of Heaven, December 21, 1539*
>
> "Ring Out, Wild Bells" from *Three Pieces after Tennyson* (for TTBB or SATB chorus and instruments)

Unit 9: Additional References and Resources

Blum, David. *Casals and the Art of Interpretation*. Berkley, Los Angeles, CA: University of California Press, 1977.

Cope, David. *New Directions in Music*. Seventh edition. Prospect Heights, IL: Waveland Press, 2000.

Dallin, Leon. *Twentieth Century Composition*. Third edition. Dubuque, IA: William C. Brown Company Publishers, 1974.

Dvorak, Thomas L., Robert Grechesky, and Gary Ciepluch. *Best Music for High School Band*. Brooklyn, NY: Manhattan Beach Music, 1993.

Fennell, Frederick. *Time and the Winds*. Kenosha, WI: LeBlanc Educational Publications.

Harnsberger, Lindsey C. *Essential Dictionary of Music*. Second edition. Los Angeles, CA: Alfred Publishing Co., Inc., 1997.

Labuta, Joseph A. *Teaching Musicianship in the High School Band*. Ft. Lauderdale, FL: Meredith Music Publications, 1977.

Lisk, Edward. *The Creative Director: Intangibles of Musical Performance*. Ft. Lauderdale, FL: Meredith Music Publications, 1996.

Miles, Richard, ed. *Teaching Music through Performance in Band*, Volume 3. Chicago, IL: GIA Publications, Inc., 2000.

Nelson, Ron. Telephone conversations with composer. September and October 2001.

Peterson, Stephen. "Profile of Composer Ron Nelson," *The Instrumentalist*, Vol. XLVIII, June 1994, p. 49.

Read, Gardner. *Modern Rhythmic Notation*. Indiana: Indiana University Press. 1978.

Rehrig, William H. *The Heritage Encyclopedia of Band Music*, Volume II. Edited by Paul Bierley. Westerville, OH: Integrity Press, 1991.

Thurmond, James. *Note Grouping*. Detroit, MI: Harlo Press, 1982.

Vandercook, H. A. *Expression in Music*. Revised edition. Chicago: 1992; Rubank, Inc., 1962.

Contributed by:

Linda R. Moorhouse
Associate Director of Bands
Louisiana State University
Baton Rouge, Louisiana

Teacher Resource Guide

Pastorale Nocturne

Bruce Yurko
(b. 1951)

Unit 1: Composer

Bruce Yurko has composed more than a dozen works for large wind ensemble or band. Performances at many regional and five national wind conductors conferences have included his works. In 1978, his *Chant and Toccata* received the first prize at the Virginia CBDNA and Southeastern Composers League Symposium III for New Band Music.

Yurko holds a Bachelor of Science in Music Education from Wilkes University in Wilkes-Barre, Pennsylvania, where he studied horn with Douglas Hill. Although Wilkes offered no composition classes, Yurko completed fifteen works there, including three for wind ensemble. While at Wilkes, he began a correspondence with Vincent Persichetti. He sent Persichetti scores and tapes of his works, and Persichetti responded with letters commenting on them. He said of Yurko's Horn Concerto, "You and I agree on how to write for percussion." Yurko also earned a Master of Music in Horn Performance with a Composition minor from Ithaca College in New York. There he was a horn student of John Covert and composition student of Karel Husa.

Yurko's works for wind ensemble include *Concerto for Wind Ensemble*, *Concerto for Horn and Wind Ensemble*, *Chant and Toccata*, *Concerto for Trombone and Wind Ensemble*, *Danza*, *Divertimento*, *Incantations*, *Night Dances*, *In Memoriam: Kristina*, *Arias*, *Rituals*, *Celebrations*, *Concerto for Percussion and Wind Ensemble*, *Elegy for Wind Symphony*, *Episodes*, *Pastorale Nocturne*, *Sinfonietta for Wind Ensemble*, *Concerto for Bassoon and Wind Ensemble*, and *Intrada*. Most of his earlier works were more complicated and appropriate for performance by the most professional wind ensembles. With *Incantations, Celebrations, Rituals, Episodes, Elegy, Night Dances, Intrada, Pastorale Nocturne,* and *In Memoriam,* Yurko's style has become simpler, triadic, and more accessible to school bands at both the middle school and high school levels. Recently, Southern Music published *Pastorale Nocturne* and Ludwig Music has published *Night Dances* and *In Memoriam: Kristina.*

Yurko directs the wind ensembles at Cherry Hill East and West High Schools in New Jersey. For nine years, he also played horn in the Philharmonic Society of Northeastern Pennsylvania as well as the North Jersey Wind Quintet. Yurko was appointed conductor of the Princeton University Wind Ensemble in September of 2000.

Unit 2: Composition

In 1996, Robert Bazzel, Director of Bands at Sterling High School in Runnemede, New Jersey, commissioned *Pastorale Nocturne* in memory of Miss Jennifer Persia. Jennifer was a clarinetist as well as a member of the marching band's color guard section.

The outer sections of *Pastorale Nocturne* serve as an elegy, while the center section has a march-like quality.

Pastorale Nocturne encompasses many of the emotions that remain from this tragedy—both the joy and the energy of Jennifer's life as well as the sadness and despair that many continue to feel.

Unit 3: Historical Perspective

Beginning with Mendelssohn's *Trauer Marsch* (1836) and Berlioz's *Symphonie funebre et triomphale* (1890), many composers have chosen large groups of winds and percussion to remember the dead. There are Requiems by Henry Brandt, Julius Fucik, Paul Gerhardt, Quincy Hilliard, Alan Hovhaness, Vaclav Nelhybel, Sepp Thaler, Fisher Tull, and Urato Watanabe. Grieg's *Trauermasche* and Wagner's *Trauersinfonie* are notable amoung the many funeral marches composed for bands.

In the twentieth century, the genre includes Warren Benson's *The Passing Bell*; Andrew Boysen's *I Am* and *Conversations with the Night*; Jacob Druckman's *Paean* and *In Memoriam Vincent Persichetti*; Walter Hartley's *In Memoriam*; David Holsinger's *Consider the Uncommon Man*; Martin Mailman's *For Precious Friends Hid in Death's Dateless Night* and *A Simple Ceremony – In Memoriam John Barnes Chance*; W. Francis McBeth's *Kaddish*; Frank Ticheli's *Amazing Grace, Postcard (to Meadville),* and *An American Elegy*; and Bruce Yurko's *In Memoriam: Kristina, Elegy,* and *Pastorale Nocturne,* all composed in memory of indivduals. Larry Austin's *In Memoriam: John F. Kennedy,* James Curnow's *J. F. K. In Memoriam,* and Ronald LoPresti's *Elegy for a Young American* were composed in memory of the fallen president.

Works in memory of fallen soldiers make up an important subgenera: James Barnes's *Lonely Beach*; Daniel Bukvich's *Symphony No. 1 (In Memoriam Dresden, 1945)*; David Gillingham's *Heroes, Lost and Fallen*; John Paulson's *Epinicion*; and James Swearingen's *The Light Eternal*. Mark Camphouse, John Barnes Chance, Gustav Holst, Karel Husa, Bin Kaneda, James Morissey, Roger Nixon, and Jack Stamp all have composed works with the term "elegy" in the title.

Unit 4: Technical Considerations

Pastorale Nocturne's instrumentation is for full wind ensemble: piccolo, 1st/2nd/3rd flute, 1st/2nd oboe, 1st/2nd/3rd B-flat soprano clarinet (divisi), B-flat bass clarinet, 1st/2nd bassoon, 1st/2nd E-flat alto saxophone, B-flat tenor saxophone, E-flat baritone saxophone, 1st/2nd/3rd/4th B-flat trumpet, 1st/2nd/3rd/4th horn in F, 1st/2nd/3rd trombone, euphonium, tuba, piano, and percussion. The score requires eight percussion players to play the following instruments: four timpani, four tom-toms, snare drum, field drum, crash cymbals, bass drum (head up), gong, xylophone, chimes, and two vibraphones (motors on, two players or one player with four mallets). Two chime players are required in several measures.

Meters of 4/4, 3/4, and 4/4 followed by 2/4 and cut-time are used. Tempo markings include *Adagio* (quarter note = 60), *subito* tempo changes of *Vivace* (quarter note = 160) and a march tempo of half note = 72+. The trumpet and trombone players must have whisper mutes. Cup mutes may be substituted, but this is not what the composer intended, as the sudden color change will be missed.

The manuscript full score was written in concert pitch. There are no key signatures in either full score or parts. All parts are written within the normal range of the high school wind ensemble or band.

Unit 5: Stylistic Considerations

Pastorale Nocturne was composed for the memory of Miss Jennifer Persia. The outer sections serve as an elegy. The solo oboe and solo flute represent Jennifer's two closest friends. "*Molto espressivo*" interpretation is required from both solo instrumentalists. They are in conversation remembering Jennifer.

The percussion "dirge" must be well balanced. The dynamic level of the gongs must be one of *piano* so as not to overshadow the timpani *glissandos* and solo oboe and flute. The chorale performance must be chorally balanced.

The center section "*alla marcia*" reflects Jennifer's love of the marching band and color guard. She had a wonderful sense of humor as well as being a very serious musician. A march-like style is presented. Dynamics, phrasing, articulations, balance, and blending of instrumental colors are of the utmost importance.

Unit 6: Musical Elements

Yurko prefers a whole consort approach to orchestration. Balance within the percussion ensemble is essential. Timpani *glissandos* must be heard. The bass drum should be in the "head up" position, and the piano lid should be removed. The placement of the two vibraphones and chimes are crucial to the "dirge" theme but should not overpower the solo oboe and flute. The chorale writing is triadic with major and minor shifts in color.

The arpeggio effect at measure 90 requires that all instrumentalists listen as they hold their particular note. With only three full scoring events for the wind ensemble (measures 119 through 126, 141 through 150, and 157 through 165), a chamber music setting is in place. At measure 215, the brass choir B-flat major chord should strive for a *diminuendo* so the clarinet choir C major chord entrance is hidden and suddenly appears.

Unit 7: Form and Structure

Measure	Event and Scoring
1–11	*Adagio* (quarter note = 60); timpani *glissandos*; bass drum introduces the "march theme"; piano arpeggio (march pitches)
12–15	Piano, vibraphone, and trumpet (whisper mutes) introduce the "dirge theme"
16–24	Oboe solo accompanied by the "dirge theme"
25–28	Flute solo accompanied by the "dirge theme" and B-flat clarinet performing the "dirge theme" (echo tone)
29–32	Clarinet solo accompanied by muted trumpet and percussion "dirge theme"
33–39	Return to oboe solo and "dirge theme"
40–71	Chorale; based upon the oboe solo motive; chorale statement presented by the clarinet choir, with addition of the flute choir, and return to the clarinet choir; second statement is presented by the brass choir, woodwind choir, horn choir, with a final return to the clarinet choir; under the chorales, bass drum continues the" march" motive
72–84	Oboe and flute duet with the return of the "dirge theme"
85–89	Original introduction (gong, timpani, and bass drum), bell choir dirge chord; tom-toms introduce new sudden tempo

MEASURE	EVENT AND SCORING
90–91	*Subito vivace* tempo (quarter note = 160); meter of 4+2; piano arpeggio at m. 6 (march pitches) for full wind ensemble; *ff* dynamic
92–93	*Subito adagio* tempo with percussion "dirge' motive and woodwind choir holding previous chord at a *piano dim.* level as background
94–99	*Subito vivace* tempo with three presentations of piano arpeggio (march pitches) for full wind ensemble
100–118	*Subito* cut-time at half note = 72+; march theme introduced by brass choir, woodwind choir with oboe and flute solos
119–126	Wind ensemble statement of march material
127–165	Trio section; mixed meter with statements from brass choir, wind ensemble, and solo tuba, with a return of the wind ensemble presenting a variant of the trio
166–181	March theme returns to solo brass (trumpet, trombone, euphonium, and tuba), oboe solo, saxophone quartet, oboe and flute duet with horn accompaniant
182–193	Wind quartet (solo flute, clarinet, bassoon, and horn) march presentation; solo flute with woodwinds and muted (whisper) trumpet and trombone, with a *ritard.* to the *adagio* tempo
194–214	*Adagio* tempo restatement of "dirge" theme with oboe and flute duet; final oboe solo and percussion entrance
215–218	B-flat chord (horn, trombone, euphonium, and tuba); bass drum march motive; hidden entrance of the clarinet choir C chord with a final bass drum march motive solo(B-flat and C chords are the first two chords of the chorale)

Unit 8: Suggested Listening

Yurko, Bruce. *Chant and Toccata.* Eugene Migliaro Corporon, West Virginia University Wind Ensemble. Tawes Theatre, College Park, MD. Crest CBDNA-77-2.

Yurko, Bruce. *Chant and Toccata.* Visions of the Twentieth Century. Eugene Migliaro Corporon, The Symphonic Band of the University of Wisconsin School of Music at Madison. Century KM-1932.

Yurko, Bruce. *Chant and Toccata*. Internal Combustion. Jack Stamp, Indiana University of Pennsylvania Wind Ensemble. Klavier.

Yurko, Bruce. *Concerto for Percussion and Wind Ensemble*. Whiplash. Jack Stamp, Indiana University of Pennsylvania Wind Ensemble. Klavier K 11115.

Yurko, Bruce. *Divertimento for Wind Ensemble*. Eugene Migliaro Corporon, University of Northern Colorado Wind Ensemble. Crest CBDNA-81-2.

Yurko, Bruce. *In Memoriam: Kristina* for Wind Ensemble. Eugene Migliaro Corporon, North Texas Wind Symphony. GIA CD 446.

Yurko, Bruce. *Night Dances* for Wind Ensemble. Eugene Migliaro Corporon, North Texas Wind Symphony. GIA CD 490.

Yurko, Bruce. *Night Dances* for Wind Ensemble. William Berz, Rutgers University Wind Ensemble.

Yurko, Bruce. *Pastorale Nocturne* for Wind Ensemble. *Diversions*. Dennis Fisher, North Texas Symphony Band. Mark Master Label 3880 MCD.

Yurko, Bruce. *Pastoralee Nocturne* for Wind Ensemble. IUP Concert Bands, 1999. Jack Stamp, Indiana University of Pennsylvania Symphony Band.

Unit 9: Additional References and Resources

"Bruce Yurko: In Memoriam: Kristina." *Teaching Music through Performance in Band*. *Compiled and edited by Richard Miles*. Chicago: GIA Publications, Inc., 1998.

"Bruce Yurko: Night Dances." *Teaching Music through Performance in Band*. Compiled and edited by Richard Miles. Chicago: GIA Publications, Inc., 1997.

Tower, Ibrook. Bruce Yurko's Concerto's for Wind Ensemble (1973–1974), for Horn and Wind Ensemble (1975), and for Trombone and Wind Ensemble (1977). Ann Arbor, MI: UMI Company, 1995.

Yurko, Bruce. *In Memoriam: Kristina* for Wind Ensemble. Cleveland, OH: Ludwig Music Publishing Company, 1997.

Yurko, Bruce. *Night Dances* for Wind Ensemble. Cleveland, OH: Ludwig Publishing Company, 1995.

Yurko, Bruce. *Pastorale Nocturne* for Wind Ensemble. San Antonio, TX. Southern Music Company, 2001.

Contributed by:

Ibrook Tower
Instrumental Music Instructor
Milton Hershey School
Hershey, Pennsylvania
and
Wind Ensemble Director
Pennsylvania Academy of Music
Lancaster, Pennsylvania

Bruce Yurko
Wind Ensemble Conductor
Cherry Hill High Schools East and West
Cherry Hill, New Jersey
and
Wind Ensemble Conductor
Princeton University
Princeton, New Jersey

Teacher Resource Guide

Puszta

Jan Van der Roost
(b. 1956)

Unit 1: Composer

Jan Van der Roost was born on March 1, 1956, in Duffel, Belgium. He is a composer, conductor, and music educator. He is married to Bernadette Johnson, and they are the parents of two sons and two daughters. Van der Roost attended the Lemmensinstituut (Leuven), where he studied trombone, music history, and music education. His studies continued at the Royal Music Conservatories of Antwerp and Ghent, where his focus became conducting and composition. He is Professor of Counterpoint and Fugue at the Lemmensinstituut in Belgium and is the conductor of the Symphonic Band. He also works as guest professor at the SHOBI Institute of Music (Tokyo).

Van der Roost is an outstanding and prolific contemporary composer. His talents as an adjudicator, lecturer, clinician, and guest conductor are recognized internationally. His compositions cover a large variety of genres and styles. His works are many and include oratorios, a symphony, several smaller works for symphonic orchestra, a guitar concerto, a lieder cycle for baritone and chamber orchestra, several works for chamber orchestra, numerous brass and wind band compositions, choral music, and instrumental solos. Many of his works have been recorded and broadcast on radio and television.

Some of Van der Roost's works for band include:

Amazonia	*Humanos*
Arsenal	*Manhattan Pictures*
Avalon	*Metalla*
Balkanya	*Minerva*

Canterbury Chorale	Nemu Susato
Condacum	Olympica
Conzensus	Poeme Montagnard
Credentium	Ponte Romano
Dynamica	Revisions
Et In Terra Pax	Rikudim
Firework	Sinfonia Hungarica
Flashing Winds	Slavia
Highland Rhapsody	Spartacus
Homage	Toccata Festival

Unit 2: Composition

Van der Roost wrote this suite in 1987, and it was published in 1988. *Puszta* is a set of four gypsy dances that will call to mind the lifestyle of the Hungarian gypsies who moved wild horses around the puszta (a great prairie). Like some of his other works, namely *Rikudim* (four Israeli dances), *Balkanya* (three Balkanese dances), *A Highland Rhapsody* (Scottish rhapsody), and *Slavia* (a Slavonic rhapsody), all themes in *Puszta* are original rather than derived from folk music. The style utilized by the composer may remind the listener of the music of Brahms, Dvorak, or Liszt. The work, full of varying character and tempi, typifies music of the gypsies.

The premiere of *Puszta* was given on December 14, 1987, by the Symphonic Band of the Belgian Guides, with Norbert Nozy conducting. The work has enjoyed numerous performances worldwide since its publication.

Movement I (*Andante Moderato* – 2:54) has a very apparent Eastern European feel in its style and harmonic structure. The fluid motion of the opening section gives way to a dance melody with a strong and regular beat. Don't be surprised if you want to shout "Hey!" following many of the phrases of this movement.

Movement II (*Tranquillo* – 2:46) is lyrical, reflective, and graceful. Beautiful instrument combinations create timbral interest.

Movement III (*Allegro Molto* – 2:11) uses a two feel similar to that of the first movement. Again, Van der Roost uses different instrument combinations to lend interest to the singable melodic line. After a somewhat frenetic dance section, the piece yields to a more reposing, lyrical section only to return to the playful music of the beginning of the movement.

Movement IV (*Presto* – 4:34) begins heavily and with great purpose, after which follows a light dance theme that gradually increases in tempo. Following a return to the slower tempo in a repeat to the beginning, the work becomes festive, almost triumphant. As though guarding against too much celebration, the heavy and somewhat ponderous material from the beginning returns yet again. But the celebratory material makes a comeback.

Duration of the entire work is approximately twelve minutes and twenty-five seconds.

Unit 3: Historical Perspective

"Puszta" means empty, bare, grassy plain. The Hungarian puszta, or the Great Hungarian Plain, is an area of arid grasslands that once covered a large part of the Alföld (plain) in eastern Hungary. Once used for cattle raising, some of the Puszta vanished as a result of irrigation and drainage in the late 1800s. An area about the same size as Holland remains in the Hortobagy region near Debrecen. It is a popular tourist site, and those who visit are treated to old customs, styles, and dances.

Unit 4: Technical Considerations

That an E-flat clarinet part plays a considerable role in this work is worthy of consideration. While some may choose to omit the part, it should be noted that the voicings and sonorities will be compromised. Additionally, the string bass plays an important part that is often different from the other bass lines. Balance is critical throughout, and isolation of instrument families will assist.

In the opening of Movement I, adherence to a slow tempo and forestalling rushed thirty-second notes will help to keep this segment deliberate. Although runs here and throughout the piece may at first appear technically challenging, Van der Roost does a good job of keeping these passages brief and scalar. Ensemble control with skillful watching of the conductor during *accelerandos* will keep the group together as the fast tempo locks in. At B, flute and piccolo may need to practice the melodic embellishment together, paying close attention to note accuracy and correct articulation. There may be a tendency for the accompaniment lines to play too heavily. This should be avoided, as these four movements constitute a set of dances. Immediate changes in dynamics and tempo will require rehearsal of phrase endings and beginnings. Rhythmic challenges are few; likewise, this work stays within a reasonable range for most instruments. Open fourths and fifths in the harmonic support throughout the middle of the work will call for discerning awareness of intonation. Styles between trumpet soloist at measure 93 and the imitation that follows in measure 101 must be matched. Tasteful performance, acute sense of balance, and precise attention to articulation nuances are the foremost technical considerations for this movement.

The beautiful ballad of the second movement, while not technically demanding, calls for a good sense of inner pulse so the tempo does not rush. Graceful and light playing across all voices is a must, as well as balance. Therefore, student musicians will need to be well in control of their instruments. Inner pulse with a focus on a sixteenth note beat division will ensure correct entrances after rests. An understanding of phrase shaping will help the ensemble convey correct expression. The use of *rubato* to assist expression will mean reinforcement of watching and listening.

In the third movement, incessant after-beat accompaniment necessitates internalizing eighth note beat division. Swift tempo may render some technical issues tricky; repeated figures in melody and accompaniment may mitigate these challenges.

The beginning of the fourth movement uses a deliberate, slow tempo. Care should be taken that the tempo is not rushed and that sixteenth and thirty-second notes are played carefully in time. A feature of all four movements, correct articulation is critical to the successful characterization of each dance. Woodwind runs in the middle of the movement must emphasize all notes in the passage. Even though the tempo is swift during these segments, the challenge of the runs is eased by their scalar nature. Finally, even the end of the work becomes rather raucous. At no point should it be performed heavily.

Unit 5: Stylistic Considerations

Stylistically, as suggested by the subtitle, these are four dance movements, and they should be played that way. Movement I begins reflectively and then falls into a dance-like section with a strong feeling of two. The entire movement (like all other movements) has a flavorful Eastern European essence that is demonstrated in the harmonic movement and familiar accompaniment technique.

Movement II is ballad-like, slow, and tranquil. *Legato* articulation sets it apart from the other three movements. It utilizes sustained and sparse accompaniment, suggesting delicate performance.

Movement III reclaims the strong feeling of two and utilizes an almost nationalistic, celebratory approach. A lighter, softer, smoother lyrical section provides brief contrast, and the music then returns to the drive and rush of the opening.

The final movement begins weightily with a deliberate tempo coupled with hesitancy in long tones and forward momentum in sixteenth and thirty-second pushes from measure to measure. In a style reminiscent of two of the three other movements, it returns to a two feel that gains in intensity with *accelerando*. This style is short-lived as the music returns to the deliberate material of the opening. However, the vacillation continues as the driving two reappears. Finally, a vibrant, brilliant concluding dance brings the piece to a splendid close.

Unit 6: Musical Elements

MELODY:

A most striking attribute of most melodies in this work is how singable they are. None are terribly complex, but all are somehow recognizable even though they are newly composed. The highly tonal singability of the melodies suggests accessibility by student instrumentalists insofar as range, expression, and technique are concerned. The director is advised to make the most of the repetition of phrases in teaching melody. While repetition will aid technique so performance of melody appears effortless, remain vigilant to stagnation that may occur. Modification of expressive qualities as suggested by the composer and as determined in interpretation by the conductor should be a focal point for teaching in rehearsal. Additionally, since there is a very apparent "vocal" quality to the melodies (that is, they are constructed in such a way that they suggest sung folk music), it will be necessary for the director to help the student musicians to recognize rise and fall, as well as temporal modifications in the phrases. Melodic dialogue occurs often in this work, giving further rise to the notion of singability. Students will need direction in listening to each other so melodic shaping and expression are matched between voice groups. It would be helpful to utilize recordings of ethnic dance music to reinforce these concepts. Of course, the director must be able to help the students make conceptual transfer from a seemingly unrelated recording to *Puszta*. In analysis prior to teaching the piece, the director must be able to identify and draw parallels between other folk/dance music and the melodic qualities of this work. In this way, the use of related recordings in rehearsal, coupled with guidance by the director regarding what to listen for and how this relates to each individual's contribution to the ensemble in this work, will be invaluable.

HARMONY:
Harmonically, this work is clear-cut with tonalities focusing on major, minor, and occasionally modal structures. As the director teaches the work, it will be important to emphasize accurate performance of altered tones (accidentals) in melody as well as supporting lines. These devices often function as harmonic variation.

RHYTHM:
Puszta maintains an achievable rhythmic structure, primarily due to its dance form. Offbeats are employed at various times and will require a good sense of beat internalization. Acute attention to expressive score markings will assist the student in the precise performance of rhythmic units and will help them to preserve tempo and steady beat. Tempi across the four movements are more prone to immediate modification rather than gradual change or the use of *rubato*. Again, this is attributable to the dance-like nature of the work. The director should have prepared the piece in advance so tempo changes are not surprising and the ensemble might prepare in advance of a change that may not utilize gradual transition. It will also be beneficial for players to be aware of the smallest beat division at all times. This awareness will assist in keeping steady beat and entrances/releases that occur before or after a beat. There are several moments of syncopation that function playfully in the work. Warm-up

exercises that focus on this rhythmic device are transferable into the work.

TIMBRE:

There is really nothing out of the ordinary in the sonorities present in *Puszta*. Van der Roost relies on instrument family dialogue throughout. This creates aural interest for the listeners while challenging the performer to match quality, balance, and style. His interspersing of solo instruments, often to introduce sections, is an appealing method for contrast. It is important to adhere to the octave placement in the writing of this work. Avoid allowing students to change octaves for the sake of making the piece somehow "easier." The voicing placement is purposeful and functions to alter timbre in effective ways. Adjustment of voicings will have an impact on the intended color of the work.

Unit 7: Form and Structure

SECTION	MEASURE	EVENT AND SCORING
Movement I: Introduction	1–8	*Andante moderato* (quarter note = 72); 4/4; eight-measure phrase with melodic material of the first subphrase nearly repeating itself; mm. 1–4 E-flat and 1st clarinet perform wistful melody; three main accompaniment figures are deliberate with slow moving rhythm; mm. 5–8 melody fortified with additional instrumentation (piccolo, flute, oboe, 2nd clarinet); mainly *legato* articulations; although measured, sextuplets at m. 8 give cadenza-like feel; *fermata* ends in a lift prior to A
	9–24	*Andante moderato* (quarter note = 60, with accelerando to m. 138); 2/4; statement of the first dance theme centers on C minor and is characterized with recurring rhythm: ♩ ♩ |♪♩ ♪|♩ ♩ |♪ ; light accompaniment in first rendering (mm. 9–24) uses unadorned quarter movement in lower voices with offbeat punctuation in trombone and tambourine (later joined by horn and snare drum); B section of the theme (mm. 17–20) moves into restatement of

SECTION	MEASURE	EVENT AND SCORING
		A with a lift-off of 1 and heavy accent on 2 (m. 20); melody primarily in alto/ tenor voices but includes soprano as instrumentation is augmented through the section (this practice is repeated in mm. 25–40)
	25–40	Constitute a complete restatement of the theme with the addition of embellishment of the melody in piccolo, flute, E-flat clarinet, and B-flat clarinet
	41–60	Brief key change to C major in mm. 41–44 (repeated); quarter note = 152; new melody in the eight-measure major interlude rendered by brass with timpani and tambourine; return to C minor at m. 45; melody A is presented here in variation, mm. 45–60; first half of phrase by brass joined by saxophone and English horn, increased percussion; fuller texture in second half of phrase with tutti ensemble playing; countermelodic imitation in horn, 1st trombone, and baritone
	61–76	Same material as mm. 25–40
	77–108	Horns unison in new, sharply articulated melodic material, mm. 77–84; while melody is present in C major, homophonic accompaniment in trombone and baritone moving in open fourth and fifths between C and B-flat major, suggesting mixolydian mode
		In the next statement of the same melodic material (mm. 85–92), harmonic movement stays the same and melody now mirrors harmony with flatted seventh; instrumentation of melodic line increases to include all

SECTION	MEASURE	EVENT AND SCORING
		trumpets, horns, 2nd trombone, and baritones; drone accompaniment now increases to include all woodwinds and string bass; percussion tacit (mm. 77–92)
		New melodic material at mm. 93–100 (performed by solo trumpet) changes character in key (C major) and articulation (lyrical); smooth articulation in accompaniment supports character of melody; accompanying voices in bass clarinet, saxophone family, string bass, and bells perform descending half-note line while 1st clarinet and alto clarinet add eighth note arpeggios; same melodic material performed by piccolo, flute, oboe, English horn, and bassoon at mm. 101–108; half-note accompaniment is retained in other woodwind lines, minus alto and tenor saxophone, with bells retaining the arpeggiation and bass line rendered by string bass
	109–124	Same material as mm. 9–24
	125–140	Same material as mm. 25–40
Movement II:		
	1–16	Tranquil (quarter note = 60); 24; first four measures of the simple folk-like melody is stated by solo flute with equally simple sustained accompaniment in woodwind voices; second half of the primary melodic phrase is reinforced by 1st horn and bells while 1st oboe adds a moving line to complement the melody; mm. 9–16 constitute a restatement of the theme fortified with additional instrumentation and the similar accompaniment; dynamic levels throughout are relatively soft and with flowing articulation

SECTION	MEASURE	EVENT AND SCORING
	17–24	B section of the main melody is stated; very light accompaniment that results in lighter texture; contrary sixteenth note motion between melodic voices in the first two measures provides an interesting dialogue feature, a contrast to the first sixteen measures of the work; the dialogue continues in the last four measures of this section between 1st clarinet, answered on beat two by 3rd clarinet, alto clarinet, and alto saxophone
	25–33	A theme of the first section returns and is performed by all clarinets except bass; a trill in piccolo, flute, and oboe adds an idyllic quality; suspension and resolution in 2nd alto saxophone and 1st trumpet across mm. 27 and 28 should be emphasized; bells added to the descending sixteenths (mm. 29 and 30) should also be brought out to ensure shimmer
	33–42	The melodic herein is shared, stated in the first two measures by trumpet with half-quarter accompaniment in the brass minus trombone, and taken over in the next two measures by bassoon, alto and bass clarinet, baritone saxophone, baritone, and tuba; this change in voicing obviously changes the timbral focus; midsection of this phrase enjoys a suspension as in the phrase that preceded (flute, 2nd oboe, 2nd horn) and should be stressed; timbral focus changes further in the next two measures (mm. 37–38) as the sixteenth note figures are assumed by oboe, English horn, and 1st trumpet with the melody finally soaring in the upper woodwinds in the last moments

SECTION	MEASURE	EVENT AND SCORING
		of the phrase; final measures of this section serve as a tag that brings back a triadic fragment of the melody
	43–56	*Poco piu mosso* (quarter note = 76); contrasting section moves more decidedly; while retaining some of the rhythmic motives of the first section, the melodic material is new and freshly stated in solo oboe; dynamic level stays soft as it has been to this point; accompaniment is generally sustained although the string bass rhythm ♩ ♪ ♪♩ ♪ ♪ help to maintain momentum; during the first four measures of this section, the interjection of many accidentals would suggestion movement towards a change of key, but the tonal center settles back into C at m. 47; close harmony in the trombone voices in mm. 47–52 will require intonation work; directors should note an error in the piccolo/flute part in m. 50: the printed B-flat should be changed to a B-natural to match the C-sharp in 1st clarinet and 1st trumpet; first ending of this section repeats back to m. 43 and the work concludes softly, reiterating the descending/ascending melodic triad
Movement III: Introduction	1–2	Solo clarinet performs strong cadenza-like scalar passage leading to slow cadential prologue to the first theme
	3–18	Allegro molto (quarter note = 152); 2/4; percussive, rhythmic style characterizes this quiet yet spirited theme with this recurring rhythm ♪♪♪ ♪♪ ♪♪♪ ; the eighths in the second measure of the rhythmic motive lead the music into the next measure definitively each time it is played; the

SECTION	MEASURE	EVENT AND SCORING
		"boom-chick" accompaniment gives urgency to this dance rhythm and punctuates the phrase pause with a syncopated tag (mm. 9–10); the second half of the phrase (mm. 11–18) is ushered in with a sextuplet ascending scalar flourish in the upper woodwinds and alto saxophone; mm. 3–18 repeat
	19–38	The music goes through some modification at this juncture; dynamic level rises; syncopation observed briefly in the first section now plays a prominent role in the melodic rhythm; this change in rhythm may prompt the director to choose to conduct one beat per measure across four measures as if each measure were one beat in a four pattern; the new melodic material is performed regally with unaccompanied trumpet and 1st trombone, with percussion interjection at the phrase midpoint and end (mm. 22 and 26); the brass choir is extended in the second half of the phrase to include all trombones and tuba; following the first eight-measure phrase, instrumentation of the melodic line begins in middle and low brass and continues to add instrumentation through the upper instruments and woodwinds until tutti playing is achieved; this building of instrumentation is fortified with a growth in dynamic level to the end of the phrase; the next section is heralded with a scalar sixteenth note run in the entire woodwind section
	39–64	Main melody returns with its form similar to that found in mm. 3–18; sonority expanded to include full ensemble and fortification of melody

SECTION	MEASURE	EVENT AND SCORING
		through use of doubling in unison and octaves; addition of sustained trills in piccolo, flute, oboe, English horn, and alto saxophone add brilliance; dynamic level now forte; trumpet used for rhythmic emphasis; tambourine rhythm strengthens melodic rhythm
	55–70	*Meno mosso* (quarter note = 88); as the tempo slows, style moves from detached and percussive to smooth and flowing; melodic material moves primarily in stepwise fashion; upper woodwinds perform melody while other woodwinds render a sustained harmonic structure underneath; string bass, wood block, and triangle provide the only semblance of percussive sound; mm. 55–58 repeat; orchestration reorganized at m. 59 and the new melodic material of this section begins to liven with the addition of a few well-placed *staccato* articulations; altered tones in the melodic line provide colorful harmonic focus; melodic movement in the upper woodwinds (mm. 63–66) answered by saxophone, horn, and baritone (mm. 67–68) and passed on to the full clarinet family, which brings the section to a soft and slow conclusion
	71–104	In a return to the main thematic material, mm. 71–86 repeat mm. 3–18 exactly; final statement of the theme employs a high level of woodwind embellishment with all voices except bassoon, bass clarinet, and baritone saxophone performing controlled trills (sixteenths) throughout the first phrase while the melody is heard in trumpet, horn, and trombone; offbeats are now dedicated in the snare as heavy onbeat

SECTION	MEASURE	EVENT AND SCORING
		accompaniment is offered in all other bass voices and timpani; an ascending scalar flourish at m. 94 in most wind voices plus string bass *crescendos* to lead into the second half of the phrase; at m. 95, the controlled trill is now a true trill and the melodic line instrumentation increases to include some clarinet voices and tenor saxophone; the trills take on a greater harmonic role as they descend stepwise to the last two measures; dynamic level remains ff throughout; movement concludes with a two-measure accented tag
Movement IV:		
	1	*Marcato* (quarter note = 76); 2/4; pickup into first full measure (m. 2)
	2–17	Although centering on G minor, this movement begins with a feeling of "lift" due to the tempo combined with the deliberate motion of the melodic rhythm; tempo and division of beat will require keen counting and inner pulse so there is a perceived difference between sixteenth and thirty-second notes; melodic material performed by woodwinds (texture expands to include flute and oboe in second half of the phrase); a procession-like accompaniment characterizes this section; altered tonality in the harmonic accompaniment at 9 (D major) reveals the tonality heard at m. 10, where E-flat and B-flat clarinets take control of the melody, this time performed softly and against a sustained accompaniment; m. 14 returns to the motive of the opening four measures and rests on a *fermata* at the end of the phrase before breaking at A

SECTION	MEASURE	EVENT AND SCORING
	18–37 (38)	A change of tempo in this section: quarter note = 84 with gradual *accelerando* and *crescendo*; most brass voices rest, and percussion during the first eight measures includes only bells; shift to major tonality in addition to the dance-like energy of the eighth/quarter patterns sound fresh; at m. 26, tempo arrives at quarter note = 120 and the texture thins; saxophones spin the melody with sparse accompaniment until m. 30, where instrumentation expands (with the most notable timbre change in the addition of horn and low brass); a four-measure addendum at the end of the phrase allows a solo flute and bells, with sustained woodwind accompaniment, to relax the tempo in order for the music to turn around and repeat back to the beginning; at the second ending (m. 38), the section concludes as low winds sustain a unison/octave G as a preface to the *presto* segment at B
	39–62 (63)	*Presto* (quarter note = 160); now in the key of G major, a new and vibrant melody appears in trumpet with driving, accented eighth and quarter note accompaniment throughout the ensemble; artistic use of differing articulations adds precision to the music; scalar flourish in woodwinds leads into the second statement of the new melody, and at the conclusion of that phrase, the same scalar work leads to the contrasting section of the melody, proclaimed by horn, trombone, and baritone; pulsating accompaniment is abandoned for simple yet powerful punctuation; this contrasting section concludes in a bright E major; this section repeats back to m. 39

Section	Measure	Event and Scoring
	64–79	*Marcato* (quarter note = 76); material similar to the beginning of the movement (mm. 2–17) appears in the key of E minor; phrase leads back to the sign at m. 39
	39–80 (coda)	Material from m. 39 repeats and moves to the coda
Coda	81–96	From the coda, it's a dash to the end, with embellishment in upper woodwind voices against an insistent eighth/quarter accompaniment that supports a stepwise symmetrical melody that is heralded in alto saxophone, horn, and baritone; second phrase in this section acts as a response to mm. 81–88; material from mm. 81–96 repeat
Conclusion	97–102	Last five measures constitute a definitive conclusion that utilizes a comfortable cadential sequence, a predictable retard. (director should note that while predictable, it is also easy to miss since the music up to this point moves very swiftly) and a scalar flourish that stimulates the final chord

Unit 8: Suggested Listening

Bela Bartok/Gordon, *Three Hungarian Songs*

Best of 2000: Gypsy folk groups from Hungary – Austria, Hungaroton Classic, Hungaroton, 2000

Johannes Brahms/Longfield, *Hungarian Dance No. 5*

Hungarian moods – Benedict Silberman. Hollywood, CA, Capitol, 1957

Olympica – Tokyo Kosei, European wind circle, Vol. 3, 1995.

Von Weber/Rogers, *Andante and Hungarian Rondo*

Wind music of Jan Van der Roost:
    Vol. 1: De Haske Winds, 1993, 1997, DHM Records
    Vol. 2: De Haske Winds, 1997, DHM Records
    Vol. 3: De Haske Winds, 1997, DHM Records

Unit 9: Additional References and Resources

Blockmans, Willem Pieter, Gelabert González, and Juan Eloy. *Rural Landscapes*. Danbury, CT : Grolier Educational, 1994.

Dobszay, László. *A History of Hungarian Music*. Budapest: Corvina, 1993.

Dobszay, László. *Catalogue of Hungarian Folksong Types*. Budapest: Zoltan Falvy, 1992.

Kapocsy, György, and Éva Polgár. *The Hungarian Puszta*. Third edition. Budapest: Corvina, 1995.

Kodály, Zoltán. *Folk Music of Hungary*. New York: Macmillan, 1960.

Nixon, Paul. *Sociality, Music, Dance: Human Figurations in a Transylvanian Valley*. Göteborg: Göteborg University, 1998.

Vargyas, Lajos. *Folk Song in Hungary*. Kecskemét: Ujvári Lajos, 1970.

Websites:
http://hungaria.org/lists/folklor/
Hungarian Folklore List/Discussion Group – Magyar Folklór List

http://hungaria.org/lists/folklor/zene/
Hungarian Music Archives

http://www.hungary.com/corvinus/lib/timeless/chapter03.htm
The origins and development of Hungarian folk music

http://www.salamon.sk/Robert/midi/
Hungarian Folk Dance Music & Songs

http://www.tanchaz.hu/thmain.htm
Traditional Music Dance & Handicraft in Hungary

http://www.utexas.edu/students/husa/culture/culture.index.html #music
Hungarian Cultural Resources

http://www.zti.hu/:
The Hungarian Academy of Sciences Institute for Musicology

http://www2.4dcomm.com/millenia/music.htm:
The Origins of Hungarian Folk Music

Contributed by:
Deborah A. Sheldon
Ester Boyer College of Music
Temple University
Philadelphia, Pennsylvania

Teacher Resource Guide

Serenade for Band
Vincent Persichetti
(1915–1987)

Unit 1: Composer

Vincent Persichetti has become one of the most admired and performed American composers of the twentieth century. Born in Philadelphia, Pennsylvania, on June 6, 1915, Persichetti began his music life at the age of five, first studying piano and then organ, double bass, tuba, theory, and composition. By age eleven, he was performing professionally as an accompanist, radio staff pianist, church organist, and orchestra member. His earliest published works, written at age fourteen, exhibit a mastery of form, medium, and style.

Persichetti received his Bachelor of Music in Music Education from Combs College of Music in 1935. Upon his graduation, he was simultaneously head of the theory and composition departments at Combs College, conducting student of Fritz Reiner at the Curtis Institute of Music, and piano student of Olga Samaroff at the Philadelphia Conservatory. He received a diploma in conducting from the Curtis Institute, and his Master of Music and Doctor of Musical Arts from the Philadelphia Conservatory.

In 1941, Persichetti was appointed head of the theory and composition departments at the Philadelphia Conservatory. He joined the faculty of the Juilliard School of Music in 1947 and was appointed chair of the composition department in 1963. He was the recipient of three Guggenheim Fellowships; the first Kennedy center Friedheim Award, grants from the National Foundation on the Arts and Humanities, and the National Institute of Arts and Letters; the Juilliard Publication and Symphony League Awards; The Blue Network and Columbia Records Chamber Music Awards; and citations from the American Bandmasters Association and the National Catholic Music Educators Association. Among some one hundred commissions were those from the Philadelphia Orchestra, the New York Philharmonic, the St. Louis and Louisville Symphony Orchestras, the Koussevitsky Music Foundation, the Martha Graham Company, and the Juilliard Musical Foundation.

In addition to his compositional efforts, Persichetti wrote one of the definitive books on modern compositional techniques, *Twentieth Century Harmony: Creative Aspects and Practice* (W. W. Norton, 1961). He also co-authored a biography of William Schuman (G. Schirmer, 1954). Persichetti died in Philadelphia on August 14, 1987.

Unit 2: Composition

Serenade No. 11 for Band, Op. 85, is Persichetti's fifth work for wind band. It was composed in 1960 as the first of two commissions from the Ithaca High School Band (Ithaca, New York), Frank Battisti, director. The work, written in five movements, was first performed by the Ithaca Band on April 19, 1961, with the composer conducting. The eleventh in a series of serenades for miscellaneous instrumental groupings, each of the five short movements, "Pastoral," "Humoreske," "Nocturne," "Intermezzo," and "Capriccio," are representative of Persichetti's compositional style. Each reflects the moods of a summer evening. The first movement, "Pastoral," has a lyrical, flowing melody that is reminiscent of a carefree rural or idyllic scene. "Humoreske" is full of jocundity, with a graceful woodwind melody over a *staccato* bass and chordal accompaniment. "Nocturne" is dreamily romantic with its sentimental expression about the beauty of the night. The fourth movement, "Intermezzo," uses two short and simple melodic ideas to provide a transition to the last movement, "Capriccio," which is a spirited 6/8t movement reflecting the joy of the moment and youthful exuberance.

Unit 3: Historical Perspective

The Persichetti *Serenade* was written during a pivotal time in the history of the wind band. During the 1940s and 1950s, some of the most respected composers in the world were encouraged to write for the wind band medium. Along with composers such as Darius Milhaud (*Suite Francaise*, 1945), Morton Gould (*Ballad for Band*, 1946; *Symphony for Band*, West Point, 1952), H. Owen Reed (*La Fiesta Mexicana*, 1949), Virgil Thomson (*A Solemn Music*, 1949), Robert Russell Bennett (*Suite of Old American Dances*, 1950; *Symphonic Songs*, 1957), Walter Piston (*Tunbridge Fair*, 1950), Paul Hindemith (*Symphony in B-flat*, 1951), Peter Mennin (*Canzona*, 1951), William Schuman (*George Washington Bridge*, 1951), Howard Hanson (*Chorale and Alleluia*, 1954), Paul Creston (*Celebration Overture*, 1954), Clifton Williams (*Fanfare and Allegro*, 1956), and Joseph Willcox Jenkins (*American Overture for Band*, 1959), Persichetti wrote original works now considered to be the nucleus of the wind band repertoire. Before this time, only a few respected composers (Gustav Holst, Ralph Vaughan Williams, Gordon Jacob, Florent Schmitt, and Percy Grainger) had written original works for the band.

Persichetti composed a wealth of literature of significant importance for the wind band. Among his fourteen works for winds are *Divertimento for Band, Op. 42* (1950), *Psalm for Band, Op. 53* (1951), *Pageant, Op. 59* (1953), *Symphony No. 6 for Band, Op. 69* (1956), and *Masquerade, Op. 102* (1965).

In the 1964 Autumn issue of *The Journal of Band Research*, Persichetti wrote, "Band music is virtually the only kind of music in America today (outside the pop field) which can be introduced, accepted, put to immediate wide use, and become a staple of the literature in a short time." Persichetti's contributions to the wind band's literature, teachings, and twentieth century harmonic practices continue to have a lasting and profound influence on the music world.

Unit 4: Technical Considerations

The writing throughout this work is idiomatic, without extremes in range, making this one of Persichetti's more technically accessible works for high school band. The work has no key signatures, so accidentals abound, and there are no meter changes after the beginning of each movement. There are both *staccato* and *legato* articulations requiring careful control of contrast. Control of pitch within the polytonal harmonies will also require careful listening skills. *Serenade* is representative of Persichetti's compositional style; thus, the use of polytonality with triads juxtaposed at the intervals of the second, fourth, and fifth is pervasive. The melodies exist above the undulating polychordal accompaniment, and the transparent scoring and chamber-like sections (small group and sectional writing) help to achieve clear tonal colors and textures. Persichetti seldom wrote for full (*tutti*) ensemble, so students must play with initiative. While Persichetti was known for his innovative use of percussion instruments as a textural fabric to the band, the demands here are modest with only five parts: timpani, suspended cymbal, snare drum, tenor drum, and bass drum.

Unit 5: Stylistic Considerations

The first, third, and fourth movements feature *legato* and *cantabile* styles, the fifth movement utilizes mostly a *staccato/marcato* style, and the second movement features a graceful, *legato* melody in the woodwinds with a *staccato* accompaniment in the brass and percussion. The fifth movement requires flexibility, good clarity of articulation, and a strong sense of rhythm. Since the majority of articulations deal with the tongue, a clear understanding of accent, *staccato*, and *marcato* is necessary. The slower movements require good tonal control, a strong sense of phrasing, and an understanding of the transparent textures. Conductors are encouraged to address each articulation in scale and arpeggio warm-up exercises. By focusing on these articulations outside the music, students can focus on the sound quality of each articulation and begin to discriminate each articulation both aurally and technically. Encourage the players to "speak" each articulation out loud. ("If they can say it, they can play it.") Because of the polyphonic scoring, care must be taken to achieve proper balance. W. Francis McBeth discusses how to teach proper balance and blend in his book, *Effective Performance of Band Music* (Southern Music, 1972). All ranges of dynamics are expected to be employed for convincing contrast.

Unit 6: Musical Elements

Melody:

The melodies from each of the five movements are diatonic, although leaps as large as a major sixth occur. These leaps will challenge players to maintain connection between the notes with the air stream. To help achieve a smooth connection between intervallic leaps, prepare a teaching strategy focusing on air movement and finger technique. This could be done on any major or minor scale by performing intervallic exercises, both slurred and tongued. For example, using a B-flat major scale: B-flat to C, B-flat to D, B-flat to E-flat, B-flat to F, B-flat to G, B-flat to A, B-flat to octave B-flat—then reverse the pattern. Students could also learn to solfege these exercises for better pitch awareness.

Harmony:

The harmonic texture of the work is primarily homophonic with some contrapuntal elements. Homophonic texture is identified by a single melodic voice with harmonic accompaniment support. When two or more melodies of equal importance occur, the texture is considered contrapuntal. Students should become familiar with these terms and be able to identify these textures in any composition. One of the hallmarks of Persichetti's harmonic style is his use of polytonality. In *Serenade*, polytonality is always present with triads juxtaposed at the intervals of the second, fourth, and fifth. As intervals are stacked within various harmonic passages, players must be confident in performing their pitch against dissonant tones from other players. Persichetti was quoted as saying this regarding his compositional style: "My music varies, it goes from gracious to gritty very often. Sometimes it has a lot of serial in it; other pieces have less of that and are more tonal. It's a mixture." *Serenade* exploits both the "gracious and gritty" sides of Persichetti's harmonic style.

Rhythm:

The basic rhythmic structure found in *Serenade* should not be difficult for a high school player. An understanding of whole, half, quarter, eighth, and sixteenth note subdivision is required. The fifth movement is the most challenging of the five, with an understanding of the rhythmic precision necessary for playing 6/8. The tied eighth notes followed by *legato* or *staccato* eighth notes may need some extra attention for precision and clarity. An acute awareness of horizontal independence and rhythmic (vertical) alignment will be integral. Students should be able to count each rhythm, and they should practice specific rhythmical units with the aid of a metronome. Conductors are encouraged to have the students clap and say their parts while the metronome provides a steady beat. Reinforce this exercise with the students fingering their parts. When they can perform this exercise with accuracy, have the students "sizzle" their parts by using the correct fingerings while producing an air stream and correctly articulating that air stream. These activities assist students in the cognitive and kinesthetic aspects of making music.

TIMBRE:

The timbre of any Persichetti composition involves a series of rapid color changes while the melody weaves from one voice to another. Players are required to perform contrasting styles simultaneously. Attaining proper balance between woodwind, brass, and percussion voices is essential for an artistic performance. Students must isolate melody, countermelody, and accompaniment to understand and demonstrate appropriate tone color and balance. Conductors are encouraged to create a "flowchart" of each movement, diagramming precisely where melodies and rhythmic passages are found and who plays them. This teaching aid could be done as a class activity and, in such a collaborative setting, would help the students achieve a more insightful performance.

Unit 7: Form and Structure

MEASURE   EVENT AND SCORING

Movement I: "Pastoral"
(half note = 88)

1–6	Lyrical theme introduced by flute and clarinet; harmonic accompaniment primarily in woodwind choir
6–10	Theme in horns; harmonic support in woodwind choir
11–14	Theme in clarinet with harmonic support in woodwinds, shifting to trombone choir
14–23	Developmental material primarily in woodwinds
24–41	Theme returns in piccolo and clarinet with harmonic support in low brass; theme alternates from horn, flute, E-flat clarinet, clarinet, horn, and ends in flute and piccolo with shifting harmonic choirs

MEASURE   EVENT AND SCORING

Movement II: "Humoreske"
(quarter note = 96)

1–2	Flowing theme introduced by upper woodwinds
3–9	Theme in clarinet; *staccato* accompaniment in brass
10–19	Developmental material with increased texture, culminating in first full *tutti* statement
20–28	Theme returns in woodwinds; leads to chordal statement in brass
29–37	Flowing theme returns to woodwinds with *staccato* accompaniment in brass

Movement III: "Nocturne"
(quarter note = 63)

1–2	First phrase in woodwind choir with muted cornet
3–4	Second phrase continuing in woodwind choir
5–8	Third phrase in woodwind choir
9–11	Fourth phrase in woodwinds with low brass harmonic support
12–15	Fifth phrase in woodwind choir with low brass support
16–19	Theme in cornet with thin textures
20–22	Seventh phrase in woodwind choir
23–27	Alternating melodic thoughts in cornet and woodwind choir

Movement IV: "Intermezzo"
(quarter note = 112)

1–9	First theme in clarinet; developed in woodwind choir
10–15	Second theme in brass choir with flute embellishment
16–19	First theme in clarinet
20–27	Second theme returns in brass choir and finishing *pianissimo* in clarinet choir

MEASURE   EVENT AND SCORING

Movement V: "Capriccio"
(dotted-quarter note = circa 100)

1–3   Staccato introduction in brass and upper woodwinds

4–9   Theme in clarinet with *staccato* accompaniment in
                 woodwind choir

10–16   Theme in cornet with harmonic support in brass choir
                 leading to second *tutti* statement (mm. 15–16)

17–24   Theme in woodwinds with thin harmonic support

25–29   *Staccato* accompaniment returns with theme in woodwinds

30–35   Theme in upper woodwinds with *staccato* accompaniment
                 in brass

36–42   Theme in cornet with harmonic support in brass choir...
                 leading to third *tutti* statement

43–57   Coda in full ensemble

Unit 8: Suggested Listening

Any of the fourteen works for wind band by Vincent Persichetti.

Unit 9: Additional References and Resources

Battisti, Frank. *The Twentieth Century American Wind Band/Ensemble: History, Development and Literature.* Fort Lauderdale, FL: Meredith Music Publications, 1995.

Dvorak, Thomas L., Robert Grechesky, and Gary Ciepluch. *Best Music for High School Band.* Brooklyn, NY: Manhattan Beach Music, 1993.

Hilfiger, John Jay. "A Comparison of Some Aspects of Style in the Band and Orchestra Music of Vincent Persichetti." Ph.D. dissertation, University of Iowa, 1985.

Morris, Donald Alan. "The Life of Vincent Persichetti, with Emphasis on his Works for Band." Ph.D. dissertation, Florida State University, 1991.

Morris, Donald, and Jean Oelrich. "Vincent Persichetti Remembered: Music from Gracious to Gritty." *The Instrumentalist*, XLVII/4, November 1992, pp. 30–8.

Rehrig, William H. *The Heritage Encyclopedia of Band Music.* Westerville, OH: Integrity Press, 1991.

Contributed by:
Richard Anthony Murphy
Middle Tennessee State University
Murfreesboro, Tennessee

Teacher Resource Guide

Slava!

Leonard Bernstein
(1918–1990)

Unit 1: Composer

Leonard Bernstein was born on August 25, 1918, and died on October 14, 1990. He was a prolific composer, conductor, and music educator throughout his career. He attended Harvard University, where he studied composition with Walter Piston, Edward Burlingame-Hill, and A. Tillman Merritt, among others. At the Curtis Institute of Music in Philadelphia, he studied piano with Isabella Vengerova, conducting with Fritz Reiner, and orchestration with Randall Thompson. He continued his conducting studies at the Tanglewood Institute (founded by the Boston Symphony) with its conductor, Sergei Kouusevitsky.

Bernstein was a leading advocate of American composers, particularly Aaron Copland. The two remained close friends for life. Bernstein composed three symphonies that were inspired by his Jewish Heritage: *Symphony No. 1* (*"Jeremiah"*), *Symphony No. 2* (*"Age of Anxiety"*), and *Symphony N. 3* (*"Kaddish"*). His numerous theatrical works made Bernstein famous among a worldwide audience, the most famous being *West Side Story* and *Mass*.

Bernstein struggled throughout his career with being a composer or a conductor. Most agree that he was exceptional as both, and the last twenty-five years of his life were dedicated to music education.

Unit 2: Composition

Slava! was composed for the appointment of Mistlav Rostropovich, "Slava," as the music director and conductor of the National Symphony Orchestra. The piece is a celebratory piece with dance-like music in duple and mixed meter.

The composition begins as a vaudevillian-style work with sliding trombones, growling trumpet solos, and quirky modulations. The second section is a 7/8 dance that is heard first as a solo and then in canon between high and low voices of the band. The introduction interrupts the dance in 7/8 and the themes return in reverse order, with the 7/8 dance first followed by the vaudevillian tunes. The band yells "Slava!" at the close, which means "glory" in Russian (homage to the conductor, Mistlav Rostropovich).

Unit 3: Historical Perspective

Many works of Bernstein can be divided into two categories: 1) the serious Hebrew music and 2) the show tune and swing sounds of the 1940s and 1950s. *Slava!* is definitely in the second category. The piece seems to fit perfectly as if it were taken from the taunting of Officer Krupke in *West Side Story* with its immediate sounds of the whip cracks, slide whistles, and rhythmic motives.

Unit 4: Technical Considerations

Slava! is intended for mature bands. Each part poses different technical problems. The trumpets must be able to play a clear, in-tune high D, as well as shake and growl for effects in the first section. Clean ability to play the full range of most of the woodwind parts is key to the correct sound scored out by Clare Grundman. Many parts in the introduction contain leaps of descending ninths. The key centers give the piece a certain brightness that will require mature players to control their intonation.

Unit 5: Stylistic Considerations

Slava! requires a very good band to make this piece sound good. The maturity of the group will also determine the correct style of playing in the opening vaudeville style tune. An example would be the trombone solo with a plunger and trumpet solo with a plunger and growls. The transition between the first theme and the 7/8 theme is tricky due to constancy of the tone needed for the ascending eight notes in the woodwinds. The parts begin to trade off groups of two eighth notes in a soft but important rocket motive that leads to a wood block solo, and then the 7/8 dance. Playing in time is the most important aspect of this transition so the eighth notes sound like one line changing timbre. The 7/8 dance melody is controlled by a grouping of 2+2+3 in 7/8 time. This motor must be very steady, especially when the upper voices have an eighth rest at the beginning of the measure. Otherwise, this will begin to phase and rush. The 7/8 background or rhythmic motor must also stay light from the low voices through the more active voices. If the motor is light and consistent, the melody will not have any trouble floating on top. The balance between the upper and lower canonic voices must also stay light and yet push forward with energy. Articulations must be adhered to exactly as Bernstein or Grundman indicate.

Unit 6: Musical Elements

Slava! contains some interesting scoring. The saxophone section is divided into four, with alto saxophone doubling on B-flat soprano saxophone. The piece also requires the use of an electric guitar. The coloristic points of interest come from the percussion that must perform on slide whistle, police whistle, whips, tambourine, and triangle, as well as the standard keyboard percussion and timpani.

Unit 7: Form and Structure

SECTION	MEASURE	EVENT AND SCORING
Introduction	1–10	Key center G
Theme A	11–18	1st trombone
	19–21	Trumpet solo
	22–36	Full band
	37–46	Solo trumpet and trombone
	47–54	Full band
Transition	55–60	Recap introduction
	61–75	Woodwinds trade eighths
Theme B	76–79	Motor in 7/8
	80–95	Soprano saxophone with Theme B
	90–91	Motor/inevitable counterpoint to high voices
	92–114	Canon between clarinet and French horn
Retransmission	114–121	Introduction material returns in 2/4
Theme B	122-133	Canon between high woodwinds and trombone; all other voices run the 7/8 motor
Extension	134–137	Theme B is extended four measures
Retransition	138–149	Woodwinds quote middle section of Theme A
Theme A	150–177	Recapitulation of Theme A
Extension	180–185	
Theme B	186–189	Final full band chorus of the 7/8 dance
Introduction	190–197	Music from introduction returns

Unit 8: Suggested Listening
Leonard Bernstein:
> *A Musical Toast*
> *Chichester Psalms*
> *Jeremiah, "Profanation"*
> *Jubilee Games*
> *On the Town Dances*
> *West Side Story*

Contributed by:
Jim Colonna
Laramie County Community College
Cheyenne, Wyoming

Teacher Resource Guide

Songs Without Words

Dan Welcher
(b. 1948)

Unit 1: Composer

A native of Rochester, New York, composer-conductor Dan Welcher has created a substantial body of work in many genre including opera, concerto, symphony, vocal literature, chamber music, and piano solos. Born in 1948, Welcher's initial training was as a pianist and bassoonist. He earned degrees from the Eastman School of Music and the Manhattan School of Music, and joined the Louisville Orchestra as principal bassoonist in 1972, remaining there until 1978. He joined the Artist Faculty of the Aspen Music Festival in the summer of 1976, teaching bassoon and composition there for fourteen years. In 1978, he accepted a position on the faculty of the University of Texas, where he created the New Music Ensemble and served as assistant conductor of the Austin Symphony from 1980 to 1990. He currently holds the Lee Hage Jamail Regents Professorship in Composition at the School of Music at the University of Texas–Austin, where he teaches composition and orchestration, and serves as director of the New Music Ensemble.

In 1990, Welcher was appointed Composer-in-Residence with the Honolulu Symphony Orchestra through the Meet the Composer Residency Program. This three-year residency was distinguished by an award-winning radio series entitled *Knowing the Score* (which has had a second life on KMFA-FM in Austin, winning the 1999 ASCAP-Deems Taylor Broadcast Award), a statewide program teaching elementary school children the basics of musical composition. In addition, he conducted over thirty concerts with the Honolulu Symphony and inaugurated a series of new music concerts entitled *Discoveries*.

Welcher has won numerous awards and prizes from institutions such as the Guggenheim Foundation (a Fellowship in 1997), the National Endowment for the Arts, the Reader's Digest/Lila Wallace Foundation, the Rockefeller Foundation, the MacDowell Colony, Yaddo, the American Music Center, and ASCAP. Award-winning compositions include *Zion* for symphonic wind ensemble, which won the American Bandmasters Association Ostwald Award in 1996. Recent orchestral works include *JFK: The Voice of Peace*, a 55-minute oratorio for choirs, orchestra, narrator, solo cello, and soloists, premiered by the Handel and Haydn Society of Boston; and the orchestral version of *Zion*, commissioned by the Utah Symphony and premiered by that orchestra under the direction of Keith Lockhart in September 1999.

Unit 2: Composition

Songs Without Words: Five Mood Pieces for Wind Ensemble was commissioned by the College Band Directors National Association with funds provided by a consortium of twenty-two member colleges and universities. The work was premiered by the National Small College Intercollegiate Band, Allan McMurray, conductor, on February 24, 2001, at the Winspear Concert Hall at the Murchison Performing Arts Center on the campus of the University of North Texas. The performance was part of the College Band Directors National Association's thirty-first National Conference.

The composer writes, "Since the very nature of a piece entitled *Songs Without Words* would be destroyed by too many words about the piece, it seems best to let the movement titles speak for themselves. Mendelssohn's celebrated set of piano pieces in this genre establishes a precedent for short, mood-oriented works with simple titles attached (although in Felix's case, it was the publisher who invented the titles). I began this composition by imagining five moods that could be portrayed in wind, brass, and percussion colors—then expanded on the idea by linking the separate motives together in the fifth "song." The effect would be one of looking at separate elements of a personality, then looking at the whole person.

"Manic" was originally titled *Almost Too Happy* (like Schumann's *Almost Too Serious* in *Kinderscenen*). It is very short and over the top in terms of energy.

"Reflective" was inspired by a series of days in which it never stopped raining. The motion-driven craziness of the previous movement is completely taken over by an introspective mood. The effect is somewhat like sitting in a Zen garden listening to the tiny waterfall.

"Giddy" is pure silliness and good humor. A middle section allows the brass and timpani to indulge in some vaudevillian high jinks. But as the music gallops to what feels like a happy climax, it is suddenly interrupted.

"Stunned" is what happens in life when we aren't looking. The carefree mood is shattered, almost like running into a brick wall. At length, a melody in the solo saxophone mourns some unspoken loss.

The finale is "Confident," but it doesn't start quite that way. Emerging from the unsettled final chord of "Stunned," a repeated chord begins tapping at our consciousness as if trying to pull us out of our despair. A trumpet intones a hopeful tune as the music becomes faster and more assured. "Manic," "Reflective," and "Giddy" are heard briefly. The personality is reassembling itself after the tragedy. When the main theme of "Confident" returns again, there is a sense of wholeness and a healthy spirit. The piece ends in a buoyant cloud of optimism.

Unit 3: Historical Perspective

Songs Without Words is a work that portrays short, mood-oriented impressions through wind, brass, and percussion timbres. Many such works were composed in the romantic era, mostly for pianoforte, and were referred to as "character pieces." Such compositions were usually quite short and were designed to portray a specific mood or character. Many of these works were in ternary form (ABA), with A and B representing contrasting moods. Robert Schumann wrote large and demanding compositions consisting of a number of character pieces to be played in succession (character cycle) and organized around a unified idea, for example, *Pappillons*, *Carnival*, *Kreislerianna*, and *Davidsbundler*. While these titles often suggest extra-musical poetic fancies, Schumann, on his own admission, usually composed the music before he thought of the title. Other precedents include Felix Mendelssohn's forty-eight short pieces issued in six books under the collective title *Songs Without Words*. The names now attached to many of these pieces were supplied by the publishers.

Unit 4: Technical Considerations

Songs Without Words for wind ensemble contains medium to medium-advanced technical demands. High schools, honors bands, and college and university ensembles will benefit musically from performing this work. It utilizes the following instrumentation: piccolo, two flutes, two oboes, three B-flat clarinets, bass clarinet, two bassoons, contrabassoon or contrabass clarinet, two E-flat alto saxophones, B-flat tenor saxophone, E-flat baritone saxophone, four horns in F, three B-flat trumpets, three trombones, euphonium, tuba, contrabass, timpani, four percussion, piano, and celesta. Lyrical solos are required of bassoon, tenor saxophone, and alto saxophone in "Reflective" (bassoon and tenor saxophone cross-cued in euphonium), French horn in "Stunned" (cross-cued in alto saxophone), alto saxophone in "Stunned," euphonium and trumpet in "Confident." Of these solo passages, perhaps the most difficult is for the French horn and alto saxophone due to the phrasing, control, and endurance required.

Piano and celesta writing is of modest difficulty and, although not independently scored, adds a great deal of color. The percussion section is expanded but judiciously and musically employed. Technical requirements are moderate but require sensitivity. Instruments include glockenspiel, xylophone, marimba, vibraphone, chimes, snare drum, four tom-toms, two bongos, snare drum, bass drum, timpani, five temple blocks, three wood blocks, five cowbells, three suspended cymbals, sizzle cymbal, brake drum, tam-tam, ratchet, castanets, and tambourine. The composer specifies mallet types as hard, soft, and metallic.

Tonal areas and scale formations include C-natural minor; F major; C, F, and G mixolydian; E-flat minor; G and C lydian; and D/A-flat and E/G bitonality. "Manic" is organized around several twelve-tone rows consisting mostly of alternating seconds and thirds. Mixed meter is utilized in "Reflective," but the moderate tempo (quarter note = 84) and repeated structure negate most difficulties here. Woodwinds must be able to perform sustained sixteenth note figures in 4/4 at quarter note = 116 and 138. "Giddy" contains substantial sections in 6/8. Also, several wide leaps and glissandi will present technical difficulties for young performers. Unmeasured tremolos and fluttertonguing are other extended techniques. Straight and cup mutes are required of brass, including tuba and euphonium. All brass are required to fluttertongue with an extensive passage utilizing this technique for trombones in "Manic." Double tonguing is needed by the trumpets in "Manic." Upper-register playing is required but not extreme (for example, trumpets never exceed written B ii).

Perhaps the most difficult technical issue has to do with exposure. There are few full ensemble *tutti* passages except near the end of the final movement. This clarity of scoring requires sound tone production basics for individuals and sections.

Unit 5: Stylistic Considerations

One of the most challenging aspects of this work is in the area of style. Consistent demands are placed on the performers to be very exact in the area of articulation, expressive *legato* playing, and control, as well as sudden dynamic variation. Transparent, coloristic moments pervade "Reflective" and "Stunned." Passages in "Manic" and "Giddy" are often rhythmically independent and overlapping. "Confident" requires aspects of all these as material from previous movements is revisited, altered, extended, and layered with new material. A listing of terminology and performance suggestions by movement will reflect the wide range of styles needed by performers of this work.

"Manic" . . . . . . .wired, barking, very rigid and clock-like, like vulgar laughter, humorous, raucous, spiky

"Reflective" . . . .unhurried and steady, gently flowing but always rhythmic, pulsing, lonely, hushed

"Giddy" . . . . .boisterous, with infectious good humor, snappy, incisive, grotesque, vulgar, raucous, always very clipped and dry

"Stunned" . . . . . . .glacially slow and tragic, very somber, dark, unhurried, mournfully

"Confident" . . . . .a bit tentative, growing in security, steady and sure, proudly, with a pure and singing tone, stately, in full command, shining

Unit 6: Musical Elements

Songs Without Words contains a diverse amount of musical material, which has the potential to deepen each performer's musical understanding. Listening skills will be challenged as each conductor and instrumentalist comes to terms with the feelingful imagery demanded by the wide variety of styles contained in each movement. The following is a brief summary of several teaching possibilities presented by this work.

MELODY:
- Twelve-tone melodic construction consisting of major and minor thirds

- Diatonic, stepwise melodies, lyrical motion, compact tessitura, based on natural minor, major, lydian, and mixolydian scales

- Angular constructions with wide leaps

- Very slow, sustained, expressive melodies in minor keys

HARMONY:
- Twelve-tone row presented at multiple pitch levels, third inversion major chords, root movement by third

- Major, minor, modal linear and chordal configurations, mixolydian, lydian, natural minor, major

- Bitonality, A-flat/D, E/G

RHYTHM:
Many teaching possibilities are present in the rhythmic content of this work. A major feature is the independent nature of the individual parts. Every player will be challenged to be self-initiating in this regard.

TEXTURE:
There is a wide variety of color and spacing. Orchestration is clear with idiomatic instrumental usage. There is a tendency to employ pure colors.

Foreground, middleground, background roles are apparent, and clear balances are inherent in the score. The teaching challenge will be to create a clear, subtle, nuanced performance. Melody plus accompaniment and layering technique are the predominant textural ideas.

Unit 7: Form and Structure

Songs Without Words is in five movements. Movement III, "Giddy," segues into Movement IV, "Stunned," into Movement V, and "Confident" follows after a brief pause. Material from the first four movements returns in the final movement.

SECTION	MEASURE	EVENT AND SCORING
Movement I: "Manic" (quarter note = 138+; wired)		
A1	1–12	Motive 1; falling minor third, presented in overlapping entrances and varied registers; accents displaced; harmonized as major chords in third inversion, D-flat–B-flat, melodically, six tones of twelve-tone row
Transition	13–18	Woodwind *ostinato* in half steps
A2	19–32	Motive 1 varied in trumpet; woodwind *ostinato* continues; horn presents Motive 1 in augmentation
A3	33–59	Trombone presents Motive 1 in raucous style; woodwinds answer with twelve-tone row at six pitch levels; interplay continues as Motive 1 is developed
A4	60–70	Full ensemble presents twelve-tone at multiple pitch levels then in retrograde followed by version *fff*; grand pause abruptly halts motion
Transition	71–78	Descending pyramid on Motive 1 leads to a brief percussion solo
Coda	79–87	Piccolo, flute, vibraphone present motive in augmentation; all fade as trumpet states opening motive, D-flat–B-flat chords

SECTION MEASURE EVENT AND SCORING

Movement II: "Reflective"
(quarter note = 84; unhurried and steady)

This movement follows an unchanging metric pattern of 5/8, 2/4, and 3/4 in the outer sections. Variety is achieved through overlapping, canonic entrances, differing scale formations, points of color in percussion, and poignant bassoon and saxophone solos.

Section	Measure	Event and Scoring
A1	1–9	Clarinet, vibraphone, and wood block present fixed metric pattern; C-natural minor; continuous eighth note motion
A2	10–18	Bassoon solo; lonely; eighths continue
A3	19–27	Solo continues; *ostinato* continues
A4	28–36	Tenor saxophone joins bassoon; *ostinato* increases with canonic entrances; F mixolydian
A5	37–45	Solos continue; ostinato gets more complex; C pedal leads to transition
Transition	46–49	Metric pattern replaced by continuous 3/4; scoring and dynamic taper
B	50–71	Pulsing eighth note figures; hushed chords; flute and celesta alternate; dreamlike passage
A6	72–80	*Mf* dynamic accompanies brief E minor; metric pattern returns
A7	81–89	Bassoon solo returns; G-natural minor
A8	90–98	Solo; *ostinato* continues
A9	99–107	Alto saxophone solo
A10	108–116	Solo continues; C major/minor
Coda	117–125	B recollected
	126–132	Gradual thinning of texture

SECTION	MEASURE	EVENT AND SCORING
Movement III: "Giddy"		
(dotted-quarter note = 92; boisterous; 6/8)		
A	1–16	Main theme in bassoon, baritone saxophone, euphonium; wide leaps with *glissandi*; woodwind *ostinato* accompanies, G-major7 chords; lydian scale in melody
A2	17–34	Clarinet presents main theme in F; other winds join on B-flat
B	35–48	Horn soli accompanied by percussion, tuba, and contrabass
A3	49–61	Main theme in original key
Trio	62–108	Meter shifts to 2/4, 3/4, descending eighth note figures with triplet interjections; marked grotesque and vulgar, imitates laughter; quarter note = 138
A4	109–125	Return of main theme in original key; abruptly shortened as it is interrupted by Movement IV, "Stunned"
Movement IV: "Stunned"		
(half note = 46; glacially slow)		
Section 1	1–7	Abrupt *ff*; E-flat minor; large registral space; horn and saxophone have non-harmonic tones against chordal background; tapers to *p*
Section 2	8–19	Horn solo against shifting woodwind; percussion sonorities; harmonic sequence B A; C minor; timpani on "heartbeat" motive
Section 3	20–32	A-flat major against alto saxophone solo in D major, then D minor
Section 4	33–41	Clarinet and marimba in E major against alto saxophone solo in G major; chimes intone "Taps"

SECTION	MEASURE	EVENT AND SCORING
Section 5	42–54	A-flat major returns against D major; tempo slows; texture thins; timpani reiterates "heartbeat"

After a brief pause, segue to "Confident"

Movement V: "Confident"
(quarter note = 96)

SECTION	MEASURE	EVENT AND SCORING
Introduction	1–13	Introductory material; C major; euphonium intones Motive 1; tentative, quarter note = 96
A	14–32	Main theme in trumpet solo; C lydian; Motive 1 interspersed; quarter note = 112; gaining in strength
A2	33–51	Main theme in upper woodwinds and trumpet; eighth note *ostinato* accompanies; B-flat major; introductory theme interspersed; accelerates and gains energy; main theme in canon
B	52–65	Material from Movement I ("Manic") returns; one-half step lower than original
C	66–79	Material from Movement II ("Reflective") returns; horn and percussion accompany in expanded form
D	80–104	Movement III material overlaid with main theme of Movement V
A3	105–119	Introductory theme now marked stately, in full command, then main theme, *ff*
A4	120–130	Accelerates, gains momentum; main theme in canon
Coda	131–141	C major; full chords; expanded woodwind figures; final chords refer to Movement I but in C major

Unit 8: Suggested Listening
Other works for concert band and wind ensemble by Dan Welcher:
Arches: An Impression for Concert Band (1985)
Spumante for Wind Ensemble (1999), transcribed by Paul Bissell
Symphony No. 3: Shaker Life (1997)
    I. Laboring Songs
    II. Circular Marches
    Movements are available individually – *Convergence*: North Texas Wind
        Symphony, Eugene Corporon, conductor: Klavier CD 11110
The Yellowstone Fires for Wind Ensemble (1988)
Zion for Wind Ensemble (1994), score and parts
    Published by Elkan-Vogel, Inc., *Tributes*: North Texas Wind Symphony,
    Eugene Corporon, conductor: Klavier CD 11070

Additional works by Dan Welcher:
Abeja Blanca (1973), Jan De Gaetani, Mezzo-soprano; Philip West, English
    horn; Robert Spillman, piano: Bridge Records CD BCD9048
Brass Quintet (1982), American Brass Quintet: Summit Records CD DCD-
    187
Castle Creek Fanfare (1989), Summit Brass: Summit Records CD DCD-127
Evening Scenes: Three Poems of James Agee (1985), Paul Sperry , tenor, with
    Voice of Change Ensemble, Dan Welcher, conductor: Crystal Records
    CD 740
Haleakala (1991); *Prairie Light* (1985); *Clarinet Concerto* (1989), Honolulu
    Symphony Orchestra, Donald Johanos, conductor, with Richard
    Chamberlin, narrator and Bill Jackson, clarinet: Marco Polo CD
    8.223457
Tsunami (1991), New World Records CD 80559-2

Nineteenth century character pieces for piano:
Ludwig van Beethoven, *Bagatelles*
Felix Mendelssohn:
    Children's Pieces
    Songs Without Words
Robert Schumann:
    Album for the Young
    Carnaval
    Davidsbundler
    Fantasiestucke
    Intermezzi
    Kindescenen
    Kreisleriana
    Novelletten
    Papillons

Unit 9: Additional References and Resources

For information on early American hymnody, Shaker music, and the
    development of American musical styles, consult:

Chase, Gilbert. *America's Music: From the Pilgrims to the Present.* Revised
    third edition. Urbana and Chicago: University of Illinois Press, 1987.

Watkins, Glenn. *Soundings: Music in the Twentieth Century.* New York:
    Schirmer Books, 1988.

For a general discussion of nineteenth century piano music, consult:

Grout, Donald Jay, and Claude Palisca. *A History of Western Music.*
    Fifth edition. New York: W. W. Norton and Company, 1996.

For more specific information on nineteenth century piano repertoire,
    consult:

Stewart, Gordon. *A History of Keyboard Literature: Music for the Piano and Its
    Forerunners.* New York: Schirmer Books, 1996.

For a complete listing of works by Dan Welcher as well as a discography, consult www.presser.com/welcher.html. Biographical information used in Unit 1
of this teaching guide was adapted from this source.

Contributed by:

Scott Carter
Director of Bands
East Carolina University
Greenville, North Carolina

Teacher Resource Guide

Symphonic Dance No. 3 ("Fiesta")

Clifton Williams
(1923–1976)

Unit 1: Composer

Born in Traskwood, Arkansas, in 1923, James Clifton Williams had an immense impact on the standard of literature for school, college, and military concert bands. Having pursued piano lessons as a child, he became a horn player in the Little Rock High School Band and Orchestra under the baton of L. Bruce Jones. After high school, he attended Louisiana Tech University for one year before joining the United States Air Force as a bandsman in 1942. He played horn in the Air Force Band, was drum major for the marching band, and began to compose for various Air Force Ensembles.

When World War II ended, Williams returned to Louisiana State University, where he studied composition with Helen Gunderson. His college ensemble conductors were Louis Hasselmans and his former high school director, L. Bruce Jones. Williams completed his Master of Music degree at the Eastman School of Music in 1949, where he had the opportunity to study composition with Bernard Rogers. Upon graduation, he accepted a position at the University of Texas at Austin, where he taught horn and composition.

Williams played horn and guest conducted the San Antonio Symphony for twelve seasons, and also played horn in the Austin Symphony Orchestra for five seasons. In 1966, he was appointed chairman of the department of theory and composition at the University of Miami, where he remained until his death from cancer in 1976. Williams was the teacher and mentor of wind band composers such as W. Francis McBeth, Lawrence Weiner, and John Barnes Chance.

Unit 2: Composition

Symphonic Dance No. 3 is a single-movement work, approximately six minutes and twenty seconds in length. The form of the work consists of three major thematic areas distributed in the form of Introduction–A–B–C–A–Coda.

Harmonically, the work incorporates bitonality and chromaticism. Metric modulation is employed throughout the work, and syncopated patterns are essential in both melodic and accompaniment writing. Contrasts in texture and orchestration contribute to the work's originality and effectiveness. John Wojcik provided the following summary: "The modal characteristic, rhythms, and finely woven melodies depict what Williams called the pageantry of Latin American celebrations—street bands, bullfights, bright costumes, the colorful legacy of a proud people."[1]

Unit 3: Historical Perspective

By 1957, Williams began to receive national acclaim as a composer of serious music for wind band. His work *Fanfare and Allegro* received the first American Bandmasters Association/ Ostwald Award for composition in 1956. Williams also received the award in 1957 for his *Symphonic Suite.*

In 1963, Williams was commissioned to write a group of five works to celebrate the twenty-fifth anniversary of the San Antonio Symphony Orchestra. Between 1963 and 1965, he wrote five *Symphonic Dances*, none of which were published in the orchestral version. The composer rescored all five dances for concert band, and the second ("The Maskers," 1968) and third ("Fiesta," 1967) were published by Sam Fox Publishing Company.

Symphonic Dance No. 3 was first performed by the San Antonio Symphony Orchestra in 1965. Williams conducted the first performance of the band version with the University of Miami Concert Band in 1967. This unique position as an active composer for wind band and orchestra in the 1950s and 1960s is significant. Although *Symphonic Dance No. 3* was written for orchestra, it was published only for wind band and is appropriate for both high school bands and advanced ensembles.

Unit 4: Technical Considerations

The demands of range, articulation, and irregular meter make *Symphonic Dance No. 3* challenging for young players. The parts for English horn, alto clarinet, E-flat contra alto clarinet, and string bass are doubled in other parts. This allows the work to be performed without these instruments as necessary.

Members of the ensemble are asked to play in the keys of A-flat minor; E, G, A-flat, D-flat, and C major; and F and B-flat lydian. Because the score and parts of *Symphonic Dance No. 3* do not utilize a key signature, players must be proficient in reading accidentals.

---

1 John Wojcik, "Bitonal Harmonies in Clifton Williams' Fiesta," *The Instrumentalist*, May 1996, p. 28.

Brass players are required to execute rapid articulations in upper ranges during the work. Articulations must remain clear and non-accented tones light. Balance and intonation of chords must be approached consistently throughout to work to execute bi-tonal elements. Woodwinds are required to maintain pitch during long, sustained tones and phrases with extensive chromaticism.

Unit 5: Stylistic Considerations

The themes in *Symphonic Dance No. 3* are principally conjunct, and the melodies are characterized by syncopation and accents. Accents enhance syncopated melodic and accompaniment lines. The sixteenth note triplet motive is central to the introduction, coda, and three thematic areas of the work. Triplet figures are written as ornaments of the principal melodic pitches. In addition, double dotted-quarter notes are employed in the introduction.

Establishing the appropriate tempo in each section of the work is essential to the development of each theme's individual character. Careful consideration of the markings (*drammatico*, *allegretto con grazia*, and *pesante e rubato*) provides direction for the treatment of articulations, dynamics, note lengths, and releases. For example, *molto meno mosso* and *piu mosso* markings at letter D indicate those sections of the trumpet solo that proceed in and out of tempo; the corresponding section at measure 135 is marked *andante rubato*. *Fermatas* highlight important structural points, create dramatic impact, and allow for flexibility of interpretation. Breath marks contribute to both phrasing and musical effect.

It is difficult to successfully execute the percussion parts of *Symphonic Dance No. 3* without five players. In addition, the introduction is effective with doubling of the Latin percussion instruments. Percussion *ostinati* enhance the character of the melodic writing and contribute to its rhythmic vitality. The 3/4 section of the coda, letter N, features a percussion interlude.

Unit 6: Musical Elements

Williams uses bitonality to create indistinct harmonies without atonal dissonance. There is extensive harmonic and melodic use of the minor second. An effective teaching strategy could include the isolation of individual tonalities in bi-tonal sections in order to isolate members of distinct chords.

Williams's orchestration contrasts full ensemble with solo, sectional, and chamber writing. These textural contrasts are generally accompanied by distinct contrasts in style, tempo, dynamics, and articulations. Each of the thematic areas should be compared and contrasted to establish the appropriate style indicators within the sections. For example, the trumpet solo at measures 44 through 51 should be rehearsed alongside the parallel structural section in measures 135 through 142. The A theme at measure 17 should be rehearsed with attention to its second appearance in measure 119.

Williams employs metric modulation throughout the work, and syncopated patterns on the anacrusis of beats two and four are an essential compositional element. Both duple and triple division of the beat is employed. The coda, beginning at letter M, employs canonic imitation and increased harmonic and rhythmic activity. The conductor may consider incorporating visual images with each new character or theme of the work to facilitate interpretation.

The dynamic range of the work extends from *piano* to *sforzando*. Williams carefully notates accents, *tenuto* markings, and *staccatos*, and the articulations solidify the character of each of the three themes. These articulations should be altered according to the tempo and style of the thematic areas. Specific focus on articulations and note lengths at a variety of tempi will assist in the establishment of style and the vital role of the accent.

Unit 7: Form and Structure

Section	Measure	Event and Scoring
Introduction	1–10	*Drammatico*; brass fanfare; melodic motive based on the interval of A minor second (B-flat to B-natural)
	10–16	Second motive in A-flat minor appears in low reeds and brass; trombone and saxophone accompaniment in E major
A	17–43	Theme 1 in G major; 5/4 meter (AAB form, three four-measure phrases); low reeds and brass provide accompaniment in F lydian (note B-natural)
	44–52	Trumpet solo in 4/4 meter (two four-measure phrases) in *rubato* style
	53–70	Principal theme returns in woodwinds and horn, then woodwinds, trumpet, and baritone with rhythmic modulation between 5/4 and 4/4 meter
B	71–84	*Allegretto con grazia*; Theme 2 in D-flat major (flute) with accompaniment patterns in G-flat major; modulation to C-flat major with D-flat major accompaniment in m. 79

SECTION	MEASURE	EVENT AND SCORING
	85–96	Second presentation of Theme 2 with increased instrumentation; modulation to A-flat major
C	97–118	*Pesante e rubato*; Theme 3 derived from melodic material in mm. 1–2 (melodic minor second, F to G-flat primary); B-flat pedal in upper woodwind voices
A	119–134	Theme 1 returns in 5/4 meter with transition in 4/4 meter; melody is in C major, while accompaniment is in B-flat lydian (dense orchestration)
	135–142	Melodic woodwind unison parallel to trumpet solo in mm. 44–52
	143–156	Principal theme returns in 4/4 meter (dense orchestration returns)
Coda	157–163	Descending melodic line emphasizes the dominant to tonic relationship, modulating from F major to C major; C pedal in upper woodwind, trombone, and bells parts
	163–172	Bitonal elements; modulation from C to C-flat major followed by percussion interlude in 3/4 meter
	173–182	Repetition of mm. 163–172 with added trombone *glissandi*
	183–188	Syncopated unison phrase ends on F; trombone *glissandi*, m. 185, in F lydian reminiscent of Theme 1

Unit 8: Suggested Listening
Aaron Copland, *El Salon Mexico*
Morton Gould, *Santa Fe Saga*
Roger Nixon, *Fiesta Del Pacifico*
H. Owen Reed, *La Fiesta Mexicana*
Clifton Williams:
> *Caccia and Chorale*
> *Dedicatory Overture*
> *Fanfare and Allegro*
> *Symphonic Dance No. 2 ("The Maskers")*
> *Symphonic Suite*
> *Variation Overture*

Unit 9: Additional References and Resources

"Clifton Williams, Caccia and Chorale." *Teaching Music through Performance in Band.* Compiled and edited by Richard Miles. Chicago: GIA Publications, Inc., 1997.

Daniel, Joe Rayford. "The Band Works of James Clifton Williams." Ph.D. dissertation, University of Southern Mississippi, 1981.

Rehrig, William H. *The Heritage Encyclopedia of Band Music.* Westerville, OH: Integrity Press, 1991.

Siler, John Robert. "The Non-formalized Pitch Rhythm Ostinato in Band Works of Clifton Williams: A Categorization of Patterns." Ph.D. dissertation, University of South Carolina, 1985.

Smith, Norman E. *Program Notes for Band.* Chicago, IL: GIA Publications, Inc., 2001.

Wojcik, John. "Bitonal Harmonies in Clifton Williams' Fiesta." *The Instrumentalist,* May 1996, pp. 28–34.

Contributed by:
Wendy McCallum
Doctoral Conducting Associate
University of North Texas
Denton, Texas

Grade Five

Teacher Resource Guide

Aegean Festival Overture

Andreas Makris
(b. 1930)

Unit 1: Composer

Andreas Makris was born in the Aegean seaport of Salonika, Greece, in 1930. He was a prize student at the National Conservatory of Greece. At the age of twenty, he came to America, where he was a scholarship student at Phillips University, the Kansas City Conservatory, and the Mannes School of Music in New York City. He did post-graduate work at the Aspen Music Center and studied composition in Paris with Nadia Boulanger.

The bulk of his career was spent as a first violinist in the National Symphony Orchestra in Washington, DC. He had the distinction of becoming the first contemporary composer to have his music performed at the Kennedy Center for the Arts under the direction of Conductor Antal Dorati. In addition, Mstislav Rostropovich appointed him to the post of Composer-in-Residence for the National Symphony and sought his advice in selecting new works to program with the orchestra.

His numerous works include two string quartets, *Quintet for Soprano and String Orchestra, Concerto for Strings, Viola Concerto, Anamneses* (for orchestra), *Concertino for Trombone and Strings, Efthymia* (for orchestra), *Fantasy and Dance for Saxophone, Mediterranean Holiday* (for concert band), and *Chrometekinesis* (for orchestra).

Unit 2: Composition

Aegean Festival Overture was written for the National Symphony Orchestra and premiered in 1967 by the Symphony under the direction of Howard Mitchell at the Kennedy Center in Washington, DC. The composition was supported by a grant from the National Endowment for the Arts. The popularity of the work attracted the interest of the United States Air Force Band and its conductor, Colonel Arnold Gabriel. The chief arranger for the U. S. Air Force Band, Major Albert Bader, collaborated with Makris to produce a transcription to be used on subsequent tours by Col. Gabriel. The arrangement was so successful that it has since become a staple of the wind band repertoire.

Major Albert Bader is a native of St. Louis who was trained at the St. Louis Conservatory. Prior to his appointment to the Air Force Band in Washington, Major Bader was the chief instructor at the U. S. Air Force School of Music, where he designed curricula and taught conducting, arranging, and theory. During his tenure in Washington, Major Bader was also the assistant conductor for the U. S. Air Force Band. He has contributed several outstanding transcriptions to the wind band repertoire, including Samuel Barber's *School for Scandal Overture*.

This composition is approximately ten minutes in length and is a terrific showpiece to highlight the virtuosic characteristics of the modern wind band. The exotic nature of the melodies combined with the rhythmic energy produced by the asymmetrical meter make this work an outstanding curtain-raiser for any concert setting.

Unit 3: Historical Perspective

Contemporary orchestral compositions during the 1960s were dominated by composers who stretched the musical boundaries and experience levels of their audiences. Composers such as Xenakis, Cage, and Stockhausen were less concerned with establishing a relationship with their audience; rather, they were more concerned with the purity of the artistic process and expression. This often left audiences alienated and frustrated by contemporary music programmed by orchestras around the world during this time period.

The appearance of *Aegean Festival Overture* in 1967, supported by a grant from the National Endowment for the Arts, must have been a welcome change for patrons who recoiled at the appearance of any piece of music written after 1940. This music is tuneful, with a relentless rhythmic drive that immediately made a favorable impression with audiences. The Greek folk-like character of the middle section suggests the work of early twentieth century composers, such as Bartok, Kodaly, Holst, and Vaughan Williams, who utilized indigenous folk music in their serious orchestral works. Furthermore, the classical form of *Aegean Festival Overture* allowed audiences to process the exotic melodic material in such a manner that it was more easily accessible than most of the contemporary music of the day.

This orchestral work lends itself very well to a transcription for winds. The rhythmic nature of the "A" section translates easily to wind instruments, and the lyrical solos in the "B" section are straight from the original orchestration.

Unit 4: Technical Considerations

This work demands a thorough understanding of the relationship between pulse and subdivision in asymmetric meter. The constancy of the eighth note pulse as it winds through the various mixed meters is paramount. Ensemble problems develop rhythmically when performers compress eighth notes grouped in three and then tend to slow down eighth notes grouped in two. Time and effort must be spent on teaching how to deal with this rhythmic concept. The antiphonal use of winds versus brass through these passages also poses ensemble problems. Tempo inaccuracies occur when rests are subdivided improperly, which causes subsequent entrances to enter late.

The challenge for the conductor in this piece is to establish the right tempo and spirit of the piece without upsetting the rhythmic flow for the players. The piece can settle into a "groove" that swings quite naturally. Extraneous gestures and over-conducting can quickly sap the rhythmic energy of the piece and make it very difficult for the players to maintain the tempo and style.

Virtuosic technical passages occur in each section. A thorough knowledge of phrygian modes, chromatic, and diminished scales is required of everyone. Stylistically, the ensemble must be able to produce a pristine, light *staccato* style. The melodies (especially in the "A" section) will not sparkle unless lightness in articulation can be produced.

The "B" section requires strong independent soloists on all woodwind instruments. The prominent solos demand excellence in musicianship from piccolo, flute, oboe, clarinet (extended cadenza), bass clarinet, bassoon, and alto saxophone performers. The E-flat clarinet solos are cross-cued in the solo clarinet part, and the lack of an English horn may require cross-cueing of this part for the alto saxophone. However, the color contrast loss due to the cross-cueing may take away some of the sparkle of the orchestration.

Unit 5: Stylistic Considerations

The exuberant nature of the "A" section requires a sophisticated approach to articulation. To maintain tempo, each instrument and family must be able to produce a light *staccato* style. The natural attack of a xylophone performing eighth notes in the upper register or a small triangle would be a good example to portray the style intended by the composer for the students.

The "B" section is much more reflective and somber. The performers must be free to shape the musical line individually to reproduce the most expressive interpretation of the phrase. This requires a basic understanding of the concept of "tension and release" in phrasing. Also, the connection between notes of upward melodic intervals is crucial to the success of the individual solos. This effect is very similar to the use of *portamento* in string technique.

Unit 6: Musical Elements

The combination of classical form (A–B–A), exotic Greek folk-like melodies, and the relentless rhythmic activity make for an interesting study of compositional technique. The construction of the piece is a large A–B–A arch form. Within each major section, another arch form (a–b–a) appears. Consequently, the composition makes structural sense intellectually and perceptually to the listener during the initial hearings.

The melodies are constructed around major modes, chromatic scales, diminished scales, and minor phrygian modes. The texture is basically homophonic, with a brief section of polyphony in the "b" section of the first "A" statement. The chordal structure is common practice harmony with dissonant chromaticisms and polychords tossed in to create tension and forward motion.

The rhythmic treatment is the most engaging facet of the composition. Constant metrical and asymmetrical shifts, along with the usage of hemiola and shifting accents, create an air of expectancy and excitement throughout the piece.

Unit 7: Form and Structure

SECTION	MEASURE	EVENT AND SCORING
A	1–9	Introductory material; *tutti* dotted-eighth note and sixteenth triplet figures; woodwinds play sixteenth note scalar passages
	10	Transition; *staccato* eighth note passage in clarinet and bassoon establishes F major as tonic
a	11–18	Theme 1; performed by E-flat clarinet, flute, and alto saxophone in F major
	19–27	Theme 1a; performed by low brass and low woodwinds
	28–36	Theme 1a; continued by low brass and woodwinds; melodic fragments tossed about hocket-style in woodwinds
	37–46	Retransition; *tutti* chromatic melodic and rhythmic fragments in hemiola
	47–54	Theme 1 returns in upper brass and woodwinds

SECTION	MEASURE	EVENT AND SCORING
b	55–56	Transition material; *staccato* eighth notes in clarinet provides rhythmic ground for next theme
	57–66	Theme 2; piccolo solo in B phrygian; asymmetrical meter; triangle and xylophone accompany
	67–72	Theme 2; E-flat clarinet in E-flat phrygian; brass interjections at phrase ending
	73–78	Theme 2; E-flat clarinet passes phrase to piccolo; oboe and English horn conclude phrase
	79–87	Theme 2; alto saxophone passes theme to clarinet in B-flat phrygian; piccolo performs figurations *obbligato*
	88–95	Theme 2a; trumpets develop material from Theme 2 chromatically in asym metric meter
Fugal development	96–105	Theme 2 performed by low woodwinds and bass in C-sharp phrygian
	106–115	Theme 2 performed by clarinet in D phrygian; countersubject stated by bass clarinet, bassoon, and euphonium
	116–124	Theme 2 performed by clarinet in B phrygian
	125–131	Theme 2a; *tutti*; motive developed chromatically
	132–141	Theme 2; performed by upper woodwinds in B phrygian; pulsing eighth note figures in brass reinforce feeling of tonic
Codetta	142–148	Closing material; woodwinds develop motive from Theme 2; dominant pedal-point on C helps return tonal center to F major

SECTION	MEASURE	EVENT AND SCORING
a	149–156	Theme 1 returns in upper brass and woodwinds (F major)
	157–163	Theme 3 appears in D major; *tutti*; asymmetric meter gives theme dance-like quality
Coda	164–177	D major chord in woodwinds is juxtaposed with B-flat major chord in brass antiphonally; tone cluster by flute heightens tension as section comes to a close
	178–180	Tone cluster by flute descends chromatically; rising *glissando* by timpani introduces clarinet cadenza
B	181–182	Percussion establish rhythmic *ostinato*
	183–191	Theme 4 introduced by bassoon in E-flat minor
	192–193	Brass take over rhythmic *ostinato*
	194–199	Theme 4 performed by flute
	200–203	Theme 4, Motive 1 passed between oboe, bass clarinet, clarinet, and bassoon
	204–217	Theme 4 performed by woodwinds in D minor accompanied by horn
	218–222	Theme 4, Motive 2 developed by a chromatic sequence in clarinet
	223–228	Theme 4, Motive 2 developed by a chromatic sequence in oboe and flute; saxophone and clarinet conclude phrase
	229–240	Theme 4 performed by segmented phrase in bassoon, alto saxophone, English horn, and bassoon in D minor
A	241–244	Transition; clarinet performs a combination of diminished and chromatic scale figurations.

Section	Measure	Event and Scoring
	245–250	Return of introductory material in woodwinds
	251	Transition; *staccato* eighth note passage in clarinet and bassoon establishes F major as tonic
a	252–259	Theme 1; performed by E-flat clarinet, flute, and alto saxophone in F major
	260–269	Theme 1a; performed by low brass and woodwinds; melodic fragments tossed about hocket-style in woodwinds
	270–278	Retransition; *tutti* chromatic melodic and rhythmic fragments in hemiola
	279–286	Theme 1 returns in upper brass and woodwinds
b	287–288	Transition material; *staccato* eighth notes in clarinet provides rhythmic ground for next theme
	289–298	Theme 2; piccolo solo in D phrygian; asymmetrical meter; triangle and xylophone accompany
	299–304	Theme 2; E-flat clarinet in G-flat phrygian to flute in G phrygian; brass interjections at phrase ending
	305–316	Transition; Theme 2 phrase segments passed among low woodwinds
	317–324	Theme 1; piccolo plays first phrase with flute and triangle accompaniment in F major; second half of phrase performed *tutti*
	325–334	Theme 3 reappears in D major; *tutti*
Coda	335–339	D major chord in woodwinds is juxtaposed with B-flat major chord in brass antiphonally

SECTION	MEASURE	EVENT AND SCORING
	340–344	D major/B-flat major polychord; octave D concert sustained while brass create tension with stacked triads underneath
	345–350	Raucous percussion brings piece to a close in D major

Unit 8: Suggested Listening

Bela Bartok:
Concerto for Orchestra
The Miraculous Mandarin
Leonard Bernstein:
The Jeremiah Symphony (Profanation)
"Symphonic Dances" from *West Side Story*
Michael Hennagin, *Dance Scene*
Andreas Makris:
Mediterranean Holiday
Intrigues for Solo Clarinet and Wind Ensemble
Alfred Reed, *Armenian Dances*, Part 1
Nikos Skalkottas, *Greek Dances*
Igor Stravinsky, *L'Histoire du Soldat*

Unit 9: Additional References and Resources

Baker, Theodore. *Baker's Biographical Dictionary of Music and Musicians*. Sixth edition. Revised by Nicolas Slonimsky. New York: Schirmer Books, 1984.

Bernstein, Leonard. *Findings: Fifty Years of Meditations on Music*. New York: Simon and Schuster, 1982.

Smith, Norman, and Albert Stoutamire. *Band Music Notes*. Chicago, IL: GIA Publications, Inc., 2001.

National Band Association Selective Music List for Bands

Rehrig, William H. *The Encyclopedia of Band Music*. Edited by Paul E. Bierley. Westerville, OH: Integrity Press, 1991.

Contributed by:

Leslie W. Hicken
Director of Bands
Furman University
Greenville, South Carolina

Teacher Resource Guide

Bacchanale, Op. 20

Rolf Rudin
(b. 1961)

Unit 1: Composer

Rolf Rudin, a native of Frankfurt, Germany, received his formal music training in music education, composition, conducting, and theory in Frankfurt and Würzburg. During his academic studies, the Bavarian Ministry for Cultural Affairs awarded him a scholarship with a six-month sabbatical and sojourn in Paris, France, where he studied at the Cité Internationale des Arts. Upon completion of his studies in 1992, Rudin began working as a freelance composer, and since 1993, he has also taught music theory at the Frankfurter Musikhochschule.

Rudin has written well over fifty works for a variety of performance media, and several of his pieces for chamber ensembles, choir, and orchestra have won prizes in national and international competition. However, Rudin is an outspoken advocate for the symphonic wind orchestra, and since 1989, he has concentrated a great deal of his energies on composing for band.[1]

Rudin's first two pieces for band, *Imperial Prelude, Op. 15*, and *Bacchanale, Op. 20*, were premiered in 1990. Since that time, Rudin has composed at least one major work for band each year. He has enjoyed a steady stream of commissions, and his pieces have been premiered by some of the finest bands in Europe.

---

1 Rudin, Rolf. Biographical Notes in *Bacchanale für Sinfonisches Blasorchester, Op. 20*. Germany: Edition Flor, 1990.

Unit 2: Composition

Although Rudin found it difficult to decide on an appropriate title for *Imperial Prelude*, his first work for band, he found it quite easy to name his second band composition. In fact, the first piece was entirely completed before a title had been selected, but Rudin writes that the title *Bacchanale* "came to mind almost involuntarily when I was working with the score."[2]

Bacchus was the Greco-Roman god of wine, and the original Latin term "bacchanal" referred to an ancient Roman festival to honor or worship the god. Later, the term came to insinuate a boisterous, drunken party. So, the term "bacchantic" can be taken to mean boisterous and exuberant. This is the atmosphere into which musicians and listeners find themselves catapulted at the beginning of this piece.

The piece has three major formal divisions, but because of the two interludes that foreshadow the third section, one might initially hear five formal events. The composer describes the foreshadowing passages as mere interludes, with the melodic and harmonic material in the first two sections building to a pure apogee, or apex, in the third section. While the first two sections are very rhythmic and energetic, with a quick tempo, the closing section is very romantic in thematic and harmonic material, with a slow and resolute tempo. With a duration of approximately eleven minutes and thirty seconds, the piece provides a great deal of musical material to engage both the performers and the listeners in developing concepts of thematic progression, growth, and formal design.[3]

Unit 3: Historical Perspective

Rudin has emerged as one of a generation of composers who have chosen to write music for wind ensemble (or as he calls it, "symphonic wind orchestra") because of its viability as an expressive, artistic, and powerful performance group. He does not see himself as a "band composer." Having become familiar with the timbres, technical abilities, power, and finesse available from a band of proficient players, Rudin simply chooses the wind ensemble, from many available options, as a vehicle by which he wishes to communicate his musical ideas. He is one of several composers who, since the advent of the Eastman Wind Ensemble in 1952, has gained recognition and acclaim not only for his band works, but also for the compositions he has written for other mediums.[4] The popularity of works by Rudin, Jan Van der Roost, Johan de Meij, and other European composers provides evidence that the reputation of the symphonic wind band is growing in many parts of the world. So while the

---

2 Ibid.

3 Ibid.

4 Interview with the composer. 1999 World Association of Symphonic Bands and Ensembles (WASBE) convention. http://www.bandandorchestra.com/html/AV_html/Rudin.htm.

musical ideas of this piece may reflect an atmosphere or environment of ancient Greco-Roman culture, the musical elements of melody, harmony, rhythm, and tonal design are clearly reflective of a full-scale symphonic wind composition from the second half of the twentieth century.

Unit 4: Technical Considerations

Expanded instrumentation is an issue that must be addressed in the programming of this work. Rudin's instrumentation seems to have evolved from traditional European military band scoring. A large clarinet section will be needed, including an E-flat soprano and at least three players on each of the three remaining B-flat soprano clarinet parts. In addition, three flugelhorn parts are scored independently of the three traditional trumpet parts, so the flugelhorn parts cannot be doubled by the trumpet players. The piece also calls for three euphoniums in divisi, and it will take approximately seven proficient percussionists to play all of the percussion parts.

The most challenging aspect of the opening section of this piece is the rhythmic construction. It is written in cut time, *alla breve*, with several measures of 5/4, 3/4, and 1/2 incorporated into phrases. Additionally, because of the frequent use of half note triplets and quarter note triplets, the performers must become comfortable with seamless transitions in and out of simple and compound subdivision. This means that at times there is a constant pulse with changing subdivision and at times the pulse is changed by a constant subdivision. In a very effective way, this keeps the listener from being able to identify an exact pulse or time for the opening section, but the notation for the performers is quite clear. Although it will take fairly mature players to be able to perform these multi-metered passages, the phrases occur in a repetitive pattern, so these are skills that could actually be learned and developed through the rehearsal process.

The second section of the piece is quite brisk, and for the most part, it is in simple compound meter (4/4) with eighth note triplet subdivision. The woodwind parts contain a significant amount of chromatic motion, and most of the upper brass will need to be able to triple-tongue in order to play the fanfare passages. Again, pulse and rhythmic skills will be important because the melodic and harmonic material is often treated in a hocket fashion. In addition to the polychordal harmonic writing, this middle section of the piece has a great deal of polyrhythmic moments—with triplets against straight eighth notes and sixteenths.

The final section of the piece is beautiful and lyrical, with a variety of exposed solo timbres in the melodic line and carefully scored color changes in the supporting harmonic material. Additionally, all throughout the piece there is a wide range of dynamic contrast. This bacchanale will require mature tone quality throughout the ensemble.

Unit 5: Stylistic Considerations

Harmonically, this is a contemporary piece of music, but from a melodic perspective it is written in the romantic tradition. A sense of *rubato* and freedom of expression are necessary for the lyrical aspects of the piece to be communicated. It also requires a wide variety of dynamic contrast. In the opening section of the work, the two contrasting motivic ideas are presented in unison, delineated by different articulations and dynamic levels. However, as each of the two ideas is repeated, additional chord tones are added. By the time the climax of the opening section arrives (at measure 78), the theme is voiced in a thick polychordal texture. The woodwinds must be able to play spaced *staccatos* with a strong "front" on each note, and the *marcato* accents should have the same front, with a full-valued duration. The dynamic build throughout the opening section is integral to a well-paced and musically prepared climactic phrase beginning in measure 78.

As noted earlier, the middle section of the piece will require a precise pulse and accurate rhythmic subdivision for the driving tempo to remain constant and energetic. The *staccato* notes must be dry and crisp to achieve balance and clarity between the various voices. Trills, tremolos, and fluttertongued passages are part of the devices used to create polychordal sound screens behind the aggressive rhythmic melody.

The two lyrical interludes and the closing section are based melodically and harmonically on a circle-of-fifths progression. As the melody slowly unfolds and moves through different voices, the harmonic progression continues to build dramatically. The piccolo solo above the brass chordal section is dramatic, and it will require a very advanced musician. In the last seven measures of the piece, there is a brief but formally significant polychordal progression that precedes a very clear cadential ending on an E-flat major triad.

Unit 6: Musical Elements

The harmonic language of the piece is polychordal, with several overlapping triads occurring in what Rudin calls "bitonal architecture."[5] The most prevalent tonal center in the opening section is A major, which is actually the first triad performed in the piece. After the arrival at the climactic event of the first section, measures 78 through 97, with a thick polychordal texture, the A major triad emerges in a cadential fashion at the end of the first section. The middle section also contains passages of quarter note polychords, usually functioning as harmonic material, but closely related to the polychordal passages from the opening section. The final section of the piece is centered in triadic harmonies, but there is the brief polychordal "remembrance" of previous material that occurs in the final seven measures of the piece.

---

5 Rudin. Notes in *Bacchanale, Op. 20*.

There are several ways an ensemble can become accustomed to balancing, centering, and tuning these bitonal or polychordal passages. With a major or minor triad as a starting point, additional major or minor thirds could be stacked above and below the triad, creating a variety of polychordal textures. Most bands are familiar with the "Remington" warm-up, which begins on concert F in all voices and descends by half steps, returning to the F in between each descending pitch. One might divide an ensemble into two groups, with one group holding a constant triad (for example: C, E, G) while the other group starts on that triad and then proceeds through the Remington pattern. This would result in a unison C major triad, followed by a C major triad/B major triad, back to a unison C major triad, followed by a C major/ B-flat major triad, C major triad, followed by a C major/A major triad, and so forth. Although this exercise may originally sound extremely dissonant, with emphasis placed on connecting to common harmonics, it could prove very beneficial to tuning and balancing polychordal and bitonal writing.

The middle section of the piece requires that the ensemble be able to play technical passages together and in time. Much of the writing centers around triple-tongued passages in the brass and whole-tone scale patterns in the woodwinds, both in triplet subdivision. One teaching technique might include writing out different whole-tone scales, with eighth note triplets occurring on each pitch of the scale. The brass players could practice their triple tonguing, and the woodwinds could practice the scalar passages and finger patterns. Once the whole-tone scales are mastered, ascending and descending, the patterns could be increased in speed. One might also have the whole-tone scales played in sixteenth notes, and combine the sixteenth note patterns with the eighth note triplets at the same time so one group is playing compound subdivision against the duple subdivision of the other group.

The performing ensemble should understand the melodic and harmonic role that the circle of fifths plays in the two interludes and the final section, the apogee of the piece. Perhaps simply playing a circle of fifths progression, in unison, on whole or half notes would establish familiarity with the interval of the perfect fifth and the pitch tendencies of the circular melodic movement. If an exercise were to be written that involved moving from one triad to the next, adding the dominant seventh of the chord before each new triad, the players could concentrate not only on pitch but also on the chromatic motion and resolution from the third of the triad (which is the leading tone to the next triad) and the downward chromatic movement of the dominant seventh to the new third.

Unit 7: Form and Structure

Section	Measure	Event and Scoring
A	1–101	Opening motive ideas in unison; patterns repeating three times through letter A; triadic harmonies incorporated beginning at m. 24, building harmonically to polychordal apex at m. 78; full scoring
Interlude 1	102–118	Foreshadows Section C; solo voicing in several instruments; one on a part during ensemble passages; begins in tonal area of C and cadences on B major triad at beginning of Section B
B	119–228	At times, contrasting ideas voiced in choirs, but mostly aggressive full ensemble scoring; technically demanding; wide dynamic range necessary
Interlude 2	229–236	Foreshadows Section C
B1	237–293	Begins with soft solo scoring, building quickly to full tutti rhythmic and polychordal harmonic climax at m. 278; controlled and measured dissonant resolution to E-flat major triad in mm. 286–293
C	294–end	Melody initially scored for solo voices with ensemble harmonic support; dramatic subito piano and emerging piccolo solo at m. 311; dynamics continue to build through the circle of fifths progression to a dynamic climax at m. 319; polychordal "reminder" in mm. 329–332; piece cadences and ends resolutely on E-flat major triad

Unit 8: Suggested Listening

Michael Colgrass, *Urban Requiem* – University of Miami Wind Ensemble (Troy 212 Albany Records)

Jacques Ibert, *Bacchanale* – Louisville Orchestra (LS-702)

Ron Nelson, *Rocky Point Holiday* – Dallas Wind Symphony (Reference Recordings RR-76CD)

Rolf Rudin:

Bacchanale, Op. 20 – University of North Texas Wind Symphony, (Klavier KCD-11098)

The Dream of Oenghus, op. 37. University of North Texas Wind Symphony, (Klavier KCD-11089)

Camille Saint-Saëns, "Bacchanale" from *Samson and Delilah* – Philadelphia Orchestra (Columbia Masterworks MS6624)

Unit 9: Additional References and Resources

"About the Works for Symphonic Wind Orchestra by Rolf Rudin." Erlensee, Germany: Edition Flor, 1999.

Edition Flor. "Rolf Rudin: Works for Symphonic Wind Orchestra." St. Louis, MO: Shattinger Music Co., 1998.

Interview with Rolf Rudin at the 1999 World Association of Symphonic Bands and Ensembles (WASBE) convention. http://www.bandandorchestra.com/html/AV_html/Rudin.htm

Rudin, Rolf. *Bacchanale, Op. 20.* Erlensee, Germany: Edition Flor, 1998.

Tower, Ibrook. "Lied ohne Worte (Song without Words), by Rolf Rudin" in Blocher, Corporon, et al. *Teaching Music through Performance in Band,* Volume 3. Edited by Richard Miles. Chicago: GIA Publications, 2000, pp. 238–44.

Contributed by:

Brian Lamb
Director of Bands
University of Central Oklahoma
Edmond, Oklahoma

Teacher Resource Guide

Bugs

Roger Cichy
(b. 1956)

Unit 1: Composer

Roger Cichy has a diverse background as both a composer/arranger and a music educator. He holds a Bachelor of Music and Master of Arts in Music Education from The Ohio State University.

As a music educator, Cichy was a very successful band director in Mars, Pennsylvania, covering grades five through twelve in instrumental music. He served as Associate Director of Bands at the University of Rhode Island and Iowa State University. Since 1995, he has devoted full time to composing and arranging. He has over 275 compositions and arrangements accredited to his name, and major college and professional bands around the world have performed his works. Recent works include *Divertimento for Winds and Percussion*, *Galilean Moons*, *Colours*, *Make a Joyous Sound*, *BBC Forever!*, *Wisconsin Soundscapes*, *First Flights*, *Festival!*, *T.Rex*, and *Wizards*.

Unit 2: Composition

Bugs is an engaging work in six movements that takes the performers and listeners through numerous musical styles that allude to pictorial representations of various insects. Cichy writes:

> The concept for *Bugs* had been in the back of my mind for a number of years and this commission seemed right for this piece. Several years back when I came up with the idea for the piece, I visited the Field Museum in Chicago and "researched" the bugs. I came back with a long list of possibilities for the movements. I had not intended on writing an introduction, which I humorously titled

"Prelude," but it just popped out when I started working on the piece. The other bug movements were chosen based on a variety of musical styles that would ultimately make up the piece. The final movement was completed and delivered to St. Thomas less than a month before the premiere.

Unit 3: Historical Perspective

Bugs is the result of a commission from the University of St. Thomas Wind Ensemble and its conductor, Matthew George. It received its premiere at the Midwest Regional CBDNA Conference in Spring 2000 at Central Michigan University. Since its premiere, it has received numerous performances throughout the United States and abroad, and has been recorded by the University of North Texas Symphonic Band on MARK MCD 3880, released 2001.

Unit 4: Technical Considerations

Movement I: "Prelude"

This brief introduction to the work (one minute and thirty seconds) is somewhat precocious in nature, perhaps suggesting the comings and goings of various insects exploring a stationary object or person. The introduction centers around three solo snare drums played with brushes and punctuated by claves, as if slapping at the bugs. The three solo parts become intertwined and serve as the "glue" throughout the movement. The first melodic material is provided in hocket fashion in high woodwinds and muted brass. The driving nature of the movement is soon transferred to the *tutti* ensemble. It continues to retain a *staccato* and vibrant style. The high woodwinds and percussion begin an improvised "bug noise" section that layers over the top of a quasi "jazz rhythm section." The movement closes with a fervent ascending scoring that results in C/C-sharp dissonant punctuations.

Movement II: "Dragonfly"

This movement seems to extend the flighty, *staccato* style that was introduced in the "Prelude." The initial tempo is only slightly faster (160) than the "Prelude." The movement's "A" section provides the most metric challenges in the piece for the ensemble and conductor. It includes meters of 3/4, 4/4, 9/8, and 5/8, with numerous syncopations and duple/triple rhythmic combinations. The "B" section is a little slower (138) and continues the metric diversity of the "A" section. This section contains the primary melodic material for the movement and heavily utilizes the tritone influence. High woodwinds provide *staccato* punctuation over the top of low reed and brass melody throughout this section. Percussion and piano continue to weave in and around both musical ideas.

MOVEMENT III: "PRAYING MANTIS"

This movement is marked "Religioso" at MM 60 and serves as a beautiful and reflective contrast to the previous two movements. The opening eight measures present a brass quartet consisting of horn, trombone, euphonium, and tuba. The "A" section of the theme is repeated by oboe/flugelhorn with lush, low brass chordal accompaniment. The bridge, or "B" section, is a little faster and features solo flute with solo horn *obbligato* over clarinet accompaniment. Alto saxophone joins the flute at the conclusion of the section. The opening hymn returns with oboe and flugelhorn melody and concludes with a lullaby reference in the horn. The primary technical challenges in this movement result from intonation issues that are inherent with the key of C and in equal temperament tuning of the winds to the fixed pitch piano and keyboards throughout.

MOVEMENT IV: "BLACK WIDOW SPIDER"

The composer describes the style of this movement as "Swinging, cool (and HOT!)" at MM 152. This programmatic movement is very much "big band"-oriented with pianistic right hand/left hand concepts throughout. It describes a "cool" black widow spider slowly crawling across its web. The melody is in eights—for the eight legs it has. In addition, there is a fragmentized dodecaphonic scale from the octave working inward, simulating a web. The heavy jazz influence in this movement is obvious in its rhythmic and driving percussive nature. The primary melodic theme is introduced in clarinets over the top of "cool" finger pops, ala *West Side Story*. Consider expanding the number of performers doing the finger pops to maximize the effect. This fifteen-beat melody continues to vamp five times as additional layers of activity, countermelody, and counter-countermelody join. According to the composer, this section suggests the spider sensing some prey and an eventual meal, gradually moving towards it. After a fatal bite and a losing struggle on the part of the prey, the spider enjoys a good meal. Again, Cichy cleverly hockets transition material along with right hand/left hand jazz piano concepts throughout. The ending section depicts the spider relaxing with an after-dinner smoke and pondering its next victim. This movement is perhaps the most rhythmically demanding of the piece and requires that every performer fully understand how their role in the music interacts with others. As in the previous movement, the key center of C predominates.

MOVEMENT V: "TIGER SWALLOWTAIL"

This movement is a result of Cichy responding to his mother's love of butterflies. He chose the title for this movement as a result of a book he was reading at the time he was composing it that referred to the Tiger Swallowtail as a "flying flower."

This movement is scored for woodwinds, 1st/2nd horn, and percussion only. The primary percussion voices are vibraphone and piano. The opening, marked "mystically" at MM 80 is scored for solo flute and vibraphone. The composer suggests miking the flute with a high level of reverb as an option. The primary melody is introduced in solo alto saxophone with reed and horn accompaniment. Piano arpeggios utilizing duple/triple rhythmic combinations play a key role throughout and must be heard. It may be necessary to amplify piano slightly to achieve this. Principal players in all the high woodwinds get an opportunity to carry the melody. Cichy uses duplet, triplet, and quintuplet note groupings throughout to push and pull the music effectively. The movement closes similarly to the beginning with flute and vibraphone, this time including clarinet. Based in E-flat, this movement provides numerous solo opportunities within the woodwind section.

MOVEMENT VI: "ARMY ANTS"
The final movement is constructed in march style with primarily 12/8 meter throughout. It is set in three tempo stages, each slightly faster and more agitated. The title appropriately suggests the style and mental imagery needed for the movement. Again, Cichy uses a right hand/left hand approach for much of the accompaniment throughout. Unison muted trumpet fanfare sets up the first melodic theme in flute and saxophone accompanied by *staccato* horn chords. The bridge passes to oboe and clarinet. Each part must clearly articulate the markings throughout to capture the style accurately. High woodwinds have several rhythmic interjections that are technically challenging. The trio of the march begins the building of intensity to the end. Using the key centers of D minor and G minor, the movement miniaturizes the march style. As in all previous movements, percussion plays a key role throughout. Keep your eyes and ears open for the tarantella (tarantula?) imbedded in the movement.

Unit 5: Musical Considerations
Bugs is a challenging work for all sections of the ensemble. It requires mature musical and technical facility, strong rhythmic concepts, and focused listening concepts.

MOVEMENT I: "PRELUDE"
Percussion, especially solo snare drum, is very closely integrated. The sounds of each drum must be distinct. Spatial separation of the instruments provides a very nice contrast. The *staccato* nature of the sounds in the winds is very important and must be maintained in all voices. The woodwinds should begin their improvisations more slowly and in a lower register so there is room for them to grow in agitation. The notes creating dissonance throughout the conclusion must be equal.

MOVEMENT II: "DRAGONFLY"
Maintaining the tempo without rushing at the beginning is crucial. The

rhythm of triplet and then duplet in the opening clarinet and piano is very important. Accuracy of articulations of long/short notes throughout in all voices must be maintained. Care must be taken with the end of the "A" section for rhythm and tempo accuracy in all voices. The chromatic sixteenth notes in woodwinds in the transition must be brought out. Take care to balance snare drum (with brushes) with all other percussion voices.

MOVEMENT III: "PRAYING MANTIS"

The opening provides an opportunity for the chamber quartet to set the mood for the movement through phrase shape and musical nuance. Because of the scoring and chord structure, it is essential that all four players play with warm and rich tone, and match pitch and balance. For the best texture, the oboe/flugelhorn duet must be played on those instruments rather than substituting trumpet. When the solo flute takes over the melody, that voice must dominate, with solo horn playing a slightly secondary role. The syncopated pulsation in the clarinets must be clear, but only supportive and not dominant. The quintuplets in the melodic line seem to serve as a means of "stretching" a part of the phrase and is Cichy's way of letting the performers know how he felt the musical nuance of the phrase shape. Caution must be taken against letting pitch rise at the end in the woodwinds as they play softer in the key of C, and tuning must be to the fixed pitch keyboard instruments.

MOVEMENT IV: "BLACK WIDOW SPIDER"

Rhythmic integration between voices, articulation accuracy, and the "swing" feel is paramount throughout this movement. Even though Cichy notates the movement in 4/4, he intends for it to feel 12/8. This presents a few concept problems for the players playing rhythmic syncopation. The conductor must take care in pacing the building section so it doesn't peak too soon. Also, the balance of being able to hear the countermelodies in flute/oboe and trumpet/trombone is essential. Increasing the heaviness of the backbeats in snare drum at measure 61 helps to provide conclusion to the vamp section. The long, slow *glissando* must go through the measure and not end too soon. This movement takes on the characteristics of *West Side Story*, and modeling that stylistic concept will help students conceive the appropriate style and feel.

MOVEMENT V: "TIGER SWALLOWTAIL"

Balance between the flute and vibraphone in the beginning is very important. The vibraphone should pedal with the phrase markings and have the motor on for maximum effect. The piano is crucial to ebb and flow of the phrases. The pianist must be accurate with duple/triple relationships and almost feel independent of the melody voices musically. Whenever solo voices are in octaves, the "joining" or lower voice should color the original voice, not cover or replace it. As the flute hands off the melody to the clarinet at the end, it should be seamless. Use the vibraphone as the primary voice. Flutes must articulate clearly at the end for the rhythm of the E to match the vibraphone. Selection of mallets for the vibraphonist is very important with consideration to the instrument, placement, etc. One interesting note from the composer in the middle section, beginning at measure 20, is loosely based on the "B" section of *Greensleeves*. The chord progression is duplicated and the melodic line descends from its highest point here.

Movement VI: "Army Ants"
Again, the rhythmic hocket in 12/8 is very important. Take care that the euphonium and bassoon don't begin to play two sixteenth notes. Using the snare drum as the key here will be very helpful. The marching machine sound must be fairly prominent throughout. All rhythms of dotted-eighth/sixteenth should be stylized with emphasis on the length of the dotted-eighth. They should not fall into the 12/8 triplet feel. Care should be taken to emphasize the individual eighth note before the dotted-eighth/sixteenth and not let it take on the flavor of the dotted rhythm. The sixteenth note moving slurred passages in inner and upper woodwinds should be strong enough to color the sound and not get lost in the sound of the ensemble. Individual percussion interjections must be taken at face value for maximum effect. Clearly define tempi at the *animato* and *accelerando* for optimum pacing through the end.

Unit 6: Musical Elements
Many diverse musical elements make up this charming and engaging work. Virtually all types of articulations are included and must be played accurately. The concept of hocket and interrelationships between voices plays a very large role in this piece. It is imperative that each player knows his or her individual role and how it relates to other voices throughout. Extended chord structures of major sevenths, minor ninths, and tritones abound throughout the piece.

Unit 7: Form and Structure

Section	Measure	Event and Scoring
Movement I: "Prelude"		
Introduction	1	Solo snare drum (brushes) and claves
	8	Time begins without interruption; addition of 2nd solo snare (lower in pitch) and 3rd solo snare (lowest in pitch); all should be equal in volume and separated for maximum effect

SECTION	MEASURE	EVENT AND SCORING
A	17	Oboe, clarinet, piano, flute over snare drum trio; melody passes into muted trumpet/trombone, saxophone, and into *tutti* ensemble Errata – m. 17, 1st clarinet: C-natural
Transition	40	Transition into improvised sounds in flute, clarinet, keyboard percussion, oboe
B	48	Improvisation continues over low brass/low reed driving jazz style bass line
	53	Quadruple forte trumpet trill interrupts line to set up ascending scalar line to concluding syncopated ending
Movement II: "Dragonfly"		
Introduction	1	*Tutti* brass in 3/4 soft to loud *crescendo* Errata – mm. 1–2, baritone saxophone: B-flat
A	3	Solo clarinet, piano, flute, vibraphone alternating melodic line
	8	Trombone/bassoon/muted trumpet/oboe syncopated answer to theme
	9	Rhythmic variation of introduction
A	12	Solo woodwinds return, ending with euphonium extension
Development	23	Development of introduction through mixed meter concluding with tam-tam, ringing through a *quasi caesura*
Transition	33	Descending high woodwind sets up hint of Theme B, m. 38
B	47	Theme in low brass/woodwinds; high brass/woodwinds continue with material developed from mm. 33–37
	61	Solo 1st clarinet; Theme B fragment

SECTION	MEASURE	EVENT AND SCORING
	66	Clarinet, flute, alto saxophone recap Theme A
Ending	72	High woodwinds/brass bring back material introduced in B; unison C in low brass/woodwinds conclude the movement following decay of vibraslap

Movement III: "Praying Mantis"
(2nd flute, tenor saxophone, baritone saxophone, 2nd/3rd trumpet tacit throughout movement)

A	1	Horn is melodic voice with trombone, euphonium, tuba; quartet; C major tonality
A	9	1st oboe, flugelhorn unison over *tutti* low brass chorale accompaniment; addition of piano arpeggios
	16	Cadential extension
B	18	Solo flute with solo horn countermelody over clarinet accompaniment over F (subdominant) tonality
A	36	1st oboe, flugelhorn unison over *tutti* low brass chorale
	45	Flute, clarinet, bells, piano recap theme motif
	46	Lullaby motif in bass clarinet and horn

Movement IV: "Black Widow Spider"

A	1	B-flat contrabass clarinet/tuba ascending in half steps from C; saxophone/bassoon descending in half steps from C in alternating rhythm over high hat and snare (brushes)
	5	Clarinet introduces theme motif 2 with jazz punctuation in saxophone and muted trombone (cup)

SECTION	MEASURE	EVENT AND SCORING
	13	Trumpet joins trombone/saxophone in punctuation—bring out
	14	Repeats beginning with 2nd bassoon joining all tubas; bass clarinet, bass trombone joining 1st bassoon and baritone saxophone
	17	1st clarinet, saxophone, trombone imitate m. 12 and extend with trumpet; all clarinets, horns, euphonium, vibes, piano joining with an extended *diminuendo* to *mezzo piano*
	22	Flutes imitate m. 1 in variation
	23	Original instruments imitate m. 1 in variation
	26	Big band style *tutti*
	30	*Tutti* imitation of m. 1
	31	Vibraslap decays into theme ending in flute, 1st clarinet, vibraphone, bass clarinet, 1st bassoon, bass trombone (mute)
	34	Triplet set-up of jazz style hit in mm. 35–36
A	37	Recap of m. 1 over finger snaps (extend finger snaps to all others not playing for balance and effect)
B	45	1st/2nd clarinet melody over vamp from m. 37 and finger snaps
	48	2nd/3rd clarinet, alto saxophone, and vibe lead-in
	49	Theme B repeats with addition of flute and oboe countermelody
	52	2nd/3rd clarinet, trumpet lead-in
	53	Theme B repeats with addition of horn and vibes on melodic line with clarinet

SECTION	MEASURE	EVENT AND SCORING
	57	Theme B repeats with addition of second countermelody in 1st trumpet, 1st trombone; snare drum adds backbeats
	61	Final time through Theme B with backbeats in snare drum very heavy
	62	Tom-toms lead into jazz hits
	67	Long fall through the measure; hi-hat must stay strong to be heard
A	70	Variation of Theme 1 in bass clarinet, 1st bassoon, contrabass clarinet/2nd bassoon, and hi-hat/snare drum; 2nd flute, 1st clarinet, and xylophone continue; xylophone plays the composite
	74	Piccolo and piano begin recap of m. 32
	78	Low reeds recap m. 34 in diminution leading to m. 79
	79	Low brass and woodwinds set up ending
	80	Bass clarinet, contrabass clarinet, bassoon, tuba, timpani, percussion, and piano punctuate hemiola rhythm on pitch C with a *crescendo* to the end

Movement V: "Tiger Swallowtail"
(trumpet, 3rd/4th horn, all low brass are tacit throughout the movement)

SECTION	MEASURE	EVENT AND SCORING
Introduction	1	Solo flute and vibraphone; vibraphone must pedal with flute phrasing
	7	1st oboe, 1st clarinet unison melody with chordal accompaniment in other clarinets, low reeds, and horns
A	11	Solo alto saxophone melody with clarinet, low reeds, and horn chordal accompaniment; piano arpeggios must balance

SECTION	MEASURE	EVENT AND SCORING
B	20	2nd flute, 1st clarinet, and horn have melodic line with wind accompaniment
	24	1st flute replaces 2nd flute in melodic grouping; horns are out
B	34	Oboe repeats theme with only clarinet, horn, and piano accompaniment
	37	1st flute and 1st alto saxophone take over second half of phrase
Ending	38	Flute, clarinet, and vibraphone; compressed version of the introduction
	47	Clarinet, piano provide repeated chords with flute/vibraphone playing repeated E-flats

Movement VI: "Army Ants"

SECTION	MEASURE	EVENT AND SCORING
Introduction	1	Contrabass clarinet/tuba, 1st bassoon, euphonium introduce rhythmic vamp over snare drum and marching machine
Fanfare	9	Trumpets (muted) have fanfare motif over continued vamp expanded to include bass clarinet, tenor saxophone, bass trombone
A	16	Piccolo, flute, alto saxophone melody over low reed/brass accompaniment
B	24	Second half of theme in 1st oboe, clarinet, tenor saxophone, xylophone
	25	Timpani, bass drum must be heard
	27	Bring out 3rd clarinet and bass clarinet
	28	Timpani, bass drum must be heard
A	30	Piccolo, flute, 1st clarinet, trumpet melody
	38	Bring out oboe, 2nd/3rd clarinet, piano
B	38	1st trumpet and 1st/2nd horn melodic line; high woodwinds alternating sixteenth triplet must be heard

SECTION	MEASURE	EVENT AND SCORING
	44	Rhythmic vamp in low woodwinds and brass; timpani/bass drum *forte*
	45	Timpani/bass drum *fortissimo*; Theme A motif in flute, alto saxophone, xylophone with marching machine
Trio	51	Imitation of introduction; typical trio modulation to subdominant key signature, but tonally remains in D minor
	54	Timpani solo link sets up tonal modulation to G minor
C	56	*"Animato"* tempo indication should be slightly faster but not too fast; clarinet, bass clarinet, alto saxophone, xylophone melody over 12/8 rhythmic accompaniment
	58	Trumpet (cup mute) colors melodic line
	64	*Accelerando* to new tempo
C	66	Repeat of trio theme with added melodic instruments of oboe and 1st/2nd trumpet
	67	Bring out piccolo, flute, 1st clarinet, and 3rd trumpet "answer"
	68	Bring out accent on beat 4
	73	M. 73 and beats 1 and 2 in m. 4 should feel as if in 3/4; beats 3 and 4 in m. 74 return to previous feel
	75	Prominent *rallentando*

Unit 8: Suggested listening

Roger Cichy:

Bugs – Diversions, University of North Texas Symphonic Band: MARK
MCD 3880

Divertimento for Winds and Percussion – Tributes, University of North Texas
Wind Symphony: Klavier KCD 11070

First Flights – Milestones, University of Georgia Wind Ensemble: Summit
DCD 281

Galilean Moons – New Lights, University of Georgia Wind Ensemble: MARK
MCD 2550

Unit 9: Additional References and Resources

C. Alan Publications, Greensboro, North Carolina.

Cichy, Roger. Correspondence with the composer.

Contributed by:

Dennis W. Fisher
Associate Director of Wind Studies
University of North Texas
Denton, Texas

Teacher Resource Guide

Danceries

Kenneth Hesketh
(b. 1968)

Unit 1: Composer

Danceries is a delightful, fresh composition from the pen of Kenneth Hesketh, a native of Liverpool, England. It is full of color and charm, and each movement has a unique character that is refreshing in content.

Hesketh studied at the Royal Conservatory of Music in London with Edwin Roxburgh, Simon Bainbridge, and Joseph Horovitz. Prior to attending the Royal College of Music, Hesketh had already written commissions for the Royal Liverpool Philharmonic Orchestra, the National Youth Orchestra of Great Britain, and the National Children's Orchestra. He has also composed occasional music for a ballet score for the English National Ballet, a fanfare for the inauguration of the Prince of Wales as President of the Royal College of Music, as well as numerous Christmas Carols. Hesketh recently finished a commission for Sir Simon Rattle and the Birmingham Contemporary Music Group.

Unit 2: Composition

According to the composer, "*Danceries* can be found in a copy of Playford's *Dancing Master,* which is an extensive collection of folk and popular tunes of the seventeenth century and earlier. This publication was used by master fiddle players to teach the various dance steps of the day to a noblemen's house or a King's court." It is the intention of the composer to, indeed, set the feet tapping.

Hesketh decided to adapt some of the melodies along with his own original melodies to formulate this composition. He freely intersperses new material, and his harmonies bring something new to these wonderful themes from the past while adding new musical drama to their content.

MOVEMENT I: "LULL ME BEYOND THEE"

The first movement is "Gentle and lilting," almost a barcarole in its style. Hesketh refers to it as a "reverie," and the original tune had the name "Poor Robin's Maggot." The term "maggot" in the seventeenth century simply meant "whim" or "fancy." This particular theme may also be found in *The Beggar's Opera* of John Gay, though under the title "Would You Have a Young Lady."

The structure of the first movement (see Unit 7) is easily understood. The piece opens with a two-measure introduction that sets the tone for the entire movement. Prominent is the sense of hemiola established by oboe. The off-pulse entrance of low reeds, bass, and string bass lends to the motion as the tonality of D major is established. The two sixteenth note anacrusis in alto saxophone at the end of measure 1 is a premonition of the importance of this particular figure to the melodic line in Movement 1.

The general structure of the melody is a–a–b–b, and the formal structure is most easy to follow in the score. One of Hesketh's exceptional abilities is in the choices he makes for the instruments selected to carry the melodic line to achieve textural clarity. The first phrase (a) combines 1st flute, E-flat clarinet, and cornet, and the combination works beautifully together. His talent for writing interesting harmonic backgrounds requiring good balance and musicality is also notable, and this will be borne out through careful study of all four movements. Much of what makes his work so very excellent relates to the subtle manner in which he constructs the harmonic background and the countermelodies in his music. It is done with great craft and attention to detail.

The second presentation of "a" (measures 12 through 19) keeps the flute color intact on the melodic line, though with the addition of euphonium two octaves below. Here, there is more sense of a sustained harmonic background in support of the melodic line. Creative scoring appears at every turn, and it is an interesting study to observe how the composer alters harmonies within the divisi 1st and 3rd clarinet parts. The relationship of these four parts to the bass line is most revealing as to the harmonic plan of the composer and well worth careful study. Vibraphone continues to play an important arpeggiated role in support of the texture, outlining the harmony used in support of the melody line.

The third phrase of the melody begins at letter B (measure 20), where the composer utilizes the oboe as the carrier of the melodic line. Variety is achieved by adding other instruments to the melody every two measures, and the glockenspiel outlines essential notes of the melodic line. The harmonic support is written in a creative manner.

The importance of the dotted-eighth/sixteenth/eighth note figure is not lost upon the conductor or the listener in establishing the lilting style referred to by the composer in the program note. The oboe takes it up as the sole proprietor of the melodic line for two measures beginning at measure 20, and the composer cleverly adds other colors over the course of the next eight measures. Hesketh's knack for treating the ensemble in chamber-like fashion is also evident here, and it is partly the transparency of his ideas that brings the music much of its inherent charm. Interesting is his approach to the clarinet scoring, whereby the first part is playing the lowest voice in the chords beginning at measure 20. Glockenspiel is used to outline the melodic line in a simple, effective manner.

The phrase presented at letter B is repeated beginning at measure 28, now within a fuller texture. Strong root movement is present in the bass instruments, and this tends to focus the harmony clearly in a manner that emphasizes the key center of D major. The introductory material of the first two measures reappears at measure 36 and serves to bridge the music to the next appearance of the theme.

The theme begins anew at measure 38, with the melody solidly entrenched in piccolo, 1st flute, and E-flat clarinet. The lilting sensation established right from the very beginning of the movement is reestablished at measure 38 with string bass, baritone saxophone, and bass clarinet gently pulsing on the third subdivision of each beat. At measure 46, the sixteenth note accompaniment in clarinet and glockenspiel add momentum to the melody, and the fuller bass line tends to firmly establish the harmonic content. Care should be taken that the bass line does not slow down to achieve the firm harmonic support called for by the composer.

The "b" portion of the theme at letter D will be heard easily with oboe, cornet, and 1st trumpet sounding the joyful tones of the melody. The more difficult task is establishing the sweeping passages in flute and clarinet. The key to achieving adequate sound during execution is to request additional volume, especially as the instruments sweep downwards to the lowest part of their register. In short, woodwinds must *crescendo* as the line moves lower.

The suspension at measure 59 is highlighted by the *ritardando* in the previous measure, the *mf/p* dynamic, and the sostenuto of the stacked triads that provide the harmonic basis for the *arpeggio* in 1st clarinet and vibraphone. The final two measures of the phrase are sounded gently in measures 61–62 before the coda begins.

The coda begins quietly with the anacrusis to measure 63, and only the first three notes of the theme are used to foreshadow what is to come. At letter E, the theme begins anew, accompanied by piccolo and bells, slowly melding into the E-flat clarinet picking up the sixteenth note passage where piccolo leaves off at measure 67. The dominant appears in the bass at measure 68, though the harmony above seems bent upon moving elsewhere. Hesketh resolves deceptively to a creatively scored B minor7 with an added ninth and eleventh for good measure. There is a feeling of inconclusiveness to the ending, though the sounding of the "b" in string bass and timpani in measure 70 brings the music to a hauntingly beautiful close.

MOVEMENT II: "CATCHING OF QUAILS"

"A colorfully buoyant *scherzo* on an original melody. The thematic material is shuttled around through the band with full-bodied *tuttis*. The last few measures fade away to almost nothing, it seems, until a final surprise."

Incessant octave Cs open this movement, and the introduction has barely established the tempo before the melody begins in measure 5. The 3/8 meter is conducted in one, and the tonal center of the melody seems to be centered upon C major at the beginning, though the "A minor" harmonies in support of the melody belie this fact. The "A minor" contains extended harmonies utilizing the seventh and ninth in harmonic support of the melody. The melody, introduced by flute, oboe, and 1st clarinet, literally propels itself forward with its energetic character. Phrasing is relatively simple, as the structure of the theme falls into an a–b–a1–b pattern. As in Movement I, the creativity of the orchestration relates to the subtle means by which the composer modifies the accompaniment to achieve variety. Second and third clarinet, divisi, provide the bulk of the harmonic substance, and it will remain a critical issue to maintain these parts in good balance. Hints of hemiola come and go in this wonderful music, and the composer uses this interplay of "two versus three" throughout the movement.

The "B" portion of the thematic material begins at letter A, and its structure is easily identified as c–d–c1–d. As in the earlier thematic material, the composer modifies the material and, in this instance, it is more through the subdivision feeling of "one...three one..." Variety is also achieved by passing the melody freely among other instruments after it has been introduced.

At letter B, while it may be a brilliant effect to hear the thematic material in four octaves, it is the "bell-tone" accompaniment effect that captures our attention in trumpet and trombone. This sets up a pedal point of sorts that stays with the listener for the first eight measures of the return, and the tonal center sounds in the tonal center of "a" rather than the earlier presentation due to the accompaniment. The second repetition of a1–b is supported by an "a pedal point" in low brass and reeds, and the hemiola provided by the snare drum triplet/eighth beginning in measure 45 clouds the bar line emphasis.

At letter C, there is a semblance of new material, though one could just as readily state that it bears close resemblance to earlier material. The second measure of the melody in trombone and euphonium has an inverted pattern (measure 54), and the series of harmonies supporting the melody contain hints of polytonality. It is intriguing to analyze such material in several different ways, but the important issue is how the music sounds to the ear in performance. As quickly as the music passes, here it simply sounds as if two chords are being played simultaneously. In other measures, such as measure 61, the harmony sounds more or less as an extended harmony, E minor7 with an added ninth and eleventh. As in earlier sections, the percussion parts are scored as essential parts, sometimes rhythmic, other times as complementary melodic material. Their appearance, as in the case of the string bass *pizzicato* throughout, is essential to establishing the character of the work.

At letter D, Hesketh truly diverges from his original melodic plan. There is just enough similarity that the listener can almost be deceived into believing that this is music that has been heard previously. The structure bears similarity in its e–f–e1–f pattern, and the rhythmic patterns of the accompaniment have been heard in previous passages. The key of A minor and its related harmonies are the province of this particular section. The composer makes good use of varying the thematic material with slightly altered articulation and slur patterns, but more importantly, it is the variety of texture that brings this music to life. It is joyful music, and care should be taken to balance the accompaniment in each phrase to reveal it as such.

The final appearance of the original theme occurs at letter E, and as it is scored in the *cor anglais*, bassoon and horn, the sixteenth note *obbligato* part in the upper woodwinds catches our attention at the *fortissimo* dynamic level. Percussion is left out of this presentation, with the exception of sporadic accented bursts, such as the occurrence at measure 93. The earlier pattern of a–b–a–b remains true, and the "B" portion of the theme remains the same as well. Note the subtle addition of hemiola in the melodic line at measures 103 and 104 in the upper woodwinds. The crossing harmonic effect of 2nd and 3rd clarinet beginning at measure 101 is worthy of study by the conductor. Horn and alto saxophone countermelody should not be lost to the ear within this passage. At measure 109, the hemiola pattern is emphasized in the beaming of the sixteenth notes in the upper woodwinds.

As the movement comes to conclusion, Hesketh uses an extension of the melodic idea beginning at measure 117. This eases the music into the coda beginning at measure 121, and the principal idea is repeated and accelerated until the abrupt halt in measure 128. Measures 129 through 132 provide nothing more than a folk-like "4–3" suspension resolution with an "A" harmonic emphasis on the final subdivision of each measure. The 4/8 measure following presents a reminiscent modal melody, simple and folk-like in content. It is shared by flute and bassoon two octaves distant, and the flat seventh present in the line adds rest to the music. The surprise A major chord brings this music to a startling conclusion.

MOVEMENT III: "MY LADY'S REST"

Movement III begins in the most benign way imaginable. A series of repeated tones on D for two measures serves as the dominant of the eventual key of G minor/major. Measure 3 adds the tonic G to the bass line, serving as the supporting foundation for a *soli* between bass clarinet and 1st bassoon. This melodic idea has a tendency toward a modal character and sounds somewhat improvisational in its effect upon the listener. This duo completes the four-measure introduction as the melancholy entrance of oboe at letter A begins the thematic material.

The structure of theme beginning at letter A is a–a–b–b–a. The composer has marked it appropriately *Andantino con sentimento* and adds to the mood with the *espressivo* designation. The texture of the accompaniment is thinly scored, allowing the necessary transparency for oboe to be easily audible. Bass clarinet and 1st bassoon continue in the style of the introduction, and the trills lend a marked quaintness to the line. First and second clarinet provide much of the harmonic rhythm within the orchestration, and the vibraphone has an integral part that lends to the mood. The first four-measure phrase is repeated with little change in texture in measures 9 through 12.

As the third phrase of the music (b) begins at letter B, the texture is modified only through the addition of flute doubling the melodic line with oboe. Clarinet adds the third part, and through use of divisi the composer has six separate accompaniment parts present. E-flat clarinet doubles oboe for the second presentation of "b" beginning at measure 17, and there is a firm establishment of the key center of G with the prominent addition of the F-sharp in measure 20. The fifth phrase of the theme picks up at letter C; it is a modified version of the original phrase from measure 5.

Hesketh reestablishes the introductory bass clarinet and bassoon material in measures 26 and 27 prior to repeating the thematic material. There is somewhat of a deceptive feeling in the timpani roll at measure 26 in that it seems like the composer is about to modulate. This does not occur, as the focus remains clearly in G as the theme begins its second presentation, with fuller scoring of the ensemble. Percussion remains tacit until the fourth phrase, and there are interesting lines abounding within the individual parts of the ensemble. The dynamic curve of the melody has increased considerably, and the designation of *Teneramente* at letter D allows the conductor to add to the expressive quality of the music. The second repetition of the "b" phrase at measure 39 brings with it new accompaniment in piccolo and flute, delicately magnified in glockenspiel. *Cor anglais* and 2nd clarinet engage in a beautiful countermelody that must be musically highlighted from within the texture.

Though most of the ensemble is playing during the return of the "a" at measure 43, the marking of *pianissimo* clearly reveals the composer's intent— remarkably rich tone played very softly. The composer chooses to elongate the melody this time with a second repetition of the theme played even more softly beginning at measure 47, marking the passage *ppp sub.* The gentle trills of the divisi 1st flute and clarinet lend a simple, gentle quality to the conclusion of the theme.

Bassoon and euphonium are joined for what sounds closely like an improvisatory presentation of material based upon the first phrase of the melody as the theme begins its third and final repetition. The thinnest of accompaniment is provided as the music casts a pleasant spell upon the listener. Individual lines in oboe and *cor anglais* must be carefully balanced to achieve the transparency called for in this passage. This music is theatrical; it creates images in the mind of the listener that seem "extra-musical," and the conductor should take the time to ensure all musical elements contribute to the musical ambiance.

Letter H finds the solo 1st flute picking up the thematic material (b), with nothing more than a few woodwinds providing a thinly scored accompaniment that is decidedly "soprano" voice in nature. It is one more means used by Hesketh to create the musical imagery that he desires for his theme, and the addition of vibraphone and glockenspiel to the texture at measure 63 highlights this effect. The final phrase (a) begins at letter I, and the *crescendo* that precedes it announces the first full ensemble sound of the entire movement. Care should be taken by the conductor to ensure that the thicker texture does not cover the melodic line in the desire to achieve the musical climax that is so apparent.

Measure 71, the *Poco meno mosso rall.*, begins a brief coda, though it happens in such subtle fashion that the listener is scarcely able to believe it is not a repetition of the "b" portion of the theme. The dynamic rapidly increases up to the *fermata* on beat 6, receding quickly in the next measure for musical effect. Measure 73 uses the final cadential material borrowed from "a" and placed in duple meter to add a natural *ritardando* to the music. In the 9/8 measure, the composer implies that the music will cadence in G minor, though the arpeggio at the end of the measure places the music clearly in G major. The sustaining perfect fifth in 1st flute and trumpet ties directly to the beginning of the fourth movement without break.

MOVEMENT IV: "QUODLING'S DELIGHT"

The final movement of *Danceries* combines one of the melodies from "Playford's Dancing Master" (under the title *Goddesses*, used as Theme 1) with an original melody by Hesketh (Theme 2). The *Allegro Vivace* with which this music is set in motion is a most appropriate tempo for the delightful music to follow. Bass instruments prepare the tempo with their rhythmic punctuation in the opening measures. Trombone and other brass follow with a musical pyramid, while upper woodwinds engage in rapid sixteenth note scale patterns preparing for the introductory thematic material presented in trumpet and horn at measure 7. Bridge material follows at measures 14 through 15, leading directly to the presentation of the first theme.

Theme 1 appears at letter A in simple, forthright form, loosely centered in G minor. It is shared by solo 2nd flute and solo oboe, accompanied by little more than long tones in clarinet, bassoon, horn, glockenspiel, and vibraphone. It falls into a periodic structure of 4+4 in terms of phrasing, though Hesketh is unable to resist extending the first presentation by four measures beginning at measure 24. The character of this theme is accented and whimsical, certainly one of great charm. All harmonic and rhythmic elements must be balanced in a manner that allows the music to propel forward at great speed. Theme 1 is repeated a second time at letter B with melody in flute, clarinet, and cornet. All other voices punctuate the melody with massive eighth note chords, and the structure of the theme is very cohesive.

Theme 1 appears for the third time at letter C in a considerably lower octave. Second clarinet, 1st alto saxophone, and 1st bassoon are combined to achieve the low register mixture, and flute and oboe are engaged in a rapid *obbligato* that lends even more impetus to the melody. The bass line offbeats are the key to maintaining precision in this section, and brief splashes of color in trombone and xylophone must not slow the pace of the music. It is important that as the melody shifts to the euphonium (measure 40) and finally to horn and upper woodwinds (measure 42), the tempo remains constant and full of energy. A brief two-measure bridge, similar to the one found at measures 14 and 15, connects the music at measures 44 and 45 to Theme 2.

The structure of Theme 2 is metrically uneven in conception, though it does not impede the flow of the music at hand. There are four four-measure phrases (c–c1–d–c2); the first phrase concludes with a measure of 2/4, and the second phrase with a measure of 3/4. The composer continues to center upon a G minor tonal center, and the sliding harmonies of clarinet are delightfully reminiscent of the music of Percy Grainger. The bar line seems to disappear as the composer skillfully cadences and continues with ease. The constancy of the eighth note and the rapid harmonic changes that result propel this music forward smoothly and fluidly. The composer makes use of an offbeat G pedal point at measure 49 and later at measure 59 to emphasize the importance of the G within the tonal structure of the movement.

The second appearance of Theme 2 at letter E at first sounds as if the composer has simply rescored the melody for a larger ensemble than in the first appearance. The composer doubles the melody over a four-octave span, adding euphonium on the lowest octave. The second phrase is altered for the sake of variety, and the composer continues to change the length of the theme by altering the meter to accommodate his or her ideas.

The manner in which Hesketh achieves variety for his repetitions of the thematic material is the crux of the creative approach he applies to the craft of orchestration. He does not score for more instruments than are absolutely necessary, and this is readily apparent at letter F, the fourth appearance of the first theme. Piccolo, flute, and oboe all share in the melodic line, and the accompaniment is nothing more than a rapid series of eighth note clusters played by muted trombone and trumpet. The entire eight measures contain a tremendous range of orchestrational variance, and it is this variety that lends interest to the music. The "b" phrase sounds decidedly as if the composer has finally arrived in B-flat major at measure 78, though the respite is brief.

Letter G begins yet another appearance of Theme 1, solidly placed in G minor along with G pedal points and supported by the tam-tam. The theme is extended at measure 90, and the snare drum paired with cornet playing punctuated rhythm sets the tone for the escalating pyramid at measure 94, introductory material that first appeared at measure 3. The pyramid drops to *subito piano* to begin a second pyramid. The content of this second pyramid is the same sixteenth note material supported by a bass line that has moved up a half step from D to E-flat. This leads to the stark, augmented theme beginning at letter I, which is nothing more than Theme 2 in augmentation. What makes the music so poignant is that all rhythmic intensity, the prevalent force up to this point, has completely dissolved for this moment. It captures our rapt attention through its vivid contrast. The rapid eighth notes in clarinet and horn at measure 109 provide a return to the incessant momentum we have come to expect. Hesketh continues to carry on in augmentation, including the two-measure trumpet fragment at measures 126 and 127 prior to his musical *accelerando* beginning at measure 128.

If it is possible to vary the nature of the first theme through variance of tempo, Hesketh has done this equally well as through creative and varied orchestration. The tempo marking at letter K of quarter note = 160 (*Piu mosso, agitato ed energico*) pushes the ensemble to the edge of technical clarity. The accommodating dynamic drop to *piano* is indeed welcome to assist in maintaining precision at the higher tempo. It is the accuracy of the accompaniment that will hold this music together rather than the technical performance of the melody; so ample time must be spent on the background.

This exciting music is further enhanced by one more leap in tempo at letter L to quarter note = 168. Now we find all performers engaged at the *fortissimo* level, and the ensemble must avoid playing in a *pesante* style so as to avoid a slowing of the excitement generated by the extreme rapid tempo. An extension is added to the thematic material at measure 146 in preparation for the coda at letter M. The extension feels as if it shifts to another metric pulse, though this has been achieved through beaming the eighth notes across the bar line at measure 147.

The coda is a dash through melodic material at a tempo marked *Con Fuoco*, though the actual tempo will be determined by the ability of the performers to accommodate the technique required to play the passage. At measure 154, there is a final recollection of the fanfare-like material first presented in trombone at measure 7, and following is a massive *crescendo* to the final G major punctuation that concludes this magnificent work.

Unit 3: Historical Perspective

Danceries is a delightful, fresh composition from the pen of Hesketh, a native of Liverpool, England. It is full of color and charm, and each movement has a unique character that is refreshing in content.

Hesketh has created a musically dynamic and expressive work for the wind band. *Danceries* has also been orchestrated for brass band and used as a test piece within British brass band circles, and an orchestral version has been released by the publisher as well. At times, one senses Hesketh's roots in the British musical traditions of Gustav Holst and Ralph Vaughan Williams, utilizing his own strikingly original ideas and harmonies. Not once does the music lack for vitality, and the composer has an uncanny ability to maintain interest through simple, effective melodic repetition accompanied by marvelous orchestration. Derived from 17th century melodies from Playford's *Dancing Master*, it is clear that the composer wishes to infuse these delightful dance melodies from the distant past with new life and vigor using contemporary harmonic treatment. One must be impressed by how well the composer has bridged the two styles required: the quaint quality of the seventeenth century dance and the interesting, lush harmonic palette of the modern composer.

Danceries is a welcome addition to the repertoire and well worth the time spent in preparation. The program note within the score proper indicates

> *Danceries (Set 1)* were transcribed for symphonic wind band for the Faber Wind Band Series. The first performance was given by the Royal Northern College of Music Wind Orchestra, conducted by Clark Rundell, at The Brown Shipley at the Royal Northern College of Music, Manchester, as part of the BASBWE/RNCM International Wind Festival on 14 April 2000.

Clearly, the purpose of Hesketh's composition was to capture the dance flavor of old English dances. It is this melding of the dance form of the seventeenth century with the harmonic language of the twentieth century that gives the work its delightful appeal. The rich influences of the British school of composition are apparent in this music, and it is the penchant for beautiful melody that forms the bond with his predecessors. Hesketh's orchestration shows a maturity that belies his years, and it is his ability to treat the symphonic band in transparent fashion that captures the attention of the listener.

While the British affinity for the folk song is readily apparent in *Danceries*, the quality of the orchestration clearly stands out as one of *Danceries'* greatest strengths. There is a tendency to score only what is required to reflect the composer's intent, and this characteristic has roots in the transparent music of *First Suite in E-flat* of Gustav Holst. One only needs to examine the delicate balances in the thinner variations of the "Chaconne" movement to note the similarity. It is this ability to provide wonderful music with limited numbers of parts that is the strength of the music, and Hesketh has mastered this very early in his career. Ralph Vaughan Williams demonstrates this same trait in the "I'll Love My Love" movement of the *English Folk Song Suite* as well. Even a cursory examination of the scoring practices of these two remarkable British composers will reveal their unmistakable talent for creative scoring.

More recently, the music of Guy Woolfenden should be examined in light of the work of Hesketh. Both have the uncanny ability to draw the listener into extra-musical images. In the case of Woolfenden, this imagery is based on the imaginary Shakespearean land of Illyria. The suite of three dances of Woolfenden, *Illyrian Dances*, is written for an imaginary land referenced in Shakespeare's *Twelfth Night*, Act I, Scene 2. It is a land of make-believe, and the idea of writing music for such a place is what intrigued Woolfenden. It is in the transparent scoring that one sees the resemblance to Hesketh. Also present is the graceful manner in which the music moves forward.

Credit must be given to the orchestrational style of Malcolm Arnold as well. In Arnold's *Four Scottish Dances*, one notes the ease with which the composer moves between the styles of the various movements as well as the effectiveness of the scoring in support of each movement. Arnold is able to capture the essence of each movement and present it in a manner that leaves no room for question regarding what the music portrays. Hesketh has developed this ability as well and is able to place the listener in the character of each dance with an unusual level of skill. This particular characteristic may be observed and contrasted equally well in Arnold's movement three of the *Four Scottish Dances*, as well as in Hesketh's "My Lady's Rest."

Unit 4: Technical Considerations

Each movement of *Danceries* presents unique problems to the musicians. Movement I begins in the key of D major, which presents fingering problems and intonation issues for those ensembles rarely performing in this vibrant key. Percussion is not the only instrument family assigned responsibility for maintaining the pulse, and instruments such as bassoon, euphonium, and tuba must have the inner ability to maintain accurate subdivision at a fairly slow tempo if the music is to have a flowing character. Two excellent mallet players are necessary to play the movement well, and clarinet must be able to maintain smooth, repeated sixteenth note passages in divisi parts with no break in the soothing flow of the music. There are difficult scalar passages in piccolo, flute, E-flat clarinet, and B-flat clarinet that will require adequate attention.

Movement II is a light, buoyant movement, and the 3/8 meter is conducted one beat to the measure to achieve this character. Thematic material appears to be centered in C major, though the frequent appearance of F-sharp within the melodic line gives the melody a sense of moving back and forth from C major to G major within a short span of time. Accompaniment harmonies utilize sevenths and ninths with great frequency, and the occasional use of seconds and fourths lend distinctive qualities to the harmonic function. Importantly, the harmony in support of the thematic material moves freely in related keys, such as A minor and A major.

Hesketh writes the melody in four octaves at letter B and uses bell-tone accompanimental effects in support of the theme. First and second trombone must have the ability to read in the tenor clef in order to play these passages. Hemiola technique is used in exchange between the winds and percussion, and there is ample use of pedal point in the bass voices. Poly-chordal effects are noted at letter C, requiring the ensemble to develop the ability to play in tune in a more mature fashion. Melody is doubled between piccolo, oboe, E-flat soprano clarinet, and xylophone, requiring excellent musicianship from these performers. Ample dependence is required within the clarinet section, as all three parts use divisi frequently to create unusual harmonic effects. The dotted-eighth/sixteenth/eighth rhythm is prevalent throughout the movement and must be executed with precision for the movement to maintain its lighter character. This movement comes to a cadence point in the key of A major after a series of suspensions.

Movement III begins in G minor. Bass clarinet and 1st bassoon contain challenging rhythmic introductory passages in unison. The 6/8 meter is conducted with the eighth note as the unit of beat, and the phrasing of the solo lines is critical to the musical flow of this movement. Four-mallet technique is required for the vibraphone part. The ability of instruments within the same family to maintain rhythmic independence is important, and excellent balance at the softer dynamic levels is necessary to achieve an excellent musical performance. There is a quasi-improvisatory section (written out) between 1st bassoon and euphonium that requires musical maturity. Multiple mallet parts are provided and must be performed precisely rhythmically.

Movement IV is pitched in G major. Strong unison horns are required to play the principal melodic material. The tempo of quarter note = 144 presents technical challenges for some of the parts, and fluttertonguing is required in 1st flute. Light articulation is required of flute and oboe at letter C in support of the thematic material. Cor *anglais* is required and is provided with a challenging part. The 2nd oboe receives an important solo in octaves with piccolo, and meters move freely from 4/4 to 2/4, 5/4, and 6/4 time. Thin textures abound requiring great sensitivity to the issues of balance and chord quality. Augmentation is utilized later in the movement in the woodwind colors, and rhythmic acceleration is used to prepare for the energy required for the higher tempo that concludes the piece. The technical issues required to play this music at quarter note = 168 must be considered in setting the tempo for the conclusion of this movement.

Unit 5: Stylistic Considerations

Movement I requires the melodic line to be performed *espressivo* and *cantabile* at a moderately slow tempo. This presents a greater challenge to the accompanimental parts than to the melodic parts. Light articulation is required much of the time to maintain the delicate balance between melody and accompaniment. In addition, the ability to play the dotted-eighth/ sixteenth/eighth rhythm accurately while both tonguing and slurring is absolutely essential. Upper woodwinds must be able to play rapid thirty-second note passages in unison in an elegant sweeping fashion. Percussionists have musically challenging parts for glockenspiel and vibraphone in terms of accurate relationship to the upper voices.

Movement II is marked *Vivace con vigoroso*, and performers are challenged by the 3/8 meter played one beat per measure. The rapid changing of the underlying harmonies and achieving their clarity is essential. The upper woodwinds are occasionally scored in four-octave unisons requiring care in maintaining the same style between the highest and lowest voices. Flowing sixteenth notes passages exchanged between *divisi* parts in the flutes and clarinet families creates some challenge as well since maintaining the continuity of this accompaniment is important.

Movement III is simply a challenge to maintain musical intensity at a slow tempo. Great phrasing must be maintained between the unison bass clarinet and 1st bassoon. Excellent balance must be maintained between solo oboe and the slurred inner voices of the B-flat clarinet. While full ensemble writing is infrequent, good balance and clarity of line must be achieved when the fuller textures are utilized. In general, all musicians must be capable of subdividing the beat with precision in order to hear the relationship of the individual voices and to play together with musical precision.

Allegro vivace is the opening style marking in Movement IV. The rapid scale passages present no problems for mature performers in the upper woodwinds, but they do provide great challenges to younger musicians. Bold, *marcato* style is required form the unison horns in the fanfare-like presentation at measure 7. Rapid dynamic changes are necessary at times, and stopped horns must be played well in tune. Extremely accurate melodic lines shared between various instrument families must be carefully defined through the use of light articulation and excellent balance. Tempo plays a major role in the success of the ensemble in achieving this parity. Soloistic playing abounds in this movement, and great confidence is required. The ability to maintain musical intensity while the tempo is increasing is critical to achieving an exciting musical climax at the end of the movement.

All of the movements are based upon dance themes borrowed by the composer. Hence, the primary compositional technique used in *Danceries* is one of a theme repeated using varied and creative orchestration for each appearance. The challenge comes in the form of achieving excellent musical continuity throughout each of the movements.

Unit 6: Musical Elements

Each movement of *Danceries* presents thematic material that may be utilized by the entire ensemble to teach interpretation. It would be advantageous for each member of the ensemble to have a copy of the principal theme for each movement, easily accomplished by using any of the music editing software packages currently available.

MELODY:

The theme from Movement I is marked *Dolce*, and it is easy for the performers to see the sequential nature of the theme. Encourage small *crescendos* as the sequential nature of the thematic material increases the range of the melody. Note should be made of the effect of the grace notes upon the interpretation of the melody as compared to the interpretation of the melody when the grace notes are absent.

Movement II has a light buoyant quality, and rehearsing the melody with appropriate accent on the fourth measure of each phrase is required, as indicated by the composer. Though marked *piano*, clearly there is intent to shape the melody as it weaves its way forward. A small *crescendo* at the measure 4 followed by a small *diminuendo* at measure 8 is musically appropriate. A slightly more aggressive character is appropriate for the latter portion of the theme, as implied by the use of both *marcato* and *sforzando*.

Movement III presents the difficult task of allowing the performers flexibility in their approach to the theme. While the conductor's interpretation of the melody is important, room should be allowed for the oboist to shape the nuance to some degree. The important issue is the use of the word *sentimento* in the style marking; this will mean markedly different ideas to different performers. Importantly, the accompaniment must follow the flow of the dynamic nuance of the soloist, hence requiring good listening skills from members of the ensemble. The second theme (measure 27) will require more leadership from the conductor due to the fact that it is scored among several voices. Similar dynamic nuance must be encouraged from the various colors sharing the melody.

The first theme presented by the unison horns should be rehearsed diligently so as to achieve a true unison *marcato* style. The key component of achieving musical excellence is adherence to good intonation and uniform attack and release. The second theme (measure 16) is marked *Energico*, and this characteristic must be maintained while flute and oboe are playing lightly. Small *crescendos* are in order during the repetitive sixteenth notes that occur. Extensions of the melody must lift the music dynamically upward from the sense of rest provided at the cadence point.

HARMONY:

While Hesketh provides tonal centers for each movement, rarely does he use block harmonies in support of his thematic material. Examination of Movement I harmonic material in measures 3 and 4 reveals much about his intent. Passing tones and insistent perfect fifths are the means of establishing the key center. Mallet instruments play arpeggiated material highlighting the harmonic language, but it is the interaction with other voices that creates the "harmonic palette" that supports the melodic material. Another point that should be observed is the unusual independence of the inner. Clarinets are often divisi in all three voices, and the harmony is simply not complete when voices are missing or underplayed.

Movement II contains many extended harmonies (note the A minor7 that supports the entrance of the theme in measure 5), and these are often very transparent. Notable is the lack of doubling among the various voices. This creates truly delightful clarity in the harmonic accompaniment. Sevenths and ninths are frequently added to triads, and the use of seconds and fourths further enhance the harmonic palette of the composer. Hesketh alters the harmony used in each presentation of the melody to achieve variety, creating a unique freshness to his music.

Movement III is as remarkable for what is not present harmonically as for what is present. Opening with a series of the note D sounding in various instruments, the addition of the G in measure 3 provides an open fifth that creates space for the bass clarinet and bassoon unison passage. The G remains as a pedal point for nine measures, and the harmonies above imply G minor, though the slow changing nature of the individual lines creates a constantly changing sense of harmonic rhythm. Light trills in bass clarinet and bassoon further cloud the direction of the music. Vibraphone provides the barest skeleton of the harmonic intent with occasional arpeggiated tones. The accompaniment should be rehearsed as if it were as important as the theme to bring home the importance of the individual lines.

Movement IV establishes the G tonal center through scalar passages in the woodwinds and the use of pyramid effects within the brass. When the horns appear on the fanfare-like material at measure 7, the accented chords in the full ensemble are clearly extended harmonies, though not always with the root of the chord as the bottom note. Ensemble rhythmic unison is the mode of presentation, and parallelism is prevalent. The appearance of the second theme at measure 16 is supported by nothing more than the note D repeated in numerous octave transpositions, eventually expanding to more fully extend harmonies. Again, it is the sporadic entrances of key voices that create the harmonies rather than a block harmony approach that creates the musical interest. As in earlier movements, each time the theme appears, the harmony and orchestration is varied.

RHYTHM:

The rhythmic impulse of Movement I is subtle and only achieved by the accurate offbeats provided by low reeds and brass. The conductor should create a series of exercises where half of the ensemble enters on beat 1, and the other half enters on the sixth subdivision. A secondary exercise should be created using the primary rhythm of the melody (dotted-eighth/sixteenth/eighth) and having the students alternate between articulating and slurring the exercise. The slurred version is often played less accurately, and its exactness is essential in the performance of movement I. A third exercise would be to play steady sixteenth notes using the tongue/slur pattern played by 2nd clarinet at measure 12. Finally, an exercise that utilizes the two-sixteenth note *anacrusis* should be developed as well.

Movement II requires that the ensemble play comfortably "in one" and all of the various sixteenth note subdivisions that are applied. Exercises should be developed that switch from strong beat emphasis to "one-three" beat emphasis. Hemiola appears in the percussion parts at measure 45, and this two-against-three metric feeling should be practiced as written so the wind players understand the relativity of the percussion section to the totality. All of the ensemble must capture the sensation of playing off the beat in a light, forward-moving way. If the music becomes heavy, it loses the character intended by the composer.

The difficulty of Movement III rests in the slow-moving pace of the eighth note. It is easy for this music to become lacking in vitality and intensity; hence, developing exercises where the conductor is able to stress the intensity between beats 1, 3, 4, 6, and 1 is critically important. This applies to both the harmonic rhythm and the melodic line as well. The occasional use of the tied eighth to the dotted-eighth requires some attention, and writing out global exercises for the entire ensemble will help solve this problem (see measure 41).

Movement IV requires a steady eighth note that maintains the support of the melodic line. The entrance of series of eighth notes off the beat presents small problems, and exercises may be developed to reinforce its importance (rest-and-two-and). Steady scale passages for the woodwinds are in order, as seen in the introduction, and this may be solved in a multitude of ways. The simplest is to exercise the ensemble on such passages articulating the notes at a slower tempo to ensure accuracy of finger placement. Gradually increase the tempo as the precision improves, adding the slurs to the passage as the improvement is noted.

TIMBRE:

Hesketh has presented his music with excellent craft as it relates to the use of pure and mixed timbres. Melodic lines are often presented in combination with instruments that create a unique combined timbre. For example, the very first theme of Movement I combines flute, E-flat soprano clarinet, and cornet in a two-octave presentation of the melody. By contrast, the accompaniment emphasizes clarinet color with some bass instruments highlighting the off-beat pulse. Finally, the use of oboe alone on a simple descending countermelody is the perfect choice to contrast with the other combinations.

At other times, Hesketh uses a layering effect to achieve his melodic intentions. Again in Movement I, oboe begins the phrase at measure 20. Two measures later, oboe is joined by E-flat soprano clarinet, and in measure 24 flute and 2nd cornet add the parallel sixth. This layering effect adds to the intensity as well as to the volume in a manner that highlights the increasing intensity of the line over these six measures of music.

Moving to Movement III, the composer takes the purest form of presentation possible by giving the theme to the solo oboe in measure 5. At letter B, the third phrase begins and Hesketh adds solo flute to the oboe to achieve effective contrast. To further contrast the single tone color, the composer removes flute and adds E-flat soprano clarinet to the fourth and final phrase. The color of the accompaniment through these opening measures remains markedly similar, and the composer has elected to achieve his intent by varying the combination of tone colors to carry forward the melody. Important is how well the clarity has been achieved using delicately balanced tone colors.

A notable section that stands out for its differences appears in Movement IV. At letter I, there is a clear point of woodwind choir writing. Seven independent voices appear (eight if one counts the pedal point in bass clarinet). It presents such a delightful change to the manner in which Hesketh has scored much of his music that it is simply highlighted by this fact. The unison melody that follows in measure 109 with the simplest of all accompaniments, repeated eighth notes, demonstrates clearly the degree of comfort the composer has in his ability to maintain musical interest using a minimum of musical resources.

Unit 7: Form and Structure

Each of the four movements of *Danceries* follows a relatively simple plan seen in the diagrams provided below. Hesketh follows the pattern of introduction followed by presentation of the theme. At this juncture, it is his creative approach to orchestration that takes over as he varies the accompaniment in support of the theme. Melodic material is rarely repeated without a varied accompaniment, and this leads to a feeling that each movement is richly rewarding in every measure. There simply is no unnecessary filler in the scoring.

Formal Structure
Movement I: "Lull Me Beyond Thee"

Intro	Theme (1x)	Intro (modified)	Theme 2x	Coda
Hemiola	Barcarole	Hemiola	(shortened)	Fragments of "a"
Key: D major	a–a1–b–b1		a–a1–b	
mm. 1–2	mm. 3–35	mm. 36–37	mm. 38–62	mm. 63–70

Formal Structure
Movement II: "Catching of Quails"

Intro (A–B)	Theme (A–B)	Theme 2x (A–B)	Theme	Theme 3x
Key:	Scherzo		based on previous	
a minor.	A = a–b–a1–b1	a–b–a1–b1	material	a–b–a1–b1
tonal ctr	B = c–d–c1–d1	c–d–c1–d1	e–f–e1–f1	c–d–c1–d1
	mm. 5-36	mm. 37–68	mm. 69–84	mm. 85–116
Extension	Coda	(cont.)	(cont.)	Final chord
based on d	based on theme	4–3 susp A major	peasant theme (scale)	
mm. 117–120	mm. 121–128	mm. 129–132	mm. 133–134	mm. 135

Formal Structure
Movement 3: "My Lady's Rest"

Intro	Theme	Intro material	Theme 2X	Theme 3X
Key:	Andantino		Teneramente	(Develop.)
G minor	a–a–b–b–a1		a–a–b–b–a (echo)	a–a–b–b–a
mm. 1–4	mm. 5–24	mm. 25–26	mm. 27–50	mm. 51–70

Coda
Based b/a
Extension
mm. 71–75

Formal Structure
Movement IV: "Quodling's Delight"

Intro	Intro (cont.)	Intro (cont.)	Intro (cont.)	Theme 1–1X
Key: G	Pyramid	Trumpet FF	Bridge	a–a–b–b
				(extension)
mm. 1–2	mm. 3–6	mm. 7–13	mm. 14–15	mm. 16–27

Theme 1–2X	Theme 1–3X	Bridge	Theme 2–1X
Accent chords	WW *obbligato*	Offbeats	c–c1–d–c2
mm. 28–35	mm. 36–43	mm. 44–45	mm. 46–59

Theme 2–2X	Theme 1–4X	Theme 1–5X	Intro.
c–c1–d–c2	a–a–b–b	a–a–b–b (extens.)	Pyramid 1X
mm. 60–73	mm. 74–81	mm. 82–93	mm. 94–97

Intro.	Theme 2	Theme 1–X	Theme 1–7X
Pyramid 2X	Augmentation	a–a–b–b	a–a–b–b (extens.)
mm. 98–101	mm. 102–129	mm. 130–137	mm. 138–148

Coda (FF fragment)
Con Fuoco
mm. 149–157

An examination of the structural diagrams reveals that the composer utilizes an introduction to each movement and closes each movement with a coda. Each theme has its own structural uniqueness based upon the formal properties of the original dance tunes used by the composer. Phrase structures are very strict, with an occasional extension/modification provided by Hesketh.

Each of the first three movements is based upon a single theme, some old and some new. The fourth movement is based upon a theme from the original Playford's *Dancing Master* entitled "Goddesses." This is contrasted by the composer's original second theme.

Unit 8: Suggested Listening
Malcolm Arnold, *Four Scottish Dances*
Percy Aldridge Grainger, *Lincolnshire Posy*
Gustav Holst:
  First Suite in E-flat for Military Band
  Second Suite in F for Military Band
David Stanhope, *Folk Song Set No. 2*
Ralph Vaughan Williams, *English Folk Song Suite*
Guy Woolfenden, *Illyrian Dances*

Unit 9: Additional References and Resources

Hesketh, Kenneth. *Danceries* for Symphonic Wind Band. Published by Faber Music, 2000.

Contributed by:

Barry E. Kopetz
Director of Bands
Capital University, Conservatory of Music
Columbus, Ohio

Teacher Resource Guide

Dies Natalis

Howard Hanson
(1896–1981)

Unit 1: Composer

Howard Harold Hanson was one of the most important figures in the American music world. He exerted widespread influence as a composer, conductor, philosopher, educator, and administrator. From 1924 to 1964, he helped build the Eastman School of Music into a first-class institution, and he was a champion of American music throughout his lifetime.

Howard Hanson was born in Wahoo, Nebraska, the son of Swedish immigrants Hans and Hilma Christina (Eckstrom) Hanson. He learned piano with his mother, began composing at age six, and later became an excellent cellist. He studied at Luther College, University of Nebraska, Institute of Musical Art (now Juilliard School of Music), and Northwestern University. At the age of twenty, Hanson joined the faculty of the College of the Pacific. Three years later he was named dean of its Conservatory of Fine Arts. In 1921, Hanson received the Prix de Rome and was the first composer to enter the American Academy in that city. Upon his return to the United States in 1924, he became director of the Eastman School of Music, a position he held until hisretirement forty years later.

Hanson's awards are numerous, including the Pulitzer Prize (in 1944 for his *Symphony No. 4*), membership in the American Academy of Arts and Letters, and thirty-six honorary doctorate degrees.[1]

---

1 Norman E. Smith, *Program Notes for Band*. Chicago, IL: GIA Publications, Inc., 2001, p. 270.

Unit 2: Composition

Dies Natalis for band is in the form of an introduction, a chorale, five variations, and a finale, based on the ancient and beautiful Lutheran Christmas chorale-tune celebrating the birth of Christ. It was performed for the first time in the Eastman Theatre on April 7, 1972, by the Eastman Wind Ensemble, under the direction of Donald Hunsberger, for the fiftieth birthday of the Eastman School of Music.

Hanson has the following to say about the chorale-tune:

> I used to sing it as a boy in the Swedish Lutheran Church of Wahoo, Nebraska. This Chorale has, without doubt, been the greatest single musical influence in my life as a composer. Traces of the chorale appear in my early orchestral work, *Lux Aeterna*, and in sections of my opera, Merry Mount. The chorale form has also influenced my *Chorale* and *Alleluia* for band and my fourth and fifth symphonies for orchestra.[2]

The performance time of the composition is approximately fifteen minutes in length.

Unit 3: Historical Perspective

Hanson's music has frequently been termed neo-romantic. His compositions are often melodious and dramatic, and his harmonic vocabulary is tonal in the mid-twentieth century sense of the term. Hanson wrote a text, *Harmonic Materials of Modern Music: Resources of the Tempered Scale*, that sheds light on his compositional style. Although the work was written in 1972 for the Eastman Wind Ensemble, the score calls for a large (four-part) clarinet section and split cornet and trumpet parts, possibly indicating that the work is also appropriate for a large symphony band.

The Lutheran chorale tune upon which *Dies Natalis* is based is known to many as "How Brightly Shines the Morning Star." J. S. Bach used this chorale in *Cantata No. 36*, and many settings of this chorale are widely available.

Unit 4: Technical Considerations

With a performance time of fifteen minutes, endurance is a primary concern for all wind players. No key signature is indicated, but the primary key center is G major with several complex excursions. Security and facility in all keys is necessary for successful performance. The upper range of the soprano instruments is frequently exploited, including in the finale. Frequent meter changes occur in the Gregorian chant variation (Variation 3), and the *Allegro Feroce* section (Variation 4) has very rapid sixteenth note passages for woodwinds and cornet. Variation 2 includes many rapid and awkward

---

2 Howard Hanson, Dies Natalis (New York: Carl Fischer, 1973), program note.

fingering patterns for clarinet. Percussion demands are modest compared to many contemporary works of this magnitude.

Unit 5: Stylistic Considerations

The prime requisite for performance of this work is an ensemble capable of projecting the emotion and drama of the neo-romantic style. The extensive chorale statements demand the utmost in tone quality, intonation, balance, and blend. Variation 3 ("in the Gregorian manner") requires strong solo double reeds capable of creating the illusion of rhythmic freedom in spite of the complex meter changes. This variation also includes a lyrical tuba line that reaches the top of the bass clef staff.

Unit 6: Musical Elements

MELODY:
Predominantly lyrical, in chorale style.

RHYTHM:
Simple duple meter is the predominant framework throughout the composition. Variation 3 alternates 2/4 and 3/8 measures to create a sense of rhythmic freedom.

HARMONY:
Neo-tonal, with extended tertian sonorities and distant key relationships.

TEXTURE:
Predominantly homophonic, with many chorale textures. Scoring is generally quite thick, producing a romantic "blended" sound.

DYNAMICS:
The work utilizes the full dynamic range. Dramatic effect is central to the success of the composition.

Unit 7: Form and Structure

SECTION	REHEARSAL NO.	KEY CENTER	EVENT AND SCORING
Introduction	Beginning	G	*Maestoso*; pedal G; timpani solo
Chorale	1	G	*Maestoso*; harmonic structure and chorale statement
Variation 1	8	G-sharp minor	*Poco piu mosso*; imitative texture; lyrical setting
Variation 2	10	F-sharp minor; D minor	*Ancora piu mosso, un poco agitato*; quarter note chorale statement with rapid accompaniment

SECTION	REHEARSAL NO.	KEY CENTER	EVENT AND SCORING
Transition	11	Undefined	*Molto meno mosso pesante*; steady quarter note pulse with dramatic *sforzando* whole notes
Variation 3	13	A minor; F minor	*Andante calmo, nel modo Gregoriano*; 2/4 to 3/8 alternation; transparent textures; neo-Gregorian mood
Variation 4	15	Rapid key shifts	*Allegro feroce*; sixteenth note rhythmic surface; *marcato*
Variation 5	19	G; E minor	*Larghetto semplice*; 3/4 placid statements; eighth note rhythmic surface
Finale	21	E minor; G	*Maestoso, Tempo di comminciando*; chorale statements; homophonic texture; cadential closing figures

Unit 8: Suggested Listening

J. S. Bach, *Cantata No. 36*, "Schwingt freudig euch empor" (BWV 36)
Howard Hanson:
> *Chorale and Alleluia*
> *Dies Natalis* (band and orchestra versions)
> *Symphony No. 1* (Nordic)
> *Symphony No. 2* (Romantic)

Jean Sibelius, *Symphony No. 5*

Unit 9: Additional References and Resources

Bach, J. S. *Cantata No. 36*, "Schwingt freudig euch empor" (BWV 36). Gachinger Kantorei Stuttgart, conducted by Helmuth Rilling. Hanssler #92012, 1999. Compact disc.

Hanson, Howard. *Dies Natalis*. Eastman Wind Ensemble, conducted by Donald Hunsberger. Centaur #2014, 1996. Compact disc.

_____. *Dies Natalis*. Seattle Symphony Orchestra, conducted by Gerard Schwarz. Delos #3160, 1994. Compact disc.

_____. Harmonic Materials of Modern Music: Resources of the Tempered Scale. New York: Appleton-Century-Crofts, 1960.

Johnson, Barry Wayne. "An analytical study of the band compositions of Howard Hanson." Ed. D. dissertation, University of Houston, 1986.

Rehrig, William H. *The Heritage Encyclopedia of Band Music*. Edited by Paul E. Bierley. Westerville, OH: Integrity Press, 1991.

Smith, Norman E. Program Notes for Band. Chicago, IL: GIA Publications, Inc., 2001.

Contributed by:
Darin Schmidt
Director of Bands
Lakeview School District
Battle Creek, Michigan

Teacher Resource Guide

Divertimento

Ira Hearshen
(b. 1948)

Unit 1: Composer

Ira Hearshen is one of the most sought-after orchestrators in Hollywood. A graduate of Wayne State University (Michigan), Hearshen also studied orchestration at the Grove School of Music in Los Angeles. His principal teachers include film composers Albert Harris and Allyn Ferguson. His 25-year career has afforded him the opportunity to collaborate with other notable Hollywood giants: Hearshen served as Lalo Shifrin's principal orchestrator for the film *Rush Hour*, he teamed up with Randy Newman in Disney's blockbuster animated film, *A Bug's Life*, and he was the principal arranger for the NBC mini-series *Atomic Train*. He currently serves as the principal arranger for the Miss America Pageant.

Hearshen's original compositions and arrangements have been premiered at the Detroit Symphony's Pine Knob Summer Series, The Summer Pops Series for John Denver, and educational conferences around the world. Other orchestrations include music for the feature films *Guarding Tess*, *The Three Musketeers*, *All Dogs Go to Heaven 2*, the television series *Beauty and the Beast*, and the Broadway production *Into the Light*.

Hearshen has done a great deal to perpetuate the American musical tradition for concert bands. Inspired by the composers who precede him, Hearshen has produced works that illustrate and incorporate many different American musical styles. His inspirations can be traced to the earliest masters—from John Philip Sousa and Scott Joplin to the pioneers of the Broadway musical stage.

Unit 2: Composition

Hearshen's *Divertimento* was written using American composer Vincent Persichetti's *Divertimento for Band, Op. 42*, as a model. Hearshen employs traditional American compositional and harmonic devices in this five-movement work, but he did so with a twist: modern be-bop harmony pervades the "Ragtime" and "Blues" movements. The third movement, "Mambo Loco," is based on a rhythmic structure designed to make the concert band swing in the manner of Leonard Bernstein. "Susan's Song" is named for and dedicated to Hearshen's wife, and the final movement, "Children's Dance," exploits the universally recognized (minor third) interval used by children all over the world—the "Naa-Naa" interval.

Unit 3: Historical Perspective

Divertimento was commissioned by the United States Air Force Heritage of America Band stationed at Langley Air Force Base, Virginia; however, the piece was released to the United States Air Force Concert Band, Washington, DC, and premiered by this ensemble in April 1998 under the direction of Colonel Lowell Graham.

The first movement harkens back to the piano rags of Scott Joplin (1868–1917). The second movement, titled "Blues," loosely mirrors a twelve-bar blues format while "suggesting" various keys throughout the course of the movement. The third movement is inspired by the "Mambo" from Bernstein's *West Side Story*. The fourth movement features solo trumpet and is reminiscent of the "Soliloquy" from Persichetti's *Divertimento for Band*. The final movement, "Children's Dance," is a spirited theme and variations.

Unit 4: Technical Considerations

The key areas of G major, C major, D major, D-flat major, and F major are utilized throughout the composition. There are several sixteenth note passages for the woodwinds in "Ragtime," "Mambo," and "Children's Dance." "Susan's Song" contains exposed solo parts for trumpet, horn, oboe, and flute; and the "Blues" movement requires players to perform melodic and accompaniment figures containing wide leaps, contrasting articulations, and dynamic contrasts all within the context of a swing style. "Ragtime," "Blues," "Mambo," and "Children's Dance" demand a high degree of facility and rhythmic consistency from the players, despite moving from one genre to the next. The conductor may want to consider using snare with brushes in the second movement.

Unit 5: Stylistic Considerations

Hearshen's *Divertimento* requires the ensemble to play in a variety of different styles. The "Ragtime" movement should be performed in a lilted manner with a relaxed tempo, giving careful consideration to note lengths in the melody and accompaniment. *Staccato* markings indicate separation (not necessarily short), and a syncopated approach should be maintained throughout the movement.

The "Blues" movement should have a consistent swing feel, allowing triplet figures to be played in a relaxed style. Passages without specific articulation markings should be played *legato*, and accented and *marcato* markings can have added emphasis and/or weight.

The rhythmic nature of the "Mambo Loco" drives this particular movement forward, and special consideration should be taken not to slow down in the B section.

"Susan's Song" requires expressive playing from the soloists, and all of the *molto expressivo* lines should sing through the texture. Also, the conductor should be aware how the overall dynamic shape of this movement mirrors the form.

Finally, "Children's Dance" must maintain a bright and humorous style on each repetition of the melody, despite an increase in rhythmic and harmonic intensity.

Unit 6: Musical Elements

The first movement focuses around the key of G major and C major. The melody is straightforward and has a limited range. Traditional harmonies are utilized in the B section of the movement, and the harmonic rhythm is characteristic of a standard piano rag.

The melodic material in the "Blues" movement outlines a pentatonic scale, hinting at the keys of B-flat and E-flat. The melody is initially presented in a "question and answer" fashion and typically resolves on B-flat at the end of each phrase. The predominance of D-flat at measure 13 is a typical use of blues harmony (i.e., III b in the key of B-flat).

The "Mambo" centers around the keys of D Major and B-flat major. The movement contains thick textures and complex rhythms that increase in density as the melody progresses in either duple or triple.

"Susan's Song" utilizes dominant, diminished, polychordal, and cluster harmonies. The melody outlines wide leaps (to include major sevenths) followed by more diatonic and chromatic stepwise motion.

The melody in "Children's Dance" centers around the interval of a minor third, or C to A. Each repetition of the melodic material contains an increased harmonic tension and/or contrapuntal complexity.

Unit 7: Form and Structure

SECTION	MEASURE	EVENT AND SCORING
Movement I: "Rag"		
Introduction	1–9	G major
AA	10–25	Theme in clarinet and bassoon
B	26–33	Theme in oboe, saxophone, piccolo
A	34–45	Theme in clarinet and euphonium; countermelody in flute and saxophone
CC	46–61	Theme in trombone, 1st alto saxophone, and upper woodwinds; countermelody in flute, bassoon, and euphonium
D	62–69	Retransition
Da Capo	1–44	G major
Coda	70	G major
Movement II: "Twelve-Bar Blues"		
Introduction	1–2	Two measures of time; cluster chords imply a dominant function
First statement	3–14	Twelve-bar phrase; use of hocket in melody; implies keys of E-flat and B-flat
Second statement	15–26	Twelve-bar phrase; imitation of melodic fragments at different pitch levels (D-flat, C, E, G, B, A); uses standard-step blues progression in mm. 21–23
Interlude	27–42	Sixteen-bar bridge; cycles through four key areas (G, E, D-flat, and A); imitation of melodic fragments; span of orchestration increases
Third statement	43–52	Eight-bar phrase with two-bar extension; melody in piccolo, English horn, bassoon, and 1st alto saxophone; countermelody in clarinet

SECTION	MEASURE	EVENT AND SCORING
Fourth statement	53–62	Eight-bar phrase with two-bar extension; half-step blues progression returns in mm. 53–55 and mm. 57–59

Movement III: "Rondo"

A

First statement	1–8	D major; melody in trumpet and woodwinds
Second statement	9–16	Thirds added above melodic line
Transition	17–21	

B

Introduction	22–25	D major
First statement	26–31	*Legato* melody in trumpet
Second statement	32–37	Horns added to melodic line; ad-lib timbales and conga
Transition	38–41	
Third statement	42–47	Abbreviated statement of melodic material
Retransition	48–51	Brief harmonic shift from A-flat to E-flat

A

Third statement	52–59	D major; ad-lib percussion more active

C

Introduction	60–67	B-flat major
First statement	68–76	Melody in trombone; add marimba; uses A material in English horn, 2nd/3rd clarinet, and 4th/5th trumpet

A

Fourth statement	77–85	D major; melody in imitation
Fifth statement	86–95	Span of orchestration increases; add timpani

SECTION	MEASURE	EVENT AND SCORING
B Fourth statement	96–101	D major; melody in trumpets, euphonium, and woodwinds; additional voices in accompaniment
Fifth statement	102–107	Melody in horn, woodwinds, and euphonium
Transition	108–111	
A Sixth statement	112–123	D major

Movement IV: "Modified Song Form"

A First statement	1–18	Melody in trumpet; countermelody in tenor saxophone and euphonium; span of orchestration increases throughout phrase
Second statement	19–26	Melody in euphonium, tenor saxophone, and bassoon; legato countermelody in woodwinds and horns
B First statement	27–34	Melody in flute; accompaniment in clarinet and low brass/low woodwinds
Second statement	35–46	Melodic material presented in horn, flute, clarinet, oboe, trumpet, etc.; A material briefly recalled in m. 43

Movement V: "Theme and Variations"

Introduction	1–11	Chord cluster followed by sixteenth note "screen" in the woodwinds; C and A are predominant Tones
Theme	12–19	F major; oboe presents the "naa-naa" interval of a minor third in melody; accompaniment in clarinet
Variation I	20–27	F major; melody in piccolo, 1st alto saxophone, and tenor saxophone; imitation in flute and trombone

SECTION	MEASURE	EVENT AND SCORING
Variation II	28–35	Melody repeated; new accompaniment in clarinet and saxophone "implies" different key areas; phrase ends on F major
Variation III	36–43	Theme presented in hocket using trumpet, horn, and saxophone; dissonant unison lines in woodwinds
Variation IV	44–51	Three-part canon of melodic material
Variation V	52–59	Melody in low brass/low winds; contrapuntal use of material; juxtaposition of rhythms to include triplets against eighth notes; alternating unisons between trumpet and horn
Variation VI	60–67	Melody in upper woodwinds; major/minor harmonies presented in trumpet, horn, and trombone; span of orchestration increases to include additional percussion; triplet countermelody continued in low brass/low winds
Codetta	68–71	F major

Unit 8: Suggested Listening

Leonard Bernstein, *West Side Story*
Roger Cichy, *Divertimento*
Ira Hearshen, *A Patriotic Overture*
Scott Joplin, *Maple Leaf Rag*
Vincent Persichetti, *Divertimento*
Jack Stamp, *Divertimento*

Unit 9: Additional References and Resources

Ira Hearshen, *Divertimento for Band. American Premieres* compact disc recording, United States Air Force Band, Colonel Lowell Graham, conductor.

Fennell, Frederick. "Vincent Persichetti: Divertimento for Band." *BD Guide*, September/October 1984, p. 1.

Contributed by:
Captain Keelan Edward McCamey
Deputy Commander
United States Air Forces in Europe Band
Sembach, Germany

Teacher Resource Guide

Fanfare and Allegro
Clifton Williams
(1923–1976)

Unit 1: Composer

One of the most influential and important composers of band music in the twentieth century, James Clifton Williams contributed many serious works to the repertoire. While Williams composed music for many genres, his dedication to writing serious music for both amateur and professional bands helped to shape the medium.

Born in Traskwood, Arkansas, Williams attended secondary school in Little Rock, where he played horn in the school band and orchestra, and began experimenting with composing for instrumental ensembles. He attended Louisiana Tech University for one year prior to joining the U.S. Army Air Corps as a bandsman in 1942. After World War II, Williams finished his bachelor's degree in music at Louisiana State University before attending the Eastman School of Music. At Eastman, he studied composition with Bernard Rogers, and was influenced by Howard Hanson, completing his Master of Music degree in 1949. Williams taught for seventeen years at the University of Texas, also playing horn professionally in the San Antonio and Austin Symphonies. In 1966, he became chairman of the Theory and Composition Department at the University of Miami. Williams lost his long battle with cancer in 1976.

Unit 2: Composition

Fanfare and Allegro, composed in 1956, is dedicated to R. Bernard Fitzgerald and the University of Texas Symphonic Band. The work won the first Ostwald Award for composition from the American Bandmasters Association and was premiered by the U.S. Air Force Band, William F. Santleman, conductor, at the 1956 ABA convention.

Although composed in two separate and distinct sections, the work is performed as one piece, with a timpani roll connecting the two parts. Scored for standard concert band instrumentation, performance time is approximately six minutes (the "Fanfare" is two minutes and thirty seconds; the "Allegro" is three minutes and thirty seconds). Originally published by the Summy-Birchard Company, the work is now available from Warner Brothers.

Unit 3: Historical Perspective

Williams's name was forever etched in the history of the modern concert band when he not only won the first American Bandmasters Association Ostwald Award for composition but also the second. Having received the 1956 award for *Fanfare and Allegro*, his *Symphonic Suite* was awarded the 1957 prize. The ABA/Ostwald Award was the first competition for band compositions in America and is one of the most prestigious awards in that field. At a time when the concert band was still struggling for acceptance as a serious medium for making music, Williams made a significant impact for many reasons. Not only did he continue to write music for bands after winning his awards, he also wrote music at various levels and in many styles. Thirty-one of Williams's works for band are published. As a university professor, he also influenced the music and careers of many other band composers, including W. Francis McBeth and John Barnes Chance.

Fanfare and Allegro has remained a staple of the modern concert band repertoire. The work is consistently found on lists of standard wind band literature, such as the National Band Association's "Selective Music List for Bands." Frank Battisti lists *Fanfare and Allegro* on his "Recommended Twentieth Century Literature for the University, School of Music, Professional Contemporary Wind Band/Ensemble" and on his "Recommended Twentieth Century Repertoire for the Contemporary High School Wind Band/Ensemble."

Unit 4: Technical Considerations

While there are no solo passages in this work, one of the principle challenges of *Fanfare and Allegro* is the unison melodic and rhythmic playing required of most sections within the band. The cornet section is featured throughout the work, beginning with the opening fanfare and continuing with short passages in the "Allegro." The horn, trombone, and euphonium sections join the cornets for many of these interludes. First cornet performers are required to play in the upper register much of the time, with notes written to C above the staff. The upper woodwinds must play repetitive, rhythmic *ostinato* passages, often at very fast tempi. The percussion section uses standard traditional instruments, and performers must be comfortable playing independently. All instruments are asked to perform *ostinato* patterns, *legato* melodic lines, and *marcato* fanfare-like figures at various times. Rapid rhythmic passages, utilizing dotted-eighth and sixteenth note combinations, are also frequently found, as well as rapid intervallic leaps of thirds, fourths, and fifths. The use of lydian scales within the melodic lines, as well as octatonic scales and unusual note groupings in some of the woodwind passages, will require technical preparation. Upper woodwind performers are asked to play half-step trills.

While the majority of the work is written using cut-time, the second half of the fanfare section is in a *L'istesso tempo* 4/4. The cornets, as well as various other sections, are required to perform some of the fanfare-like figures in quarter note triplets against the cut-time pulse.

Unit 5: Stylistic Considerations

Characteristic of Williams's compositional style, *Fanfare and Allegro* is very declamatory in nature. Williams relied heavily on the brass and percussion sections to provide the necessary power for a brilliant and exciting composition. Long, sustained phrases are juxtaposed against the many rhythmic *ostinati* and fanfare-like figures. Throughout the work, Williams utilizes a fairly small range of dynamics and articulations, which are reflective of the style and mood of this music. With the exception of the last few measures of the piece, he generally uses only the *staccato* and accent articulations throughout the composition.

The dynamic range is consistently within the *mezzo-forte* to *fortissimo* levels. The only use of *piano* level dynamics are found at the end of the "Fanfare" section. The work utilizes a small metronomic range of half note = 100–116. While *Fanfare and Allegro* is a tonal work, the bitonality and the use of altered scales definitely cast the work in the style of similar music written during the middle of the twentieth century for band. The piece presents a very majestic, serious, and dramatic mood throughout.

Unit 6: Musical Elements

Fanfare and Allegro firmly established the components of music often found in the band works of Williams. Rather than writing long phrases, Williams generally concentrated on developing themes by combining short motives. Motivic development, and elisions between sections, are also hallmarks of his style. His continual use of rhythmic *ostinato* figures contribute to creating forward motion in the work.

Clearly a tonal piece, *Fanfare and Allegro* utilizes a tonal center of B-flat while presenting many examples of bitonality. In his dissertation analyzing the compositional characteristics of Williams's music, William Richardson reveals many of the techniques common in Williams's music. Motivic transformation and coupling, augmentation, diminution, and retrograde are evident in this work and are devices found consistently in the compositions of Williams.

Richardson believes the manipulation of these techniques, rather than the techniques themselves, are what is most relevant.

When reviewing a list of compositional characteristics prepared by John Siler for his dissertation involving the music of Williams, almost all are evident in *Fanfare and Allegro*. These include his use of modality, employing chords in parallel harmony often built on altered scale tones, and the use of tritone relationships, especially at cadence points.

Unit 7: Form and Structure

SECTION	MEASURE	EVENT AND SCORING
Movement I: "Fanfare"		
	1–19	Cut-time, *Allegro non troppo* (half note = 100–108); cornet presents an opening fanfare punctuated by interludes from the percussion section; concert F fermata by cornet connects to the next section
	20–44	Beginning with a *tutti* ensemble chord, this section continues the cornet fanfare with chords punctuated by the entire ensemble; upper woodwinds present the first occurrence of the dotted-eighth/sixteenth note rhythmic figures before being transferred to saxophone, horn, trombone, and euphonium; cornet fanfare becomes a quarter note triplet figure echoed by alto and tenor saxophone, horn, trombone, and euphonium
	45–55	4/4, *L'istesso tempo* (quarter note = half note); various rhythmic ostinati in woodwinds and low brass; *legato* melody presented by piccolo, flute, oboe, and 1st clarinet
	56–76	Timpani and snare drum *ostinato* figures are added; new melody presented by piccolo, flute, alto saxophone, tenor saxophone, and horn; several melodic and harmonic ideas are juxtaposed

Section	Measure	Event and Scoring
	77–86	Ending passage of the "Fanfare" (*poco a poco rit. e dim. al fine*); F major *pianissimo* chord for all winds except cornet and saxophone; timpani rolled *crescendo* F *Lunga* to the *"Allegro"* section
Movement II: "Allegro"	87–93	Cut-time, *Drammatico*; brass and percussion *forte-piano* chords
	93–110	*Allegro non troppo* (half note = 108–116); m. 93 ends the *Drammatico* section and provides the pickup half note for the beginning of fugue; fugue begins with 2nd/3rd trombone and tuba; fugue continues with horn, 1st trombone, and euphonium; last fugue section is played by cornet
	111–126	Low woodwinds and low brass half note background harmonies transition from D major to D minor; melody is played by piccolo, flute, English horn, E-flat clarinet, 1st clarinet, tenor saxophone, 1st cornet, and euphonium, with 2nd/3rd clarinet, alto saxophone, and horn eventually added; *ritardando* in mm. 125–126 with *diminuendo*
	127–132	Fanfare-like figure in English horn, alto saxophone, tenor saxophone, and horn
	133–150	Rhythmic interplay between various sections; upper woodwinds play repetitive quarter note figures of descending perfect fifths ending with trills and eighth note triplet figures propelling toward the next section
	151–158	Fanfare-like transition in low woodwinds and low brass

SECTION	MEASURE	EVENT AND SCORING
	159–178	Rhythmic ostinati in low woodwinds, low brass, and percussion; restatement of fugue subject originally presented in m. 93 played by piccolo, flute, oboe, E-flat clarinet, clarinet, and cornet; rhythmic interjections from English horn, alto clarinet, alto saxophone, and euphonium; builds toward a cornet and horn fanfare
	180–197	Fanfare-like figure in upper woodwinds continually concluded by cornet and 2nd/3rd trombone; rhythmic *ostinati* in low woodwinds, saxophone, euphonium, tuba, and timpani
	198–202	Transition section presents rhythmic figure in woodwinds and horn leading to next section
	203–207	*Molto allargando*; quarter note triplet fanfare figures played by cornet, trombone, and snare drum; fanfare figure echoed by English horn, alto s axophone, tenor saxophone, horn, and euphonium
	208–225	*Piu mosso* (half note = 100–108); *ostinato* quarter notes in low woodwinds and low brass combined with rhythmic ostinato dotted-eighth/sixteenth note patterns played by flute, E-flat clarinet, and 1st clarinet; new *legato* melody presented by oboe, English horn, 2nd/3rd clarinet, alto clarinet, alto saxophone, tenor saxophone, and baritone saxophone
	226–244	Fanfare-like figures continue with English horn, alto saxophone, tenor saxophone, baritone saxophone, horn, and euphonium

SECTION	MEASURE	EVENT AND SCORING
	245–250	*Meno mosso (accel. e cres. al Tempo I)*; *subito piano crescendo* to *forte* building toward the last section
	251–266	Tempo I (*accel. al Vivace*); *tutti* ensemble playing quarter notes or dotted-eighth/sixteenth note *ostinato* patterns; concludes with B-flat major chord

Unit 8: Suggested Listening

Clifton Williams:
  Caccia and Chorale (1976)
  Dedicatory Overture (1963)
  The Sinfonians (1960)
  Symphonic Dance No. 3, "Fiesta" (1967)
  Symphonic Suite (1957)
  Variation Overture (1961)
British and American Band Classics. Eastman Wind Ensemble, Frederick
  Fennell, conductor: Mercury 432 009-2, 1959
Fanfare and Allegro. Tokyo Kosei Wind Orchestra, Frederick Fennell, con-
  ductor: Kosei KOCD-2811, 1984

Unit 9: Additional References and Resources

Battisti, Frank. *The Twentieth Century American Wind Band/Ensemble.* Ft.
  Lauderdale, FL: Meredith Music Publications, 1995.

Birdwell, John Cody, ed. *Selected Music List for Bands.* Eighth edition.
  Nashville, TN: National Band Association, 2001.

Daniel, Joe Rayford. "The Band Works of James Clifton Williams." Ph.D.
  dissertation, University of Southern Mississippi, 1981.

Kerr, Stephen P. "A Brief Biography of James Clifton Williams." *The Journal
  of Band Research,* Volume 34, No. 1, Fall 1998, pp. 25–37.

Rasmussen, Richard Michael. *Recorded Concert Band Music, 1950–1987.*
  Jefferson, NC: McFarland Press, 1988.

Rehrig, William H. *The Heritage Encyclopedia of Band Music.* Edited by Paul
  E. Bierley. Westerville, OH: Integrity Press, 1991.

Richardson, William Newell. "An Analysis of Selected Compositional
  Characteristics of Three Works by James Clifton Williams." Thesis,
  University of Mississippi, 1983.

Siler, John Robert. "The Non-formalized Pitch-Rhythm Ostinato in Band Works of Clifton Williams: A Categorization of Patterns." Ph.D. dissertation, University of South Carolina, 1985.

Smith, Norman. *Program Notes for Band.* Chicago, IL: GIA Publications, Inc., 2001.

Contributed by:

James Popejoy
Director of Bands
University of North Dakota
Grand Forks, North Dakota

Teacher Resource Guide

French Impressions
Guy Woolfenden
(b. 1937)

Unit 1: Composer

English composer and conductor Guy Anthony Woolfenden was born on July 12, 1937, in Ipswich. His early music studies were received at Westminster Abbey, where he served as senior chorister. He completed his Master of Arts at Christ's College, Cambridge (1959), and continued his training at Guildhall School of Music, where he studied conducting with Norman Del Mar. During the 1960–61 season, he performed as a professional horn player with the Sadler's Wells Opera before joining the music staff of the Royal Shakespeare Company at Stratford-upon-Avon. For the next thirty-five years (1963–1998), Woolfenden served as head of music and resident composer for this internationally known theater group. He composed more than 150 scores for the company's productions. During this same period, he won the Ivor Novello Award and the Society of West End Theatre Award for the best British musical of 1976, *The Comedy of Errors*, a production based on the Shakespearean play of the same title. Equally well regarded for his conducting, Woolfenden has served as conductor for Morley College (1968–1978), Liverpool Mozart Orchestra (1970–1992), and the Warwickshire Symphony Orchestra (beginning 1972). In addition, he has worked with the London Symphony Orchestra, Halle Orchestra, Chelsea Opera Group, Scottish Opera, and the Kirov Ballet.

The fact that Woolfenden is respected and honored by his colleagues and peers is evidenced by his awards and positions of leadership. In 1990, he was awarded a Fellowship of the Birmingham Schools of Music for his service to music. He is an honorary member of the London College of Music and Media, a licentiate of the Guildhall School of Music, chairman of the British Association of Symphonic Bands and Wind Ensembles, president-elect of the Incorporated Society of Musicians, and an honorary associate artist of the Royal Shakespeare Company.

Woolfenden's compositional output includes works for orchestra, chamber orchestra, wind orchestra, chamber ensembles, concertos (oboe, clarinet, horn, bassoon), voice, music theater, film scores, music for television, and educational pieces. His wind orchestra compositions include *Gallimaufry* (1983), *Deo Gracias* (1986), *Illyrian Dances* (1986), *S.P.Q.R.* (1988), *Mockbeggar Variations* (1991), *Curtain Call* (1997), *Birthday Treat* (1998), *Rondo Variations* (a version of his Clarinet Concerto, Movement 2, arranged for clarinet and concert band, 1998), and *French Impressions* (1998). Woolfenden and his family own and operate Ariel Music.

Unit 2: Composition

Commissioned by the Metropolitan Wind Symphony, *French Impressions* was premiered by that ensemble in Boston, Massachusetts, on November 7, 1998, with music director David Martins conducting. The inspiration for the work came from four paintings by French artist Georges Seurat (1859–1891). Seurat, along with several other young artists, helped to establish the *Société des Artistes Indépendants*, a democratic group at the center of the neo-impressionistic movement. Although the Seurat paintings provided the stimulus for *French Impressions*, there is no musical correlation between the artist's pointillistic style and Woolfenden's compositional techniques. Rather, the colors, tone, and mood of the artworks are the impetus for the composition.

The first movement, "Parade," contrasts Seurat's *La Parade de Cirque* (1888): Invitation to the Sideshow and *Une baignade, Asnières* (1883–1884): A Bathing Place, Asnières. The artistic difference in the two works is readily apparent. *La Parade de Cirque* features a centralized figure playing the trombone with a trio of accompanying musicians on one side and the ringmaster and clown balancing the opposite side. The russet colors and shadowy figures of this gas-lit arena serve to create a somewhat sinister feeling. In normal light, the faces of the figures appear to be orange, but when viewed under gas lighting, these same visages become flesh colored. In contrast to this murky setting is the almost overly bright seaside scene of *Une baignade, Asnières*. A grassy shore hosts several white-skinned bathers in various stages of dress. The sunny afternoon and blue waters ought to establish an idyllic mood, but the presence of smoky factory chimneys in the background again remind the viewer that all is not as it seems.

The second movement, "Can Can," offers musical images based on Seurat's *Le Cirque* (1890–1891), unfinished due to Seurat's untimely death at the age of thirty-two from virulent diphtheria, and *Le Chahut* (1889–1890).

Alike in the energy conveyed by the characters, *Le Cirque* features a circus performer atop a galloping white horse creating a whirling dervish-like image, while *Le Chahut* depicts four can-can dancers accompanied by a lively pit orchestra. The word *chahut* means "horseplay," and *faire du chahut* means "to make a racket." There is no question that these paintings portray the gaiety and rhythmic energy of the circus and the dance hall. Woolfenden has captured this spirit and the different settings in "Can Can."

French Impressions is dedicated to Bob and Esther Piankian, who are affiliated with the Metropolitan Wind Symphony. Bob Piankian is vice president of the group, and his wife has the distinction of being the principal trombonist. The work is listed as a grade 4.5 (advanced) and is approximately ten minutes in duration. "Parade" is the longer of the two movements at seven minutes. *French Impressions* is published by Ariel Music.

Unit 3: Historical Perspective

The inspiration behind the composition of a particular piece may come from anywhere. Sounds, events, nature scenes, buildings, stories, individuals, feelings, and creatures are just a few potential sources that may motivate a composer. As Modest Mussorgsky's *Pictures at an Exhibition* (1874) so clearly illustrates, paintings too may provide a strong stimulus for musical ideas.

The paintings that inspired Woolfenden's *French Impressions* are among a group of six large pictures by Georges Seurat that are regarded as his major works. In a period in art history when impressionism was the reigning style, Seurat's dotted brushwork and flat figures represented a more primitive art. The artist deliberately turned from the tradition of the day, and when *Un dimanche après-midi à l'île de la Grande Jatte* was exhibited in May 1886, neo-impressionism (as it was dubbed in September of that same year) began. Although the artist lived a mere thirty-two years, his contributions to the world of art are significant.

Woolfenden's musical impressions pay tribute to the paintings that inspired the composition. So it is appropriate that his style of writing is suggestive of that of the French impressionistic composers. Impressionism is defined as "...a style of musical composition in which lush harmonies, subtle rhythms, and unusual tonal colors are used to evoke moods and impressions."[1] The style is most evident in the works of Claude Debussy (1845–1924) and is characterized by the use of whole-tone scales, unresolved dissonances, triads with added color tones, use of tritones, winding melodies, parallel motion in supporting chords, and avoidance of the leading tone. While many of these elements are found in *French Impressions*, the composition is more readily compared to works by Maurice Ravel (1875-1937). In comparison to the

---

1 "Impressionism." *Webster's Encyclopedic Unabridged Dictionary of the English Language*. New York: Gramercy Books, 1994.

works of Debussy, Ravel's music tends to be less dense with cleaner melodic lines and more functional harmonies. *French Impressions* is akin to this model.

Unit 4: Technical Considerations

French Impressions is scored for wind band. The set of parts includes multiple copies of flute and clarinet parts; one copy each of piccolo, 1st/2nd oboe, bassoon, all saxophone, F horn, trombone, euphonium, and percussion parts; two copies of each trumpet part; and four copies of the tuba part. Additional horn parts in E-flat and treble clef trombone, euphonium, and tuba parts are supplied. European wind orchestra parts, such as E-flat tuba parts in treble and bass clefs, are available on request. The published set of parts indicates that this work is best performed by a wind ensemble rather than the full symphonic band, and analysis of the score supports this reasoning.

Although the technical demands of range and rhythm are not extensive for most instruments, the exposed solo lines, slow tempi, and rich impressionistic harmonies make this work more difficult than its grade 4.5 categorization might suggest. Solo parts for two flutes, oboe, E-flat clarinet, two B-flat clarinets, bass clarinet, alto saxophone, horn, three trombones, and euphonium will require players with mature, well-developed tone and breath support. The tuba part provides the most challenging range concerns with a *tessitura* from g1 to d4. Euphoniums will need to play with security from g2 to a4. The first flute part has numerous sections that employ g6 and a6 in rapid but brief sixteenth note passages. If these notes are in the players' comfortable playing range, then isolation of the section to work out the technical demands of the fingering patterns will be the only concern. There is an alto clarinet part that is cross-scored in various other voices, but the composer prefers that an actual alto clarinet be used whenever possible. The four percussion parts provide more color than rhythmic substance. Consider using very light brass mallets for the glockenspiel, and experiment with various tambourines to achieve the color that most enhances the French quality of the music. The harmonic structure offers additional challenges with many color tones and parallel fifths in supporting voices.

"Parade," the first movement, has tempi ranging from quarter note = 60 in 4/4, to dotted-quarter note = 56, 40, and 36 in 6/8. Although the rhythmic patterns are basic combinations of quarter, eighth, and sixteenth notes, the slow tempi with their subsequent divisions of beat demand control from both players and the conductor. The transparent scoring and interplay of solo lines provide opportunities to focus on balance, intonation, and musical expression. As the title of the work implies, the delicate melodies should be performed in a French-like manner, light and relaxed.

The challenge in "Can Can," the second movement, is the interplay of rhythms and dynamic control. The basic tempo is quarter note = 126 with *accelerandos* and *rallentandos*. The dynamics, ranging from *piano* to *fortissimo*, are well conceived and scored in a manner that allows for maximum success in achieving the composer's intent. The beauty of the movement is found in the contrasts of styles, dynamic levels, and various timbres created by the orchestration.

Unit 5: Stylistic Considerations

The style of *French Impressions* is reminiscent of the works of Ravel and Milhaud. "Parade" is particularly similar in color and orchestration to the impressionistic works of these composers. Listen to Ravel's *Le Tombeau de Couperin* (orchestral and/or wind quintet versions) for an aural model. The horns are scored in a symphonic manner, with 1st and 3rd horns being the upper voices, and 2nd and 4th horns generally playing a lower part. When only two parts are required, the composer relies on 1st and 2nd horns.

French Impressions offers challenges for the performers and conductor. The beautifully crafted lines of the "Parade" are set at a slow tempo but flow in two. According to the composer, measure 104 should be conducted in six and measure 105 in eight. Consider working the 6/8 sections in six to establish the interworkings of the musical lines before bringing the music up to tempo. As the students feel more secure with how the different parts fit together, it will be easier to establish the feeling of two and to maintain the necessary delicate balance of voices and tone color.

The "Can Can" is uplifting and fun as the music alternates between the delightful circus-like music and the gloriously bawdy *Le Chahut* dance hall theme. The energy comes from staying on top of the beat, not by increasing the tempo beyond the suggested quarter note = 126. The composer indicates that he makes a significant *molto rallentando* before "L" (measures 154 through 157) and conducts measure 157 in four. Measure 158 ("L") should be conducted in a slow two, and then use the next eight measures to get back to the *tempo primo*. (Think grand finale dance number!)

Unit 6: Musical Elements

MELODY:

The melodic material in the first movement of *French Impressions* is scored for solo voices. The introductory measures provide musical foreshadowing of the primary melody of this section. A solo flute, supported by other solo woodwind voices and two horns, establishes the four-note motif that will permeate this movement: an ascending minor seventh followed by a descending pair of seconds, one major and one minor (G–F–E- flat–D). At rehearsal letter B, 1st oboe presents the haunting seven-measure melody (Theme A) as a solo horn provides an underlying melodic echo. Because this melody is used throughout the movement with gentle modifications at each subsequent entrance, a handout would allow a comparison of the melodic variations. Develop ear-training skills by having solo players perform the melody so the band may hear the differences. Ask the students to identify which version of the melody is being performed.

Phrasing is written into the melody itself. The seven-measure melody allows for breaths in the second and fourth measures. When an eighth note is followed by an eighth rest on count one, a slight lift is appropriate. (Think "duh dah" with a slight break between the two.)

Theme B is found in the 6/8 sections, and comparable settings may be found in Ravel's *Le Tombeau de Couperin*. Treat this melody lightly and gently, with the delicate written *crescendo* and *decrescendo* apparent within each two-measure section.

"Can Can" contrasts circus music with that found in a dance hall. The intertwining of woodwind runs needs to sound seamless. This will be most readily accomplished by helping the students identify how the melody travels through the ensemble. Rehearse the melody without the accompanying figures. The melody should be buoyant, with a natural dynamic flow that coincides with the melodic direction. The *staccato* notes at the ends of phrases must have a resonant lift. *Staccato* phrases must bounce. Strive for lightness and bounce throughout these sections by staying on the softer side of the dynamics (rehearsal letters A, B, C, F, H, I, J, and K). In contrast to the graciousness of the circus theme, the raucous dance hall theme is loud, heavy, and irreverent. Achieve this feeling by emphasizing the accented and *tenuto* notes within the melodic line and establishing good balance. The accompaniment must never overshadow the melody in volume or in articulation. Try having the students clap the supporting rhythms as the melody is played. Once there is a sense of how the accompaniment fits into the section, have the students sing these parts. Record the group as they perform this *forte* and *fortissimo* section. A playback coupled with careful listening will identify other balance issues. Avoid the temptation to phrase this melody as 4+2+2. It is an eight-measure phrase, and students will need to be reminded of this.

HARMONY:

French Impressions is a tonal work scored with written key signatures of E-flat, C, and A-flat. However, these define tonal centers and modes rather than harmonic structure. Theme A of "Parade" is composed in the phrygian mode, a church mode characterized by a pattern of half step–whole step–whole step–whole step–half step–whole step–whole step (G–A-flat–B-flat–C– D–E-flat–F–G.). Have students play this phrygian scale. Begin with the known: play a concert E-flat scale. Next ask the students to play the same scale tones but start on the third of the scale, concert G. It will be helpful to play this scale on a keyboard instrument so students may hear the unique pattern of whole steps and half steps associated with this mode.

Much of the harmonic structure is scored in open chords with frequent fifths and sevenths. Tune these in segments beginning with any octaves and then the fifths. The impressionistic quality of the harmonic structure is best achieved by thinking and tuning the fifths within the seventh chords rather than taking a chordal approach. For example, even though the chord may be a seventh chord of C–E-flat–G–B-flat, approach the tuning through the fifths of C–G and E-flat–B-flat. Students will be more aware of the fifths and will tune that interval rather than the thirds.

The harmonic structure of Theme B (rehearsal letters C and K) in the 6/8 sections is also impressionistic in character. With its supporting open harmonies and clouded tonal center, the section appears to be in dorian mode (on C), another church mode with half steps between the second and third degrees and the sixth and seventh degrees. However, a case could be made for G minor, especially since the movement ends on a G major chord.

The dorian mode differs from the natural minor in its placement of the second half step. The natural minor scale has a half step between the fifth and sixth degrees of the scale, whereas the dorian mode finds this half step between the sixth and seventh degrees.

Compare:

Dorian –

C	D	E-flat	F	G	A	B-flat	C
1	2	3	4	5	6	7	8

Natural minor –

G	A	B-flat	C	D	E-flat	F	G
1	2	3	4	5	6	7	8

The melody alone supports the G minor concept, but the added C–G–D arpeggiated figure in bassoon gives substance to the modal approach. Use this information to stimulate discussion about analysis of the harmonic structure of twentieth century works.

The intricacies of "Can Can" are predominately found in the supporting chords and rhythms. This rollicking second movement opens in the key of C major and then moves to A-flat and E-flat. The melody remains within the key, but the supporting harmonies are rich and varied with frequent use of seventh chords and color tones. The resultant major seconds and minor s evenths will require attention to adjust the intonation. Work to keep the minor seventh on the lower side. When serious intonation concerns arise, it will be beneficial to help the students identify the harmonic function of their notes. A simple reminder to lower the third in major chords and to raise the third in minor chords will be insufficient if the students cannot identify the chord or the position of the written note within the chord.

RHYTHM:

The rhythmic concerns in "Parade" are primarily based on the divisions of 4/4 versus 6/8. Players will need to move freely from the duple to triple pulses with rhythmic accuracy. Consider using a basic tonguing exercise as part of the warm-up. Set the metronome at quarter notes = 60 and have the band play a measure each of half notes, quarter notes, eighth notes, eighth note triplets, sixteenth notes, and a whole note. Listen for accuracy as the band changes to the new division of the beat. The exercise may be used in conjunction with the scale of the day. Repeat the rhythmic tonguing pattern on each note of the scale. Complete focus of the player's attention will result in a better awareness of these shifts in rhythms.

Since many of the players' 6/8 entrances follow an eighth or a sixteenth note rest, it would be helpful to work this into another warm-up exercise. Set the metronome at dotted-quarter note = 56. Use the triplet division on the metronome to set the 6/8 and have the players say "–2–3–4–5–6." Count one (1) should be silent. Do the same thing with the sixteenth rest: "–+2+3+4+5+6+" or "–2+ 3+." Once the students can say the rhythm with clarity and accuracy, have them say the rhythm and finger the part. Repeat this procedure with the metronomic markings of dotted-quarter note = 40 and 36.

Create a handout that demonstrates the vertical alignment of the more intricate measures. It need not be elaborate, but it should show how the parts line up (measures 53 and 54 in "Parade").

The exciting and somewhat tongue-in-cheek "Can Can" will benefit from rehearsal with a metronome. The composer indicates a tempo of quarter note = 126, with interjected *rallentandos* and *accelerandos*. The effectiveness of these deviations from the established pulse will be enhanced if the basic tempo remains consistent. Use a counting system and ask the students to say their rhythms with the metronome clearly maintaining the tempo. This will be quite easily accomplished if it is initially approached from a more conservative tempo. Use of the metronome will help students to internalize the pulse and allow them to hear how the various rhythmic figures combine, especially in the *tutti* sections at rehearsal letters D, E, L, and M.

Timbre:

To create the best tone color for *French Impressions*, have the students listen to examples of impressionistic music. Ravel's orchestrated version of *Le Tombeau de Couperin* will offer insight to the tonal structure of "Parade." There are a variety of settings for this work, including a woodwind quintet version that will be quite helpful. Recording information is included in Unit 9.

Players will need to have developed a good characteristic tone and should be able to play at softer dynamic levels with control. Develop this capability through the use of long tones, chorales, and works set at slower tempi. Challenge students to perform longer phrases within the chorales and to learn to control the amount of air that goes through the instrument. Use compositions that do not present range or rhythmic difficulties so the ensemble may focus on beautiful tone and phrasing.

Excellent tone and tone colors cannot be easily achieved on inferior equipment. Encourage students to purchase quality instruments and consider developing a basic recommendation sheet for mouthpieces and reeds. Regional professional musicians are a wonderful source of information concerning all aspects of performance and quality equipment. Take advantage of this resource through master classes and a private lesson program. Music Educators National Conference offers a list of funding opportunities.

ERRATA:

"Parade": In measures 41 and 42 of the score, the 1st horn part is missing notes. The player's part is correct, and those notes need to be written into the conductor's score.

"Can Can": Be aware that in measure 83 of the score, the printed rest for 3rd trumpet is easily misinterpreted as a tie over 2nd trumpet's first two notes. The printed "1." is also misleading. The 2nd trumpet's individual part is correct: all notes are *staccato*, and it is a solo.

Unit 7: Form and Structure

SECTION	MEASURE	EVENT AND SCORING
Movement I: "Parade"		
Introduction	1–9	Solo horn; solo woodwinds in 4/4
	9–18	*Tutti* woodwinds in 6/8; establishes meters of the two themes; 4/4 returns with muted trumpet and two solo flutes supported by two horns and four clarinets
Theme A	19–28	Solo oboe with solo horn response; transition to 6/8
Theme B	29–37	Flute melody with bassoon, bass clarinet, clarinet, and string bass
Theme B'	37–45	Antithesis of B melody in oboe and woodwinds
Transition	44–47	4/4 resolves B and introductory material for return of A
Theme A	47–55	Solo trombone with low brass and horn
	55–63	Full band; *forte*

SECTION	MEASURE	EVENT AND SCORING
	63–69	Oboe, E-flat soprano clarinet, and trumpet with woodwinds; alto saxophone response to melody
	71–74	Solo oboe with woodwinds
Transition	75–87	Woodwinds provide hints of B
Theme A	87–93	Solo oboe with woodwinds and trombone
Introduction	93–95	Return of 6/8; introduction to B
Theme B	95–106	Flute with bassoon, bass clarinet, and string bass; solo trombone plays Theme A four-note motif

Movement II: "Can Can"
Theme A = Le Cirque (circus)
Theme B = Le Chahut (can can/racket music)

Introduction	1–17	Percussion, bass clarinet, bassoon, muted trombone, saxophone, muted trumpet, and horn; pyramid effect through full band
	17–21	Glockenspiel and flute provide introduction to Theme A
Theme A	21–44	Circus music; clarinet and oboe; flute
Theme B	45–61	"Can Can" music; melody in 1st trumpet, 2nd/3rd clarinet, and piccolo with countermelody in euphonium, tuba, and string bass
	61–81	Low brass and low woodwinds
Theme A	85–101	Clarinet and other woodwinds
	101–109	Euphonium solo
Transition	109–122	Woodwinds and horn accompaniment
Theme A	122–158	Woodwinds, solo alto saxophone; tuba
	154–158	*Molto rallentando* into return of can can music

Section	Measure	Event and Scoring
Theme B	158–166	*Accelerando;* low brass and low woodwinds melody with full band
	166–174	Tempo primo
	174–185	Trumpet and clarinet melody
Coda	189–end	Circus and can can themes interspersed in woodwinds and brass to a rousing conclusion

Unit 8: Suggested Listening

Claude Debussy, *Nocturnes*
Norman Dello Joio, *Scenes from "The Louvre"*
Martin Ellerby, *Paris Sketches*
Ira Hearshen, *A Patriotic Overture*
Darius Milhaud, *La Cheminee Du Roi Rene*
Modest Mussorgsky, *Pictures at an Exhibition*
Maurice Ravel, *Le Tombeau de Couperin*
    Guy Woolfenden:
    Gallimaufry
    Illyrian Dances
    Suite Française

Unit 9: Additional References and Resources

Abbado, Claudio, conductor. *Ravel Orchestral Works.* Deutsche Grammophone CD-459439, 1999.

Apel, Willi. *Harvard Dictionary of Music.* Second edition. Cambridge, MA: The Balkan Press of Harvard University Press, 1970.

Colley, Stephen C. *Tuneup: CD-Based Intonation Training System,* Richmond, VA: TuneUp Systems, 2001.

Corporan, Eugene Migliaro, conductor. "Woolfenden's French Impressions." *Rendezvous.* North Texas Wind Symphony. Klavier CD, K-11109, 2000.

Durrant, Sabine. "Music at the Close." *The Independent* (London), 24 June 1992, Arts Page, p. 18.

Grout, Donald Jay. *A History of Western Music.* Third edition. New York: W. W. Norton & Company, 1980.

Hampton, Wilborn. "A Little Shakespearean Traveling Music." *New York Times,* 19 May 2001, late edition, p. B10.

Herbert, Robert L. *Georges Seurat 1859–1891*, New York: Harry N. Abrams, Inc., 1991.

Miles, Richard, ed. *Teaching Music through Performance in Band*, Volume 2. Chicago: GIA Publications, 1998.

Ravel, Maurice. *"Le Tombeau de Couperin."* The Scandinavian Wind Quintet, ASIN CD B0000015AN, 1999.

Woolfenden, Jane. Email correspondence with author. 27 September 2001.

Website:
www.arielmusic.co.uk

Contributed by:
Susan Creasap
Assistant Director of Bands
Morehead State University
Morehead, Kentucky

Teacher Resource Guide

Gloriosa

Yasuhide Ito
(b. 1960)

Unit 1: Composer

Yasuhide Ito is a native of Hamamatsu, Shizuoka Prefecture, Japan, born December 7, 1960. His early music study included childhood piano lessons, and he began to study composition as a high school student. He received his advanced musical training at Tokyo University of Fine Arts, majoring in composition and receiving his graduate degree in 1986. The winner of numerous composition awards, including the Japan Music Competition, the Competition for Saxophone Music, and the Bandmasters Academic Society of Japan, Ito currently teaches at Tokyo University of Fine Arts and Music, Sakuyo Music College, and Tokyo Conservatoire Shobi. He also serves as the regular conductor of the Tsukuba University Band. Ito has composed thirty-eight works for band, has authored *Kangakki no Meikyoku Meienso (The Masterpieces and Great Performances of Wind Instruments)*, and has translated Frank Erickson's *Arranging for the Concert Band*.

Unit 2: Composition

Gloriosa is a symphonic poem for wind ensemble, set in three movements ("Oratorio," "Cantus," and "Dies Festus") and inspired by the music of the "hidden Christians" of Kyushu, who secretly practiced their faith after the abolition of Christianity in 1614 by the Tokugawa government in present-day Tokyo. The music of *Gloriosa* is based on Gregorian chants sung by Christians during their two hundred years of underground religious practice. Commissioned by the Sasebo Band of Japan Maritime Self-Defense Force and published in 1990 by Ongaku No Tomo Sha Corp. (distributed in the United

States by Theodore Presser Co.), the piece is approximately nineteen minutes and thirty seconds in duration. The piece may be purchased in two parts: Movement 1 alone or Movements 2 and 3 together. Each set comes with a full score for all movements; however, the full score is not available for purchase separately.

Unit 3: Historical Perspective

In the sixteenth century, Portuguese Catholics introduced Christianity to Japan. For approximately fifty years, the religion flourished, but in 1614, the Tokugawa government abolished the practice of Christianity in Japan and expelled all missionaries. In spite of the laws against Christianity, nearly 150,000 believers continued to practice their faith secretly in the Nagasaki and Shimabara areas of Kyushu for the next two hundred years. During this time, the original melodies and Latin words of the Gregorian chants used in Christian worship were altered to reflect traditions of Japanese music and culture. These "Japanized" versions of the chants formed the basis of the music for *Gloriosa*.

Unit 4: Technical Considerations

Gloriosa is scored for the following instrumentation: piccolo, two flutes, oboe, bassoon, E-flat clarinet, three B-flat clarinets (two players each), bass clarinet, two alto saxophones, tenor saxophone, baritone saxophone, three B-flat trumpets, four horns, three trombones, euphonium (two players), tuba (two players), and string bass. Percussion scoring calls for four players and includes timpani, glockenspiel, xylophone, snare drum, three toms, vibraphone, bass drum, tambourine, triangle, cymbals, tam-tam, chimes, vibraphone, xylophone, suspended cymbal, ratchet, and sleigh bells. The second movement calls for a *ryuteki* (Japanese flute), which can be played by piccolo. Special notation in the piccolo part indicates the use of microtones for an authentic ryuteki sound. Percussion scoring in the second movement calls for the use of a *gyoban* (percussion instrument), which can be substituted by a large rectangular wooden board and hammer, and the special technique of "bowed vibraphone" is required. All trombone and euphonium parts necessitate the ability to read tenor clef.

The scoring for winds requires players of well-developed technical proficiency who have full command of the entire range of the instrument. *Gloriosa* explores a variety of styles and forms, including chants and chorales that require superb *cantabile* style and energetic *allegro* sections that demand clarity and precise articulation from all players. The first movement, *Oratorio*, opens with a chant melody that is to be sung by all available male voices.

Unit 5: Stylistic Considerations

Each of the three movements of *Gloriosa* is based on a Gregorian chant, thus establishing a flowing style as the basis for each movement. Movement 1, "Oratorio," begins with vibraphone and chimes, evoking the image of church bells. It evolves from a simple statement of the chant, marked *Moderato religioso, nello stile del canto gregoriano*, through a series of thirteen variations gradually building in volume, intensity, and tempo. As the musical energy increases, the stylistic demands move from *legato* to *marcato*. With the exception of a brief interlude of chorale-style passages in the ninth and tenth variations, the rhythmic and stylistic energy continue through the final variation, followed by a return to the church bells from the beginning of the movement.

Movement 2, "Cantus," begins with a ryuteki (piccolo) solo, unaccompanied, which is based on the chant *San Juan-sama no Uto*; it should be played in a free, recitative style. If played on the piccolo, care must be taken to observe the microtone indications, giving the melody the characteristic sound of the authentic Japanese instrument. The solo is joined by delicate percussion and then by sustained low clarinets, also requiring musical sensitivity. The first entrance of the horns must be played strongly, with weight and passion, as the chant reflects the martyrdom of Japanese Christians who were murdered for their faith. A tender, more reflective statement of the theme follows in the woodwinds before returning to the heavy, driving full ensemble scoring. The movement ends with a return to the sparse scoring of piccolo, low clarinet, and delicate percussion.

The final movement, "Dies Festus," based on the Japanese tune *Nagasaki Bura Bura Bushi*, begins with a fast, rhythmic motive scored for the full ensemble, which requires accuracy of rhythm and precision of articulation. Following a percussion interlude that sets up an *ostinato* pattern to drive the movement forward, the melody is presented in the trombones, with interjections from high woodwinds and brass. A harmonized statement of the theme that follows demands the same crisp style of articulation. The middle section of the movement presents a contrast of style, with the woodwinds playing sustained, lyrical lines based on the *Gloriosa* theme of the first movement, followed by a brass choir chorale and, finally, a full ensemble scoring of the chorale. The next section of the movement returns to the percussion *ostinato* with the *Nagasaki* theme, again demanding driving energy and precise, crisp articulation. A fugue on the same theme requires proper note spacing and evenness of rhythm to achieve vertical clarity. The movement closes with a chorale on the *Gloriosa* theme in a grandiose, brilliant style.

Unit 6: Musical Elements

MELODY:

Each of the three movements is based on varied forms of a Gregorian chant sung by the hidden Christians during their time of persecution. Melodic opportunities are spread throughout the ensemble, with the only prominent solo being that of the ryuteki (piccolo), which opens and closes the second movement.

HARMONY:

Gloriosa is predominated by modal and major tonalities. Each of the three chants used as a basis for the three movements is a dorian melody with a tonic/dominant relationship (D and A dorian). Harmonizations of the melodies appear in a number of forms, including chorale settings, canons, and countermelodies. Motives written for the high brass and woodwinds that augment the main melodies are frequently scored in fourths and fifths, giving the music an authentic Japanese sound.

RHYTHM:

The rhythmic demand in *Gloriosa* is fairly straightforward, utilizing standard rhythm patterns throughout the piece. The highest difficulty would be found in the timpani and toms parts, where the composer uses syncopated patterns abundantly. In the wind parts, several unison patterns of sixteenth notes after the beat ("e-and-a-two," etc.) require strict attention to the division of the beat into four equal parts.

TIMBRE:

Gloriosa presents a variety of tonal colors in its scoring. Single-line melodies in the low brass are harmonized by flowing lines in the woodwind choir. Mid-voice melodies are harmonized within the horn/saxophone choir and accompanied by contrapuntal lines in trombone and euphonium. High brass and low brass choirs answer in canon, accompanied by running scale passages in the upper woodwinds and by accented rhythmic figures in the rest of the ensemble. The opening of the second movement, scored for ryuteki (piccolo) accompanied by low clarinet and percussion, offers a tranquil, yet haunting sound in contrast to the energy of the first movement. The final movement utilizes single-line melodies in the low brass accompanied by interjections from the high woodwinds and brass, as well as alternating woodwind and brass choirs. The piece closes with a chorale scored for the full ensemble in the key of D major, creating a brilliant closing to the music.

Unit 7: Form and Structure

Section	Measure	Event and Scoring
Movement 1: "Oratorio" (thirteen variations in the form of a Chaconne)		
Introduction	1–10	Vibes, chimes with timpani pedal, D dorian
1	11–19	Trombone/euphonium/male voices with timpani pedal; D dorian
2	20–31	Low brass continue; trumpet/horn countermelodies; D dorian
3	32–46	Switch to woodwind colors; bassoon and low clarinet melody with high brass/woodwind interjections; D dorian
4	47–60	Harmonized horn/saxophone melody with contrapuntal line in tuba/trombone/low reeds; D dorian
5	61–74	Canon at the octave, one measure apart, by low brass/reeds and trumpet/horn; contrapuntal eighth note lines in high woodwinds; D dorian
6	75–88	Variation on the first interval of the theme; D dorian
7	89–102	Trombone/euphonium melody with rhythmic accompaniment; canonic entrances by horn/trumpet; D dorian
8	103–117	Upper woodwind variation of the theme; rhythmic accompaniment continues; D dorian
9	118–131	Woodwind chorale; F major shifting to D major
10	132–144	Full scoring of chorale; F major and D major
11	145–158	Rhythmic variation; D dorian

SECTION	MEASURE	EVENT AND SCORING
12	159–166	Brass canon at the tritone, one measure apart, with percussion *ostinato*; chromatic tonality
13	167–183	Sustained woodwinds with rhythmic brass, followed by sustained brass with rhythmic woodwinds; D dorian
Coda	184–190	Vibes/chimes, as in the introduction; D dorian

Movement 2: "Cantus"
(A–A?–B–A)

A	1–15	Ryuteki (piccolo), unaccompanied; A dorian
A?	16–34	Ryuteki continues, with percussion and clarinet accompaniment; A dorian
B	35–66	Horn melody with chordal accompaniment in saxophone/low brass; F minor
A	67–74	Ryuteki solo, with percussion and clarinet accompaniment; A dorian

Movement 3: "Dies Festus"
(A–B–A–C–Coda)

Introduction	1–2	Rhythmic motive; D dorian
A	3–41	Melody in trombone/euphonium with high brass and woodwind interjections; harmonized melody in woodwinds and horn; canon at a sixth, one beat apart between low brass and upper woodwinds; D dorian
Bridge	42–45	Bell tones on four-note motive from the theme
B	46–62	Woodwind chorale on first movement theme; C major shifting to F major
B (continued)	63–100	Brass chorale on first movement theme; F major shifting to D major

SECTION	MEASURE	EVENT AND SCORING
A	101–127	Melody in trombone/euphonium with high brass and woodwind interjections; harmonized melody in woodwinds and horn; canon at a sixth, one beat apart between low brass and upper woodwinds; D dorian
Bridge	128–131	Bell tones on four-note motive from the theme
C	132–165	Fugue on the first movement theme; D dorian
Coda	166–195	Chorale on the first movement theme; D dorian shifting to D major

Unit 8: Suggested Listening

Toshio Akiyama, *Japanese Songs for Band*
James Barnes, *Impressions of Japan*
Ray Cramer, *Fantasy on "Sakura, Sakura"*
Yasuhide Ito:
> *Festal Scenes*
> *Funa-Uta for Band*
> *Interlude to an Unfinished Opera*
> *"La Vita" Symphony in Three Scenes*
> *Melodies for Wind Instruments*
> *Variations from the Northern Sea*

Soichi Konagaya, *Japanese Tune*
Alfred Reed, *Fifth Symphony (Sakura)*
Bernard Rogers, *Three Japanese Dances*

Unit 9: Additional References and Resources

Brain Music Co. Ltd.: Hiroshima, Japan.

Bravo Music, Inc.: Hiroshima, Japan, and Deerfield Beach, FL.

Ito, Yasuhide. Gloriosa. Tokyo, Japan: Ongaku No Tomo Sha Corp., 1990.

Ito, Yasuhide. *Gloriosa*. University of North Texas Wind Symphony, Eugene Corporon, conductor. Compact disc KCD 11077, 1996.

Rehrig, William H. Supplement to *The Heritage Encyclopedia of Band Music*. Edited by Paul E. Bierley. Westerville, OH: Integrity Press, 1996.

TRN Music Publisher, Inc.: Ruidoso, NM.

Waterhouse, David. "Japan: 16th and 17th century Christian music." Sadie, Stanley, ed. *The New Grove Dictionary of Music and Musicians*. London: Macmillan Publishers Ltd., 2001.

Contributed by:

C. Kevin Bowen
Director of Bands
Wake Forest University
Winston-Salem, North Carolina

Teacher Resource Guide

Music for a Festival
Gordon Jacob
(1895–1984)

Unit 1: Composer

Gordon Percival Septimus Jacob, a native of London, was educated at Dulwich College and the Royal Conservatory of Music, where he studied under Stanford and Howells in the years immediately following World War I. In 1926, he joined the faculty of the conservatory and taught theory and composition. His pupils included Malcolm Arnold, Imogen Holst, Antony Hopkins, Colin Horsley, Elizabeth Maconchy, and Bernard Stevens. As a composer, his orchestral and choral works include a ballet, a concert overture, two symphonies, numerous concertos for wind and string instruments, many pedagogic works for piano and for chorus, and a variety of chamber works, songs, and film music.

In addition to composing, teaching, writing, and conducting, Jacob continued his interest in several societies, including the Incorporated Society of Musicians and the Worshipful Company of Musicians. His particular interest in instrumentation resulted in a textbook on scoring and transcription, *Orchestral Technique* (London, 1931). In 1948, he undertook the editorship of the Penguin scores, and he also contributed to various works of reference and textbooks.

Jacob wrote, "I dislike an 'academic' outlook, but by style is deeply rooted in the traditions in which I was trained and which, by inclination, I followed."[1] Everything he composed is marked by sterling craftsmanship and by clarity, economy, and directness. His main interest is in the musical

---

1 *The New Grove Dictionary of Music and Musicians.* Edited by Stanley Sadie.

material and it exploitation in the chosen medium rather than in the expression of a particular sentiment or the representation of non-musical ideas. He has been particularly drawn to wind instruments.

Unit 2: Composition

In a review of the Chicago Chamber Brass and the Dallas Wind Symphony for *Fanfare* magazine (May/June 1988), music critic Benjamin Pernick wrote,

> Gordon Jacob, the long-lived and prolific Briton, composed *Music for a Festival* for the 1951 Festival of Great Britain. Befitting its title, it is a grandiose, vibrant, sonorous work. Originally scored for Berliozan-proportioned forces of military band plus fanfare trumpets, it is played here in an uncredited arrangement with a septet of four trumpets, horn, trombone, and tuba replacing the trumpet ensemble. As Berlioz did in his *Requiem*, Jacob marshals his forces carefully, with loud, heaven-storming passages used sparingly. Only in the finale of the eleven-movement work do the septet and band play together; the odd number movements are given to the brass, while the full band plays in the even numbered sections. Jacob draws on renaissance and baroque forms (e.g., movements designated *intrada, round, madrigal*). Stylistically, much of the music is rooted in the British band tradition as filtered through Elgar, Vaughan Williams (especially *The Wasps* and *Folk Song Suite*), and Walton.

Unit 3: Historical Perspective

Jacob ranks as one of the foremost contributors to the expanding repertoire of original works for band through his compositions for military band—the English term for a wind group of complete instrumentation as opposed to the British brass band. Two notable works are *An Original Suite*, which is a worthy companion to the Holst suites and the Vaughan Williams suite for band, and a monumental work, *Music for a Festival*, commissioned by the Arts Council of Great Britain for the Festival of Britain in 1951. In addition, he set two of William Byrd's delightful keyboard pieces for wind band: *The Battell* may be classified an arrangement, but according to Frederick Fennell, "in no way can his scoring of the *William Byrd Suite* be considered an arrangement of Byrd's music."[2]

From 1928 when he composed *An Original Suite* to the final period of commissioned works, Jacob's band compositions have spanned a period of over fifty years. Latter pieces for band include *Concerto for Band, Flag of Stars, Giles Farnaby Suite, Symphony for Band "A. D. 78," Tribute to Canterbury, Fantasia for Euphonium and Band, Miscellanies for Alto Saxophone and Band, and Cameos for Bass Trombone and Band.*

---

2 Band Music Notes. Frederick Fennell and John Wakefield.

Unit 4: Technical Considerations

The writing for brass calls on several resources: brilliance, fullness and, at times, delicacy and choral style. Highest written notes for brass instruments are as follows: Trumpet I: C above staff; Trumpet II: G on top of staff; Trumpet III: G on top of staff; Horn I: A above staff; Trombone I: high C five spaces above staff; Euphonium: A above staff.

This work is not technically difficult (except for the "Scherzo"). A mature, well-developed ensemble sound is necessary to fulfill the musical textures that are predominant in all of Jacobs's wind compositions. The percussion writing is very moderate.

Unit 5: Stylistic Considerations

Due to the varied number of movements, many stylistic dimensions are asked of the performing ensemble. The challenge is to be able to change character as the movements unfold. The music demands full, sustained playing by *tutti* ensemble, and then can immediately change asking for rhythmic independence in highly polyphonic passages.

Unit 6: Musical Elements

Although written in a classical suite style, all melodic material in this piece is original. Jacob explores the standard forms of the renaissance, baroque, and classical periods: "Intrada," "Overture," "Round of Seven Parts," "Air," "Interlude," "March," "Saraband," "Scherzo," "Madrigal," "Minuet and Trio," and "Finale."

Unit 7: Form and Structure

SECTION	EVENT AND SCORING
	"Intrada" – B-flat; *Grave e maestoso* (quarter note = 56) / *Allegro* (quarter note = 112); 4/4; brass choir; opens with a sustained but well-marked chordal statement in a majestic style, followed by a rhythmic *marcato* section
2	"Overture" – B-flat; *Allegro vivace*; quarter note = 152; 3/4; full band; quite lively and energetic; consists of three themes, ending with a short coda; scoring is contrasting choirs
3	"Round of Seven Parts" – E-flat; *Allegro moderato*; quarter note = 126; 3/4; brass choir; written in the round technique (by four measures); ends with a soft two-chord transition, which segues into No. 4

SECTION	EVENT AND SCORING
4	"Air" – F; *Adagio*; eighth note = 58; 3/4 beat in 6; full band; very slow, smooth movement, supported by a basso *ostinato* featuring solo cornet and clarinet in the melodic line, then ending with full ensemble texture
5	"Interlude" – G minor; *Adagio*; quarter note = 54; 4/4; brass choir; this number is sixteen measures long and uses the opening motive of the "Intrada" as the main melodic material; material is stated at *p* dynamic level in a *legato* style; answered in chords by trumpet
6	"March" – C minor/A-flat/C minor; Vivace alla marcia; quarter note = 132; 2/4; full band; written in an ABC section form; Theme I of the A section is stated in cornet with an answering motive in clarinet; Theme II is a syncopated melody for full band; contrasting B section (Trio) has a flowing lyrical melodic theme; closing C section juxtaposes melodies from each of the previous sections
7	"Saraband" – G minor; *Lento alla Sarabanda*; half note = 44; 3/2; brass choir; very slow and lovely sustaining movement written primarily in half notes
8	"Scherzo" – E-flat; *Molto allegro e brillante*; quarter note = 144; 2/4; full band; written in ABA form, based on a three-note motive (E-flat, G, B-flat); A section is light and delicate with intricate interplay amongst voices; B section contrasts in tempo (slower) and style (*legato*) to the A section
9	"Madrigal" – A-flat; *Allegro*; half note = 84; 2/2; brass choir; written emulating the style of the sixteenth century English composers, a group Jacob in particular held in high regard; Jacob employs both homophonic and contrapuntal textures as well as terraced dynamics; this beautiful spirited movement contrasts dramatically to No. 10
10	"Minuet and Trio" – E-flat/A-flat/E-flat; *Tempo di Menuetto non troppo lento*; quarter note = 104; 3/4; full band; smooth flowing lightly scored "Minuet" is followed by the "Trio" marked with *staccato* and *marcato* passages

Section

11

Event and Scoring

"Finale" – B-flat; *Grave e Maestoso* (quarter note = 56; 4/4); *Fuga* (quarter note = 112; 4/4); *Grave e maestoso* (quarter note = 56; 4/4); brass choir and full band; begins with a fanfare from the brass, using the motive from No. 1; full band enters, followed by the brass, with both groups finally playing together; this is followed by a fugue section that uses stretto and augmentation techniques; piece closes with a return of the slow powerful Grave section (from No. 1)[3]

Unit 8: Suggested Listening
Gordon Jacob:

Music for a Festival – The Brass and the Band, Chicago Chamber Brass, Dallas Wind Symphony, Howard Dunn, conductor: Crystal CD (431)

Original Suite: Intermezzo – Tokyo Kosei Wind Orchestra, Frederick Fennell, conductor: KOCD 3576

William Byrd Suite – British and American Band Classics, Eastman Wind Ensemble, Frederick Fennell, conductor: Mercury CD (432 009-2)

Unit 9: Additional References and Resources

Dvorak, Thomas L., Gary M. Ciepluch, and Robert Grechesky. *Best Music for High School Band*. Brooklyn, NY: Manhattan Beach Music, 1993.

Jacob, Gordon. *The Composer and His Art*. Westport, CT: Greenwood Press, 1986.

Kreines, Joseph. *Music for Concert Band*. Tampa, FL: Florida Music Service, 1989.

Rehrig, William H. *The Heritage Encyclopedia of Band Music*. Edited by Paul E. Bierley. Westerville, OH: Integrity Press, 1991.

Thompson, Kevin. "Gordon Jacob—I Aim at Greater Simplicity Nowadays." *The Instrumentalist*, XXXVIII, September 1983, pp. 38–9.

Thompson, Kevin. "Gordon Jacob in Conversation." *Journal of the British Association of Symphonic Bands and Wind Ensembles*, Volume 1. Spring 1982, pp. 3–4.

Wetherell, Eric. *Gordon Jacob, A Centenary Biography*. London: Thames Publishing, 1995.

---

3 (Compiled from *Music for Concert Band* by Joseph Kreines and *Best Music for High School Band* by Thomas L. Dvorak, Robert Grechesky, and Gary M. Ciepluch).

Whiston, J. Alan. "Gordon Jacob: A Biographical Sketch and Analysis of Four Selected Works for Band." Ph.D. dissertation, University of Oklahoma, 1987.

Website:
www.gordonjacob.co.uk

Contributed by:
Kevin L. Sedatole
Associate Director of Bands
University of Texas
Austin, Texas

Teacher Resource Guide

Pastime

Jack Stamp
(b. 1954)

Unit 1: Composer

Jack Stamp was born in Washington, DC, in 1954, and grew up in the nearby Maryland suburbs. He received a his B.S. degree in Music Education from Indiana University of Pennsylvania in 1976, his M.M. degree in Percussion Performance from East Carolina University in 1978, and his D.M.A. degree in Wind Conducting from Michigan State University in 1988, where he studied with Eugene Corporon. His primary composition teachers were Robert Washburn and Fisher Tull. More recently he has worked with Joan Tower, David Diamond and Richard Danielpour.

Stamp is currently Professor of Music and Director of Band Studies at Indiana University of Pennsylvania, where he conducts the wind ensemble and symphony band, and teaches courses in graduate and undergraduate conducting. He is a member of the American Bandmasters Association and founder and musical director of the Keystone Wind Ensemble, a professional recording group dedicated to the advancement of American concert band music.

Unit 2: Composition

Pastime, subtitled "A Salute to Baseball," is based upon the well-known tune, *Take Me Out to the Ballgame*. The work is dedicated to avid baseball fan and band conductor legend, Frank Battisti. The work is loosely woven around two musical phrases of the classic song: "Take me out to the ballgame," and "Buy me some peanuts and Crackerjacks." The work, written for the Santa Clara County Band Directors Association (near San Francisco), pays homage to the

1962 San Francisco Giants. Written during the fabulous 1998 baseball season, this work also pays homage to that great homerun race.

Unit 3: Historical Perspective

The work was premiered on January 24, 1999, with the composer conducting. Works based on familiar tunes are not uncommon to composers or, in particular, band music. One only needs to be reminded of Robert Jager's *Variations on a Theme of Robert Schumann*, or the use of *London Bridge* by Charles Ives and Alfred Reed. However, this may be one of the first concert works, particularly for band, based upon a "song" about a sport.

Unit 4: Technical Considerations

The work is highly contrapuntal. In particular, the tuba and low reed parts are demanding. The work is highly modal, so there is no key signature and the extend harmonies create a lot of accidentals in the music. The work is rhythmically challenging as well, with many meter changes and syncopated rhythms. In particular, the section from measures 102 through 108 for trumpet and 1st trombone is challenging in the areas of rhythm and independence. Ranges are not extreme, though the 1st trumpet part is taken to high C a few times.

Unit 5: Stylistic Considerations

Due to its highly contrapuntal nature, the work demands linear musical thinking and must be played with a forward motion. There is demand on individuals for clarity in articulation so all the lines in the fugal sections can be heard. There are major contrasts from the fugal sections to soft, homophonic sections. The notation "tongued, but connected" appears several times in the work.

Unit 6: Musical Elements

The entire work is motivically conceived, so emphasis on projecting the two motives used is imperative. The work also highlights the 1962 Giants and the 1998 baseball season. Players are saluted as their jersey numbers correspond to measure numbers. In measures 60 through 72, the 1998 homerun race is saluted. Detailed explanations appear in the score's program notes.

Unit 7: Form & Structure

The work is based upon two phrases from the well-known baseball tune *Take Me Out to the Ballgame*: "Take me out to the ballgame" and "Buy me some peanuts and Crackerjacks." The first phrase appears in fragment form eighteen times, and the second appears seventeen. In addition, there are two fugues based upon the phrases: Phrase 1 fugue (measures 73 through 92) and Phrase 2 fugue (measures 126 through 136). Interspersed between these sections are the salutes to the 1962 Giants and the 1998 baseball season (detailed in the program notes).

Unit 8: Suggested Listening
Usually band works are suggested in this unit of the resource guide.
However, I am suggesting that the following "baseball tunes" be listened to:
 Soundtrack: *Baseball*, a film by Ken Burns – Nonesuch Records
 Baseball's Greatest Hits – Rhino Records

Unit 9: Additional References and Resources
Rehrig, William H. *The Heritage Encyclopedia of Band Music*. Edited by Paul
 E. Bierley. Westerville, OH: Integrity Press, 1991.

Contributed by:
Jack Stamp
Director of Band Studies
Indiana University of Pennsylvania
Indiana, Pennsylvania

Teacher Resource Guide

Santa Fe Saga
Morton Gould
(1913–1996)

Unit 1: Composer

Morton Gould was one of the most prolific American composers of the twentieth century. His enormous contribution to American music includes works for band, symphony orchestra, ballet, chamber music, solo works, chorus, and soloists, as well as music for Broadway, television, and films. Early in his career, Gould recognized the importance of the wind band as a serious performance medium. He often used what is today referred to as "roots music" with distinctly American flavors, such as folk tunes, traditional spirituals and gospel, country and western, jazz, and blues. He received commissions from major American symphony orchestras as well as the New York City Ballet, Library of Congress, Chamber Music Society of Lincoln Center, and the American Ballet Theatre. His music has been performed by all of the major symphony orchestras in the United States under the leadership of Arturo Toscanini, Sir Georg Solti, Eugene Ormandy, Fritz Reiner, and Leopold Stokowski.

As a conductor, Gould has worked with orchestras and bands worldwide while making over one hundred recordings. His recording of Charles Ives's *First Symphony* with the Chicago Symphony Orchestra won a Grammy Award in 1966 and was a catalyst for the renewed interest in Ives's music. In 1994, Gould was selected to receive the Kennedy Center Honor, and he also received the Pulitzer Prize in Music the following year. Other awards included election to the American Academy of Arts and Letters and twelve Grammy Award nominations. For thirty-six years, Gould was a member of ASCAP's Board of Directors, including eight years as the organization's president.

Unit 2: Composition

Commissioned for the American Bandmasters Association by Edwin Franko Goldman in 1955, *Santa Fe Saga* was premiered at the Association's annual convention held that year in Santa Fe. Programmatic in nature, it is through-composed and consist of four distinct sections: "Rio Grande," "Round Up," "Wagon Train" and "Fiesta." It is written to evoke the history and images of indigenous culture in and around Santa Fe, New Mexico. The score uses standard concert band instrumentation and includes English horn, separate cornet and trumpet parts, four trombone, and added percussion instruments to produce the "Western sounds. The score is notated in concert pitch, but the parts are transposed. Parts are available for D-flat piccolo, E-flat horn, and baritone treble clef. The piece is approximately nine minutes in duration.

Unit 3: Historical Perspective

Santa Fe, New Mexico, has a rich history that includes cultural influences of Native American and Mexican peoples. In addition, many of the cowboy traditions of the Old West are still respected today. The American Bandmasters Association's decision to hold their convention in this city prompted Gould to compose this tribute to the rich cultural heritage of the region. Composed using all original material, Gould was able to evoke the image of the southwestern United States with realism and excitement. His use of tonal material suggestive of American themes is one reason that his work is often referred to as "American music."

Unit 4: Technical Considerations

This piece is technically demanding for all instruments. In addition to the level of difficulty for each player, the constantly changing meter and rhythmic variety present additional challenges. Key and meter changes occur frequently. Solo lines occur in many instruments and are not limited to first parts. Maintaining a light, crisp quality in the energetic rhythmic passages requires that attention be paid to the air pulse element of articulation. Precision is essential to the rhythmic clarity of the piece, and proper balance must be sought especially when the scoring is dense. Because the melodic material moves so quickly from instrument to instrument, decisions must be made regarding the relative importance of a particular phrase and which portions of each phrase must be emphasized.

Unit 5: Stylistic Considerations

Santa Fe Saga presents different stylistic challenges in each of its four sections. A wide variety of articulations are required throughout. Contrast is a key element in the work as a whole. In "Rio Grande," warmth of sound and lightness of articulation are required to provide the grace and delicacy requested by the composer. The accents present later in this section must be tempered to ensure that the light quality is maintained. Very aggressive air pulses assist in creating the energy necessary for "Round Up." Dynamics should be tempered, allowing the rhythmic energy to create the *forte* as indicated at letter L. Only at letter M should a true *forte* be achieved. The indication for "bells up" in the horn will create a more brilliant sound. The opening of "Wagon Train" requires large musical gestures. Exaggeration will make each of these gestures most effective. "Fiesta" is similar to "Round Up" in the sense that rhythmic energy and precision are fundamental concerns. Attention must be paid to the emphasis placed on accented notes. The agogic stress inherent in many of these lines must be correctly interpreted.

Unit 6: Musical Elements

MELODY:

One of the most challenging aspects of this work is the independence of musical line throughout the piece. All instruments are challenged on a technical and melodic level, as evidenced by the bassoon and bass clarinet lines from measures 70 through 76. Shifting accents and slur groupings contribute to the characteristic sound of the indigenous music of the Southwest. The eighth note groupings at measure 309 imply a 6/8 rhythmic feel alternating with the traditional groupings of the indicated 3/4 time signature.

HARMONY:

Gould uses frequent changes of tonal center throughout the work, the result of which is a feeling of constant motion. Arrival points often feature stable tonal centers and driving rhythmic emphasis of the harmonic area. The use of stacked fourths and major seconds, such as in measures 259 through 262, emphasize the transitional nature of the introduction of "Fiesta." This avoidance of triadic harmony reinforces the stability of the following material. Gould's use of techniques such as these greatly enhances the effect of the constant harmonic flow.

RHYTHM:

Perhaps the most interesting use of rhythm in the piece is the way Gould presents the movement of time in "Wagon Train." The stretching of sustained notes followed by brief splashes of rhythmic action and silence create a lurching effect in the music. Once a more regular flow of time is underway, the choice of 5/4 continues the uneven feeling of motion. Constantly changing accents and driving rhythmic activity are present in each section. Hemiola figures are created by such rhythmic displacement. For example, the figures in measures 41 through 42 for the upper clarinets are embellishments of a line, which suggests characteristics of the Mexican mariachi style. Another example of this style may be found in the "Fiesta" section, where Gould alternates note groupings: eighth notes in groups of three followed by groups of two. Displaced accents also create hemiola figures in measures 367 through 374, yet not always in the same part of the measure.

TIMBRE:

A wide variety of scoring techniques are used. The opening flute solo floating above very soft reeds creates a transparent texture, which gradually thickens. Special effects are created by a combination of orchestration and rhythm. For example, the bird-like fluttering in several woodwinds contrasts with the long cornet line in measures 23 through 27. Also very effective is Gould's use of the whip crack in the "Wagon Train" section of the piece. Stopped horn and extensive use of brass mutes in this work demonstrate the colorful tonal palate of this composer.

Unit 7: Form and Structure

MEASURE	EVENT AND SCORING
"Rio Grande"	
1–13	Flute solo opens the piece; cluster chord builds as accompaniment; joined by muted cornet; tom-toms provide pitched percussion tones
14–21	Letter B; brief melodic fragments from single clarinet, horn, and baritone in *soli*
22–27	Letter C; pair of cornets in solotone mutes continue "distant" texture with brief pointillistic fragments interspersed by bass clarinet, B-flat clarinet, and flute solos
28–35	Letter D; lyrical style with *legato* rhythms as underscoring
36–68	Flowing 3/8; transparent texture; muted brass
69–76	Letter H; clarinet and alto saxophone melody contains syncopations based upon the slur markings and the accents
77–85	Letter I; asymmetrical 5/8 combines with syncopations within the second half of each measure
"Round Up"	
86–95	Letter J; suddenly fast and rhythmically aggressive; muted brass and low woodwinds begin; texture thickens
96–108	Letter K; no transition; "Brash and rowdy" indicated in the score; cornet and trumpet with melody joined by trombone and baritone

MEASURE	EVENT AND SCORING
109–133	Letter L; *tutti* with rhythmic intensity; call and response in the scoring from measure to measure
134–135	Letter N; transition; rhythmic modulation from 3/4 measures into 3/8, upper woodwinds only
136–141	3/8 introduction to new material
142–156	Letter O; clarinet, and later all woodwinds, state melodic material
157–164	Letter P; bell-tone effects beginning with low instruments and moving to higher voices
165–172	Letter Q; 3/8 continues, with the rhythmic activity building
173–190	Letter R; instrumental combinations and textures are varied; scoring becomes thicker
191–211	Letter S; repetitive rhythmic patterns predominate often with alternating dynamics

"Wagon Train"

212–220	Letter U; large musical gestures are used to create a feeling of lurching forward: mixed meter and silence interrupted by whip cracks
221–229	Letter V; flowing 5/4 in woodwinds interrupted by "rips" in brass
230–250	Letter W; combinations of alternating 3/4 and 2/4 measures melding into 5/4 continue the feeling of unevenness

"Fiesta"

251–258	Cornet solo requiring rapidly articulated sixteenth notes; repeated jagged rhythmic figures in upper woodwinds begin
259–262	Jagged figures intensify, joined by swift cornet line
263–308	Letter Aa; alternating aggressive rhythmic figures and flowing lyric lines above a steady rhythm in tuba and horn
309–317	Letter Ff; alternating measures of syncopation and straight time, all of which is in 3/4
318–321	Letter Gg; syncopated rhythmic feel continues

Measure	Event and Scoring
322–338	Letter Hh; syncopation occurs both in fundamental rhythms and melodic voices
339–356	Letter Ll; suddenly soft; triplets predominate; building in intensity and thickness of scoring
357–366	Letter Nn; arrival point; triplets continue softer and more soloistic
368–374	Letter Oo; rhythmically aggressive, rapidly alternating loud and soft, two against three syncopations creating the feeling of hemiola
375–386	Letter Pp; three large gestures using trumpet, horn, and baritone to state a dramatic melodic statement slowly ("held back") followed by intense rhythmic activity in woodwinds (*A tempo*)
387–399	Letter Qq; tempo returns with dramatic *tenuto* melodic figures in the brass juxtaposed against repetitive rhythmic figures in the woodwinds
400–409	Letter Ss; 5/4 time with rips returns briefly followed by intense rhythmic activity to the end of the piece

Unit 8: Suggested Listening

Morton Gould:
>   *Centennial Symphony* ("Fiesta" movement)
>   *Cowboy Rhapsody*

Aaron Copland:
>   *Appalachian Spring*
>   *Rodeo*

Leonard Bernstein, "America" from *West Side Story*

Unit 9: Additional References and Resources

Battisti, Frank. *The Twentieth Century American Wind Band/Ensemble: History, Development and Literature*. Fort Lauderdale, FL: Meredith Music Publications, 1995.

Band Music Guide. Evanston, IL: The Instrumentalist Company, 1983.

Dvorak, Thomas L., Robert Grechesky, and Gary M. Ciepluch. *Best Music for High School Band*. Edited by Bob Margolis. Brooklyn, NY: Manhattan Beach Music, 1993.

Nettle, Bruno. *Folk Music in the United States: An Introduction*. Third edition. Detroit, MI: Wayne State University Press, 1976.

Rehrig, William H. *The Heritage Encyclopedia of Band Music*. Edited by Paul E. Bierley. Westerville, OH: Integrity Press, 1991.

Sadie, Stanley, ed. *The New Grove Dictionary of Music and Musicians*. London: Macmillan Publishers Limited, 1980.

Slonimsky, Nicolas. *Baker's Biographical Dictionary of Musicians*. Eighth edition. New York: Schirmer Books, 1992.

Websites:
http://www.schirmer.com/composers/gould_bio.html
http://www.ascap.com/press/gould-22196.html

Contributed by:
Sean Flanigan
Assistant Director of Bands
Drake University
Des Moines, Iowa

Teacher Resource Guide

Southern Harmony
Donald Grantham
(b. 1947)

Unit 1: Composer

Donald Grantham earned his Bachelor of Music degree from the University of Oklahoma and his D.M.A in Composition from the University of Southern California. His composition teachers have included Halsey Stevens, Robert Linn, and Nadia Boulanger.

Grantham is the recipient of numerous awards and prizes in composition, including the Prix Lili Boulanger, the Nissim/ASCAP Orchestral Composition Prize, First Prize in the Concordia Chamber Symphony's Awards to American Composers, a Guggenheim Fellowship, three grants from the National Endowment for the Arts, three First Prizes in the NBA/William Revelli Competition, two First Prizes in the ABA/Ostwald Competition, and First Prize in the National Opera Association's Biennial Composition Competition. His music has been praised for its "elegance, sensitivity, lucidity of thought, clarity of expression, and fine lyricism" in a citation awarded by the American Academy and Institute of Arts and Letters. In recent years, his works have been performed by the orchestras of Cleveland, Dallas, and Atlanta, and the American Composers Orchestra, among many others. He has fulfilled commissions in media from solo instruments to opera. His music is published by Piquant Press, Peer-Southern, E. C. Schirmer, and Mark Foster. A number of his works have been commercially recorded.

Grantham currently resides in Austin, Texas, and is Professor of Composition at the University of Texas at Austin. With Kent Kennan, he is co-author of *The Technique of Orchestration* (Prentice-Hall).

Unit 2: Composition

Grantham's 1998 suite, *Southern Harmony*, is based on tunes collected by William Walker and published in an 1835 anthology of the same title. The work was commissioned by the Southeastern Conference of Band Directors. Others have drawn inspiration from the same source, but Grantham's signature harmonic vocabulary is present, especially in the fourth and final movement.

The four movements, titled "The Midnight Cry," "Wondrous Love," "Exhilaration," and The Soldier's Return" (also includes "Thorny Desert"), are based on actual pieces found in the musical companion published in 1854. The original tunes are singable, memorable, and mostly three-part with the melody in the tenor. The pentatonic scale is commonly employed. Grantham's contemporary settings do preserve the energy and integrity of the originals, but they present the tunes in a way that exploits the qualities of the wind ensemble. The use of complex harmony, suspensions, bitonal tensions, and extensive percussion are characteristic.

Southern Harmony is approximately ten minutes and thirty seconds in length. It is published by Grantham's publishing company, Piquant Press. At the time of this writing, the work is available for rental only.

Unit 3: Historical Perspective

The use of hymn songs, sacred tunes, or anthems is prevalent in the wind band repertoire. The setting of tunes from *The Southern Harmony* is of interest due to the publication's unique place in the history of music in America. While there are several books of this nature, including the more popular Davisson's *Kentucky Harmony* of 1816 (on which Grantham also based a work) and Jeremiah Ingall's *Christian Harmony* of 1805, none has achieved the place of *The Southern Harmony*. Each year in Benton, Kentucky, the Big Singing, a large festival preserving the performance practices of the mid-nineteenth century, takes place. *The Southern Harmony* is the sole document used for this gathering.

Known as "fasola notation," the shaped-note style of writing includes the use of four note shapes to represent the then-popular four syllables used in the scale. The right triangle represents *fa*, the circle *sol*, the square *la*, and the diamond *mi*. Many great tunes have come from this shaped-note tradition, including *Amazing Grace, Foundation, Pisgah, Beach Spring, Land of Rest,* and *Wondrous Love*.

The Southern Harmony was published by William Walker, but many accounts suggest that he compiled the book with his brother-in-law Benjamin Franklin White. In addition to the work of these men, the great religious fervor of the time must also be credited with the development of tune books in general. The camp meetings that were so common along the

Kentucky/Tennessee border often brought together thousands of people and created a tremendous need for such a publication.

The importance of Grantham's work is that it preserves this truly American music in a way that makes it accessible to students, conductors, scholars, and audiences. Some 140 years after the originals were published, Grantham wrote a work that captures the excitement and heartfelt manner in which these tunes would have been sung by fervent worshipers.

Unit 4: Technical Considerations

Southern Harmony's four movements each present unique challenges for performers and conductors. Grantham's unique style of composition creates interesting melodic, harmonic, and rhythmic activity that must be considered.

MOVEMENT I: "THE MIDNIGHT CRY"

Movement I is written in 2/2 in the key of A-flat. Blocked statements by the brass answered by woodwinds require that attention be paid to uniformity of articulation. Rapid woodwind flourishes demand clarity in articulation and finger dexterity. The movement is entirely diatonic.

The tune is set in three verses: call and response, a chamber music or "soloistic" presentation, and finally a full setting. Oboe, English horn, and bassoon are scored alone in the second verse accompanied by vibraphone and orchestra bells. Pyramid entrances in the brass and full chordal sonorities must be balanced carefully to ensure clarity in the very active and rapid woodwind lines. Trumpets are required (for only one measure) to execute difficult trills in three parts based on the tonic triad.

Consistency of interpretation and articulation should be the focus of attention in the first movement to guarantee uniformity within each section, within woodwind and brass choirs, and within the ensemble as a whole.

MOVEMENT II: "WONDROUS LOVE"

Written in 2/2 (6/4), with the half note marked at 42 beats per minute, this movement presents some unique challenges in regard to performance of subdivisions. The composer strikes a well-crafted balance between new material derived from the theme and the chorale-like original melody. Grantham himself draws a comparison to many Bach Chorale Preludes that include independent or new material, along with the thematic material on which the piece is based. In general, the new material or accompanimental music reflects the 6/4 (or two groups of three) subdivision, while statements of the chorale *Wondrous Love* are presented in 2/2. Exposed, soloistic writing is common in this movement and present in all three B-flat clarinet parts.

Balance should be a concern throughout the movement to ensure that the more active new material does not overshadow the sustained statements of the tune in low brass and low reeds. Balance is particularly important during the fugue-like section beginning in measure 57. This movement requires control at the extremes of the dynamic range.

MOVEMENT III: "EXHILARATION"

Movement III is notated in the key of G, is primarily pentatonic, and reflects a ternary structure that, according to the composer, "picks up on the country-fiddle nature of the original." Traditional scoring for woodwinds and horn is utilized. The remainder of the brass section, double bass, and timpani are scored as "hand clappers," for which the composer has provided a part. The hand clapper parts are, at times, divided between stage left and stage right. The rhythmic content of the hand clapping part is not extensive but will require rehearsal to achieve clarity in the ensemble. The tempo marking is "very crisp," with the half note suggested at 84 beats per minute.

Grantham's careful and thorough marking of the score requires that much attention be paid to articulation. Extensive marking and note groupings that create hemiola are prevalent. The woodwinds are required to play in rhythmic unison for a major part of the movement's sixty-three measures. The four horn parts are written in unison throughout. Range of the horn line is very reasonable. The woodwind parts are very active and at times require the performance of rapid articulated patterns in the upper register. The last four measures in particular include a challenging passage for flute and especially piccolo.

MOVEMENT IV: "THE SOLDIER'S RETURN"

The longest and most challenging movement in terms of technical demand and overall complexity is the fourth movement. The opening ten measures are written in 2/2 and marked *tranquillo, rubato* (half note = 60). Woodwinds, percussion instruments, and two trumpet parts accompany a trumpet solo marked *molto legato*. The dynamic markings throughout this section are *pp* and *ppp*. Execution of quarter note triplets in 2/2 should be the focus. The opening statement of the theme is immediately followed by a section that is marked *vivace* (dotted-quarter note = 138) and written in 6/8. The march theme presented in this section is the basis for the modified rondo form. The third element in the final movement is the use of a new theme, "Thorny Desert," which is set in 9/8.

Of particular technical concern in this movement is the harmony. The notated key is concert A-flat. At times, the tonality is solidly diatonic. However, the use of chromaticism and dissonance creates a sense of transient harmony throughout.

Due to the technical demand created by the constantly changing tonal center, in combination with a significant amount of notated accidentals, the woodwind parts are especially challenging. In addition, at measure 255 the tempo marking changes to *Presto* (quarter note = 160).

Throughout the movement, the woodwind parts surpass those of the brass in terms of difficulty, but both include passages of angular, rapid patterns. Trills, accidentals, note groupings, difficult fingerings, and tempo demands will require mature players to achieve a quality performance. The brass writing is exciting, with many demands in regard to accents, articulation, and full sonorous sections that must be balanced within the brass choir and against the woodwind writing. Mutes are required for trumpet and trombone. Hand stopping is included in the horn parts. The timpani part is demanding both in regard to technique and tuning.

The complex harmonic writing in the last movement will require careful attention on the part of the conductor as well as the players in regard to the development and presentation of the various lines and gestures. Maneuvering the asymmetrical scalar patterns will require discipline and a great deal of individual effort to achieve an ensemble performance that is marked by clarity and integrity. Movement IV demands intellectual, mechanical, and musical effort on the part of every performer to a greater degree than any of the other movements. It is extremely well crafted and quite complex.

Unit 5: Stylistic Considerations

Each of the four movements of *Southern Harmony* contains distinctive stylistic elements. Grantham's ability to capture the fervor and excitement as well as the reflective and almost prayerful nature of the music must be the focus of performance. The wind ensemble and its individual performers must rely upon physical means to achieve musical ends. Through tone quality, phrasing, articulation, and dynamics, the emotional elements of the music can be sustained.

MOVEMENT I:

The text speaks of salvation, the coming of the end of the world as we know it and the preparation to go on to heaven. It is a noble text full of conviction and steadfast belief. This would have been performed with the same confidence and intensity depicted in the text. Grantham writes the opening of this movement with three accent markings on each note in the brass choir. To portray the appropriate style, attention should be given to the weighted style of the articulation. Uniformity of articulation is of the utmost importance throughout. The woodwind flourishes, as well as the many trills, should be played with a great deal of intensity and must not carry through to the rest. The release of each of these gestures must be accurate to align with and enhance the *sforzando* markings in the brass. In the setting of the tune in the brass, the notes should not be played too *staccato*. Each must be full-bodied and resonant to properly reflect the style and intent of the original.

MOVEMENT II:

Marked *Lento, cantabile ed espressivo*, this movement provides an opportunity for lyrical, connected playing by soloists and the ensemble. Performers should strive to achieve the most beautiful tone possible during the long, sustained phrases. The text for the original tune states:

> What wondrous love is this, Oh my soul!
> Oh my soul! What wondrous love is this?
> That caused the Lord of bliss, to bear the dreadful
> curse for my soul, for my soul, for my soul,
> To bear the dreadful curse for my soul.

Wondrous Love, the inspiration for this movement and the chorale tune on which it is based, is a lamentation. It is introspective and contemplative. The melody must be played *molto cantabile* to appropriately reflect the prayerful if not mournful nature of the original. This is important in both the new material created by the composer and the settings of the original tune in the low brass and low reeds. Throughout the movement, dynamic shading and shaping should be employed to create direction in the moving lines. Balance should be the focus when the scoring becomes full at measure 48 so sonority is chosen over volume. Control will be needed at all dynamic levels to achieve an excellent performance of this movement. Movement II provides contrast with the movements that surround it. If prepared with this idea in mind, the appropriate style should be achieved.

MOVEMENT III:

Exhilaration was written to depict the excitement and zeal of a religious camp meeting. One might imagine worshipers gathered together singing and clapping hands with great joy. This movement, employing woodwinds and horn accompanied by hand clappers, makes an attempt to recreate the sound of one of those events.

Through the fast tempo, active passages, and articulate character of the tune, a great deal of excitement is generated. Clarity of articulation will be the single most important factor in the preparation of this movement. Woodwind parts are often in the upper register and will require a substantial degree of facility in all parts. The composer was diligent in the marking of accents to create rhythmic or agogic stress on the appropriate beats. Exaggeration of these markings should be encouraged. Written in a "hoedown" or "fiddle" style, Movement III relies on rhythm to create its character. The hand clapping must be very accurate, and performers should be reminded to enter aggressively after rests to ensure proper timing.

The horns perform the more *legato* portion of the melody. The melody is written *ff* in a unison *soli* style. The approach here should be, in the words of Grainger, "to the fore" to achieve excitement, energy, and direction. Solo for piccolo at measure 37 and *soli* for flute and piccolo at measure 60 will require consideration. The melody is scored for low reeds at measure 49, and ensemble balance must be addressed to provide for the register in which they are written.

MOVEMENT IV:

In terms of style, the final movement is the most contemporary in nature. The original hymn is the most "modern" sounding of those selected. Grantham's own harmonic vocabulary is more present in this movement than the others and creates a unique style that presents traditional melodies in a distinctive manner. *The Soldier's Return* is paired with *Thorny Desert*. In addition, a march-like melody in 6/8 is the basis for the majority of the movement.

Performance of *legato* passages present the usual challenges associated with that style and should be prepared consistent with the character of the second movement. After the opening fifteen measures, the meter changes to 6/8 and the melodic lines are characterized by dissonance, leaps, and trills. Performance of the woodwind parts especially will be technically and visually challenging. The written key is A-flat, but the use of accidentals is prevalent. Brass parts require confidence in counting of rests and syncopated entrances that are often meant to mirror fragments of an existing melody. Brass parts also include the use of mutes, dynamic effect, and fluttertonguing. Trumpet parts ascend to written D-flat above the staff, and the horn parts contain written B-flat above the staff. Percussion parts in the fourth movement require the most attention. The piano part should not be considered difficult but is very effective and important to the overall color of the work.

Rapid articulation in all sections is required. Brass parts require a great deal of independence and are at times very angular. Due to range and use of chromaticism, the woodwind parts should be considered very challenging.

Unit 6: Musical Elements

Southern Harmony, like all great works for winds, contains teaching opportunities and challenges in regard to each of the four major musical elements. The work is unique due to the inherent qualities of the original tunes and because of the composer's characteristic style.

MELODY:

Teaching Concept – using existing melodies for a new composition
  Strategies:
  - Cover historical aspect of tune(s) and culture.
  - Explain the art of transcription.
  - Discuss transposition to instrumental setting.
  - Demonstrate orchestration techniques used by the composer as part of the rehearsal

Concept – pentatonic melodies
  Strategies:
  • Discuss difference between diatonic, pentatonic, and chromatic scales.
  • Teach pentatonic scale in several keys.
  • Discuss origin of shaped-note system and "fasola" notation.

Concept – form in music
  Strategies:
  • Analyze form of original melodies in Southern Harmony.
  • Discuss the varied forms used by the composer (song, ternary, rondo, modified rondo)
  • Prepare diagrams that visually represent form.

Concept – augmented/diminished intervals (Movement IV)
  Strategies:
  • Rehearse march theme from Movement 4.
  • Create unison scale patterns that focus on certain problem intervals.
  • Write out the difficult melody for the entire group to play (in rehearsal) to instill an understanding of the intervals and/or writing style.

HARMONY:

Teaching concept – counterpoint
  Strategies:
  • Highlight "chorale prelude" style of Movement II.
  • Illustrate independence of opening counterpoint material in Movement II and its eventual harmonic role within the context of the work.
  • Discuss writing in double reeds from measures 29 through 32.
  • Consider the point-counterpoint relationship between woodwinds, hand clappers, and horns in Movement III.
  • Review the complex counterpoint in the Movement IV at measure 99 during the presentation of *Thorny Desert*.

Teaching concept – canon
  Strategies:
  • Discuss the most basis technical aspects of canon and apply it to warm-up patterns or scales with the ensemble; use measures 54 through 63 in Movement II to illustrate canon. Canonic entrances are used again beginning in measure 13 of Movement III but in a much different style.

Teaching concept – bitonality
  Strategies:
  • Demonstrate bitonality by using two different keys simultaneously during warm-up.

- Consider the accompanimental parts during Movement IV.
- Analyze stacking of chords throughout Movement IV that imply extended chords and/or two tonal centers being used at once.
- Discuss juxtaposition of different thematic material used as a vehicle for this technique.

Teaching concept – consonance versus dissonance
  Strategies:
- Utilize warm-up material or other works that contain suspensions, retardations, appoggiatura, and other non-harmonic tones to create dissonance. Draw a comparison between the original settings from The *Southern Harmony* and Grantham's arrangement.
- Draw a comparison between the sound of the first three movements and Movement IV.
- Encourage confidence when dissonance is present in a particular part to enhance this compositional technique.

RHYTHM:
Teaching concept– agogic/rhythmic stress through meter
  Strategies:
- Discuss the interpretation of the 2/2 meter as opposed to a "common time feeling" in Movement I.
- Address the combination meter in Movement II and the "forced" relationship between the triple subdivision in 6/4 and the duple subdivision in 2/2.
- Consider the "back-beat" feel of Movement III and the necessary strength of the offbeats in this style.
- Illuminate the relationship between the duple 6/8 and triple 9/8 in the final movement and how the composer varies the style along with the meter.

Teaching concept – subdivision in varied time signatures
  Strategies:
- Discuss the use of thirty-second notes in Movement I and their brilliance in the "slower feeling" 2/2 meter.
- Consider how the interpretation of the piece might be changed if Movement I were written in 2/4 (one subdivision lower).
- Highlight the concept of "two against three" as it exists in Movement II.
- Rehearse the 6/4 parts and 2/2 parts independently to achieve accuracy in the rhythm.
- Utilize 6/4 versus 2/2 patterns during warm-up exercises with scales, etc.

- Consider the use of quarter note triplets in the final movement (measures 1 and 2) and the notation of the same motive as eighth notes in 6/8 later in the work (measures 29 through 31).

TIMBRE:

Teaching concept – orchestration

Strategies:

- Discuss challenges present during transcription of vocal music to winds.
- During rehearsal, highlight the variety of instrumentation choices in the work.
- Encourage and develop listening skills to improve intonation despite the orchestration selected.
- Develop awareness among players in regard to unique pairing of instruments in the work.
- Consider the utilization of the brass, woodwind, and percussion ensembles within the band and their own inherent characteristics.

Teaching concept – *tessitura*

Strategies:

- Consider the characteristic sounds of certain instruments in the various ranges.
- Discuss the impact of high and/or low tessitura on intonation.
- Include the appropriate registers in the group warm-ups and ensemble exercises.
- Prepare for the challenges of extreme tessitura as it relates to endurance.

Teaching concept – tone color as it relates to key

Strategies:

- Consider the use of key signatures in the work to create color.
- Discuss and demonstrate through exercises how the quality of the band sound is affected by key.
- Create exercises within the keys selected by the composer.

Unit 7: Form and Structure

SECTION	MEASURE	EVENT AND SCORING
Movement I:		
Theme	1–12	Antecedent-consequent scoring between brass and full band
Transition	13–24	New material derived from the tune
Theme	25–40	Woodwinds, with focus on double reeds

SECTION	MEASURE	EVENT AND SCORING
Transition	41–49	New material based on three-note motive; gradual re-introduction of brass playing accompanimental figures based on the thematic material in augmentation
Theme	50–65	Brass written in blocked chorale style with woodwind flourishes in accompaniment
Ending	66–69	Four-measure ending based on three-note motive
Movement II: Introduction	1–14	Freely composed new material in E-flat
Theme	15–35	Euphonium, tuba, and double bass present reharmonized statement of the theme in 2/2 while free polyphonic material continues in the woodwinds in 6/4
Transition	36–39	Polyphonic material continues in 6/4; harmonies become more extended
Theme	40–52	Scored in the brass in the key of A-flat; begins with trombone quartet with tuba and gradually adds all brass and eventually all winds
Theme and fugue	53–64	Statement of chorale tune in a *fugato* style utilizing woodwinds, euphonium, tuba, and double bass
Ending	65–68	6/4 feel returns in solo 1st/2nd clarinet; ends in B-flat minor
Movement III: Introduction	1–2	Hand clapping scored in brass, double bass, and timpani
Theme	3–12	Woodwinds present theme based on A and B sections of original tune
Transition	13–20	Pyramid entrances based on a five-note pattern derived from the theme

SECTION	MEASURE	EVENT AND SCORING
Theme	21–24	Full statement of the four-measure B section of the original tune
Theme	25–28	Horns state second half of B section while woodwinds play offbeat patterns and hand clappers continue
New material	29–46	Developmental section based on fragments of the theme sections; oboe and piccolo are central
Three-part canon	47	Hand clappers return for one measure after a sudden stop in melody and a silence determined by conductor; canon begins with second entrance in inversion
Theme	48–55	Melody in low reeds with upper woodwinds playing counterpoint based on A section of theme
Theme	56–end	Final statement of the B section of theme by horn with woodwinds and hand clapper accompaniment
Movement IV: Introduction	1–3	Woodwinds play quarter note triplets in 2/2; key of A-flat
Theme	3–10	Trumpet solo plays first two phrases of The Soldier's Return
March introduction	11–15	Meter changes to 6/8; snare drum with brass punctuation
March theme	16–28	Clarinets present march theme while accompaniment continues in brass and snare drum
Interjection	29–33	Interruption of march theme by flute presenting new material based on a three-note motive
March theme	34–64	March theme continues in clarinet with interjections by other woodwinds; other parts join with thematic fragments

SECTION	MEASURE	EVENT AND SCORING
Development	64–73	Begins with timpani solo and continues with blocked chords in the brass accompanied by woodwind flourishes
Development	74–77	Woodwinds present running eighth note passages while brass continue blocked statement of chords
Development	78–98	New 3/4 material builds in brass; trumpet takes over eighth note activity; woodwinds rejoin to complete modulation to E
New theme/ episode	99–105	Thorny Desert theme is introduced in woodwinds written in 9/8
Interjection	106–108	Trumpet presents material derived from the 6/8 section in a fanfare or martial style
New theme	109–127	Woodwinds revisit moving eighth note pattern; Thorny Desert theme presented in brass
March returns	128–154	Percussion; blocked chords in brass return; written key returns to A-flat
Development	155–160	Material derived from both themes; highly chromatic, dissonant, "transient" harmony
March theme	161–173	Scored in woodwinds over accompaniment in double bass, piano, and gradually the brass section
Interjection	174–178	Flute revisits previous material
March theme	179–205	Return in woodwinds
Transition	206–211	Timpani with rhythmic punctuation in brass, percussion, and piano
Return of A	212–223	Return of "soldier's theme" and a solid return to A-flat; trumpet presents the melody in a march-like manner

SECTION	MEASURE	EVENT AND SCORING
Interjection	224–227	Trumpet revisits fanfare material; woodwinds play accompaniment derived from 6/8 march music
A continues	228–254	Trombone, euphonium, and eventually trumpet continue presentation of A theme
Coda	255–303	Tempo change to presto; new material derived from themes in fragmented style builds to end

Unit 8: Suggested Listening

Donald Grantham:
>   Bum's Rush
>   J'ai ete au bal
>   Kentucky Harmony

Unit 9: Additional References and Resources

Grantham, Donald. *Southern Harmony*. Eugene Migliaro Corporon and the North Texas Wind Symphony, 1999. Compact Disc "Sojourns," 1999.

Donald Grantham. Correspondence with William Stowman, 10 August 2001.

Sadie, Stanley, ed. *Norton Grove Concise Encyclopedia of Music*, New York and London: W. W. Norton & Company; London: Macmillan Press, 1988.

Walker, William. *The Southern Harmony and Musical Companion*. Edited by Glenn C. Wilcox. Lexington, KY: The University of Kentucky Press, 1987.

Website:
www.piquantpress.com

Contributed by:

William Stowman
Director of Bands
Messiah College
Grantham, Pennsylvania

Teacher Resource Guide

Southwestern Sketches

Samuel Adler
(b. 1928)

Unit 1: Composer

Samuel Adler was born in Mannheim, Germany, in 1928 and came to the United States in 1939. He holds a Bachelor of Music from Boston University, a Master of Arts from Harvard University, a Doctor of Music (honorary) from Southern Methodist University, a Doctor of Fine Arts (honorary) from Wake Forest University, a Doctor of Music (honorary) from St. Mary's College (Indiana), and a Doctor of Music (honorary) from Saint Louis Conservatory. During his tenure in the U.S. Army, Adler founded and conducted the Seventh Army Orchestra, and because of the orchestra's great psychological and musical impact on the European cultural scene, he was awarded the Army's Medal of Honor.

Adler's catalog includes over four hundred published works in all media, including five operas, six symphonies, eight string quartets, eight concerti (organ, piano, violin, cello, flute, guitar, saxophone quartet, woodwind quintet), many shorter orchestral works, works for wind ensemble and band, chamber music, and a great deal of choral music and songs. He has published three books: Choral Conducting, an anthology (Holt, Rinehart and Winston, 1971), including second edition (Schirmer Books, 1985); Sight-Singing (W. W. Norton, 1979, 1997); and The Study of Orchestration (W. W. Norton, 1982, 1989), as well as numerous articles in major magazines and reference books here and abroad.

Since 1966, Adler has been professor of composition at the Eastman School of Music and chairman of the composition department since 1974. In 1984, he was made a mentor of the University of Rochester. Previous to this, he was professor of composition at North Texas State University (1957–1966) and music director at Temple Emanu-El in Dallas, Texas (1953–1966). From 1954 to 1958, he was music director of the Dallas Lyric Theater.

Adler has been a guest composer or conductor at over three hundred universities and colleges worldwide. He retired from Eastman in 1994 to become Professor Emeritus of that institution. Since then he has taught at Ithaca College, University of Cincinnati, Bowling Green State University, University of Missouri (Kansas City), University of Utah, and others. He is currently on the faculty of the Juilliard School of Music in New York City.

Adler has received commissions and grants from the National Endowment for the Arts (1975, 1978, 1980, 1982), the Ford Foundation, the Rockefeller Foundation, the Barlow Foundation, the Koussevitzky Foundation, the Dallas Symphony Orchestra, the Rochester Philharmonic, the Fine Arts Quartet, the Pro Arte Quartet, the Kentucky Arts Commission, the Sinfonia Foundation, the City of Jerusalem, the Cleveland Quartet, the Welsh Arts Council, Oklahoma City Symphony, Cincinnati Symphony, and many others. Adler has been awarded many prizes, including a 1990 award from the American Academy and Institute of Arts and Letters, the Charles Ives Award, the Lillian Fairchild Award, etc. In 1983, he won the Deems Taylor Award for his book on orchestration. In 1984, he was appointed Honorary Professorial Fellow of the University College in Cardiff, Wales, and was awarded a Guggenheim Fellowship for 1984–85. He was a MacDowell Fellow for five years between 1954 and 1963. In 1986, he received the Distinguished Alumni Award from Boston University. Also, the Music Teachers' National Association selected Adler as its Composer of the Year 1986–87 for Quintalogues, which won the national competition. In the 1988–89 year, he was designated Phi Beta Kappa Visiting Scholar. In 1989, he was awarded the Eastman School's Eisenhart Award for distinguished teaching, and he has been given the honor of Composer of the Year (1991) for the American Guild of Organists. During his second visit to Chile, Adler was elected to the Chilean Academy of Fine Arts (1993) "for his outstanding contributions to the world of music as composer, conductor, and author."

Adler's works have been performed by major symphonic, choral, and chamber organizations in the United States, South America, Europe, Asia, and Israel, including the New York Philharmonic, the Chicago Symphony, the Philadelphia Orchestra, the Dallas Symphony, the Boston Pops, the Houston Symphony, the Detroit Symphony, and the orchestras of Kansas City, San Antonio, Ft. Worth, New Orleans, Cincinnati, St. Louis, Los Angeles, and others.

Adler has also appeared as conductor with major orchestras both here and abroad, and his compositions have been recorded on RCA, Vanguard, Crystal, CRI, Lyrichord, Mark, Turnabout, Gasparo, and Golden Crest Records.

Unit 2: Composition

Southwestern Sketches was written in 1960 on a commission from the New Mexico State University in honor of the fiftieth anniversary of statehood of the state of New Mexico. It was premiered in 1961 by the Wind Ensemble of New Mexico State University, with Ray Tross conducting.

From the composer's notes:

> In the late 1950s, I was asked by the Dallas, Texas Theatre Center to compose music for a play called "Joshua Beene and God," starring Burl Ives. This was a play similar to the Elmer Gantry story about a "holy man" operating in the southwest. The play was very successful and was to go to Broadway, but circumstances beyond anyone's control kept it from taking that leap.
>
> The music was characteristic of the Southwest, but it was entirely an original score—not using any indigenous folk song material—though Burl Ives did sing several songs which I composed during the play. The only actual quote is the hymn "Fairest Lord Jesus," which occurs at the end when the congregation that has condemned the "holy man" sings this hymn to purify themselves.
>
> After the show had closed and I received this commission, I felt the music for the play would be a good starting point for a band piece. Therefore, I used fragments of it and composed a work which is sectionalized but is in one continuous movement. The feeling of it is one of exuberance and truthfulness with a great deal of energy, but also having many sudden contrasts built in. I have always felt that the southwest of our country is a most exciting place, but one of many dichotomies. Nature itself is a changing phenomenon and the changes are not gradual at all, but there are sudden contrasts as there are also in the people. I hope that this work reflects these contrasts and gives an idea and a feeling which I have always received from living in the southwestern United States.

This twelve-minute, grade five work is published by Oxford University Press.

Unit 3: Historical Perspective

Landscapes and their nationalistic and cultural associations have provided many composers the inspiration for musical settings. Pieces as diverse as Milhaud's *Suite Francaise*, Sibelius's *Finlandia*, Coates's *London Every Day*, Smetana's *The Moldau*, and Husa's *Music for Prague 1968* attempt to capture musical, geographic, cultural, social, and political impressions of various locales.

The American West and Southwest have captured the imagination of countless composers of art music and music for film. The spaciousness and wonder of the land and its people (from the Frontier to the current day) have been most notably depicted by Aaron Copland (*Tender Land, Billy the Kid, The Red Pony, Rodeo*, among others). Ron Nelson's "holidays" for wind band (*Rocky Point Holiday, Aspen Jubilee, Sonoran Desert Holiday*) are musical impressions of favorite vacation spots.

Unit 4: Technical Considerations

Southwestern Sketches is scored for "complete band," including two bass trombone parts, two baritone (euphonium) parts, and string bass. There is no baritone saxophone part, although the composer calls for contrabassoon and contrabass clarinet. Percussion includes timpani, snare drum, bass drum, bongos, gong, xylophone, glockenspiel, and celesta. With the exception of the rambunctious section at measure 135, scoring is sparse (reminiscent of the *Sinfonietta* by Ingolf Dahl) and requires careful attention to rest counting and complete accuracy.

There is some extremely challenging E-flat clarinet solo work (register and intonation issues require an advanced performer), and confident soloists are needed in piccolo, flute, oboe, clarinet, saxophone, and cornet. Because of the disjunct intervallic leaps and contemporary harmonies, a mature ensemble is required for successful performance of this work.

There are a few "special effects" (e.g., fluttertonguing in trumpet and horn at measure 125, rim shots in the snare at measure 135); otherwise, performance techniques are fairly straightforward.

Southwestern Sketches contains both tuneful folk-like melodies and dissonant harmonies, often simultaneously. There are occasional cadential points, but functional harmony is not the language of this work. Rather, it is liberal in its use of bitonality, cluster chords, and free dissonance. Additionally, shifting compound meters, imitation, and colorful, virtuosic instrumental combinations give the work a distinctly contemporary feel.

Unit 5: Stylistic Considerations

Like the southwestern United States landscape, this piece is one of contrasts, demonstrated by Adler in nearly every area of musical style. Emotionally, an ominous introduction, a proclamatory passage, a gentle melodic section, and a soft cadence, all leading to a rollicking opening *allegro*, take place in the first two minutes of the piece. Rehearsal markings (in groups of ten) do not necessarily coincide with formal divisions, so it is helpful to mark the score with more practical spots.

Articulation ranges from sustained lyricism to punchy, dry, Stravinsky-esque punctuation. Some of the more energy-charged moments demand an aggressive, gritty approach. Breath accents in compound meters will help the listener discern agogic accents, and space between syncopated notes will bring out the rhythmic differences. Dynamics run the gamut and should be exaggerated, especially on the low end.

Because of the rapidly changing palette of instrumental colors, balance issues must be observed sensitively by all players. The *tutti* sections are sometimes homophonic, so a lightness is required even when the texture seems "heavy." Imitative passages require equality in projection and sameness in style.

Unit 6: Musical Elements

MELODY:

Melodic structure and design include a mix of diatonicism, chromaticism, pentatonicism, conjunct/scalar and disjunct intervallic leaps, and imitation (usually not strict). Inversion is used at measure 65 in continuation of the phrase, and a hymn quotation occurs at measure 241. The final section implements augmentation of melody underneath the melody in "normal time."

HARMONY:

There is a similarly varied vocabulary of harmonic practices in *Southwestern Sketches*. While it is decidedly not "common practice period" harmony, it is not exclusively atonal.

There is frequent use of bichords, often where a triad is scored above an open fifth whose root is a major second below the root of the triad. Additionally, entire passages tend toward bitonality (see measure 47, with melody in D major, timpani in G major and A major). Intentional clashing minor seconds occur at measure 43 (A and A-sharp), and the entire melodic line at measure 141 is harmonized with half steps, creating significant dissonance.

Clusters also occur throughout the piece. When cluster chords occur with a tune, melody is given prominent voicing so it is audible, but harmonies are spicy and non-tertian (and non-functional). The use of unison (see opening), contrary motion (see measures 51 through 53), multi-polyphonic layering (see measure 180), and imitation (see measure 21) contribute to a number of interesting harmonic techniques.

RHYTHM:

Tempo, metric, and rhythmic variety add further variety to this piece. Generally speaking, with the exception of the quick-moving section at measure 160, rhythmic patterns themselves are relatively non-complex—the challenge is often in the successful blending of multiple musical lines. In the *Allegro* section, compound (sometimes uneven) meters change frequently (eighth note constant) to fit the melody. Hemiola occurs at measure 185 (3/4 feel in 6/8), and syncopation occurs regularly, often emphasizing counts 2 and 5 in 6/8.

698

TIMBRE:

Southwestern Sketches is a highly colorful composition. Adler alternates unison *tuttis*, large sections (all woodwinds or all brass), and chamber groupings throughout the piece. Interesting combinations include piccolo/bassoon/celesta (see measure 15), flute/muted cornet (see measure 21), alto saxophone with muted horns (see measure 67), muted bass trombone/trumpet accompaniment under woodwinds (see measure 94), all brass (see measure 183), and more. He frequently writes in "families," utilizing the entire horn section, all woodwinds, and flute/oboe/clarinet trio, among other combinations.

There is also great variety in texture, as demonstrated by *tutti* homophonic sections (opening, measure 30), polyphonic writing (see measure 75), and imitative lines (see measure 167).

Unit 7: Form and Structure

MEASURE	EVENT AND SCORING
Opening	*Adagio*; unison E-flat and half step punctuated by drum; roll *tutti* woodwind proclamation (bitonal); trumpet/trombone/tuba response
11	Oboe solo, accompanied by horn
15	Lyrical eighth notes in piccolo and bassoon in contrary motion; triangle and celesta add color; alto saxophone pentatonic melody
21	Muted trumpet and flute in imitation—extension of saxophone melody
26	Cadence in clarinet on F-sharp major; oboe solo in C major; section cadences and *decrescendos*
30	*Allegro vivace* (quarter note = 144); full ensemble with simple scalar melody; meter shifts into 6/8, 7/8, 5/8, 4/4, and 3/4
38	Descending minor third motive in muted cornet, flute, and piccolo; more shifting meter
43	Woodwind/cornet playful melody with clashing minor seconds; transition to m. 47
47	Return of main melody in piccolo, flute, clarinet, and trumpet; tonic-dominant timpani accompaniment

MEASURE	EVENT AND SCORING
51	Bombastic transition to next section; unison E-flat major diatonic scalar patterns in horn and low brass/low woodwind
54	Soft *legato* accompaniment in clarinet; light downbeats alternating in bassoon and bass clarinet; occasional glockenspiel; oboe solo; more shifting meters
62	Melody doubled in piccolo and oboe; begins in inversion from original statement at m. 56
67	Bouncy dotted-figure alto saxophone melody accompanied by light muted horn, then by light trumpet
75	Before saxophone line (with muted bass trombone finishing touch) is over, flute and oboe return in counterpoint on a varied version of the oboe tune; bassoon accompanies with quick *staccato* eighths
80	E-flat clarinet plays the bouncy melody in upper register; B-flat clarinets in counterpoint; colorful sound blotches
85	Pseudo-waltz (with meter changes) begins (oom-pah-pah in bass drum and flute/piccolo); displaced downbeat in horn
93	Stravinsky-esque dry accompaniment in bass trombone, muted trumpet, and timpani; second half of oboe tune sounded in piccolo, flute, oboe, and bassoon; transforms into the bouncy saxophone tune; increased activity in brass
100	*Tutti* transition; block unison in brass and saxophone; repeated eighth note patterns (alternating major seconds) in woodwinds
104	Return of main melody
112	Return of descending minor third motive; transition to full stop at m. 123; cadence on B-flat/C/F
124	*Very slowly* (quarter note = 50); chromatic runs and trills in piccolo, flute, oboe, and clarinet punctuated by *sff* muted and fluttertonguing trumpet and horn
126	Descending chromatic patterns; oboe, bassoon, and clarinet play a fragment of the bouncy melody and cadence on an open B-flat/F; four *tutti* cluster chords are sounded

MEASURE	EVENT AND SCORING
135	*Fast and rhythmic* (quarter note = 132); timpani, bongos, bass drum, and snare rim shots with syncopated tuba and quarter notes in contrabassoon; new, gritty, simple dance melody in trumpet and cornet (clustered in minor second relationships: D/E-flat and G/A-flat for the first notes of the melody); infusion of 5/8 and 7/8
146	Dance melody at a higher pitch level and added instruments (baritone, horn, clarinet, oboe, and flute); percussion plays fragments of introduction as accents; highly dissonant; "cadence" on cluster in m. 151 (3/8)
152	Dissonant chords sounded by the familiar flute/oboe/clarinet/cornet/horn grouping; percussion continues patterns with rim shots
156	Piccolo/flute/oboe/bassoon/saxophone (with clarinet later) sound dissonant chords in shifting meters (one per measure, with the pattern 5/8, 7/8, 5/8, 6/8, 5/8, 4/8, 5/8, 4/4); "add-on" *tutti* descending pattern to C unison at m. 167
167	Canonic section (E-flat clarinet, flute, clarinet, bassoon); counterpoint in oboe; section continues with fragments and *stretto*
183	Cornet/trumpet/horn countermelody; trombone and tuba in canon, all still under the woodwind fragment
188	*ff* cluster chord in *tutti* brass; unison *staccato* figurations in woodwinds; shifting meters; xylophone solo; and short "hits" that lead to four more slow cluster chords (similar to those that began this section); *fermata* and release
200	*Fast and rhythmic* (quarter note = 132); percussion rim shots start again, now with a lyrical, dissonant line in horn, bass clarinet, clarinet, English horn, and oboe; dissonant dance tune is heard again in trumpet and cornet; pedal bass (dissonant) in tuba and baritone is added; restatement of the tune in horn, cornet, trumpet, and upper woodwinds; more shifting meters; cadence on a cluster and *molto rallentando*
218	Much slower; woodwinds on syncopated, descending, dissonant figures; cadence on unison C; horn, bass trombone, and baritone echo the "winding down" pattern and cadence on B-flat minor (held trumpet on C)

MEASURE	EVENT AND SCORING
225	*Largo* (quarter note = 52); trumpet solo with horn solo in loose imitation, accompanied by sustained tuba and two baritones; oboe takes tune, English horn takes counterline, flute and bassoon complete the phrase; alto saxophone returns with opening pentatonic melody with tenor saxophone sustained notes
241	"Reverently"; quote of *Fairest Lord Jesus* (hymn tune "St. Elizabeth"); melody in bassoon and oboe, harmonized by oboe, bassoon, and muted horn; flute takes mid-phrase with clarinet and alto clarinet; baritone and horn continue with melody, while trumpet provides counterline; cadence on open C/G, then pedal F enters in tuba and bass trombone to create a quintal chord
259	*Allegro* (quarter note = 120, *alla breve*); scalar contrary motion runs in flute and clarinet; xylophone adds short hit points in the rests
269	New, cheery folk-like dance tune (with a syncopated twist in the middle) in piccolo, oboe, bassoon, and bass clarinet; runs continue; timpani echoes melodic contour
285	Tune continues, now with counterline in cornet, trumpet, and imitative line in horns (at one measure); rhythmic activity increases in clarinet and bass clarinet
300	Pedal muted B concert in trumpet; disjunct oboe melody above playful lines between English horn, oboe, and trumpet
310	Clarinet solo over muted trombone, then taken by muted trumpet over clarinet
317	Bassoon and xylophone with the tune; light scoring with dissonance and different fragments of the tune (solos in piccolo, oboe, E-flat clarinet)
336	Clarinet family with *staccato* melody over sustained bass clarinet line; bassoon joins, and then flute and piccolo
349	Sudden hits in the bass drum and short, accented horn/low brass notes; transitional material in horns and low brass leading to m. 361

MEASURE	EVENT AND SCORING
361	*Tutti* texture; melodic material in oboe, English horn, bassoon, cornet, and trumpet; contrary motion eighth notes in piccolo, flutes, clarinet, and bass clarinet; augmented melody in trombone, bass trombone, and tuba; pyramidal effect to final cadence on a unison G

Unit 8: Suggested Listening

Wind Visions: The Music of Samuel Adler, The Keystone Wind Ensemble, Jack Stamp, conductor: Citadel Records, 1997

Other wind music of Samuel Adler:
A Little Night and Day Music
Brass Fragments
Double Visions
Festive Prelude
Symphony No. 3, ("Diptych")
The Force of Credulity

Music that evokes Southwestern United States landscapes and culture:
Aaron Copland:
Billy the Kid
Rodeo
Tender Land
The Red Pony
Morton Gould, *Santa Fe Saga*
Ferde Grofé, *Grand Canyon Suite*
Ron Nelson:
Aspen Jubilee
Holiday
Rocky Point Holiday
Sonoran Desert

Unit 9: Additional References and Resources

Paynter, John P. "New Music Reviews." *The Instrumentalist*, 25, November 1970, p. 71.

Smith, Norman, and Albert Stoutamire. *Band Music Notes*. Revised edition. San Diego: Kjos West, 1979, p. 3. Note contributed by Gene C. Smith.

Teacher Resource Guide

The Final Covenant
Fisher Tull
(1934–1994)

Unit 1: Composer

Fisher Aubrey Tull was born in Waco, Texas, on September 24, 1934. He graduated from North Texas State University in 1957 with degrees in music education, trumpet performance, and theory. While at North Texas, Tull served as an assistant to trumpet teacher John Haynie as well as staff arranger for the North Texas Lab Bands. He returned to North Texas in 1962 to study composition with Sam Adler. Tull spent his teaching career at Sam Houston State University, where he was Distinguished Professor of Music and chairman of the Department of Music.

Tull completed over forty commissions for various ensembles including service bands, professional music organizations, and major symphony orchestras. Some of the awards he received include the 1970 ABA Ostwald Award for *Toccata*, the Arthur Fraser Memorial Award for *Three Episodes for Orchestra*, and the Walter Beeler Award. He is the recipient of nine ASCAP awards and won First Prize in the Texas Composers Guild five times. Tull appeared as a guest composer, conductor, and lecturer throughout the United States and Germany.

Some of the works composed for band by Tull include *Accolade, Antiphon, Credo, Prelude and Double Fugue, Reflections on Paris, Sketches on a Tudor Psalm*, and *Toccata*.

Unit 2: Composition

The Final Covenant was commissioned by the New Jersey Music Educators Association. It was premiered by the New Jersey All-State Wind Ensemble, conducted by Richard Castiglione, at the Eastern MENC meeting in Atlantic City in February of 1979. This piece is scored for symphonic band and lasts eight minutes.

Unit 3: Historical Perspective

A covenant is an agreement, in this case between God and mankind. A dear friend of the composer who was terminally ill at the time inspired this composition. It expresses a deep religious emotion through a slow tempo, warm melodies, and dark harmonic structure. This piece is appropriate on a program as concert music or in memoriam.

Unit 4: Technical Considerations

Technical issues in *The Final Covenant* are limited. The conductor and performers need to be concerned with musical maturity and balance of line. Ranges will not be a problem for most bands. First trumpets play as high as written B-flat. French horn, trombone, and euphonium each play up to their written high G. Instrumentation requirements call for two oboes, English horn, E-flat alto clarinet, B-flat bass clarinet, contrabass clarinet, string bass, and four percussion plus timpani. Important parts with little or no cross-cueing are written for these instruments. Additionally, solos for piccolo, E-flat clarinet, bassoon, trumpet, and horn will require strong players on each part. Sections with multiple parts will need strong players throughout as Tull's writing within sections is very independent.

Unit 5: Stylistic Considerations

The Final Covenant requires *legato* style for almost the entire piece. Ensembles will be challenged to maintain the *legato* style while attaining rhythmic precision. Phrases are often long, connected lines passed among various sections. Dynamic contrasts are frequent and vary from being quite subtle to drastic. The thick writing used by Tull makes attention to dynamics and balance between melody and accompaniment parts crucial. Themes are often passed between instruments, making it difficult for the listener to follow the melodic line unless the performers are careful with that exchange.

Unit 6: Musical Elements

MELODY:

The Final Covenant has two main themes. The first theme begins with solo horn in mm. 4. It must be balanced against four percussion parts. First clarinet joins the horn on the first theme at measure 9 before it moves to solo trumpet at measure 12 and upper woodwinds at measure 16.

Oboe and English horn introduce the second theme at measure 27. Flute and clarinet join at measure 30. This theme is an imitative duet, with the second part playing exactly an eighth note behind the first. The desired effect is to be an echo. Both parts must use just enough decay to hear the next entrance without losing the echo effect.

HARMONY:
There are no keys indicated, and while cadences do exist, tonal centers are rarely established. Tull uses thick harmonies of multiple colors to establish the desired mood. There is constant tension and release, which maintains listener interest without becoming predictable. Harmonies and melodic themes are complex and sound serial in construction, although they are not.

RHYTHM:
Tull is known for writing in mixed meter, although metric modulation is not difficult in this piece. Rhythmic precision without losing *legato* style will be a challenge for any ensemble. Tull makes frequent use of duple versus triple rhythms. Beginning in measure 2, he has percussion playing half and quarter note triplets against straight eighth notes. In measure 9, 2nd clarinets play quarter note triplets while 3rd clarinets play eighth notes.

Syncopation is also used frequently. The chimes foreshadow this at measure 2 in conjunction with the duple versus triple. The secondary theme at measure 27 achieves its echo effect when 2nd oboe is syncopated, moving entirely on the second halves of the beat. Piccolo and bassoon repeat this effect in measure 66, separated by a quarter note. Tull adds to the rhythmic interest with his use of quintuplets and dotted-sixteenths with thirty-second notes. Another rhythmic device used in this piece is the fragmented melodies played by woodwinds in measure 55 and brass in measure 74. The effect is to be a continuous line in spite of the broken voicing (see Figures 1 and 2).

TIMBRE:
The overall mood of *The Final Covenant* is very dark. Although it begins with bright percussion instruments, they help to create a lasting atmosphere of longing and solemnity with the solo horn and accompanying lower wood-winds. The conductor must pay attention to phrase beginnings and endings to ensure a seamless transfer without missing the changes in color, which are often gradual. In measure 9, clarinet joins horn almost without being noticed. That duet continues at measure 13, but solo trumpet takes the main line. However, after only two measures, the listener's ears must immediately be drawn to oboe and clarinet. After another two measures, flute and E-flat clarinet play the melody. This kind of rapid yet subtle transfer of line typifies the piece. There are moments of illumination and brilliance, such as the "ring-off" effect in measure 82, but these events are limited only to points of climax.

Unit 7: Form and Structure
The Final Covenant is a single-movement work with clear sectional breaks and development of previous material. Even what appears to be a direct quote of

an earlier theme usually does not quote exactly. Tull wrote the following in his score notes:

> Two thematic elements are employed: the first, a dramatic proclamation, is introduced by horns and subsequently taken by trumpets and woodwinds; the second plaintive theme, in the manner of a supplication, is presented by oboes followed by flutes and clarinets. The first theme returns leading to a climactic section by the full ensemble. A development section focuses on fragments from the principal theme culminating in a brief brass fanfare based on the earlier accompanying motives. The recapitulation of the principal theme brings the work to a quiet and peaceful close.

MEASURE	EVENT AND SCORING
1	Percussion introduction; pay special attention to balance of all instruments; although not notated, Tull suggests E and F struck together for crotales
4	Horn introduction of Theme I; appropriate to use multiple players with a larger section; there should be no break in the line until m. 8
9	First clarinet joins horn on Theme I; low woodwinds join percussion on the cross-rhythm accompaniment
12	First trumpet continues Theme I, but should become secondary from mm. 15–18 when upper woodwinds take Theme I; timbre color gradually changes due to *pianissimo* low brass entrance
20	Semi-climax
21	Natural *diminuendo* occurs as register becomes lower and brass exit
27	Tull's "plaintive subordinate theme" begins in canon with oboes separated by an eighth note, thus creating an echo effect; Tull asks for more defined articulation from 2nd oboe to emphasize the syncopation
30	Flute continues plaintive subordinate theme; due to low register, additional players may be used on the 2nd flute part; continue defined articulations in second part
34	Alto and bass clarinet should be at equal volumes; if necessary, add 3rd clarinet to the alto clarinet part; use contrabass clarinet in the absence of string bass

MEASURE	EVENT AND SCORING
27 and 34	Tull notes that these tempo markings in the score were added upon proofreading and are not included in the parts
40	Baritone and tuba reintroduce Theme I; continuous line is again important as the theme is passed up to the higher brass through m. 53
52	Tull states it is "difficult to imagine too much stretching of the beats"; final beat of m. 52 should be marked *molto tenuto*
53	First major climax; Tull calls it the "abortive climax" due to the *subito piano* in m. 54 and prefers the effect be enhanced with a slight pause at the end of m. 53
55	Woodwinds begin fragmented soloistic passage; players must enunciate their parts clearly and then make way for subsequent entries through m. 61; Tull wants this to be a pointillistic effect when all parts are played consecutively (Figure 1)

Figure 1: Fragmented Woodwind Melody (mm. 55–62)

62	Upper woodwinds have homophonic writing
66	Canon between piccolo and bassoon separated by three octaves
70	Entire woodwind section returns with homophonic writing; Tull again requests no break in line
74	Brass has fragmented soloistic passage similar to woodwinds in m. 54 (Figure 2)

Figure 2: Fragmented Brass Melody (mm. 74–78)

82	"Ring off" effect requiring full sonority from woodwinds, with weight and length from brass; antiphonal effects in mm. 84–85 should not be separated
91	Preface to recapitulation using fragmented material and cross-rhythms
94	Only a few low brass instruments play Theme I
99	Begins building towards ultimate climax
105	Ultimate climax; unlike abortive climax at m. 53, the ensemble should continue to the downbeat of m. 106 for the point of greatest intensity
107	Tension gradually subsides until conclusion; cross-rhythms, contrapuntal entrances similar to fragmented passages, and reduced instrumentation lead to the final cadence; Tull suggests breath attacks from brass on final two chords as well as a staggered release on the final measure, leaving only flute, clarinet, and bassoon to fade away one beat later than the rest of the ensemble

Unit 8: Suggested Listening

John Barnes Chance, *Elegy*
Norman Dello Joio, *Variants on a Medieval Tune*
Fisher Tull:
    Prelude and Double Fugue
    Sketches on a Tudor Psalm
    Toccata

Unit 9: Additional References and Resources

Dvorak, Thomas L., Robert Grechesky, and Gary Ciepluch. *Best Music for High School Band*. Brooklyn, NY: Manhattan Beach Music, 1993.

Grout, Donald, and Claude Palisca. *History of Western Music*. Fourth edition. New York: W. W. Norton & Co., 1988.

Randel, Don Michael. *The New Harvard Dictionary of Music*. Cambridge, MA: Harvard University, 1986.

Rehrig, William H. *The Heritage Encyclopedia of Band Music*. Westerville, OH: Integrity Press, 1991.

Smith, Norman, and Albert Stoutamire. *Band Music Notes*. Lake Charles, LA: Program Note Press, 1989.

Tull, Fisher. "The Final Covenant." *The School Musician*. October 1980, pp. 8–9.

Contributed by:

Mark Duker
Scullen Middle School
Naperville, Illinois

Teacher Resource Guide

The Red Pony: Film Suite for Band

Aaron Copland
(1900–1990)

Unit 1: Composer

The work of Aaron Copland has left an indelible mark on American art music. His works touched nearly every genre, including works for the ballet, film, radio, and concert hall. His significant contributions as an educator, conductor, and author place him in a select group of artists who significantly impacted the way we listen to and think about music. Copland's compositions encompass a wide spectrum of influences, including jazz rhythms (*Concerto for Piano* and *Music for the Theater*), abstract works (*Piano Variations* and *Statements for Orchestra*), folk-inspired themes (*Appalachian Spring* and *Rodeo*) to twelve-tone composition (*Connotations* and *Inscape*). His books, including *What to Listen for in Music* and *Music and Music and Imagination*, have become staples in the training of music educators around the world. Copland's dedication to teaching at the Berkshire Music Center and at universities around the world have produced scores of celebrated composers. His life's work has been recognized through such honors as the Pulitzer Prize, the Guggenheim Foundation, the American Academy of Arts and Letters, the Medal of Freedom, the Kennedy Center Honors, and the National Medal of the Arts.

Unit 2: Composition

The Red Pony: Film Suite for Band is an adaptation of a film score that Copland wrote for the film The Red Pony. The film was based on a novel of the same name by noted American author John Steinbeck. In the process of composing the music for the film, Copland was approached by Efrem Kurtz, newly appointed conductor of the Houston Symphony. Kurtz wanted a composition from Copland to perform in his first season as music director, so Copland arranged the music from the film into an orchestral suite. This concert version was first performed by the Houston Symphony on October 30, 1948. In 1966, Copland made an arrangement of the orchestral suite for band. Of the six original movements, only four were suitable for transcription: "Dream March"/"Circus Music," "Walk to the Bunkhouse," "Grandfather's Story," and "Happy Ending." The first performance of this work was scheduled to be premiered by the U.S. Navy Band under the direction of Anthony Mitchell at the Mid-West Band and Orchestra Clinic in December of 1968.

Unit 3: Historical Perspective

The Red Pony was written during a period in which Copland wrote several film scores, including *The City* and *Of Mice and Men* (both in 1939), *Our Town* (1940), *North Star* (1943), *The Cummington Story* (1945), and *The Heiress* (1948). Copland's final film score was *Something Wild* (1961). These works came from a rather prolific period in his life, during which he wrote *Rodeo* (1942), *Lincoln Portrait* (1942), *Appalachian Spring* (1944), and *Third Symphony* (1946).

Unit 4: Technical Considerations

In this adaptation of his orchestral suite, Copland pushes nearly every instrument to its limit in terms of technique, range, endurance, and intonation. The trumpet and cornet parts are frequently written above the staff, ascending to d3 in places. The clarinet parts are often very high, especially in the solo and 1st clarinet parts. A full clarinet choir, including alto and contrabass clarinets, is required, as there are no cross-cues for any of the clarinet parts. Separate parts for piano and harp are included in the score, although Copland marks these instruments as ad-lib.

Unit 5: Stylistic Considerations

The Red Pony gives opportunities for players to display different moods: anger, joy, sadness, and laughter, among others. These moods are accomplished by careful attention to rhythm, intonation, articulation, and tone color. Copland's score is very clearly marked to many of these details but still leaves ample room for individual interpretations.

Unit 6: Musical Elements

The Red Pony contains primarily homophonic material throughout. Key centers are often used to dictate sections of the form in each movement. There are numerous examples of modal writing, in particular mixolydian mode.

Unit 7: Form and Structure

SECTION	MEASURE	KEY	EVENT AND SCORING

Movement Ia: "Dream March

A	1–34	D major	
	35–50	E-flat major	Second statement of A
	51–70	B-flat major	Third statement of A
	71–86	E major	Fourth statement of A
	87–131	D major	Fifth statement of A

Movement Ib: "Circus Music"

A	132–164	G major	
B	165–175	E-flat major	
C	176–207	C major	
A	208–241	G major	

Movement II: "Walk to the Bunkhouse"

A	1–20	C major	
B	21–23	C major	
A	24–59	C major	
B	60–71	C major	
A	72–96	C major	

Movement III: "Grandfather's Story"

A	1–13	G major	
A	14–28	G major	
B	29–61	A/C major	
A	62–70	G major	

Movement IV: "Happy Ending"

Introduction	1–9	F major	
A	10–27	F major	
B	28–53	C major	
A	54–81	C major	
A	82–110	F major	
Reprise	111–121	F major	Reprise of introduction

Unit 8: Suggested Listening

Leonard Bernstein, *On the Waterfront*
Aaron Copland:
    Our Town
    The Heiress Suite
Sergei Prokofiev, *Lieutenant Kije Suite*

Unit 9: Additional References and Resources

Copland, Aaron. *What to Listen for in Music*. New York: McGraw-Hill, 1957.

The New Music: 1900–1960. New York: W. W. Norton & Co., 1968.

Music and Imagination. Cambridge: Harvard University Press, 1952.

Copland on Music. New York: W. W. Norton & Co., 1963.

Copland, Aaron, and Vivian Perlis. *Copland Since 1943*. New York: St. Martin's Griffin, 1989.

Morton, Lawrence. "*The Red Pony*: A Review of Aaron Copland's Score." *Film Music Notes*. February 1949, pp. 2–8.

Pollack, Howard. *Aaron Copland: The Life and Work of an Uncommon Man*. New York: Henry Holt and Company, 1999.

Sternfeld, Frederick. "Copland as Film Composer." *Musical Quarterly* 37, 1951, pp. 161–75.

Contributed by:

Jason Worzbyt
Assistant Professor of Bassoon
Conductor of Concert Band
Indiana University of Pennsylvania
Indiana, Pennsylvania

Teacher Resource Guide

The Sword and the Crown
Edward Gregson
(b. 1945)

Unit 1: Composer

Edward Gregson is one of Britain's most versatile composers whose music has been performed, broadcast, and recorded worldwide. Gregson studied composition and piano at the Royal Academy of Music (1963–1967), winning five prizes for composition. Early success was achieved with his *Brass Quintet*, which was broadcast and recorded as well as being a finalist piece in the 1968 BBC Young Composer's Competition. This was followed by many commissions from the English Chamber Orchestra and the York Festival, among others. Since then, he has written orchestral, chamber, instrumental, and choral music, as well as music for theatre, film, and television.

Gregson's concerti for wind instruments are established repertoire in many countries (*Trumpet Concerto* of 1983 has received performances from the Detroit and Louisville Orchestras, as well as the Rotterdam Philharmonic and BBC Scottish Symphony Orchestras). Other major orchestral works include *Music for Chamber Orchestra* (1968), *Metamorphoses* (1979), *Contrasts* (1983), and *Blazon* (1992). His output also includes two brass quintets, an Oboe Sonata (1965), a Piano Sonata (1983), a Sonata for Four Trombones (1984), many works for brass and wind bands, and three choral works: *In the beginning* (1966), *Missa Brevis Pacem* (1987), and *Make a Joyful Noise* (1988). He has recently completed commissions for the Royal Liverpool Philharmonic and Bournemouth Symphony Orchestras, as well as a Clarinet Concerto for Michael Collins and the BBC Philharmonic, premiered in Manchester in 1994.

His music for theatre includes commissions for the York Cycle of Mystery Plays (1976), *The Plantagenets* (1988), and *Henry IV*, Parts I and II (1990), which were commissioned by the Royal Shakespeare Company for performances in Stratford-upon-Avon and London. In 1988, Gregson was nominated for an Ivor Novello Award for his title music for BBC Television's Young Musician of the Year programs, for which he has also regularly acted as a jury member.

A noted conductor of contemporary music, Gregson has held numerous academic posts, including professor of music at Goldsmith's College and University of London, and visiting teacher and conductor at the Royal Academy of Music. He was recently appointed principal of the Royal Northern College of Music.

Unit 2: Composition

The Sword and the Crown was commissioned by the Royal Air Force Services for the British tour of the Massed Bands of the Royal Air Force in 1991. It received its first performance, conducted by the composer, at the Free Trade Hall in Manchester (England) on October 18, 1991. Further performances on the tour followed, including the Royal Albert Hall, London and Symphony Hall, Birmingham.

Program notes by the composer:

In 1988 I was commissioned by the Royal Shakespeare Company to write the music for The *Plantagenets* trilogy, directed by Adrian Nobel in Stratford-upon-Avon. These plays take us from the death of Henry V to the death of Richard III. Later, in 1991, I wrote music for Henry IV, parts 1 and 2, again in Stratford. All of these plays are concerned with the struggle for power (the crown) through the use of force (the sword), and they portray one of the most turbulent periods in the history of the British monarchy.

When the Royal Air Force Music Services commissioned me to write a work especially for their British tour in 1991, I immediately thought of turning to this music and transforming some of it into a three-movement suite for symphonic band.

The first movement opens with a brief fanfare for two antiphonal trumpets (off-stage), but this only acts as a preface to *Requiem aeternam* (the Death of Henry V) before changing mood to the English army on the march to France; this subsides into a French victory march, but the English army music returns in counterpoint. Finally, a brief reminder of the *Requiem* music leads to the triumphal music for Richard Plantagenet, Duke of York, father of Edward IV and Richard III (the opening fanfare transformed).

The second movement takes music from the Welsh Court in Henry IV (part 1), which is tranquil in mood; distant fanfares foreboding battles to come are heard, but the folk tune is heard three times in different variations and the movement ends as it began with alto flute and gentle percussion.

The final movement starts with two sets of antiphonally placed timpani, drums, and tam-tam, portraying the "war machine" and savagery of battle. Trumpet fanfares and horn calls herald an heroic battle theme which, by the end of the movement, transforms itself into a triumphant hymn for Henry IV's defeat of the rebellious forces.

The fifteen-minute, grade six work is dedicated to Adrian Noble and the Royal Shakespeare Company, and was published in 1993 by Studio Music Company.

Unit 3: Historical Perspective

Shakespeare has been the inspiration for more musical creations than any other single author in history. His comedies, tragedies, and histories provided material for tone poems, symphonic works, and opera libretti once his plays were in circulation in Europe and abroad.

While Handel and Bach did not compose using Shakespearean themes (scholars debate whether Bach had even heard of the playwright), scores of composers throughout history have used the Bard's dramas as the point of inspiration, if not the basis, for compositions. They include Beethoven, Bellini, Berlioz, Bloch, Britten, Bruch, Debussy, Dvorak, Elgar, Faure, Gounod, Humperdinck, MacDowell, Mendelssohn, Nicolai, Prokofiev, Purcell, Rossini, Schumann, Shostakovich, Sibelius, Smetana, Strauss, Tchaikovsky, Vaughan Williams, Verdi, and Walton, among others.

The Sword and the Crown creates impressions of the British monarchy as portrayed in Shakespeare's histories. Gregson draws upon his experience with brass bands as well as the resources of the modern wind ensemble. The three primary instrumental groupings (notably absent are the saxophones, perhaps too "modern" for a period piece) remind the listener of what music might have been experienced in medieval and renaissance England: brass (fanfares and military bands), woodwinds (harmoniemusik ensembles for court entertainment), and percussion (military drums). The presence of simple melodies, modal harmonies, folk tunes, battle music, and heroic themes add to the programmatic nature of this composition.

Unit 4: Technical Considerations

While saxophones are absent from the piece, Gregson calls for an expanded brass section (four onstage trumpets, two of which double piccolo trumpet, and two antiphonal trumpets off-stage) plus alto flute, string bass, harp, and piano throughout the piece. Eight total percussionists are needed to cover the sizeable percussion complement, including two antiphonally placed timpani. Full requirements include snare drum, small medieval drum, two tenor drums, bass drums, tom-toms, suspended cymbal, clashed cymbals, bowed cymbal, antique cymbal, small oriental clashed cymbals (finger), two tam-tams, metal wind chimes bell tree, triangle, chimes, hand bells (on frame), crotales, glockenspiel, and vibraphone. There are also parts for piano, harp, and string bass.

Advanced playing and endurance are required for all brass, but especially for the off-stage trumpets, who must navigate a series of challenging fanfare figures, often in close, complex counterpoint.

Gregson specifically requests rauschpfeifen or shawms at letter E of the first movement, but "raucous" (overblown) oboes are listed as an ample substitute.

Players are required to sing in the opening of the first movement. Gregson notes that "as this work was originally written for the theatre as an accompaniment to some spectacular scenes, and was then turned into a symphonic suite for massed bands, the larger the group playing it the better. Doublings can be employed freely. However, care should be taken that the full forces be used only in the climaxes. There is ample opportunity for delicate chamber-style playing in the slow movement."

The pitch material is often modal (especially aeolian and mixolydian) and explores bitonality and lack of key establishment for long passages. Much of the composition centers around F major, but significant key areas found elsewhere include D aeolian (opening), a modulatory first movement fanfare section, a B-flat major dance, a return to D aeolian in the second movement, a shift to F minor, movement back to D major (P), and back to D aeolian. The third movement is ambivalent in key establishment, but centers on F at rehearsal W. The piece ends in C major.

Rhythm presents a significant challenge, especially in fanfare figures, which appear in groupings of two, three, four, five, and six. Meters change frequently, but the true difficulty is the counterpoint, which adds complex layerings to many sections of the piece.

The texture oscillates frequently between *tutti* passages and light chamber sections.

Unit 5: Stylistic Considerations

The outer movements of *The Sword and the Crown* contain fanfares and martial gestures, all of which require significant separation between notes, confident (but not too heavy) accents, and forward-moving intensity. Fanfare trumpets and other brass may need to spend time in sectional rehearsals to clarify same styles of entrance, weight, intonation, sustaining, and release. The conductor will also need to allot sufficient rehearsal time in the performance hall to ensure appropriate placement of off-stage trumpets for optimal balance and effect.

The middle (and opening chant sections), by contrast, demands a smooth connectedness and long, sustained phrasing.

Unit 6: Musical Elements

MELODY:

Much of Gregson's fanfare material involves ascending and descending leaps of fourths and fifths, while the lyrical folk-like melodies and florid runs tend to be diatonically scalar. The fanfares provide a sense of unity throughout the work, punctuating and separating large sections from each other.

The final heroic theme is in mixolydian mode, with the "flat" seventh occurring at the apex of the melodic phrase.

HARMONY:

Gregson gives listeners a taste of early modal harmony with frequent use of parallel fifths, although the use of bitonality, harmonizations of seconds and tritones, and other dissonance give the piece a distinctly modern bent. Still, frequent allusions to music of earlier times occur: for example, the use of the horn fifth technique (pitches 1–2–3 harmonized with pitches 3–5–1) and parallel thirds in the section eight measures after F.

Superimposition of themes, creating a fascinating polyphonic layering effect (see I-J), also propels the piece into bitonal regions (primarily centered in B-flat and F simultaneously). The stacking of ascending fifths at different pitch levels, most common in the fanfares, creates shifting, simultaneous tonal centers as well.

Much of this music "breaks the rules" of common practice period harmony (modality, parallel movement, non-leading tone cadences, and more), which accounts for the work's historical flavor and appeal.

RHYTHM:

Frequently changing meters (all simple 2, 3, 4, and 5) add variety to the overall metrical structure, although none pose a formidable challenge to the players.

At the beat level, Gregson presents a variety of divisions of two, three, four, five, and six, sometimes simultaneously. This creates dizzying counterpoint that requires confident musical independence.

Military-style patterns in the percussion (snare and field drum) create the mood of conflict and also stabilize the various musical lines in the winds. Sicilian *ostinati* at letter W provide a static (yet exciting) rhythmic accompaniment to the main melody.

TIMBRE:

The Sword and the Crown is a highly colorful piece in terms of instrumentation, utilizing alternation of thin scoring with chamber-like texture and full ensemble sections. The relatively low incidence of loud *tuttis* makes for highly effective climaxes.

One of the most striking timbral effects is the use of off-stage trumpets. Muted effects (horns after letter N, trumpets after letter P and at letter R) and stopped horns (before letter Q) also add to the myriad of brass colors that are produced in the work.

The softer middle section exploits some colorful instrument combinations, including alto flute, English horn, and harp, frequently over the *mysterioso* wash of glissandi in the glockenspiel, bell tree, wind chimes, and crotales. The use of clarinet family *tutti*, piano, and timpani duo contribute to the unique instrumental combinations found throughout the piece.

Unit 7: Form and Structure

REHEARSAL   EVENT AND SCORING

I: "Henry the Fifth, too famous to live long! England ne'er lost a king of so much worth"

Opening	Antiphonal off-stage trumpets
A	Introduction of *Requiem aeternam* in voices; light commentary in low brass; climax of *Requiem* motive at m. 20
B	March; introduced by percussion; fanfare figure in horn and trombone (harmonic fifths and fourths); military percussion persists throughout (to letter E); *staccato* antecedent phrase in woodwinds
C	Entrances of the fanfare rhythm in *stretto* and different pitch levels
D	Increased activity and intensity; m. 53 bombastic fanfare in brass, then dies down

"Advance our waving colours on the walls; Rescu'd is Orleans from the English"

E	Meter change to 6/8 with military-like percussion; rauschpfeifen/shawms sound a blaring French victory march
F	Horn section accompanies, then continues the march
G	*Tutti* statement of march
	Original fanfare returns in horn and trombone; 2/4

REHEARSAL	EVENT AND SCORING
H	Superimposition of march tune with *staccato* antecedent phrase (now in muted trumpet)
I	*Tutti* bitonal superimposition of fanfare and march
	Fragments of the fanfare and march appear with a decrease in instrumentation and intensity
J	A *tempo* (3/4); return of *Requiem aeternam* and chant-like texture; off-stage trumpets introduce new fanfares over the chant

"Rise, Richard, like a true Plantagenet, and rise created princely Duke of York" (Henry VI, part 1)

	Horns, all trumpets, and trombone play a transformed version of the opening fanfare
K	*Tutti* ensemble fanfare

II: "She bids you on the wanton rushes lay you down, and rest your gentle head upon her lap, and she will sing the song that pleaseth you..." (Henry IV, part I)

	Indeterminate (ten seconds) opening with *glissandi* in glockenspiel, bell tree, wind chimes; alto flute solo
L	English horn solo, accompanied by clarinet, harp, and percussion; folk song
M	Flute and horn take over solo, accompanied by tuba, bassoon, and harp; English horn resumes, with stopped horn and distant chiming sounded by the harp, crotales, and chimes
N	Transition with block chords in the low brass and fanfare motives from the entire horn section; *Tempo primo*: clarinet solo on the folk song with clarinet family accompaniment (eighth note movement)
O	Oboe solo on the folk song with pedal C in tuba and bass; glockenspiel and piano add twinkling effect modal cadence (D-flat major to G major) in low brass
P	Fanfare transition; faster (quarter note = 120), D major established; on-stage and off-stage trumpets present fanfares; "steadier" (quarter note = 100 indicated), D minor established

REHEARSAL	EVENT AND SCORING
Q	Return to *tempo primo* (quarter note = 76); flutes on folk song; increased activity in accompaniment: running scalar figures in oboe and clarinet, steady eighth notes in bassoon, muted horn, arpeggiating harp, and mark tree
R	Climax of middle section; meter change to 3/4; *tutti* ensemble: melody in horn and euphonium
S	Indeterminate ("senza tempo") section (approximately ten seconds) of quiet *glissandi* in glockenspiel, crotales, bell tree, bowed cymbal, and wind chimes; alto flute cadenza-like solo; open fifth on D sounds in piano and harp; bass drum roll (*attacca* into Movement III)

III: "...and here draw I a Sword, whose tempter I intend to stain with the best blood that I can meet withal in the adventure of this perilous day... Sound all the lofty instruments of war..."

	6/8 established, quarter note = 100; percussion introduction: timpani duet (indicated to be on opposite sides of the stage)
T	Off-stage trumpets introduce fanfare with a Sicilian rhythm and *stretto* fanfare ensues with on-stage (standing) trumpet; tom-toms add to the rhythmic activity
U	Timpani duet returns; "bells up" horns sound melodic fifth horn call, then break into *stretto* on the fanfare figure with trombone; snare and tenor drum join
V	Fanfare motives continue in brass while woodwinds and glockenspiel play canonic figures; increase in rhythmic activity and instrumentation *crescendos* to letter W
W	Climactic "*sempre marcato*"; open fifth *ostinato* on F in all woodwinds and piano; heroic/triumphant victory march played in unison by some on-stage trumpets, horns, trombones, and euphonium; short response in horns, low woodwinds, tuba, and string bass; woodwind swirls
X	Open fifth *ostinato* on C; march again appears, this time with the addition of clarinet, horn, and all trumpets
Y	Timpani duet over tom-tom and snare rolls at *fortissimo*

REHEARSAL	EVENT AND SCORING
Z	"Bells up" horn call; fanfares in *stretto* in all trumpets and then upper woodwinds; full percussion battery join; m. 361 hit point, *"l'istesso tempo"*; horn call with heavy low percussion accents

"Rebellion in this land shall lose his sway, meeting the check of such another day, and since this business so fair is done, let us not leave till all or own be won" (Henry IV, part I)

AA	"Majestically" and sustained (quarter note = 52); C pedal established in string bass and contrabassoon; melodic fourths and fifths
BB	Quarter note = 92; cadence on C
CC	Slower (quarter note = 84)
	Final note recedes and swells to winds-only finish

Unit 8: Suggested Listening
"Paradigms" – Cincinnati College, Conservatory of Music Wind Symphony, conducted by Eugene Corporon

Royal Northern College of Music Wind Ensemble and Manchester Cathedral Choir Boys, conducted by Timothy Reynish and Edward Gregson

"The Glorious Sound of Brass" – The Philadelphia Brass Ensemble and New England Brass Ensemble with E. Power Biggs, organ "Two Renaissance Dance Bands" and "Monteverdi's Contemporaries" – Early Music Consort of London, conducted by David Munroe

Other wind band music by Edward Gregson:
Celebration
Concerto for Tuba and Wind Ensemble
Festivo

Unit 9: Additional References and Resources
Graham, Arthur. *Shakespeare in Opera, Ballet, Orchestral Music, and Ballet.* New York: Edwin Mellen Press, 1997.

Wilson, Christopher. *Shakespeare and Music.* New York: Da Capo Press, 1977.

Contributed by:
Scott A. Stewart
Emory University
Atlanta, Georgia

Teacher Resource Guide

Variations on a Theme by Robert Schumann

Robert Jager
(b. 1939)

Unit 1: Composer

Robert Jager was born in Binghampton, New York, on August 25, 1939. He received his education at Wheaton College and University of Michigan. From 1963 to 1965, while serving in the U.S. Navy, he was a staff arranger at the Armed Forces School of Music. He directed the band at Old Dominion College and taught composition and theory at Tennessee Technological University.

To date, Jager has 122 published works to his credit. He has won several awards for his works, including two Roth awards, three Ostwald awards, and the Distinguished Service to Music medal (Kappa Kappa Psi). He has written for chamber groups, orchestra, and concert band, and has fulfilled many commissions for works for high school and college music groups. He has also conducted and lectured throughout the United States, Canada, Europe, Japan, and the Republic of China. Jager is now retired from university teaching and is Professor Emeritus at Tennessee Technological University in Cookeville, Tennessee.

Unit 2: Composition

Variations on a Theme by Robert Schumann was written as a result of a commission by conductor Warren Mercer and the North Hills High School Band of Pittsburgh, Pennsylvania. The premiere performance took place at the 1969 Eastern Region Music Educators National Conference meeting in Washington, DC. The piece was composed in 1967, while composer Jager was a graduate student at the University of Michigan. He indicates that the inspiration for the piece came about while he was walking on the campus one day. He was absently humming a tune when he stumbled and automatically adjusted the meter of the tune to fit his extra steps. The odd meter change to the melody proved intriguing to the composer. He later wrote down his idea and realized that the tune he had been humming was *The Happy Farmer*. This later became the sixth variation in *Variations on a Theme by Robert Schumann*, and Jager began to add five other variations, working backwards to the theme itself.

The theme used as the basis for the variations is the song *Frölicher Landmann, Op. 68, No. 10*, written by the romantic composer Robert Schumann in 1848, and known to young piano students as *The Happy Farmer*. This composition is the sophisticated metamorphosis of a theme through six variations. In the score, the composer outlines the basic structure as follows:

Theme:	*The Happy Farmer*
Variation I:	The theme is juxtaposed throughout "solo" voices in a Haydn-esque fashion.
Variation II:	Flutes outline theme in scherzo-like style.
Variation III:	Free variation on rhythmic values.
Variation IV:	Melodic and intervallic variation.
Variation V:	Distortion of melodic line in rhapsodic variation.
Variation VI:	Rhythmic variation of theme.

A performance of this composition will take approximately nine minutes and twenty-five seconds. The composition is really chamber music for the concert band and will require a musically mature ensemble in order to deal with the challenges presented by the neo-romantic style and transparent scoring. For example, the different variations require solos from alto saxophone, bassoon, clarinet, oboe, flute, and tuba, and also feature a woodwind quartet, flute trio, saxophone quartet, and tuba duet, among others. Indeed, some fifty-eight measures are performed before the entire band is finally heard together, well into the second variation. *Variations on a Theme by Robert Schumann* is listed as a grade five piece and will require a musically sensitive and accomplished ensemble to meet the challenges of this engaging composition.

Unit 3: Historical Perspective

Theme and variation form came into being as a musical form in the early sixteenth century. It was a common practice to borrow a theme from another composer (e.g., Brahms's *Variations on a Theme of Haydn*, Copland's *Variations on a Shaker Melody*, Vaughan Williams's *Variations on a Theme of Thomas Tallis*) and set a number of variations to it. The borrowed theme was usually a short, simple tune in binary form. The eight-measure theme used by Robert Jager in this piece comes from a piece in Robert Schumann's *Album for the Young*, entitled *The Happy Farmer*, written for young pianists in 1848. The theme and variation form that Jager has used in this piece is consistent with the "character variations" (evoking the ideals and imagery of the romantic period), which romantic composers Mendelssohn, Weber, and Schumann himself were using. Utilizing many of the same devices that romantic composers were developing to achieve variety in this form, Jager has written a neo-romantic work for band that also utilizes more contemporary techniques, such as mixed meters and a very fluid harmonic language.

Unit 4: Technical Considerations

The composition presents technical challenges as well as musical challenges in equal measure. There are many solos, and only two cross-cues are provided. The instrument ranges are all consistent with the demands of a grade five piece. Therefore, players can expect parts that will require them to play with facility near the extreme ranges for their instrument. The conductor should study the score carefully to ensure that there are accomplished performers in each section to play the exposed passages and several solos.

Variations IV and VI will require a high degree of technical preparation due to the fast tempi, shifting meters, and rhythmic challenges. Because of the chromaticism and shifting key centers, there are no key signatures used in the parts. The resulting frequent use of accidentals will require careful part preparation by individual members of the ensemble.

Intonation will need to be carefully addressed throughout due to the exposed passages. The initial statement of the theme in F major is performed by a solo alto saxophone. The succeeding variations then employ numerous key centers, which set up mediant relationships. In other words, a movement from B-flat major to D-flat major would then move directly to G-flat major, treating D-flat as the dominant of G-flat major. Enharmonic relationships are also frequently utilized, treating G-flat as an F-sharp, the mediant of D minor, for example. Modal passages and chromaticism are used frequently.

The piece is written in several accessible meters, including 2/4, 3/4, 4/4, 5/4, 2/8, 3/8, and 6/8. Metrically, Variation VI is the most challenging, with frequent shifts of meter, hemiola, and syncopations. Variations II, IV, and VI all require placement of accents on weak beats at fast tempi.

Precise and specific articulations are called for throughout the piece from all instruments. The piece will require four percussionists, using timpani, xylophone, vibraphone, bells, chimes, gong, and standard drums and small percussion instruments. As much of this piece is rooted in a chamber music style, it may prove productive to consider programming small ensemble works on the same concert. This would allow for focus on chamber music skills in rehearsal and provide opportunity to strengthen the necessary listening and musical skills required to perform in small ensembles.

Unit 5: Stylistic Considerations

Variations on a Theme by Robert Schumann will require the band to be familiar with both the elements of romantic music style and theme and variation form. The piece features *rubato* playing, frequent harmonic modulation, chromaticism, tuning idiomatic chords (such as diminished sevenths and German sixths), and sustaining musical intensity when the melodic line is shared between various soloists or small ensembles. The wide variety of tone colors achieved through the many solos and small groupings found in this composition is a style initiated during the romantic period. Other romantic traits exhibited in this piece include a wide emotional range, a large harmonic vocabulary, and the careful shaping of phrases of varying lengths.

In addition to listening to a recording of Schumann's original piano piece, the band should also listen to romantic compositions such as Brahms's *Variations on a Theme of Haydn*. This will logically lead to a discussion of variation processes used in this form and in this particular piece, such as ornamentation of the theme melody, thickening of the texture, variety in tone color, rhythmic modifications to the theme, harmonic variety, and changes in character of the theme personality. An effective teaching and rehearsal technique would be to provide multiple copies of the score for band members so they can study and then perform sections where these techniques are used. After the presentation of the theme by the alto saxophone (marked quarter note = c. 80, *moderato e semplice*), the variations alternate between slow and fast tempi in the following manner:

Variation I:	*L'istesso tempo*
Variation II:	*Allegro vivace* (quarter note = c. 152)
Variation III:	*Andante sostenuto* (quarter note = c. 80)
Variation IV:	*Presto* (quarter note = c. 160)
Variation V:	*Andante sostenuto* (quarter note = c. 64)
Variation VI:	*Allegro con brio* (quarter note = c. 152)

Unit 6: Musical Elements:

Preparation of this piece will afford an excellent opportunity to discuss the musical element of form with the ensemble. Theme and variation is one of the most accessible of compositional forms. In exploring the theme, focus can be given to the elements of melody, rhythm, harmony, and timbre. The initial statement of *The Happy Farmer* theme in this piece is given to a solo alto saxophone. To facilitate discussion of the various ways in which this melody is manipulated during the course of the piece, have the other sections of the band learn to transpose this theme into the appropriate key for their instruments so the band might rehearse the theme statement in unison. In addition, the band should sing the melody together to strengthen listening skills across the ensemble. Reinforcement of the melody line in this manner will later benefit intonation stability. In dealing with the aspect of rhythm in the variations, focus should be given to the contrast between Variation III and the remaining three variations. Note that in Variation III, the composer manipulates the theme through varying note values within the structure of a consistent triple meter. Variations IV, V, and VI, however, all use at least three different time signatures, utilizing different meters and accent patterns to manipulate the theme rhythmically.

Many examples of hemiola and syncopation can be found in the last variations, and members of the band could be directed to find examples of these in their study scores. In dealing with the technical challenges these complex rhythms may present to players (e.g., Variation VI), encourage the players to simplify rhythms by marking each beat in their part with a vertical pencil slash, drastically slowing the tempo, and eliminating ties when first reading passages. Another useful technique in dealing with the rhythmic challenges of Variations VI and IV would be to have sections rehearse very slowly and play only the notes in their parts that are marked with accents, with equivalent values of rests for the eliminated notes. Repeating the passage and increasing the speed will reinforce the accent pattern of the rhythm. When the part is then played as written, the accent pattern should be consistent and accurate throughout the ensemble. Harmonically, the composition uses a wide range of tonalities.

Using copies of the score, players could explore the uses of chromaticism, the mediant key relationships, the use of enharmonic relationships used to change key centers, and identify idiomatic chords such as diminished sevenths and German sixths. Listening to recordings of theme and variation compositions by romantic composers (e.g., *Variations on a Theme of Haydn*) and comparing the harmonic language of those compositions with that of this piece would lead to a more thorough understanding of the harmonies utilized in this composition. The treatment of the theme is mostly homophonic throughout the theme statement and the variations. In keeping with its romantic roots, the treatment of timbre in this piece will offer wide-ranging rehearsal opportunities.

The many small ensembles within the larger structure should be rehearsed separately, with the players addressing correct balance within their duet, trio, or quartet. The many solos will require careful listening and balance from the accompanying instruments. Those players accompanying soloists in the different variations should listen and attempt to "place" their sound inside that of the soloist to achieve correct balance and blend. It is also recommended that players listen to professional recordings of soloists on their instruments to develop characteristic, mature tone within each section. As well, listening to a recording of a quality performance of *Variations on a Theme by Robert Schumann* would also help develop the correct concepts of balance, blend, and tone color for this piece.

Unit 7: Form and Structure

SECTION	MEASURES	EVENT AND SCORING
Theme	1–8	Marked *moderato e semplice*, quarter note = c. 80; theme is stated by 1st alto saxophone in F major; accompaniment limited to trombone, tuba, and piccolo; meter is common time
Variation I	9–27	*L'istesso tempo*; woodwind quartet of bassoon, oboe, clarinet, and flute trade fragments of the theme, with a brief chromatic B section from all woodwinds and cornet; overall structure ABA, F major; meter is common time
Variation II	28–122	*Allegro vivace*, quarter note = c. 152; rondo-like structure of this variation is a–a1–b–a2–b–a; flute trio in a section, with added woodwinds, added brass in a1; bravura-like b sections in the style of a Galop feature first use of full band in the piece; a2 section shares melodic variation between saxophone quartet and tuba duet; meter remains in 2/4 throughout; harmonies built around key centers of F and D-flat; frequent chromaticism
Variation III	123–159	*Andante sostenuto*, quarter note = c. 80; elegiac-style variation through-composed; bassoon and oboe solos; texture thinly scored throughout; tonality suggests several minor keys, much use of chromaticism; meter is 3/4
Variation IV	160–202	Marked *presto*, quarter note = c. 160; meters alternate between 2/4, 3/4, and 6/8; sweeping chromatic passages for all instruments; ABA structure

SECTION	MEASURES	EVENT AND SCORING
Variation V	203–237	*Andante sostenuto*, quarter note = c. 64; rhapsodic variation with modal tonal center on E; meter is primarily 3/4, with some 4/4 and 5/4; alto saxophone and clarinet solos, thinly scored in the accompanying instruments; very *rubato* and expressive style throughout; through-composed with unifying elements in the alto saxophone solos
Variation VI	238–356	*Allegro con brio*, quarter note = c. 152; key centers move through mediant relationships and enharmonic minor relationships; highly chromatic passages, floating tonality; meters shift between 3/4, 2/4, and 4/4 until m. 287; *Poco meno mosso* and *Alla valse* to m. 315; meter shifts between 2/8 and 3/8 until *tempo I* at m. 316; meters used until m. 339 are 2/4, 3/4, 3/8, and 4/4; mm. 339–343 is a single, adagio statement of *The Happy Farmer* theme shared between solo alto saxophone and solo oboe in F major; coda m. 343 to the end is marked *presto*, quarter note = c. 160, in 3/4; extensive syncopation and use of hemiola throughout this movement

Unit 8: Suggested Listening

James Barnes, *Fantasy Variations on a Theme by Niccolo Paganini*
Johannes Brahms, *Variations on a Theme of Haydn*
John Barnes Chance, *Variations on a Korean Folk Song*
Norman Dello Joio, *Variants on a Medieval Tune*
Charles Ives/Rhoads, *Variations on "America"*
Robert Jager:
  Diamond Variations
  Variants on the Air Force Hymn
Arnold Schoenberg, *Theme and Variations for Wind Band, Op. 43a*
Robert Schumann, *The Happy Farmer* (from *Album for the Young, Op. 68*)

Unit 9: Additional References and Resources

Apel, Willi, ed. *Harvard Dictionary of Music*. Second edition. Cambridge, MA: The Belknap Press of Harvard University Press, 1970.

Dvorak, Thomas L., Robert Grechesky, and Gary M. Ciepluch. *Best Music for High School Band*. Edited by Bob Margolis. Brooklyn, NY: Manhattan Beach Music, 1993.

Einstein, Alfred. *Music in the Romantic Era*. New York: W. W. Norton & Co., Inc., 1947.

Jager, Robert. Telephone interview with the composer, August 2001.

Miles, Richard, ed. *Teaching Music through Performance in Band*, Volume 3. Chicago: GIA Publications, Inc., 2000.

Rehrig, William H. *The Heritage Encyclopedia of Band Music*. Edited by Paul E. Bierley. Westerfield, OH: Integrity Press, 1991.

Sadie, Stanley, ed. *The Grove Concise Dictionary of Music*. London: Macmillan Press Ltd., 1994.

Smith, Norman E. *Program Notes for Band*. Chicago, IL: GIA Publications, Inc., 2002.

Williamson, John E. *Rehearsing the Band*. Edited by Kenneth L. Neidig. Cloudcroft, NM: Neidig Services, 1998.

Robert Jager's personal website:
www.rjager.com

Contributed by:
Dennis Beck
Director of Bands
Unionville High School
Markham, Ontario, Canada

Teacher Resource Guide

Vesuvius

Frank Ticheli
(b. 1958)

Unit 1: Composer

Frank Ticheli is an Associate Professor of Composition at the University of Southern California. He received his master's and doctoral degrees in composition from the University of Michigan, where he studied with William Albright, George Wilson, Leslie Bassett, and William Bolcom. Ticheli was Composer-in-Residence with the Pacific Symphony Orchestra from 1991 to 1998. His awards include the Charles Ives Scholarship and Goddard Lieberson Fellowship, both from the American Academy and Institute of Arts and Letters, First Prize in the Texas Sesquicentennial Orchestral Composition Competition, the Frances and William Schuman Fellowship from the MacDowell Colony, and the Ross Lee Finney Award. His compositions for winds have been performed widely throughout the world and have been awarded several prizes, including the 1989 Walter Beeler Prize and First Prize in the eleventh annual "Symposium for New Music" held in Virginia.

Ticheli has received numerous commissions and grants, including those from Chamber Music America, The American Music Center, Pacific Symphony Orchestra, University of Michigan, and the Indiana Bandmasters Association. He was also commissioned by the students of Columbine High in Littleton, Colorado, to write a piece of music (*An American Elegy*) honoring and commemorating those affected by the shooting tragedy there in April 1999. Other Ticheli band and wind ensemble works include *Amazing Grace*, *Blue Shades*, *Cajun Folk Songs*, *Fortress*, *Gaian Visions*, *Music for Winds and Percussion*, *Pacific Fanfare*, and *Postcard*.

Unit 2: Composition

Vesuvius, composed in 1999, was commissioned by The Revelli Foundation for The Paynter Project. In composing *Vesuvius*, Ticheli "started with the main theme, which was left over from an earlier work, *Radiant Voices*, and sat around for years until I found the right piece for it. It suggested the image of a bacchanal in ancient Rome."[1] This wild, uninhibited form of dance could have represented a last celebration during the final doomed days of Pompeii when Mount Vesuvius, in A.D. 79, erupted with such force and fury that it completely engulfed the city. The work is approximately nine minutes in length.

Unit 3: Historical Perspective

Ticheli's music for winds reflects the work of a composer, active and much sought-after, whose music appeals to a wide variety of players and listeners. His compositions range from simple and quickly accessible (settings of *Amazing Grace, Shenandoah, Cajun Folk Songs*), to accessible yet challenging for both performers and audiences (*Pacific Fanfare, Postcard*), to works of large, complex tapestries (*Music for Winds and Percussion, Gaian Visions*).

While the twentieth century music was an eclectic, broad range of compositional styles where sounds, effects, textures, and esoteric formulas were favored, composers in the last fifteen to twenty years have returned to more familiar and understandable compositional means hoping to pique the interest of, and communicate with, listeners immediately. A prominent feature of Ticheli's style is his use of melodies and themes that form the foundation of the growth and development of a work's progress. Whether they are familiar tunes (*Amazing Grace, Shenandoah*, or *Cajun Folk Songs*) or original melodies or motives (*Postcard*), the composer's reliance on these understandable musical elements allows the listener to follow their progress of transformation and development through the course of the piece.

In *Vesuvius*, Ticheli's use of melodic and harmonic motives, at first hinted at early in the piece and then more fully developed as the work unfolds, is reminiscent of the forms and procedures of classical music. Other classical elements include key relationships (A phrygian to D aeolian, for example), a formal rondo structure, a variety of developmental inventions (canon, imitation, varieties of instrumentation), and contrasting masculine and feminine thematic subjects. On the other hand, the expressiveness displayed through the wide range of dynamics, the energy and fury of the primary theme juxtaposed with the soft lyricism of the B section theme, and the instrumentation for large symphonic band (including eighteen percussion instruments divided between three players) certainly suggest a turbulent,

---

1 John Thomson and Matthew Baumer, "Exploring Vesuvius with Frank Ticheli," *The Instrumentalist* 55, June 2001, p. 22.

romantic style of composition. Undoubtedly, the overall effectiveness of this work draws from both the classical and romantic styles of music.

Unit 4: Technical Considerations

The modal harmonic and melodic foundation of *Vesuvius* is an excellent study of scalar patterns that are increasingly being used by composers. Modes in the piece include phrygian (A), aeolian (D), lydian (B-flat), dorian (A), and a touch of major and minor. Appropriate lessons with an ensemble could include the study of both the formulas for composing each mode and the extramusical emotions and feelings each portrays. Since the harmonic foundation of these modes is presented in either tonic pedal tones or open fifths, intonation is a challenge. Additionally, intonation and ensemble tone color are greatly affected by the frequently loud dynamics and articulations.

Shifting mixed meters and uneven divisions of measures present a pulse and rhythm challenge. Measures in 9/8 (for example, the meter of the primary theme) are divided 2+3+2+2, forming a sort of uneven 4/4 measure. A challenge even for seasoned musicians, keeping the eighth note pulse constant and not turning the second beat into a triplet becomes an exercise in developing good counting skills.

Wide contrasts in dynamics and instrumentation are a prominent feature of *Vesuvius*, not just in *tutti* scoring but also in shifting combinations of instruments. A good relative sense of dynamic range, the technique to play with good tone and fast tempo, and the expressiveness to project subtle as well as overt dynamic expression are challenges for every ensemble member. Percussion colors abound, so in addition to maintaining a solid inner pulse, percussionists also need to have a firm grasp of a variety of techniques on their instruments. Also, with percussionists handling a minimum of five instruments (Percussion I, seven; Percussion II and III, five each), the section needs to be placed where there is adequate room for set-up and movement. (The composer assigns the variety of percussion instruments to three players but adds that two players could more easily manage the Percussion I part.)

Unit 5: Stylistic Considerations

To capture an older or "ancient" style of tonal center, the themes and harmonies in this work are based on a mixture of aeolian, dorian, lydian, and phrygian modes. These modes are easily understood by comparing the root notes of each mode with that of a C major scale. For example, the dorian mode is the scale that, using the notes of the C major scale, begins on D. The phrygian mode is the scale that begins on E, lydian on F, and aeolian on A. These modes, while not often encountered in many works for winds, are a refreshing variety to major or minor tonalities and can be introduced to musicians in this context where the modal sound is clearly heard in both the melodic and harmonic elements of this piece.

Two styles of playing dominate the work: an energetic, almost frenetic character that is occasionally accented and featured in a wide variety of dynamics, and a smooth, *legato* texture that moves almost as quickly as the 9/8 tempo. The driving, rhythmic nature of the first theme, masculine and forceful in nature, is a definite challenge for most ensembles. The 9/8 time signature is not felt as it usually is (three groups of three eighths, 3+3+3) but rather as an uneven four-beat pattern (2+3+2+2). The subdivision of eighth notes is essential to keep the second beat (three eighths) steady so it does not become a triplet rhythm. The composer, in a preface to the score, states,

> *Vesuvius* is, above all, a furious dance. In order to preserve the work's fiery energy, players must clearly communicate all indications of stress (e.g., accents, sfz markings). In addition, the tempo must not drag! In the premiere performance, we found that the energy could be effectively heightened by playing at an even faster tempo than is marked in the score [quarter note equals 168]. The players should keep in mind at all times that this is a dramatic work, both in the loud and quiet passages.[2]

Unit 6: Musical Elements

The melodic material is based on four distinct themes, with all four introduced in either the opening introduction or the first presentation of the A section. All themes are constructed upon, and supported harmonically by, various forms of phrygian, aeolian, dorian, and lydian modes, an interesting aural flavor of this piece. Classical forms of development of the themes include imitation of motives and motivic fragments, canonic imitation of themes, and the central tonic/dominant relationship of A phrygian and D aeolian. As can be expected in modal harmonies, intervals of a perfect fifth are a distinct feature of the harmonic texture. Instrumental textures vary greatly throughout the work, creating a challenge for maintaining a consistent, uninterrupted tempo. Interesting scoring in the work includes the rhythmic onomatopoeic use of "ch-ch" in the A section, the colorful variety of percussion instruments and effects, and the often drastic contrasts in dynamics. The latter requires a mature approach to independent playing, where one section or family of instruments might be in opposition to the dynamic textures of another. Finally, a strong inner pulse and consistency of tempo is a goal for the entire ensemble. The forward-moving, frenetic motion of the work is dependent on musicians who do not simply rely on the conductor for the beat but who have a strong, solid inner sense of keeping eighths and quarters steady and metronomic.

---

2 Frank Ticheli. *Vesuvius*. New York: Manhattan Beach Music, 1999.

Unit 7: Form and Structure

Section	Measure	Event and Scoring
Rondo Form: A–B–A–C–A		
Introduction	1–46	A phrygian, pedal point; hints of Themes 3 and 4; energetic 4/4 meter
A	47–103	9/8 meter (2+3+2+2); D aeolian tonality; first and second themes presented; "ch-ch" vocal effect in ensemble
Transition modulation	104–139	Change in texture to a slower, smoother rhythmic flow; instrumental effects include fluttertonguing in flute and a cymbal played on the head of a *glissando*/pedaled timpani
B	140–216	Shift in tonal center to A phrygian, dorian, and major; new meter in 3/4, with a tempo feeling "in one"; introduction of new Theme 3 in its entirety; tempo and texture changes
Transition	217–240	Eighth note motives in canon, drawing from material from introduction
A	241–279	Return to A section material, with a brief added modal shift to B-flat lydian
C	280–335	Juxtaposition of Themes 3 and 4; modal centers of A phrygian, C-sharp major, F phrygian, and ending the section in D minor
A	336–368	Final return of A material, with canonic variations of Theme 1; modal shifts between D and A aeolian
Coda	369–388	Fragments of Theme 1; unison ending in D aeolian

Unit 8: Suggested Listening

Amazing Grace – Timepieces, DePauw University Band, Craig Paré, conductor: Mark Records MCD 2877

Amazing Grace, Blue Shades, Cajun Folk Songs, Cajun Folk Songs II, Fortress, Gaian Visions, Pacific Fanfare, Songs of Tagore – "Blue Shades": The Music of Frank Ticheli, Michigan State University Wind Ensemble, John Whitwell, conductor: Mark Records MCD 2744

Blue Shades – Deja View, North Texas Wind Symphony, Eugene Migliaro Corporon, conductor: Klavier Records KCD 11091

Concertino for Trombone and Wind Ensemble – Suncircles, Baylor University Wind Ensemble,
Michael Haithcock, conductor: Mark Records MCD3

Pacific Fanfare – Bird Songs, North Texas Wind Symphony, Eugene Migliaro Corporon, conductor: Klavier Records KCD 11071

Postcard – Postcards, Cincinnati Wind Symphony, Eugene Migliaro Corporon, conductor: Klavier Records KCD 11058

Music for Winds and Percussion – Ithaca College Wind Ensemble, Rodney Winther, conductor: Mark Records MCBS 35891

Vesuvius – 1999 WASBE, North Texas Wind Symphony, Eugene Migliaro Corporon, conductor: Mark Records MCD 3144

Unit 9: Additional References and Resources

Battisti, Frank. *The Twentieth Century American Wind Band/Ensemble: History, Development, and Literature.* Fort Lauderdale, FL: Meredith Music Publications, 1995.

Corporon, Eugene, and David Wallace. *Wind Ensemble/Band Repertoire.* Greeley, CO: University of Northern Colorado, 1984.

Dvorak, Thomas L., Robert Grechesky, and Gary M. Ciepluch. *Best Music for High School Band.* Edited by Bob Margolis. Brooklyn, NY: Manhattan Beach Music, 1993.

Dvorak, Thomas L., Cynthia Crump Taggart, and Peter Schmaltz. *Best Music for Young Band.* Edited by Bob Margolis. Brooklyn, NY: Manhattan Beach Music, 1986.

Farkas, Philip. *The Art of Musicianship.* Bloomington, IN: Musical Publications, 1976.

Garofalo, Robert J. *Guides to Band Masterworks.* Fort Lauderdale, FL: Meredith Music Publications, 1992.

_____. *Instructional Designs for Middle/Junior High School Band.* Fort Lauderdale, FL: Meredith Music Publications, 1995.

Kreines, Joseph. *Music for Concert Band*. Tampa, FL: Florida Music Service, 1989.

Manhattan Beach Music:
http://members.aol.com/mbmband/index.html

Rehrig, William H. *The Heritage Encyclopedia of Band Music*. Edited by Paul E. Bierley. Westerville, OH: Integrity Press, 1991.

Stolba, K Marie. *The Development of Western Music*. Dubuque, IA: William C. Brown Publishers, 1990.

Thomson, John, and Matthew Baumer, "Exploring Vesuvius with Frank Ticheli," *The Instrumentalist* 55, June 2001, pp. 22–6.

Watkins, Glenn. *Soundings*. New York: Schirmer Books, 1988.

Contributed by:

Craig T. Paré
Associate Professor of Music
Director of University Bands
DePauw University School of Music
Greencastle, Indiana

Teacher Resource Guide

Yiddish Dances

Adam Gorb
(b. 1958)

Unit 1: Composer

Adam Gorb, currently Head of School of Composition and Contemporary Music at the Royal Northern College of Music in Manchester, England, started composing at the age of ten. A selection of his set of piano pieces (*A Pianist's Alphabet*) that he composed at the age of fifteen was performed on BBC Radio 3 in 1976. Gorb graduated in 1980 from Cambridge University, where he studied with Hugh Wood and Robin Holloway while he earned his Masters of Music from the Royal Academy of Music with highest honors, including the Principal's Prize.

Recent compositions include a Viola Concerto written for Martin Outram and the Docklands *Sinfonietta; Metropolis for Wind Band,* which has won several prizes including the Walter Beeler Memorial Prize in the USA in 1994; *Prelude, Interlude and Postlude* for piano, which won the Purcell Composition Prize in 1995; *Kol Simcha* (1995), a ballet given over fifty performances by the Rambert Dance Company; a Violin Sonata premiered at the Spitalfields Festival in 1996, *Awayday* for wind band, which has had several hundred performances since its premiere in 1996, and a Percussion Concerto given its first performance by Evelyn Glennie and the Royal Northern College of Music Wind Ensemble, also in 1998.[1]

Yiddish Dances was written in 1998 for the sixtieth birthday of Timothy Reynish, conductor of the Royal Northern College of Music Symphonic Wind Orchestra. The work was premiered by Mr. Reynish at Royal Northern College of Music in Manchester, England, on March 9, 1998.

---

1 Adam Gorb, telephone interview, October 2001.

Unit 2: Composition

As Gorb indicates, *Yiddish Dances* is "very much a party piece. It brings together two of my abiding musical passions: the Symphonic Wind Orchestra and klezmer—the folk music of the Yiddish-speaking people."[2] In a recent conversation, Gorb indicated that the work was an opportunity for him to explore his Russian Yiddish heritage since the five-movement work is based on klezmer dances.[3]

The fourteen- to fifteen-minute work begins with the "Khosidl," or scissor dance, whose medium tempo in 2/4 meter moves freely between satire, sentimentality, and pathos. The "Terkische," an up-tempo Jewish tango, is followed by the "Doina," which is a free recitative in which various instruments have an opportunity to shine. Although the solos are written out, the intent is one of an improvisatory style that showcases the virtuosity of the performer, much like a cadenza in classical music. The "Hora" follows with a slow 3/8 time, employing a characteristically rocking rhythm. The accompaniment often plays on one and three while two is silent. The work closes with the "Frelachs," which is a very fast 2/4 time recalling the themes from the previous movements and ending in a riotous "booze-up" for all concerned, as Gorb states.[4]

Unit 3: Historical Perspective

Since *Yiddish Dances* is based on klezmer music, it is critical to understand the history of the Yiddish people and background of the music. This author highly recommends locating a klezmer expert in the community and inviting him/her to perform and clinic your ensemble. This author secured Mr. Amrom Chodos, Director of Bands at Barker High School, New York, who is a klezmer expert. His pictures, performance, and recordings were extremely helpful in understanding the culture and particularly the performance style of the repertoire.[5]

Klezmorim were either wandering minstrels who earned their living by traveling from town to town or who were part of the local shtetl band. Since there was not a standard interpretation of tunes, the wandering Klezmorim were often influenced by other ethnic styles. In the 1870s when recordings became popular, standardized versions were established.

Klezmorim performed a prescribed repertoire for the Jewish wedding with specific dances for members of the family and friends. Wedding guests who requested a dance were obliged to pay the Klezmorim. For instance, the Rumanian Hora was used to accompany the elderly members of the family

---

2 Adam Gorb, *Yiddish Dances*, Maecenas Music, 1998 preface.

3 Adam Gorb, telephone interview, October 2001.

4 Gorb, *Yiddish Dances*, preface.

5 Amrom Chodos, Klezmer expert, interview and clinic, State University of New York, Fredonia, New York, 15 October 2001.

home at the end of the wedding. Jewish musicians also played at functions such as the dedication of a new Torah, a new shul, or to accompany the Shabesklaper as he made his rounds reminding the townspeople to prepare for the Sabes.

Klezmer band instrumentation varied greatly in the seventeenth century but used primarily string instruments. The early nineteenth century saw the rise of the clarinet. Since both the clarinet and violin could emulate the voice, they were often chosen as the melodic instrument. By the end of the nineteenth century, brass instruments were added to klezmer bands. As the presence of Jewish population increased in military bands, which used considerable brass, the Jewish people who served in these bands learned to play these brass instruments.[6]

Unit 4: Technical Considerations

Technical considerations are about style rather than technique, as the style will dictate the technique. For instance, in klezmer music, the trills do not start above the pitch but rather start a minor sixth above the written pitch to imitate the cracking of the voice. The bending imitates laughing or crying. The piccolo, flute, E-flat clarinet, B-flat clarinet, oboe, bassoon, alto saxophone, trumpet, trombone, and tuba are featured in recitative solos in the "Doina." These instrumentalists must listen to and imitate the klezmer style. Scat-singing this style would certainly be an effective preparation technique.

Unit 5: Stylistic Considerations

Listening to live or at least a recording of klezmer music is essential in understanding the style. One cannot describe in words the inflections needed for a rendition with integrity. Remember that the goal is to imitate the emotions portrayed by the human voice, such as laughter, tears, love, happiness, and despair.

Unit 6: Musical Elements

MELODY:

The melodies are actually written with the klezmer ornamentation incorporated. An interesting comparison can be made between baroque and klezmer ornamentation. Just as in baroque ornamentation, many practices have been passed down through the generations prior to recordings. The performers must listen to the klezmer performance to truly understand the inflections.[7] One could also compare these musical inflections to different dialects of a language. For instance, accents of the English language can sound

---

6 Amrom Chodos, Klezmer expert, interview and clinic, State University of New York, Fredonia, New York, 15 October 2001.

7 Chodos interview.

British, southern, midwestern, Bostonian, and Canadian, but the language is still English.

HARMONY:

Klezmer is primarily modal music. While the scales used have an *oriental* feel, in Yiddish they are called *gustn*. The Freygish mode is characterized by the augmented second between the second and third degrees, while the Misheberakh employs the raised fourth scale degree.[8]

RHYTHM:

The rhythms of the "Khosidl" could be conceived as a heavy downbeat on one and an afterbeat feel on two or "boom, chuck." However, with the inflections of the klezmer scissor dance feel, an entirely different rhythmic feel emerges that must continually drive ahead both harmonically and rhythmically. The tempo indication of the "Khosidl" is eighth note = 132, but it must be conducted in two with the *backbeat feel*. The integrity and style of the subdivision must drive the Terkishe rhythm.[9]

Unit 7: Form and Structure

SECTION	REHEARSAL NO.	KEY AREA
"Khosidl"		
Introduction and A	Opening	C-sharp unison
A and A'	1	G, A, B-flat, C-sharp, D, E-flat, F-sharp
B and B'	2	
B and B'	3	
Extension	4	
A	5	
A' and Extension	6	
C	7	
C'	8	D-flat
Extension	9	
Unison	10	C-sharp
Codetta	11	G

"Terkishe"

This movement develops a melody through various orchestrations and expansions. The rhythmic underpinning begins in the snare drum and eventually becomes chordal through the orchestration of the low brass and reeds at m. 17. An answering motive is stated in the bassoon and also is reorchestrated and expanded throughout the tango. The song weaves through

8 Gorb interview.
9 Gorb interview.

the instrumentation from a unison clarinet opening to a variation in augmentation at mm. 17 and 20. An *obbligato* in piccolo and oboe joins the clarinet at m. 15 outlining the minor third.

The most significant musical element is the rhythm, which is driven by the opening snare drum measure containing a dotted-eighth followed by a sixteenth and two eighth notes. The dotted-sixteenth/thirty-second and triplet sixteenth subdivisions of the melodic line contrast this rhythm. These first melodic rhythms often outline the fifth while the triplet sixteenths outline the minor third. This interplay of rhythm creates the style of the tango, while the inflection of the minor thirds outlined by the rhythms also provides the harmony.

REHEARSAL NO.	SONG	ANSWERING MOTIVE OR B THEME	RHYTHMIC MOTIVE
Opening	Clarinet	Bass clarinet	Snare underpinning
15	Saxophone	Clarinet	Snare, low reeds, and tuba
17	Saxophone	Clarinet	Low brass and reeds; chordal
20	Upper woodwinds	1st trumpet and trombone	Low brass and horn

REHEARSAL NO.	MELODIC DEVELOPMENT
21	Development of motives
23	Canonic entrances of song motive
24	After-beat chords that drive to the end overcome pyramid entrances over rhythmic motive underpinnings

"Doina"

The next dance, the "Doina," emerges from the final chord of the previous dance through a sustained A major chord played by the stopped horns. The "Doina" is comprised of cadenzas by E-flat clarinet, trumpet, trombone, alto saxophone, and flute, with brief interjections by piccolo, oboe, trombone, and tuba. Each cadenza is accompanied by various chords, which change the accompaniment color through different orchestrations. The Yiddish scale emphasizes the upper tones of D, E, and E-flat.

"Hora"

The "Hora" is again reorchestrated throughout and driven with a rhythmic accompaniment that employs punctuating chords on one and three. The opening statement in trumpet, followed by the answering augmented phrase of the trombone and descending line in bass clarinet, summarizes most of the motives for this movement. At m. 32, the theme moves to E-flat clarinet, which is joined by B-flat clarinet countermelody. At m. 36, the dance alters between a feeling of *piu mosso* and *meno mosso*, returning to the *meno mosso* at m. 37 but then repeating the pattern at m. 38 until the good times start to subside at m. 40 as the dance returns to the simple theme at m. 42. The earlier trombone melody is often harmonized in thirds throughout the dance.

"Freylachs"

The "Hora" moves directly into the "Freylachs," which begins with a "boom-chuck" accompaniment. The "Freylachs" dance is a huge wind-up as it builds with repeated statements of the dance until it propels into the "Khosidl" tempo and melody briefly. The dances are briefly reviewed with the "Hora" return at m. 55 with an interesting turning around of the beat as the accompaniment spins into the 2/4 feeling again at m. 57. This feeling is accomplished through the use of the melodic hemiola in the bass line. The "Khosidl" tempo emerges at m. 63, but this simply sets the stage for the gradual *accelerando* to the end, which depicts parties propelling to a joyous close.

Unit 8: Suggested Listening

Klezmer! Jewish Music from Old World to Our World: Yazoo Records
Klezmer Pioneers 1905–1952: Rounder Records
Dave Tarras, Yiddish-American Klezmer Music 1925–1956: Yazoo Records
The Klezmer Conservatory Band: Old World Beat: Rounder Records

Unit 9: Additional References and Resources

Le Chaim! Attendance at an event featuring klezmer music would be the only true way to capture the meaning and style of this music. Ideally, it should be an event of Yiddish-speaking people so one could hear the wonderful inflections, which reflect the energy and passion of these people. Le Chaim! (To Life) At the very least, learn how to pronounce Le Chaim!

Contributed by:

Paula Holcomb
Director of Bands and Professor of Music
State University of New York College at Fredonia
Fredonia, New York

Grade Six

Teacher Resource Guide

American Games

Nicholas Maw
(b. 1935)

Unit 1: Composer

Nicholas Maw was born in Grantham, Lincolnshire, England, on November 5, 1935. While attending the Royal Academy of Music in London, he studied composition with Lennox Berkeley and harmony and counterpoint with Paul Steinitz. He lived in Paris during 1958 and 1959 on a scholarship from the French government, where he studied composition with Nadia Boulanger and analysis with Max Deutsch. Although he has been a full-time composer virtually all of his professional life, Maw has also taught for most of that time as well, having been associated with Trinity College Cambridge, Exeter University, Yale University, Boston University, and Bard College. Currently, he is Professor of Composition at the Peabody Conservatory in Baltimore. Among the numerous commissions and honors awarded Maw, *American Games* won the Sudler Wind Band Composition Competition Prize in 1991.

Unit 2: Composition

American Games was commissioned by the BBC for the 1991 Promenade Concerts and was premiered by the Royal Northern College of Music Wind Band, conducted by Timothy Reynish, in the Royal Albert Hall in London, on July 23, 1991. The work is published by Faber Music Ltd., and a study score (ISBN 0 571 51444 8) is available for purchase. The parts, along with a large score, are available on rental. *American Games* is comprised of an introduction, seven movements, and a coda, which are connected without pause for a total duration of approximately twenty-two minutes. The work is scored for a slightly expanded orchestral wind section: three flutes (2nd doubling alto flute, 3rd doubling piccolo), three oboes, E-flat clarinet (which may optionally be doubled with the alto saxophone part), three clarinets in B-flat and A, alto saxophone, two bassoons, contrabassoon, four horns, three trumpets in B-flat, two tenor trombones, bass trombone, euphonium, two tubas, timpani, and three percussionists. While the work is masterfully orchestrated, Maw chose not to employ instruments such as English horn, bass clarinet, piano, harp, or string bass; the percussion requirements also do not include instruments that would generally be regarded as exotic. In terms of difficulty, using whichever yardstick one might choose to apply—technique, range, rhythm, meter, and especially musical maturity—*American Games* requires outstanding players and, thus, is clearly a grade six work.

Unit 3: Historical Perspective

Both the older and most recent *New Grove* articles on Maw discuss his compositional style at some length, and these articles should be consulted. As is true of many composers whose professional life has spanned the second half of the twentieth century, Maw's musical language has undergone evolution and change in pursuit of his personal voice. In Maw's case, one work displays much of this evolution. *Odyssey*, a work for large orchestra that Maw wrote between 1972 and 1987, is an aural map of his development as a composer; the title refers not to the Greek myth but to Maw's personal journey as he composed the piece over this unusually long span of time. The work is almost one hundred minutes of continuous music and is believed to be the longest purely orchestral piece in existence. Although *American Games* does not often "sound like" *Odyssey*, this author believes nonetheless that listening to the latter would be of great benefit in studying the former. *Odyssey* is, for instance, both more dense texturally and less consonant harmonically than *American Games*, but one can hear in *Odyssey*, particularly in the central slow movement, the kind of melodic beauty and deft chord spacing that allows the slow movements of *American Games* to "sing" so beautifully. Rather than assign a label to a work or a composer to understand them, something Maw himself abhors,[1] perhaps the best way to place *American Games* in context is to listen to as much of Maw's music as possible, certainly including *Odyssey*, and decide for oneself. Finally, it is interesting to note that *American Games* was written within the same twelve-month period as *Ceremonial* by Bernard Rands and *Three City Blocks* by John Harbison. This connection is made explicit by Daniel Gordon's review of these three works in the endnotes to this resource guide. Since these works are arguably three of the most important wind band pieces composed in the 1990s, and since these composers are virtually contemporaneous, listening to and studying Rands and Harbison in tandem with *American Games* might prove fruitful.

---

1 Byrne, Frank. Program notes to the United States Marine Band recording, USMC-13, 1997.

Unit 4: Technical Considerations

As previously mentioned, *American Games* requires musically mature performers with advanced technical ability. The most technically demanding movements are I, IV, and VII, and although much of the difficulty in these movements is arpeggio or scale-oriented, some of the writing employs the use of sharps and double sharps in combinations that even experienced players will have to work out slowly and carefully, particularly in the first movement. Maw does not use key signatures, but the local tonic areas are easy to discern and identify, making it possible for the conductor (or the players) to isolate problems and devise exercises to surmount them, if desired. One example in this regard would be the extended bassoon *soli*, which begins the seventh movement. Although the passage is extremely rapid, the pitch content oscillates between D major and F major, making it somewhat reasonable to work out and master.

Unit 5: Stylistic Considerations

The harmonic language of *American Games* is clearly pitch-centric throughout; Movement II is the most chromatic and employs extended tertiary harmonies that sound bi-tonal. Movement VI, which Maw describes as "my version of a Baptist hymn,"[2] employs functional, common-practice tonality. Even with three slow movements and an introduction that might strike some listeners as somber, the overall spirit of the work is ebullient, as Maw's inscription, "affectionately...to our friends in Washington, DC,"[3] might imply. The piece contains different types of both slow and fast music; thus, there are multiple styles and effects present in the work. As a whole, *American Games* should quickly appeal to both audience and ensemble, while possessing enough depth to reward continuing study.

Unit 6: Musical Elements

MELODY:

Much of the melodic material in *American Games* is diatonic, as one might expect in a work that is so clearly pitch-centric. Because the pitch centers shift rapidly in the faster movements—a process once called "phrase modulation"—the fingers and ears of the players will have to become accustomed to these changes to be convincing. The slower movements present the more usual demands of projection, expressive playing, and tonal control.

HARMONY:

The preponderance of triadic harmony means that advanced ensembles, or those that work regularly on chorales or other tonal material, should not have undue difficulties in this area. The chords in the second movement will

2 Ibid.
3 Maw, Nicholas. *American Games*. London: Faber Music Ltd, 1996.

require close inspection by the conductor; this is perhaps the one place in the work where discussing the vertical sonorities in rehearsal would be helpful to the players.

RHYTHM:

No rhythms in *American Games* should be problematic for the caliber of ensemble that would be performing the work, with the important exception of the fifth movement, which is almost entirely in the meter of 5/16+2/8. Since the given tempo is quarter note = 126, most conductors will conduct this using a slightly imbalanced two pattern. This difficulty is somewhat mitigated because an *ostinato* pattern recurs throughout which, if performed accurately, can anchor the movement. Movements I and VII contain 15/8 and 18/8 meter. While this is not difficult conceptually, it may require a brief explanation to the players once the conductor has decided which patterns are appropriate.

TIMBRE:

As previously mentioned, Maw eschews several instruments that could be called "color" instruments, but that does not mean the work is not orchestrated with imagination and care. Indeed, Maw's approach to scoring could properly be called "orchestral" in the same way Ingolf Dahl used that term when writing about his *Sinfonietta*: a play of pure colors. For instance, although the alto saxophone is used sparingly, the few prominent solos given to it seem absolutely "right." Also of particular note is the third movement; a careful examination of the voicing and spacing of the chordal accompaniment will reveal Maw's skill in providing rich and resonant harmonic support while allowing the solo voices ample room, sonically, to be heard.

Unit 7: Form and Structure

American Games is unified at the largest level by the D major tonality, which emerges in the introduction and concludes the entire work. The opening trumpet and horn statements also return at the end, adding to the cyclic effect. Most of the variations have forms that are discernible, which are given in the table below. Although the work as a whole is not a theme and variations, the third movement is based on the introductory material; the alto saxophone solo that begins the movement is quite closely related, and each successive phrase moves farther away from that theme. Some of the variations are clearly in a key, while others shift very rapidly or have an ambiguous sense of pitch center. The chart below is no substitute for an in-depth flowchart, which should be done for the entire work, but it should provide a brief overview of the organization of *American Games*.

	Tempo	Primary Meter(s)	Form	Primary Pitch Centers	Important Solos or *Soli*
Introduction	Half note = 60	2/2	Two long phrases	D	Trumpet Horn
I	Dotted quarter note = 144–152	9/8 12/8 15/8 18/8	ABA'	Several	Virtually entire ensemble
II	Quarter note = 58	4/4	Two long phrase groups	Unstable	1st flute Alto flute
III	Quarter note = 44, 54	12/8	Variation	D	Alto saxophone 1st oboe 1st flute 1st/2nd clarinet Horn a4 1st trumpet
IV	Quarter note = 152	4/4 3/4	ABA'	Unstable	Most of the ensemble
V	Quarter note = 126	5/16 2/8	Strophic	Several	Trombone 1st flute 1st oboe
VI	Quarter note = 100	3/4	ABA'	F	1st flute Euphonium
VII	Dotted-quarter note = 144–152	9/8 12/8 15/8 18/8	Free sectional	Several	1st bassoon Bassoon a2 *soli*
Coda	Half note = 60	2/2		D	1st trumpet 1st horn

Unit 8: Suggested Listening

Nicholas Maw:

American Games – CCM Wind Symphony, Eugene Corporon, conductor: Klavier: KCD 11047, 1993

American Games – "American Games: Twentieth Century Classics for Winds." United States Marine Band, Timothy W. Foley, director: USMB-CD-13, 1997

Odyssey – City of Birmingham Symphony Orchestra, Simon Rattle, conductor: EMI Classics CDS 7-54277-2, 1991

Unit 9: Additional References and Resources

Gordon, Daniel. "Band Music." *Notes,* Volume 55, No. 1, 5 September 1998, pp. 199–201.

This article is a review and comparison of three works for wind ensemble: *American Games, Three City Blocks* by John Harbison and *Ceremonial* by Bernard Rands.

Sadie, Stanley, ed. *The New Grove Dictionary of Music and Musicians.* London: Macmillan Publishers Limited, 1980. S.v. "Nicholas Maw," by Bayan Northcott.

The New Grove Dictionary of Music and Musicians. Second edition. London: Macmillan Publishers Limited, 2001. S.v. "Nicholas Maw," by Andrew Burn.

While the information in the newer *Grove* article is obviously more current, reading both articles provides an interesting overview of Maw's work from two complementary perspectives.

Websites:
Information regarding Nicholas Maw is also available on several websites, including those maintained by the Peabody Conservatory (www.peabody.jhu.edu) and Boosey & Hawkes (www.boosey.com), publisher of Maw's early works. The most recent and extensive information, however, is available on the site of Faber Music Ltd. (www.fabermusic.co.uk), Maw's publisher since 1980.

Contributed by:

Gary Speck
Professor of Conducting
Miami University
Oxford, Ohio

Teacher Resource Guide

Canvas

George Theophilus Walker, Jr.
(b. 1922)

Unit 1: Composer

George Theophilus Walker, Jr., was born on June 27, 1922, in Washington, DC. He was born into a musical family, and it was important to his parents that he and his sister had exposure to good music throughout their youth. While a student at Dunbar High School, Walker studied piano with Lillian Baskerville Mitchell Allen at the Howard University School of Music Junior Preparatory Division. Having entered Oberlin College at the age of fourteen, Walker graduated with a Bachelor of Music in Piano, with highest honors, in 1941. At Oberlin, he studied piano with David Moyer, organ with Arthur Croley and Arthur Poister, and composition with Normand Lockwood. After doing some graduate work at Oberlin, Walker entered the Curtis Institute where, in 1945, he would became the first black graduate. There he studied piano with Rudolph Serkin and Mieczyslaw Horszowski, composition with Rosario Scalero, orchestration with Gian Carlo Menotti, and chamber music with Gregor Piatigorsky and William Primrose. Walker earned Artist Diplomas in both piano and composition. He went on to earn an Artist Diploma in piano from the American Academy in Fontainbleau in 1947, where he studied with Robert Casadesus. A man of many "firsts," Walker became the first black student to earn the Doctor of Musical Arts degree from Eastman in 1956, where he studied with José Echániz. After Eastman, Walker spent two years in Paris studying with Nadia Boulanger, supported by a Fulbright and a John Hay Whitney Fellowship.

Walker's New York debut recital at Town Hall in 1945 was one of his early performing triumphs. Two weeks later he appeared with Eugene Ormandy and the Philadelphia Orchestra, performing Rachmaninoff's *Third Piano Concerto*. This performance was the result of winning the Philadelphia Youth Auditions while a student at Curtis. The premiere of Walker's first important composition, *Lament for Strings* (later called *Lyric for Strings*) was in 1947, the same year he performed Brahms's *Piano Concerto in B-flat Major* with the Baltimore Symphony. Throughout the 1950s and 1960s, Walker appeared in solo recitals with leading symphony orchestras throughout the United States and Europe. After developing an illness while on his first tour, he began to have doubts about his ability to perform frequently. It was at this time that he considered putting his efforts toward composing and teaching.

Walker has held teaching positions in piano, composition, and music theory at a number of universities including Dillard University, Dalcroze School of Music, New School for Social Research, Smith College, University of Colorado at Boulder, Peabody Institute Conservatory, University of Delaware, and Rutgers University. He did most of his teaching at Rutgers from 1969 until his retirement in 1992, teaching piano, theory, music history, and composition. From 1975 to 1977, he was chairman of the music department at Rutgers.

Walker's composition output is prodigious. His published catalog (MMB Music, Inc.) exceeds seventy works, which include instrumental and vocal solos, chamber music, and orchestral, wind, and choral music. In addition to his *Lyric for Strings*, he is also known for his *Sonata No. 2 for Piano, Music for Brass (Sacred and Profane), Folk Songs for Orchestra, Poem for Soprano and Chamber Ensemble*, and *Lilacs. Lilacs*, for voice and orchestra, received the Pulitzer Prize for Music in 1996. Walker was the first black composer to be so honored. In addition to the Pulitzer, he has received numerous awards, including an American Academy and Institute of Arts and Letters Award (1982), two Koussevitsky Fellowships (1988, 1998), two Guggenheim awards (1969, 1988), and several Rockefeller awards, MacDowell Colony Fellowships, and National Endowment for the Arts grants.

Unit 2: Composition

Canvas was commissioned by the College Band Directors National Association Consortium in the Fall of 1999 for the CBDNA Biennium National Conference at the University of North Texas in February of 2001. The University of North Texas Wind Symphony, conducted by Eugene Migliaro Corporon, premiered the work on February 22, 2001, in the Murchison Performing Arts Center in Denton, Texas.

Canvas, which is dedicated to Walker's parents, is comprised of three substantial movements that can be performed together or separately. Extract 1, Landscape ("The View Below") is seven minutes in length and is composed for winds alone. Extract II, Commentary ("Voices in the Corridor") is five minutes in length and utilizes five narrators in addition to winds. Extract III,

Psalm 121 ("The Horizon and Beyond") is seven minutes and thirty seconds in length and is composed for SATB chorus and winds. Total performance time is approximately twenty minutes. The work is scored for piccolo, three flutes, alto flute, two oboes, English horn, E-flat clarinet, two B-flat clarinets, bass clarinet, alto saxophone (only used for one measure!), two bassoons, contrabassoon, four horns, four C trumpets, two trombones, bass trombone, tuba, timpani, celesta, harp, and contrabass. There is a considerable amount of percussion writing. Percussion instruments include: glockenspiel, xylophone, vibraphone, marimba, chimes, triangle, wood blocks, temple blocks, claves, maracas, castanets, tambourine, suspended cymbal, anvil, timbales, snare drum, bass drum, roto-toms, tam-tam, and glass wind chimes.

Canvas is an extremely challenging work due to the nature of Walker's complex pointillistic scoring and rhythmic sophistication, the coordination of the narrators, and the difficulty of the divided choral parts. Walker considers *Canvas* considerably more complicated than *Lilacs*, for which he won the 1996 Pulitzer Prize for Music. He states, "I have expended an enormous amount of time and thought on it, more than with any work in years."

Unit 3: Historical Perspective

Walker, who has often been described as an "eclectic" twentieth century composer, combines modern techniques with a traditional romantic spirit. His music, which appeals to a wide variety of listeners, is comprised of traditional musical materials, serial techniques, complex rhythms, and engaging melodies. Some of his music is infused with a sometimes subtle and other times obvious use of black folk, jazz, and popular idioms. His compositional style melds the techniques of Schoenberg, Stravinksy, and Hindemith through the use of twelve-tone melodic conception, motivic development, rhythmic and scoring complexity, and counterpoint. Much like Debussy and Ravel, Walker's pianistic background shapes his instrumental composition.

Canvas falls into a category of its own in regard to wind music. Walker is one of few Pulitzer Prize composers and one of the only African-American composers to have composed a piece of this scope for the medium. *Canvas* is also one in a handful of works for winds that involve a full chorus and narrator.

Unit 4: Technical Considerations

Canvas requires a great deal of independent and soloistic playing. Doublings are relatively rare, and performers must be able to understand the role of their seemingly isolated part within the composite structure of the contrapuntal texture. Therefore, sufficient rehearsal time is needed to realize the "chamber-like" integration of the work. Although the tempi throughout the piece are decidedly slow, much of the rhythmic activity occurs at the sixteenth note and thirty-second note level. Due to this and the prevalence of irregular meter, much of the first and second movements must be conducted at the eighth note. Tempo control is critical for the conductor—for when there is relaxed rhythmic activity, the tempo is usually marked under 50 beats per minute (at the quarter note). Ranges for the brass are quite reasonable, which is more than made up for by exposed and technically challenging motives. Most of the woodwinds and brass are asked to double tongue at various times, although Walker has given "his blessing" to single tonguing in clarinet and oboe.

Extract II requires five narrators who must possess a high degree of musical literacy. The rhythm of the text is specifically notated and quite complex. In addition, the pacing of the "free" text must be performed within the context of surrounding changing metrical structure. Walker expressly requests that the five narrators (soprano, two tenors, baritone, and bass) be actors, that each have a microphone, and that they are positioned on the stage in a specific arrangement. A reverb unit is to be used for the baritone. It is critical that the narrators are able to read a complex score. It should be pointed out that the saxophone's only musical contribution in the work is comprised of seven notes at the end of this movement. Unavailability or availability of a saxophonist should not be a factor in selecting this work.

The concluding movement, Extract III, is the least difficult movement for the instrumentalists. Most of the technical concerns center around the SATB choir. Walker's choral writing is highly syncopated and dissonant. The parts are slow and sustained, and often split. Ranges are reasonable, although the short tenor solo includes a high B-flat. The choral parts are rarely doubled, and there is an extended *a cappella* section midway through the movement.

Unit 5: Stylistic Considerations

Walker's mosaic of sound created by his pointillistic style of composition is quite specifically marked. Articulations and dynamics are well defined. The key stylistic consideration is the understanding of role of individual points of sound within a composite melodic line or harmony. Wind players must mimic the accents, note length, and decay of the percussion instruments that are integrated within the musical texture. The use of mutes in the brass instruments requires some modifications in dynamics and articulation style. A rhythmically precise approach is required to maximize the complex scoring. The narrators in Extract II must perform the text poetically within a defined rhythmic structure. Syllable and word accent is not marked and must be defined by the conductor and performers. The pacing of free text segments is often very fast and must be coherent. Because this pacing is defined by the wind and percussion writing, certain modifications may be made to start the free text sections slightly earlier or later than marked. Because of the use of microphones, the wind and percussion writing is not accompanimental. The voices and instruments can be considered one organic whole. There are very often soaring melodic lines that exist within an angular texture. Care should be taken to differentiate between the styles. Aware of Walker's fondness for jazz and popular musical devices, it is appropriate for the saxophone melody in the second movement to be a bit "jazzy." Stylistic considerations for Extract III consist mainly of the sustained gestures and the need for diction and textural clarity in the choral parts. As in the instrumental parts, the choral parts are well articulated.

Unit 6: Musical Elements

The melodic material in *Canvas* is mainly comprised of short motivic devices that are often passed between voices. Many times these short melodic ideas are the result of hocket scoring. Variations of these motives are combined in different ways throughout the work. The final choral movement is designed in much the same manner, though the choir retains most of the melodic material.

The harmonic language is decidedly twentieth century. Walker employs serial and motivic devices to create relative tonal areas. The intervallic relationships within the melodic motives themselves determine perceived harmony which, in turn, helps achieve a coherent unity within each movement.

Rhythmic materials are of a highly complex and subdivided nature. The abundance of asymmetrical and polyrhythmic devices are often unified by forward moving *ostinati*. These *ostinati*, which are most prevalent in the first and second movements, function as both melodic motives and motoring rhythms. The organic manner in which melodic and rhythmic motives are morphed into each other is the foundation of *Canvas's* compositional logic.

The timbral unification of wind and percussion sounds is a hallmark of the work. The thin texture and chamber group scoring achieves an amazing clarity and variety of tone color. Timbral modification of melodic motives is used throughout as a device of variation.

Unit 7: Form and Structure

EXTRACT I, LANDSCAPE ("THE VIEW BELOW")
Extract I is in a two-part form, which is organized by "cells" of motivic ideas. The cells, which are quite short at the outset of the movement, gradually increase in size and complexity. Many of these cells are marked by *fermatas*, changes in tempo, or changes in meter. The ten cells in the first half of the movement are quite distinct, becoming more organically integrated into large "cell areas" in the second half.

SECTION	MEASURE
Part I	1–47
Cell 1	1–2

Section	Measure
Cell 2	3–7
Cell 3	8–14
Cell 4	15–16
Cell 5	17–25
Cell 6	26–29
Cell 7	30–33
Cell 8	34–35
Cell 9	36–40
Cell 10	41–47
Part II	48–112
Area 1	48–55
Area 2	55–78
Area 3	79–102
Area 4	103–112

EXTRACT II, COMMENTARY ("VOICES IN THE CORRIDOR")
The motivic cells of movement one are continued throughout the second movement as well. The importance of the melodic motive as a unifying device for each cell is overshadowed by the rhythmic pacing of the narration. After an introduction, the narration is presented in two sections, separated by a short instrumental interlude.

Section	Measure
Introduction	1–9
Part I	10–28

Baritone:	If I were you…
Tenor 1:	It's just a thought, mind you, just a thought.
Tenor 2:	Pure speculation, I would say, that stretches even my imagination.
Tenor 1:	Clearly a hypothetical factor when measured on a scale of one to nine hundred sixty-eight and a half with only a 2 percent margin of error.
Baritone:	The old cheese, is still, still porous!
Bass:	Hah, he's at it again—there's obviously a message that he wants to send.
Tenor 2:	Whatever's on his mind may augur something important in due time.
Tenor 1:	Consider, if you will, certain issues that remain unchanged and unresolved still.

SECTION	MEASURE		
		Baritone:	Think about it!
		Tenor 1:	Certain attitudes that persist towards persons displaced, excluded and stigmatized by race should be excised now, if we insist.
		Tenor 2:	Fill us in, brother!
		Baritone:	We could converse on many subjects like this, even worse.
Interlude	29–38		
Part II	37–67		
		Tenor 1:	It can be said with some assurance, that may be perceived by some as arrogance, that if we are determined to obliterate the strata of inequity that victimizes the dispossessed, and if we repudiate the polarizing patterns embedded in years of sanctioned neglect, and if we voice our objection to the propagation of the violent activity that threatens to destroy the moral fabric of our society...
		Soprano:	Let's not forget those pandering, posturing, political puppets!
		Tenor 1:	I'm sure that you understand the drift of this...
		Tenor 2:	It can be said, yes, it should be said, and certainly must be said...
		Baritone:	Another word to be heard?
		Tenor 1:	With this, I venture to say, regarding other matters of extreme gravity— there's more to be said; but, we must move ahead.
		Soprano:	I must confess—this leaves me more than a little bit distressed.
		Bass:	May I ask, who will be challenged by this task?
		Tenor 2:	It's just a thought, just a thought, mind you.
		Baritone:	If I were you...

SECTION	MEASURE	
Bass:		A premise, in this case, to be considered another time—another place.

EXTRACT III, PSALM 121 ("THE HORIZON AND BEYOND")
The final movement is organized by the choral text. After a very brief introduction, each section is comprised of two lines of Psalm 121. The repetition of the final line of the text serves as the coda.

SECTION	MEASURE
Introduction	1–4
Part I	5–28 I will lift up mine eyes unto the hills, from whence cometh my help. My help cometh from the Lord, which made heaven and earth.
Part II	29–42 He will not suffer thy foot to be moved: He that keepeth thee will not slumber. Behold, He that keepeth Israel shall neither slumber nor sleep.
Part III	43–53 The Lord is thy keeper: the Lord is thy shade upon thy right hand. The sun shall note smite thee by day, nor the moon by night.
Part IV	54–76 The Lord shall preserve thee from all evil: He shall preserve thy soul. The Lord shall preserve thy going out and thy coming in from this time forth, and even for evermore.
Coda	77–85 The Lord shall preserve thy going out and thy coming in from this time forth, and even for evermore. *Credo in unum deum.*

Unit 8: Suggested Listening

Albany Records has produced several CDs of George Walker's music:

George Walker (Troy 154) includes *Piano Sonata No. 2, Sonata for Cello and Piano, Poem for Soprano and Chamber Ensemble, Sonata for Violin and Piano No. 1, Music for Brass, Sacred and Profane.*

Canvas – Time Pieces, North Texas Wind Symphony, Eugene Migliaro Corporon, conductor: Klavier 11122 (2001)

George Walker: A Portrait (Troy 136) includes *Five Fancies for Clarinet and Piano Four Hands, Antifonys for Chamber Orchestra, An Eastman Overture, Variations for Orchestra, Cantata for Soprano, Tenor, Boys Choir and Chamber Orchestra, Three Pieces for Organ.*

George Walker (Troy 270) includes *Serenata for Chamber Orchestra, Lyric for Strings, Orpheus for Chamber Orchestra, Poème for Violin and Orchestra.*

Unit 9: Additional References and Resources

Clague, M. "George Theophilus Walker, Jr." *International Dictionary of Black Composers*, Volume II. Edited by Samuel A. Floyd, Jr. Chicago: Fitzroy Dearborn Publishers, 1999, pp. 1169–78.

Ramsey, Jr., Guthrie P. "George (Theophilus) Walker." *The New Grove Dictionary of Music and Musicians 27.* Second edition. Edited by Stanley Sadie. New York: MacMillan Publishers Limited, 2001, p. 31.

Sims, D. Maxine. "An Analysis and Comparison of Piano Sonatas by George Walker and Howard Swanson." *The Black Perspective in Music* 4, No. 1, Spring 1976: pp. 70–81.

Southern, Eileen. *Biographical Dictionary of African American and African Musicians.* Westport, CT: Greenwood Press, 1982.

Terry, Mickey Thomas. "An Interview with George Walker." *The Musical Quarterly* 84, No. 3, Fall 2000, pp. 372–88.

Walker, George. "Let's Consider the Listener." *Music Journal* 19, No. 1, January 1961, pp. 40, 104.

Contributed by:

Ryan Nelson
Doctoral Conducting Associate
University of North Texas
Denton, Texas

Teacher Resource Guide

Ceremonial

Bernard Rands
(b. 1934)

Unit 1: Composer

Bernard Rands was born in Sheffield, England, in 1934 and immigrated to the United States in 1975, becoming a citizen in 1983. His initial studies were in English literature and music at the University of Wales, where he became interested in Celtic lore. His literature studies have also included intensive research in the works of James Joyce. As a result of his linguistic studies, Rands is fluent in French, Italian, and Spanish. His musical training continued with composition and conducting study with Roman Vlad in Rome, Luigi Dallapiccola in Florence, and Pierre Boulez and Bruno Maderna at Darmstadt. Later, he studied electronic music with Luciano Berio in Milan. Rands has been on the faculties at the University of York, University of California at San Diego, Boston University, and the Juilliard School. He is currently the Walter Bigelow Rosen Professor of Music and the Walter Channing Cabot Fellow at Harvard University. He has been Composer-in-Residence at the Aspen and Tanglewood festivals, and with the Philadelphia Orchestra from 1989 to 1996. His many commissions include works for the New York Philharmonic, the Boston Symphony Orchestra, the Los Angeles Philharmonic, the Philadelphia Orchestra, the Eastman Wind Ensemble, and the Chicago Symphony. Since immigrating to the United States, Rands has been the recipient of awards from the American Academy of Arts and Letters; the Guggenheim Foundation; the National Endowment for the Arts; the Barlow, Fromm, and Koussevitzky Foundations; the Pew Trust; and Carey Trust, as well as many others. In 1984, Rands was awarded the Pulitzer Prize in Music for his *Canti del sole* for tenor and orchestra. His compositions include works for orchestra, chamber ensembles, keyboard, solo instruments, and vocal/ instrumental ensembles.

Unit 2: Composition

Ceremonial was composed in 1982 for the Symphony Band at the University of Michigan and is dedicated to H. Robert Reynolds, its music director and conductor. Its premiere was at the CBDNA National Conference in Columbus, Ohio, in February 1993. Helicon Music Corporation published this work in 1983. In the liner notes to the recording of *Ceremonial* by the Cincinnati Wind Symphony (KCD-11059), conducted by Eugene Corporon, the composer is quoted regarding the composition:

> *Ceremonial* is a monothematic composition in which a single, extended melody is repeated ten times during the course of the work. The melody, first stated by a solo bassoon, is subsequently played by various combinations of instruments, always increasing in density and in complexity of timbre. This latter quality is the central concern of the work, which employs unusual and unconventional mixtures of instrumental groups—sometimes in extreme registers— in order that the melody is continuously transformed. Each statement of the melodic theme is separated from the next by a dense harmonic idea, which serves to interrupt the forward motion of the melodic and rhythmic flow. At the outset, both harmonic and melodic ideas float free of any discernible meter or pulse. As specific rhythmic ideas are introduced and accrue in the percussion section, the music gradually takes on a regular pulse, which propels it to its concluding climax. The mood and pace of the music is comparable to a ceremony which gradually, deliberately, and inevitably moves through its rituals.

This thirteen-minute, single-movement work is scored for a symphonic wind band consisting of piccolo, two flutes, oboe, English horn, bassoon, contrabassoon, three clarinets, bass clarinet, two alto saxophones, tenor saxophone, baritone saxophone, three trumpets, four horns, three trombones, two euphoniums, two tubas, timpani, and five percussion.

Unit 3: Historical Perspective

Ceremonial is actually the third in a series of identically titled compositions. The other two were written for large orchestra in 1986 and 1991 and, though composed before the work for winds, are titled *Ceremonial 2* and *Ceremonial 3*, respectively, in the composer's catalog of compositions. The formal structure of this monothematic work has its roots in the ground bass technique commonly used in sixteenth and seventeenth English music. This is a technique in which a bass line is continuously repeated throughout the course of the composition. Later, in chaconnes and passacaglias, the repeated line could appear in voices other than the bass line. *Ceremonial* is related to this type of writing. Two well-known works in this style are *Bolero* by Maurice Ravel and *Passacaglia and Fugue in C minor* by J. S. Bach. Rands actually pays homage to Bach by inserting the B(B-flat)–A–C–H(B) theme into *Ceremonial*.

Unit 4: Technical Considerations

The recurring melody of the work is twenty-one measures in length, using all twelve chromatic tones. It ties together duple rhythms with quarter note, eighth note, and sixteenth note triplets within a duple meter to create a melodic line that seems ambiguous in pulse. It is accompanied by a snare drum *ostinato* which, while being quite regular in its repetitions, contributes to the ambiguity. Each time the melody is played, the snare drum rhythm accompanies it in exactly the same way. The two elements are always heard together. The relationship of these two elements to each other requires that the ensemble maintain a very precise pulse, which is made difficult because of the various triplet patterns. While this work was written for one player per part, some judicious may be considered for the sake of maintaining proper balances. The dynamic contrasts are quite extreme, as are some of the range requirements for the wind players. The brass use a variety of mutes (harmon, straight metal, cup), and the trombones need a well-controlled glissando technique. The percussion requirements for this work include timpani (five drums), two vibraphones, snare drum, bongos (two pair), three tom-toms, chimes, bass drum, and tam-tam.

Unit 5: Stylistic Considerations

This work requires the performers to maintain control over a very wide range of dynamics, which must be sustained over long passages. Of particular importance is that the overall dynamic progression from *ppp* (after the initial loud entrance) to *fff* is a steady progression from beginning to end as if the piece were one long *crescendo*. Another concern is the length of the melodic line. The melody is twenty measures long in six irregular phrases. The phrases, however, must have a sense of connection, and the performers should strive to consider the longer line as being of utmost importance. An even more important concept is the way in which Rands adds instruments to each repetition of the melody. In each repetition, he creates a new timbre for the melody by combining the timbres of multiple instruments. For instance, in the second statement of the melody, he combines the sound of the oboe, English horn, and two bassoons. Instead of hearing each of these instruments as a distinct timbre, the ensemble should listen for the new timbre (singular) created by this combination. This will require a very careful balancing of the voices and a matched approach to articulations and phrases. Beginning with the sixth repetition of the melody, the composer adds contrapuntal lines (based on the B–A–C–H theme). The snare drum *ostinato*, which accompanies each repetition of the melody, is also added to by bongos and tom-toms, which combine to create a more elaborate *ostinato*. The score indicates the tempo as quarter note = 72, but a slightly slower or faster tempo may be needed based upon the particular ensemble and acoustics. However, the conductor must be certain to maintain a very clear and steady tempo throughout.

Unit 6: Musical Elements

MELODY:
As mentioned, the single melody of this composition is an important feature. Rands creates a set of variations—not of the melody but of the timbre. Within this melody, he uses all twelve chromatic pitches but still allows a semblance of tonality by stepwise motion and intervals with harmonic implications. It is important that the six irregular phrases be seen as one longer unit. The individual phrases provide no true sense of harmonic progression. With each repetition, the focus must be on the new timbre. The melody is eventually scored for every wind instrument in the ensemble with the exception of euphonium and tuba. There are two other melodic ideas that Rands includes in *Ceremonial*. The first is the B-A-C-H theme (sometimes in an altered sequence), which he uses as counterpoint to the main melody. The second is a four-note descending theme, which is also used as a contrapuntal idea.

HARMONY:
The harmonic vocabulary of this work is tonally based but only hints at a specific tonal center. Rands often superimposes triads: major triads an augmented fourth apart, diminished triads a major second apart, minor triads a minor second apart, etc. These triadic harmonies most often appear in the vibraphone parts as single quarter note figures. As the work moves steadily toward its climax, the harmonies become increasingly dense.

RHYTHM:
The meter signature is 3/4 and the tempo indication is quarter note at 72 beats per minute. These two elements establish the framework for a perceived rhythmic ambiguity. The work begins with somewhat static harmonies in the introduction, with only the snare drum contributing anything that sounds like a regular rhythm. The first statement of the melody presents the listener with a line that includes simple half note, quarter note, and eighth note rhythms interspersed with quarter note, eighth note, and sixteenth note triplet figures. These are often connected with ties, making for a rhythmically complex melodic line, which draws the listener's ears away from the fact that there truly is a regular pulse underlying the entire line. The performers must be diligent in keeping the internal pulse consistent, particularly with the

addition of more instruments with each repetition of the melody. It is imperative that the conductor possesses a clear technique.

TIMBRE:

One of the most important elements of this composition is its use of timbral change. Each repetition of the melody utilizes a different combination of instruments, making it essential to be diligent regarding balance so each new combination creates the desired composite timbre. The same holds true for each of the dense harmonic interruptions, as they also each have a change of timbre. Rehearsing the melodic episodes alone and then perhaps the interruptions should help the performers to grasp the concept of how each timbral change transforms the music.

Unit 7: Form and Structure

Ceremonial is built on a fairly simple structural concept: dense harmonic episodes alternating with the primary melody increasing in timbral density. The first forty measures are an introduction in which Rands develops the dense harmonic idea that separates each repetition of the primary melody. He begins with just two pitches and then uses triadic figures that continually increase in density. Each repetition of the primary melody is twenty-one measures in length, and each interrupting episode is seven measures in length.

MEASURE	EVENT AND SCORING
1	Introduction; full ensemble in alternating groups; increasing harmonic density
40	Melody I; 1st bassoon/snare drum
61	Episode I; based on material from introduction; flute/ clarinet/saxophone/ contrabassoon/brass/vibraphones
67	Melody II; oboe/English horn/1st and 2nd bassoon/snare drum
88	Episode II; triplet motives from melody bassoon/ saxophone/brass/ timpani/vibraphones
94	Melody III; oboe/English horn/1st and 2nd bassoons/1st clarinet/1st also saxophone/snare drum/bongo
115	Episode III; similar to Episode II; all winds (except piccolo)/ timpani/vibraphones
121	Melody IV; 2nd flute/1st and 2nd oboe/English horn/1st and 2nd bassoon/1st and 2nd clarinet/1st alto saxophone/snare drum/bongo

MEASURE	EVENT AND SCORING
142	Episode IV; similar to Episode II; flute/oboe/clarinet/ saxophone/brass
148	Melody V; 2nd flute/1st and 2nd oboe/ English horn/1st and 2nd bassoon/1st and 2nd clarinet/1st alto saxophone/1st and 2nd horn/snare drum/bongos (two pair)/ tom-toms
169	Episode V; opening material; 1st and 2nd oboe/English horn/1st and 2nd bassoon/bass clarinet/1st alto saxophone/ brass/timpani/vibraphones
175	Melody VI; 2nd flute/1st and 2nd oboe/English horn/2nd and 3rd clarinet/2nd alto saxophone/ 1st and 2nd horn/snare drum/bongos/tom-toms; add B–A–C–H theme, 1st flute/1st clarinet/1st alto saxophone/tenor saxophone/ vibraphones; add four-note descending theme, bass clarinet/baritone saxophone/1st and 2nd trumpet/1st and 2nd trombone
196	Episode VI; introductory material plus four-note descending theme; 1st and 2nd flute/1st and 2nd oboe/bassoon/clarinet/ 1st alto saxophone/brass/timpani/vibraphones
202	Melody VII; 1st and 2nd flute/1st and 2nd oboe/English horn/1st and 2nd clarinet/horn/snare drum/bongos/tom-toms/timpani; add B–A–C–H theme, 3rd clarinet/bass clarinet/2nd alto saxophone/tenor saxophone/vibraphones; add four-note descending theme, 1st and 2nd bassoon/ baritone saxophone/1st and 2nd trumpet/1st and 2nd trombone
223	Episode VII; opening material and triplet figures; *tutti*
229	Melody VIII; piccolo/1st and 2nd flute/clarinet/ alto saxophone/snare drum/bongos/tom-toms/timpani; add B–A–C–H theme, 1st and 2nd oboe/English horn/1st and 2nd bassoon/tenor saxophone/chimes; add four-note descending theme, trumpet/trombone; add sixteenth note interjections, contrabassoon/baritone saxophone/ euphonium/tuba
250	Episode VIII; similar to Episode VII; *tutti*

MEASURE	EVENT AND SCORING
256	Melody IX; piccolo/1st flute/1st and 2nd oboe/English horn/1st and 2nd bassoon/1st and 2nd trombone/snare drum/bongos/tom-toms/timpani; add B–A–C–H theme, 2nd flute/1st, 2nd, and 3rd clarinet; alto saxophone; chimes; add four-note descending theme, trumpet/horn; add sixteenth note interjections, contrabassoon/bass clarinet/ tenor saxophone/baritone saxophone/euphonium/tuba; add sixteenth note triplet figures, trumpet
277	Episode IX; opening material; piccolo/flute/oboe/English horn/1st and 2nd bassoon/1st, 2nd, and 3rd clarinet/alto saxophone/horn/trombone/ euphonium/tuba
283	Melody X; piccolo/flute/tenor saxophone/baritone saxophone/trumpet/ horn/snare drum/bongos/tom-toms/ timpani; add B–A–C–H theme, oboe/English horn/1st and 2nd bassoon/1st clarinet/alto saxophone; chimes; add sixteenth note triplet figures, 2nd and 3rd clarinet/bass clarinet; add interjection (*sfz/p–crescendo–ff*) contrabassoon/ trombone/euphonium/tuba
304	Coda; various triplet figures and *glissandi*; *tutti*

Unit 8: Suggested Listening

J. S. Bach, *Passacaglia in C minor*
Gustav Holst, *First Suite in E-flat (Chaconne)*
Gordon Jacob, *William Byrd Suite (The Bells)*
Ron Nelson, *Passacaglia (Homage on B-A-C-H)*
Maurice Ravel, *Bolero*

Unit 9: Additional References and Resources

Battisti, Frank. *The Twentieth Century American Wind Band Ensemble: History Development and Literature*. Fort Lauderdale, FL: Meredith Music Publications, 1995.

Guskin, Amy. *Bernard Rands – Composer*. 9 August 2001: http://www.bernardrands.com/

Lebrecht, Norman. *The Companion to Twentieth Century Music*. New York: Simon & Schuster, 1992.

Bernard Rands. European American Music Distributors, LLC. 9 August 2001: http://www.eamdc.com/08.html

Rands, Bernard. *Ceremonial: for Symphonic Wind Band* (full score). Miami: Helicon Music Corporation, 1993.

Rands, Bernard. *Ceremonial*, Cincinnati Wind Symphony, Klavier KCD-11059.

Rands, Bernard. *Ceremonial*, New England Conservatory Wind Ensemble, Albany Troy 340.

Schwartz, Elliott, and Daniel Godfrey. *Music Since 1945: Issues, Materials, and Literature*. New York: Schirmer Books, 1993.

Struble, John Warthen. *The History of American Classical Music: MacDowell Through Minimalism*. New York: Facts on File, 1995.

Contributed by:

Donald G. Lovejoy
Director of Bands
Winona State University
Winona, Minnesota

Teacher Resource Guide

Dream Sequence, Op. 224

Ernst Krenek
(1900–1991)

Unit 1: Composer

Spanning seven decades of the twentieth century, Ernst Krenek's compositions reflect nearly every trend from the 1910s through the 1980s. Frequently criticized for his nomad-like stylistic changes, Krenek credits the contradictory tendencies in his personality for not only the diversity in his aggregate compositional output but also the variety within the individual specimens. Stravinsky noted the composer's contrasting personality traits in an interview with Robert Craft, published and co-authored in *Dialogues and a Diary*. Stravinsky states, "Krenek is an intellectual and a composer, a difficult combination to manage, and he is profoundly religious, which goes nicely with the composer side, less nicely with the other thing." Krenek himself admits that his desire for pure, uncompromising creation has been met with an opposite need to be practical.

Krenek's first teacher, Franz Shreker, was associated with the expressionistic movement characterized by the use of pathological and morbid subject matters. Krenek's works from this period (1910–1921) are patterned in the spirit of post-romantic German polyphony, spiced with impressionistic devices of French and Italian origin.

Seeking new direction after Shreker, Krenek was attracted by Béla Bartók's music through dispensation of traditional tonal relationships and use of dissonant polyphony and extended motoristic rhythmic *ostinati*. Later in the 1920s, he was attracted by the equilibrium, poise, grace, and clarity of French music. This view also placed him closer to the tenets of *gebrauchsmusik*, which demanded that music fit the community for which it was written.

Krenek's neo-classic creative efforts in the 1920s, influenced by Igor Stravinsky and *Les Six*, did not last long. His close friend, Edward Erdmann, influenced Krenek in the music of Franz Schubert that resulted in a song cycle patterned after Schubert's *Die Winterreise*. Krenek's neo-romantic phase and stated desire to be comprehended by a wide audience was manifested in the opera, *Johnny spielt auf* of 1925–1926. International acclaim was accorded Krenek for this jazz opera, which included modern stage devices such as the telephone, trains, and a taxi. With the financial success of *Johnny spielt auf*, Krenek was finally in a position to look internally for artistic principles. The shift to the idealistic component of his character led to exploration of twelve-tone technique, which was to remain a consistent thread throughout many changes to come. His first major twelve-tone composition was the opera, *Charles V*, which was to be performed at the Vienna Opera House but was canceled due the politically sensitive nature of the subject amidst the rise of Adolf Hitler to power. The 1933 opera was finally premiered at the Vienna State Opera in 1984.

Krenek immigrated to the United States in 1939 and taught music theory at Vassar College. In 1942, he was appointed head of the music department of Hamline University in St. Paul, Minnesota. Krenek's composition output in America continued with twelve-tone technique dominated by manipulation procedures, a technique utilized in "Puzzle," the third movement of Dream Sequence. As with serialists Olivier Messiaen, Karlheinz Stockhousen, and Pierre Boulez of the 1940s and 1950s, Krenek applied serialism to rhythms, timbre, and dynamics. When the realm of predetermination includes control of pitch, rhythm, dynamics, and timbre, the aural perception of these complex events becomes similar to chance music, which by design has unpredictable results. In 1961, Krenek experimented in this vein with the television opera, *Ausgerechvet und verspielt*. Even the subject of this opera deals with chance when the main character strives to outwit chance at roulette through the use of a computer. Ironically, the computer overloads in working to find a winning number and creates a musical tune in despair. The melody eventually is revealed to be a twelve-tone combination that contains the solution to the game. Through the plot, music is symbolically placed at a higher status than mathematics and pure logic.

In 1966, Krenek moved to Los Angeles, California, where he resided until his death in 1991. During the latter part of his life, Krenek's music was celebrated at festivals from Graz and Vienna to the California cities of Santa Barbara, Palm Springs, and San Diego. In 1992, his remains were transferred to an honorary grave in Vienna, Austria.

Unit 2: Composition

Dream Sequence, Op. 224, the College Band Director's National Association's 1975 commission of Krenek, entered the band repertoire in a decade marked by continuing awareness by CBDNA leadership of the need for pursuing major composers of the century to write for concert band. The world premiere by the Baylor University Wind Ensemble, Richard Floyd, conductor, took place on March 11, 1977, during the national conference of the CBDNA on the University of Maryland campus. The composition is published by Universal Edition (catalog number UE 16627NJ).

Krenek's note in the preface to the score states,

> The title *Dream Sequence* hints at the imagery that may loosely be associated with the music. It does not mean that the music describes any particular dreams or narrates any story. *Nightmare* and *Pleasant Dreams* indicate the general character of the music. *Puzzle* is a strictly constructed serial piece (perhaps the result of a sleepless night than of any dream…). The last movement is evocative of the sentiments that accompany the familiar *Dream About Flying*.

In analysis, tonality or pitch is secondary to texture, *tessitura*, rhythm, dynamics, and timbre. Joan Tower's terminology for analysis in determining energy lines and space or dimension seems most appropriate.

Unit 3: Historical Perspective

Dream Sequence is a psychological tone poem reflecting expressionist elements similar to Alban Berg's opera *Wozzeck*, with depiction of the inner mind through dream episodes and a wide emotional palette. *Dream Sequence* also reflects the more abstract serial world associated with music of Arnold Schoenberg, Anton Webern, and Karlheinz Stockhausen. The third movement, "Puzzle," even approaches complete serialism. However, the music is not abstract in its emotional portrayal of dream-states. Interesting as well is that the composition fits into the German symphonic tradition with its four-movement structure, cyclic nature, and tightly developed motivic framework. While the neo-classic multi-movement design provides a large structure to follow, the internal structure is more elusive since through-composed continual development overrides longer segments of phrase repetition. As the title suggests, the music reflects a stream of consciousness with unexplained shifts of mood rather than classical strains of logical phrases. Unity is perceived in the existence of small motivic elements similar to a fabric of wild design that is unified by the color of thread within that design. The listener is kept interested by the unpredictability of events and wide variety of mood and color.

Unit 4: Technical Considerations

Dream Sequence is scored for full ensemble (minus euphonium), piano, and harp. There are two tenor saxophone and three baritone saxophone parts that, along with a few judicious cues in bass clarinet and contrabass clarinet, are achievable. The ten trumpet parts in the original are also playable by six trumpets with the edited parts by Richard Floyd. There are extreme demands technically for individuals, most of which also require a keen ear for non-tonal patterns. The scoring is transparent, placing solo-like demands on many individuals and need for control at soft dynamic levels. Few measures utilize the *tutti* ensemble. The need for bringing character to a few notes or measures requires performers to broaden their listening to sensitively play in the larger context of the phrase. It may be important to note that the outer movements have been programmed separately and, for some conductors, stand alone as worthy statements. These unique challenges offer rich opportunities from which individuals can learn by reframing their knowledge and experience.

Units 5 and 6: Stylistic Considerations/Musical Elements

While Krenek refers to his output as a varied collection and a metaphor for his ever-changing life, *Dream Sequence* seems stylistically aligned with the expressionist movement that included painters Vincent Van Gogh and Paul Gaugin. Expressionism may be defined as an artistic style in which the artist seeks to depict not objective reality but rather the subjective emotions and responses that objects and events arouse in him. Krenek's *Dream Sequence* fits this style more than impressionism and abstractism. Consequently, stylistic traits include exaggeration, distortion, primitivism, and fantasy. Krenek imposes his own personal and spontaneous self-expression in vividly portraying violence, surprise, and many other wide-ranging emotions. In this emotional context, form is less important than achieving the highest intensity of expression. In other words, the performer is invited to exaggerate dynamics and articulations to portray the emotional content as vividly as possible. Keep in mind that exaggeration includes gestures associated with subtlety and confusion in addition to the bold gestures associated with nightmares. The floating, polyphonic episodes of *Pleasant Dreams*, for instance, stand in contrast to the jagged, knife-like figures of the first movement. In summary, this music invites the performers to insert their own reality to represent the real meaning of the experience.

Unit 7: Form and Structure

SECTION	MEASURE	EVENT AND SCORING
Movement I: "Nightmare"		
Introduction I	1–8	Static; slipping into dream-state through timbral modulation from low to high registers
Introduction II	9–16	Progressive to regressive; jagged melodic shapes in polyphony suggest disruptive, disjointed feeling; silence

SECTION	MEASURE	EVENT AND SCORING
A	17–26	Expository, stable; four-note germ cell emerges
	27–33	Anticipatory; germ cell developed; jagged shapes and long notes return from the introduction
	34–36	Regressive, winding down; silence interrupts
B	37–50	Developmental; germ cell, jagged shapes, long notes associated with timbral modulation
	51–54	Regressive; winding down, but no silence
C	55–62	Anticipatory; transitional; long notes of "winding down" replaced by *ostinato* sixteenth notes; germ cell fragmented; driving to apex of movement
	63–66	Apex reached; note values accelerate as shapes descend
	67–79	Stable; jagged shapes return; germ cells return
	80–89	Regressive; winding down in descending shapes; germ fragment leads to a *glissando*-like dissolving of sound
Coda	89–97	Anticipatory; germ cell transformed to rising figures before falling and ending with one extended germ cell statement

Movement II: "Pleasant Dreams"
The eight note tone row is a rising alternation of skips followed by half steps that ends with a three-note descending chromatic. The jagged shape of the first part of the row relates to similar shapes in the first movement. The articulation of *staccato* eighth notes and rests at the end of each statement is connected to the four-note germ cell of the first movement.

A	1–6	Expository; eight-note tone row stated in various forms; monophonic to polyphonic texture; rhythmic utterances punctuated by hesitant rest as in four-note germ cell of "Nightmare"

SECTION	MEASURE	EVENT AND SCORING
Interlude I	7–8	Almost static chorale texture (rhythm is related to germ cell of "Nightmare"); rising chromatic bass line used as cadence signal
B	10–13	Progressive, free atonal; polyphonic and rhapsodic "night music"
Interlude II	14–15	Static chorale texture; chromatic bass line used again as cadence figure; similar color and tessitura of Interlude I
AB	16–24	Stable, then anticipatory; serial and free atonal material combined; eight-tone row used in rhapsodic manner of "B"; polyphonic texture
Interlude III	25–27	Regressive; winding-down effect of falling intervals and decreasing note values; homophonic texture
A	28–31	Return of eight-note serial material in polyphonic texture
B	32–33	Free atonal material more rhapsodically treated; approaching the character of "Nightmare"; "falling" gesture
"Nightmare"	33–38	Recalls "Nightmare" introduction; jagged shapes and long-note timbral modulation; climbing high again before "falling"
Interlude IV	39–43	Brass chorale of eight-note chords from expansive intervals to closed; homophonic movement; static ending
B – Interlude	44–49	Begins rhapsodically with free atonal material; recalls climbing material before regressing to static chorale
A+B+Nightmare	50–54	Combination of eight-note tone row, interlude chorale, and "Nightmare" climbing and falling effects

SECTION	MEASURE	EVENT AND SCORING
Codetta	55–56	Eight-note tone row with rhapsodic free atonal figures
	57–63	Clarinet choir imitates brass chorale from Interlude IV; then woodwinds state a winding-down cadential event
	64–66	Eight-note tone row truncated to seven pitches before a three non-pitched eighth note and rest pattern punctuates the statement (related to germ cell); a downward (falling) glissandi timpani closes the movement

Movement III: "Puzzle"

The form of this unusual movement follows a matrix of five events, which are rotated in a pre-determined order:

I	II	III	IV	V
V	I	IV	II	III
III	V	II	I	IV
IV	III	I	V	II
II	IV	V	III	I

All I's are identical or similar, as are the remaining four musical events. The individual events are labeled in the score, and the five larger sections are separated by double bars. Five events in five large sections adds up to twenty-five events, and Krenek utilizes that formal number as the number of serial pitches per event.

The title "Puzzle" most likely refers to the composer's plight in making each of the events twenty-five tones or two statements of the twelve-tone row: F–D–E–C-sharp–G-sharp–D-sharp–F-sharp–C–G–A–B–A-sharp plus the beginning tone F. The II event, since beginning on F, utilizes the inversion of the original row. The II event ends with F, A-flat, dictating that III begins with the original row transposed a minor third up (A-flat, F). The remainder of the piece is constructed according to these principles, with minor adjustments necessitated by the fact that both character and position of the concluding elements are premeditated qualities. Krenek remarks in the prefatory note of the score that this movement is a "…strictly constructed serial piece, perhaps more the result of a sleepless night than of any dream…."

SECTION	MEASURE	EVENT AND SCORING
Movement IV: "Dream About Flying"		
Introduction or take-off	1–12	Rising, free atonal, fluttertongued pitches gather in altitude, strength of rpm's, and speed before lifting off; final two measures suggest the extreme space between flight and the ground (bass drum); ends with an eerie simulation of fast air by a bowed tam-tam *fermata*
A	13–19	Shaky flight; register differentiation of high and low becomes more extreme as highs become more elevated; keyboard instruments have rapidly accelerating and decelerating figures; out-of-control feeling
	19–23	Melodic figure (trumpet) attempts to assume more control; woodwinds add to the tension with two rapid, jagged-shape rising and falling frenetic figures; final measure upward *glissando* lifts to a more secure elevation
B	24–52	Stable feeling assimilates material from other movements; chorale interlude (II), tone-row steady rhythm (II), germ cell shapes (I), jagged "nightmare" shapes (I), rising bass line (III), "Puzzle" cadence from event I, brass chorale (II), winding-down cadence material (I), and three-note ending from "Pleasant Dreams," ending from Puzzle" event I
Retransition	53–64	Two-measure *ostinato* figure in piccolo and glockenspiel signals ending as a rising bass figure recalls the "Puzzle" event IV; tempo accelerates to silence

SECTION	MEASURE	EVENT AND SCORING
Coda	65–69	Brass chorale interlude material from "Pleasant Dreams" combines with "Puzzle" I rising cadence and *fermata*
	70–73	Final winding-down cadence from "Nightmare" movement
	74–75	Send-off into space at warp speed with accelerating, rising, and *glissandi* figures in free-form notation

Unit 8: Suggested Listening

Alban Berg, *Three Pieces for Orchestra*, Op. 6, *Wozzeck*
Arthur Honegger, *Rugby*
Ernst Krenek, *Three Merry Marches*, Op. 44
György Ligeti, *Atmosphéres*
Arnold Schoenberg, *Five Piano Pieces*, Op. 23
Anton Webern, *Symphony*, Op. 21

Unit 9: Additional References and Resources

Krenek, Ernst. *Horizons Circled: Reflections on My Music*. Berkeley, CA: University of California Press, 1974.

Krenek, Ernst. *Music Here and Now*. New York: W. W. Norton & Co., 1939.

Ogden, Wilbur Lee. *Series and Structure: an Investigation into the Purpose of the 12-Tone Row in Selected Works of Schoenberg, Krenek, and Leibowitz*. Ph.D. dissertation, Indiana University, 1955.

Reynolds, H. Robert. *The CBDNA Commissions Ernst Krenek. The Instrumentalist*, January 1978, pp. 48–9.

Tubb, Monte. *Textural Constructions in Music*. Journal of Music Theory Pedagogy 1, No. 2, Fall 1987.

Wakefield, William K. *Ernst Krenek's Dream Sequence, Op. 224, for Concert Band: An Analysis and Discussion of Performance Problems*. DMA Treatise, University of Texas at Austin, 1990.

Contributed by:

William K. Wakefield
Director of Bands
University of Oklahoma
Norman, Oklahoma

Teacher Resource Guide

Et exspecto resurrectionem mortuorum pour Orchestre de Bois, Cuivres et Percussions Métalliques

Olivier (Eugène Prosper Charles) Messiaen
(1908–1992)

Unit 1: Composer

Olivier Messiaen exercised a remarkable influence over composers both in his native France and elsewhere, although his own work is unique in its individuality. He was born in Avignon the son of Pierre Messiaen (a scholar of English literature and of the poet Cicile Sauvage), and spent most of his life in Paris. He began composing at the age of seven and taught himself to play piano. A devout Christian throughout his life, Messiaen entered the Paris Conservatoire at the age of eleven, where his teachers included the great French organist Marcel Dupré and the composer Paul Dukas. He became principal organist of La Trinité in Paris after graduation in 1930, and except for 1939 to 1942, he regularly played for masses there until his death in 1992. In 1932, Messiaen married Claire Delbos. In 1936, with composers André Jolivet, Daniel Lesur, and Yves Baudrier, he founded the group *La Jeune France* ("Young France") to promote new French music. He taught at the Schola Cantorum and the Icole Normale de Musique from 1936 until the outbreak of World War II in 1939. As a French soldier, he was taken prisoner by the

Germans and interned at Görlitz (Stalag VIIIA) in Silesia (now in Poland), where he wrote *Quatuor pour la fin du temps* (Quartet for the End of Time). Repatriated in 1942, Messiaen resumed his post at La Trinité and taught at the Paris Conservatoire until his retirement in 1978. He also is said to have invented rhythmic serialism in 1948 (or thereabouts) with a piano etude. In 1967, he was elected to the Institut de France, and in 1971 he was a recipient of the Erasmus Prize

One of the most original French composers since Debussy, Messiaen created a new musical language that profoundly influenced twentieth century music. Messiaen's musical language is derived from a number of varied sources, including Greek metrical rhythms, Hindu tradition, the serialism of Schoenberg and Debussy, and bird song, with his whole work and life deeply influenced by the spirit of Catholicism. Messiaen was self-admittedly a synesthete, as is quite well detailed in his own writings and in interviews. Many of his compositions, such as *Oiseaux Exotiques*, *L'ascension*, and *Couleurs de la cite celeste*, are directly based upon his, in a sense, trying to "produce pictures" via sound, writing specific notes to produce specific color sequences and blends. He used bird song as the basis of many of his melodies; he traveled the world to hear exotic birds in their native habitats. Before him, both Handel and Beethoven imitated the cuckoo and the nightingale, and Rameau mimicked bird song in his harpsichord pieces.

The influences found in Messiaen's music were very much a part of his life as a student of Greek poetry and an accomplished amateur ornithologist. In his book, *The Technique of My Musical Thought*, Messiaen pronounces the dictum that music should communicate "lofty sentiments...and in particular, the loftiest of all, the religious sentiments exalted by the theology and truths of our Catholic faith." True music was "an act of faith" to him.

He wrote for most musical forms, including symphonies, chamber music, and opera, but much of his oeuvre was for the organ. His pieces span the whole of his sixty-year composing career, from *La Banquet Céleste* (written when he was twenty) to the huge organ cycle *Livre du Saint Sacrement* of 1984. All his music expressed theological ideas or rejoiced in the splendor of creation or a kind of revelation of God.

Unit 2: Composition

Messiaen was one of the giants of twentieth century composition. *Et exspecto resurrectionem mortuorum* (And I await the resurrection of the dead) was composed in 1964. The title quotes the Nicene Creed in the Roman Catholic Mass in reference to the Last Judgment, as described in the *Book of Revelations*. Messiaen has not undertaken merely to represent the end of the world but to create something of an analogue in sound to an event the immensity of which is beyond comprehension. Although he had created works of religious mysticism before and would again, there is nothing else quite this vast in conception, an undertaking supported, Messiaen indicated, by his contemplation of other gigantic achievements, in ancient architecture, the writings of St. Thomas Aquinas, and the Alps. There are five movements, each prefaced and inspired by a biblical quote (see Unit 7: Form and Structure).

Notes translated from French in the score:

Et exspecto resurrectionem mortuorum (And I await the resurrection of the dead) was composed and orchestrated in 1964 for a commission from Andre Malreaux. Its instrumentation intends it for vast spaces: churches, cathedrals, even in the open air, as on mountain heights.

It is, perhaps, useful to recall that, at the time he was writing his score, the composer gladly surrounded himself with strong and simple pictures of the stepped pyramids of Mexico, the temples and statues of Ancient Egypt, Romanesque and Gothic churches; that he re-read the texts of St. Thomas Aquinas on "The Resurrection" and "The World of the Resuscitated"; that he worked in the high Alps facing those powerful landscapes that are his true homeland.

The orchestra comprises three ensembles: woodwinds, brass, and metallic percussion instruments. The woodwinds are written in four parts (three oboes and one English horn—three bassoons and one contrabassoon), and five parts (two piccolos and three flutes—one E-flat clarinet, three clarinets, one bass clarinet). That which allows the blocks of sound can quickly and continuously transform the general color. The brass instruments are equally numerous (in addition to the three trumpets is the shrillness of the piccolo trumpet in D), the six horns playing six-note chords, giving even more movement to the complex colors, in addition to the three trombones comes the bass-register of the bass trombone, tuba, and bass saxhorn in B-flat. The percussion consists of three large sets of cencerros (Mexican chimes) who unite with the chimes, six gongs, three tam-tams, ranging from medium-high to very low. These play rhythmic counterpoints, reinforce the basses and envelop the rest of the orchestra, reinforce the greatness of the symbols and the sacred reverence by terrible *fortissimi* or mysterious resonances.

It is in five movements. Each movement carries a passage of text from the Holy Scripture.

Details of the first three performances:
The premiere took place in the presence of André Malraux in Paris, on 7 May 1964 at La Sainte Chapelle. In this marvelous church built at the orders of St. Louis, King of France—where the crown of thorns rests, where the blues, the reds, golds, violets resound in each

window alongside the music. This space was perfect for the work, in such a way that the marriage of the complex sonorities with the blossoming of the colors as much as the cross-resonances circling around the windows. It was 11 a.m., and the sun also played his role, transporting this-and-that spots of colors with the rebounding sounds. The orchestra was directed by Serge Baudo. The musicians were specially selected from the best in France—here are some of their names:

1st piccolo: Jean Chefnay – 1st flute: Jacques Castagner - 2nd flute: Christian Lardé – 3rd flute: Alain Marion – 1st oboe: Claude Maisonneuve – E-flat clarinet: Marcel Naulais - 1st clarinet: Guy Deplus – 2nd clarinet: André Fournier - trumpet in D: Roger Delmotte – 1st trumpet: Pierre Thibaud – 1st horn: André Fournier – 1st trombone: René Allain – bass trombone: Camille Verdier – tuba: Pierre Daudin – bass saxhorn: Jeam Appelghern – cencerros: Georges Van Gucht, Claude Ricou, Jean Batigne – chimes: Jean Paul Finkbeiner – gong: Gabriel Bouchet – tam-tams: Diego Masson.

The second performance was at Chartres, in the cathedral of Notre Dame de Chartres (Sanctuaire Marial, famous throughout the world for the beauty of its architecture, its statutes, and its stained-glass windows). It was Sunday, 20 June 1965, at the closing of the Grand Mass, in the presence of M. Michon, bishop of Chartres, and of General Charles de Gaulle, president of the Republic of France. The orchestra was seated in the Choir, under the direction of Serge Baudo. M. Michon and the priests of the cathedral occupied the south crossing [*the *Croisillon* is the bit of the church that runs usually north/south], and G. de Gaulle and his invited guests in the north crossing. André Malraux, and all the ministers, occupied the first rows of the Nave. The public was seated in the Nave and the rest of the church.

Even without the same mystic splendor, the third performance was no less glorious. It was at the Odéon, Theatre of France, on 12 January 1966 in the evening, as part of the Concerts du Domaine Musical created by Pierre Boulez, where one could hear the most beautiful performances of contemporary music from France and the rest of the world. The orchestra was under the direction of Pierre Boulez. The orchestra was the "Orchestre du Domaine Musical" and the "Groupe Instrumental a Percussion de Strasbourg"—it was basically (more or less) the same instrumentalists as the first performance.

For the conductor:
Make sure that the instrumentalists observe all the dynamic markings, especially during the mixing and superimposition of contrasting markings. Follow the indicated metronome markings. Stay constant during fast passages (especially for the song of the Alouette Calandre in the fourth piece). Strictly follow the slow tempi, and the extra-slow tempi. Respect the silences and the breaths, do not cut off the immense resonances of the tam-tam in the third piece. Finally, to properly articulate the silences and the breaths placed in the pieces which are so dear to their construction, in addition to the normal silence that would separate the pieces, the composer demands, in between each piece, a silence of about one minute.

Messiaen said, "The brass chorale represents the glory of the Heavenly City. The birds of the xylophones, the woodwinds, the piano solo, symbolize the joy of the resurrected, assured of being always near to Christ" (although *Et exspecto resurrectionem mortuorum* does not use xylophone or piano). Through the creative use of instruments, Messiaen leaves little doubt as to the programmatic content of the work: the Roman Catholic belief in the Resurrection of the Dead and the second coming of Jesus Christ. The work is approximately thirty-three minutes long and is a grade 6+ difficulty. It is published by Alphonse Leduc, Paris (23.681); Robert King Music is the American subsidiary.

The percussion instruments required include six pitched gongs, three tam-tams, chimes, and three and one-half octaves of cencerros (essentially pitched cowbells). These very unique requirements alone may prove daunting to any ensemble considering performing the work.

Unit 3: Historical Perspective

Although integral serialism-composition according to exclusively serial principles was developed mainly by composers who reached maturity after World War II, its history within a European context begins with Messiaen, a member of the previous generation. As an established figure by the end of the war, and as a teacher at the Paris Conservatoire from 1942, he influenced three generations of composers. His theories of melody, harmony, and rhythm, drawing on medieval and oriental music, have inspired contemporary composers such as Pierre Boulez, Karlheinz Stockhausen, Iannis Xenakis, Jean Barraqué, Betsy Jolas, Tristan Murail, George Benjamin, Alexander Goehr, Karel Goeyvaerts, and William Albright (all of whom were his students), as well as the noted musicologist Roland Jackson).

From his early years, Messiaen favored a rigorous and objective approach to composition, which he eventually documented in the book *Technique de mon language musical* (1944). He discusses his inclination to treat the individual attributes of musical sound—pitch, rhythm, dynamics, timbre—as separable components, each with its own specific structural characteristics.

Another important aspect of Messiaen's compositional method is the "borrowing" of pre-existent material and its transformation through what the composer calls the "prism" of his own musical awareness. Messiaen sought inspiration from sources distantly removed from modern Western music. Not only are his rhythmic theories influenced by his study of Hindu music, but he actually used Hindu rhythmic formulas frequently. Another source is Gregorian chant.

Most of Messiaen's works use bird song or refer at least briefly to bird calls, and some derive virtually all their melodic content from this source. For most of his life, Messiaen notated the songs of birds encountered during his extensive travels. As with other borrowings, his intention is not to imitate the source but to transform the bird calls so they become musically meaningful. Messiaen said, "Among the artistic hierarchy, the birds are probably the greatest musicians to inhabit our planet."[1]

A final ingredient of Messiaen's musical character is his deeply mystical and religious nature, which contributes to the expressive detachment and structural rigor of his work. For Messiaen, music constituted not only a means of personal expression but also an objective representation of the beauty and perfection of God's universe. The composer's description of plainchant applies equally well to his own work: music that is "truly religious because it is detached from all exterior effect and from all intention." Further, he said, "Music does not express anything directly. It can intimate, cause a feeling, a state of the soul, touch the subconscious, or increase the dream faculties, and this is where it has immense capacities. It cannot absolutely 'state,' or inform with precision."

Unit 4: Technical Considerations

This work is extremely difficult and demands advanced study because of the notational style. All of the parts are very difficult. Instruments are required to play independently, and specific sections are frequently featured and exposed. The piece has no key signatures, so accidentals abound. There are many changes of meter, some very complicated (2/16 to 2–3/32 to 3–3–2/32…, etc.), and most meters occur on the eighth, sixteenth, or even thirty-second note level. There are articulations of every kind. All instruments are essential. Ranges are difficult, dynamics are frequently extreme, there is little triadic harmony, and large intervallic leaps occur throughout parts. The conductor and ensemble must have a clear conceptualization of the piece and its presentation to successfully perform the work. Because of these reasons, and

---

1 Claude Samuel, *Conversations with Olivier Messiaen*, p. 51.

its duration of thirty-three minutes, only very advanced ensembles (and audiences) will find this work accessible.

Unit 5: Stylistic Considerations

Articulations should be as accurate as possible. The intensity and movement of the music should be equal to the phrasing, articulation, rhythms, and principles of the notation. This is a twentieth century work with twentieth century sounds; it should be approached with a straightforward interpretation that attempts to replicate the score's intention as closely as possible.

There are parts in the score containing instructions that require specific balances between woodwinds and brass. Tempo relationships between sections are important. Contrasts between sections of each movement are vital. Also important is the use of silence and decay (particularly in the metallic percussion resonance).

Unit 6: Musical Elements

Only the highest-performing ensemble should consider approaching this work. The conductor would best spend the ensemble's time assembling the different parts—that is to say, teaching the players everyone else's parts. Along the same lines, the audience to whom this work will be performed should also be considered since the sounds are all very non-traditional and the work is lengthy; a pre-concert lecture might help the audience's appreciation of the work. With that in mind, there are some general comments to make about Messiaen's approach to composition and to the piece specifically:

Melody and Harmony:

It is difficult to address melody and harmony separately in the music of Messiaen. In Messiaen's music, melody is often disassociated from consistent rhythmic identity, and harmony is almost entirely coloristic. Messiaen's music of the post-World War II period moves toward a dissociation between melody and rhythm.[2] Pitch relationships, though still based upon various kinds of artificial scales (whole-tone, octatonic, etc.) are treated in a systematic manner. One of his compositional devices is the use of chromatic "modal" scales, from whose notes many of his melodies are formed and whose notes played at the same time form many of those characteristic "Messiaen chords" in his harmonies. Symmetric sets are comparable to what Messiaen called "modes of limited transposition," which are seven symmetric sets that can each be transposed to alternative pitch levels only a few times before the set repeats itself. The whole-tone scale, Messiaen's first mode of limited transposition, is a simple example: it can be transposed up one semitone and render a new set of six pitches, but if it is transposed up two (or any even

---

2 Robert T. Kelley, *Tradition, the Avant Garde, and Individuality in the Music of Olivier Messiaen*, website.

number) of semitones, it will produce the same collection of pitches as the original.

Et exspecto resurrectionem mortuorum is almost entirely homophonic; there is little, if any, counterpoint to be found in the entire piece. Rather, the impact and resonance of the sounds generated by rhythm, meter, and durations takes precedence.

RHYTHM:

Rhythm is perhaps the most difficult aspect of Messiaen's music to perform, interpret, or comprehend. His writing of complicated rhythms is addressed in his own statement about rhythm: "Most people believe that rhythm means the regular values of a military march. Whereas, in fact, rhythm is an unequal element following fluctuations, like the waves of the sea, like the noise of the wind, like the shape of tree branches."[3] Electing to "replace the notions of 'measure' and 'beat' by the feeling of a short value (the sixteenth note, for example) and its free multiplication," he moves toward an essentially "ametrical" idea.

Messiaen's works are experiments in rhythm in which notes are shortened or lengthened by half a beat, these augmented or diminished rhythms then being repeated or reversed and set symmetrically next to each other. His rhythmic system (using deci-tâlas, augmentation, and diminution of values) invites being interpreted as a method to approach the complexity of divisions of time found in nature. The accuracy of his transcriptions is widely acknowledged.

His slow movements seem to dissolve in timeless contemplation, in which hypnotic slowly changing chords accompany a melismatic melody in an irregular rhythm that seeks to "banish the temporal." In contrast, his fast movements are dances of joy depicting God's pleasure in his creation.

TIMBRE:

Messiaen's works are distinguished by variety of color. This is achieved by his use of sumptuously sensual harmonies and by his varied orchestration and organ registration. He was innovative in using the organ to its full capability, frequently using unusual combinations of stop timbres, often involving very high- or low-pitched pipes, and giving melodies to the pedals played at high pitch (freeing them from their traditional role of bass accompaniment). Messiaen also said, "It is possible to make sounds on a piano that are more orchestral than those of an orchestra."[4]

Unit 7: Form and Structure

In form, Messiaen presents blocks (sections of form) without development

---

3 Samuel, p. 78.
4 Roger Nichols, *Messiaen*.

that contrast with other blocks around them in a "non-narrative" temporal organization.[5] Although Stravinsky called Messiaen a "juxtaposer, not a composer," this form was used by Stravinsky himself (*Symphonies of Wind Instruments*) and by Varèse, among others. English translations of Messiaen's descriptions in the score of each movement are provided below, followed by a form analysis, followed by translations of instructions found in each movement:

MOVEMENT 1:
"Out of the depths have I cried unto thee, O Lord; Lord, hear my voice."
(Psalm 130:1, 2)

The church used this psalm for the souls of those in Purgatory, who are cast from heaven, and for all of those (living and dead) who await the Resurrection. A rising theme in low brass harmonized by six horns—"cry from the abyss!"

MEASURE	EVENT AND SCORING

Très lent (♪ = 36 or ♪ = 72) unison statement

1	Bassoon, bass trombone, tuba, saxhorn, tam-tams; harmonized statement
2	Add English horn, clarinet, bass clarinet, horn
5	Plus lent (♪ = 63) "cry from the abyss"; *tutti*, all in 4/8; principal melody in trombone, tuba, and saxhorn; but one must hear absolutely the colored harmonies of the winds and horn, without reinforcing 1st horn and 1st clarinet; all of the notes of these chords carry the same importance
	Here, the cries of the abyss; one must hear absolutely the chords of clarinet and oboe, then flute, oboe, clarinet who attack these grace note before-the-beat chords *fff*

MOVEMENT 2:
"Christ being raised from the dead dieth no more; death hath no more dominion over him." (Romans 6:9)

The resurrected Christ, who lives and lives forever in his body and in his soul. He is "the first born to confront the dead" (Saint Paul)...the man-god reborn, he is at once the nearest and most fundamental cause of our resurrection (St. Thomas of Aquine).

---

5 Jonathan Cross, *The Stravinsky Legacy*, chapter 2.

Several fast notes; the same melody played by successive deletion of pitches (the ends of the sounds give the contour); the same melody again from solo oboe, solo clarinet, and the echoes of flute. Cencerros, chimes, and gongs play through an Indian "deçi-tâla"—the Simhavikrama (the lion-force). This rhythm combines the fourth Greek Epitrite and the Hindu Vijaya (victory) and is dedicated to Shive thanks to his 15 Matras (3 times 5), and Shive represents the death of death: all of these symbols placed together can signify the victory over death; thus, the choice of the Simhavikrama.

With the Simhavikrama comes a melody played by trumpet, who calls into attention the colors of the woods (like Matthias Grunewald's Resurrected Christ, who seems enveloped in a rainbow made of his own light). Several silences, as important as the music. Conclusion by solo clarinet and English horn.

The composer mentions a *mélodie par manques* (i.e., by successive deletion of pitches) near the opening and a Hindu rhythm in the percussion following a woodwind melody.

MEASURE	EVENT AND SCORING
1	Vif – piccolo, flute, oboe, English horn, clarinet
2	Très modéré (♪ = 72) – piccolo, flute, oboe, English horn, clarinet
2	Très lent (♪ = 72) – flute, oboe, English horn, clarinet, bassoon, horn
3	Presque lent (♪ = 52) – 1st oboe, 1st clarinet, English horn, 1st flute solos
6	Bien modéré (♪ = 80) – percussion
7	*Tutti*
9	Presque lent (♪ = 52) – 1st oboe, 1st clarinet, 1st flute, gongs solos
11	Bien modéré (♪ = 80) Simhavikrama – percussion
12	*Tutti*
14	Vif (♪ = 88) – piccolo, flute, oboe, English horn, clarinet
2 (14)	Très modéré (♪ = 72) – piccolo, flute, oboe, English horn, clarinet
15	Très lent (♪ = 72) – flute, oboe, English horn, clarinet, bassoon, horn

MEASURE	EVENT AND SCORING

16   Presque lent (♪ = 52) – 1st clarinet, 1st flute, English horn solos

Melody by successive deletion of pitches; one must hear neatly the ends of each sound. The instrument that is going to end must make a light *crescendo*, almost at the point of stopping, without exaggeration.

The little grace notes —slightly slower and before the beat.

Principal melody in trumpet; play *mf*, and reinforce the harmonics of the winds; by contrast, the winds should play *f*; one most hear the rainbow of all their chords' colors.

The gong counterpoint—mysterious, but audible.

The gongs play a brusque *mf*.

MOVEMENT 3:
"The hour is coming when the dead shall hear the voice of the Son of God." (John 5:25)

This voice is the symbol of the signal of the resurrection: divine order, whose execution is imminent, like the enhancement of grace from the sacraments. This voice has tripartite symbolism, as well. First symbol—given to a group of winds, the song of the Uirapuru. The Uirapuru is a famous bird: the musical embodiment of Amazonia (a large region that makes up the states of Para, Amazonas, Acre, and the territories of Amapá and Rondonia). The bird's mysterious song with magic timbres surprises and engages the ear with its disjointed melodic jumps, its changes of color, and its dynamic contrasts. It is said that one hears this song at the moment of death. The other symbols are more terrible. Second symbol—silence, and the permutations of chimes. Third symbol—a very long and very powerful stroke of the tam-tam.

MEASURE	EVENT AND SCORING

1   Modéré (♪ = 176) Uirapuru, bird of the Amazon – woodwinds

4   Très lent (♪ = 36 or ♪ = 72) - chimes

5   Très vif (♪. = 144) – *tutti*

6   Très lent (♪ = 36 or ♪ = 72) – low woodwinds, low brass, tam-tams, gongs

7   Modéré (♪ = 176) Uirapuru, bird of the Amazon – woodwinds (lower)

MEASURE	EVENT AND SCORING
10	Très lent (♪ = 36 or ♪ = 72) – chimes
11	Très vif (e. = 144) – *tutti*
12	Très lent (♪ = 36 or ♪ = 72) – low woodwinds, low brass, tam-tams, gongs

In this whole passage of Uirapuru, winds must observe with care with slurs, the *détaché* markings and, above all, the different dynamic markings.

The articulations in horn and trumpet—clean, short, well marked.

The trills of the gong and tam-tam should obtain a point of extreme force (*fffff*) at the end of the measure; at the end, let both instruments resonance; the resonance of the tam-tam will ring alone, stretching out, and will last a very long time (wait until the sound has completely died).

MOVEMENT 4:
"They shall be raised in glory, with a new name, when the morning stars sing together, and all the sons of God shout for joy." (I Corinthians 15:43; Revelations 2:17; Job 38:7)

During this age of scientific precision, in light of all the theories surrounding the expansion of the universe, it seems as if the Bible always tells the truth—that the number of stars is really unknowable, and also that the stars "sing." In effect, certain stars are gaseous, functioning like organ pipes—and one can witness their vibrations.

In this second-to-last piece, the three mysterious elements, the three resonances, the pianissimo and fortissimo tones of the tam-tam that continuously interrupt the musical discourse symbolize at once the name of the Trinity, the solemn moment of the resurrection, and the distant melodies of the stars. The Easter Introit of the chimes and the cencerros, the Alleluia of the trumpets with its halo of harmonics, symbolize one of the qualities of the heavenly body: the gift of clarity. The Alouette Calandre, found in Greece and Spain, is a remarkable singer. Different from the melodious delirium of the Field Alouette, and of the chromatic poetry of the Lulu Alouette, his song is characterized by a great rhythmic variety, a fast tempo, a rich timbre, and a contrasting lightness. Given to flute, oboe, clarinet, bassoon, the song means joy and the gift of agility.

And then all these themes battle one another. We find again the Easter Introit in the tubular bells, the Alleluia in the trumpets, the Simhavikrama tala in the six gongs and, at the same time, the theme of the first segment proclaimed by the trombones. The angels and the stars unite in their glory to acclaim the resurrection while superimposing four musics, four explosions of color, four complex sonorities. Ending with three strokes of the tam-tam, whose resonances is augmented by that of the gongs, it develops and defines itself by the great, prolonged chords of the winds and the brass.

Three long tam-tam resonances, in progressively louder recurrences, interrupt a melodic process that consists of Gregorian chant melodies (bells have the Easter Introit, trumpets the Alleluia) and the song of a lark (woodwinds, symbolizing joy); then all sound simultaneously joined by the Hindu rhythm (gongs) again.

MEASURE	EVENT AND SCORING
1	Lent – 3 tam-tam hits
2	Bien modéré (♪ = 84) (Easter Introit) – cowbells, chimes
3	(Easter Alleluia) – trumpet; *tutti*
5	Lent – three tam-tam hits
6	Un peu vif (x = 200) (Alouette Calandre, bird of Greece and Spain) – woodwinds
12	Lent – three tam-tam hits
13	Bien modéré (e = 84) (Easter Introit) – cowbells, chimes
14	(Easter Alleluia) – trumpets; *tutti*
5 (14)	Sihavikrama – gongs
18	Lent – three tam-tam hits
19	Un peu vif (♪ = 200) (Alouette Calandre, bird of Greece and Spain) – woodwinds
27	Lent – three tam-tam hits
28	Bien modéré (♪ = 84) (Easter Introit & Alleluia) – *tutti*
5 (28)	Sihavikrama – gongs
29	Thème de la première pièce – horn, trombone, tuba, saxhorn
37	Lent – gongs and tam-tams
38	Eight *fermata* whole notes; *tutti*

MEASURE   EVENT AND SCORING

The winds play *ff*, on the other hand, so one can hear each chord-color; one must also hear the theme in the chimes and cencerros.

In this whole "Alouette Calandre" passage, the winds must observe with great care the slurs, détachés, and most of all the different dynamic markings; work on rhythmic exactness here.

One must hear all trumpets and trombones, who play *ff*; but these two musics have their colored harmonics, which one must also hear (winds and horns); third music (chimes and cencerros) must also be heard equally; as for the fourth music (gongs), respect all of the dynamic markings.

One must hear the three hits, and the three resonances; try to avoid allowing one of the gongs or one of the tam-tams to dominate the others; this must sound like a chord of resonances.

MOVEMENT 5:
"And I hear the voice of a great multitude." (Revelations XIX: 6)

"Like the motions of the great waters"—song of the worship of saints, whose book of Revelations describes a solemn power. The repeated percussion of the gongs, the low brass, and the orchestral *tutti* are made to play the chorale: an enormous *fortissimo*, unanimous and simple.

The apocalyptic vision is evoked by a *fortissimo* musical procession of transcendental simplicity.

MEASURE	EVENT AND SCORING
1	Très lent (♪ = 66) first statement – unison low brass, percussion
2	Second statement – harmonized *tutti*
3	First statement repeated (last two measures changed slightly) – unison low brass, percussion
4	Second statement repeated up M second – harmonized *tutti*
5	First statement repeated (some pitch changes) – unison low brass, percussion

MEASURE	EVENT AND SCORING
6	Second statement repeated down m second – harmonized *tutti*
8	Conclusion long notes – harmonized *tutti*

Very slowly until the end.

Throughout the piece, trumpet, trombone, tuba, and saxhorn must breathe on each note (while giving the illusion of a *legato*).

For the gongs, hit with force—each hit must be of the same intensity. Let them ring throughout the whole piece.

Unit 8: Suggested Listening

Et exspecto resurrectionem mortuorum; *La Ville d'en haut*, Cleveland Orchestra, Pierre Boulez, conductor

Et exspecto resurrectionem mortuorum; *Couleurs de la cité céleste*/Messiaen *Symphonies of wind instruments*/Stravinsky

Yvonne Loriod, piano (second work); group instrumental à percussion de Strasbourg (first and second works); Orchestre de Domaine musical (first and second works); New York Philharmonic (third work); Pierre Boulez, conductor. New York: Sony Classical, p1995.

Et exspecto resurrectionem mortuorum; *Couleurs de la Cité céleste*; *La Ville d'en haut*; *Oiseaux exotiques* – Peter Donohoe, piano, Netherlands Wind Ensemble, Reinbert de Leeuw, conductor

Et exspecto resurrectionem mortuorum; *La Ville d'en haut*; *Oiseaux exotiques* – Yvonne Loriod, piano, Berlin Radio Symphony Orchestra, Karl Albert Rickenbacher, conductor

Et exspecto resurrectionem mortuorum – Emory Wind Ensemble, Steven Everett, conductor

Couleurs de la Cité céleste; *Oiseaux exotiques* – Yvonne Loriod, piano, Ensemble InterContemporain, Pierre Boulez, conductor

Oiseaux exotiques – Terry Metzger, piano, Meadows Wind Ensemble, Jack Delaney, conductor

Quatuor pour la fin du temps; *Et exspecto resurrectionem mortuorum* – Royal Concertgebouw Orchestra, Bernard Haitink, conductor: Philips CD 446 578-2

Unit 9: Additional References and Resources

Alphonse Leduc (music publisher). 2000. *Alphonse Leduc*. [online] Accessed 12 August 2001.
http://www.alphonseleduc.com/english/index_main_neu.htm

Baker, Theodore, and Nicolas Slonimsky. *Baker's Biographical Dictionary of Musicians*. Simon & Schuster, March 1992 (ISBN: 0028724151).

Bell, Carla Huston. *Olivier Messiaen*. Boston: Twayne Publishers, 1984.

Bell, Carla Huston. *A structural and stylistic analysis of representative compositions of Olivier Messiaen*. Ed. D. Thesis, Columbia University, New York City, 1977.

Benitez, Vincent. 2000. *A Creative Legacy: Messiaen as Teacher of Analysis*. [online]. Accessed 14 August 2001. http://www.music.org/ProfActiv/Pubs/Sym/Vol40/articles/Benitez.html

Bernard, Jonathan. "Messiaen's Synaesthesia: The Correspondence between Color and Sound Structure in his Music." *Music Perception* 4, Fall 1986, pp. 41–68.

Boucourechliev, André. "Olivier Messiaen." In *The New Grove Dictionary of Music and Musicians*, Volume 12. Edited by Stanley Sadie. London: Macmillan, 1980, pp. 204–10.

Bruhn, Siglind. *Messiaen's Language of Mystical Love*. New York: Garland, 1998.

Bruhn, Siglind. "Religious Symbolism in the Music of Olivier Messiaen." *The American Journal of Semiotics* 13, Nos. 1–4, Fall 1996 (1998), pp. 277–309.

Covach, John. *The Musical Mechanics of Mysticism*. [online]. Accessed 15 August 2001. http://www.ibiblio.org/johncovach/messiaen.htm

Cross, Jonathan. Chapter 2 – "Block Forms," *The Stravinsky Legacy (Music in the Twentieth Century)*. Cambridge: Cambridge University Press, 1998.

Forte, Madeleine. *Olivier Messiaen, the Musical Mediator: a Study of the Influence of Liszt, Debussy, and Bartók*. Madison, NJ: Fairleigh Dickinson University Press, 1996.

Griffiths, Paul. "Olivier Messiaen." *The New Grove twentieth century French masters: Fauré, Debussy, Satie, Ravel, Poulenc, Messiaen, Boulez*. New York: W. W. Norton & Co., 1986.

Griffiths, Paul. *Olivier Messiaen and the Music of Time*. Ithaca: Cornell University Press, 1985.

Halbreich, Harry. *Olivier Messiaen*. Paris: Fayard, 1980.

Hamilton, David. "The New Releases." *High Fidelity*, 18, March 1968, p. 88.

Hill, Peter, ed. *The Messiaen Companion*. London: Faber and Faber, 1994.

Hill, Peter, ed. *The Messiaen Companion*. Portland, OR: Amadeus Press, 1995.

Hsu, Madeline. *Messiaen The Musical Mediator*. Madison: Farleigh-Dickinson University Press, 1996.

Indiana University. 05 April 2001. *Olivier Messiaen Annotated Bibliography*. [online]. Accessed 13 August 2001. http://theory.music.indiana.edu/t556/messiaen.html

Johnson, Robert Sherlaw. *Messiaen*. London: J. M. Dent & Sons Ltd., 1975.

Kelley, Robert. 19 April 2000. *Tradition, the Avant Garde, and Individuality in the Music of Olivier Messiaen: Musical Influences in Méditations sur la mystère de la Sainte-Trinité* [online]. Accessed 13 August 2001. http://www.geocities.com/Vienna/3624/messiaen.htm

Kennedy, Michael. *The Oxford Dictionary of Music*. Second edition. Oxford University Press: 1997 (ISBN: 0198691629.)

Malko, Jonathan. 23 April, 1999. *Olivier Messiaen*. [online] Accessed 13 August 2001. http://www.emory.edu/MUSIC/ARNOLD/messiaen2_content.html

Messiaen, Olivier. *Et exspecto resurrectionem mortuorum, pour orchestre de bois, cuivres, et percussions métalliques*. Paris: Alphonse Leduc, 1964.

Messiaen, Olivier. *The Technique of My Musical Language*. Volume 1/Text; Volume 2/Musical Examples. English translation by John Satterfield. Paris: Alphonse Leduc, 1956.

Messiaen, Olivier. *Music and Color: Conversations with Claude Samuel*. Edited by Claude Samuel. Trans. by E. Thomas Glasow. Portland, OR: Amadeus Press, 1994.

Messiaen, Olivier. *Traité de Rythme, de Couleur, et d'Ornithologie (1949–1992)*. Book 5, Volume 1, "Chants d'Oiseaux d'Europe." Paris: Alphonse Leduc, 1999.

Morgan, Robert P. *Twentieth Century Music*. New York: W. W. Norton & Company, 1991, pp. 335–40.

Muncy, Thomas R. *Messiaen's influence on post-war serialism*. M.M. thesis, North Texas State University (Denton, TX), 1984.

Nichols, Roger. *Messiaen*. Oxford Studies of Composers (13). London: Oxford University Press, 1975, pp. 70–4.

Sadie, Stanley, ed. *The New Grove Dictionary of Music and Musicians*. St. Martins Press, September 1995 (ISBN: 1561591742).

Samuel, Claude. *Conversations with Olivier Messiaen*. Trans. by Felix Aprahamian. London: Stainer & Bell, 1976, pp. 97–8.

Shepard, Brian K. "The Symbolic Elements of Messiaen's Work for Wind Ensemble, *Couleurs de la cité céleste*." *Journal of Band Research*, 18, Fall 1982, pp. 52–9.

Simeone, Nigel. *Olivier Messiaen: A Bibliographical Catalogue of Messiaen's Works*. Musikbibliographische Arbeiten, 14. Tutzing: Hans Schneider, 1998.

Simms, Bryan R. *Music of the Twentieth Century: Style and Structure*. New York: Schirmer Books, 1986, pp. 403–9.

Slonimsky, Nicolas. *Music Since 1900*. Schirmer Books, July 1994 (ISBN: 0028724186).

Sun, Shu-Wen. "Birdsong and Pitch-Class Sets in Messiaen's L'Alouette Calandrelle." D.M.A. dissertation, University of Oregon, 1995.

Thomas, Neil, and Bruce Hembd. 1999. *Robert King Music Sales*. [online] Accessed 12 August 2001. http://www.rkingmusic.com/

Troup, Malcolm. "Orchestral Music of the 1950s and 1960s," *The Messiaen Companion*. Edited by Peter Hill. Portland, OR: Amadeus Press, 1994.

Von Gunden, Heidi Cecilia. *Timbre as symbol in selected works of Olivier Messiaen*. Ph.D. thesis, University of California (San Diego, CA), 1977.

Wallendorf, Paulette Sue. *The role of textural design in the music of Olivier Messiaen: a study of Couleurs de la cité céleste*. MM Thesis, North Texas State University (Denton, TX), 1981.

Contributed by:

Matthew Mailman
Director of Bands and Associate Professor of Music
Oklahoma City University
Oklahoma City, Oklahoma

Teacher Resource Guide

Fascinating Ribbons

Joan Tower
(b. 1938)

Unit 1: Composer

Joan Tower was born in New Rochelle, New York, grew up in South America, and received her professional training at Bennington College and Columbia University, where she earned her doctorate in composition. Tower is currently the Asher Edelman Professor of Music at Bard College, where she has taught since 1972. She serves as Composer-in-Residence for the Orchestra of St. Luke's, co-artistic director of the Yale/Norfolk Chamber Music Festival, and Composer-in-Residence at the Summit Institute for the Arts and Humanities in Utah. During her three-year residency (1985–1988) with the St. Louis Symphony, Tower wrote *Silver Ladders*, which won the prestigious 1990 Grawemeyer Award for Music Composition. Her music has been performed by orchestras all over the world, including St. Louis, New York, San Francisco, Minnesota, Tokyo NHK, the National Symphony, and London Philharmonic.

Unit 2: Composition

The composer writes:

> *Fascinating Ribbons* was commissioned by the College Band Directors National Association in 2000 with a consortium of thirty-one bands. It is dedicated to Jack Stamp, that intrepid "stalker" of composers who will not give up until he gets a band piece from them. (I should know: it took him five years to get me to write one!) Since this was my first foray into the band world, I decided that a short piece would be the wisest course. One of the rhythmic motives was taken from

George Gershwin's "Fascinating Rhythms" and many of the contours of motives in the piece are shaped in curved "ribbon" patterns—hence the title of the work. I am happy to be finally entering the band world—a generous and hardworking one that has generated so many excellent wind, brass, and percussion players. It seems also to be a place of people that actually love living composers! I hope that my piece will live long enough for me to get to know this world a lot better.

Unit 3: Historical Perspective

The quest to have major composers already established in the "orchestral world" write for the wind band is not a new idea. In 1932, Edwin Franko Goldman stated:

> The one greatest drawback to bands is the fact that most of the music which they perform is music that was originally written for orchestra...through the influence of the American Bandmasters Association—the great composers of the world are now writing original works directly for band.

Goldman was instrumental in urging major composers to write works for band. A sample list appears below:

A Solemn Music by Virgil Thomson (1949)
A Walt Whitman Overture by Norman Lloyd (1960)
Canzona by Peter Mennin (1951)
Celebration Overture by Paul Creston (1956)
Chorale and Alleluia by Howard Hanson (1954)
Huntingtower Ballad by Ottorino Respighi (1932)
Mademoiselles by Robert Russell Bennett (1952)
March with Trumpets by William Bergsma (1957)
Night Fantasy by Robert Ward (1962)
Pageant by Vincent Persichetti (1953)
Praeludium and Allegro by Vittorio Giannini (1958)
Santa Fe Saga by Morton Gould (1957)
Singing Band by Henry Cowell
The People's Choice by Douglas Moore (1959)
The Power of Rome and the Christian Heart by Percy Grainger (1948)
Tunbridge Fair by Walter Piston (1950)

Selected works written for the Goldman Band with premiere dates:
A Glorious Day by Albert Roussel (June 19, 1933)
A Legend by Paul Creston (July 16, 1942)
Divertimento by Vincent Persichetti (June 16, 1950)
Prelude and Fugue by Wallingford Riegger (June 16, 1943)

Spring Overture by Leo Sowerby (June 27, 1942)
Theme and Variations by Arnold Schoenberg (June 27, 1946)

The College Band Directors Association continues the pursuit of established composers to write for the wind band.

Unit 4: Technical Considerations

The instrumentation of *Fascinating Ribbons* is not unique, but it does require the following instruments: English horn, soprano saxophone (in place of 1st alto), trumpet in C, and piano, along with the traditional band complement. The work is a rhythmic challenge for all players. The "ribbon" activity requires woodwind players to play sixteenth note "ribbons" at both loud and soft volumes. The saxophone section has an extended cadenza-like section that "dialogues" with the percussion section. The low brass has two challenging sections (measures 90 through 117 and 139 through 155). They are exposed and difficult, particularly in the sustaining of intensity. Though range demands are not extreme, 1st trumpet is required to "hover" above the staff quite often. Finally, the work is equally challenging for the conductor to conduct. The many stylistic and tempo changes, coupled with the plethora of meter changes, will require some practice.

Unit 5: Stylistic Considerations

The work exhibits a wide range of stylistic demands that require the players to perform with great control. The prominence of the dotted-eighth/sixteenth rhythm is the organic rhythmic device in the work. The ensemble must possess the ability to change from powerful rhythmic "barbarism" to lyrical linear statements when "ribbon" activity begins. The scoring also presents many opportunities of "hand-offs" or "dove-tailing" that need to be performed with seamless perfection.

Unit 6: Musical Elements

The entire work is about contrasts between the driving dotted-eighth/sixteenth rhythm and the "ribbon" interludes. However, within this framework is a driving energy that is a challenge to sustain, particularly in the "ribbon" sections. Particularly in the slow sections, instrumental color is explored. Most importantly, the musical elements in *Fascinating Ribbons* are those elements found in all of Tower's music. Careful study of several of her orchestral works will glean valuable insight to the conductor.

Unit 7: Form and Structure

MEASURE	EVENT AND SCORING
1–18	Slow; introduction of rhythmic motive
19–51	Rhythmic motive grows into "ribbon-like" passages
52–89	Combination of rhythmic motive and "ribbons"
90–117	Low brass statement; "Stravinsky-like" barbarism
118–138	"Ribbon" interlude
139–155	Low brass statement returns, accompanied by the rhythmic motive
156–177	Juxtaposition of "ribbons" with rhythmic motive
178–183	Saxophone section "cadenza" with answers by full ensemble with the rhythmic motive
184–202	Saxophone cadenza continues as a dialogue with the percussion section
203–end	Coda based upon rhythmic motive

Unit 8: Suggested Listening

Joan Tower:
> *Concerto for Orchestra* – Colorado Symphony, Koch
> *Sequoia* – St. Louis Symphony, Nonesuch
> *Silver Ladders* – St. Louis Symphony, Nonesuch

Unit 9: Additional References and Resources

Hitchcock, H. Wiley, and Stanley Sadie, eds. *The New Grove Dictionary of American Music.* New York: MacMillan Press, 1986.

McCutchan, Ann. *The Muse that Sings.* Cary, NC: Oxford University Press, 1999.

Contributed by:

Jack Stamp
Director of Band Studies
Indiana University of Pennsylvania
Indiana, Pennsylvania

Teacher Resource Guide

J'ai été au bal
Donald Grantham
(b. 1947)

Unit 1: Composer

Donald Grantham is a native of Duncan, Oklahoma, where he grew up in a musical household and studied piano and trumpet in his formative years. During his high school years, he studied theory and composition from faculty at (then) the Oklahoma College of Liberal Arts and Midwestern State University. He received his Bachelor of Music from the University of Oklahoma in 1970 and then moved to California, where he pursued both his master's and DMA degrees at the University of Southern California. His principal teachers there were Ramiro Cortés, Robert Linn, and Halsey Stevens. Further studies were undertaken in 1973 and 1974 in Fontainebleau, France, with Nadia Boulanger. Currently, Grantham is Professor of Composition at the University of Texas at Austin.

Co-author of *The Technique of Orchestration* (a text which, in an earlier edition, had a marked musical effect on him in his youth), Grantham has won the Prix Lili Boulanger, the Nissim/ASCAP Orchestral Composition Prize, the NBA/William Revelli Composition Award on two occasions (for *Bum's Rush* in 1995 and for *Fantasy Variations* in 1998), and three awards from the National Endowment for the Arts. He was awarded the 1999 ABA/Ostwald Composition Award for *J'ai été au bal*.

Grantham currently resides in Austin, Texas, and publishes his music privately through his own company, Piquant Press.

Unit 2: Composition

J'ai été au bal is a composition of ten minutes' duration, commissioned in 1999 by the University of Texas–Austin Wind Ensemble. The conductor (Jerry Junkin) gave no restrictions to Grantham as to length, difficulty, or scope in the commission, but Grantham knew from the outset that he wanted to include some Cajun/Zydeco music in the composition. As the title implies, the composition is associated with dancing and is comprised of three large, connected sections. The first and last sections rely heavily on Cajun folk song, and the middle third of the composition is built around early twentieth century jazz music of New Orleans. The instrumentation calls for:

Piccolo (3rd flute)	4 horns	Crash cymbals
2 flutes	4 trumpets	3 snare drums
2 oboes	4 trombones	Spoons (3 sets)
English horn	Euphonium	Trap set
E-flat clarinet	Tuba	Maracas
3 B-flat clarinets	Double bass	Bells
Bass clarinet	Timpani	2 Suspended cymbals
2 bassoons	Piano	Guiro
Contrabassoon	Celesta	Tam-tam
B-flat soprano saxophone	Vibraphone	Mark tree
E-flat alto saxophone	2 bongos	Triangle
B-flat tenor saxophone	2 congas	Small triangle
E-flat baritone saxophone	2 xylophones	Cowbell
	Slapstick	Washboard
	Chinese cymbal	4 brake drums

Even though the orchestration is for expanded wind ensemble, it should be noted that, with the lone exception of contrabassoon, all other wind instruments have unique voices in the scoring. With the exception of horn, all of the winds and string bass have solos. Due to extreme demands of technique, *tessitura*, and tonal quality, *J'ai été au bal* may perhaps be performed well by only the best college and professional wind ensembles. Regardless, the high quality of compositional technique and scoring already cause many conductors and listeners to consider it one of the masterworks for wind ensemble.

Unit 3: Historical Perspective

Started in 1998 and completed in early 1999, this recent work for wind ensemble is part of a contemporary pattern of composition in the last twenty years. In the past two decades, ensembles have increasingly relied on commissions (paying composers to write specific works for a particular group, ensemble, and/or occasion) to have new works performed. As more ensembles and conductors wish to add to the wind ensemble repertoire, fees for compositions have increased dramatically. It is now common for well-known composers to charge $10,000 to $20,000 (and even more) for a single composition. In conjunction with these trends, the technical and endurance demands on wind ensembles have also risen dramatically. From the standpoint of the compositional process, the organic unity present in *J'ai été au bal* (see Unit 7) through folk song is as prevalent as the modern wind band itself. Examples of such organic unity through folk influences can be found in such disparate compositions as Holst's *Suite in E-flat*, H. Owen Reed's *La Fiesta Mexicana*, and Husa's *Music for Prague 1968*. The use of popular music in the compositional process is not new to Grantham; he has written three other works for band with some degree of jazz or popular music influence. In a 1997 interview, he recalled the origins of this recent trend:

> I guess about ten years ago I wanted to incorporate some popular elements, some more obviously American elements into my instrumental music than I had done before. That also ties in with the Robert Chandler sort of thing. Particular jazz elements from that period appealed to me.[1]

Unit 4: Technical Considerations

The technical challenges in *J'ai été au bal* are very difficult and are based on tempo, rhythm, chromaticism, syncopation, and *tessitura* throughout the composition. The first 103 measures (quarter note = 69, quarter note = 138, and quarter note = 144) are only moderately difficult in comparison to the rest of the composition. The technical challenges in this first section are related to the shifting time signatures of +, ", and Z, though it should be noted that these meter changes occur in the first thirty-six measures and at a slow tempo. The middle third of the composition (measures 104 through 231) is in C at a tempo of (at least) 96 to the half note. At that tempo, the use and prevalence of swing eighth notes makes the technique very challenging. Even the initial tuba solo of this section is a precursor of the advanced technical challenges to come. (All musical examples are given in written pitches.)

---

1 James Robert Tapia, "Donald Grantham's *Bum's Rush*: A Conductor's Analysis and Performance Guide." DMA dissertation, University of Texas–Austin, 1997, p. 12.

Example 1: mm. 115–127

The tuba solo is repeated as a duet with euphonium. What follows is a shout chorus for brass punctuated by a woodwind *obbligato*:

Example 2: mm. 147–151

Starting with measure 237, the time signature is + at a tempo of quarter note = 138. From there until the end, there are many challenging parts with sixteenth note passages, especially for the woodwinds. Typical of this section is the opening "hoe-down," first introduced by the clarinet in a chorus of twelve measures:

Example 3: mm. 240–253

Rhythmic challenges are moderate and are in two areas. Since the middle third of the composition is notated "…in light swing rhythm," students must be made aware of the performance practice and stress involved in swing eighth notes. The triplets from example 2 are indicative of the woodwind counterpoint used throughout the middle third of the composition. This rhythm, combined with speed and chromaticism, make for very difficult passages. The use of syncopation is a prominent compositional device, and both director and students must be aware of the individual and section role in rhythmic ensemble. These roles are made more difficult by the frequent pointillistic nature of the counterpoint, where different sections share the melodic and harmonic roles in alternating phrases. Instrumental ranges are quite extreme for upper woodwinds; piccolo, flute, oboe, and clarinet play much of the composition above the staff. Below is a summary of highest written pitches for selected instruments:

Piccolo: *altissimo* B-flat   Trumpet 1: high D
Flute 1: *altissimo* C   Horn 1: high B-flat
Flute 2: *altissimo* B-flat   Trombone 1: high B-flat
Oboe: high E-flat   Euphonium: high A-flat
Clarinet 1: *altissimo* F-sharp   Tuba: C above bass clef
Clarinet 2/3: *altissimo* E

Unit 5: Stylistic Considerations

The use of articulation is consistent with the form of the composition. The opening thirty-six measures are written primarily in a detached style, which contrasts greatly with the lyric writing of measures 38 through 103. These measures are based directly on a Cajun song "Allons danser, Colinda," which is presented in the woodwinds. Example 4 shows the lyrical writing and the detail of instruction Grantham gives to the phrasing:

Example 4: mm. 38–47

Greater attention must be paid to the middle third of the composition, which is a quasi-Dixieland jazz ensemble of expanded proportions. All members of the ensemble must know the proper rhythmic interpretation of swing eighth notes, as measures 104 through 231 rely primarily on that interpretation. The clarinets (and later, the saxophones) have a *soli* melody in unison at measures 172 through 191 that is reminiscent of bop in both rhythm and melodic content. The clarinet, tenor saxophone, baritone saxophone, trumpet, trombone, euphonium, tuba, and string bass soloists have significant roles within a Dixieland style; it is suggested that individual coaching and listening to recordings take place with these players. The percussion writing of measures 168 through 188 and 253 through 269 is intended to simulate a Zydeco band; suitable recordings should be made available to the percussion for the use of spoons along with an actual washboard. In the final third of the composition, players should be aware that a stylistic layering technique is used. The lyrical song from the first third of the composition (Allons danser, Colinda) is combined with "Les flammes d'enfer" and elements from the beginning of the composition. For a successful performance and understanding of *J'ai été au bal*, students must be familiar with the styles of (Louisiana) folk song, Dixieland jazz, bop, and swing.

Unit 6: Musical Elements

From a tonal view, C major, E-flat major, A-flat major, and G minor are the primary scalar and tonal resources. These scales are rarely shown in their unaltered form; Grantham usually presents them in chromatic variants. His preference is for octatonic or blues forms of these scales. For example, the blues scale on C is:

C – D – E-flat – F – (F-sharp) – G – A-flat – B-flat – C

The octatonic (alternating whole- and half-steps) version of this scale is:

C – D – E-flat – F – F-sharp – G-sharp/A-flat – A – B – C

or

C – D-flat – E-flat – E – F-sharp – G – A – B-flat – C

Notice the similarities between both types (blues and octatonic) of scales. Harmonically, Grantham uses much of the complex vocabulary of jazz and prefers either extended sonorities (seventh and ninth chords with chromatic alterations) or "split" chords to pure triads. For example, a C major chord with a split root would have both the "normal" root and the raised root (in this case: C, C-sharp, E, G). Again, these types of harmonic and melodic constructions are consistent with blues and octatonic scales. In the area of rhythm, Grantham uses a wide palette that includes layering of duplets and triplets simultaneously. There is a high degree of pointillism throughout the composition, both between sections of the ensemble and even within the same section. Thematic material is frequently broken up so sections alternate motives or phrases with melodic and accompanimental roles. For a greater understanding of the composition in the rehearsal, it is recommended that the following terms be familiar to both conductor and student:

Augmentation
Blues scale
Diminution
Dixieland band (instrumentation)
Fugato
Jazz harmonic alteration: raised/lowered ninth, eleventh, and thirteenth
Mediant relationships (keys)
Motive: rhythmic, melodic, and harmonic
Octatonic scale
Pointillism
Polyrhythm
Shout chorus
Simultaneous recapitulation
"Split" chords (root, third, or fifth)
"Walking" bass
Zydeco

Unit 7: Form and Structure

Note that the introductory motive and its accompaniment (Example 5) are the source of much of the harmonic, accompanimental, and contrapuntal material, particularly the motives marked A and B:

Example 5: mm. 1–3

SECTION	MEASURE	EVENT AND SCORING
Macro form: Introduction–A–B–C–Coda		
Introduction	1–37	E-flat
Fanfare	1–6	Starts in C
a	7–14	E-flat blues
b	15–26	
c	27–37	
A	38–103	E-flat
A1	38–47	Flute
A2	48–55	
A3	56–63	
Transition	64–72	
A1	73–78	Clarinet
A2	79–84	
A3	85–93	
Codetta	94–103	
B	104–232	A-flat
Introduction	104–115	Percussion
Chorus	116–127	Tuba solo
Chorus	128–139	Tuba/euphonium duet
Bridge	140–145	
Shout Chorus 1	146–159	
Bridge	160–167	
Transition	168–171	Percussion
Fugato	172–191	Clarinet; G minor
Development	192–209	
Transition	210–215	Bop style; A-flat major
Shout Chorus 2	216–226	

SECTION	MEASURE	EVENT AND SCORING
Codetta	227–232	Dixieland style
C	233–382	C
Introduction	233–240	
Counterpoint	241–252	Clarinet
Verse 1	253–268	
Verse 2	269–284	F major
Interlude	285–292	Brass
Verse 3	293–324	A-flat minor
Transition	325–348	
Recapitulation	348–382	C major; A material plus music from m. 241
Coda	383–401	C; "Les flammes d'enfer" plus Interlude material

Unit 8: Suggested Listening
Donald Grantham:
> *Bum's Rush* (1994)
> *Don't You See?* (2001)
> *Fantasy on Mr. Hyde's Song* (1998)
> *Fantasy Variations* (1997)
> *Farewell to Gray* (2001)
> *Fayetteville Bop* (2002)
> *Kentucky Harmony* (2000)
> *Northern Celebration* (2001)
> *Phantasticke Sprites* (2002)
> *Southern Harmony* (1998)
> *Variations on an American Cavalry Song* (2001)

Frank Ticheli, *Cajun Folk Songs I and II*

Recordings:
Grantham, Donald. *J'ai été au bal* – Texas A&M University Commerce Wind Ensemble (Dallas, TX): Bandmaster BM-1012, 2000
Grantham, Donald. *J'ai été au bal* – University of Florida Wind Ensemble (Clarence, NY): Mark Records 3490-MCD, 2000
Grantham, Donald. *J'ai été au bal* – University of North Texas Wind Ensemble (Boca Raton, FL): Klavier KCD-11109, 2000
Grantham, Donald. *J'ai été au bal* –University of Texas at Austin Wind Ensemble (Clarence, NY): Mark Records 3680-MCD, 2002

Unit 9: Additional References and Resources

Blank, Les, and Chris Strachwitx. *J'ai été au bal (I Went to the Dance): the Cajun and Zydeco Music of Louisiana.* El Cerrito, CA: Brazos Films, 1989. Videocassette (84 minutes).

Dempsey, Tom. *Origins of Zydeco and Cajun Music.* Seattle, WA: 1996. www.scn.org/rec/zydeco/origins.html.

Emge, Jeffrey. "Third-Stream Music for Band: An Examination of Jazz Influences in Five Selected Compositions for Winds and Percussion." DMA thesis, University of Cincinnati, 2000.

Hanna, Scott Stewart. "*J'ai été au bal*: Cajun Music and the Wind Band in the Late Twentieth Century." DMA treatise, University of Texas–Austin, 1999.

Lindberg, Kathryn. "Third Stream Music in Twentieth Century American Wind Band Literature." PhD dissertation, University of Florida, 2000.

Tapia, James Robert. "Donald Grantham's *Bum's Rush*: A Conductor's Analysis and Performance Guide." DMA dissertation, University of Texas–Austin, 1997.

Contributed by:

Jeffrey Emge
University of Texas at Tyler
Tyler, Texas

Teacher Resource Guide

Les Couleurs Fauves
(Vivid Colors)

Karel Husa
(b. 1921)

Unit 1: Composer

Over the last several decades, the wind band world has known no better friend than Karel Husa. His contributions to the band's repertoire have helped to define the medium as a viable force in the modern art-music world, capable of performing contemporary compositions of the highest artistic integrity and technical complexity.

Karel Husa was born in Prague, Czechoslovakia, in 1921. Although guided by his parents toward a career in engineering, he was also permitted to take lessons in painting and music. In 1941, he was able to avoid deportation by the Nazis by gaining admission to the Prague Conservatory. This occurred after the technical institute in which he was initially enrolled was closed following a student protest in 1939. From 1946 to 1948, he attended the *Ecole normale de musique* in Paris, and he attended the Paris Conservatory from 1948 to 1949. It was during his Paris years that he studied composition with Nadia Boulanger, Arthur Honegger, and Darius Milhaud. He also studied conducting with Jean Fournet, Eugene Bigot, and André Cluytens. An early but quite notable accomplishment for conductor Husa was his production of the first recording of Bartók's *Miraculous Mandarin*.

After immigrating to the United States, Husa joined the faculty of Cornell University (Ithaca, New York) in 1954 at the invitation of American musicologist Donald Jay Grout. He taught at Cornell until his retirement in 1992. In addition to teaching music theory and composition, he was also responsible for conducting the university orchestra (until 1975). He obtained American citizenship status in 1959.

Husa was strongly influenced by the neo-classicism of Honegger and Stravinsky, and the use of folk music idioms by Bartók and Janácek. By the end of the 1950s, he was trying a more atonal and experimental style that included serial procedures. Husa had codified his multiple influences and musical theories in the form of the *Concerto for Alto Saxophone and Concert Band* in 1967. The Concerto evidenced the formal clarity of neo-classicism but also incorporated a harmonic and melodic vocabulary more characteristic of serialism.

Husa's *String Quartet No. 3*, written in 1968, was honored with the 1969 Pulitzer Prize. Other important recognitions include the 1993 Grawemeyer Award for Music Composition (worth $150,000) for his *Cello Concerto*, and the first Sudler Award for Composition in 1983 for his *Concerto for Wind Ensemble*. He has received the Czech Republic's highest civilian recognition, the State Medal Award of Merit, First Class. This was bestowed upon Husa by Czech President Vaclav Havel in October 1995. In 2000, the distinguished composer donated his personal library to the Ithaca College of Music. He has conducted many of the world's greatest orchestras and regularly appears on university campuses as a guest artist.

Unit 2: Composition

About *Les Couleurs Fauves*, Husa wrote:

> I have always been fascinated by colors, not only in music but also in nature and art. The paintings of the Impressionists and Fauvists have been particularly attractive to me, and their French origin accounts for the French title of my piece. The two movements ("Persisting Bells" and "Ritual Dance Masks") gave me the chance to play with colors—sometimes gentle, sometimes raw—of the wind ensemble, something John (Paynter) also liked to do in his conducting.
>
> John has been a wonderful friend since we met for the first time in 1968, when we both taught summer courses at Northwestern University. At that time I had written only one work for band, the Saxophone Concerto. John's devotion to wind ensembles made a great impression on me and certainly influenced me to write more for these instrument combinations. His honesty and dedication to the art of music and to teaching was exemplary. He had first-class baton technique and communicated to the players, as well as to the audiences, in a very moving way: powerful, passionate, or delicate and gentle, as the score required. I was reminded of those French painters whom I admired as a young student in Paris. They called themselves fauvists (vivid, wild), for they used bold, often powerful strokes of brushes with unmixed colors. Their paintings, though, breathe with sensitivity, as his conducting had these characteristics,

and hopefully Les Couleurs Fauves will remind you of them. I am most grateful to Dr. Mallory Thompson and all performers for their devoted work on my composition.

Unit 3: Historical Perspective

Les Couleurs Fauves was commissioned as a tribute to John Paynter, the retiring director of bands at Northwestern University to honor the fortieth anniversary of his appointment to the faculty. Lamentably, Mr. Paynter, who was widely recognized as a strong advocate of new music, died before the work's premiere. The commissioning was underwritten by Mr. and Mrs. Charles T. Urban, Jr., with support from alumni and friends of the Northwestern University School of Music. It was premiered by the Northwestern University Symphonic Wind Ensemble with Karel Husa guest conducting on November 16, 1996, in Pick-Staiger Concert Hall in Evanston, Illinois. It is just over sixteen minutes in duration. The second performance of *Les Couleurs Fauves* occurred at the Mid-West International Band and Orchestra Clinic on December 18, 1996, in Chicago. The performing ensemble was the United States Navy Band, and it was conducted by the composer.

Unit 4: Technical Considerations

Les Couleurs Fauves is intended for a large wind ensemble or symphonic band. In addition to what might be considered a normal instrumentation, the score includes parts for four trumpets in C, four trombones, two euphoniums, bass saxophone/B-flat contrabass clarinet, double bass/contrabassoon, four percussion and timpani, and alto clarinet, which has at least several measures not doubled with any other voice. To maximize the coloristic intentions of the composer, it would be best to attempt *Les Couleurs Fauves* with all parts covered as requested in the score, even if doubled.

Husa's compositions typically make formidable demands upon the players in terms of range, rhythmic complexity, note density, and harmonic structure. There are also many requests for special effects, including *glissandi*, note-bending, free *accelerando*, fluttertonguing, rapid articulation patterns (perhaps requiring double and triple tonguing ability by brass players), and aleatory passages for woodwinds. In addition to advanced wind players, *Les Couleurs Fauves* requires four strong percussionists who are quite proficient on mallet instruments and a near virtuoso timpanist. Five timpani are necessary to cover the pitch requirements.

Unit 5: Stylistic Considerations

This work is fully characteristic of many advanced twentieth century compositional techniques. It is demanding from just about every possible standpoint. Although one would be tempted to identify it as atonal and serialistic, it is the author's contention that this work does not easily lend itself to those characterizations. There are more than several places where a tonal center appears to be present, and structure seems to be more derived from the composer's intention to achieve broader coloristic effects than those that might be dictated from a strict serial procedure. Although pitch-class analysis would no doubt be useful toward gaining a more complete understanding of melodic and harmonic structure, it is not necessary to obtain a generalized feel for the nature of the composition.

Crucial toward accomplishing the composer's expressive aims is an understanding of the dynamic shape of each movement and how it drives toward particular arrival locations. The first movement represents an arch of sound, with the climax occurring just past its mathematical center (perhaps in deference to the Golden Mean). The second movement contains two larger sections. The first section itself is actually divided into two parts, each representing a long *crescendo* to the maximum density for the particular thought being developed. The second larger section is a kind of homage to Ravel's *Bolero,* with its long *crescendo* driven by the addition of different instrumental timbres that thicken the texture contrapuntally, all above a quasi-bolero rhythm in the percussion. Performers must be extremely conscientious about obtaining the exact effect requested by the composer, especially in areas where he specifies bell-like articulations, brassy or reedy timbres, or sounds of great intensity.

Unit 6: Musical Elements

MELODY:

Melody is organized by sets or cells of selected pitches. It tends to be both smooth (conjunct) and extremely angular (disjunct), often in close proximity. When in slower tempi, the pitch density is often quite thick, containing figures similar to baroque-style ornamentation. When tempi are fast, melodic material tends to stay closer to the basic division of the beat in terms of density, but the variety of intervals present (as dictated by pitch set utilized) continues to be very diverse. Strong soloists are required on oboe, English horn, piccolo, and clarinet for certain passages. The disjunct nature of many passages, along with the sometimes atonal pitch order, make accurate performance difficult. It is vital that performers attempt to hear the correct note before playing. Since pitch is carefully controlled, it follows that correctness of pitch (and intonation) is critical. This is too often overlooked in certain twentieth century music.

Melodic demand and presence also varies with texture throughout the work. Monophonic, homophonic, and polyphonic textures are used to highlight or intensify melody as well as other elements. Some very effective polyphony occurs in the second half of "Ritual Dance Masks" during the quasi-bolero section (second half of the movement). To achieve maximum sound presence and dissonance, however, Husa favors more homophonictextures, as evidenced by the powerful chorale-type statement at the end of the work.

In unpublished performance notes from the composer, he offers the following suggestions regarding pitch concerns to enhance the performance:

> In the first movement, "Persistent Bells," during measures 38 through 39, trombones and euphoniums must bring out the descending notes: E, D-sharp, C-sharp, B, and E. At measure 40, trumpets and trombones must be heard, probably with "bells up" from measures 40 to 53 for trumpets and 40 to 49 for trombones. Beginning in measure 51, low voices must strongly bring out the descending notes: B, B-flat, A-flat, G-flat, F-flat, and D-flat. Saxophones must play at their most intense level when a fortissimo dynamic is requested. From measure 73, woodwind releases must end precisely as notated (not too long or short).

HARMONY:

The method of deriving harmony in *Les Couleurs Fauves* is the result of combining notes from the melodic sets or cells of pitches. Often, the resulting harmonies are clusters of major and minor seconds or thirds placed within the same or contrasting instrumental timbres, depending upon the degree of dissonance desired. Maximum dissonance is achieved as the composer builds vertical structures that include minor seconds in a homogenous timbre. The effect of dissonance is softened when close intervallic structures are assigned to voices of contrasting color. In several places, a major/minor ambivalence appears to have been established, such as in the opening of "Ritual Dance Masks." There, the trumpets alternate three pitches: E-flat, B, and D. This might be perceived as a reference to B major/minor, although the intention is confounded by a pedal E-flat in low reeds, and then a pedal D in low brass. Another interesting structure may be found at the end of the second movement where, following a massive chorale of dissonant affect, a dominant/tonic relationship may be found as a quasi-cadence moves to a final chord that is essentially a G tonic.

RHYTHM:

Husa uses a tremendous variety of rhythmic figures in *Les Couleurs Fauves*, often superimposed. It would be common to find simple and compound division occurring simultaneously, and for diverse levels of rhythmic density to be utilized in close proximity to achieve extreme complexity in the texture. Furthermore, the work includes many rhythmic notations/figures not commonly encountered in other wind music. There is extensive syncopation in compound division and frequent changes of pitch on divisions and subdivisions of the beat. Although the intent is to produce micro-moments of tension/release, the effect is to challenge the players to be constantly internalizing subdivision while performing this music. Rhythm is also extensively used to achieve textural aims. A characteristic technique employed by Husa is to write an *ostinato* rhythm that is divided among different voices to achieve a texture of color. A good example of this may be found in the percussion part in Movement II, measures 89 through 118.

Les Couleurs Fauves is an outstanding example of contemporary rhythmic notation, not only from the standpoint of creating texture with rhythm but also the technique of notating diverse rhythmic figures that exist contrary to the prevailing division.

In "Persistent Bells," the composer suggests that the keyboard percussionist perform rather freely, with little *accelerando* and *ritard.* as felt by the performers. At measure 35, the rhythm must be precise. From measure 59 to the end, the percussionist may again play *liberamente*. In "Ritual Dance Masks," Husa makes the following further recommendations:

> I conduct in 2 at the beginning and then in measures 11 through 15 switch progress into one beat per measure, then at measure 40 (or measure 39) go into two beats, and after measure 50, into one again. Same at measures 79 through 90 and 118 through 132 approximately. At measure 257, not too slow. I believe one has to keep the tempo going ahead; otherwise, the players may slow it down progressively. At measure 365, trumpets and later (mm. 382-383) trombones, baritones, and tubas [should] think of the triplet as if written in 3/8 or 6/8, or as in the first movement of Beethoven's Seventh Symphony, but with the first note long. There is a tendency, if one thinks it as [a] triplet, that one gets slower.

TIMBRE:

Timbre is the principal concern or driving force for the construction of this work. In *Les Couleurs Fauves*, Husa extensively explores different combinations of instruments for coloristic effect. Brass are often pitted against woodwinds, and control of dynamic levels is essential to achieve the composer's sonic objectives. In several locations, measures 34 and 35 in "Persistent Bells" for example, woodwinds are asked to *crescendo* past the brass, creating a shift of color. This technique is found throughout the work. Moreover, Husa is also unusually specific when compared to many other composers regarding the type of mute or the kind of stick to be used to obtain a particular sound. He is likewise very specific and generous in his use of descriptive terminology.

An advanced musical concept that may be explored would be control of dissonance through the use of instrumental timbre. *Les Couleurs Fauves* is simply full of examples of different instrumental combinations for coloristic effect. The impact of rhythmic, textural, and pitch organization on timbre is easily illuminated in various sections of this work. It is a veritable orchestration textbook for wind and percussion writing.

In unpublished performance notes from the composer, he offers the following suggestions regarding pitch concerns to enhance the performance:

In "Ritual Dance Masks": From the beginning until the trumpets, later saxophones, at m. 111 woodwinds and trombones, as well as the percussion, will be dominating until m. 172, but the swellings in the low winds have to be brought more and more in evidence as music progresses. At m. 257, the snare drum could be even covered for some time until approximately m. 301 and vibraphone also has to be very soft to start with. On the other hand, the clarinet, piccolo soli very dramatic (like 2 fighting birds). Short notes (horns in m. 308, saxophones in m. 310, trombones in measures 312 through 313 and all others should be very powerful and *forte*.

Unit 7: Form and Structure

Les Couleurs Fauves is a two-movement work, with the second movement divided into two broad sections of approximately the same length. The first of those two sections is itself divided into two smaller parts that may be identified by the contrast of beat division in brass voices (the first part compound, the second part simple). The composition may be diagramed as follows:

Total composition time: ca. 16:00

SECTION	MEASURE	EVENT AND SCORING

Movement 1: "Persistent Bells" (4:45)
3/4 time, *Moderato molto* (quarter note = 56–60)

	MEASURE	EVENT AND SCORING
	1–9	Solo oboe above sparse accompaniment by glockenspiel; piano
	10–20	Addiction of 2nd oboe with chimes and vibraphone
	20	Addition of English horn
	20–30	Texture thickens with addition of more woodwinds and percussion, some brass
	31–39	Substantial addition of brass; increase in percussion density and a significant *crescendo*
	40–54	Area of greatest sound with several climactic figures or events; this is the top of the dynamic arch; some shifting of time signature to produce compound division notation more easily

SECTION	MEASURE	EVENT AND SCORING
	55–72	Controlled *diminuendo*; not a mirror image, but the decrease of voices is similar to the order of addition used in the *crescendo*
	67–69	Important tuba solo, disjunct
	73–end	Piccolo solo with sparse accompaniment

Movement II: "Ritual Dance Masks" (11:25)

Section 1 – two long *crescendos*, the first emphasizing compound division figures, the second emphasizing simple subdivided figures (5:45)

Part 1:
6/8 time, *Vivace* (dotted-quarter note = 144)

	1–10	Opening statement in trumpet; *forte*
	11–39	Temple block maintains disjunct *ostinato* against a long note accompaniment in low reeds first, then low brass
	40–49	Second wind statement; fragmented eighth note idea presented in trumpet and horn, with overlapping dissonant intervals
	50–78	Percussion answer with multiple low tom-toms and temple blocks; similar long note accompaniment but more dense
	79–89	Third wind statement, this time with trumpet, horn, saxophone, and euphonium
	89–117	Same kind of percussion answer but with the addition of high tom-toms and more voices on sustained notes
	118–131	Fourth wind statement, with trombone and clarinet added
	132–169	Percussion answer with timpani added along with more voices on sustained notes; maximum dynamic level achieved at m. 169

SECTION	MEASURE	EVENT AND SCORING
	169–172	Sudden *diminuendo* as volume is reset for a second long *crescendo*
Part 2:	173	Beginning of an aleatory section for upper woodwinds that will continue to m. 213
	173–197	Introduction of two main ideas: a sub-divided simple figure in trombone and horn (loud), and a compound division lyric nuance found in trumpet (soft)
	198–212	A second reset of both figures, each becoming more insistent, but with the greatest dynamic growth in the lyric figure
	213–235	The third reset of both figure; in this statement, the figure introduced by trombone becomes dominant, as simple division takes over in 6/8 time
	236–256	Final statement (total of four as in first part); most insistent yet, but with an interjection of eighth notes in compound division at mm. 244–247, before simple division has the final word

Section 2 – 3/4 time, *Andante ritmico* (quarter note = 66); a long *crescendo* ala Ravel's *Bolero* (5:40)

	257–274	Clarinet solo with bolero-like snare accompaniment, sparse vibraphone; soft
	275–295	Addition of piccolo; small interjections from various other voices
	296–304	Entrance of flute (a2) and E-flat clarinet; texture continues to thicken with small nuances added in different voices
	305–343	Introduction of an important structural figure in trumpet and timpani that is developed to a major climax; principal melodic interest is confined to woodwinds in increasingly longer note values

SECTION	MEASURE	EVENT AND SCORING
	344–362	Woodwinds perform melodic material homophonically above a dissonant, rhythmic *ostinato* in trumpet with a surging long note harmonic accompaniment in lower voices; *ostinato* figure drops through the instrumentation while the surging figure is added at the top; ends *fortissimo*
	363–381	Tempo stays the same, but texture changes dramatically; rapidly shifting color, divisions, and location of melodic interest occurring; begins with timpani figure/*ostinato* that serves to hold section together
	382–398	Beginning of A section that becomes increasingly homophonic in texture; snare drum re-enters with the bolero rhythm at m. 392; general intensification of coloristic effects
	399–end	*Exaltando*; massive *tutti* structures, *fortissimo* to the end

Unit 8: Suggested Listening

The following is a listing of works that contain intentions or demands similar to those included in *Les Couleurs Fauves*.

Leslie Bassett:
    Designs, Images, and Textures
    Sounds, Shapes, and Symbols
Karel Husa:
    Concerto for Wind Ensemble
    Music for Prague 1968
Olivier Messiaen, *Chronochromie* for eighteen solo strings, wind,
    and percussion (1960)

Unit 9: Additional References and Resources

Battisti, Frank. "Karel Husa – Keeping Ties with Tradition." *The Instrumentalist*, XLIV, July 1990, pp. 11–15, 42.

Duff, John A. "Three Works of Karel Husa: An Analytical Study of Form, Style, and Content." Ph.D. dissertation, Michigan State University, 1982 (AAT 8308929).

Haithcock, Michael. "Karel Husa Talks About Composing." *The Instrumentalist* XXXVI, April 1982, pp. 22–5.

Hegvik, Arther. "Karel Husa Talks About His Life and Work." *The Instrumentalist* XXIX, May 1975, pp. 31–7.

McLaurin, Donald Malcolm. "The Life and Works of Karel Husa with Emphasis on the Significance of his Contribution to the Wind Band." Ph.D. dissertation, Florida State University, 1985 (AAT 8513387).

New England Conservatory Wind Ensemble, Frank Battisti, conductor. Albany, NY: Albany Records U.S., 1999 (Troy 340).

Contributed by:

John C. Carmichael
Director of Bands and Associate Professor of Music
Western Kentucky University, Department of Music
Bowling Green, Kentucky

Teacher Resource Guide

Masquerade Variations on a Theme of Sergei Prokofiev

Stephen Michael Gryc
(b. 1949)

Unit 1: Composer

Stephen Gryc was born in St. Paul, Minnesota, in 1949. He received his professional training at the University of Michigan, where he earned four degrees in music, including his Doctor of Musical Arts. He studied composition with William Albright, Leslie Bassett, and William Bolcom. He is currently Professor of Music Composition and Theory at the Hartt School of the University of Hartford, where he has served as Chair of the Composition Department, Director of the Hartt Contemporary Players, Director of the Institute for Contemporary American Music, and Co-Director of the Center for Computer and Electronic Music.

Gryc has received grants and fellowships from the ASCAP Foundation, the Connecticut Commission on the Arts, the MacDowell Colony, the Charles Ives Center for American Music, Meet the Composer, the Ucross Foundation, and the University of Hartford. His awards include the 1986 Rudolf Nissim Prize for orchestral music. His works have been performed throughout the world by such ensembles as the Kansas City Symphony and Minnesota Orchestra, and by soloists such as Philip Smith of the New York Philharmonic. Some of his other works for band include *Blue Rider, Fire Brigade Volunteers Quick March, Evensong* for solo trumpet and wind ensemble, and *Las Campanas.*

Unit 2: Composition

The composer writes,

> The Variations's small, curious theme was taken from a set of twenty short piano pieces that a young Prokofiev composed between 1915 and 1917, and to which he gave the title Visions Fugitives. I chose the second piece of the set because of its several strongly contrasting elements and moods, remarkable in a piece of such brevity, which suggested development into a much longer work. Each of the five variations assumes the character of a different musical genre or type of composition. The theme and first two variations are played without a pause. The first variation is a brassy "Fanfare," while the second variation masquerades as the frenzied Italian dance known as the "Tarantella." The slow, introspective third variation, a "Nocturne," is set off from the preceding and following variations by pauses. The fourth variation is a "Passacaglia," an ancient musical form based on a continuously repeated bass line heard at the beginning of the variation in the tuba, string bass, and timpani. Following the "Passacaglia" without pause, the fifth and final variation uses the "Tarantella" music as an introduction to another dance, a Latin-American "Danza" complete with ethnic percussion. Both "Danza" and "Passacaglia" feature strict canons, and the "Tarantella" has several. However, the real focus of the music is on instrumental color and technical brilliance. There are solos from every section of the wind ensemble. The entire piece can be considered a concerto for wind band masquerading as a set of variations.

Unit 3: Historical Perspective

Masquerade Variations on a Theme of Sergei Prokofiev was commissioned in 1997 by the University of New Mexico Wind Symphony, Eric Rombach-Kendall, conductor. It received its world premiere on the campus of the University of New Mexico on March 2, 1998, and was subsequently performed by the University of New Mexico Wind Symphony at the national convention of the College Band Directors National Association at the University of Texas at Austin on February 26, 1999.

The source material for *Masquerade Variations*, *Visions Fugitives*, *Op. 22 No. 2*, was composed by Prokofiev during a time when he was experimenting harmonically with which elements of traditional tonality are infused with "modernist" qualities, such as unresolved dissonance. *Visions Fugitives* along with *Sarcasmes*, *Op. 17* (1912–1914) are the best known of Prokofiev's character pieces for piano. Of the former, Prokofiev wrote, "A certain softening of temper may be noted in *Visions Fugitive*, *Op. 22*. The title was suggested by Balmont's poem:

In every fugitive vision I see worlds,
Full of the changing play of rainbow hues."[1]

Unit 4: Technical Considerations

Masquerade Variations is scored for the traditional American concert band instrumentation with minor variations: the addition of contrabassoon, soprano saxophone in place of 1st alto saxophone, and three trumpet parts in place of the usual three cornets and two trumpets. This is outstanding literature that is well worth the many technical challenges that the players and conductor must overcome to illuminate the beauty and depth of this music. The most pronounced technical challenges are a result of the exposed orchestration and numerous solos. Outstanding soloists on piccolo, flute, oboe, clarinet, soprano saxophone, and alto saxophone are essential, with capable soloists also needed on 2nd oboe, bassoon, contrabassoon, bass clarinet, tenor saxophone, 1st and 2nd trumpet, trombone, euphonium, tuba, string bass, and timpani.

Woodwinds encounter unusual melodic patterns and difficult fingerings throughout the piece. The most difficult passages are for the solo clarinet in the theme statement and the solo oboe in the "Tarantella." Intonation is difficult to maintain, especially for the several unison passages for upper wood-winds.

Brass players encounter some of the same unusual melodic patterns as the woodwinds. Ranges for the brass are reasonable, but some of the wide leaps require excellent control and flexibility. An excellent ear for intervals is a necessity throughout the brass section for good accuracy and intonation. Articulation demands are not excessive (single tonguing should suffice), but a good *legato* and *marcato* are required of everyone. Mutes are required for the trumpet and trombone sections, with some stopped playing required of 3rd and 4th horns.

Percussion parts are not excessively difficult but do require finesse and sensitivity to subtle shadings of timbre. The tambourine part in the "Tarantella" requires a player capable of accurate 6/8 subdivision, and the timpani part requires some difficult tuning changes in the "Passacaglia."

Even though the variations undergo several meter changes, the rhythmic challenges are quite surmountable, especially for a group that can handle the other technical difficulties. The most difficult variation rhythmically is the "Danza" with brief sections of the asymmetrical meters of 5/8 and 7/8.

---

1 Prokofiev, Sergei. *Autobiography, Articles, Reminiscences*. Moscow: Foreign Languages Publishing House, pp. 43–4.

Unit 5: Stylistic Considerations

The *Theme* section of *Masquerade Variations* is a literal statement (orchestrated for band) of Prokofiev's second piece from *Visions Fugitives, Op. 22*. Here, it is useful to have a copy of Prokofiev's piano music in hand as well as a recording for those incapable of playing the part. Only twenty-four measures long and in three sections, Prokofiev achieves a depth of expression usually reserved for much longer works.

In the first section of the piano piece, Prokofiev expresses four separate motivic ideas in the space of only six measures, and the relationship between the ideas, expressed in terms of precise balance, is essential to understanding the music (Motives A, B, C, D).

The second section (measures 7 through 12) is in stark contrast to the first section. The rapid thirty-second note figures (Motive E) stand out against the left-hand figure (Motive F) that is rhythmically identical to Motive C but with altered pitches. Measures 11 and 12 serve as a bridge to the third section.

In the third section (measures 13 through 24), Motives A, B, C, and D return with the addition of a new motive in the right hand (Motive G). The final four measures of the piece can be considered a coda (Motive H).

In Gryc's *Theme* statement at the opening of *Masquerade Variations*, the motivic ideas are given greater clarity through strongly contrasting colors in the orchestration. The oboe and soprano saxophone soloists, playing Motives A and B, should carefully consider their use of vibrato in relation to one another. The muted trombone section, playing Motive D, needs to maintain balance so the sound remains integrated with a very subtle emphasis on the 1st trombone part. The mix of sound between bassoon, horn, tuba, string bass, and timpani, playing Motive C, must be such that this idea becomes a backdrop for Motives A, B, and D.

The entrances of the solos for piccolo, flute, and clarinet in measures 7 and 8 must contrast strongly against the *misterioso* of trombone in the preceding measures.

In measures 13 through 20 of Section 3, the same issues of balance and vibrato from Section 1 are applicable, with the added dimension of Motive G. It is worth mentioning that Gryc's dynamic shadings differ from Prokofiev's in Section 3 and make it clear that Motive G should not overpower.

Considerable detail work on balance and timbre needs to be given these twenty-four measures to lend clarity to the tripartite structure and the motivic ideas of Prokofiev's music, since these are the features that Gryc uses to construct his *Variations*.

The "Fanfare" retains the tripartite structure of the *Theme*, and the required *marcato* style is straightforward.

The "Tarantella" likewise retains the structure of the *Theme* yet requires considerable subtlety of expression. The brilliance for which the tarantella is known must always be present without sounding hectic. The articulation markings must be strictly observed, and the tonguing must be light for this music to dance on its toes. The trombones in measures 88 through 89 and 107 through 108, and the brass in measures 112 through 142 must exercise caution not to give emphasis to the first note of each triplet. The texture must be seamless. Percussion must be played lightly, except where marked *forte*, and always work into the fabric of the wind sounds. The interspersed duple figures must also avoid the feeling of too much gravity, and the second note of each slur should not be clipped. The final measure of this variation must simply evaporate.

The "Nocturne" begins in a *marcato* style with Motive D found in the bass drum part. The "Nocturne" quickly settles into an expressive *adagio*, and Motive D is given to the timpani in measures 179 through 180 and to the temple blocks in measures 182 through 183. The clarinet/vibraphone screen beginning at measure 197 must be completely integrated and transparent with each melodic idea in the surrounding parts clearly heard through the texture.

In the "Passacaglia," the tripartite form of the theme is abandoned and replaced by a fourfold repetition of the passacaglia bass and melody, followed by an extended coda. In measures 221 through 243, Gryc marks the string bass one dynamic stronger than the tuba and timpani, and requests that the timpani be muted. The intent is to achieve equal balance between the players, and the interspersed percussion must work into the fabric of sound. The solo tuba must match the length and shape of notes of the timpani and string bass, and the players that follow later with the *staccato* quarter notes must have been aware of the established style. The coda, beginning at measure 271, must build gradually and not reach its dynamic conclusion until the final measure of the triple *forte*. The accented half notes at the end of this variation are to be played broadly with little separation.

Measures 292 through 319 are a transition to the "Danza." Fragments from the "Tarantella" should be played in the style of a tarantella even as the texture thickens and the dynamic increases. At measure 320, the music should explode at the *subito Meno Mosso*. The "ethnic" percussion provides interest and momentum, and should be played strictly and confidently. The clarinet solo, marked *strepitoso* (noisy, boisterous), should be just that. Rhythm is the salient feature of this final variation, and the music can border on the side of being "macho" (without overplaying the dynamics), with strong emphasis given to the indicated accents. From measures 347 through 359, balance of the counterpoint between flute/B-flat clarinet/soprano saxophone and piccolo/E-flat clarinet/xylophone must be equal. The *ritardando* from measure 448 to the end is intended to increase the tension that has been building for some time. A slight increase of intensity as the tempo slows can be inferred.

Unit 6: Musical Elements

About the compositional process of writing *Masquerade Variations* Gryc writes, "I take a deconstructionist attitude toward the theme, taking the original elements and building new pieces rather freely. The successive variations aren't necessarily "progressive" as they might be in a set of variations by Mozart or Beethoven, and they contrast markedly with one another more in the manner of a suite of pieces rather than a string of variations."

MELODY:

Melodic material in the theme statement and each of the variations is fairly easy to identify even though the material is developed rather freely. Melodic material is more instrumental rather than vocal in character due to the angularity of the melodic motives from Prokofiev's piano piece. While this angularity does not pose great difficulty for the pianist, it does for the wind player. Each time the winds encounter melodic material in a *legato* style but with wide intervallic skips, the challenge is to maintain the *legato* without exposing the angles and corners of the melody. The payoff is that if the player is successful at maintaining the *legato* despite the difficulty and tension created by wide intervals, so much greater is the expression (measures 233 through 243).

One of the most interesting features of *Masquerade Variations*, and Gryc's music in general, is the well-crafted counterpoint. Examples of counterpoint can be found in each of the variations:

Variation 1	"Fanfare"	measures 26–36
Variation 2	"Tarantella"	measures 92–101
Variation 3	"Nocturne"	measures 215–220
Variation 4	"Passacaglia"	measures 259–270

The counterpoint in measures 259 through 270 is especially interesting in that there are two themes superimposed with the long note theme also expressed in canon at the minor third below.

Variation 5	"Danza"	measures 347–355

HARMONY:

Prokofiev's *Visions Fugitives, Op. 22, No. 2,* is filled with harmonic tension in each of its twenty-four measures. In the opening four measures, the tension is created by the D diminished triad outlined in the left hand reacting against the non-harmonic tones of the right hand. The tension resolves briefly in measure 4. In measures 5 and 6, the tension is heightened by the dissonance of the intervals combined with their close proximity on the keyboard. Here, the tension resolves only on the fourth beat of measure 6. In measures 7 through 10, further tension is created through the dissonance of the C-sharp against the C-natural, the rapid thirty-second notes, the *subito* dynamic change to *forte* in the right hand, and the wide spread of the range to more than four octaves—especially dramatic following the compact range and *misterioso* of the previous beat. The final two measures build an eight-note ascending "pyramid" chord (A-flat, F, C, G, A-sharp, C-sharp, E, F-sharp) that is highly unstable.

The active nature of the harmonic material, often heightened by elements of dynamics, register, and speed, provided Gryc excellent material with which to create a piece filled with intensity and momentum. Prokofiev's harmonic material can be found in some fashion in nearly every measure of *Masquerade Variations*. Some of the most recognizable examples follow:

Measures 66–69	The ascending chord is derived from measures 23 and 24 of Prokofiev.
Measures 173–174	The polytonal chord (G/D-flat/d) is derived from measure 1 of Prokofiev with the addition of A-natural.
Measures 433–435	The chord that is built down from the top comprises all of the notes from measures 1 and 2 of Prokofiev with the addition of the top B-flat.
Measures 452–456	The piece ends with the same chord that ends the Prokofiev.

RHYTHM:

The rhythmic constructs of *Masquerade Variations* are mostly Gryc's creation and are the result of the types of musical genres he has chosen for the variations. Therefore, the "Fanfare" uses many triplets and sixteenth notes (rhythms commonly found in fanfares), the "Tarantella" is in 6/8 meter, the tempo of the "Nocturne" is slow as would be expected, and the "Danza" frequently uses the rhythmic pattern typical of this urban Cuban dance.

TIMBRE:

One of Gryc's strengths as a composer is his ability to use orchestration and the resultant timbre to illuminate important musical ideas and add to the expressive content of the music.

His use of orchestration in the opening measures of the *Theme* to highlight the various musical motives has already been discussed in Unit 5: Stylistic Considerations. Subtle touches of orchestration can be found throughout the work and lend great beauty and meaning to the music. The importance of these subtleties should not be overlooked. For example, the marimba in measures 7 and 10 reinforces the first note of the piccolo solo, calling attention to the change of mood while making apparent that this is an important place in the form. At the same time, the marimba, rather than some other instrument, lends a quality that is at once percussive and resonant, much like the piano from Prokofiev's work would be in this register.

There are several other ways musicians can consider the orchestration in *Masquerade Variations* that will assist in revealing its beauty. First, one can consider the variety with which each family of instruments is treated. For example, flute and piccolo play a soloistic role in the *Theme* and most of the "Tarantella" and "Nocturne," but as integrated members of the upper woodwind section in the "Fanfare" and "Passacaglia." In measures 113 through 125, solo piccolo and solo flute are combined in four-octave unison with solo bassoon, solo contrabassoon, and solo string bass, creating a beautiful contrast of high and low frequencies.

Second, one can consider the unusual or innovative use and combinations of instruments. The muted trombones in measures 5 through 6 and 17 through 18 with the melody of 1st trombone imbedded between 2nd and 3rd trombone is the perfect timbre to represent the *misterioso* Prokofiev had in mind. The orchestration of the "Passacaglia" is rife with examples of beautiful combinations of instruments and timbre used to create contrast. The combination of solo tuba, *pizzicato* string bass, and muted timpani playing the *staccato* bass line against the *legato* melodic line in horn and euphonium in measures 233 through 244 is one such example. Adding to the beauty is the contrasting section of two solo oboes in counterpoint against the passacaglia bass that immediately follows from measures 244 through 258. The constant variety of timbre that Gryc uses highlights the structure of the music and gives it motion.

Third, one can consider which instruments the composer has chosen to leave out. While many band compositions suffer from orchestration where all players play most of the time, *Masquerade Variations* strikes a good balance between sections of "chamber music" and sections of large ensemble playing. In fact, the first time where everyone in the band plays together is not found until the final twenty measures of the work when all the forces are needed to bring the work to a rousing climax. This "holding in reserve" of players is perhaps the most outward example of orchestration used to create an expressive effect.

Unit 7: Form and Structure

The large-scale form of *Masquerade Variations* is readily apparent from the score, as the theme and each variation are clearly marked.

The composer provides the following detailed analysis:

SECTION	MEASURE	EVENT AND SCORING
Theme		Literal statement of Visions Fugitives
	1–6	Presentation of Motives A, B, C, D
	7–12	Presentation of Motives E, F
	13–20	Return of Motives A, B, C, D; presentation of Motive G
	21–25	Coda; presentation of Motive H; one-measure extension
Variation 1: "Fanfare"		
	26–29	Trumpet presents Motive A
	30–38	Reordering of Motive A notes; trombone presents version of Motive D as counterpoint to trumpet; pyramid chord represents Motive C with added pitch of B
	39–48	Saxophone plays downward moving line from Motive E; trombone and trumpet invert the saxophone passage; bassoon and low brass play Motive D
	49–56	Upper woodwinds reiterate Motive A while brass counterpoint is made up of all the notes of Motive C
	57–65	Trumpet reiterates Motive A; trombone plays Motive H over pedal
	66–69	Loud reiteration of last pyramid chord from the Theme
Variation 2: "Tarantella"		
	70–79	"Tarantella" melody played by oboe combines all the melodic elements of the first six measures of the Theme (see Figure 1); tambourine provides rhythm

SECTION	MEASURE	EVENT AND SCORING
	80–87	"Tarantella" melody transposed down a perfect fourth by soprano saxophone with alto saxophone in canon four measures later and down another perfect fourth
	88–91	Trombone presents 6/8 version of Motive D followed by harmonized duple version in horn
	92–101	Four-part canon in a series of ascending perfect fourths at a distance of two measures between entries
	102–106	Upper woodwinds use the downward moving cadence figure from the "Tarantella" melody (mm. 78–79) against a rising figure in saxophone from the second measure of the "Tarantella" melody
	107–112	Trombone and horn reiterate Motive D
	113–125	Melodic line based on reordered elements of Motive E as 1st clarinet interjects elements of the "Tarantella" melody
	125–141	Saxophone reiterates preceding melodic line
	142–151	Triple canon on "Tarantella" melody at the octave and at the distance of one measure (note how canons become closer together as piece progresses)
	152–172	Motive D reiterated, gradually shortened to one beat and thinned to one piccolo against percussion interjections; string bass re-establishes A-flat pedal and descends an octave, using tail of "Tarantella" melody, to cadence on low A-flat; cadence achieved by motion to highest and lowest registers of ensemble

Section	Measure	Event and Scoring
Variation 3: "Nocturne"		
	173–180	Introduction comprises three superimposed triads: G major, D-flat major, D minor; triads are suggested by Motive A; rhythmic idea in bass drum, timpani derived from Motive D
	181–190	Temple block continues Motive D; Motive G appears in bells with piccolo and flute, alto saxophone plays Motive E
	188–197	Solo flute plays elaborated Motive E
	197–198	Clarinet chords are reminiscent of opening two chords of "Nocturne"
	199–201	Oboe solo derived from Motive D
	201–207	Melodic line starting in the string bass rises up through bassoon, horn, and trumpet in successive measures in a version of Motive D; alternating transpositions of this melodic idea are a tritone apart and overlap nicely since the last note of the D transposition is also the first note of the A-flat transposition
	208	Climax note of the brass line takes over pedal G from the piccolo and E-flat clarinet
	209–212	Five-octave descent that terminates on low G in bass clarinet
	212–214	Motive E in bass clarinet
	215–218	Alto saxophone plays version of Motive D while timpani plays closing A-flat pedal articulated in the rhythm of motive D
	219–220	Last chord of the "Nocturne" is the F–C dyad from Motive H

SECTION	MEASURE	EVENT AND SCORING
		While the "Nocturne" begins and ends with references to Motive A, it is chiefly constructed of elements from Motives D and E. Though the perfect fifth is identified with the end of the "Nocturne," as it is in the Theme, Motive G is found near the beginning of the "Nocturne" while it is associated with the return of Motive A in the Theme. Thus, I call the "Nocturne" a distortion of the form of the Theme.
Variation 4: "Passacaglia"		In the "Passacaglia," the form of the Theme is abandoned and replaced by a fourfold repetition of the passacaglia bass and melody, which is followed by an extended coda
	221–230	Passacaglia bass is presented alone; based on Motive C
	233–243	Passacaglia bass is repeated below melody in horn and euphonium that is derived from Motives A, B, D, E; the bass line and melodic line present all the principal elements of the Theme
	244–255	Bass line repeated with melodic line inverted; 2nd oboe has counterpoint derived from original passacaglia bass and then proceeds as a loosely inverted imitation of 1st oboe
	255–258	Flute and clarinet imitate end of 1st oboe line to form a brief interlude
	259–271	Passacaglia bass contrapuntally inverted to become top-sounding line with a canon of the melodic line below at the minor third
271–287		Coda to this variation; trombone plays a version of Motive A over a pedal C in timpani, repeated seven times; woodwinds add a line of free counterpoint

SECTION	MEASURE	EVENT AND SCORING
	287–291	Trumpet plays two shortened versions of Motive A by omitting every other pitch as other brass harmonize them
Variation 5: "Danza"		
	292–319	Transition to "Danza" that provides an acceleration in tempo and a motion from a C pedal to an A-flat pedal; A-flat is reached through a rising line in euphonium, bassoon, and bass clarinet (mm. 299–302) taken from the end of the "Passacaglia" melody, which is itself linked to Motive E; soprano and alto saxophone in mm. 295–298 play a fragment from "Tarantella," and the idea is taken up by clarinet playing continuously overlapping versions (mm. 303–319); idea from Motive E played by flute, oboe, and muted trumpet, starting in m. 307, while Motive G is played by piccolo and bells
	320–328	*Ostinato* pattern that forms much of the background for the "Danza" is first heard in trombone, horn, and tuba (mm. 320–323); ostinato is a truncated version of the chordal background of the entire theme (Motive C), with its arpeggiation of the D diminished triad (mm. 1–6) to move to the E–C-sharp dyad (mm. 7–11) and back to the D diminished triad (m. 13)
	329–340	The primary melody of the "Danza," first heard in solo clarinet, is derived mostly from Motive A with hints of Motives B and E
	341–343	Solo trumpet and solo trombone figures are derived from Motive D and form a short interlude before the reiteration of the "Danza" melody; as in the "Tarantella," each of the three parts of

SECTION	MEASURE	EVENT AND SCORING
		the "Danza," corresponding to the three parts of the Theme, are repeated with significant additions to achieve a longer movement
	344–358	Repetition of the "Danza" melody featuring a canon in which E-flat clarinet, piccolo, and xylophone follow B-flat clarinet and flute at a distance of one beat and at the transposition level of one octave higher
	359–366	Second interlude where solo trumpet and solo trombone reiterate Motive D, which is then taken up by tenor saxophone and used to sequence down to a concert G
	367–379	Measure 367 starts the section of the "Danza" that corresponds to m. 7 of the Theme; flute and marimba play an *ostinato* on C-sharp and E, the notes of the accompanying chordal figure in mm. 7–11 of the Theme; oboe line is derived from Motive E, specifically mm. 7–8 of the Theme; alto saxophone takes up Motive E in m. 375 and is joined by other woodwinds in m. 378 playing a line taken from mm. 7–8 of the Theme
	380–390	Oboe's melody is repeated with added instrumentation and is again followed by alto saxophone and upper woodwinds, which play the five- and six-note figures they played before, and add a seven-note figure
	391–401	The chord that is built up and then repeated in the woodwinds is derived from the arpeggio figure in m. 9 of the Theme

Section	Measure	Event and Scoring
	402–426	The "Danza" melody is reprised and then repeated again at m. 414 with a counterpoint in piccolo, flute, and xylophone taken from Motive E (mm. 416–420) and Motive G (mm. 422–423); horn, euphonium, and tuba add another line of free counterpoint (mm. 415–426)
	427–432	Trombones reprise Motive D (mm. 427–428), and another version of Motive D is passed from low brass (m. 429) to 1st/2nd trombone (m. 430) to 2nd/3rd trumpet (m. 431) to upper woodwinds (m. 432)
	433–436	The chord that is built down from the top comprises all of the notes of Motive A with the addition of the top B-flat, the last note of Motive D
	437–451	Trumpet and trombone repeat the F–C dyad of Motive H against Motive G in upper woodwinds; bass instruments reestablish the A-flat (m. 441) and then use Motive D (mm. 442–448) to circle around and return to it
	452–456	The piece ends with the same chord that ends the Theme

Unit 8: Suggested Listening

Stephen Michael Gryc, *Evensong* – Philip Smith, trumpet, and Eric Rombach-Kendall, conductor, University of New Mexico Wind Symphony. Fandango. Summit Records, DCD 271

Stephen Michael Gryc, *Masquerade Variations on a Theme of Sergei Prokofiev* – Eugene Migliaro Corporon, conductor, North Texas Wind Symphony. Convergence. Klavier, K-11110

Stephen Michael Gryc. John Wion, flute, and Bert Lucarelli, oboe. New Music for Flute and Oboe. Opus One CD, 166.

Sergei Prokofiev, *Visions Fugitives, Op. 22* – Michael Berhoff, piano. Prokofiev: The Five Piano Concertos. EMI Classics, CDZB 7 62542 2

Unit 9: Additional References and Resources

Minturn, Neil. *The Music of Sergei Prokofiev*. New Haven: Yale University Press, 1997.

Contributed by:

Eric Rombach-Kendall
Director of Bands
University of New Mexico
Albuquerque, New Mexico

Teacher Resource Guide

Mosaic

Michael Tippett
(1905–1998)

Unit 1: Composer

Sir Michael Tippett, one of England's most important twentieth century composers, was born in London on January 2, 1905. His parents were open-minded and instilled in their children an attraction to unorthodox ideas, an appreciation of independent thinking, and a love of travel.

The family moved to Suffolk, where Michael had little contact with music, although he did take piano lessons and participated in amateur theatrical productions. As a teenager, he heard an orchestral concert conducted by Malcolm Sargent and decided to become a composer. He entered the Royal College of Music in London in 1923.

Upon completing his studies at the Royal College of Music in 1928, Tippett involved himself with amateur music making, immersed himself in studying music that interested him (from all stylistic periods, but especially Beethoven), and began comprehensive studies in counterpoint with R. O. Morris.

With the onset of the Great Depression, Tippett was drawn into social activism, which included forming and conducting the South London Orchestra of Unemployed Musicians, and a brief flirtation with Communism. His activities during the Depression and the declaration of war in 1939 led to his first major work, *A Child of Our Time* (1939–1941), an oratorio that deplored persecution and tyranny and which has become his most performed work. It also illustrated his wide-ranging musical interests by including Negro spirituals. Throughout World War II, Tippett embraced pacifism and registered as a conscientious objector. His uncompromising commitment to pacifism led to a prison term in 1943.

From 1940 to 1951, Tippett served as music director at Morley College, a position once held by Gustav Holst. His work revitalized the music program, and Morley College became a center for the performance of new music and a showcase for emerging performers. He was also active as a composer, producing his *Symphony No. 1* (1945) and his first important opera, *The Midsummer Marriage*, a work that took six years to complete (1946–1952), and represents a watershed in his career.

After 1951, Tippett devoted himself almost exclusively to composition, producing a series of large-scale works. Of special note was his opera *King Priam* (1958–1961), which introduced a number of significant stylistic changes. Declamation replaced lyricism; his harmonic usage, previously essentially tonal, embraced atonality; and most important, he began to use the orchestra as a collection of small ensembles instead of one homogenous group—a process the composer himself has called a "mosaic of musical gestures" (Clarke, 2001, 509).

Tippett's international reputation was secured during the 1960s. After 1965, he made many visits to the United States to present lectures, to work with other composers, and to conduct. He developed a special appreciation for the American landscape, its people, and its culture. This rapport was fruitful since two important commissions, *Symphony No. 4* (1976–1977; Chicago Symphony) and The *Mask of Time* (1980–1982; Boston Symphony), came from the United States. Tippett remained highly productive throughout the final decades of the twentieth century, composing, conducting, and traveling extensively. His ninetieth birthday in 1995 stimulated an outpouring of accolades, including a series of recordings, radio programs on the BBC, and a month-long Tippett festival in London. Late in 1997, Tippett journeyed to Stockholm to attend the largest retrospective ever of his music. He fell ill and returned to London, where he died quietly on January 8, 1998.

Tippett's works for winds include *Sonata for Four Horns, Praeludium for Brass, Bells and Percussion*, five fanfares for brass (some with, some without percussion), *Festal Brass with Blues* for brass band, and *Triumph* for concert band, another American commission.

Unit 2: Composition

Mosaic is the first movement of Tippett's *Concerto for Orchestra*, written in 1962–1963 and dedicated to Benjamin Britten "with affection and admiration in the year of his fiftieth birthday." This three-movement work employs winds, percussion, piano, and harp for the first movement; strings, piano, and harp for the second; and both ensembles combined for the third. The composer has certified performance of the first movement by itself. Interestingly, the original score provides no specific title for this first movement, but the designation adopted is an apt description of the compositional process involved in its creation.

Mosaic consists of nine separate ensembles, each with its own distinctive music. The nine "musics" are presented in three groups of three, with each grouping unified by a particular musical principle.

1. 2 flutes (piccolo) and harp
2. Tuba and piano   Line and Flow
3. 3 horns
4. Timpani and piano
5. Oboe, *Cor Anglais*, bassoon, contrabassoon   Heroic and Martial
6. 2 trombones and percussion
7. Xylophone and piano
8. Clarinet, bass clarinet, piano   Speed and Energy
9. 2 trumpet and snare drum

(Bowen, 1982, 112)

The work has essentially three "expositions," each of which introduces one of the groupings above. In the first exposition (measures 1 through 66), ensembles one, two, and three are presented in sequence, followed by a short section combining all three. Expositions two (measures 67 through 124) and three (measures 125 through 185) follow a similar pattern in introducing ensembles four through six, and seven through nine. During the expositions, the ensembles are juxtaposed without separating cadences, but they do not overlap. Texturally they progress in complexity, with the final group (ensembles seven through nine, representing speed and energy) being the most intricate. Ensemble seven (xylophone and piano) launches animated music that is imitative at a close-time interval; ensemble eight (clarinets and piano) presents a frantic inverted canon between the clarinets; ensemble nine (trumpets and percussion) is playful and comprises several contrapuntal devices including sequences and canon.

With all his material introduced, Tippett begins what might be called "development" (measures 186 through 291), in which the nine ensembles are combined, contrasted, and superimposed in an apparently random selection—Tippett's "mosaic of musical gestures." All nine are never used at once. Usually three or four are being heard at any one time. The development separates into three subsections, which are built around the three phrases of the wistful flute and harp music of ensemble one. The first two subsections cadence on a single tuba note (measures 224, 255), the third reaches the work's major climax (measures 286 through 290), which is marked by dense, dissonant counterpoint and a tam-tam stroke—the only one in the piece (Kemp, 1984, 382).

"Recapitulation" occurs at measure 291 with the restatement of the opening motives of the first three ensembles. Measures 322 through 331 are an exact repetition of measures 115 through 124, and since these measures lead (as they did in the exposition) to a brilliant solo passage for ensemble seven (xylophone and piano), they considerably reinforce the feeling of recapitulation. The passage presented by ensemble seven at this point, which begins as a unison canon at the rhythmic distance of an eighth note at a fast tempo, seems to occupy the place of the "cadenza" in traditional concerted works. Another recall of ensemble one at measure 339 is apparently the coda, which leads to the work's "non-ending." The initial motives of ensembles one and eight simply fade to silence as if listeners are "to go on hearing the various instrumental *concertini* combine and juxtapose in our minds long after the musicians have stopped playing" (Bowen, 1982, 114).

While an overall structure can be ascertained, it must be pointed out that these formal elements only approximate sonata principles. The work's energy originates in the sharp contrasts of timbre and texture, not in the usual interactions of the components of sonata form. Tippett has provided a suggested stage set-up that should be employed in performance since it offers antiphonal effects that enhance the timbral contrast and, at the same time, allows performers to hear each other easily.

Only two closely related tempi appear: tempo one is two-thirds as fast as tempo two. Like the relationship among the ensembles, tempo changes are abrupt with no transitions. Only ensembles seven through nine (speed and energy) employ tempo two. When these ensembles are integrated with others during the development, which employs tempo one almost exclusively, the rhythm is adapted to permit this material to be presented at its original tempo, resulting in some very complex rhythmic superimpositions.

Mosaic is approximately twelve minutes and thirty seconds long.

Unit 3: Historical Perspective

Tippett was an avid student of all musics past and present, including all forms of popular music. *Mosaic* displays contrapuntal devices such as imitation and various forms of canon, which have their origin in the Middle Ages. The highly syncopated music of ensemble nine (trumpets and percussion) sounds jazz influenced. Tippett was also keenly aware of developments in the art music of his time. His manipulation of tempo in *Mosaic* is similar to the "tempo modulation" technique of Elliott Carter (Kemp 1984, 333). Several writers have suggested that the apparently random selection of ensembles in *Mosaic* may have been influenced by "indeterminacy," as practiced by composers like John Cage and Witold Lutoslawski.

In the context of his *oeuvre*, this work appears at a critical time. Tippett had recently finished the opera *King Priam* and was still working out the implications of the stylistic change necessitated by that watershed work. *Mosaic* clearly illustrates the extended tonal vocabulary and the "mosaic scoring" that were features of the opera. Interestingly, Tippett omitted the strings entirely from Act II of *King Priam* (Bowen, 1982, 64), perhaps another precursor of *Mosaic*.

Tippett had worked diligently to master Beethovenian developmental techniques, which he had turned to regularly as a means of structuring large-scale movements (Clarke 2001, 510). In *King Priam* and subsequent works, he abandoned these procedures in favor of "statement, counterstatement, thematic superimposition and juxtaposition" (Bowen 1982, 64). In *Mosaic*, a distant echo of sonata form is present, but the material that comprises it has progressed far from any Beethovenian reference.

The concept and construction of *Mosaic* was unique in concert music at the time of its composition. Tippett continued to develop and refine the principles involved in many of his subsequent works.

Unit 4: Technical Considerations

Any successful performance of *Mosaic* requires accomplished performers. Not only are individual lines demanding, but every instrument is, in effect, a soloist. Confident, experienced players who are well in command of their instruments are necessary.

The melodic construction is often angular as a result of the harmonic content, which frequently employs all or nearly all of the chromatic aggregate. Flute, tuba, trombone, and clarinet in particular must phrase over wide, dissonant intervals, which often extend into register extremes. Ensembles seven, eight, and nine must deal with very fast passagework. The music presented by ensemble seven (xylophone and piano), in addition to the swift pace, is also imitative and sometimes canonic at a very narrow time interval. The clarinets of ensemble eight contend with a frantic inverted canon that explores the highest registers of both instruments. The trumpets of ensemble nine must also deal with a very fast canonic passage.

During the initial presentation of material in the three expositions, the rhythm is rather straightforward, although marked by considerable shifting meter and syncopation, especially in the trumpets. However, at the development, the rhythmic context becomes very complex. Most of this section is at tempo one. When ensembles seven, eight, and/or nine (which appear at tempo two in their exposition) are used, their rhythm must be altered to allow them to play at their original tempo. The resulting rhythmic superimpositions produce involved rhythms under triplet sigla.

The musical conception of this piece requires that each ensemble maintain its own character. During the developmental episodes, as many as four may be used at any one time, creating complicated issues of balance. Only experienced, proficient players are likely to have the highly developed listening skills that are required.

The piano part demands special attention. This player participates in no fewer than five of the ensembles, and the demands vary considerably from group to group. In ensemble two, the piano is in a rather traditional accompanying role in relation to the tuba. However, it also provides an element of linkage with ensemble one in assuming a similar figuration to that of the harp in the previous measures. In ensemble four, the piano presents almost exclusively a single line becoming, in effect, a second timpani (the score instructs the player to imitate the timpani). It also plays in triplet rhythms against the timpani's duplets, requiring a player with very secure rhythmic skills. A single line appears again in ensemble seven, but in this case at a rapid tempo and in close imitation. As before, the player must have a highly developed sense of pulse and subdivision. In ensemble eight, the piano contributes only a few notes that highlight accents in the clarinets, and in ensemble nine it appears briefly in an accompanying role. On a few occasions during the development, Tippett uses fragments from as many as three of the above ensembles in close rhythmic proximity, requiring the pianist to change style very quickly. At measures 281 through 282, the pianist must participate in two ensembles simultaneously. The right hand is playing with the xylophone of ensemble seven while the left hand accompanies the trumpets of ensemble nine.

Unit 5: Stylistic Considerations

Mosaic does not participate in any of the defined stylistic periods into which music history is normally divided. In fact, it was unique at the time it appeared, essentially creating its own stylistic parameters as one of the first works to employ "collage" as a compositional element.

However, if the work does not conform to traditional stylistic principles, it does have a rigid internal stylistic integrity. Each of the nine ensembles has its own style, which needs to be consistently interpreted throughout the piece. Contrast of style, timbre, and texture is the most important aspect of the musical dialogue. Juxtaposition and superimposition of distinctive and fixed ideas has replaced traditional developmental technique. Any successful performance must ensure that as each of the individual "musics" appear, it is readily identifiable by listeners. Achieving this clarity requires a firm adherence to its own distinctive style, as established during the expositions. Perhaps most important in this regard is ensemble one, since the music of this ensemble defines much of the form.

An effective way to ensure consistency might be to establish descriptive terms for each style. For example:

Ensemble one.............."wistful"
Ensemble two.............."pensive"
Ensemble three.........."searching"
Ensemble four.............."steady"
Ensemble five.............."austere"
Ensemble six ...."forceful"
Ensemble seven.........."animated"

Ensemble eight...........“frantic”
Ensemble nine............“playful”

Obviously, the above terms are suggestions only. Conductors are encouraged to find words that speak clearly to them and to their ensembles.

Unit 6: Musical Elements

MELODY:

Only some of the “musics” making up this work can be considered melody and accompaniment. In most cases, even in these ensembles the melody involves more than a single player, although the texture varies from ensemble to ensemble. The flutes of ensemble one and the clarinets of ensemble eight are in an imitative relationship, while the trombones of ensemble six are coupled in unison rhythm and the trumpets of ensemble nine employ both textures, coupling and imitation. Only the tuba and piano of ensemble two are in a simple melody and accompaniment texture.

In the other ensembles, such as the three horns of ensemble three, the double reeds of ensemble five, and both percussion/piano ensembles, all the voices have an equal role, and it is usually difficult to assign the melody to any particular part.

Melodies throughout are angular and often chromatic. Many use as many as ten different pitches. Lyrical melodies require phrasing over wide intervallic leaps; faster melodies present smoother profiles. Phrase lengths are always irregular and, as is common in atonal music, are defined by rhythm and dynamics rather than by harmony. Players need to be encouraged to enhance phrase endings with slight relaxations of tempo and volume.

HARMONY:

The harmonic context is consistently complex, using all twelve tones of the chromatic set. However, since the texture is highly contrapuntal, harmony appears to be subservient to line, texture, and timbre. In the development, the superimposition of the ensembles seems to be in random order, indicating no attempt to control or limit the harmonic context. Certain ensembles do employ harmonic devices as unifying elements. The horns return over and over to the same chord in fifths, and the trombones feature almost consistent harmonic seconds.

RHYTHM:

As observed earlier, the rhythmic context during the expositions is relatively straightforward, although marked by frequent simple meter changes and considerable syncopation. At the development, rhythmic activity becomes much more complex. Since tempo one is two-thirds the speed of tempo two, Tippett has accomplished the integration of the two tempi by writing the music for ensembles seven through nine under triplet sigla, resulting in complex notation. Interpretation of rhythm is much more complicated for the players in these three ensembles than for anyone else.

TIMBRE:

Timbre is a fundamental compositional principle in this work. The distinctive timbral mixes of each ensemble must always be clearly perceivable. Careful control of balance is essential, both within the individual ensembles and among the ensembles whenever they are combined. In some cases, blend is also very important, such as between the flutes of ensemble one, the horns of ensemble three, the double reeds of ensemble five, the trombones of ensemble six, and the trumpets of ensemble nine. In other cases, the instruments appear to have been chosen for their timbral contrast, such as the tuba and piano of ensemble two, the timpani and piano of ensemble four, the xylophone and piano of ensemble seven, and the clarinet and bass clarinet of ensemble eight. Issues of balance and blend are especially important in the development, where the relationships among the ensemble become extremely intricate.

TEACHING CONCEPTS AND STRATEGIES:

Since only accomplished players will be capable of performing this work, there will be little need for instruction on basics. Conductors will need to focus their attention on more advanced issues, such as stylistic consistency, balance, and interpretation.

It seems obvious that each ensemble needs to be rehearsed on its own before all ensembles are put together. Several particular issues need to be addressed in these individual ensemble rehearsals. The interpretation of ensemble one needs to be assured, since this music has a crucial structural role. Ensembles two and seven through nine must deal with tempo modulation, which needs to be carefully rehearsed not only to secure the two speeds but also to avoid the accentuation that often accompanies the playing of complex, syncopated rhythms. Despite the complicated notation that appears in the development, this music must sound exactly as it did in the exposition so listeners recognize it instantly.

At the larger level of interpretation, performers should be introduced to the mosaic as it exists in architecture, through the showing of slides. Perhaps an art historian could be invited to a rehearsal to explain the principles of its construction. Mosaic is largely a practice of the ancient world, although contemporary artists have continued to create in this medium and have vastly expanded the range of materials used. The principle of construction, however, is still the same: the juxtapositioning of pieces unrelated by color, shape, or material. Clearly, this is also the concept of Tippett's composition.

In recent writings, the term "mosaic" has assumed a new meaning, as a synonym for plurality or multi-culturalism in society. In many ways, this definition is a better model for the understanding of this work. As in a pluralistic society, this composition embraces many distinctive voices that sometimes speak alone, sometimes in conversation, and sometimes in a cacophony of different voices sounding simultaneously. In this sense, Tippett's *Mosaic* is a microcosm of many twentieth century societies, especially those in North America.

Unit 7: Form and Structure

In the descriptive analysis below, terms associated with sonata form are employed for clarity and convenience. However, the music that makes up this work does not follow traditional sonata technique, which depends on harmonic and thematic contrast, developmental principles that explore diverse key areas while blending fragments of recognizable themes, and readily identifiable recapitulation. In Tippett's composition, a sonata-influenced form organizes the largest elements of the work, but the "collage" that fills the frame is unlike anything that preceded it. At the same time, certain hints of conventional development technique do appear. Motives are repeated at different transpositions and are occasionally shared among the various ensembles. The rare instances when music associated with one ensemble is played by another (e.g., measures 244–247, the oboe and bassoon of ensemble five double the clarinets playing material from ensemble eight) seem to have been necessitated by practical matters rather than aesthetic considerations—Tippett apparently was concerned about the balance among the voices and added more weight to the woodwind sound.

SECTION	MEASURE	EVENT AND SCORING
Exposition 1: (Tempo one)		
	1–21	Ensemble one; "wistful"; three phrases with cadence divided 6+4+9+2-measure cadence
	22–40	Ensemble two; "pensive"; four phrases divided 5+4+7+3
	41–57	Ensemble three; "searching"; two phrases divided 9+8; climax of exposition one at mm. 53–57 in a powerful canon at the second
	58–66	Development and combining of the opening motives from the three initial ensembles
Exposition 2: (Tempo one)		
	67–79	Ensemble four; "steady"; three phrases divided 4+4+6

SECTION	MEASURE	EVENT AND SCORING
	80–97	Ensemble five; "austere"; four phrases divided 4+3+4+7
	98–114	Ensemble six; "forceful"; five phrases divided 3+3+5+4+2
	115–124	Combining and development of motives from ensembles four through six; trombone motives are very short and are not drawn exactly from earlier music; climax of this exposition at m. 115; at mm. 123–124 clarinet and flute are added apparently in a harmonic function since they hold long notes
Exposition 3: (Tempo two)		
	125–136	Ensemble seven; "animated"; three phrases divided 2+2+8
	137–150	Ensemble eight; "frantic"; no clear phrase breaks because of canonic texture
	151–175	Ensemble nine; "playful"; five phrases divided 3+7+5+5+5; percussion covers some phrase breaks in trumpet
	176–185	Combining and development of motives from ensembles seven through nine; more developmental than previous expositions clarinets reverse parts; trumpet motives are not exactly as in earlier music but develop similar ideas through sequence and canon; climax of this exposition at m. 176
Development section, Part 1:		(Tempo one, structured around motives from the first phrase of ensemble one)
	186–190	First motive of ensemble one, ensemble five, and hints ensembles four, nine, and seven
	191–192	First motive of ensemble one transposed, ensemble five continues, ensemble nine, hints of seven

SECTION	MEASURE	EVENT AND SCORING
	193–198	Second motive of ensemble one, ensemble two, three, five, hints of eight and nine
	199–203	Second motive of ensemble one transposed, ensemble nine, two, three, five, hints of eight and nine
	204–207	Third motive of ensemble one, ensemble two continues, ensemble three, nine, hints of six
	208–213	Ensemble two continues, ensemble six, seven, eight, hints of five
	214–223	Ensemble two continues, ensemble nine, five, eight, hints of three
Development section, Part 2:		(Tempo one, structured around the second phrase of ensemble one)
	224–227	Phrase two of ensemble one, ensemble three
	228–230	Phrase two of ensemble one transposed, ensemble three continues
	231–238	Ensemble five, seven, hints of three
	239–243	Ensemble six, nine, two
	244–255	Ensemble two continues, ensemble eight, five, hints of four; at mm. 244–247, ensemble five and eight play music associated with ensemble eight— the first time in this piece that one ensemble has borrowed from another
Development section, Part 3:		(structured around the third phrase of ensemble one)
	256–266	Tempo one; third phrase of ensemble one extended and developed, ensemble five, six, four, hints of ensemble nine
	267–285	Ensemble six continues, ensemble seven, nine; tempo two at mm. 276–285

SECTION	MEASURE	EVENT AND SCORING
	286–290	Tempo one; climax of the work; ensembles three, five, and seven present the powerful canon at the second first stated by ensemble three at mm. 53–57 prominent tam-tam stroke; in this section of the development, several ensembles present music exactly as it appeared in one of the expositions (e.g., trombone, mm. 262–270 are exactly like mm. 104–112; trumpet, mm. 271–280 are exactly like mm. 161–170; xylophone/piano, mm. 276–282 are exactly like mm. 125–133); these precise restatements are clearly intended to prepare for recapitulation
Recapitulation	291–297	Ensemble one first phrase, ensemble two first phrase, ensemble three first measure
	298–306	Tempo two; ensemble two continues extension of phrase one, ensemble eight second phrase from initial presentation in exposition three, mm. 304–306, oboe and bassoon from ensemble five join clarinet presenting ensemble eight material in unison, ensemble nine
	307–321	Tempo one; ensemble one development of first phrase, ensemble three development similar to first phrase, ensemble nine
	322–331	Exact restatement of mm. 115–124
	332–338	Tempo two; cadenza ensemble seven, begins as an exact canon between piano and xylophone; later canonic but not exact
	339–340	Tempo one; ensemble one first two measures, ensemble eight

Section	Measure	Event and Scoring
	341–350	Tempo two; ensemble eight continues, ensemble nine
	351	Tempo one; ensemble one first measure, ensemble eight m. 137 (first measure of ensemble eight in exposition three)
	352	Silence

Unit 8: Suggested Listening

Béla Bartók, *Concerto for Orchestra*
Franco Cesarini, *Mosaici Bizantini*
Edward Gregson, *Celebration*
Michael Tippett:
> *Concerto for Orchestra* (three movements)
> *Festal Brass with Blues* (this work may be especially applicable to the study of *Mosaic* since it is a particularly good illustration of Tippett's combining of disparate elements. It restates a short section of *Symphony No. 3*, where a quotation from the last movement of Beethoven's Ninth Symphony is juxtaposed with blues)
> *King Priam* (excerpts)
> *Ritual Dances from The Midsummer Marriage*

Recordings:
Cincinnati College Conservatory of Music Wind Symphony, Eugene Corporon, conductor: Klavier Records CD; KCD 11067; 1996

Unit 9: Additional References and Resources

Bowen, Meirion. *Michael Tippett*. London: Robson Books, 1982.

Clarke, David. *Tippett, Sir Michael (Kemp)* in *New Grove Dictionary of Music and Musicians*. Second edition. 29 volumes. Edited by Stanley Sadie. London: Macmillan Publishers Ltd., 2001. Vol. 25, pp. 505–20.

Clarke, David, ed. *Tippett Studies*. Cambridge: Cambridge University Press, 1999.

Harding, Catherine. *Mosaic* in *The Dictionary of Art*. 34 Volumes. Edited by Jane Turner. London: Macmillan Publishers Ltd., 1996. Vol. 23, pp. 154–166.

Jordan-Bychkov, Terry. *The Human Mosaic*. Eighth edition. New York: Longman, 1999.

Kemp, Ian. *Tippett: The Composer and His Music.* London and New York: Eulenburg Books and Da Capo Press, 1984.

Osborne, Harold, ed. *Mosaic* in *Oxford Companion to Art.* Oxford: Oxford University Press, 1979, pp. 742–8.

Theil, Gordon. *Michael Tippett: A Bio-Bibliography.* Westport, CT: Greenwood Press, 1989.

Whittall, Arnold. *The Music of Britten and Tippett.* Cambridge: Cambridge University Press, 1990.

Website:
www.michael-tippett.com

Contributed by:
Keith Kinder
McMaster University
Hamilton, Ontario, Canada

Teacher Resource Guide

Myaku

David Dzubay
(b. 1964)

Unit 1: Composer

David Dzubay was born in Minneapolis, Minnesota, in 1964 and was raised in Portland, Oregon. He attended Indiana University, earning his B.S. in 1986, his M.M. in Composition and Trumpet in 1988, and his D.M. in Composition in 1991. His principal teachers have been Donald Erb, Frederick Fox, Eugene O'Brien, Lukas Foss, Oliver Knussen, Allan Dean, and Bernard Adelstein.

Formerly on the faculty at the University of North Texas, Dzubay is now Associate Professor of Music at the Indiana University School of Music in Bloomington, Indiana. He is also director of the New Music Ensemble, and he teaches composition. From 1995 to 1998, he served as Composer-Consultant to the Minnesota Orchestra, where he coordinated reading sessions for works by composers of Minnesota.

Dzubay's compositions have been performed by orchestras and wind bands throughout the nation and internationally. Dzubay has also received numerous commissioning projects for various organizations and ensembles, including the National Endowment for the Arts, the National Repertory Orchestra, and Voices of Change. He has received many awards, including the NEA Individual Artist Grant (1992, 1993), ASCAP Young Composer Awards (1988, 1989, 1990), BMI Student Composer Awards (1987, 1988), Barlow International Competition for Orchestra Music (1995), Tanglewood (Koussevitsky Fellowship), the 2000 Wayne Peterson Prize, and the 2001 Walter Beeler Memorial Prize for *Myaku*. He has written numerous instrumental works, including *Projectus* for solo trumpet and wind octet, *Two Celebratory Fanfares* for six trumpets, *...as filaments of memory spin...* and *Incantation* for wind band.

Unit 2: Composition

Myaku is a lively and rhythmic set-based composition that continuously pushes to a dramatic conclusion. Dzubay writes,

> Opening with gentle waves of woodwind oscillations and building to powerful repetitive arpeggios near the end, this fanfare for wind band takes two main ideas as themes: *Pulse* (*Myaku* in Japanese) and the number seven (representing the celebration of the seven decades of existence of the Musashino Academy of Music). The pulses occur on many levels, often as groups of seven evenly spaced articulations, but also as rhythmic underpinnings. The number seven works into the composition in different ways, such as the number of sections and the tempo markings of quarter note = 140, 168, and 77.
>
> The principal musical motive is a four-note subset of a pentatonic scale: A, B, D, and E. There is also extensive use of diatonic clusters (built by stacking up transpositions of the above motive) and the ascending melodic minor scale.

The piece is four minutes and forty seconds in length, and the score is in C with no key signatures.

Unit 3: Historical Perspective

Myaku was commissioned jointly by the Indiana University Wind Ensemble, under the direction of Ray Cramer, and by the Musashino Academy of Music in Tokyo, Japan, in honor of its seventieth anniversary. Ray Cramer conducted the premiere performances of the work in April and May of 1999 with the Indiana University Wind Ensemble and the Musashino Academy of Music Wind Ensemble. Dzubay writes,

> *Myaku* is dedicated to Ray Cramer, Director of Bands at Indiana University and tireless supporter of contemporary music for wind band. I send the fanfare to the Musashino Academy with best wishes for another seven decades of fine music making.

Unit 4: Technical Considerations

Myaku is scored for:

Piccolo	E-flat baritone saxophone
Oboe 1, 2	C trumpet 1, 2, 3, 4
Flute 1, 2	F horn 1, 2, 3, 4
English horn	Trombone 1, 2
Bassoon 1, 2	Bass trombone
E-flat clarinet	Euphonium 1, 2
B-flat clarinet 1, 2, 3	Tuba
B-flat bass clarinet	Timpani

E-flat alto saxophone 1, 2   4 percussion
B-flat tenor saxophone

1: vibraphone, crash cymbals, bass drum (shared with Percussion 4)
2: marimba, small suspended cymbal
3: glockenspiel, xylophone, snare drum, large suspended cymbal,
   tubular chimes (with Percussion 4)
4: tubular chimes, 4 tom-toms, bass drum

Harp (optional)
Piano (optional)
String bass (optional)

As *Myaku* features multiple rhythmic layers, perhaps the work's greatest challenge is to achieve an exact vertical alignment. The work begins in 3/4 but in its short duration traverses through time signatures of 9/8, 12/8, 6/8, 10/16, 15/16, 5/8, and 7/8. Mixed meters are complicated by Dzubay's use of syncopation and unusual subdivisions in five parts.

Woodwind technical requirements are extremely demanding, with B-flat clarinet range extended to b3. Brass scoring features extended *tessituras* (C trumpet, b2; horn, b2) and angular leaps through a gauntlet of polymeters. Skilled and sensitive mallet percussionists are a necessity, as balance issues with woodwind oscillating figures must be dealt with throughout the work. Although Dzubay lists harp, piano, and string bass as optional, the work is a stronger presentation when these colors are present. *Myaku* works well in both wind ensemble and large band combinations.

Unit 5: Stylistic Considerations
Syncopated rhythms throughout the piece are difficult and will need careful rehearsal in order to layer the primary rhythmic devices and balance the instrumentation. Dzubay's manipulation of rhythmic and metric variance will require strict adherence to reproduce the seamless quality of the work. An overall characteristic of high energy and aggressiveness must be maintained.

Unit 6: Musical Elements
Myaku is a contemporary set-based composition for large wind ensemble or symphonic band. The primary melodic content of *Myaku* is derived from the four-note subset of the pentatonic scale, (A, B, D, E), and the transpositions of this set. When put in *normal order*, this motive is represented in numbers (as 9, 11, 2, and 4) by their scale degrees. The *prime form* of this set is 0257. The majority of the melodic material is based on this and/or transpositions of this set. Occasionally there is use of the ascending melodic minor scale and other modes.

The chordal harmony is often based on the stacking of the set vertically and/or horizontally, which creates diatonic clusters (Figure 1).

Figure 1

In Figure 1, taken from measure 30, the prime form (0257) is stacked vertically as transpositions of the set move horizontally. This technique creates many major seconds, major and minor thirds, and perfect fourths and fifths, which gives the work a diatonic sound. Because the set is transposed several times and is stacked vertically to create harmony, a true tonal center does not seem obvious. That being said, the pitches A and F-sharp seem to hold the closest resemblance of a tonal center because they appear as strong pedal tones in the low voices or as roots in scalar passages. Dzubay also makes use of the ascending melodic minor scale and the lydian and phrygian modes.

Dzubay explains that the number seven is important to the work in that it represents the seventy years of the Musashino Academy of Music in Tokyo, Japan. It appears in groups of accented articulations, number of sections, and the metronome markings of quarter note = 140, 168, and 77.

Pulse, *Myaku* in Japanese, is of equal importance to the piece as the number seven. It occurs on many different levels in the work; from full ensemble articulated passages to accented *ostinato* figures that line up other rhythmic textures. The most powerful use of pulse is when it is combined with the seven accented articulations. This first appears in the introduction beginning in measure 14 with the low brass (Figure 2), and variations of the articulated pulse exist through the end, where the piece draws its conclusion with the percussion marking the last seven pulses (Figure 3).

Figure 2

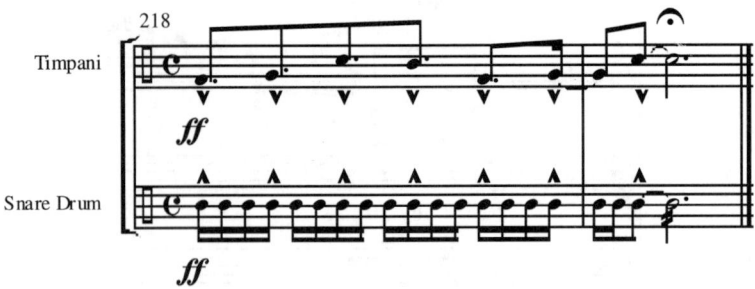

Figure 3

Myaku is composed of several rhythmic motives. One motive may be introduced alone, or more than one may be layered throughout the texture. With the many levels of rhythmic motives occurring, it will be difficult to line up the many articulations that create the pulse. The rhythmic motives go through constant development and never repeat. Figures 4a, 4b, and 4c offer a few examples of these continually evolving motives.

Figure 4a   **Figure 4b**   **Figure 4c**

Unit 7: Form and Structure

Myaku is composed of several sections that, aside from two seven-measure transitions, do not entirely relate to each other. A graph of the form is shown below (Figure 5) .

	Section 1	Trans.	Section 2	Section 3	Section 4	Section 5	Section 6	Section 7	Trans.	Coda	
mm.	1–23	24–30	31–58	59–88	89–145	146–151	152–158	159–197	198–204	205–219	

Figure 5

SECTION	MEASURE	EVENT AND SCORING
1	1–23	Introduction; in 3/4; marked by oscillating woodwind waves, the seven accented pulses and transposition of the four-note pentatonic subset; quarter note = 140
Transition	24–30	Seven-measure transitional material that leads to section two and the development of the piece
2	31–57	Meter shifts to 9/8 and rhythmic motives begin passing through variations; meter shifts to 12/8 in preparation for Section 3; woodwinds and brass share texture
3	58–88	Texture is dominated by the brass for the first eleven measures; m. 69 begins a sharing of the seven articulated pulses, with woodwinds playing four of the accents and brass completing the motive with the following three; section ends with the full ensemble, *forte* and *tutti*; meter shifts through 12/8, 9/8, and ends in 6/8
4	89–145	Meter changes to 3/4 and the close, rapid rhythms seen before are now augmented and less pulsing; dynamics and texture dissipate, leaving only families of instruments to play oscillating waves of the transposed and harmonized set; as the section closes, the texture rebuilds to a powerful lead into Section 5; there are several meter changes, such as 6/8, 10/16, 15/16, and 9/8, which help to propel building textures
5	146–151	This is the first of two small sections that brings a return to the strong articulated pulses that drive to the end of the piece; in 9/8 and 12/8

SECTION	MEASURE	EVENT AND SCORING
6	152–158	The second of the smaller sections; meter shifts back to 3/4, and the strong articulated pulse drives the piece to the final section
7	159–197	Marked *piu mosso*, this is the first tempo marking change to quarter note = 168; this section features power ascending arpeggios of the prime form set and transpositions of it; arpeggios start in low voices and grow through the texture, juxtaposed throughout the orchestration but always with the accents lining up; the section ends with a *molto ritardando* and *diminuendo* with the last two measures holding the other different tempo marking of quarter note = 77
Transition	198–204	This seven-measure transition marks the only material of the piece that is actually repeated though not exact, it closely resembles the transitional material in mm. 24–30; both transitions seem to bookend the piece, separating the introduction and coda from the main body; marked Tempo I in the score, the meter signature returns to 3/4 and tempo marking of quarter note =s 140 reappears
Coda	205–219	The coda concludes the piece with flourishes from woodwinds and a final fanfare from horns and middle voices; after meter shifts through 6/8, 12/8, and 9/8, Myaku ends in 4/4 with the last two measures offering the final seven articulated pulses that finally complete the work

Unit 8: Suggested Listening
David Dzubay, *Labyrinth* for chamber ensemble
Lubos Fiser, *Report*
Karel Husa, *Al Fresco*
Cindy McTee, *Soundings*

Unit 9: Additional References and Resources

Dzubay, David. "Myaku." *Convergence.* Corporon/North Texas Wind Symphony. Klavier 11110, 2000.

Dzubay, David. "Labyrinth for chamber ensemble." *New Music from Indiana University – Volume II.* Dzubay/Indiana University Music Ensemble. (IUSM-08), 1998.

Contributed by:
Joseph P. Missal
Director of Bands
Oklahoma State University

Monte Grisé
Master's Conducting Associate
Oklahoma State University

Teacher Resource Guide

Propagula
Robert Linn
(1925–1999)

Unit 1: Composer

Born in San Francisco, California, on August 11, 1925, Robert Linn was an esteemed pianist, composer, and arranger whose music has been performed on six continents. As a composer, he created vocal and chamber pieces, works for orchestra, piano, and a number of successful works for wind ensemble and band. His compositions and arrangements range in style from *Little Brown Jug* and the *March of the Olympians* (performed at the Los Angeles Olympic Games in 1960 and 1984) to more formal concertos for flute, piano, and soprano saxophone.

Linn was educated in his home state, studying with Darius Milhaud at Mills College and later at the University of Southern California, where he received a Master of Music degree. During that time, his principal teachers were Halsey Stevens, Roger Sessions, and Ingolf Dahl. Beginning in 1957, Linn taught composition and theory at University of Southern California, and from 1973 to 1990, he served as department chair for the University of Southern California Thornton School of Music. In 1992, he was named Professor Emeritus, continuing to compose until his death on October 28, 1999.

Unit 2: Composition

Propagula was commissioned by the *Alpha Psi* Chapter of *Kappa Kappa Psi*, West Texas State University, and was premiered in 1971 by the West Texas State University Band, directed by Gary Gardner. "Propagula" (pronounced pro-PAG-u-la) is a botanical term referring to the regenerative parts of a plant, such as the shoots and buds. The composition may be described as a collection of variations growing out of the musical "buds" introduced in the opening measures. Seven contrasting sections following the theme imply the styles of a march, waltz, dirge, scherzo, fanfare, chorale, and fugue. This exciting and rigorous composition features challenging moments for soloists and small groups within the ensemble. Minimal twentieth century performance techniques (free-time arpeggios and *glissandi*) are employed successfully in the final fourteen measures of the piece, creating an exciting closing to this twelve-minute work.

Unit 3: Historical Perspective

Propagula (1971) was composed during a period of expanding compositional activity for wind bands. This was the result of an increase in the number of commissions from high schools, universities, band associations, and other enlightened organizations. While not all of the works have become a part of the band repertoire, the creation of this literature helped to elevate the wind band from its historically utilitarian role to a more aesthetic one. Works from the same period ranged in style from the conventional to the adventurous. Howard Hanson (*Dies Natalis*), Alfred Reed (*Armenian Dances*), John Zdechlik (*Chorale and Shaker Dance*), Vincent Persichetti (*Parable IX, Op.121*), Karel Husa (*Apotheosis of This Earth*), Barney Childs (*Supposses: Imago Mundo*), and Donald Erb (*The Purple Roofed Ethical Suicide Parlor*) were composers who premiered works in the early 1970s.

Historically, much of Linn's compositional style has been characterized by elements of lyricism, consonance, and nontriadic harmonies enclosed in traditional, well-balanced forms. This is evident in the theme and variations of *Propagula*, where the composer explores the unique color combinations available in the wind band palette. Some of this piece is also quite aggressive, especially the brass writing in the march, fanfare, and fugue sections.

Unit 4: Technical Considerations

A successful performance of *Propagula* requires strong independent playing from the entire ensemble. The opening musical "buds" are solo motives for flute, bassoon, trumpet, alto saxophone, horn, and B-flat clarinet, as well as alto flute and English horn (cues provided). Throughout the piece individual colors sparkle and small ensembles play important roles. Examples include, but are not limited to, a trumpet trio in measures 109 through 113, a bassoon trio in measures 113 through 118, a tuba duet in measures 118 through 121, a euphonium duet in measures 122 through 129, and an oboe trio in measures 187 through 194. Meeting the requirements of rhythmic independence, attention to details of articulation, and knowledge of one's function in the surrounding musical environment is a must. Trumpets are challenged to play in the upper register and to sustain these pitches with accurate intonation and quality tone. The scherzo section beginning at measure 155 is an opportunity for an impressive performance from the percussion section. Meeting these challenges will help ensure a performance of this work that shimmers with unique timbres and rhythmic vitality.

Unit 5: Stylistic Considerations

Front notes to the score of *Propagula* describe the work as "...a set of free variations consisting of eight sections with contrasting moods: theme, march, waltz, dirge, scherzo, fanfare, chorale, and fugue." It should be noted that these sections are stylized versions of these traditional terms. While it is important to recognize the various interpretative principles associated with these descriptors, it will take added study to be able to perform the sections in the correct style dictated by the composer. Those who would wish to dance the waltz, march the march, or sing the chorale will be disappointed. The fresh spin that the composer puts on these sections is one of the things that makes the work worthy of performance.

Performers will want to pay close attention to the various articulations. The tendency to perform the articulation ∧ and the same sign with a *staccato* mark as a percussive attack and immediate decay often leads to a heavy, overblown style of playing. Thinking of this marking as a bell-like articulation will help. Be sure to consider the individual parts within the context of the rest of the ensemble to ensure appropriateness of articulations and a homogeneity of sound.

Unit 6: Musical Elements

The process of taking a musical idea and modifying or varying it in some manner is one of the oldest compositional devices. *Propagula* is based on a series of short motives rather than a sustained theme, but the methods used to progressively develop a musical idea while retaining some constant elements are still variations of melody, texture, rhythm, and timbre.

MELODY:

In the opening section of *Propagula*, a series of melodic motives (musical buds) are sounded by various solo instruments. These individual cells are extended and combined vertically and linearly to create a veil of continuous sound. The section is highly chromatic; however, in the opening, the various cells are all quite delicate in their dissonance. Identifying the various cells and their development in the opening and throughout the piece is an important exercise.

Motive 1: mm. 1–2

Motive 2: mm. 2–3

Motive 3: mm. 5–6

Motive 4: mm. 8–9

Motive 5: mm. 10–11

HARMONY:

Harmonic techniques and textures in *Propagula* are of two types. Some sonorities are the result of the contrapuntal combinations of the various lines. Others are blocks of sound used to emphasize rhythmic structures and cadence points. Both allow for the exploitation of the wind band's large sonic palette. Many instances of sonorities created through a combination of various lines of melodic material occur. The resulting chords do not function in a traditional way. Instead, the techniques of voice leading, control of tension, and relaxation through the use of dissonance and consonance, and other techniques developed in the last half of the twentieth century provide an alternate process for the succession of musical events.

RHYTHM:

The rhythmic shape of the various motives is important in the construction of *Propagula*. There is a rhythmic similarity to the motives in that they all proceed from shorter to longer duration values. In general, the variations maintain this rhythmic idea. The longer note at the end of the motives and phrases allows the creation of engaging vertical sonorities. Rhythmic interest is also created through the use of syncopated entrances and accents. The use of rhythmic phrases across the bar line (from weak to strong metric units) helps to maintain forward motion throughout the piece.

TIMBRE:

The manner in which Linn utilizes tone color is one of the most salient features of this composition. Because there is a limited amount of melodic material, there is a need to emphasize other musical elements. The contrasting timbres of the solo instruments, small ensembles, and instrument families effectively provide original and stimulating units of sound for the listener. The employment of the motivic material in the extreme ranges of the instruments and a wide spectrum of dynamic levels serve to emphasize the timbral contrasts as well.

Unit 7: Form and Structure

Propagula is a set of sectional variations. Each section is clearly defined by shifts in style, tempo, texture, dynamics, or other musical elements.

SECTION	MEASURE	EVENT AND SCORING
Theme	1–28	*Adagio*; opening motives are presented by solo instruments; these motives gradually expand into short phrases; some phrases are played by trios of similar instruments (three clarinets, three saxophones, three flutes), but the soloistic nature of the section remains intact throughout
March	29–82	*Allegro*; motives and phrases of the opening section are offered in a more rhythmic style; various instrumental groups present phrases punctuated by block chords; scoring is much fuller as the imitative entrances, concluding with sustained tones, create dissonant sonorities; texture thins at m. 75 in preparation for the next variation
Waltz	82–121	*Moderato*; a lighter and softer section beginning with solo trumpet and featuring small ensemble textures reminiscent of the opening measures; a bassoon and oboe duet, an oboe trio, a flute trio, a trumpet trio, a bassoon trio, and a tuba duet are all featured

SECTION	MEASURE	EVENT AND SCORING
Dirge	122–154	*Andante;* this variation begins with a baritone horn and tuba quartet, which is joined by a solo horn in m. 126; dirge theme is repeated by the flute choir with an accompanying obbligato played by alto saxophone, bells, and vibraphone; a more intense statement of the dirge by the full ensemble follows; the variation ends with a six-part pronouncement of the lament by trombone accompanied by augmented motives in flute and alto saxophone
Scherzo	155–254	*Allegro scherzando;* xylophone, vibraphone, snare drum, and four drums of graduated pitch (two bongos and two tom-toms are suggested) announce the beginning of the scherzo variation; there is little in the way of playfulness in this movement, but the lively motion, marked rhythms, and unexpected twists and turns qualify as "scherzo-like"; at m. 244, the tempo slows as an eleven-measure transition signals the close of the section
Fanfare	255–264	Opening motives work well as incipits for each entrance of the fanfare's six solo trumpets; each entrance adds energy by strengthening the volume and extending the upper register; this regal variation exploits the noble nature and brilliant timbre of the trumpet section
Chorale	264–278	*Maestoso;* this is not a traditional chorale; thickly scored, it is more rhythmically active, metrically varied, and at a higher dynamic level than expected in a chorale section; the majestic, fully scored polychords are a continuation of the style of the previous fanfare section

SECTION	MEASURE	EVENT AND SCORING
Fugue	279–363	*Allegro;* the final section of this piece begins with the statement of a theme by the flute choir and xylophone; more in the form of a canon than a fugue, oboe, English horn, and tenor saxophone take up the theme in m. 284; imitative fragments of the theme, as well as complete statements, are used to develop the highly contrapuntal conclusion of this work; in the closing measures, the opening motives reappear one final time, harmonized as thickly scored block polychords; adding to the excitement of the finale are clarinet arpeggios (m. 350), random bongo and tom-tom fills (m. 356), and trumpet and trombone *glissandi* (m. 359), all played as rapidly as possible

Unit 8: Suggested Listening

Robert Linn:

Concerto for Soprano Saxophone and Wind Ensemble – The Chicago Saxophone Quartet, Indiana State University, John Boyd, conductor

Concerto for Violin and Wind Octet – Crystal Chamber Orchestra, Robert Kraft, conductor: Crystal Records, 1972

Dithramb – I Cellisti, Jerome Kessler, conductor: Orion Records, 1971

Divertimento for Oboe, Two Horns, and Strings – members of the Southwest Chamber Music Society: Cambria Records, 2000

Propagula – University of Illinois, Harry Begian, conductor

Quintet for Brass Instruments – Fine Arts Brass Quintet: Crystal Records, 1980

Saxifrage Blue – Mark Walters, baritone saxophone: Crystal Records, 1979

Vino – Goldman-Brown Duo: Orion Records, 1976

Wind Quintet – Westwood Wind Quintet: Crystal Records, 2001

Unit 9: Additional References and Resources

Casey, Patrick. "Errata Corner: Propagula by Robert Linn." *CBDNA Report.* Fall 1996, pp. 9–11.

Hitchcock, H. Wiley, and Stanley Sadie, eds. *The New Grove Dictionary of American Music.* New York: Grove's Dictionaries of Music, Inc., 1986. S.v. "Robert Linn," by David Cope.

Smith, Norman. *Program Notes for Band.* Chicago: GIA Publications, 2000.

Contributed by:

James Chesebrough
University of Connecticut
Storrs, Connecticut

Teacher Resource Guide

"Red Cape Tango" from Metropolis Symphony Michael Daugherty

(b. 1954)

transcribed by Mark J. Spede

(b. 1962)

Unit 1: Composer

Michael Kevin Daugherty was born in Cedar Rapids, Iowa, in 1954. He grew up in a musical environment: his father played drums for country and lounge bands, and his four brothers are also professional musicians. Daugherty played piano and drums while growing up, and he attended North Texas State University (now the University of North Texas) in Denton, Texas, playing piano in the jazz lab bands. He supported himself as a pianist in local bars and lounges, and wrote his first orchestral work while an undergraduate. After graduating from North Texas State University, Daugherty studied at Boulez's IRCAM (Institut de Recherche et Coordination Acoustique/Musique) in Paris as a Fulbright Fellow, where he composed music for computer. He completed his doctoral studies in composition at Yale University in New Haven, Connecticut, where he studied with Earle Brown, Jacob Druckman, Bernard Rands, and Roger Reynolds. He lived in Hamburg, Germany, from 1982 to 1984 and studied composition with György Ligeti. In 1986, he was appointed to the faculty at Oberlin (Ohio) College. In 1991, he joined the faculty of the University of Michigan in Ann Arbor, where he is currently Professor of Composition.

---

1 Michael Daugherty, *Metropolis Symphony*, Baltimore Symphony Orchestra, David Zinman, conductor. CD liner notes (Argo recording 452 103-2, 1995), pp. 4–5.

In 1999, Daugherty began a four-year tenure as Composer-in-Residence with the Detroit Symphony Orchestra. He has received numerous awards for his music, including the Stoeger Prize from Lincoln Center, recognition from the American Academy and Institute of Arts and Letters, and fellowships from the Guggenheim Foundation and National Endowment for the Arts. His works for winds include *Desi* (1991), *Bizarro* (1993), *Red Cape Tango* (1993/trans. by Spede, 1999), *Motown Metal* (1994), *Timbuktuba* (1996), *Niagara Falls* (1997), *UFO* (1999/trans. by Daugherty, 2000), *Rosa Parks Boulevard* (2001), and *Bells for Stokowski* (2002).

Mark J. Spede was born in Brooklyn, New York, in 1962. His degree work includes a Bachelor of Music in Percussion Performance (with distinction) from the University of Michigan (1984), a Master of Music in Instrumental Conducting from Ball State University (1988), and a Doctor of Musical Arts from the University of Texas at Austin (1998). From 1989 to 1995, Spede was employed on the faculty of the University of Florida in Gainesville as Assistant Director of Bands and Professor of Percussion. He also has served on the faculty at the University of Texas, and recently worked as a freelance composer and arranger in New York City. He currently resides with his wife and son in Austin, Texas, and is the staff arranger for the University of Texas Bands.

Unit 2: Composition

"Red Cape Tango," the last movement of the *Metropolis Symphony*, continues a trend by Daugherty of composing concert music inspired by contemporary American popular culture—or as he calls them, "American Icons." The first such work, *Desi*, was written in 1991 for orchestral winds and percussion and was inspired by the 1950s icon Desi Arnez of "I Love Lucy" fame. "Red Cape Tango" was commissioned by the Albany (New York) Symphony Orchestra and completed in the summer of 1993. At the time, the DC Comics hero Superman had just been killed in the comic strip, leading to worldwide media coverage. Daugherty used "Red Cape Tango" as a metaphor for the death of a simpler time, and based the motivic material of the work on the plainsong melody *Dies irae*. By the sixteenth century, secular music had entered the Roman Mass, and tropes and sequences had corrupted existing plainsong. The Council of Trent (1543–1563) sought to restore the original plainsong, and *Dies irae* was one of only four sequences retained, usually as part of the Requiem Mass (Mass for the Dead). Many composers have been drawn to the mournful quality of its dorian mode, as well as its connection to the supernatural and images of the Judgment Day. These include Berlioz, Liszt, Saint-Saëns, Moussorgsky, Tchaikovsky, Mahler, Rachmaninoff, Richard Strauss, Vaughan Williams, Respighi, Miaskovsky, Khatchaturian, Honegger, and Dallapiccola. Two other works by Daugherty that make use of the *Dies irae* are *Beat Boxer* (1991) and *Dead Elvis* (1993), which was composed during the same summer as "Red Cape Tango" and bears a strong resemblance to it. In

"Red Cape Tango," Daugherty uses a tango bass line and tango rhythms as the backdrop for the melody, infusing the work with the smooth and slow nature of the dance interrupted by sudden, swift motions. Daugherty writes:

> I began composing my *Metropolis Symphony* in 1988, inspired by the celebration, in Cleveland, of the fiftieth anniversary of Superman's first appearance in the comics. When I completed the score in 1993, I dedicated it to the conductor, David Zinman, who encouraged me to compose the work, and to the Baltimore Symphony Orchestra. David Zinman and the Baltimore Symphony Orchestra later gave the *Metropolis Symphony* its New York (Carnegie Hall) and Baltimore premieres in January 1994.
>
> The *Metropolis Symphony* evokes an American mythology that I discovered as an avid reader of comics in the fifties and sixties. Each movement of the symphony—which may be performed separately—is a musical response to the myth of Superman. I have used Superman as a compositional metaphor in order to create an independent musical world that appeals to the imagination. The symphony is a rigorously structured, non-programmatic work, expressing the energies, ambiguities, paradoxes, and wit of American popular culture. Like Charles Ives, whose music recalls small-town America early in our century, I draw on my eclectic musical background to reflect on late twentieth century urban America. Through complex orchestration, timbral exploration, and rhythmic polyphony, I combine the idioms of jazz, rock, and funk with symphonic and avant-garde composition.
>
> "Red Cape Tango" was composed after Superman's fight to the death with Doomsday and is my final musical work based on the Superman mythology. The principal melody, first heard in the bassoon, is derived from the medieval Latin death chant *Dies irae*. This dance of death is conceived as a tango, presented at times like a concertino comprised of a string quintet, brass trio, bassoon, chimes, and castanets. The tango rhythm, introduced by the castanets and later by finger cymbals, undergoes a gradual timbral transformation, concluding dramatically with crash cymbals, brake drum, and timpani. The orchestra alternates between *legato* and *staccato* sections to suggest a musical bullfight.[1]

The band transcription was completed in early 1998 and was first performed by the University of Texas Wind Ensemble on March 30, 1998, Mark Spede, conductor.

Unit 3: Historical Perspective

Daugherty's method of composition may be unique among composers in that he makes use of technology in an unusual way. The basic equipment he uses includes two of the latest Macintosh computers, a number of midi-keyboard controllers and synthesizers, and four Emulator digital samplers, one for each section of the orchestra (woodwinds, brass, strings, and percussion). This technology allows him to immediately hear what he has composed using sounds that closely resemble an actual orchestra. This method of composition often manifests itself as an audible layering of the melodic material, and his frequent use of *stretto* entrances leads to ever more complex textures.

Daugherty's usual method is to present the material in a simple form and then to begin layering other voices and textures against the original. The listener can keep track of the material because he or she is familiar with it by the time the additive process comes into play. An example of this process can be seen and heard at measure 21 of "Red Cape Tango." The solo bassoon continues the basic statement of the *Dies irae*, joined in measure 30 by solo saxophone, which is offset by two beats and pitched a minor tenth higher. Different textures and layers are added until, by measure 61, there are ten distinct ideas occurring simultaneously. Another feature of Daugherty's music that stems from his use of digital samplers is the use of block orchestration. Frequently families of like instruments will have one musical idea, while a contrasting idea is presented in another group of like instruments. An example of this is found at measure186, where the high woodwind motive is countered by brass interjections.

Unit 4: Technical Considerations

As a grade six work, "Red Cape Tango" presents challenges to almost all of the players. Before programming the piece, the conductor should note the following. Two secure horn players (one is offstage) are needed for the two duets. It would be wise to have two strong bassoonists, although the first part is the true solo part. The E-flat clarinet part gets quite high in range, and the player needs to have very secure intonation (most of the part is cued in piccolo flute). The 1st soprano saxophone goes to a written F-sharp above the treble clef numerous times, with an 'a' five spaces above treble clef as the top note. Brass players are required to enter at *fortissimo* dynamics in upper registers following prolonged rests, and there is some double-tonguing as well. There is a brief trombone solo that returns a few times. There are numerous chromatic runs in the woodwinds, often in odd groupings (such as five or seven notes per beat). The climax of *Red Cape Tango* is loud and sustained, so the brass players will have to pace themselves. The work requires five percussionists plus a timpanist, and there is a suggested set-up to maximize some stereophonic interplay (notably crash cymbals and finger cymbals), which can present phasing difficulties. A five-octave marimba is required for the bass line.

Unit 5: Stylistic Considerations

Daugherty's musical language is rooted in tonality; rarely is there a moment in his music when the tonal center seems unclear. His roots in jazz and popular music are very evident as well.

In measure 279, the brass play a chord that is marked "jazz fall"; this chord may be analyzed using jazz nomenclature as an A9 with an added flat ninth and sharp thirteenth. A distinctive stylistic feature of much of Daugherty's music is his use of hemiola, syncopation, and metric displacement (see Unit 6 for discussion). Since the tango is such an integral element of *Red Cape Tango*, familiarity with that style would improve the conductor and ensemble performance.

Unit 6: Musical Elements

MELODY:

"Red Cape Tango" is filled with musical portrayal of emotions, and it is the job of the conductor to bring these to the forefront. The use of *Dies irae* in secular music has precedent; part of this is due to the tune's minor mode and mournful quality. A teaching segment on the use of *Dies irae* in other compositions and/or listening to those compositions would place *Red Cape Tango* in historical perspective. The tune itself in its basic form is important to point out:

Dies irae (on 'e' tonic):

HARMONY:

As discussed in Unit 5, Daugherty makes use of jazz and pop harmonies in this piece. Have the ensemble play and hold the chords at measures 168 and 279 to demonstrate these examples.

Jazz chord interruption from Red Cape Tango:

Jazz fall from *Red Cape Tango*:

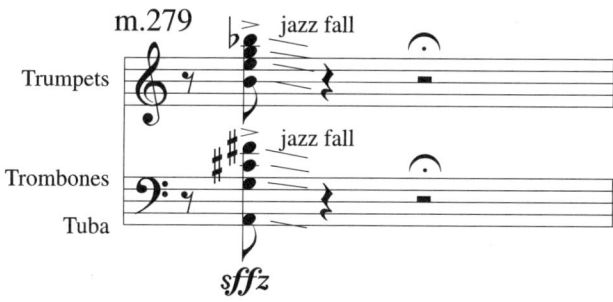

RHYTHM:

The moments when the tango bass and rhythm first make their appearance (at measures 18 and 22, respectively) should be pointed out to the ensemble. As a teaching lesson on the piece, the director might play examples of tangos that use a similar bass line and show a video of a representative tango dance (see Unit 9).

Tango bass and rhythm from *Red Cape Tango*:

The opening horn duet is an expansion of hemiola (three against two). An example of syncopation can be found beginning in measure 300. Melodic instruments have a rhythmic variation of the *Dies irae*, a group of dotted-quarter notes repeated four times followed by two quarter notes in common time. This rhythm has its roots in Latin American music (such as *bossa nova*). Beneath this syncopation, the bass instruments have an example of metric displacement using the pitch material of the *Dies irae*. Here the rhythm is a repeated pattern of six eighth notes, implying a meter of 3/4 time against the overall common time of the melody. This departure and return to the 4/4 barline takes four repetitions of the bass pattern over three measures, resulting in a large phrase that aligns with the treble clef melody every six measures.

Use of syncopation and metric displacement in *Red Cape Tango*:

The section at measure 234 provides another illustration of Daugherty's use of metric displacement. The woodwind trio plays a fragment of the *Dies irae* containing seven pitches, two equally spaced pitches for every measure of 3/4 meter. In measure 248, the second and third clarinets begin a six-note fragment of the tune, joined every four measures by a new voice. The composite layers form a complex metric displacement of seven against six against four against three. The different timbre of each layer allows them to remain aurally distinct.

TIMBRE:

The orchestration of the *Dies irae*, which frequently places it in the upper register of an instrument, adds to the mournful quality of the tune. Examples can be found in bassoon (measure 21), E-flat clarinet (measure 44), flute (measure 52), and piccolo (measure 152). The conductor could have those solo instruments play the tune down an octave to see how it might affect the character. An interesting percussion orchestration occurs near the end of the piece (measure 341) when the tango rhythm appears in the brake drum. Ask the students why this choice was made.

Unit 7: Form and Structure

The formal structure for *Red Cape Tango* is a twentieth century sectional form based on pitch material from *Dies irae*. There is a sense of departure and return provided by the return of the introductory horn duet (measure 132), as well as the return of *Dies irae* and fast motivic development sections. Although the work begins with E as tonic, A and D compete beginning at measure 186, with A as the final tonic. The partnership of *Dies irae* and the tango at the beginning of *Red Cape Tango* dissolves into a battle, with the tango eventually winning in a triumphant and very loud climax.

SECTION	MEASURE	TONIC	TEMPO	EVENT AND SCORING
A	1	e	60	Horn duet (*rubato*)
B	17	e	92	*Dies irae*
C	79	a	160	Motivic development
A'	132	e	60	Horn duet (*rubato*)
B'	141	e	96	*Dies irae*
C'	186	a–d	160	Motivic development
B"	276	d/a	88/152	*Dies irae*
Coda	341	a	72	Tango

ERRATA:

m. 8	Horn 3 – Rhythm should be half note, quarter note under triplet bracket.
m. 37	Flute 1 – Last sixteenth under "7" groupings on beats 3 and 4 should be D's (match m. 38)
m. 41	Piccolo, Flute 2 – Downbeat of beat 2 should be A-sharp (chromatic run).
mm. 67–72	Clarinet 1-a – Beat 3 half note should be F-sharp.
mm. 74, 76	Clarinet 1-a – Beat 3 half note should be F-sharp.
m. 77	English horn – Should have straight chromatic scale up; culminate on F-sharp, not G.
m. 135	Horn 3 – Rhythm should be half note, quarter note under triplet bracket.
m. 189	Clarinet 1–3, sax, percussion 5, piano – Beat 3 should have a courtesy A-natural.
m. 190	Horn 1 – All bottom E's need a flat sign.
m. 194	Flute 1–2, E-flat clarinet, clarinet 1–3, saxophone, percussion 5, piano – Beat 3 should have a courtesy A-natural.
m. 195	Horn 1 – All bottom E's need a flat sign.
m. 199	Clarinet 1–3, saxophone, percussion 5, piano – Beat 3 should have a courtesy A-natural.
mm. 200–213	Horn 1 – All bottom E's need a flat sign.
mm. 203–213	Horn 1–4 – Open symbol not needed.

m. 207	Clarinet 1–3, saxophone – Second and sixteenth should be E-flat.
m. 214	Percussion 3 – Should be marked "Tambourine with knee."
mm. 260–275	Horn 1 – All bottom E's need a flat sign.
m. 269	Percussion 3 – Should be marked "Tambourine."
mm. 303, 307	Trombone, tuba – Remove slur beats 3 to 4.
mm. 308–315	Piano – Pedal marking should continue in two-measure sequences.
mm. 308–315	Contrabass – Change to *glissando*.
mm. 316, 318, 320	Trumpet 1–2 – Concert E-natural.
mm. 316, 318, 320, 322, 324, 326	Trumpet 3–4 – Concert E-natural.
m. 320	Trumpet 1–2 – Concert B-natural.
m. 329	Trombone 1 – Solo should say "*gliss.*" over diagonal line; notes should have NO "+" or "o" over beats 2 and 3.
m. 339	English horn – Should have straight chromatic scale up (missing numbers after beat 2).
m. 349, 351	Trumpet 1–2 – Concert A on downbeats.
m. 351	Trumpet.

Unit 8: Suggested Listening

Benjamin Britten, *Sinfonia da Requiem*
Michael Daugherty:
    Beat Boxer
    Dead Elvis
    Metropolis Symphony
Jacob Druckman, *Brangle for Orchestra*
Gyorgy Ligeti, *Concerto for Violin*
Various, *The Story of Tango*. Compact Disc Metro Blue/Capitol Records 7243 8 55646 2 8, 1997.

Unit 9: Additional References and Resources

Azzi, Maria Susanna, Simon Collier, Artemis Cooper, and Richard Martin. *Tango! The Dance, the Song, the Story.* London: Thames and Hudson Ltd., 1995.

Britten, Benjamin. *Sinfonia da Requiem, Op. 20.* London: Boosey and Hawkes Music Publishers Limited, 1942.

Caldwell, John, and Malcolm Boyd. "*Dies irae.*" *The New Grove Dictionary of Music and Musicians.* Edited by Stanley Sadie. London: Macmillan Publishers, 1980.

Daugherty, Michael. Liner notes, *Metropolis Symphony.* Baltimore Symphony Orchestra, David Zinman, conductor. Argo 452 103–2, 1996.

Jurgens, Dan, Jerry Ordway, Louise Simonson, and Roger Stern. *The Death of Superman.* New York: DC Comics, 1993.

Potter, Sally. *The Tango Lesson.* Hollywood, CA: Columbia TriStar Home Entertainment, 1997. Videocassette (105 minutes).

Spede, Mark James. "Michael Daugherty's *Red Cape Tango:* A transcription for band." Dissertation, University of Texas at Austin, 1998.

Veloz, Frank, and Yolanda Veloz. *Tango and Rhumba: The Dances of Today and Tomorrow.* New York: Harper & Brothers Publishers, 1938.

Wanninger, Forest Irving. *Dies irae: Its Use in Non-Liturgical Music from the Beginning of the Nineteenth Century.* Dissertation, Northwestern University, 1962.

Werner, Eric. *The Sacred Bridge.* New York: Columbia University Press, 1959.

Websites:
http://www.fabermusic.co.uk
http://www.michaeldaugherty.net/

Contributed by:

Mark J. Spede
University of Texas at Austin
Austin, Texas

Teacher Resource Guide

Rocky Point Holiday

Ron Nelson
(b. 1929)

Unit 1: Composer

Ron Nelson was born in Joliet, Illinois, on December 14, 1929. As a child, he was influenced by his mother, who played the piano by ear. He began piano lessons at the age of six and had ambitions of becoming an organist. About his piano lessons, Nelson states, "I found it more fun and easier to make up pieces than learn others. My teacher taught me notation and insisted that I write down what I improvised. It was good discipline." Nelson became a paid church organist at age thirteen. He has remarked that his organ studies taught him the basic concepts of orchestration. Nelson played string bass in the Joliet Township High School band.

Nelson was accepted to the Eastman School of Music, where he studied with Howard Hanson and Bernard Rogers. About Hanson's influence, he states, "Hanson's genius was to create an environment where you couldn't wait to write something for the next class. He was a source of inspiration, a mentor, and one of the reasons that I stayed at Eastman." After earning his Bachelor of Music (1952) and Master of Music (1953) from Eastman, Nelson studied at the Ecole Normale de Musique and the Paris Conservatory on a Fulbright Grant from 1954 to 1955. He returned to Eastman, completing his Doctor of Musical Arts in 1956.

In 1956, Nelson accepted a position at Brown University and served as Chair of the Music Department from 1963 to 1973. He retired from this position and was granted Professor Emeritus status in 1993.

Nelson has gained wide recognition for his diverse musical style and has composed music for band, orchestra, and choir. His ever-growing list of works currently includes a mass, a cantata, and an oratorio, two operas, commercial music for film and television, as well as many other choral and instrumental compositions. He has received commissions from the Rochester Philharmonic Orchestra, the Rhode Island Philharmonic Orchestra, the United States Air Force Band, the Brevard Music Center, and the Aspen Music Festival. His music has received recognition with awards from the American Bandmasters Association, the National Band Association, and the Sudler International Wind Composition Competition.

Unit 2: Composition

About *Rocky Point Holiday*, Nelson states, "It was commissioned in 1965 by Frank Bencrisutto for the University of Minnesota Concert Band's Russian tour. Frank wanted an 'American' piece to open the program. This was a pivotal moment in my notion of wind ensemble scoring, in which I focused on orchestrating in an extremely transparent way. Others have commented that they felt *Rocky Point* marked a change in the overall philosophy of scoring for wind band."

He continues, "This style had its genesis at Eastman. I came from huge, Revelli-style bands in Joliet and had that sound in my ear. Then I got to Eastman and heard this very tight, sinewy sound in the form for the Eastman Wind Ensemble under Frederick Fennell. This sound was seeping into my musical consciousness and it was not until I got away from it that I realized how important this experience was."

Rocky Point Holiday was composed while Nelson was vacationing with his family at a Rocky Point seaside resort in Rhode Island.

Unit 3: Historical Perspective

Nelson has become a master of a variety of musical genres. Leonard Slatkin has stated, "Nelson is the quintessential American composer. He has the ability to move between conservative and newer styles with ease. The fact that he's a little hard to categorize is what makes him interesting."

Rocky Point Holiday is one of eight compositions in a series of overtures written by the composer. This genre began in 1953 with *Savannah River Holiday* and, according to Nelson, has ended with *Sonoran Desert Holiday*, composed in 1994 for the Air Force Band of Flight.

Many feel the compositional techniques represented in these eight overtures has defined Nelson's musical style. About this the composer states, "I have long ago accepted being typecast as a composer of flashy, high energy overtures. I would like listeners to understand that I do not 'arrange' my lighter pieces. I really feel this music. These are two distinct aesthetic tracks in my musical personality, and I believe that both are composed and orchestrated equally well." *Rocky Point Holiday* was the second, and perhaps most popular, composition written in this genre.

Unit 4: Technical Considerations

Rocky Point Holiday is a showcase for the concert band. It was one of the earliest works to expand the coloristic use of the percussion family. The score requires as many as ten percussionists, including a significant celesta/piano part. The marimba writing is particularly extensive and virtuosic. Harp adds to the coloristic nature of the music and should be included even if synthesized. A challenge for the conductor will be to maintain a dynamic balance between the percussion and the full ensemble while clearly hearing individual percussive colors and motives.

Nelson has written many florid woodwind passages requiring advanced technique throughout the clarinet section. Some divisi writing appears in the woodwinds, requiring rhythmic precision in passing figures within various sections. A light, rapid *staccato* style is required in several passages in the woodwinds and trumpets. For woodwind instruments pitched in B-flat, scale, arpeggio, and thirds exercises in all sharp keys (especially E, B, and F-sharp) will help provide a technical foundation for this work.

Unit 5: Stylistic Consideration

Shifting textures will be an important consideration throughout the work. Nelson frequently contrasts *tutti fortissimo* passages with more soloistic, chamber-like textures. Many short, jazz-like rhythmic motives are used throughout the work, both for color and for unifying and transitional purposes. Care must be given to project these rhythmic motives without overshadowing longer melodic lines. Nelson uses melodic augmentations in several passages. Care should be given to highlight such material, especially when scored in the lower voices of instrumental families. Precise and accurate articulations are an important stylistic element in Nelson's writing. As in the music of Stravinsky, detailed attention to accents, *sforzandi*, *staccato* markings, and abrupt dynamic shifts is required.

Unit 6: Musical Elements

Important musical elements in *Rocky Point Holiday* include the relationship between long, sweeping melodic lines and the development of short rhythmic motives; the use of timbral contrasts; and the innovative use of percussion colors. Specific teaching concepts are provided below.

MELODY:
- Teach the phrasing and architecture of long melodic lines, with special attention given to interpreting the dynamic direction of longer notes (Theme A, measures 12 through 47).

- Teach how a second theme (Theme B, measures 107 through 137) can be drawn from repetition of notes from Theme A.

- Teach how melodies can be augmented (Theme A, measures 201 through 229).

HARMONY:

- Teach how composers can create energy through rapid modulations (measure 1 opening with D-flat major scale leading to G-flat, E-flat minor arriving at C major by measure 5).

- Teach how composers can create harmonic interest through arpeggiated treatment of material (measures 47 through 60 in clarinets).

- Show how composers can use a pedal point to musically unify sections (measures 47 through 60 in horn).

- Show how composers can chromatically modulate (measures 70 through 96).

- Demonstrate the harmonic use of higher number chords (measures 138 through 161 in percussion and harp).

RHYTHM:

- Teach how composers can use short rhythmic motives (measures 5 through 24 in clarinets) for continuity and unity in the music (measures 196 through 210 in trumpets).

- Show how composers can create added motion by shifting the speed of accompanimental figures (measures 47 through 60).

- Demonstrate how composers can use syncopations for heightened energy (measures 25 through 28 in the trumpets).

- Demonstrate how composers can use several layers of rhythmic activity simultaneously (measures 201 through 225).

TIMBRE:

- Teach how composers can vary timbral sounds between pitched and non-pitched percussion instruments (measures 84 through 100).

- Show how composers can use mallet percussion instruments to harmonically unify large sections of material (measures 100 through 137, use of marimba and vibraphone).

- Demonstrate the unique timbral quality created by combining the sixteenth note arpeggio figures in the woodwinds with the harp glissandi (measures 195 through 225).

- Demonstrate the coloristic use of stopped and muted brass instruments to generate additional contrasts (measures 241 through 265).

- Demonstrate the coloristic and timbral contrast created by introducing maracas, bongos, and anvil to the score (measures 321 through 350).

Unit 7: Form and Structure

SECTION	MEASURE	EVENT AND SCORING
Introduction	1–11	D-lat leading to C major
Section 1, Theme A	12–28	Long, lyric themes in upper woodwinds, accompanied by two sixteenth/eighth motive (Motive 1)
Theme A1	28–46	Presentation of second half of Theme A; introduction of syncopated eighth/quarter/eighth figure (Motive 2)
Theme A restatement	47–61	Theme A with broken arpeggiated sixteenth figure in clarinet
Theme A1 restatement	61–73	
Closing	73–96	Modulating closing based upon material from A1
Transition	96–99	Percussion over C-sharp pedal
Section 2, Introduction	100–106	Textural contrast over C ostinato figure in double bass
Theme B	107–137	Long, lyric melody based on Theme A; tonality revolves around F minor and A minor contrapuntal treatment of Theme B
Theme B restatement	138–171	Change of accompaniment to a two-sixteenth figure based upon Motive 1; introduction of Motive 2 derived from Theme A
	154–171	Contrapuntal treatment of Theme B; added rhythmic layers developed in the percussion
Closing	172–194	Theme B with added motive material from Theme A

SECTION	MEASURE	EVENT AND SCORING
Section 3, Introduction	195–200	Textural contrast with sixteenth note arpeggios set against harp *glissandi*
Theme A	201–265	Return to C major; Theme A in augmentation; contrapuntal material in percussion
Theme A1	265–305	
Transition	305–320	Modulatory
Introduction	321–327	New rhythmic treatment for return of Theme B; introduction of exotic percussion
Theme B	328–346	Interjections of melodic motives for Theme A
Closing	356–361	Theme A in augmentation accompanied by arpeggiated sixteenth note figure and harp *glissandi*
Coda	362–367	F major

Unit 8: Suggested Listening

Ron Nelson:
Aspen Jubilee
Lauds (Praise High Day)
Morning Alleluias for the Winter Solstice
Savannah River Holiday
Sonoran Desert Holiday

Unit 9: Additional Referenced and Resources

Byrne, Frank. Program notes for "Holidays and Epiphanies...the Music of Ron Nelson." Dallas Wind Symphony, RR-76CD.

Peterson, Stephen. "Profile of Composer Ron Nelson." *The Instrumentalist*, June 1994, p. 49.

Pfenning-Berning, Kristina. Program notes for "Images." United States Air Force Band of Flight, Department of Air Force.

Smith, N., and W. David Richardson. Program notes for "When the Trumpets Call." University of Georgia, Summit Records.

Contributed by:
Edward C. Harris
San Jose State University
San Jose, California

Teacher Resource Guide

Symphony No. 4
David Maslanka
(b. 1943)

Unit 1: Composer

David Maslanka was born in New Bedford, Massachusetts, in 1943. Trained in his youth as a clarinetist, he holds an undergraduate degree in music from the Oberlin College Conservatory and graduate degrees in composition from Michigan State University. He also studied at the Mozarteum in Salzburg, Austria. His composition teachers include Joseph Wood and H. Owen Reed. He has been a member of the faculties at the State University of New York at Geneseo, Sarah Lawrence College, New York University, and Kingsborough College of the City University of New York. He currently resides in Missoula, Montana.

Maslanka has composed numerous works for wind band including *Concerto for Piano, Winds, Brass, and Percussion* (1974–1976), *Rollo Takes a Walk* (1980), *A Child's Garden of Dreams* (1981), *Symphony No. 2* (1985), *In Memoriam* (1989), *Concerto for Marimba and Band* (1990), *Golden Light* (1990), *Symphony No. 3* (1991), *Montana Music: Choral Variations* (1993), *Laudamus Te* (1994), *Tears* (1994), *Variants on a Hymn Tune* for Solo Euphonium and Band (1994), *A Tuning Piece* (1995), *Mass* (1996), *Symphony No. 5* (2000) and *Song Book for Flute and Wind Ensemble* (2001). He has also composed works for orchestra, choir, and a variety of chamber music.

Unit 2: Composition

For many of his compositions, Maslanka draws inspiration from his appreciation of nature and the environment as well as his deep spiritual convictions. These sources provide a background for his examination through music of the "connection of the conscious mind to unconscious power." He cites the music of Johann Sebastian Bach as personally significant and indicates that Bach's numerous chorales provide a "deep connection to things as they are." A highly thoughtful and reflective individual, Maslanka notes that the writings of psychologist Carl Gustav Jung are another key source of inspiration.

Symphony No. 4 is based on original thematic material along with the hymn tune *Old Hundred*. The work is constructed as one continuous movement in contrast to the traditional practice of multiple, independent movements. Conceptually, the symphony is considered by Maslanka to be a "connected series of dreams" (or episodes) about *Old Hundred*. This episodic approach provides interesting possibilities for the development of thematic material, and Maslanka makes use of the technique to take both performer and listener on an unpredictable emotional journey. The presence of *Old Hundred* is important to the overall form, not only for the symbolism it represents but also as a unifying element across the various episodes. Likewise, many of the original themes are hymn-like in nature and, thus, provide consistency to the overall form.

The composer draws additional inspiration for the symphony from his life-long fascination with Abraham Lincoln. Maslanka's admiration for the late President is evident in the preface to the score, where he states that Lincoln "remains a model for this age" because he "maintained in his person the tremendous struggle of opposites raging in the country in his time." The composer notes that Lincoln embodied the "unshakable idea of unity of all the human race" as well as "the unity of all life with all matter, with all energy" and the "unfathomable mystery of our origin." There are further references to the funeral procession and the long lines of Americans who waited to view the body of the slain Chief Executive. Maslanka quotes Carl Sandburg to note that *Old Hundred* was played by a brass band during a stop in Columbus, Ohio, as the body journeyed to its final resting place in Springfield, Illinois.

Maslanka writes that the symphony rises out of the "impulse to shout for the joy of life." This impulse takes form across the entire symphony through a variety of orchestrations and the use of extreme dynamic indications. From the opening statement of the solo horn (a single voice) to the majestic ending (many voices), Maslanka uses the instruments of the band to create an impressive palette of sound intended to express his personal view of life as a series of dualities—conflict and resolution, chaos and quiet, yearning and fulfillment. The ending, in particular, is a powerful statement using dynamics in the extreme range. For most of the final 188 measures, the winds are required to play no less than *fortissimo*, and the final measure implies an even louder dynamic range.

One of the more interesting elements of *Symphony No. 4* is the use of the clarinet mouthpiece to achieve a realistic emulation of crying babies. The players are instructed (at measure 712) to remove the mouthpiece and barrel from the body of the instrument and insert a finger into the barrel. The finger is then used as a "slide" to control pitches. Specific notes are provided across the three clarinet parts, but no rhythms are indicated and durations are set in free time (ad-lib). Like the trombone or violin, some practice is required to achieve the indicated pitch, but in reality a less-than-perfect pitch center actually makes the effect more realistic. The "cry" alternates with two-measure statements of the hymn tune *Christ Who Makes Us Holy* performed by flute choir and harp. This alternation continues until measure 721 when the "babies" and accompaniment are combined. (At this point, the "babies" are notated with standard rhythms.) Maslanka gradually expands the instrumentation until the hymn ends in measure 731.

Symphony No. 4 was commissioned in 1993 by the band programs at the University of Texas at Austin, Stephen F. Austin University, and Michigan State University. The score and parts are available from Carl Fischer. The full score is a photocopy of the handwritten manuscript (in concert pitch) and may be purchased from the publisher. The parts (transposed as necessary) are computer-generated and available for rent.

Unit 3: Historical Perspective

The symphony as a musical form has been popular among composers for several centuries. The name is borrowed from the Italian word "sinfonia." Typically, the modern symphony is a large instrumental work in multiple movements, but there are numerous exceptions. Composers have always felt free to experiment with the symphony, and their work is often a reflection of the times (musical and otherwise) in which they live.

Influences on the modern symphony are found in the instrumental forms commonly used during the baroque period: trio sonata, suite, concerto, French overture, and Italian sinfonia. An early precursor to the modern symphony was the late baroque *ripieno concerto* that established a traditional form (fast–slow–fast) across multiple movements. The popular *dance suite* expanded this form to the more familiar four movements. Important composers during this period include Arcangelo Corelli (1653–1713), Antonio Vivaldi (1678–1741), George Friedrich Handel (1685–1759), and Giovanni Battista Pergolesi (1710–1736). The first true concert symphonies were established in "pre-classical" form by 1740.

Franz Joseph Haydn (1732–1809) wrote over one hundred symphonies, and the development of the form can be traced across these works. His early symphonies are pre-classical in nature, his middle symphonies are genuinely classical, and his late symphonies display a mature style with elements of experimentation. Likewise, the development of the symphony from pre-classical to classical form is evident across the symphonies of Wolfgang Amadeus Mozart (1756–1791). The nine symphonies of Ludwig van

Beethoven (1770–1827), especially *Symphony No. 9*, are considered benchmark compositions having influence over composers for decades.

During the romantic period, the symphony received somewhat less attention from composers but nevertheless followed two tracks of development. One track followed the line of traditional development established by Haydn, Mozart, and Beethoven's early symphonies. The other track followed a more expansive model in the style of Beethoven's later symphonies. Many composers have created symphonies, including Ludwig Spohr (1784–1859), Carl Maria von Weber (1786–1826), Franz Schubert (1797–1828), Felix Mendelssohn (1809–1847), Robert Schumann (1810–1856), Cesar Franck (1822–1890), Anton Bruckner (1824–1896), Johannes Brahms (1833–1897), Camille Saint-Saëns (1835–1921), Peter Tchaikovsky (1840–1893), Antonín Dvovak (1841–1904), Edward Elgar (1857–1934), and Gustav Mahler (1860–1911).

The wide variety of styles and influences within the twentieth century resulted in many variations on the symphony as a form for instrumental music. While it is not possible to list all of the composers writing symphonies, some important names include Igor Stravinsky (1882–1917), Ralph Vaughan Williams (1872–1958), Jean Sibelius (1865–1957), Sergei Prokofiev (1891–1953), and Dmitri Shostakovich (1906–1975). Numerous band composers have utilized the symphony as a form for their larger works. Two of the most respected pieces in all of band literature are the *Symphony in B-flat* (1951) by Paul Hindemith (1895–1963) and *Symphony No. 6* (1956) by Vincent Persichetti (1915–1987). Symphonies for wind band have also been composed by Alan Hovhaness, Vittorio Giannini, Warren Benson, Morton Gould, and John Barnes Chance, with recent contributions by James Barnes, Jerry Bilik, and David Stanhope, among others.

Unit 4: Technical Considerations

By any definition, *Symphony No. 4* requires a high degree of technical expertise. Conductors should consider carefully the inherent technical demands before programming this work. Excellent solo players are required in virtually every section. Ranges are extreme throughout, and some individual parts require technique at the professional level. The piccolo trumpet solo (measures 370 through 393), with its rapidly articulated notes in the upper register, is a good example of the high level of technical proficiency needed for a successful performance. Due to the length of this work (919 measures; approximately thirty minutes), endurance may be a problem for young performers.

A variety of professional-level instruments are required, some of which may not be available to school-based ensembles. These include piccolo trumpet, alto flute, contrabassoon, harp, and organ. Additionally, the work requires an abundance of quality percussion equipment. These include bull roar; five non-pitch specific gongs (small to large); a variety of cymbals, tom-toms, bongos, and snare drums in different sizes; tam tam; shaker; anvil; crotales; wood block; bass drum; timpani; and the standard percussion keyboards. (Bows are required for some of the mallet parts.)

The piano part is critical, so a quality instrument must be available. The harp and string bass parts include solo passages. It is possible to substitute an electronic keyboard for the organ if high-quality organ sounds are available. (The organ sounds on many electronic keyboards are designed for popular music and may not be suitable for this work.)

In addition to the technical demands noted above, *Symphony No. 4* presents numerous ensemble challenges, with the most important being balance. Maslanka indicates that the work is for "symphonic wind ensemble." This suggests an ensemble of one or two players per part, or something in between a "one-per-part" wind ensemble and a full symphonic band with many players per part. All things considered, a two-per-part configuration might be ideal for this work. Given the high *tessitura* of the brass, two per part will allow players to alternate and rest during sections of extreme range. Likewise, two per part in the woodwinds will contribute to better balance against the extreme dynamics of the brass. Of course, the work can be successfully performed by a one-per-part wind ensemble or a large symphonic band, but care must be taken to ensure proper balance.

Unit 5: Stylistic Considerations

Maslanka's voice is unique among wind band composers. Always full of imagination, his large-scale compositions are quite unpredictable in terms of orchestration. At one moment, the score may require powerful *tutti* forces, likely followed by solo instruments performing in a chamber music setting. *Symphony No. 4* is consistent with this approach and encompasses a broad range of contemporary styles. Intense and energetic themes are contrasted with beautiful, sustained melodies resulting in numerous challenges for both conductor and performer.

Maslanka has provided ample articulations across the entire work. Most sections are clearly marked, leaving little doubt as to the intentions of the composer. Conductors should note that there is liberal use of the term *simili* (abbreviated "sim."), which is often used as a shorthand device when writing music by hand. Since the full score is in Maslanka's own hand, the use of *simili* makes sense. Unfortunately, the computer-generated parts retain this shorthand convention. This could produce ambiguity in performance. Careful attention to articulation in these sections is essential. (Once a very common marking, the recent use of computer software to create scores and parts has made the *simili* abbreviation virtually obsolete, and young musicians may need to be reminded of the correct articulation across numerous rehearsals.) Maslanka also uses *simili* to shorthand the notation of triplets (measures 427 through 500), leaving out the familiar bracket and numeral for most of the section. Again, this shorthand makes sense in the handwritten score, but the retention of this in the parts is without justification. An examination of the 1st flute part, for example, reveals the correctly notated triplet at measure 441, but the bracket and numeral are dropped in measure 442. These appear again in measure 468 but are left out between measures 485 and 501 despite an extensive section of rest and without any obvious reference to the previous triplet pattern. This unfortunate practice could contribute to confusing rehearsals and sloppy rhythmic performance.

One of the most challenging aspects of *Symphony No. 4* is the tremendous stylistic contrast required across the various hymn tunes and original melodies. Each episode features a unique theme setting crafted for maximum emotional impact. Quiet, reflective melodies alternate with themes that stir feelings of restless anticipation. The long, sustained themes require expressive phrasing and maturity of tone color, while the contrasting fast themes require precise rhythmic control and an energetic approach to articulation. A good example of the stylistic challenge is found in the intriguing saxophone solo (measures 504 through 562). Performed by solo alto (and briefly taken over by solo French horn), this theme is both familiar and mysterious. With its long, sustained tones, unpredictable intervallic skips, and rhythmic phrase endings, this theme requires a mature conceptualization on the part of both performer and conductor. Its pivotal position in the center of the symphony functions as a "resting place" between the episodes of intense energy and emotional drive that occur before and after. Further complicating the stylistic challenge is the crisp eighth note accompaniment used by Maslanka to punctuate the melodious solo.

Much of the inherent energy of *Symphony No. 4* is generated by rhythmic accompaniment. Repeated chords (scored across a variety of instruments) are often used to achieve a percussive effect. The quarter note accompaniment between measures 249 and 272 is typical of this technique. Maslanka marks these notes with accents *and staccatos* indicating weight and separation. Scored for upper woodwinds, upper brass, piano, and mallet percussion, these chords could easily become over-accented and mask the melody performed by unison low brass and woodwinds. (This becomes especially important since most school bands have many more "high" instruments than "low" instruments.) Extreme care must be taken to ensure proper balance without disruption of the intrinsic energy. Correctly performed, the effect of this technique is hypnotic.

Tempo will also have an enormous effect on the resulting articulation. The tempo indications are appropriate as indicated, and conductors should not try to compensate for a perceived "lack of energy" by increasing tempo. (One section, measures 792 through 839, with a tempo marking of circa 172 beats per minute, would become impossible to perform if increased.) Students should instead be sensitized to the presence of the melody and the role the articulation plays in creating a "percussive" effect. Recordings of rehearsals may prove useful to accomplish this task. It is further suggested that wind students listen carefully to the changes in tone color created by using different mallets (yarn, hard rubber, etc.) on the various percussion keyboards. The conductor should then relate these changes in color to the desired articulation.

The most interesting stylistic challenge is also perhaps the most unexpected—the surprising appearance of an original "jazz riff" that is used to accompany a jazz variation of *Old Hundred*. (The setting of a hymn tune in jazz style is certainly a contradiction of sorts, but it is precisely this sort of duality that fascinates Maslanka and permeates much of the entire piece.) The riff, which first appears in measure 633, is made challenging by large intervallic skips performed in quick rhythmic succession. Maslanka has marked carefully the precise articulation to be used, and strict adherence to these markings is essential. Maslanka states that this episode was inspired by his days of living in New York City, and the musical reference to the energy of jazz is intentional.

Unit 6: Musical Elements

There are numerous musical elements that serve to reinforce important concepts for the student performer. These include the following: time signatures (2/4, 3/4, 4/4, 5/4, 2/2, 3/2, 4/2, and 6/2), written dynamics (*pianissimo*, *piano*, *mezzopiano*, *mezzoforte*, *forte*, *fortissimo*, plus the extended markings of "*ppp*" and "*fff*"), phrase markings, terminology (numerous performance indications in English and Italian), articulations (standard accents, *staccato*, etc.), and the graphic representation for *crescendo* (expanding lines) and *decrescendo* (contracting lines). The compositional devices of fragmentation, augmentation, and canon are employed.

Without doubt, *Symphony No. 4* should be considered as advanced literature. As such, only the most mature and technically proficient students will be capable of performing this work. Despite this fact, there are numerous musical concepts that are likely to be introduced for the first time to young musicians. These include null key signature, improvisation, free-time notation (free rhythm to pitches as indicated), and uneven rhythmic subdivision (for example, measures 42 and 748). Maslanka indicates some of the compound rhythms as ratios (e.g., 3:2 and 4:3). There is also extensive use of the dotted-sixteenth/thirty-second note rhythm, which is rarely encountered in school-based ensemble literature.

Unit 7: Form and Structure

Any work the size and magnitude of *Symphony No. 4* offers many possibilities for analysis. The following analysis of form and structure is but one potential analysis. There are undoubtedly many other ways to subdivide the work for teaching purposes. It is hoped that the analysis provided here will serve as a starting point for conductors who wish to bring their students to the highest level of musical understanding.

The first theme, stated by solo French horn (measures 1 through 29), can be broken down into three segments: "a" segment, measures 1 through 9; "b" segment, measures 10 through 16; and "c" segment, measures 17 through 29. Each segment is used, in whole or part, in subsequent episodes.

SECTION	MEASURE	EVENT AND SCORING
Section I	1–29	Introduction; horn solo; initial statement of first theme; quarter note = 128–132
	30–62	Low woodwinds and low brass; statement of first theme with some rhythmic variation; "c" segment developed and extended in mm. 50–62
	63–83	*Tutti* winds; partial statement of first theme; *accelerando* mm. 76–88
	84–87	Transition (*accelerando* continues)
	88–106	Woodwinds and string bass; sequential chord progression in quasi-tremolo (sixteenth notes) style; quarter note = 152; *accelerando* mm. 103–106
Section II	107–114	Introduction to second theme; dotted-half note = 62 (quarter note = 186)
	115–132	Initial statement of second theme by piano, bassoon, and contrabassoon; strict eighth note accompaniment in oboe, alto and baritone saxophone, 1st horn, and bass trombone; changing meters: 2/4 and 3/4
	133–140	*Tutti* winds and percussion; second statement of second theme
	141–157	Extension of second theme motifs (development)
	158–176	Transition

Section	Measure	Event and Scoring
	177–207	Second theme (third statement) in canon; harp, alto flute, flute, clarinet, vibraphone, piano, piccolo, and xylophone with organ and percussion accompaniment
	208–248	Transition; fragments of second theme and extension motifs in development
	249–286	*Tutti* winds and percussion; fourth statement of second theme
	287–308	Closing based on section material (theme and development)
	309–333	Transition; clarinet and xylophone
	334–359	Solo horn partial restatement of first theme; harp arpeggios; closing chords in horn, low brass, and some woodwinds; tempo begins to decrease in m. 333
Section III	360–405	First statement of *Old Hundred* by solo flute (m. 372); "dots" of tone color provided by various winds and percussion (pointillism); quarter note = 80
	406–419	*Tutti* winds and percussion; multiple statements of *Old Hundred* in canonic form using syncopated and displaced rhythms to obscure strong beats of second and third voices; half note = 80
	420–426	Transition; development of motifs from *Old Hundred*
Section IV	427–502	"New" theme closely related to "b" segment of first theme; low brass and low woodwind melody; changing 2/4 and 3/4 meters; strong triplet pulse in accompaniment; quarter note = 76

SECTION	MEASURE	EVENT AND SCORING
Section V	503–561	Third original theme stated by solo alto saxophone; briefly restated by solo horn (mm. 529–542); *staccato* eighth note accompaniment throughout; quarter note = 124
	562–569	Closing material; cadential extension; piano solo
Section VI	570–571	Introduction to new section; *tutti* winds and percussion
	572–588	Transitional theme ("heroic") performed by horn, upper woodwinds, and low saxophone; punctuated chords used as accompaniment; tempo indicated as "suddenly a bit slower" (suggested tempo: quarter note = 90)
	589–605	Transitional theme ("frantic") performed by low brass and low woodwinds; upper woodwind accompaniment; battery percussion in sixteenth note runs; *poco accelerando* begins at m. 604
	606–627	Closing transition material; quarter note = 124
Section VII	628–632	Introduction to "jazz" section; "swing" style
	633–645	"Jazz riff" in various combinations of brass, woodwinds, and percussion; improvisation in some percussion; accompaniment consists of accented chords in syncopation
	646–647	Snare drum solo
	648–653	Repeated single note "jazz" piano solo riff; percussion accompaniment quasi-drum "fill" with sustained bass

SECTION	MEASURE	EVENT AND SCORING
	654–658	Jazz variation of Old Hundred in block chords; piano, upper woodwinds, saxophone, trumpet, and vibraphone with sustained bass instruments; *sempre staccato*
	659	Upper woodwind "jazz lick"
	660–661	Return of single-note "jazz" piano riff with trumpet and vibraphone
	662–665	Jazz variation of Old Hundred by solo clarinet; rhythmic pedal note (C) in trumpet, trombone, and vibraphone; piano block chords
	666–667	Brief return of "jazz riff"
	668–671	Jazz variation of Old Hundred by horn, trumpet, upper woodwinds, and xylophone; snare drum accompaniment (same rhythm as melody)
	672–678	Transition using a fragment of material from introduction to this section
	679–683	"Jazz riff" in canon; *tutti* winds and percussion
	684–686	Unison "jazz riff" with "walking bass" accompaniment; tutti winds and percussion
	687–692	Extension and repetition of "jazz riff" elements
	693–696	Return of Old Hundred in jazz variation by flute, clarinet, and vibraphone
	697–700	Return of "jazz riff" in xylophone solo; piano "walking" bass line; brass block chords
	701–704	Final statement of Old Hundred in jazz variation by solo flute and vibraphone

Section	Measure	Event and Scoring
	705–710	Closing material; "jazz" piano chords
	711	Grand pause
Section VIII	712–731	Statement of Christus, der uns selig macht by woodwinds and harp (selected brass added); clarinet mouthpieces removed and used as baby's cry; includes sections with indicated pitches only (player provides rhythm; free time); quarter note = 52
Section IX	732–763	*Tutti* winds and percussion; hymn-like theme alternating with fragments of initial theme (all segments) developed; quarter note = 96 with *accelerando* (mm. 750–753) to 132
	764–769	Cadential extension and transition
	770–791	*Tutti* winds and percussion; continuing restatement of initial theme; quarter note = 132 with *accelerando*
	792–801	Transition; quarter note = 172
	802–839	*Old Hundred* in augmentation; trombone and tenor saxophone melody with *tutti* wind and percussion accompaniment
Section X	840–865	Closing material (A); clarinet, alto saxophone, tenor saxophone, horn, and euphonium melody; sustained chords in low brass, low woodwinds, and organ; dotted-half note = 60
	866–886	Cadential extension and closing chords; *tutti* winds and percussion
	887–892	Closing material (B); horn, trumpet, euphonium, organ, and timpani melody; sustained chords in low woodwinds; MM: half note = 60
	893–909	Closing material (B) continued; *tutti* winds and percussion

SECTION	MEASURE	EVENT AND SCORING
Coda	910–919	*Tutti* ending

Unit 8: Suggested Listening

John Adams, *Short Ride in a Fast Machine*

Warren Benson, *Symphony II: Lost Songs*

Philip Glass, *The Canyon*

Paul Hindemith, *Symphony in B-flat*

David Maslanka:

> *Live at All-State 1996*, University of Arkansas Wind Symphony (Warren)
>
> *Live from the College of Creative Arts*, West Virginia University Wind Symphony (Wilcox)
>
> *Sounds, Shapes, & Symbols*, Ohio State Wind Symphony (Mikkelson)
>
> *Symphony No. 4*
>
> > *1994 TMEA Concert*, University of Texas at Austin Wind Ensemble (Junkin)

Vincent Persichetti, *Symphony No. 6, Op. 69*

Unit 9: Additional References and Resources

Jung, C. G. *Memories, Dreams, Reflections*. New York: Pantheon Books, 1961.

Sandburg, C. *Abraham Lincoln: The War Years*. New York: Harcourt, Brace & Company, Inc., 1939.

Stedman, P. *The Symphony*. Englewood Cliffs, NJ: Prentice-Hall, Inc., 1979.

For more information on David Maslanka and his music, visit his website: http://www.davidmaslanka.com

Maslanka's publisher, Carl Fischer Music, also maintains information on the composer at its website: http://www.carlfischer.com/maslankabio.html

Portions of this resource guide were taken from an interview with David Maslanka by the author, October 2001.

Contributed by:

Patrick Dunnigan

Florida State University

Tallahassee, Florida

Teacher Resource Guide

Symphony on Themes of John Philip Sousa

Ira Hearshen
(b. 1948)

Unit 1: Composer

Ira Hearshen received his Bachelor of Music in Music Theory and Composition from Wayne State University in Detroit. In 1972, he moved to Los Angeles to study orchestration at the Grove School of Music and with film composer Albert Harris. He also studied counterpoint with Allyn Ferguson. Hearshen has served as arranger for the Detroit Symphony Orchestra, the Jacksonville Symphony, and the Air Combat Heritage Band. His Hollywood credits include major television shows and film scores.

Unit 2: Composition

Hearshen has provided the following comments on this work:

> Stirred and fascinated by the music of John Philip Sousa since childhood, I still get a chill upon hearing the piccolo *obbligato* in the trio of "The Stars and Stripes Forever." While the thought of transforming popular march music into a legitimate piece for the concert stage had a lot of intellectual appeal, I figured that any attempt I made to pay homage to Sousa would be misunderstood. But artistic challenge won out and I started working on what was to become the second movement of the symphony in the winter of 1990–91.

The work was completed in 1995 and is published by Ludwig Music.

Unit 3: Historical Perspective

The four marches used in the symphony are among Sousa's most popular and enduring. *The Washington Post* was written in 1889 to help promote an essay contest sponsored by the newspaper. It remains one of Sousa's most popular marches. Sousa dedicated *The Thunderer* (also written in 1889) to the Knights Templar of Washington, DC, after his induction into that organization. It was Mrs. Sousa's favorite march. *The Fairest of the Fair* (1908) was inspired by a pretty girl who worked at the annual Boston Food Fair. It is generally regarded as one of Sousa's finest and most melodic marches. *Hands Across the Sea* of 1899 is one of Sousa's most outstanding works. In the *Great Lakes Recruit* of March 1918, Sousa discussed the justification of the Spanish-American War and quoted a line by Frere: "A sudden thought strikes me—let us swear an eternal friendship." Sousa then added, "That almost immediately suggested the title *Hands Across the Sea* for that composition, and within a few weeks that now-famous march became a living fact."[1]

Unit 4: Technical Considerations

The work presents significant technical demands. A wide variety of keys are explored in the various movements. The woodwinds are presented with some challenging technical passages throughout the work, including many exposed parts. The brass parts require strong players. In addition to numerous solo lines in the brass, the 1st trumpet part is particularly demanding. The percussion demands are substantial. A full battery, as well as an array of mallet instruments and auxiliary percussion, is required. The percussion parts present a technical challenge.

Unit 5: Stylistic Considerations

In this symphony, themes and motives from the four Sousa marches are cast in a wide variety of stylistic guises. The work explores numerous styles, from the rhythmic activity of the outer movements and the scherzo (Movement III) to the beautiful lyricism of Movement II. It is important that each style (accented, *staccato*, *legato*, *tenuto*) be carefully taught and that the energy and character of these styles be maintained throughout the work.

Unit 6: Musical Elements
MELODY:

Hearshen states, "Sousa's melodies are all strong and of a wide variety of architectural styles. They range from complex (*Hands Across the Sea*), to simple (*Washington Post*), and all are stirring, intense and, above all, really fun to listen to." The melodic elements of the four Sousa marches appear in every

---

1 Paul E. Bierley, *The Works of John Philip Sousa*. Westerville, OH: Integrity Press, 1984.

conceivable guise. A unifying element appears throughout the work. Hearshen states:

> There was a four-note melodic fragment common to virtually every tune I wanted to use, the same four notes that begin the *Dies irae* portion of the Catholic Mass...In the key of C major or A minor, these notes would be C–B–C–A. This melodic motive occurs in the trios of both *Hands Across the Sea* and *Washington Post* as well as in the introduction to *Fairest of the Fair*. In fact, these are the first four notes one hears in *The Stars and Stripes Forever*.

HARMONY:
The symphony makes significant use of functional triadic harmony. Much of the work is developmental in nature, and the musical material appears in a wide variety of keys. There is also substantial use of chromatic dissonance and polytonality.

RHYTHM:
Rhythmic language ranges from the simple to the complex. There is significant use of hemiola in the waltz sections of the opening movement. Players must be extremely secure in their rhythmic execution, as rhythmic dialogue and development are integral factors in the composition of the work.

TIMBRE:
Hearshen exploits the entire range of sonic possibilities in his scoring of the work. These range from massive wind and percussion sonorities to intimate scoring for solo woodwinds and brass. The percussion section provides a strong supportive role yet also exhibits significant solo and coloristic elements. The overall effect of the scoring is a constantly changing timbral and textural fabric with a wide array of instrumental combinations.

Unit 7: Form and Structure

SECTION	MEASURE	EVENT AND SCORING
Movement I (after *Washington Post*):		
Exposition	1–206	
Introduction	1–20	Martial percussion introduction (mm. 1–4); D pedal expanding to P5 (m. 5); trumpets introduces trio motive in D minor; dissonance builds; trio motive is rhythmically altered (m. 13), recalling the opening motive of *The Stars and Stripes Forever*

First theme	21–64	Percussion *ostinato* continues throughout first theme group; low brass and woodwinds introduce trio motive as clarinet and oboe state motive from the march's introduction; counterpoint thickens as tension builds; trumpet and tuba enter (m. 36) with rhythmically augmented statements of the introduction and trio motives, respectively; climax reached (mm. 46–48) as D minor reaffirmed; energy dissipates and texture thins amid final motivic statements in woodwinds, trumpet, horn; section concludes with the open fifth (d–a)
Bridge	65–70	Horn states trio theme in B-flat major
Second theme	71–206	Meter shifts to 3/4 as clarinet begins rhythmic *ostinato*; B-flat major with F pedal; flute, piccolo, and alto saxophone state first-strain theme of march; waltz character with significant use of hemiola; tuba, euphonium, string bass enter with pointillistic interjection on F major; horn restates trio motive with trombone in imitation, again in 4/4 meter; waltz reappears (m. 102) and solo trumpet states first-strain theme (m. 109); texture builds, leading to driving eighth note figures (mm. 123–125), then thins again; sequential melodic statements appear (based on second strain of march) amid rhythmic *ostinato*; rhythmic activity increases, leading to a return to 4/4 meter and the *molto ritard.* in m. 160; closing section then ensues with final motivic statements; this is followed by a section (mm. 178–192) in which the momentum "winds down" through a series of modulations, arriving on the highly dissonant chord of m. 193 (B minor/C minor complex); sustained dissonances

follow and the exposition concludes with the four-note trio motive, now stated ominously by low woodwinds (mm. 201–206); in this context, the motive unmistakably recalls the *Dies irae*

Development	207–445	
Section 1	207–311	Horn restatement of second theme of Exposition (A major); similar statements follow in upper woodwinds, euphonium; rhythmic *ostinato* reappears in woodwinds (m. 227) and motivic fragments lead to another driving, *tutti* eighth note section, which then dissolves into motoric rhythms in clarinet and transitional statements (mm. 249–253); at m. 254, the driving rhythmic figures become more pronounced, introducing sustained B-flats in the brass and upper woodwinds; various motivic fragments appear against the relentless eighth note pulse; finally, the energy dissipates and the trio theme is restated in rhythmic augmentation in the horns (mm. 291–311)
Section 2	312–367	Fantasia section based on trio and second-strain motives; minor mode; lower voices state trio fragment as clarinet answers with melodic expansion over pedal; melodic dialogue continues; counterpoint thickens as second-strain motive appears and is passed between various voices; activity increases as trumpet insistently states the second-strain motive sequentially (mm. 340–348); brief moments of repose then alternate with motivic outbursts as the section ends with successive statements of the second-strain motive

SECTION	MEASURE	EVENT AND SCORING
Section 3	368–445	Slower tempo; E-flat clarinet thematic statement answered by tuba, euphonium, string bass interjections; activity increases until all voices join, driving to m. 376; waltz section reappears, *molto allegro*, with motivic fragments stated in various guises, increasingly distorted; waltz begins to give way to driving rhythms in the upper voices; low brass begin a series of rhythmically augmented statements (m. 396); intensity grows as statements ascend from low brass to horn to trumpet amid dissonant figures in woodwinds; climax reached at m. 430 as percussion recalls motives from mm. 1–4, now in the faster tempo; development concludes with insistent motivic statements in trumpet amid frenzied activity in upper voices; final statement in rhythmic unison leads to the recapitulation
Recapitulation	446–681	
First theme	446–463	First theme returns with the extended melodic material in horn and eighth note motive now in upper woodwinds; texture thins as final statements appear in woodwinds
Bridge	464–469	Horn restates motive of mm. 65–69; B-flat major moving to D major statement in trombone
Second theme	470–606	D major; a series of motivic fragments leads to a return of the waltz section (m. 486); texture builds leading to a brief section of driving rhythms (m. 502); texture thins again with motivic interjections in the brass; the waltz theme returns in m. 518 in B-flat major; the momentum builds again to the rhythmic unisons of mm. 538–541, and the low brass enter with the

SECTION	MEASURE	EVENT AND SCORING
		second-strain motive (mm. 542–546); a sequential series of statements ensues amid much rhythmic activity; the motive is stated in imitation in trumpet and horn (mm. 562–564), and the section builds with this motivic fragment as the pervasive element; mm. 578–584 recall the exposition material from mm. 158–165; the section shifts to 3/4 meter (m. 585) with motivic statements leading to the rhythmic *ostinato* on F of m. 593; several brilliant statements in the brass (mm. 593–600) lead to the G-flat major sonority of m. 600, and a low brass arpeggio (mm. 601–602) concludes with a dissonant pedal F-flat; final fanfare statements in B-flat follow in trumpet, and the section comes to rest on a sustained C
Coda	607–681	The opening percussion cadence reappears under a dissonant chord on G; rhythmically augmented statements of the trio motive now appear in succession, leading to a dream-like statement in upper woodwinds over sustained chords in the brass (mm. 623–624); this is answered by motivic fragments in trumpet and trombone; a similar set of statements follows in mm. 627–630; another *ostinato* appears in upper woodwinds (*poco animato*, m. 631), and brass join in as the momentum builds to m. 635 and a *diminuendo* ensues; a final dream-like statement is followed again by answers in trumpet and trombone (mm. 638–646); at m. 647, snare drum begins an *ostinato*, taken up by low brass in m. 651; upper woodwinds introduce an inverted version of the trumpet motive of m. 9, and the momentum builds in ominous fashion to the

SECTION	MEASURE	EVENT AND SCORING
		descending eighth note lines of mm. 674–678; final statements bring the movement to a close on B-flat
Movement II (after *The Thunderer*):		
A	1–12	"Trio" theme in clarinet, bassoon, euphonium; triadic harmony in A-flat major
Transition	13–16	Four-measure transition in woodwinds, horn
B	17–32	Plaintive melody in solo oboe over pulsating A minor triad in clarinet; oboe statement begins with an inversion of the trio theme; saxophone and low brass enter (m. 24) as texture builds with increased rhythmic activity; upper woodwinds join oboe in elaborating the theme; modulation toward E-flat major
A'	33–52	Trio motive returns; E-flat major; full ensemble; tension begins to build with *stringendo* leading to the *piu agitato* of m. 43; tension created by altering the intervallic structure of the trio motive (now M2–m2); momentum dissipates in mm. 47–52
Transition	53–60	Texture thins; upper woodwinds introduce theme from second strain; muted horn in imitation as if from a distance
A"	61–84	A-flat major over E-flat pedal in bass; trombone solo brings return of trio theme, now stated in its entirety; countermelodic lines in trumpet and clarinet; texture builds leading to second-strain statement in trombone (m. 77) punctuated by fanfare figures in trumpet

SECTION	MEASURE	EVENT AND SCORING
A'''	85–99	Final series of statements in A-flat major; trombone begins final statement of trio theme (m. 92) as all voices *diminuendo* and momentum dissipates
Coda	100–110	*Pianissimo* D-flat major chord in upper woodwinds prepares for final statement in saxophone, 4th/5th trumpet; brass enter and lead to resounding resolution in A-flat major (m. 107); final two measures die away as movement concludes

Movement III (after *Fairest of the Fair*):
A section

a	1–18	Four-measure introduction using motives from first strain of march; key of E-flat major; flute, oboe, introduce first-strain melody; interjections in woodwinds, brass
a'	19–26	Material of "a" section returns, now abbreviated
Interlude	27–45	Driving rhythmic figures drawn from second strain; melodic fragment returns and voices arrive on D (mm. 43–45)
A''	46–57	"a" material returns with sequential fragments of the opening theme

B section

Introduction	58–61	Slow waltz tempo; key of G-flat major
b	62–77	Lyrical tuba solo based on trio theme; woodwind interjections drawn from material of first strain
b'	78–91	Second half of trio theme in euphonium, tenor saxophone; solo trumpet joins in closing phrase; solo tuba reappears as the section concludes
Transition	92–96	Transition in 4/4 meter based on melodic fragment from the march's opening measure

SECTION	MEASURE	EVENT AND SCORING
A' section		
a	97–123	Modulatory sequence on first-strain melody; imitative statements in upper woodwinds, euphonium, horn; keys of C-flat, D-flat, F
a'	124–139	Full ensemble; key of E; trumpet, horn state first-strain motive; low brass answer with first-strain theme, which is then continued in horn, euphonium; motivic dialogue continues as section builds to its conclusion
Coda	147–171	Texture thins; eighth note rhythmic pulse in percussion; isolated melodic statements in woodwinds; texture thickens as principal motive is stated in rapid succession
	172–188	Driving, dissonant *ostinato* introduced in low brass; upper brass, woodwinds added as tension builds; motivic statement appears in 2nd trombone and tenor saxophone (E-flat major); and a series of final motivic statements brings the movement to a close

Movement IV (after *Hands Across the Sea*)
A section

Section 1	1–42	Opening motive of march in saxophone and horn, answered by lower voices; F major with frequent modulation; motivic fragments from opening strain appear at m. 5, rhythmic *ostinato* begins in m. 8; imitative fragments continue until clarinet and saxophone begin an extended canonic section (mm. 12–25) based on the march's opening material (the saxophone statement is at the major sixth below and offset by four measures); horn enters with the original motive and the texture thickens again; activity continues

SECTION	MEASURE	EVENT AND SCORING
		with sequential statements, frequent modulation; energy dissipates with *piano* woodwind statements (m. 36) then builds again, leading into m. 43
Section 2	43–129	March character; trumpet states opening melody answered by upper woodwinds; meters move from 4/4 to 2/4 and 3/4; woodwind flourishes appear at m. 54 and trumpet restates first-strain motive; voices arrive at m. 60 on rhythmic *ostinato*; trumpet introduces fanfare figure based on second-strain motive over a D pedal in bass (m. 63); imitative answers in horn, trombone; brief transition (mm. 66–69) leads to another series of fanfare statements, now over a pedal B-flat (mm. 70–73); a more extended transition ensues, with dissonant quarter note movement serving as connective material as upper woodwinds continue with first-strain motives; at m. 84, upper woodwinds and xylophone join in a unison variant of the first-strain theme as fanfare figures appear in rapid succession in horn, saxophone, and trumpet; this leads to a section (m. 90) with woodwinds exploring a second-strain motivic fragment moving to an insistent octave G as horn reinforces the tonality with a triplet-based fanfare statement (mm. 95–100); dissonant elements enter, leading to the horn statement on C of mm. 101–102 and the second-strain statement in trumpet (F major) that continues "a tempo" at m. 104; second-strain theme continues in piccolo and flute, leading to another statement (trumpet, horn, mm. 110–112), now in A-flat major; humorous elements ensue with a woodwind

SECTION	MEASURE	EVENT AND SCORING
		flourish and triplet-swells in the brass (mm. 111–114); bassoon, tenor saxophone, and euphonium briefly calm the proceedings with a lyrical thematic statement leading to a return of the movement's opening motive (m. 118); horn and saxophone now conclude on an unexpected B, and a closing section revisits various motivic fragments in a flurry of rhythmic and melodic activity
Transition	130–142	Percussion *ostinato* with sustained A pedal in low voices; horn states inverted variant of second-strain theme; minor mode; motivic fragments in upper voices lead to another horn statement (a minor second higher), now accompanied by an imitative statement in trombone (m. 136); dissonance builds; motivic fragments again conclude the phrase
B section Section 1	143–167	Low brass, bass clarinet begin *ostinato* based on horn transition figure; horns and tenor saxophone in imitation at the tritone (m. 145) offset by an eighth note; mood darkens; texture thickens and dissonance builds as voices added; upper woodwind motivic fragments begin to appear (m. 152) and begin to dominate the texture, finally leading to a final statement in clarinet and the cadence of m. 167
Section 2	168–207	Bassoon cadenza begins (mm. 168–173) by exploring opening motives of the march and concludes (mm. 174–179) with sequential use of the trio motive; cadenza cadences as voices build extended chord on F; chord resolves to B-flat (m. 180) as solo oboe presents a lyrical statement of the second-strain

SECTION	MEASURE	EVENT AND SCORING
		theme; imitative statements in woodwinds produce polytonality; oboe concludes statement on a sustained B-flat, and the section cadences in that key; bassoon, tenor saxophone, and euphonium now begin a similar statement in G-flat major (m. 191); upper woodwind flourishes create a dream-like character; upper woodwinds state the second melodic phrase as counter-melodic activity continues; penultimate measure (m. 199) is now treated sequentially, and this motive predominates to the end of the section; clarinet adds a sequential statement of the opening motive as the section concludes
A' section Section 1	208–339	Final section begins with a piccolo *ostinato* stating a first-strain fragment on A-flat; voices are added to the rhythmic *ostinato* at various intervals, producing a dissonant web; brass rise and fall with eighth note interjections (mm. 214–217), and the process begins anew in m. 218; this time the *ostinato* is answered by clarinet, followed by a trumpet statement drawn from the march's introduction (mm. 221–224); a more extended eighth note line ensues, now moving from the bass voices up through the texture to piccolo and descending again (mm. 225–230); the section finally arrives on a bass pedal and an interlude in E minor (m. 237); the motives are derived from the opening of the second strain; rhythmic activity builds, leading to another first-strain fragment (m. 246); the material now moves into D minor, the proceedings thrown off balance in 7/8, 5/8, and

Section	Measure	Event and Scoring

9/8 meters (mm. 250–252); at m. 254, the musical energy increases further with fanfare-like figures in the brass and motivic statements in the upper woodwinds; this leads to another series of mixed meters (mm. 261–265) and another fanfare section, with saxophone providing an extended melodic statement (mm. 266–271); brief march section (mm. 271–274) is interrupted by dissonant fanfare figures (m. 275–278) leading to a final statement of the first-strain motive (mm. 281–283); an extended statement in saxophone, bassoon, and clarinet grows out of this cadence, loosely based on second-strain melodic material, now in 6/8 meter; the section moves into 9/8 with the texture thickening and melodic activity increasing; trombone emphatically states a second-strain fragment (mm. 297–298), and the section concludes with a brief dialogue (mm. 300–305) based on eighth note fragments; at m. 306, the momentum increases again, now with quickly moving triplet figures *alla breve*; low brass interjections and trumpet/woodwind flourishes begin to appear (mm. 312–319) as the pace becomes frantic; triplet figures return in m. 320 leading to a series of violent *crescendi* in brass and percussion (mm. 323–325); section culminates with a series of fanfares (mm. 333–337) leading to the descending sixteenth note figures of mm. 338–339

SECTION	MEASURE	EVENT AND SCORING
Section 2	340–370	Section begins with a sustained bass pedal; F major; upper woodwind flourishes begin to appear (m. 342), leading to fanfare figures in the low brass (m. 349) and trumpet derived from second-strain material; a *molto ritard.* leads to a brass statement, *molto allargando*, of the trio theme (mm. 359–362) amid upper woodwind tremolos; melodic material in the woodwinds leads to a continuation of this brass statement (mm. 363–366); the trio theme is concluded emphatically
Coda	371–398	Introductory material from Movement I returns; D minor; martial percussion cadence introduces ominous quarter note motive; momentum quickly builds, leading to final statements from the introduction of *Hands Across the Sea* (m. 384), now in F major; a set of fanfare figures (mm. 388–392) leads to the final cadence on F, bringing the work to a close

Unit 8: Suggested Listening

"Hail, Sousa!," University of Michigan Band, William Revelli

"Strictly Sousa," Dallas Wind Symphony, Jerry Junkin

"Stars and Stripes Forever: Music of John Philip Sousa," Eastman Wind Ensemble, Frederick Fennell

"Symphony on Themes of Sousa," Tokyo Kosei Wind Orchestra, Frederick Fennell

Unit 9: Additional References and Resources

Bierley, Paul E. *John Philip Sousa, American Phenomenon*. Miami, FL: Warner Brothers Publications, 2001.

Bierley, Paul E. *The Works of John Philip Sousa*. Westerville, OH: Integrity Press, 1984.

Sousa, John Philip, ed. Paul Bierley. *Marching Along*. Westerville, OH: Integrity Press, 1994.

914

Contributed by:
Bradley P. Ethington
Associate Professor of Music
Syracuse University
Syracuse, New York

Teacher Resource Guide

The Warriors
Percy Aldridge Grainger

(1882–1961)

transcribed by Frank Pappajohn

Unit 1: Composer

Percy Grainger was born in Australia on July 8, 1882. His father was an architect from London, his mother the daughter of a London hotel manager who had come to Australia to make his fortune. His father, John Harry Grainger, was a man of some learning who was regularly away from the household supervising the construction of public works in Australia. In his absence, young Percy was doted upon by his formidable mother, the former Rose Aldridge, who supervised every aspect of his education. He was tutored at home, with a large part of his diet consisting of the Anglo-Saxon Chronicles and the Icelandic sagas. Rose Grainger was a beautiful woman with strong Nordic features (inherited by her son), but like most people of that day, she passionately disliked members of other ethnic groups, and she instilled in Percy many outrageous notions of racial superiority. On the whole, Grainger's take on life can be condensed down to a dislike of people with brown eyes and dark hair and an antipathy toward classical Roman and Greek culture. He was fascinated with primitive peoples around the world, and it became one of his life's goals to incorporate aspects of their music into his own.

When Grainger entered into public life, he adopted his mother's maiden name as his middle name. He left Australia in 1895 to study in Frankfurt for a period that lasted until 1901. At the same time, he began to compose and collect the musical folk material that was to provide the raw material for much of his greatest work. At the turn of the new century, he moved to London but toured frequently so he was always aware of the most recent innovations in the musical world. He greatly admired the composers and compositions that were scandalizing all of Europe at that time, and his letters revealed admiration for Richard Strauss, Debussy, Ravel, Stravinsky, Bartók, and Schoenberg (along with others long since forgotten). In 1914, with the outbreak of World War I, Grainger immigrated to the United States. Although he later took American citizenship, he never forgot his roots in Australia, and in the 1930s, he oversaw construction of a museum located on the campus of the University of Melbourne to house manuscripts and artifacts from his life. He died in White Plains, New York, in 1961.

Long before Grainger took up an interest in the wind band, he devoted himself to the composition of a number of large-scale works for symphony orchestra. Many of the works were sketched out at this time, only to be finished years later (*English Dance, Green Bushes, Danish Folk Music Suite,* and *Youthful Suite*). The scores that were completed and published during this period show ever more increasing mastery in the handling of orchestral forces. Among the masterful orchestral scores of his youth, one finds miniatures based on folk music (such as *Molly on the Shore* and *Irish Tune from County Derry*), original pieces in smaller forms (such as *Colonial Song* and *Mock Morris*), and two very large scores: the suite *In a Nutshell* in four movements and his largest work of any kind, *The Warriors,* to which he gave the subtitle "Music to an Imaginary Ballet."

Unit 2: Composition

The Warriors is an original work (containing no folk themes of any kind) scored for symphony orchestra of enormous proportions. Begun in London in December 1913, finished in San Francisco in December 1916 (with the bulk of the music composed in London and New York), and premiered at the Norfolk Festival in 1917, the composition is dedicated to Frederick Delius, one of the composer's greatest admirers and dearest friends. *The Warriors* evolved from discussions with conductor Thomas Beecham, an early champion of Grainger's music, who in 1913 was conducting performances by the Ballets Russes in London. Although Grainger seemed to have attempted to portray the work as if it had been commissioned by the ballet company, documents recently uncovered in the Grainger Museum indicate that Beecham had suggested that Grainger write an orchestral work prior to the composition of a true ballet to allay Grainger's concerns about his lack of experience in choreography. The implication is that *The Warriors* as we know it today was never intended to be staged as a ballet but is rather the end product of an experiment in composing something Grainger described as "danceable music," music that could later be drawn upon for an actual ballet score. In any event, the Ballets Russes were never informed of Beecham's grand plans, so in the absence of an actual scenario on which to base the composition, Grainger assembled the scored for concert performance and created the plot for an "imaginary ballet."

The composition's title is explained in Grainger's lengthy program note, a portion of which is quoted here:

> ...the ghosts of male and female warrior types of all times and places are spirited together for an orgy of war-like dances, processions and merry-makings broken, or accompanied, by amorous interludes, their frolics tinged with just that faint suspicion of wistfulness all holiday gladness wears...arm in arm in a united show of gay and innocent pride and animal spirits, fierce and exultant.

Unit 3: Historical Perspective

The first years of the twentieth century were years of artistic opulence on a scale that has seldom been repeated. With the artistic capitols of Europe enjoying undreamed of wealth as a result of the industrial revolution and the ready availability of cheap raw materials from colonial possessions, opera and ballet companies strove to outdo one another in spectacle and large forces. Large orchestral forces were the order of the day: the orchestra for Igor Stravinsky's ballet *Le Sacre du Printemps* calls for twenty woodwinds, eighteen brass, a large number of percussion instruments, and a large string section (specific numbers are not listed); larger still is the orchestra for Richard Strauss's opera *Elektra*, requiring twenty woodwinds (including Heckelphone and two basset horns), twenty brass (including four Wagner tubas, bass trumpet, and contrabass trombone), an arsenal of percussion, two harps and sixty-two strings; but the most gargantuan of all is Arnold Schoenberg's *Gurrelieder*, requiring twenty-five woodwinds (with doubling calling for four piccolos, two English horns, two each of E-flat clarinets and bass clarinets, and two contrabassoons), twenty-five brass, at least seven percussionists, four harps, celesta, and strings.

With this in mind, the number of standard orchestral players required for performance of Grainger's *The Warriors* seems quite reasonable: piccolo and two flutes; two oboes, English horn and bass oboe; two clarinets and bass clarinet; two bassoons and doublebassoon; six horns, four trumpets, three trombones and tuba; two harps, and strings. With these forces, Grainger has ample representation from three of the traditional orchestral families of sound (woodwinds, brass, and strings). It is in the fourth family of instruments that *The Warriors* breaks new ground, for Grainger demands that a percussion/keyboard section of astounding proportions be added to the traditional forces: four kettledrums, three percussionists (playing side-drum, tambourine, cymbals, bass drum, gong, castanets, and wood block), xylophone, wooden marimba (played by two performers), glockenspiel, steel marimba (played by three performers, which could be replaced by bar-piano or dulcitone), staff bells (played by three performers, or bell-piano), tubular bells, celesta, and three pianos (the composer asks for strong, vigorous players, suggesting that if the players are not strong enough, the conductor should not hesitate to double or triple each piano part). By simply counting the number of percussion/keyboard players desired, it is clear that *The Warriors* represents a unique score in which the percussion/keyboard section is required to function as a rich, colorful, and entirely self-sufficient fourth basic color within the orchestra.

Unit 4: Technical Considerations

The Warriors was conceived for an immense orchestra of professional musicians, and any faithful band transcription of this score will require a wind ensemble of similarly large proportions with technical skills on a near professional level. It is not hyperbole to state that in this score Grainger demonstrates a mastery of orchestral forces that places him on an equal footing with the greatest orchestral craftsman of the twentieth century (an elite group that numbers among its members Richard Strauss, Stravinsky, Ravel, and Respighi). Practically every orchestral device imaginable can be seen somewhere on the pages of this score.

Among the more advanced ideas is an innovation seldom seen in orchestral music: multiple conductors leading independent groups of players. At measure 292, the performing forces are divided into four distinct groups: 1) a group consisting of the majority of the performers on stage following the primary conductor in playing a languid, almost motionless chordal texture; 2) an off-stage, invisible group of six brass players (two each of trumpets, horns, and trombone, which may be drawn from the players on stage) who play march-like phrases at a tempo considerably faster than the main body of musicians under the direction of a second conductor (unseen); 3) a group consisting of 2nd piano, 2nd harp, and steel marimba, who play an *ostinato* pattern following a third conductor (who like the first conductor is situated on the stage and visible to the audience); and 4) a group consisting of wooden marimba, staff bells, celesta, 1st harp, and 3rd piano that plays independently of all of the other forces, "ignoring both conductors' beats," but later joins the group following the third conductor. It should also be pointed out that *The Warriors* is a lengthy work in one uninterrupted movement, lasting approximately nineteen minutes in performance, consequently demanding great maturity and power of concentration on the part of the members of the performing ensemble.

The Warriors, like most of Grainger's well-known scores, contains mixed meters, and though most of this mixture is of the more commonly found meters (such as 2/4, 3/4, 4/4, 2/2, 3/2, and so forth) there are a few appearances of asymmetrical meters, such as "two and one-half four."

Much, though not all, of the score is notated without key signatures, using notation common in the twentieth century of supplying all accidentals for the transposing instruments. The transcription for wind band is in the same key as the orchestral original. As the tonal center is often undefined and in a near constant state of flux, there would have been no benefit in transposing the work to a different key to suit the limitations of traditional band performance practice: any transposition would have accomplished nothing more than to have made certain of the easier portions harder in the band version while making harder sections easy.

It must be said that Grainger was a composer desperate to have his music performed, and he sanctioned compromises of the most shocking nature in most of his advanced scores. For example, although the off-stage brass players contribute greatly to the "magic" of the mid-section of *The Warriors*, Grainger allows this spectacular effect to be omitted, writing, "Should the first conductor, for any reason whatsoever, dislike the effect produced, the entire music behind the platform may be left out." It cannot be too highly stressed that the enormous forces required for performance of this score are not coincidental to the concept of this work, but are part of the essential nature of the work. Many conductors, desirous of adding *The Warriors* to their resume, might be tempted to perform this work with the elite wind ensemble drawn from the finest players at their school or university, although most of these elite ensembles tend to be rather small. Could anything be more ridiculous than for a wind ensemble of fifty-five or so players to attempt to do justice to a score that in its original conception called for an orchestra of nearly one hundred players? One could just as likely expect the full effect intended by the massive forces of Stravinsky's *Le Sacre du Printemps* to be possible from a Broadway pit orchestra. Needless to say, in addition to a very high level of skill required on the part of both ensemble and conductor(s), a great commitment of forces and rehearsal time is required for a successful performance of this score.

Unit 5: Stylistic Considerations

The Warriors requires more musical styles than any of Grainger's other works, with extremes of all types to be found. The tempi range from "*Vivace*" with blisteringly fast ideas present in many parts, to "*Lento*," where movement is scarcely perceptible (quarter note = 50) with the most delicate of nuance present. The dynamic range extends from *pppp* to *ffff*, sometimes calling for no more than two players in a gentle duet to the full ensemble assaulting the audience with all the force that can be mustered. All manner of articulations can be found, from the most brittle *staccato* to the most toneful *legato*. The score is littered with markings of the most colorful nature (in Italian and Grainger's "blue-eyed English"), such as "*marcatissimo*," "*cresc.* possible," "*feroce*," "very thumpingly," "very roughly and harshly," "very hard and sharp," "very skittishly and rhythmically," "top notes much to the fore," "gracefully, way-wardly," and perhaps the most wonderful of all: "Languishingly, *rubato*, nasal, snarling, much to the *fore*" (applied to the bass oboe solo in the middle section).

Unit 6: Musical Elements

Since *The Warriors* was originally conceived as something of a gathering of ideas that could be developed at a later date for development into separate compositions, there is a bewilderingly large number of motives, scales, juxtapositions of tonalities, and ideas that flood forth in this piece. The scope of this article is too small to allow a thorough discussion of the compositional techniques involved in this work.

Grainger was fond of using musical ideas in more than one composition (such as the lyrical melody that appears in *Colonial Song*, *The Gum-Suckers March*, and *Australian Up-Country Tune*). However, the only melodic fragment found in *The Warriors* that can also be found in any of his other pieces is the melody sang forth by the bass oboe mentioned above; this melody was sketched in 1911 and appears in a choral work entitled *The Lonely Desert-Man Sees the Tents of the Happy Tribes*, in which the singers are asked to use nonsense syllables throughout.

Unit 7: Form and Structure

In the composer's own words, *The Warriors* is built on "fifteen distinct themes and motives (none of them of a traditional or popular origin, and none of them used as 'leit-motivs' or with any 'program-music' significance of any kind) occur,...in which though cast in one continuous movement, the following divisions of mood and tempo are clearly marked and easily traced:

SECTION	MEASURE	EVENT AND SCORING
1	1–111	Fast; martial or dance-like in character
2	111–140	Slow and languorous
3	141–292	Fast; begins in the dance spirit but gradually becomes broader and more "flowing" in style; in this section, most of the thematic material of the entire work is subjected to various kinds of treatment and development
4	292–322	Slow pastoral melody on bass oboe, accompanied by [sustained chords] and by a *staccato* organ-point consisting of harp harmonics and piano strings struck by marimba mallets

Section	Measure	Event and Scoring
5	323–354	Slow, languorous music (similar to section 2) on the platform; at the same time, snatches of quick martial music are faintly heard from behind the platform
6	355–427	Dance orgy, beginning very gently but working up to a high pitch of commotion and excitement; during this section (as also in section 8), there is considerable "double-chording"—different instrumental groups simultaneously playing different chord passages that pass thru, above and below each other and are harmonically independent of each other
7	428–442	Climax; the chief theme of the composition is given forth slowly and majestically by the full [ensemble]
8	443–469	The dance orgy is resumed with vigor, but is broken off suddenly while at its height, whereupon the work ends with an abrupt anticlimax."

Unit 8: Suggested Listening

Percy Grainger:
> *Blithe Bells*
> *In a Nutshell Suite*
> *The Power of Rome and the Christian Heart*
> *Youthful Suite*

Gustav Holst, *The Planets*
Arnold Schoenberg, *Gurrelieder*
Richard Strauss, *Elektra*
Igor Stravinsky, *Le Sacre du Printemps*

Unit 9: Additional References and Resources

Bird, John. *Percy Grainger*. London, Faber and Faber, 1976.

Grainger, Percy. *The Warriors*, orchestral conductor's compressed full score. Boca Raton, FL: Edwin F. Kalmus & Co., Inc., no date.

The Warriors, dished-up (arranged) by the composer for 2 pianos, 6 hands. Mainz, B. Schott's Söhne, 1923.

Lewis, Thomas P. *A Source Guide to the Music of Percy Grainger.* White Plains, NY: Pro/Am Music Resources, 1991.

Mellers, Wilfrid. *Percy Grainger.* New York: Oxford University Press, 1992.

AUTHOR'S NOTE:

The Warriors was transcribed for wind band by Senior Master Sergeant Frank Pappajohn, principal string bassist of the United States Air Force Band. This transcription is published by Master Music Publications. This transcription was clearly tailored for the use of the Air Force Band, so the instrumentation has regrettably been reduced to reflect the available personnel in that ensemble (among many omissions, 3rd piano, 2nd harp, and celesta are omitted; the six horns requested in Grainger's orchestral score has been reduced to five; and the essential bass oboe has been omitted and its critical solo assigned to the euphonium [!]). Many of these defects could be remedied by purchasing a full set of orchestral parts and using these to restore much of the sumptuous instrumental splendor missing in this particular wind adaptation. Perhaps in the fullness of time, another transcriber will come to the fore to prepare a second, more complete rendition of this work for large wind band.

A special criticism must be made of the manner in which the score to the band transcription is presented from the publisher: Percy Grainger was one of the most thorough composers that ever lived when it comes to the subject of properly documenting the music that he wrote. Sadly, the published score to the wind band transcription omits Grainger's program note and copious performance notes, and many of Grainger's extensive performance directives (found in the original orchestral score) are severely abbreviated or have been eliminated altogether. Further, there is no listing of instrumentation or the parts provided, an unforgivable omission on the part of any publisher. The score itself has been engraved with note sizes which are so small as to be nearly unreadable. Finally, perhaps in an effort to reduce costs on an item which, due to its length and difficulty, will never be a best seller, the score has been reproduced through a photocopied process which has had the unfortunate result of a great deal of fade-out so that stems, bar lines, and staff lines often cannot be seen at all.

Contributed by:
R. Mark Rogers
Director of Publications
Southern Music Company
San Antonio, Texas

Teacher Resource Guide

Three City Blocks
John Harbison
(b. 1938)

Unit 1: Composer

John Harbison was born on December 20, 1938, in Orange, New Jersey, and was raised in Princeton, where his father was a professor of history at Princeton College. John's father, who played piano and other instruments, taught the young Harbison the basics of music, acquainted him with works of classical composers as well as popular music, and frequently took his family to concerts. While in high school in the 1950s, Harbison played piano in jazz clubs; studied tuba, voice, conducting, and composition; and began to compose. He graduated Harvard in 1960 where, along with his studies in composition, he was the conductor of the Bach Society. While completing his master's in composition at Princeton University, he was the assistant conductor of the university orchestra. In 1969, Harbison accepted a position at the Massachusetts Institute of Technology (where he is currently Class of 1949 Institute Professor of Music), and he also became the director of the Cambridge Cantata Singers.

Harbison's experiences studying and conducting Bach cantatas became integrated into his compositional style. Along with composing a large number of vocal, choral, and operatic works, the most prominent feature of his style (which is most often identified in articles and biographical entries) is the persistence of a lyrical strain, providing a singing, melodious influence to almost every phrase. He has been Composer-in-Residence with the Pittsburgh Symphony, the Los Angeles Philharmonic, the Santa Fe Chamber Festival, the American Academy in Rome, Tanglewood, the California Institute for the Arts, and Chamber Music West. Along with the 1987 Pulitzer Prize for his

924

cantata, *Flight into Egypt*, he has received the Rockefeller Foundation Award, the Brandeis University Creative Citation Award, the National Institute of Arts and Letters Award, the Koussevitzky Music Foundation Award, the American Academy of Arts and Letters Award, the National Endowment for the Arts Composer–Librettist Fellowship, the Naumburg Chamber Music Award, a Guggenheim Fellowship, and the Kennedy Center Friedheim Award. Harbison has composed in virtually every genre—from solo to chamber to symphonic music. His compositions for wind ensembles also include *Music for Eighteen Winds* (1985) and *Olympic Dances* (1997).

Unit 2: Composition

Three City Blocks was completed in 1991 at Nervi, near Genoa, on the Mediterranean coast of Italy. In 1989, Frank Battisti, the conductor of the New England Conservatory Wind Ensemble, initiated a commission consortium for a new work for symphonic wind ensemble to be composed by Harbison. Other schools in the consortium included the University of Cincinnati College–Conservatory of Music, The Ohio State University, Florida State University, the University of Michigan, and University of Southern California, and the United States Air Force Band.

The title, *Three City Blocks*, suggests a descriptive program, but the work is neither programmatic nor descriptive of any specific urban locale. Much of the musical language of the work, especially in the rhythm and harmony, is drawn from American jazz. It is through the jazz-like sounds and style of this composition that Harbison evokes the energy and vivacity of urban culture and suggests images of urban America. The program note printed in the published score implies the work represents Harbison's impression of the big city as he was growing up.

> Over the radio, in the early fifties, came sounds played by bands in hotels and ballrooms; now distant memories that seemed to a seventh-grade, small-town, late-night listener like the true pulse of giant imagined cities.
>
> Years later, these sounds—layered with real experience of some of their places of origin: magnified, distorted, idealized, and destabilized—came into contact with other sounds, some of recent origin, and resulted in these celebratory, menacing, Three City Blocks....

Performance of *Three City Blocks* calls for a large ensemble of specific instrumentation, requiring versatility from several woodwind players who double instruments and an expanded percussion section. Each of the three movements uses a variant of traditional forms. The musical structures of the forms feature clearly delineated sections. These structures may be analogous to the hard-edged, rigid glass and steel architecture of modern American cities, as suggested by the following program note Harbison wrote in 1993:

There are three blocks, each at a faster speed, each at a hotter temperature. The language is urban, the architecture is blunt and sharp.

For many years the romanticism of the rural ideal dominated American art, even as fewer and fewer people actually experienced the countryside or pursued the labors or its pleasures. But what still exists out there somewhere as a source of renewal and regeneration, or sheer escape, the rural vision has been replaced by the reality. We are ruled politically by the suburbs, which are neither here nor there, but we are haunted and challenged, terrorized and energized, by the city. So the composer who wants to deal with live material opens his ears to the sounds of downtown. These sounds cannot simply be transcribed. They must be somehow essentialized—made to stand for more.

The grand expanses of the American wind orchestra, one of our most abundant and flexible resources, seems a good place to explore both the jangle and the clarity of this powerful urban experience. Three City Blocks should suggest places we have been, places we would like to be, and places we might be afraid to be.

The first movement, in sonata form, is six and minutes and thirty seconds in length, and numbers 140 measures. Movement 2 is a sonata-rondo form, performs in four minutes and thirty seconds, and is 202 measures. The last movement is in ternary form with a coda, has 148 measures, and takes just under four minutes to perform. Performance of the three movements totals fifteen minutes.

Unit 3: Historical Perspective

Three City Blocks was premiered on August 2, 1993, by the United States Air Force Band, Lt. Col. Alan Bonner, conductor, at the Hilton Hotel Convention Center in Fort Smith, Arkansas. From the early decades of the twentieth century, composers have been incorporating sounds of jazz elements into symphonic music, for example, Darius Milhaud of France and the American, George Gershwin. *Three City Blocks*, too, relies on the sounds of jazz and, like most of the other works composed for wind ensembles, there is no improvising. These compositions use jazz-like harmonies, articulations, textures, and rhythms, but without the improvisatory element, each work presents only an impression of jazz in performance; it is not true jazz. Other works for wind ensemble that are composed with conventional techniques of Western art music but evoke big band jazz include Warren Benson's *Dawn's Early Light* (1987), Leonard Bernstein's *Prelude, Fugue and Riffs* (1950), Donald Grantham's *Bum's Rush* (1993), Gunther Schuller's *Blue Dawn into White Heat* (1996), Frank Ticheli's *Blue Shades* (1996).

Unit 4: Technical Considerations

There are no key signatures indicated in the parts or score of *Three City Blocks*. Although accidentals are abundant, performers must know the work is tonal. Most of the first movement is centered in the keys of F and C. The second movement is centered in the key of C with harmonic movement to the keys of G and F. The third movement is centered in the key of G, although after an "Amen" plagal cadence figure (IV–I, or C–G) is stated three times, the work ends with the "Amen" stated in four different keys (B–F-sharp, D-flat–A-flat, A–D, and C–G) as polychords.

Individual rhythms are not particularly difficult. It is imperative that players understand triplet rhythms, written in both quarter note and eighth note divisions. It will take concentration and time in rehearsal to work out the layering of these borrowed-time triplet figures over eighth note and sixteenth note simple-time figures. With its relationships to jazz, rhythmic syncopation permeates the composition, especially in the second movement.

There are extreme ranges written for some instruments. Harbison separates the voices in many chord structures. This scoring technique improves the clarity between instrumental groups within the wind ensemble but challenges the players' range and intonation skills. Examples include the end of the first movement where the woodwinds, including saxophone, are scored in an extreme high register with the brass separated to the lower register. At measure 24 in the second movement, the scoring encompasses five octaves from a low C (Great C) in the tuba through c''' (three-line c) in trumpet to a c'''' (four-line c) in flute. Technical considerations should also include the passages for marimba and vibraphone in the second movement that require four-mallet technique and, also in the second movement, six measures of fluttertonguing for upper woodwinds.

Instrumentation may concern ensembles desiring to perform *Three City Blocks*. The score requires four flutes with two doubling on piccolo, pairs of oboes and E-flat clarinets, four B-flat clarinets, pairs of bass clarinets (with a double on contrabass clarinet), and bassoons (with a double on contrabassoon), and pairs of alto saxophones and tenor saxophones. The brass is scored for four each of trumpets, horns, and trombones with pairs of euphoniums and tubas. Harp and piano are required along with a pair of string basses. The score calls for five percussionists to play a very large number of different instruments.

Unit 5: Stylistic Considerations

Three City Blocks draws much of its musical language from American jazz. Harbison has placed very specific articulation and dynamic markings throughout the score. The conductor must help the players understand the meanings, the levels, and the differences, albeit sometimes slight, between all of the different instructions for articulation and dynamics. Articulations signs include the indications for *martelé* or *marcato*, standard accent, *tenuto* or *legato*, *staccato*, and the words "*marcato*," "*staccato*," "*legato*," "light," "brittle," and "*secco staccato*."

Dynamic accents include the markings for "*fp*," "*sf*," "*sfz*," "*sfp*," and "*p sf*." Hairpin *crescendos* and *diminuendos* are indicated along with words and abbreviations for *piano* through *fortissimo* dynamics.

In the third movement, trumpet and trombone are instructed to use plunger mutes and must agree on the sound of "open" and "closed."

The tempi marked are as follows: Movement I, quarter note = 88; Movement II, quarter note = 176; Movement III, quarter note = 208 with dotted-half note = 69+. More helpful than the tempo markings are Harbison's instructions. The first movement's "Fervent and resolute" indication helps maintain the style of the unyielding "bluesy" triplets. The second movement's direction to be "Tough, driving" helps to sustain the vibrancy of the movement's dynamics and repetitive syncopated rhythmic motive. The third movement is marked "With relentless energy." The opening snare drum rim shots along with written instructions for the winds to play "commanding," "brilliant," "dominating," "whooping," and "brash" keep the movement electrifyingly flowing to the final climax that is marked "*tutta forza*."

Unit 6: Musical Elements

MELODY:

The melodies in *Three City Blocks* are composed of short rhythmic/melodic motives, repeated and elaborated and strung together. For example, the first movement's first theme, begun in measure 1 by trumpet and trombone, is based on a half note/triplet quarter note motive. In the five-measure melody that opens this movement, the rhythmic motive is stated three successive times and then reversed and elongated. The rhythm of the rondo theme of the second movement is written with quarter notes, dotted-eighths, and sixteenths, creating (in sixteenth note values) a 7–5–3–1 rhythmic motive that is repeated through the opening seventeen measures and, of course, in each subsequent appearance of the A section. Although notated in triple-simple time, the third movement uses a "short-long" rhythm (similar to the second rhythmic mode of thirteenth century organum). This movement's primary melody and its accompaniment are composed with the repetition of this rhythm.

HARMONY:

Three City Blocks is a tonal work. Harbison's use of harmonic structures with split thirds, absent thirds, and/or fifths, along with non-triadic construction, sustained pedal points, non-harmonic tones, and tones used as inflections of neighboring tones, all contribute to the disguising of tonality in many areas. The lowest notes of chords can usually be considered the root of the chord at beginnings and ends of phrases. The seventh chord, particularly the major-minor seventh chord, is used to harmonize much of this work. These seventh chords are used throughout *Three City Blocks* for their jazz-like sound qualities rather than for their function in a diatonic progression. The opening chords in the brass in measures 1 through 5 of the first movement illustrate such seventh chords. A cursory look at chord structures written throughout the work in the piano part will demonstrate this harmonic technique as well.

RHYTHM:

With its jazz-like qualities, *Three City Blocks* has an abundance of jazz-like rhythms, including off-beat accents and triplet figures. Harbison has meticulously written specific rhythms, and as an ensemble rehearses the work, the players must conscientiously avoid interpreting the eighth note and sixteenth note rhythms as "swing" rhythms. In learning to interpret the many tied-note rhythms in *Three City Blocks*, rehearsing with all notes articulated (removing the ties) may improve the ensemble's precision.

TIMBRE:

In most of *Three City Blocks*, Harbison's scoring techniques separate the voices of the wind ensemble. Examples from the first movement include the second melody of the first theme group at measure 10. The melody is scored in the upper range of flute, E-flat clarinet, and B-flat clarinet with the accompaniment played in the low range of the bass clarinet, contrabass clarinet, bassoon, and contrabassoon. The transition to the second theme group is scored for three disparate voices in three ranges, E-flat clarinet, alto saxophone, and tenor saxophone. The opening of the final movement illustrates another of Harbison's scoring techniques that separate the voices of the wind ensemble. Nine separate melodic and accompaniment lines appear in different instrument sections of the wind ensemble that are layered in a grand polyphonic texture. It is advantageous to rehearse polyphonic sections in a composition by allowing players to hear one line at a time.

Unit 7: Form and Structure

SECTION	MEASURE	EVENT AND SCORING
Movement I Exposition		
First theme a	1–9	Theme in trumpet and trombone with countermelody in oboe and horn stated as "call and response"
First theme b	10–20	Theme in flute, clarinet, and trumpet with countermelody in bass clarinet and bassoon stated as "call and response"

SECTION	MEASURE	EVENT AND SCORING
Transition	21–33	Triplet motive in brass and oboe with sixteenth note figures in clarinet and saxophone
Second theme c	34–47	Theme in trumpet
Second theme d	48–57	Theme in woodwinds
Development/ recapitulation	58–75	Triplet motive primarily in saxophone
First theme a	76–78	Theme in clarinet with countermelody in timpani
First theme b	79–87	Theme in bass clarinet, bassoon, and horn with countermelody in string bass and piano
Transition	88–100	Triplet motive in brass with sixteenth note figures in woodwinds and marimba
Second theme c	101–114	Theme in clarinet
Second theme d	115–123	Theme in flute and oboe
Coda	124–140	Theme c in woodwinds with steady rock beat set up in ensemble
Movement II A Theme a	1–21	Primary melodic/rhythmic theme by *tutti* with accompaniment eighth notes in saxophone
Theme b	22–36	Theme by tutti with accompaniment quarter notes in trombone
B Theme c	37–51	Eighth note accompaniment from Theme a now extended as primary material in saxophone with accompaniment in percussion, harp, and piano
A Theme a	52–60	Primary melodic/rhythmic theme by tutti with accompaniment eighth notes in saxophone

Section	Measure	Event and Scoring
C	61–76	Development of Theme a in clarinet with Theme d in bass clarinet
	77–82	Development of Theme a in brass
	83–96	Development of Theme d in clarinet with accompaniment development in saxophone
	97–102	Development of Theme a in brass
	103–114	Development of Theme a in oboe and E-flat clarinet and contraclarinet with Theme d in alto saxophone
A Theme a	115–135	Primary melodic/rhythmic theme by tutti with accompaniment eighth notes in trombone
Theme b	136–152	Theme b by tutti with accompaniment quarter notes in trombone and euphonium
B Theme c	153–167	Theme c in trombone with accompaniment in woodwinds, euphonium, harp, and piano
A Theme a	168–174	Primary melodic/rhythmic theme by tutti with accompaniment eighth notes in bass clarinet, bassoon, saxophone, trumpet, horn, and trombone
Coda	175–184	Begins with extension of Theme a
	185–194	Theme a material in woodwind
	195–202	Theme a rhythmic motive in percussion
Movement III A	1–73	A building of layers of motives and melodies
	1–8	Introductory motives in upper woodwinds and horn

SECTION	MEASURE	EVENT AND SCORING
	9–16	Add Theme a in trombone
	17–19	Introductory motives
	20–29	Theme a in trombone layered with Theme b in saxophone
	30–31	Introductory motives
	32–43	Theme a in trombone layered with Theme b in saxophone and Theme c in trumpet
	44–59	Motives extended
	60–73	Theme a in trombone layered with Theme b in saxophone, Theme c in trumpet, and Theme d in flute and oboe
B	74–97	Development of materials
	74–81	Theme a rhythm (now in quadruple meter) alternating by two measures in trumpet and trombone with Theme d motive in woodwind
	82–89	Continued alternating idea in one-measure patterns
	90–97	Return to alternating in two-measure pattern
A	98–163	
	98–103	Introductory motives
	104–111	Theme a in trombone, euphonium and tuba in canon
	112–119	Theme a now layered with saxophone Theme b
	120–127	Add layer of trumpet Theme c
	128–143	Motives extended in woodwinds and horn
	144–151	Themes a, b, and c skeletonized

SECTION	MEASURE	EVENT AND SCORING
	152–163	Motives extended
Coda	164–247	"Amen" motives
	164–175	"Amen" in flute, oboe, trumpet, trombone
	176–179	Flute, oboe, E-flat clarinet, marimba Theme a
	180–191	"Amen" in flute, oboe, trumpet, trombone layered with Theme a motive in saxophone and Theme b in clarinet
	191–197	Flute, oboe, E-flat clarinet, marimba Theme a
	198–209	"Amen" in flute, oboe, trumpet, trombone with Theme c interjected by clarinet
	210–217	Flute, oboe, E-flat clarinet, marimba Theme a
	218–240	"Amen" scored thickly and harmonized
	241–247	Tutta forza "Amen"
	248	Measure of silence

Unit 8: Suggested Listening

Warren Benson, *Dawn's Early Light* (1987)
Leonard Bernstein, *Prelude, Fugue and Riffs* (1950)
Donald Grantham, *Bum's Rush* (1993)
John Harbison:
   Music for Eighteen Winds (1985)
   Olympic Dances (1997)
Gunther Schuller, *Blue Dawn into White Heat* (1996)
Frank Ticheli, *Blue Shades* (1996)

Unit 9: Additional References and Resources

Baker, Theodore. *Baker's Biographical Dictionary of Musicians*. Eighth edition. Revised by Nicolas Slonimsky. New York: Schirmer, 1992. S.v. "John Harbison."

Bonous-Smit, Barbara. "John Harbison: His Life and Works with Piano." Ph.D. dissertation, New York University, 1996.

Condaris, Christine. "John Harbison, *Music for Eighteen Winds*." *Notes* 47, No. 3, March 1991, p. 961.

Harbison, John. *Three City Blocks*. New York: Associated Music Publishers, 1993.

Hitchcock, H. Wiley, and Stanley Sadie, eds. *New Grove Dictionary of American Music*. London: Macmillan Press, 1986. S.v. "John Harbison," by Richard Swift.

Kohlenberg, Kenneth. "*Olympic Dances* by John Harbison..." D.M.A. dissertation, University of North Texas, 1997.

Morton, Brian, ed. *Contemporary Composers*. Chicago: St. James Press, 1992. S.v. "John Harbison," by Henry Fogel.

Seabrook, Mike. "John Harbison and his Music." *Tempo*, No. 197, July 1996, p. 7.

Spittal, Robert J. "*Three City Blocks* by John Harbison." D.M.A. dissertation, University of Cincinnati, 1995.

Townell, Eric Esko. "The Symphonies of John Harbison." D.M.A. dissertation, Johns Hopkins University, 1997.

Website:
http://web.mit.edu/mta/www/music/resources/jharbison.html

Contributed by:
Kenneth Kohlenberg
Director of Bands, Professor of Music
Sinclair Community College
Dayton, Ohio

Teacher Resource Guide

Timepiece

Cindy McTee
(b. 1953)

Unit 1: Composer

Cindy McTee was born in Tacoma, Washington, in 1953, where she grew up surrounded by music. Raised in a family of amateur musicians who encouraged her interest in music and the arts, McTee began piano studies at age five with a teacher who encouraged her to improvise and studied saxophone with her mother who taught her to transpose from sheet music. This background provided a foundation for her later interest in jazz and composition.

McTee completed her undergraduate work at Pacific Lutheran University (B.M., 1975), where she studied composition with David Robbins and Thomas Clark. In the spring of 1974, she met composer Krzysztof Penderecki, as he was a guest at a contemporary music festival held at the university. This meeting resulted in the composer spending a year in Poland at the Academy of Music in Cracow (1974–1975) studying with Penderecki. McTee credits him as both a musical and professional influence, and it was Penderecki who encouraged his pupil to express humor in her music. While in Poland, McTee also had lessons with Marek Stachowski and Krystyna Moszumanska-Nazar at Cracow's Higher School of Music. She earned her master's degree from the Yale School of Music (M.M., 1978), where her teachers included Penderecki again, as well as Jacob Druckman and Bruce MacCombie. She received a doctorate from the University of Iowa (Ph.D., 1981), studying under Richard Hervig.

From 1981 to 1984, McTee taught at Pacific Lutheran University and subsequently joined the faculty at the University of North Texas, where she is Regents Professor of Music Composition. She has received a number of prestigious commissions and awards, including a Guggenheim Fellowship (2001), a Fellowship from the National Endowment for the Arts (1994), a Goddard Lieberson Fellowship from the American Academy of Arts and Letters (1992), and a Fulbright-Hayes Senior Lecturer Fellowship (1990). She is currently completing her first symphony, a commission from the National Symphony Orchestra for its 2001–02 season and European tour.

Unit 2: Composition

Timepiece denotes both the celebration of the Dallas Symphony Orchestra's one hundredth anniversary and the beginning of a new millennium. However, the title also refers to the manner in which the composer sees musical time and how that time shapes the work. According to McTee, musical time is not like ordinary clock time but "...more like the kind of time experienced when reading a story. It's almost imaginary—repeating, reversing, accelerating, decelerating, and possibly stopping."

The work begins slowly, "before" time, and then emerges into a highly energized, clock-like pulse. This energized pulse lasts for the remainder of the work's eight-minute duration. The piece begins and ends on D (for Dallas), and pitch materials are derived from octatonic and twelve-tone scales. Of *Timepiece*, McTee states:

> Much of my recent thinking about music is informed by the writings of Carl G. Jung who, in the words of Anthony Storr, "felt that the whole energy of mental function" sprang from the tension between the oppositions of conscious and unconscious, of thought and feeling, of mind and body, of objectivity and subjectivity. So too have the integration and reconciliation of opposing elements become important aspects of my work: the frequent use of circular patterns, or *ostinati*, offer both the possibility of suspended time and the opportunity for continuous forward movement; carefully controlled pitch systems and thematic manipulations provide a measure of objectivity and reason, while kinetic rhythmic structures inspire bodily motion; discipline yields to improvisation; and perhaps most importantly, humor takes its place comfortably alongside the grave and earnest. I wish both to enlighten and to entertain, to communicate wholeness and, above all, to celebrate life!

Unit 3: Historical Perspective

Premiered under conductor Andrew Litton on February 17, 2000, the original version of *Timepiece* was commissioned by the Dallas Symphony Orchestra for its one hundredth anniversary season. Later performances by the Dallas Symphony Orchestra took place in Birmingham, England, and New York's Carnegie Hall. Immediately following the first performance of *Timepiece*, a wind transcription was commissioned from the composer by a consortium of ensembles through the College Band Directors National Association. This version was premiered at that organization's national convention on February 22, 2001, by the North Texas Wind Symphony under the direction of Eugene Migliaro Corporon.

Unit 4: Technical Considerations

Timepiece may sound deceptively simple, but it is a demanding work written for mature players. Technical demands are high, but parts are idiomatic and carefully suited to the instruments. In the opening "womb" section, clarinets must manipulate subtle and sensitive dynamic changes. A piccolo trumpet solo at the end requires a player of some skill. Saxophones and clarinets often take the place of the strings in this transcription, and though this works exceptionally well, it also places some demands on the players in terms of individual technical ability and in overall consistency of playing. Several sections of the ensemble must maintain ongoing *ostinati* during the faster, "clock-like" second section, and consistency in playing is essential during these passages as well. Percussion is an integral and complex part of the work and playing must be confident and precise. A combination of sensitivity and exactness are required throughout the piece.

Unit 5: Stylistic Considerations

McTee maintains a rich yet playful stylistic palette in *Timepiece*. Sensitivity and control is required in the opening section, and an understanding of jazz nuance is necessary for much of the rest of the piece. The work is highly organic, constantly referencing itself. The composer says, "*Timepiece* represents the ticking of a clock as it ushers in the new century." This ticking combines many stylistic thoughts from the almost mechanical to the pops and shadings of jazz.

Unit 6: Musical Elements

MELODY:

The work's most important melodic pattern—minor third up, major seventh up, minor sixth down, and major seventh up—can be heard in various contexts beginning at the following measures: 134, 145, 181, 338, 357, 366, and 370. The last presentation of this tune begins in trumpet at measure 370: minor third up from F-sharp to A, major seventh up to G-sharp, minor sixth down to C. It begins again after skipping a note, with the A to G-sharp, descending a tritone to prepare the final "stretch" to D, perhaps the only melodic octave in the piece, taking that familiar major seventh to its "final resting place." Care should be made to attain clarity in this line when it appears.

HARMONY:

As stated earlier, *Timepiece* begins and ends on D (for Dallas), and though the piece is not tonal in the strict sense, this pitch is repeated and important throughout the work. Other pitch materials are derived from octatonic and twelve-tone scales. The octatonic scale is used in a variety of ways to create melodic interest. In some cases, sonorities are based on triads, and in others they are based on minor seconds, minor thirds, and tritones. To link the alternating octatonic and twelve-tone sections, the composer uses a tone row with intervallic content consisting entirely of minor seconds, minor thirds, and tritones. The scales are as follows:

Octatonic scale 1:   C – D-flat – E-flat – E – F-sharp – G – A – B-flat
Octatonic scale 2:   C-sharp – D – E – F – G – G-sharp – A-sharp – B
Octatonic scale 3:   D – E-flat – F F-sharp – G-sharp – A – B – C
Twelve-tone row: C – G-flat – F – D – A-sharp – B – D – D-flat – G – G-sharp – A – E-flat

Other important harmonic textures:

1. Articulated sixteenth notes – measures 3, 26, 39, and returning at 323

2. Sustained chords – measures 33, 53, and 70

3. Arpeggiated "flurries," used to punctuate or close a gesture – measures 95, 115, 123, 147, 173, and 319

4. *Tutti* repeated chord and "dotted" rhythm serving as points of arrival – measures 116, 125, 149, 231, and 285

5. Repeated, interlocking, forward-moving, octatonic textures – measures 96, 127, 177, 196, 292, and 344

6. Unison melodic material – measures 130, 177, 333, and 357

7. Eighth note, twelve-tone "engine" texture, used to provide "chromatic relief" – measures 151, 232, and 291

8. Pulsating vertical texture in combination with linear music; this vertical material contrasts with that which is more forward-moving and linear, causing the music to "stand up" and eventually "stand still" as it ends the piece – measures 183, 213, 303, and at 353

Isolating some of these textures during rehearsals to make certain players understand the purpose the passages serve will lead to a more confident performance and will allow performers to bring out the more important nuances.

RHYTHM:

The "timepiece" throughout the work, heard in the hi-hat, wood block, and other instruments, provides the basis for the steady pulse of the piece, set at 144 beats per minute. While the beat remains steady, time signatures change frequently, so a main rehearsal concern will be keeping the eighth note steady during some of these more complex passages in the second section. Special attention will need to be given to changes between triple and duple, and vice versa.

TIMBRE:

McTee is extraordinarily thoughtful and exact in her scoring, so it is vital to make certain that all instruments can be heard with clarity but that there is also an appropriate blend. For example, the piano often works in tandem with the keyboard percussion in providing motor. While the piano needs to be heard, it is meant to be part of the mix of the ensemble, not soloistic. There are several long passages in the second section where *ostinati* are held for long periods under the melodic material. Maintaining a proper balance will take some care and attention, as the *ostinato* may outplay the melodic work. Throughout the work, it is important to give care to both the melodic and harmonic textures pointed out in this unit and the pulse of the "timepiece" that ticks consistently. Communicating these clearly will result in a more invigorating performance.

Unit 7: Form and Structure

In the overall sense, this work is binary in form as there are two large sections that are clearly distinguishable by tempo, rhythm, and timbre. The second section is further divided into five parts that alternate between octatonic and twelve-tone harmonic structures.

SECTION	MEASURE	EVENT AND SCORING
Part 1	1–96	Approximately two minutes; the piece begins slowly, "before" time, in a womb-like state
	3–4	Three ideas presented using six of eight pitches from octatonic scale two: sustained D, highly articulated and animated sixteenth notes stressing the interval of a minor ninth, and eighth notes in brass
	6–10	Restate these materials in shortened form, surrounding and punctuating in various ways with percussion instruments; sustained D settles to a C-sharp at m. 8; additional pitches are

SECTION	MEASURE	EVENT AND SCORING
		added to eventually create a widely spaced five-note chord: G, G-sharp, B-flat, F, and C-sharp.
	22	Presents the wood block, or "time-piece," as it ticks briefly at the work's basic tempo of 144 beats per minute
		Throughout the first section, animated materials alternate with sustained sonorities, creating the tension of opposing forces that provide the necessary energy to launch the second section
Transition, Part 1	87–96	Recalls the opening, but the sustained D remains suspended so as to stretch time, creating the effect of a new beginning and the "birth" of the continuous, "living" pulse established at m. 96
Part 2	96–end	Approximately six minutes; pulse introduced in the first section takes control, providing the drive in the second section at 144 beats per minute
Section 1	96–150	Octatonic
Section 2	151–172	Twelve-tone
Section 3	173–231	Octatonic
Section 4	232–290	Twelve-tone
Section 5	291–375	Octatonic

Unit 8: Suggested Listening

Cindy McTee, "Timepiece." – *Timepieces*, Eugene Migliaro Corporon and the University of North Texas Wind Symphony: Compact disc, 2001

Other band works by the composer:
Cindy McTee:
"California Counterpoint: The Twittering Machine." – *Tributes*, Eugene Migliaro Corporon and the University of North Texas Wind Symphony: Compact disc KCD-11070, 1995

"Circuits." – *Memorials*, Eugene Migliaro Corporon and the University of Cincinnati College–Conservatory of Music Wind Symphony: Compact disc KCD-11042, 1992.

"Soundings." – *Wind Dances*, Eugene Migliaro Corporon and the University of North Texas Wind Symphony: Compact disc KCD-11084, 1997.

Other works by the composer:

Chamber – Instrumental
> *Capriccio per Krycsztof Penderecki*
> *Changes*
> *Chord*
> *Circle Music I–IV*
> *Einstein's Dreams*
> *Fantasia*
> *Images*
> *Piano Percussion Piece*
> *Stepping Out*
> *The Twittering Machine*

Chamber – Vocal
> *Psalm 142: Threnody*
> *Songs of Spring and the Moon*

Choral
> *Psalm 100*

Electro-acoustic
> *Etudes*
> "M" *Music*
> *Metal Music*

Keyboard
> *Agnus Dei*
> *Fantasia*

Orchestral
> *Circuits*
> *Elegy*
> *The Twittering Machine*
> *Timepiece*

Unit 9: Additional References and Resources

Chism, Olin. *About Cindy McTee.* www.newmusicnow.org, 1999.

Elliott, Susan. *A Conversation with Cindy McTee.* www.newmusicnow.org, 1999.

McTee, Cindy. "California Counterpoint: The Twittering Machine." *Tributes*, Eugene Migliaro Corporon and the University of North Texas Wind Symphony: Compact disc KCD-11070, 1995.

    "Circuits." *Memorials*, Eugene Migliaro Corporon and the University of Cincinnati College–Conservatory of Music Wind Symphony: Compact disc KCD-11042, 1992.

    "Soundings." *Wind Dances*, Eugene Migliaro Corporon and the University of North Texas Wind Symphony: Compact disc KCD-11084, 1997.

    Correspondence (including extensive notes and analysis) with Diana Hollinger, July/August 2001.

    Personal website: http://courses.unt.edu/cmctee

Miles, Richard, ed. *Teaching Music through Performance in Band*, Volume II. Chicago: GIA Publications, Inc., 1998.

Miles, Richard, ed. *Teaching Music through Performance in Band*, Volume III. Chicago: GIA Publications, Inc., 2000.

Reese, Kelley. "The Art and Science of Music: Cindy McTee Creates Timely Compositions." *UNT Resource*, 3 October 2000.

Contributed by:

Diana Hollinger,
DMA Student
Arizona State University,
Tempe, Arizona

Teacher Resource Guide

Urban Requiem
Michael Colgrass
(b. 1932)

Unit 1: Composer

Raised in the small town of Brookfield, Illinois, Michael Colgrass's initial cultural exposure was through the genre of movies. At age ten, he saw Ray Bauduc (drummer) and Bobby Haggart (bassist) in the movie *Big Noise from Winnetka* and was absolutely mesmerized. He soon formed his own band, the Three Jacks and a Jill, and launched his career as a self-employed musician in the Chicago area (1944–1949). He graduated from the University of Illinois (1954) in music performance and composition, where he studied percussion with Paul Price and composition with Eugene Weigel. Additional composition teachers included Darius Milhaud (Aspen) and Lukas Foss (Tanglewood). After serving almost two years as timpanist with the Seventh Army Symphony Orchestra in Stuttgart, Germany, Colgrass moved to New York City (1956), where he flourished as a freelance percussionist with such diverse ensembles as the New York Philharmonic, Dizzy Gillespie and the Modern Jazz Quartet, the original *West Side Story* orchestra, the Columbia Recording Orchestra's Stravinsky conducts Stravinsky series, and numerous ballet, opera, and jazz groups.

Colgrass's compositions have been commissioned and performed by many of the major orchestras throughout the United States, Canada, Europe, Great Britain, and Japan, as well as the Canadian Broadcasting Corporation, the Lincoln Center Chamber Music Society, the Manhattan and Muir String Quartets, the Brighton Festival in England, the Fromm Foundation and Ford Foundation, the Corporation for Public Broadcasting, and several other chamber groups, choral ensembles, and soloists. He won the Pulitzer Prize

(1978) for *Deja vu*, commissioned and premiered by the New York Philharmonic, and an Emmy Award (1982) for the Public Broadcasting System documentary *Soundings: The Music of Michael Colgrass*. Other awards include two Guggenheim Fellowships, a Rockefeller Grant, both a Fromm and Ford Foundation Award, First Prize in the Barlow and Sudler International Wind Ensemble Compositions, and the 1988 Jules Léger Prize for New Chamber Music.

Although primarily a composer, Colgrass has also been offering workshops throughout North America in performing excellence in combination with Grotowski physical training, mime, dance, and Neuro-Linguistic Programming (NLP). Most recently, he has given these sessions in Indonesia, South Africa, Brazil, Uruguay, and Argentina. These techniques were featured in his Emmy Award-winning documentary and his recently published book, *My Lessons with Kumi—How I Learned to Perform with Confidence in Life and Work*. Colgrass lives in Toronto with his wife, Ulla, where he continues to thrive in an artistically rewarding environment.

Unit 2: Composition

The following notes accompany the conductor's score:

> *Urban Requiem* for four saxophones and wind orchestra was commissioned by Gary Green and the University of Miami Wind Ensemble through its Abraham Frost Commission Series. A requiem is a dedication to the souls of the dead. *Urban Requiem* might be described as an urban tale, inspired by a diversity of random impressions. I thought of our urban area, where the saxophone was spawned, and of the tragedies and struggles that occur in this environment daily. But I was also inspired by the energy and power of our cities, and the humor inherent in their conflicts. I feel that the saxophone is particularly well suited to express the variety of emotions required for this idea, because it can be not only highly personal and poignant in character but also powerful and commanding. It can howl like a banshee or purr like a kitten. In short, the saxophone is perhaps more like the human voice than any other instrument. In my mind I heard four saxophones singing like a vocal quartet, a music that was liturgical in nature but with a bluesy overtone, a kind of "after hours" requiem.
>
> The size of the wind ensemble for *Urban Requiem* matches the non-string instrumentation of a symphony orchestra (triple winds and brasses, tuba, four horns, harp, synthesizer, timpani, and four percussion). The players are divided into four groups surrounded by the larger wind ensemble, with each sax having it own little 'neighborhood.' The soloists interact in virtuoso display and play

duets and trios with principal players in their bands. The sax players are called upon to improvise occasionally over basic material in sometimes jazz, sometimes ethnic musical traditions.

Urban Requiem is respectfully dedicated to Gary Green, whose boundless enthusiasm for its creation was a constant inspiration to me. It is written for all urban souls, living and dead, who like myself love our cities and continue to be inspired by them.

Unit 3: Historical Perspective

Written ten years after his highly successful musical fable *Winds of Nagual*, *Urban Requiem* represents another musical journey of extraordinary breadth of expression and energy. Parallels with the programmatic elements of *Winds of Nagual* are natural but only superficially describe the range of emotion and style characteristics evident throughout the *Requiem*. This is not the first time Colgrass has written for four solo voices and winds. *Deja vu* (1977) features four solo percussionists in two versions: one for wind ensemble and the second for orchestra.

Unit 4: Technical Considerations

The technical demands are considerable for both the solo saxophone quartet and accompaniment voices. The seamless nature of the events are structured with minimal transitional or linking sections. Often, the transitions must be performed suddenly with extreme contrasts in both character and energy.

Unit 5: Stylistic Considerations

This work explores several opportunities for improvisation in a variety of styles. Jazz, minimalist, and aleatoric influences are employed in both soloist and accompanimental parts. One can hear a vast array of styles from Bach to calypso, and hymns to free form. The style contrasts are either colliding or collaborating, but always speak to the strong pulse and forward momentum of the work. The inherent diversity of dynamic energy and character will demand considerable sophistication from all voices—humor and poignancy abound.

Unit 6: Musical Elements

The *Requiem* is scored for solo soprano, alto, tenor, and baritone saxophone quartet, and piccolo, flute, alto flute, oboe/English horn, E-flat clarinet, B-flat clarinet, bass clarinet, two bassoons, contrabassoon, four horns, three trumpets, three trombones, one tuba, synthesizer, harp, two contrabassoons with C extensions, timpani, and four percussion.

According to Colgrass, the piece is actually a variation form, though not in the usual sense.

> I have developed this idea I call developmental variations where the variations develop and vary within themselves, often to the point where you'll hardly recognize the melody. The melody is presented by the quartet in hocket at the beginning. The melody (in B minor) begins with the alto sax B on the fourth beat of m. 16, to the D downbeat in m. 17, then to the F-sharp–G in the soprano, down to the A-sharp in the baritone, and continues on through m. 48. The opening motive repeats then in the tenor in m. 50, now in D minor, where it dissolves. You'll recognize these opening five notes as the first five notes of Bach's *Musical Offering*, used quite unconsciously as it happens. Since the melody had a built-in modulation (up a minor third), every variation is in a different key, often but not always up a minor third.

MELODY:
Although motivic elements in the opening section subtly explore the harmonic fringes of the otherwise static harmonic rhythm, Colgrass incorporates a variety of melodic manipulation, including ambivalent modes (reflecting the major/minor quality of the harmonies), Mid-Eastern motives (both melodic and rhythmic), duets that exhibit "call and response" architecture, hocket-like exchanges, pointillism, canonic treatment in close displacement, elision of motivic ideas, aleatoric techniques, and chromaticism.

HARMONY:
Subtle alterations between chord inversions, an abundance of seventh and ninth chords, and polytonality are in evidence throughout.

RHYTHM:
Rhythmically complex statements within the framework of constant metric modulations are expressed with a variety of techniques, including Stravinsky-like layering, diminution and augmentation of melodic fragments, pointillism, and minimalism.

TIMBRE:
Characterized by muted brass, extreme ranges, and duets of contrasting instrumental color, the full spectrum of instrumental qualities of each voice is explored. The percussion voices are employed as equal partners in all elements and play an integral role in the establishment of style and genre of expression. Brass choir statements and the solo instrument writing display a thorough understanding of timbral potential and subtle nuances.

Unit 7: Form and Structure

SECTION	MEASURE	EVENT AND SCORING
A	1–62	Accompanied by synthesizer, the quartet initiates a hymn-like event characterized by mostly static harmonies (primarily seventh chords), major/minor tonalities, and an overall sense of pensive ambivalence; as described earlier, the quartet introduces the opening five-note motive in m. 16; each successive section is a variant of this melody or five-note motive in some way.
B	63–104	The B section explores a conversation between alto saxophone and alto flute with muted brass (cup) accompaniment; harmonic minor-like motivic passages are shared by both solo voices over prevailing seventh- and ninth-chord harmonies; in m. 96, the duet begins a call-and-response exchange concluding with a transitional alto saxophone statement
C	105–210	The baritone saxophone statement is characterized by Mid-Eastern motives; subsequent voice exchange between baritone saxophone and E-flat clarinet reinforce style as do upper woodwind trills, muted trumpets (harmon), stopped horns, and syncopated rhythmic accompaniment; pointillistic accompanying figures (low voices and percussion) are introduced at m. 157; the concluding climax is reinforced by a rhythmically active baritone saxophone motive and unison brass figures
D	211–297	Section D begins with a jazz-influenced soprano saxophone statement; elided exchanges continue between metal percussion, upper woodwinds, and soprano

SECTION	MEASURE	EVENT AND SCORING
		saxophone distinguished by metric diffusion and syncopated rhythms; dance-like figures (m. 246) are followed by the introduction of pans; voice exchange evolves to unison rhythms between soprano saxophone and pans in sixths displaying strong Latin influence; by m. 281, jazz phrasing is introduced followed by expanded scoring reinforcing hocket-like effect
E	298–364	At m. 298, soprano and tenor saxophone begin rhythmically active exchanges and integration of the drum set evolving into an improvisational duet between tenor saxophone and drum set; contrabassoon and low brass enter as accompaniment voices leading to a transition involving all quartet members (mm. 330–364)
F	365–386	The jazz phrasing continues while a tutti statement of the quartet employs melodic material derived from Section E; this rhythmically active event progresses to a free improvisation section "alla Coltrane"; each saxophone voice presents a solo break followed by expanded accompanimental scoring in the form of short bursts of energy culminating in a climax at m. 386
G	387–459	A calm resolution follows a thunderous ensemble statement where alto saxophone and English horn introduce a canon displaced by one and a half beats; this false return continues with a tenor saxophone and oboe duet evoking a baroque style; by m. 420, alto saxophone interrupts the harmonic serenity leading to a brief duet with English horn; tenor saxophone and

SECTION	MEASURE	EVENT AND SCORING
		oboe duet returns soon followed by alto saxophone and English horn (m. 438) with expanded accompaniment building to a short climax; in m. 444, tenor saxophone and oboe initiate a rhythmically active statement of their original duet material; however, by m. 452, a conflict of styles emerges with the reappearance of the English horn material with an altered alto saxophone version
H	460–571	A short three-measure transition introduces a march event featuring low-voice exchanges between baritone saxophone, bass clarinet, and contrabassoon; by m. 484, soprano saxophone initiates pointillistic exchanges with piccolo, E-flat clarinet, and bass clarinet; baritone saxophone introduces similar exchanges (m. 499) with bass clarinet and contrabassoon followed by a return of soprano saxophone and its previous contrapuntal partners (m. 521); after a nine-measure brass choir transition, baritone saxophone exchanges with bass clarinet and contrabassoon return followed by a restatement of the soprano saxophone pointillistic material
I	572–600	The "Hotel Band" section begins with a soprano and baritone saxophone duet (in octaves) accompanied by bassoon, trombone, tuba, and contrabass; this material digresses to "laughing" figures scored in the woodwinds and rhythmically active brass patterns; increased layering leads to another climactic transitional ensemble statement (mm. 599–600)

SECTION	MEASURE	EVENT AND SCORING
J	601–689	A sudden transition to minimalist-like layering of quartet and percussion figures builds to a second aleatoric event at m. 623; following a brass and timpani unison rhythmic statement, a call-and-response exchange begins between the quartet versus the brass and percussion resolving at m. 670; subsequent transition employs aleatoric elements in the quartet (climaxing in m. 681), gradually dissipating to a return of introductory material
K	690–806	Return-like in nature, the quartet is now accompanied by conflicting harmonies; individual cadenza statements occur in gradually descending quartet voices; return of the steel drums (m. 718) is scored with a reflective, augmented restatement of previous material with horn and harp accompaniment; solo piccolo enters in m. 756; by m. 783, both the quartet and supportive voices initiate a gradual decrease in dynamic and rhythmic energy; all voices begin continuous elided statements of *sostenuto* E-flat major seventh chords; in contrast, an ostinato vibraphone pattern alternates between arpeggiated E-flat major seventh chord members and non-harmonic A and F-sharp tones; entrance of the chime *ostinato* in m. 797 coincides with the elimination of the solo quartet, bringing the work to a gradually diminishing and reflective conclusion

Unit 8: Suggested Listening
Michael Colgrass:
    Arctic Dreams (1991)
    Deja vu (both versions, 1977)

Urban Requiem (1995)
Winds of Nagual (1985)

Unit 9: Additional References and Resources

Colgrass, Michael. *Michael Colgrass, Composer, Writer, and NLP Trainer.* Website: www.michaelcolgrass.com

Colgrass, Michael. *My Lessons with Kumi: How I Learned to Perform with Confidence in Life and Work.* Moab, UT: Real People Press, 2000.

Londeix, Jean-Marie. *150 Years of Music for Saxophone.* Cherry Hill, NJ: Roncorp, 1994.

Randel, Don Michael, ed. *The New Harvard Dictionary of Music.* Cambridge, MA: Harvard University Press, 1996.

Rehrig, William H. *The Heritage Encyclopedia of Band Music.* Edited by Paul E. Bierley. Westerville, OH: Integrity Press, 1991.

Schoenberg, Arnold. *Fundamentals of Musical Composition.* Edited by Gerald Strang and Leonard Stein. London: Faber and Faber, 1985.

Slonimsky, Nicolas, ed. *Baker's Biographical Dictionary of Musicians.* Seventh edition. New York: Schirmer, 1984.

Contributed by:

Gordon R. Brock
Director of Bands/Assistant Chair
University of North Florida
Jacksonville, Florida

Index by Title for Teaching Music through Performance in Band: Volumes 1, 2, 3, 4

Index by Publisher for Teaching Music through Performance in Band: Volumes 1, 2, 3, 4

Index by Composer, Arranger, and Transcriber for Teaching Music through Performance in Band: Volume 4

Index by Title for
Teaching Music through
Performance in Band:
Volume 4